'What Ives doesn't know... about the high politics and court life of Henry VIII's England will either never be known or is not worth knowing.'

London Review of Books

'Eric Ives achieves the notable feat of combining magisterial historical authority with a gripping style, and sets the reader's mind buzzing with debate about the complex reasons behind the astounding events of Anne's life.'

Times Literary Supplement

'[Ives] delicately pieces together a believable identity... [and] gives, too, a lucid and coherent exposition of the circumstances that led to Anne's death.'

The Guardian

'An excellent book on Anne Boleyn. Its great strength is its sophisticated understanding of aristocratic women's involvement in 16th-century politics, and precisely how this worked in practice... Ives rises effectively to the human drama of Anne Boleyn's life and in the process illuminates both the inner workings of the Tudor court and its relationship to the larger dramas of the Reformation and European politics.'

Scotland on Sunday

'What is most exciting about *The Life and Death of Anne Boleyn* is not just that it has confirmed and solidified Ives's earlier work and presented it in a more accessible format. (Like John Guy, Ives has discovered that the Starkey model really does work and that popularisation – "to place among the people" – should not be a term of opprobrium.) Rather, it is the development in methodology, the indication that cultural studies and the history of the book have provided us with new ways to evaluate evidence, to interpret the past.'

The Spectator

'Magnificently researched. Eric Ives has written the finest, most accurate study of Anne Boleyn we are ever likely to possess. He leaves no stone unturned in his quest to discover the truth. Never has the historical Anne been so satisfyingly portrayed.'

John Guy, author of *My Heart Is My Own:*
The Life of Mary Queen of Scots

ABOUT THE AUTHOR

Eric Ives is Emeritus Professor of English History at the University of Birmingham. He has written widely on Tudor history, the history of law, and on the development of modern higher education. In 2001 he was awarded an OBE for services to history and the University of Birmingham.

The Life and Death of
ANNE
BOLEYN

For Ruth

The Life and Death of

ANNE BOLEYN

'The Most Happy'

ERIC IVES

Blackwell
Publishing

BLACKWELL PUBLISHING
350 Main Street, Malden, MA 02148-5020, USA
9600 Garsington Road, Oxford OX4 2DQ, UK
550 Swanston Street, Carlton, Victoria 3053, Australia

First published 2004 by Blackwell Publishing Ltd
First published in paperback 2005 by Blackwell Publishing Ltd

SKY10037674_111722

Library of Congress Cataloging-in-Publication Data

Ives, E. W. (Eric William), 1931–
    The life and death of Anne Boleyn: 'the most happy' / Eric Ives.
        p. cm.
Includes bibliographical references (p.) and index.
    ISBN 978-0-631-23479-1 (alk. paper) — ISBN 978-1-4051-3463-7 (pbk. : alk. paper)
    1. Anne Boleyn, Queen, consort of Henry VIII, King of England, 1507–1536. 2. Great
Britain—History—Henry VIII, 1509–1547—Biography. 3. Henry VIII, King of England,
1491–1547—Marriage. 4. Queens—Great Britain—Biography. I. Title.

    DA333.B61845 2004
    942.05'2'092—dc22

                                                                  2003021527

A catalogue record for this title is available from the British Library.

Set in 10.75 on 13.5 pt Galliard
by Kolam Information Services Pvt. Ltd, Pondicherry, India
Printed and bound in the United Kingdom
by TJ International Ltd, Padstow, Cornwall

The publisher's policy is to use permanent paper from mills that operate a sustainable
forestry policy, and which has been manufactured from pulp processed using acid-free and
elementary chlorine-free practices. Furthermore, the publisher ensures that the text paper
and cover board used have met acceptable environmental accreditation standards.

For further information on
Blackwell Publishing, visit our website:
www.blackwellpublishing.com

CONTENTS

ILLUSTRATIONS

PREFACE

ONE question is asked whenever Anne Boleyn's name comes up – did she really commit adultery? Was she, while married to Henry VIII, being serviced by a stable of lovers which included the king's best friend and her very own brother? For this she was beheaded, and five men with her, but what if Anne was innocent? Henry must then be a multiple murderer. The case has been fiercely contested for the best part of five centuries and certainly makes good copy. Shakespeare put a carefully edited version of Anne's courtship and marriage on the stage, and since then, plays, opera, fiction, popular biography, film and, most recently, television have made capital of a story linking the most famous of English kings with sex, scandal and wife-killing.

So why yet another book about Anne Boleyn, beyond feeding a popular obsession, especially since I wrote about her at length twenty years ago? The answer is that Anne Boleyn was so much more important than the circumstances of her execution – a macabre story which yeomen warders of the Tower of London retail with glee to spectators at the scaffold site on Tower Green (incidentally many yards from the real spot). And awareness of that importance is steadily increasing over the years. The chronological narrative remains, but not our understanding of it. It is only a decade ago that I discovered the reason she had to die, and even less since what we knew about her life as queen was revolutionized by the publication of Henry VIII's inventory. We have also learnt and are learning more and more about the world in which she lived and particularly about the royal court which was the milieu for her success and her destruction. For instance, her preoccupation with glamour, which older historians despised as feminine weakness, has now been recognized as a concern with 'image', 'presentation' and 'message' which was as integral to the exercise of power in the sixteenth century as it is in the modern world.

Seeing Anne only through the prism of her final hours produces mani-
fest distortion but, like most people, I began there. Indeed, my interest
was not in Anne herself but in the career of one of those who died with
her, William Brereton from Malpas in Cheshire. In no way could I see him
as her 'lover' – his wife certainly did not – so I was challenged to explain
how he became involved in Anne's destruction. Enquiry revealed that the
reason for the deaths of Anne, Brereton and the others was not sexual
excess but politics. Their fate is explained by what happened not in the
bedroom, but in the corridors of power.

I have sometimes described Anne Boleyn as the third woman in my life,
after my immediate family, and it is true that once she interests you,
fascination grows, as it did for men at the time, and finally for Henry
himself. Thus, being able to explain her destruction merely provokes
another question. Why was Anne queen in the first place? Until the last
thirty years po-faced historians preferred to ignore this. The Victorian J. A.
Froude held that 'It would have been well for Henry VIII if he had lived in
a world in which women could have been dispensed with; so ill, in all his
relations with them, he succeeded.' A. F. Pollard, who dominated Tudor
history in the years before the Second World War, wrote that Anne's 'place
in English history is due solely to the circumstance that she appealed to the
less refined part of Henry's nature; she was pre-eminent neither in beauty
nor in intellect, and her virtue was not of a character to command or
deserve the respect of her own or subsequent ages.'

Yet is it credible that the woman Henry VIII pursued single-mindedly
for six years should be so worthless? And why did Henry marry one of his
own subjects? It was a virtual rule among Western monarchs to marry for
political advantage – almost always a foreign princess. If carnal desire was
what drove Henry, society had mechanisms other than marriage to deal
with that. Indeed, what baffled contemporaries abroad was his apparent
determination to marry a mistress, and the few who knew he didn't sleep
with her failed to understand why not. And was Anne, as Pollard and most
historians have implied, merely Henry's obsession; had she nothing to say
for herself? The 'other woman' in the most shattering marriage break-up
in history, she ousted an entrenched queen of many years' standing,
hugely respected. And what did she then make of that victory? Surely
there was more to the role of second wife than producing a famous
daughter and failing to produce a son.

There was also a public dimension which followed on being first
Henry's fiancée and later his queen. Under her encouragement, royal
policy took directions which continue to shape the English constitution

today. Anne was also an active and effective politician, the destroyer of Thomas Wolsey, Henry's great minister, and it was in order to avoid the same fate that the cardinal's successor, Thomas Cromwell, determined to destroy Anne first. Equally significant was Anne's personal religious commitment. It laid the foundations blocks of Protestant England and set the scene for the monumental changes that produced the religious settlement of her daughter, Elizabeth I. Pollard went wildly astray in claiming that Anne was intellectually inadequate. She read deeply in theology, the intellectual topic of the day, and her artistic taste was highly developed. She was, in fact, the first royal consort to embrace and promote the new fashion which we call Renaissance art.

Pursuing Anne gave Henry VIII years of frustration. Frustration is likewise the lot of her biographer. Anne succeeded by exploiting the rules and conventions of politics and high society, but 'influence' leaves no paper trail, no evidence of its passage. Manipulation can only be inferred from consequences. No one knows what Anne said to Henry in bed. Anne, moreover, left no journal, no memoranda and very few letters, so her inner life must similarly be inferred from externals, for instance, what she believed from what she chose to read and promote. To make matters even more difficult, Anne was such a contentious figure that much of the evidence of observers is either adulatory or bitterly hostile. Writing a biography of Anne Boleyn has all the challenge, excitement and confusion of police detection. It is no surprise that conclusions differ. Yet although we cannot recover Anne in sharp focus, she does come through as more than two-dimensional, more than a silhouette. She was the most influential and important queen consort this country has ever had. Indeed, Anne deserves to be a feminist icon, a woman in a society which was, above all else, male-dominated, who broke through the glass ceiling by sheer character and initiative.

How one would have felt about her is another matter. Captivating to men, Anne was also sharp, assertive, subtle, calculating, vindictive, a power dresser and a power player, perhaps a figure to be more admired than liked. But against that is Anne's greatest distinctiveness, something she shares with only one other English queen: she married for love. Her relationship with Henry was deeply personal in a way kings had risked only once before, and never did again until the twentieth century. The couple's attempt to have an affectionate marriage, with perceptible hints of modernity in the context of a Tudor court, explains much of the life and death of Anne Boleyn. It also means that the more we understand Anne, the more we understand the greatest puzzle of the Tudor century, the personality of her husband Henry; as the saying goes, 'it takes two to make a marriage.'

This book is structured in four parts. 'Background and Beginnings' deals with Anne's origins, her education, her launch into English court life and the reasons for the impact she made. That leads on to a discussion of the romantic relationships which she had or is supposed to have had, and hence to her agreement to marry the king. 'A Difficult Engagement' looks at the oft-told history of Henry VIII's attempt to free himself to marry, but with a focus on Anne which undermines male-dominated interpretations of tradition. Part III, 'Anne the Queen', examines Anne's marriage and consequent lifestyle, offering a picture of what it meant to be the consort of an English king at a magnification well in excess of what is possible for almost all her predecessors. Illustrating this is a nearly complete display of such visual evidence as has survived, which, in turn, supports detailed discussions of Anne's portraiture, of her role as an artistic patron, of the day-to-day context of royal living and of her mind and beliefs. The final section, 'A Marriage Destroyed', concentrates on the closing months of the queen's life, demonstrating the sudden and unexpected nature of her fall, the coup which precipitated it, the dishonesty of the case against her and the tensions of her last days.

Tudor history (especially court history) is a minefield of possible confusion arising from family names, changing peerage titles and the fluctuations of office-holding. I have therefore provided a brief explanatory list. Relationships can be equally confusing, so family trees of the royal houses of Europe, the nobility of Henry VIII's court, and the Boleyn and Howard families are also included. In the index individuals are cross-referenced to a main entry under the family name. A full bibliography of relevant material would be impossibly large, but a list of titles frequently cited and therefore abbreviated can be found before the index. Other works have been cited in full in the notes. Where the place of publication is not given, London must be understood. Spelling in quotations has been modernized.

No biographer of Anne Boleyn comes to the subject without debts. Particularly since the 450th anniversary of Anne's execution in 1986, a significant number of monographs and papers have opened or reopened issues affecting every stage of her life. Many of these contributions are discussed in the body of the text or figure in the notes, and my particular debt to James Carley and Gordon Kipling will be obvious. Not everyone is persuaded by my picture of Anne, and I am especially grateful to George

Bernard for jousts which have sharpened up my analysis. Two substantial studies within discussions of Henry VIII's complete matrimonial record deserve special mention – Antonia Fraser's *The Six Wives of Henry VIII* and, more recently, David Starkey's *Six Wives: The Queens of Henry VIII*. I do not always agree with them, but scholarship would be poorer without work of such quality. Furthermore, it is to Starkey that we owe the publication of *The Inventory of King Henry VIII*, henceforth an absolutely vital text. I have also benefited much from regular communication with Bob Knecht, particularly the chance to bounce off issues in sixteenth-century England against the situation in France and vice versa.

Many scholars and friends have helped me with particular points of difficulty, including Alan Douglas, Marguerite Eve, Joan Glanville, John Guy, Gary Hill, Richard Hoyle, Mme Nicole Lemaitre, Virginia Murphy, Geoffrey Parnell, Peter Ricketts and Barry Young. Over many years of studying the Tudor court and especially Anne Boleyn, I have also incurred considerable debts for the use of manuscripts and other material: to His Grace the Duke of Northumberland and to the archivist at Alnwick Castle, Dr Colin Shrimpton, for ready access to the Percy papers; to His Grace the Duke of Buccleuch and Queensberry for the use of the miniature of Anne Boleyn by John Hoskins; to Mr Robert Pullin for his generous help with the Hever Castle collection; to the Eyston family for access to its papers; to Patricia Collins at the Burrell Collection for introducing me to Anne's needlework. Many librarians, curators and their staffs have willingly assisted and advised, especially Miss Janet Backhouse, lately of the British Library Department of Manuscripts; the staffs of Special Collections, the Barber Institute and the Shakespeare Institute, all of the University of Birmingham, notably Miss Christine Penney and two erstwhile colleagues, Dr Ben Benedikz and Dr Susan Brock; Dr Christiane Thomas of the Österreichisches Staatsarchiv, Vienna, and Dr Christian Müller of the Kunstmuseum Basel.

Whatever merit this biography has is owed, in great measure, to the kindnesses of those named and others unnnamed. Its faults and longueurs are mine, and more than the dedicatee would have passed had she been here to subject the text to her eagle eye.

TITLES AND OFFICES

IN the nearly forty years of Anne Boleyn's story, it is inevitable that office-holders and ranks altered. The following list sets out the principal identifications; for further details, see the index and the family trees.

Archbishop of Canterbury	to 1532	William Warham
	from 1533	Thomas Cranmer
Archbishop of York	to 1530	Thomas Wolsey
Boleyn		*see:* Ormonde, Pembroke, Rochford, Wiltshire
Brandon		*see:* Suffolk
Butler		*see:* Ormonde
Cardinal	to 1530	Thomas Wolsey
Chancellor	to 1529	Thomas Wolsey
	1529–32	Thomas More
	from 1533	Thomas Audley (keeper of the great seal, 1532–3)
Controller of the household	to 1519	Edward Ponynges
	1519/20–21/22	Thomas Boleyn
	1521/22–32	Henry Guildford
	from 1532	William Paulet
Howard		*see:* Norfolk, Surrey
Legate	1528–9	Cardinal Campeggio
The legates	1528–9	Cardinals Campeggio and Wolsey
Norfolk, dowager, duchess of		Agnes Howard, née Tylney, wife of Thomas Howard (d. 1524)
Norfolk, duchess of		Elizabeth Howard, née Stafford, wife of Thomas Howard (d. 1554)

Norfolk, duke of	1514–24	Thomas Howard, d. 1524
	from 1524	Thomas Howard, d. 1554
Northumberland, countess of		Mary Percy, née Talbot, wife of Henry Percy
Northumberland, earl of	to 1527	Henry Algernon Percy, d. 1527
	from 1527	Henry Percy, d. 1537
Ormonde, earl of	to 1515	Thomas Butler
	from 1529	Thomas Boleyn
Pembroke, marchioness of	1532–3	Anne Boleyn
Percy		*see:* Northumberland
Richmond, duchess of		Mary Fitzroy, née Howard, wife of Henry Fitzroy
Richmond, duke of	1525–36	Henry Fitzroy, bastard son of Henry VIII
Rochford, Lady Anne	1532–3	Anne Boleyn
Rochford, Jane Lady		Jane Boleyn, née Parker, wife of George Boleyn
Rochford, Viscount	1525–9	Thomas Boleyn
	1529–36	George Boleyn (courtesy title only to *c.*1530)
Secretary, king's	1529–34	Stephen Gardiner
	from 1534	Thomas Cromwell
Shrewsbury, earl of		George Talbot, d. 1538
Suffolk, duchess of	1515–33	Mary, sister of Henry VIII, wife of Charles Brandon
	from 1533	Katherine Brandon, née Willoughby, wife of Charles Brandon
Suffolk, duke of	from 1514	Charles Brandon
Surrey, earl of	to 1514	Thomas Howard, d. 1524
	1514–24	Thomas Howard, d. 1554
	from 1524	Henry Howard
Talbot		*see:* Northumberland, Shrewsbury
Treasurer of the household	1519–21	Edward Ponynges
	1521/22–5	Thomas Boleyn
	from 1525	William Fitzwilliam
Wiltshire, earl of	from 1529	Thomas Boleyn

The Royal Houses of Europe.

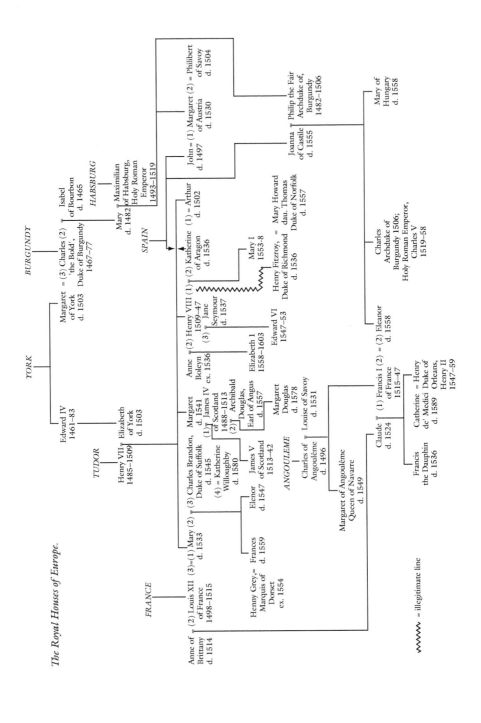

wwww = illegitimate line

The Nobility of Henry VIII's Court.

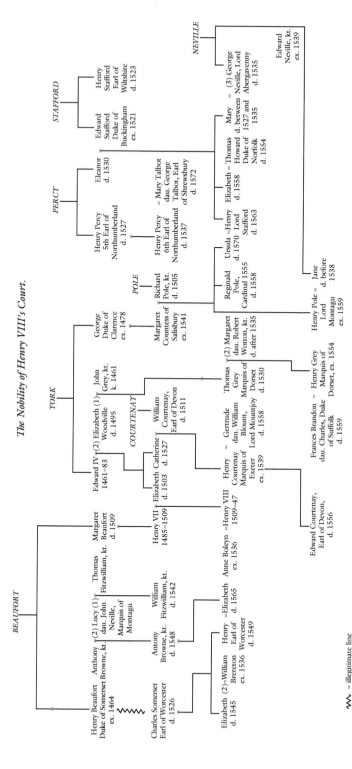

The Boleyn and Howard Families.

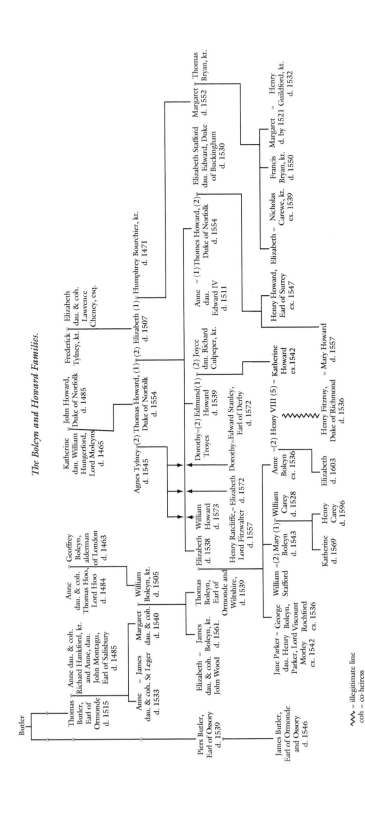

PART I

BACKGROUNDS AND BEGINNINGS

1

A Courtier's Daughter

ANNE Boleyn was born, so tradition goes, at the fairy-tale castle of Hever in the Weald of Kent. Reconstructed by the Astor family in the twentieth century, Hever remains a romantic shrine to Anne and her love affair with Henry VIII. Unfortunately for romance and tradition, Anne was in fact born in Norfolk, almost certainly at the Boleyn home at Blickling, fifteen miles north of Norwich. The church there still has brasses of the family. The Boleyns certainly owned Hever, although it was less a castle than a comfortable manor-house which her great-grandfather, Geoffrey, had built within an existing moat and curtain wall, and it did become the principal residence of her parents. But Matthew Parker, who became archbishop of Canterbury in 1559 and had earlier been one of Anne's private chaplains, was quite specific that she came, as he did, from Norfolk.[1]

Tradition also tells us that the Boleyns were a family of London merchants, and again tradition leads us astray. Anne Boleyn was born a great lady. Her father, Thomas, was the eldest son of Sir William Boleyn of Blickling, and her mother, Elizabeth, was the daughter of Thomas Howard, earl of Surrey, one of the premier noblemen in England. There was mercantile wealth in the family, but to get to that we have to go back to Geoffrey Boleyn, the builder of Hever. He had left Norfolk in the 1420s, made his fortune as a mercer in London, served as an alderman and become Lord Mayor in 1457–8. Fifteenth-century England, however, was a society open to wealth and talent. Had not William de la Pole, the most powerful man in England, been created duke of Suffolk in 1448, and his great-grandfather a merchant from Hull? It is no surprise, therefore, that Geoffrey Boleyn was able to secure as his second wife one of the daughters and joint heiresses of a nobleman, Thomas, Lord Hoo. William, the eldest surviving son of that marriage, made an equally good match with Margaret Butler, daughter and co-heiress of the wealthy Anglo-Irish earl of Ormonde, so that when their eldest son, Anne's father, married a daughter of the earl of Surrey he was continuing a tradition into the third generation. As a result – and this should finally dispel all smell of the shop – Anne's great-grandparents were (apart from Geoffrey) a duke, an earl, the granddaughter of an earl, the daughter of one baron, the daughter of another, and an esquire and his wife.[2] Anne Boleyn came, in fact, from the same sort of background as the majority of the Tudor upper class. Indeed, she was better born than Henry VIII's three other English wives. Marrying Anne did not, as has been unkindly said of Jane Seymour, give the king 'one brother-in-law who bore the name of Smith, and another whose grandfather was a blacksmith at Putney'.[3]

The Boleyns, thus, were not bourgeois, but Geoffrey's wealth had enabled his son William to establish himself as a leading Norfolk gentleman. Knighted in 1483, he became a Justice of the Peace and one of that elite of country gentlemen on whom the Crown relied in time of crisis.[4] By contrast, the position of his son and heir remained decidedly equivocal so long as Sir William lived. Thomas was the prospective successor to great wealth – the Boleyn and Hoo estates, half of the Ormonde fortune and half of the lands of the wealthy Hankford family, inherited from his Butler grandmother – but in the meantime he had to exist on an annuity of fifty pounds a year, the occupancy of Hever, and whatever his own wife had brought him.[5] That was probably not much, for the earl of Surrey had only just completed the expensive task of buying back the Howard lands he had lost after his ill-judged support for Richard III at the battle of Bosworth. With the fifty pounds and his wife's portion Thomas Boleyn was not penniless, but he had nowhere near the income to sustain his pretensions, or that high profile which was necessary if he was to achieve his full promise – even, perhaps, the revival of the Ormonde earldom in his favour. The Howard marriage and the influence of his Butler grandfather did, nevertheless, offer one immediate prospect: an entry to the traditional career of the ambitious English gentleman, royal service.[6] In 1501 Boleyn graced the marriage of Katherine of Aragon to the king's eldest son, Arthur, and in 1503 helped to escort the king's eldest daughter, Margaret, to her marriage with the king of Scotland.[7] By the time Henry VII died, in the spring of 1509, Anne Boleyn's father had risen at court to the important rank of 'squire of the body', and as he walked in the king's funeral procession, clad in his newly issued black livery, he could reflect that since his father had died in 1505 and the old earl of Ormonde was about 85, his private fortune now looked good also.[8]

Our appreciation of what it meant for Thomas Boleyn, and his daughter after him, to make a career at court is grievously impaired by our knowledge of later times, of Fanny Burney's boredom and the insipid routine of the Victorian palace. Until late in the last century, historians left court life to the writers of fiction and the imagination of Hollywood. Yet there was one great difference between later courts and those of Tudor times. The earlier court was concerned with real power, real decisions and real wealth. Though display was highly important, to be a courtier was to be at the sharp end of politics, power and profit. And since Anne Boleyn, no less than her father, was first and last a phenomenon of the court, we need to explore the milieu to which she belonged.

The starting-point is a commonplace. In the sixteenth century, power was exercised by the ruler in person, or by direct delegation. This was the reality in England and in the rest of Europe alike. Policy was what the prince laid down; advancement and honour were in his gift; his person personified the community. This is not to deny that all government was necessarily politically constrained – and in England also limited by formal structures such as parliament and the due process of law – but in practical day-to-day terms, government was a response to the will of one man. The ultimate demand on any subject was to be called to obey 'on your allegiance'.

The consequences that flowed from this 'personal monarchy' determined the shape of Anne Boleyn's life. In the first place, it meant that royal authority operated in terms of royal favour. There was no way in which men could challenge a policy when that policy was the king's will, other than themselves trying to gain the ear of the king so as to persuade him to will something different. This was precisely what Thomas More was unable to do when Henry VIII put pressure on the pope and the English Church in his effort to end his marriage to Katherine of Aragon. Open opposition would be treachery, but access to the king's mind and emotion was blocked by Anne Boleyn. Royal favour was just as vital in the exercise of power. The king gave executive authority to the men he trusted, and they acted so as to retain his trust. Thus Henry's interest in Anne had enormous implications for the government of the country at large. Favour was equally crucial in the matter of rewards. These were expressions of standing with the monarch, and it was thus of great significance when someone like Anne gained the influence which could ease her supporters into grants, offices and honours. A further consequence of personal monarchy was competition. The struggle for power was a struggle around the king's person, a battle for his favour; politics were thus court politics.

Decisions, likewise, were court decisions, and promotion and advance-ment were things achieved at court. The court made Anne Boleyn, and it would be the court which destroyed her.

To say that Thomas Boleyn and his children after him set out to be courtiers is, therefore, to say a great deal; they were taking the road to power, prestige and profit. Whether it was the road to honour is a different question, and most historians have felt that Anne's father personified all that was bad about the court. P. W. Sergeant's verdict that 'it is clearly hopeless to attempt a defence of Sir Thomas' may seem totally justified in the case of a man who, on his way to an earldom, slipped, or appears to have slipped, two daughters in succession into the king's bed.[9] Fried-mann's judgement, 'mean and grasping', is certainly correct.[10] In the autumn of 1536, when the Crown was desperately scraping up money to combat the northern rebels, Henry was delighted to be told that Cromwell had approached Boleyn for an excessive sum:

> his Grace, being very merry said there was a servant of King Edward's, his grandfather, which once made a suit unto him for 1000 oaks [so] that he might only obtain 20, and so he trusted your request to my lord of Wiltshire should purchase [bring in] £500 or such a matter by the reason it was so great, which being less would else percase [perchance] have wrought noth-ing with him.[11]

Equally warranted was the contemporary opinion that Thomas 'would sooner act from interest than from any other motive'.[12] When returning from an embassy in Spain in 1523 he brought with him an important messenger from Charles V, only to dump him when they reached London and leave the total stranger to find his own accommodation![13]

Courts and courtiers had, of course, existed since time immemorial, and in Western Europe a vigorous tradition of comment had long condemned the courtier as a self-seeking sycophant and the court as a living hell.[14] Not only did the deadly sins of sloth, gluttony and lust flourish there, but to succeed a courtier had to embrace the other four as well – pride, avarice, envy, anger – along with falsehood, flattery and servility. The wealth, power and prestige which success at court could bring attracted countless young men and women to attempt their fortunes there. But the price was their integrity, their morality, their health, their spiritual safety and their self-respect. A telling instance is provided by the love notes which passed between Henry VIII and Anne Boleyn during morning mass in the royal chapel. They wrote them in an illuminated Book of Hours, and there is something gross in the king's scrawl below the miniature of the blood-stained Man of Sorrows:

If you remember my love in your prayers as strongly as I adore you, I shall hardly be forgotten, for I am yours.

Henry R. forever.

Anne replied:

By daily proof you shall me find
To be to you both loving and kind.

And, with deliberate enticement, she chose to write this below a miniature of the Annunciation, the angel telling the Virgin Mary that she would have a son.[15]

On this view, then, the court was a Moloch that sucked in good people, body and soul, and spewed out a noisome plague of parasites – Anne among them – corrupting the community in the process. On the other hand, to the landed elite from which courtiers came, even menial duties could be intrinsically honourable. According to traditional chivalric values, still very much alive, what made service honourable was the rank of the person served. To take an extreme example, the most influential of Henry's courtiers was the man who occupied the post of 'groom of the stool' – by the time of the king's death he would be a knight and a member of the privy council – and his duty was to make provision for the king's natural functions and to attend the monarch when he relieved himself on the close stool, the royal commode.

Apologists could also stress that the courtier bore a great moral responsibility. Precisely because of the potential for corruption, it was imperative to surround a prince with good advice and men of honour. In 1536, in the northern uprising which followed the political upheavals which took Anne's life, one of her enemies, Sir Thomas Tempest, reminded the rebels of the lessons of history:

It is necessary that virtuous men that loveth the commonwealth should be of his council...such virtuous men as would regard the commonwealth above their prince's favour...In this noble realm, who[ever] reads the chronicles of Edward II [will see] what jeopardy he was in for Piers de Gaveston, [the] Spensers and such like counsellors and...Richard II was deposed for following the counsel of such like.[16]

Only the virtuous adviser could resist the potential of the court for corruption, and thereby help to make princely rule virtuous.

This line of thought appealed very much to the new, lay, intellectual fashion which we call Renaissance humanism. Since the ruler was the embodiment of the community, serving him presented the supreme opportunity to apply the moral philosophy which the humanist study of classical literature taught. As Thomas More wrote in *Utopia*, 'You, if you be disposed and can find in your heart to follow some prince's court, shall with your good counsels greatly help and further the commonwealth. Wherefore there is nothing more appertaining to your duty, that is to say to the duty of a good man.'[17] The personal qualities that humanist education inculcated were important too: effective speech, impressive appearance and manner, personal achievement and *sprezzatura*, that unique something which combined nonchalant ease with *savoir faire*; these were exactly what was needed to command attention and allow the courtier to achieve his aim 'to become the prince's instructor'. More's own entry into public service was not, as is sometimes suggested, a turning away from the ideals of humanism; it was their fulfilment.

Attitudes to the court and to courtiers were thus ambivalent. More himself was well aware that in the real world of the Renaissance court, compromise was the most that morality and honesty could hope to achieve.[18] His own career would show how difficult that was, but the dilemma was also explored at first hand in the poems of a courtier whose life was to be closely linked with that of Anne Boleyn, Sir Thomas Wyatt. Born about 1503, the son of a lifelong courtier, Thomas was at court in his early teens and, according to some stories, became Anne's lover in the 1520s. Thereafter, apart from several embassies abroad and a number of periods in the Tower or under house arrest, he spent the rest of his life in the royal household.[19] His satires are particularly revealing. Two are addressed to 'mine own John Poyntz', a minor courtier at one time in Anne's own service, and a third to Anne's cousin Francis Bryan, one of the most prominent men at court. In the first, possibly written in 1536 soon after his release from the Tower after being arrested as one of Anne's supporters, Wyatt bitterly attacks the dishonesty, the prostitution and the denial of integrity necessary for success at court and, in particular, the moral hypocrisy demanded of him:

> None of these points would ever frame in me –
> My wit is nought, I cannot learn the way.
> And much the less of things that greater be,

> That asken help of colours of device
> To join the mean with each extremity:
> With the nearest virtue to cloak alway the vice,
> And as to purpose likewise it shall fall
> To press the virtue that it may not rise,
> As drunkenness, good fellowship to call.[20]

However, Wyatt was also well aware of the attraction of the royal court:

> I grant sometime that of glory the fire
> Doth touch my heart; me list not to report
> Blame by honour, and honour to desire.[21]

His third satire is warm in its approval of Bryan's rejection of the lure of private self-indulgence:

> Likest thou not this? 'No.' 'Why?' 'For swine so groins.
> In sty and chaw the turds moulded on the ground,
> And drivel on pearls, the head still in the manger,
> [As] of the harp the ass to hear the sound.
> So sacks of dirt be filled up in the cloister
> That serves for less than do these fatted swine.
> Though I seem lean and dry, without moisture,
> Yet will I serve my prince, my lord and thine,
> And let them live to feed the paunch that list,
> So I may feed to live both me and mine.'
> By God, well said![22]

Wyatt, however, sees no escape from the courtier's dilemma, in this case, how to afford to give this devoted service. Buy friends, maintain virtue only as a front, batten on the rich and elderly, marry for money and take your pleasure on the side; if a female relative is attractive, then sell her for a good price to 'thy better', and never let friendship get in the way of advantage – this is the only recipe.[23] It was one that Wyatt, Thomas Boleyn, his daughters, indeed every courtier at some time had to follow. Yet despite his disgust, back to court Wyatt came, again and again, and it was on the way to meet the imperial ambassador and escort him to the king that he caught pneumonia and died at Sherborne in Dorset. We would describe Wyatt as a poet, but the Sherborne parish register calls him *regis consiliarius*, 'counsellor to the king'.[24]

There is no evidence that Anne's father shared Wyatt's qualms of conscience or that Anne, who did, acquired them in the Boleyn household.

Yet even if Thomas Boleyn typifies the self-seeking courtier, he did have many of the qualities a ruler looked for. He was a man of some education, far and away the best speaker of French in the Tudor court, with Latin as well, and cultured enough to commission several items from Erasmus.[25] He was, as we shall see, careful to ensure that Anne had the best available education, and he was obviously also responsible for the education of her brother, George – possibly a product of Oxford and later a recognized court poet.[26] Thomas Boleyn was also adept at courtly entertainments, notably the tournament. He fought with the king himself at Greenwich in May 1510, and nine months later he was one of the 'answerers' at the great Westminster challenge of February 1511.[27] A tournament was very much more than an occasion for martial combat. By combining display, drama and symbolism, it could approach a major art form.[28] Thus on the second day of the 1511 tilt the leading answerer, Charles Brandon, entered the lists in dead silence, concealed beneath a moving tower; when the door was unlocked, he rode out in the costume of an old, bearded pilgrim, only to cast off this disguise and appear in polished armour once the queen, in whose honour the festivity was being held, had consented to his taking part.[29] Anne's father was third into the tiltyard, alongside the marquess of Dorset, and together they continued the theme:

> like two pilgrims from St. James [of Compostella], in tabards of black velvet, with palmers' hats on their helmets, with long Jacob's staves [pilgrim staffs] in their hands, their horse trappers of black velvet, their tabards, hats and trappers set with scallop shells [pilgrims' badges] of fine gold . . . their servants all in black satin, with scallop shells of gold in their breasts.[30]

There were also indoor festivities, and at Christmas 1514 Boleyn was joined by his son in a season which included a fancy-dress dance and an indoor mêlée.[31]

This experience and skill, and his knowledge of other things courtly – horses, hawks, bowls, shovelboard – allowed Boleyn to pass anywhere and gave him the final accolade of the humanist courtier, usefulness to his prince. A man of intelligence, gifts and capacity, with a loyalty only to himself (and so to the king) and a willingness to take on a heavy workload, was a courtier worth having. For example, in the period 1519–23 Thomas Boleyn was successively Henry VIII's ambassador to the court of France, in attendance at both the Field of Cloth of Gold and the subsequent meeting with the emperor Charles V at Gravelines, a participant in the

Calais conference of 1521 (which also involved a short mission to the emperor) and finally ambassador to Spain. He clearly had the flair for diplomacy as well as the languages; Henry was to say in 1530 that there was no skilled negotiator to equal him.[32] There is a revealing scene of Boleyn at Brussels on his first embassy in 1512, shaking hands with Margaret of Austria, regent of the Netherlands, on a bet that progress in their negotiations would be achieved in ten days – her Spanish courser against his hobby.[33] One admires, too, his ability to handle Henry, the ease with which he slipped into one diplomatic report in October 1513 the remark that negotiating with Maximilian I was like tilting with a man whose horse was out of control: 'it will be long or they join well together' – just the pleasing, intimate metaphor to attract a king never fond of long epistles.[34]

Back in England, Boleyn was active on the king's council, that group of up to perhaps seventy individuals of varying importance and often fluctuating roles, which was the nearest England then had to what might later be called 'the government'. He was, indeed, one of its most active members, whether policy and administration or judicial (star chamber) business were on the agenda.[35] And there were courtly chores too, such as a six-week assignment in 1517 looking after the king's sister, Margaret, during her visit from Scotland.[36] All this brought rewards – rank (knighthood in 1509), office, wardships, some grants of land – but rewards earned the hard way. Royal favour for the really ambitious did not come cheap.

Thomas Boleyn was not the only courtier on whom the young sun of Henry VIII's bounty shone, although all were eclipsed by Charles Brandon, who succeeded in marrying the king's younger sister Mary and founding the dukedom of Suffolk. Opportunities at court were indeed particularly good at this time. In the troubles of the mid-fifteenth century, royal service in England had lost some of its kudos, but the establishment of Edward IV in 1471 as the unchallenged king ushered in a period when first the Yorkists and then the Tudors used the royal court to draw together the upper classes in support of the throne.

Political exploitation of the court was, of course, hardly revolutionary, and the model for all this was the court of the duke of Burgundy, the ruler of what is today the Netherlands, Belgium and Luxemburg, plus sizeable parts of northern France. There, in a deliberate attempt to unite these anything but coherent territories, the duke's household consciously cultivated magnificence in order to command prestige internationally as well as locally, and enrolled the arts in the service of the state. Edward IV (whose sister married the duke of Burgundy) set out to rival his brother-in-law, with results which can be seen today in the architecture of St George's Chapel, Windsor, in the pages of the earliest books in the English royal library and in the reinvigoration of the Order of the Garter. Edward's son-in-law, Henry VII, deliberately modelled his court on that of Burgundy, and his grandson did likewise.[37]

All this meant an increasing demand for able courtiers and a special premium on those with European sophistication, something which, as we shall see, lies at the heart of Anne Boleyn's success. The need for a new breed of courtier was also increased by more sober organizational changes in the English court, which created a distinctive pattern of court life for Henry VIII and his wives. For many generations kings (and great lords) had occupied that part of the 'household above stairs' known as the chamber, far away from the hustle of the kitchens and the rest of domestic life 'below stairs'. However, in the fifteenth century, the king began to desire greater privacy and to realize that the more private a monarch, the more impressive are his appearances. The result was that the chamber became divided into three parts: the privy chamber, which was a suite strictly private to the king; the presence chamber, which was open to courtiers except when the king was holding audience there; and the great or watching chamber, which was regularly accessible to all entitled to attend the household above stairs.[38]

These changes would be of only technical interest were it not for the personnel changes which followed in their wake. First, a new and exclusive group of servants was established to serve in the new privy chamber; second, because Henry VIII wanted 'pastime with good company' as well as service, such posts began to be filled by men who were first and foremost his cronies. Some years were to pass before arrangements reached their final form, but by 1518 or 1519 we can see a small establishment of such men occupying posts as either 'gentlemen' or 'grooms of the privy chamber'. In addition the king would, from time to time, invite into the privy chamber anyone who took his fancy and with whom he wished to pass the time. Such men might not have the pay of the official staff or their automatic right of access, but they were part of the privy chamber circle, and everything depended, for them as for the salaried staff, on the impression that they could make on the king. Never had a group of young men been in such a position of potential advantage since the late fourteenth century and the hated minions of Richard II. And never since that day had there been men in such a position of potential power, especially given the highly persuadable man that Henry VIII was. They gave Cardinal Wolsey nightmares – his famous Eltham Ordinance which tried (in vain) to set privy chamber numbers at fifteen was only one of a series of attempts to keep the privy chamber circle at bay – and we shall see how strife within the privy chamber circle helped to destroy Anne Boleyn in May 1536.[39]

Thomas Boleyn was deeply involved in all this. He was close to the king in the early years of the reign as one of the aristocratic group which sympathized with the ambitions of the young, warlike Henry VIII against the more sober counsels of his father's churchmen and bureaucrats. All the while, however, the brilliant new administrator, Thomas Wolsey, was advancing in royal favour, and in 1515 and 1516 he came to grips with the courtiers. One of his targets was Thomas Boleyn, whom he was certainly trying to taint with disloyalty early in 1515, although nothing came of the insinuation.[40] Indeed, for much of that year Wolsey (now a cardinal) was very much on the defensive as the champion of the clergy, who were being heavily attacked following the notorious death in church custody of a London merchant, Richard Hunne. One indication of the minister's preoccupation was that about this time Thomas Boleyn secured from the king a promise of the succession to the highly prized post of controller of the royal household whenever the existing occupant, Sir Edward Ponynges, was promoted to the senior post of treasurer.[41] Not until the autumn of 1516 did the cardinal finally triumph, or seem to triumph, though at the cost of the support of 'well nigh all' the magnates; 'the cardinal of York' was, so Sebastian Giustinian said, 'the beginning, middle and end'.[42]

'Seemed to triumph' is an important qualification, for the courtiers, defeated this time in the struggle to monopolize the king, still occupied the citadel of royal favour, the privy chamber, and continued to secure favours from the king under Wolsey's disapproving nose. When the privy chamber staff was finally organized, Boleyn had become neither a gentleman nor a groom (these posts went to somewhat younger men), but he remained in the privy chamber circle and his son George became the king's page.[43] It was probably Wolsey's suspicion of this closeness to the king, as much as Boleyn's experience in diplomacy, which brought Sir Thomas the posting to Paris in January 1519, and within weeks he was showing anxiety about the promised controllership.[44] His fears were well grounded, for in the second week in May, Wolsey wrote to say that although Ponynges would move up to the post of treasurer of the household after the 29th, Boleyn would not get the succession this time; instead, he would succeed Ponynges in due course. Boleyn's reply was an abject plea for Wolsey's support; if the minister would favour him, neither he nor the king would regret it.[45] A week later, the French king, Francis I, broke even more alarming news to him – Henry had expelled eight or nine of the privy chamber circle.[46] Pastime in the privy chamber between the king and his younger minions had been pretty free, and Wolsey had seen his chance. Henry was told that his 'minions were so familiar and homely with him, and played such light touches with him that they forgot themselves'. He reacted on cue to this slur on his dignity, and dispersed the young men to posts remote from court.[47]

Wolsey left Boleyn to sweat for four months before sending a message by word of mouth setting out his intentions about the controllership, confirming that Sir Thomas would not get it, but would become treasurer in due course. Boleyn took the hint and wrote to say that he accepted the cardinal's decision and wholly resigned his claim to the controllership to the discretion of the king and Wolsey.[48] With his abject submission thus on file and a clear recognition that while the king might promise it was Wolsey who performed – and could refuse to perform – Boleyn got the controllership after all.[49] He held it for only a short time, for Ponynges died in the autumn of 1521, whereupon he succeeded as treasurer.[50] The lesson in the political facts of life remained with Thomas Boleyn for the rest of the decade; only when his daughter was there to shield him would he be prepared to challenge Wolsey again.

Such was the heated, some might say foetid atmosphere of the court world into which Anne Boleyn was born, and such was her father. Her mother also was at court, in Katherine of Aragon's entourage, though we know less of her activities.[51] Also at court before 1520 was Anne's sister Mary, who in February of that year married William Carey of the privy chamber, with the king himself as the principal guest.[52] Her brother George had, as we have seen, played in a mummery at Christmas 1514–15 and gone on to become the royal page, but there were still some years to go before he would matter much at court.

Anne, Mary and George were the only children of Thomas Boleyn to survive to maturity, and there has been a long-running historical dispute about the date of Anne's birth and the relative ages of her brother and sister. Evidence from the later sixteenth century and the earlier seventeenth gave modern scholars the choice of a birth date for Anne of either *circa* 1501 or *circa* 1507.[53] An early letter which Anne wrote to her father would have settled the matter, but it could not be dated.[54] In 1981, however, the art historian Hugh Paget successfully demonstrated that the letter was written in 1513 when Anne Boleyn left England to become a maid of honour in the court at Brussels, a position which was open to a

12- or 13-year-old.[55] His conclusion has been challenged but is established beyond question because Anne's letter is self-evidently in the formed hand of at least a teenager (plate 14).[56] The correct date for Anne's birth is therefore *circa* 1501. This means that she was significantly older than is usually imagined. The domestic triangle which developed in 1527 was between a 36-year-old king, a wife over 40 and a mature woman of 26, not a girl of 19 or 20. Similarly, in the spring of 1536 Anne was not rejected by Henry when she was, as Catholic tradition has it, less than 29, but as a possibly ageing 35, while her supplanter, Jane Seymour, was, at 27, marginally older than Anne had been when challenging Katherine for the first time.[57] The gossip that credited Henry with a taste for younger women was evidently ill informed.[58]

Dating the birth of Anne Boleyn to 1500–1 resolved one long-running dispute, but it did not tell us about her relationship with her siblings. Here the evidence is slight, and as far as George is concerned, contradictory. His appearance in court as a juvenile and the fact that he secured his first royal grant only in 1524 would suggest that he was the youngest of the three.[59] However, a poem by Cavendish (who had certainly known him) has George saying that he had obtained a place in the privy chamber 'or years thrice nine my life had past away', and Boleyn was retired from his place there by the Eltham Ordinance of January 1526.[60] Indeed, that is only an end date, and if Cavendish is referring to George's arrival as the king's page, it could have been several years earlier. Yet even for George Boleyn to have been in his twenty-seventh year by 1526, he would have to have been born by 1499 and thus would be older than Anne.

How reliable Cavendish is on this is, however, another question. He was writing thirty years after the event, and since the dictates of the verse made the next lowest number 'years thrice eight', he may have been trying to say no more than 'about twenty-five', thus indicating a birth-date of about 1500.[61] On the other hand, after losing his post in 1525, George was restored to a full adult place in the privy chamber by the end of 1529, and it could be this that Cavendish had in mind.[62] In that case, 'or thrice nine' would, taken strictly, indicate a date of 1503–4, while 'about twenty-five' would give 1504–5. What perhaps should clinch the acceptance of this last is a remark by Jean du Bellay in 1529, suggesting that he thought George too young to be sent as ambassador to France.[63]

Mary Boleyn played much less of a part in Anne's life than did their brother. Her one claim to fame is that, for a time in the 1510s or early 1520s, she was Henry VIII's mistress. Of this there can be no doubt, despite efforts to prove the contrary. It was most tellingly demonstrated when the king himself was taxed with having slept with both Anne's sister and her mother and made the naïvely revealing reply: 'Never with the mother.'[64] The rumour of a relationship between Henry and Thomas Boleyn's wife did circulate widely, but nothing can be discovered to upset the king's denial; most probably there was some confusion of Elizabeth Boleyn with Elizabeth Blount, Henry's known mistress.[65] Later Catholic controversialists transmuted the mistake into the claim that Anne Boleyn was Henry VIII's daughter! To achieve such a feat Henry would have had to have been astute enough to escape his father's well-attested protectiveness, as well as somewhat precocious – in 1501 he was 10 years old.[66]

For Mary Boleyn there is, again, no known date of birth, but in 1597 her grandson, Lord Hunsdon, petitioned for the Boleyn earldom of Ormonde on the ground that she had been the elder sister.[67] Some historians have argued that he was mistaken, but this is totally implausible.[68] Although daughters did not normally inherit peerages, the eldest could hope that, where a title became extinct in the male line, it would be revived for her husband and their children. Thus, if Anne really was senior to Mary, any claim to the earldom belonged to her daughter, Queen Elizabeth, not her sister's son. On such a delicate matter Hunsdon must have been doubly sure of his ground.[69] Of course, if Mary Boleyn's liaison with the king could be firmly dated, this might put the issue of her priority beyond challenge. Unfortunately the first contemporary indication that Henry had slept with one of Anne's close relatives (unnamed) comes in a missive to the pope in 1527.[70] For the liaison to have begun before her marriage to William Carey in February 1520, Mary must certainly have been the elder sister, since by 1518 and possibly earlier, Henry's mistress was Elizabeth Blount. In 1519 she bore him a son, Henry Fitzroy, later duke of Richmond.[71] Moreover, for what it is worth, Mary is said to have had the reputation of 'a great wanton and notoriously infamous' when she was in France in 1514.[72] The alternative possibility – but one that says nothing about Mary's place in the Boleyn offspring – is that her affair with Henry postdated the marriage to William Carey and that she succeeded Elizabeth Blount after the latter's marriage to Gilbert, later Lord Tailbois.[73] This is the more likely. Mary used her influence to get Thomas Gardiner appointed to Tynmouth Priory not earlier than 1520 and her husband was the beneficiary of a spate of royal grants in 1522, 1523, 1524 and 1525.[74] It may also be relevant to note the long delay before she became pregnant, something which might be expected of a period when she was taken up with a man of such known low fertility as Henry VIII.

Perhaps the king had realized that it was safer to risk begetting children whose paternity could be denied than bastards who only emphasized his lack of legitimate heirs. Once Mary had begun to cohabit with William Carey, her two children came in quick succession.[75]

Whatever the date of Mary's liaison with Henry VIII, other indications confirm that Hunsdon was right in claiming that she was older than Anne. After the daughters had gone to France in 1514–15, it was Anne who remained for further training and Mary who was brought back and launched at the English court, a most curious choice if Anne were not the junior. Then there was the decision to leave Anne to make her career in France; clearly there was no place for her in Boleyn family plans. Furthermore, Anne's failure to marry while in France suggests that she was not much of a prize. Nor was a marriage for Anne discussed in England until nearly two years after Mary was Mistress Carey.[76] Here, perhaps, we can call in Sir Thomas Boleyn's own reflections in a letter to Thomas Cromwell in the summer of 1536, when his world had crashed around him, with George and Anne both dead, and most of the gains he had striven for threatened by the loss of royal favour. His early years, he recalled, had been financially straitened, not only because of the fifty pounds a year, but because his wife brought him 'every year a child'.[77] The date of his marriage is unknown, but Elizabeth Howard's jointure was settled on her in the summer of 1501, which suggests that it was relatively recent – say not before 1498.[78] If, then, we take Boleyn's memory literally, we may suppose a child in 1499, another in 1500, a third in 1501 and so on, although two children at least died before reaching adulthood.[79] Were Mary to be the eldest and born about 1499, this would make her 15-plus when going to France in 1514 and 20-plus at marriage, with an affair with the king in her late teens or, more probably, early twenties. Anne would fit in at 1500–1, firmly dated by her journey abroad in 1513; then George at about 1504, so entering the privy chamber as an adult in 1529 at about the age of 25. There are more assumptions in this than is good for any hypothesis, but it does satisfy the evidence.

Thus Anne Boleyn followed her sister into her teens and into the second decade of the sixteenth century, and in 1513 she went abroad. It was a journey that would shape her life. Ever afterwards she would stand out from the women of the English court whom she was leaving, and always would leave, far behind.

A European Education

I T was a long journey, the longest she would ever make. Through the hills of north Kent and its ancient towns, down to the sea at Dover and across the Channel. Like countless other girls of her age who would make a similar journey in later years, Anne Boleyn was going abroad to 'be finished'. We have no way of knowing what she made of the Flemish nobleman who was her escort, Claude Bouton, seigneur de Courbaron. Nor can we know what the young Anne made of the sea or of the crossing which could take anything from two or three hours to a day or more. But eventually she stepped ashore on the continent for the first time. It was 1513, and she would stay there for almost nine years.

Her destination was the Habsburg court at Mechelen in Brabant. From there Margaret of Austria ruled the Low Countries as regent for a 13-year-old nephew, Charles of Burgundy, and Anne was to join her court as one of the archduchess's maids of honour. Thomas Boleyn's decision to send his younger daughter to Margaret was clearly prompted by Anne's evident potential and her appropriate age, but even more by the opportunities which acceptance at Europe's premier finishing school would open up. True, the brilliance of the Burgundian ducal entourage was approaching its end. Through a series of vicissitudes, Burgundy was being drawn into a larger unit which would eventually bring Austria, the Holy Roman Empire, Spain, Italy and the Americas under the Archduke Charles, by his better-known name of Charles V. Yet for the moment the regent had gathered around Charles and his younger sisters a court which was still the Mecca of aristocratic and princely behaviour. Also visiting from England in 1513 was William Sidney, one of Henry VIII's favourites, while another, Edward Guildford, would arrive as late as 1518, intent on learning what the king described as 'the right way of doing things'.[1]

The opportunity for training was there because Margaret of Austria was not bringing up her Habsburg nephew and nieces in isolation. The elite of

Europe vied to place their offspring as attendants on her and her charges in the knowledge that they would effectively be educated alongside Europe's rulers of the next generation. Nowhere could a father find a better start for a future courtier. And Thomas Boleyn had something even more specific than this in mind. Henry VIII's wife, Katherine of Aragon, was sister-in-law to the regent; indeed, Margaret had taught her the French which the queen of England relied on to eke out her scanty English. If his daughter Anne could learn continental manners and good French, there was a future for her at Katherine's side, easing the way of the queen through the polite world of northern Europe, where French was the language *de rigueur*.[2] And, of course, she would be expected from time to time to put in a good word for the rest of the Boleyn family.

What gave Thomas Boleyn the chance to place Anne so advantageously was his first diplomatic posting in 1512, which was to the court of the Archduchess Margaret. As we have seen, he got on well with the regent, who agreed to take Anne as one of her eighteen *filles d'honneur*. Thus when Boleyn returned to England in the early summer of 1513 he immediately sent Anne to Margaret.[3] The regent's first impressions were good, and she wrote back to Sir Thomas:

> I have received your letter by the Esquire [Claude] Bouton who has presented your daughter to me, who is very welcome, and I am confident of being able to deal with her in a way which will give you satisfaction, so that on your return the two of us will need no intermediary other than she. I find her so bright and pleasant for her young age that I am more beholden to you for sending her to me than you are to me.[4]

Margaret was as good as her word. Anne was put to study under a tutor, one of the ducal household named Symonnet, and her first independent letter in French to her father (previous ones having been dictated by the tutor) survives in the library of Corpus Christi College, Cambridge (plate 14). Written from Margaret's summer residence at La Vure, now Terveuren, near Brussels, the letter shows that, despite the charm that had won over the duchess, Anne had no illusions as to why she was there:

> Sir, I understand from your letter that you desire me to be a woman of good reputation [*toufs onette fame*] when I come to court, and you tell me that the queen will take the trouble to converse with me, and it gives me great joy to think of talking with such a wise and virtuous person. This will make me all the keener to persevere in speaking French well, and also especially because you have told me to, and have advised me for my own part to work at it as much as I can.[5]

Unfortunately, no intelligible English translation can give the flavour of the phonetic and idiosyncratic original; Anne did certainly need to work at her written French!

Second to learning the language was the opportunity to master the sophistication of polite society. A *fille* or *demoiselle d'honneur* had no specific duties, but was under the direction of *la dame d'honneur*, the head of the female establishment. She was expected to play her part as an attendant on the duchess and to share in the intimate society of the court, to make herself useful and perform tasks on request, and to join in the serious business of court entertainment. Without the women, a court was reckoned a poor place indeed.[6] There was, as we shall see, far more to entertainment than previous generations of historians have realized; confidence in the work ethic has obscured the fact that once leisure is plentiful, managing it becomes a serious business. The elaborate dances, hunts, tournaments and festivities which fill so many pages in contemporary accounts were not peripheral elements in a Renaissance court; they belonged to the core of princely rule – and of the success of a prince's courtiers. Anne Boleyn's later achievements owed a very great deal to what she was now beginning to learn with Margaret of Austria.

The essential courtly skill was dance. All the courts of Europe danced, and being there to take part was a principal obligation on Anne and the other maids of honour. The Mechelen books of dance music are well thumbed. The staple was the bass dance, a form of couple dance which was common to aristocratic circles throughout Western Europe, so called because 'to dance it, one moves tranquilly, without agitation, in the most gracious fashion one is capable of.'[7] Dancing was also integral to the indoor pageants and formal entertainments in which the Burgundian ducal court set the fashion for the rest of polite Europe. These were a composite art form, involving drama as well as music and dance, and organized on a single theme, very often a debate between men and women, or an assault by the one on a castle garrisoned by the other. The language was the language of courtly love and the renewed chivalric fashions of the late Middle Ages – imprisoned maidens, noble knights, exotic foreigners, wild men, vices personified, mythical beasts, mountains that moved, ships in full sail, castles making music – all the conceits of the *Roman de la Rose* and more.

Such courtly disguisings were not unknown on this side of the Channel, but they had usually been extremely simple affairs. The first in anything like the fashionable continental style would appear to have been celebrated for the marriage of Prince Arthur and Katherine of Aragon in

November 1501, and the second, only weeks before Henry VII's death, to mark the betrothal of his younger daughter Mary to Charles of Burgundy. And although Henry VIII began to celebrate disguisings almost every year, by the time Anne went abroad the full elaboration of this Burgundian court form had still only been seen in England on seven or eight occasions in all.[8] In the Low Countries the tradition went back seventy or eighty years, and Margaret of Austria was an expert at it. When she had travelled in 1500 to meet her second husband, the duke of Savoy, one display prepared for her had been an assault by Venus and Cupid on the Castle of Love; in 1504, at the marriage of one Savoyard noble, she herself had appeared in the role of Queen of the Amazons, naked sword in hand, a silver cuirass studded with jewels, and a crimson head-dress topped by a great plume.[9] Anne Boleyn could have had no better mentor.

The Regent Margaret was a meticulous chaperone. Deportment and conversation had to be correct at all times, and Madame, as Margaret was called, kept a specially strict eye on the maids of honour, forbidding gossip and any by-play with the pages or gentlemen of the court. Adept as she was herself at the game of courtly love, in her household it was to be played according to the conventions. It was an attitude Anne was to imitate when she had maids of honour of her own. As Margaret wrote:

> Trust in those who offer you service,
> And in the end, my maidens,
> You will find yourselves in the ranks of those
> Who have been deceived.
> They, for their sweet speeches, choose
> Words softer than the softest of virgins;
> Trust in them?
> In their hearts they nurture
> Much cunning in order to deceive,
> And once they have their way thus,
> Everything is forgotten.
> Trust in them?[10]

Protection lay in a quick wit and a ready confidence:

> Fine words are the coin to pay back
> Those presumptuous minions
> Who ape the lover

> By fine looks and such like.
> Not for a moment but instantly
> Give to them their pay –
> Fine words!
> Word for word, that is justice,
> One for one, two for two.
> They are gracious so to converse,
> Respond yourself graciously –
> With fine words![11]

It was a lesson that Anne Boleyn learned quickly and never forgot. It carried her to the heights of courtly success only to betray her in the end, when faced by men to whom the measured conventions of Margaret of Austria meant nothing.

As well as French and the ways of the courtly world, the court of Margaret of Austria offered Anne Boleyn experience of a culture of which she could previously have perceived only pale reflections. Much though her countrymen might brag of their achievements, England was a cultural colony. Its principal debt was to Burgundy, and particularly Flanders – and for far more than the courtly expertise that she had come to absorb. For a century Flanders in particular and the lands adjacent had been the cultural heart of Europe north of the Alps. The prosperity of its cities had supported an artistic establishment which was the equal of anything in Italy. The market was threefold. First, the cities themselves: this was the era of the great cathedrals and civic buildings of the Low Countries, buildings that called for adornment. Next, as we have seen, there was the magnificent society of the duke and his court, which exploited art for princely prestige and married culture with chivalry as the *beau idéal* of every gentleman. Finally, there was the international market for painting, illumination, books and, of course, music. When Henry VIII of England turned his hand to musical arrangement, it was the Low Countries that provided his material.

In comparison with the influence of the Low Countries, the direct impact of Italy upon early Tudor England was slight. The only influence which may to any degree have challenged Burgundy was that of France. This was often the closest Englishmen got to the new ideas of the Renaissance – second-hand from France if not third-hand from the Low Countries – and there was always the allure of Paris, its style and manners. The charge against Henry VIII's minions in 1519 of undue familiarity was the more credible because they had been in France recently (and two more actually lodging at the time with Thomas Boleyn in Paris fled back to London to demonstrate that they were at heart true Englishmen).[12] But in fact the contrast between Flanders and France is easily overstated. The two were parts of one cultural entity which some critics have labelled Franco-Flemish, and the doyen of that culture was Margaret of Austria.

At the age of 3 she had been sent to France, where for ten years she was brought up as the intended bride of the future Charles VIII. There French masters taught her to paint and draw, to sing and play the lute, to dance in the style of the French court and to appreciate the music of the royal chapel there. She learned to write French verse of considerable fluency, and French books would dominate her reading throughout life. Yet when she was jilted by Charles and returned to the Low Countries, there was no break in her education. The organist of the Burgundian ducal chapel now took over as music master; it was the art collections and illuminated manuscripts of her grandmother, Margaret of York, which now fed her taste. But it was essentially the same culture that she had always known, a contrast in no more than fashion or mood. Later experience would take her to Spain and then Savoy before she returned to Mechelen, but nothing disturbed the Franco-Flemish heart of her experience.[13] This was the woman who taught Anne Boleyn.

Anne's base in the Low Countries was Margaret's palace at Mechelen. The northern range, built in stone in Renaissance fashion, was begun only after Anne had left, but the southern face, despite its nineteenth-century ill-treatment, is still much as she would have known it in 1513. Built, like all the older parts of the palace, of patterned local brick, with the occasional line of stone and a prominent string course along much of its length, it hardly seems unusual – Hampton Court near London springs at once to mind. Yet in 1513 the style was strikingly novel to the English visitor. It was less than twenty years since Henry VII had imported it for the first time for his new palace at Richmond.[14] And Anne's own palace, Whitehall, would be begun in the same style. To stand in the courtyard at Mechelen and face the southern range (plate 13) – an open arcade at ground level, now enclosed by flattened arches supported on a row of columns, the bricks laid to form a diamond pattern, rectangular windows with mullions and transoms over the prominent string course, with quoins of stone at all the angles, and dormer windows above a brick parapet making a third storey into the steep-pitched slate roof – this is to see much what Anne saw, a palace which would be recreated for her beside the Thames twenty years later.

The inventories of the household of Margaret of Austria give a vivid idea of the court the young English girl had joined. The palace was resplendent with lavish fabrics of every kind. Even though the widowed duchess now regularly wore black, the material of her clothes was always of the finest; appearances mattered. Particularly striking were the tapestries on the palace walls. Anne may well have seen some of the treasures from the looms of the Low Countries that Henry VII had painfully assembled in England. Now she could assess their real worth as she watched the court *tapissier*, Pierre van Aelst, who had produced a series in praise of the Tudor dynasty for the marriage between Arthur, prince of Wales, and Katherine of Aragon, turning his hand to five genealogical designs ordered by the Archduchess Margaret as a present for her father.[15]

We know that in later life Anne was excited by fabric and colour. She would also become the patron of Hans Holbein the younger, and this too may have owed something both to Margaret, who was passionate about painting, and to a first-hand experience of her collection which included works by masters such as Hieronymus Bosch and Jan van Eyck.[16] Anne may even have seen *The Arnolfini Marriage*.[17] In manuscript illumination, the second branch of Franco-Flemish high art, 'the Court of Savoy', as it was called, gave Anne a taste that lasted for the rest of her life. The older masterpieces there included the *Très Riches Heures du Duc de Berry*, as well as many associated with Margaret of York. There were also brilliant examples of a new style in Flemish illumination of which the Bening family from Bruges were the greatest exponents. Instead of surrounding a page of text with a patterned border, the Bening style unified the whole page, often by directing the viewer's eyes through an almost tangible frame. Thus on one folio of a Book of Hours, over a window-sill littered with the paraphernalia of courtly life – illuminated manuscript, cloth-of-gold cushion, ring, necklaces, pomander, trinket box – we watch Christ being nailed to the cross, surrounded by a crowd, half curious, half hostile.[18] When, years later, Anne exchanged love notes with Henry in a Book of Hours, it would be one in this same 'flower-scattered style'.[19] (plate 18).

Anne Boleyn would have known Margaret's collection of illuminated manuscripts almost more as *objets d'art* than as books, but one category which received considerable use was music books. Those that Margaret owned included masses, motets and chansons by composers who determined at least half of Anne's later taste. One of the duchess's favourites was Pierre de la Rue, whose lifetime in Habsburg service had culminated in his becoming her court composer. Two others were from her brief time as duchess of Savoy – Antoine Brumel and Pierrequin de Therache. The most popular composer of all was Josquin des Prés, despite the fact that it now seems certain that he was never lured back from Paris to his native

Picardy and, indeed, that he had no direct contact with the regent's court at all.

All these composers, and others, Anne certainly listened to in later years. The evidence for this is a manuscript in the library of the Royal College of Music in London.[20] It carries on page 157 the words, 'M^res A. Bolleyne', and underneath her father's motto, 'nowe thus', followed by three short and one long note of music – ♦♦♦♭.[21] Precisely what this signifies will concern us later, but the connection of the manuscript with Anne Boleyn is clear. And of the thirty items so far identified in it, half are by the favourite composers heard at Margaret's court. The line of influence seems plain. One must assume, too, that this taste was shown in Anne's own music-making, for somewhere in her education she was able to develop considerable musical skill; this is evidenced in a number of sources and may well have been an interest in common with Henry VIII, who prided himself on his own musical abilities. The Archduchess Margaret would again have been the example, for she was famous for her music, especially as a keyboard performer. Her organist, Henri Bredemers, was also well known – he had visited England in 1506 – and he taught music to Charles and his sisters. We do not know for sure that he took other pupils, but it seems reasonable to assume that he did teach Anne.

As well as absorbing the best education Europe could offer, Anne learned by observation, and learned quickly. People's memories of Anne as she was after some months at Mechelen were still vivid twenty years later – intelligent, self-possessed, wide awake, rapidly coming to grips with the French language and with the sophistication of European courts: 'la Boullant, who at an early age had come to court, listened carefully to honourable ladies, setting herself to bend all her endeavour to imitate them to perfection, and made such good use of her wits that in no time at all she had command of the language.'[22] Among those she could watch were the leaders of Europe who would so affect her later career. There was, for instance, the future Charles V. Whether he noticed the young English maid of honour is to be doubted, but she, undoubtedly, was familiar with the slight, reserved prince whose characteristic lift of the head accentuated the heavy Habsburg jaw and the open gaze of one born to command. It was probably also during her stay with Margaret of Austria that Anne was first able to observe her future husband, the far more impressive Henry VIII. Not only did Henry's 23 years make the 14-year-old Charles seem a mere youth, but the slim six-foot two-inch extrovert, who combined athletic prowess with intelligence, education, considerable musical skill and boundless energy, was hard for anyone to match.

Henry was in Europe to press a joint Anglo-imperial attack on France, which had been the prize of the negotiations between the Archduchess Margaret and Thomas Boleyn. The war had opened successfully soon after Anne's journey to the Low Countries, and on 23 August the English captured Thérouanne, south of St Omer, after defeating a French relief force in a scrambling cavalry skirmish which became dignified by the title 'the Battle of the Spurs'. Henry then marched in company with Margaret's father, the Emperor Maximilian (characteristically, at Henry's expense), to the Burgundian town of Lille, where the regent met him with her court in attendance. After three days of junketing, during which Henry made great show of his musical talents, the army moved off to besiege Tournai, which surrendered on 23 September. Maximilian sent for Margaret again to join the victors, and despite her complaint that it was not done for widows to trot about visiting armies, she came and brought her ladies with her.[23]

Even without the determination of the Habsburgs to make the greatest possible show, Anne would have been an obvious person to summon to Lille and Tournai, for her father was with the English army and French speakers were at a premium.[24] This fact comes out clearly in the story of the great scandal of the encounter, the flirtation between Margaret of Austria and Henry VIII's boon companion, Charles Brandon. The two of them played the game of courtly love with an enthusiasm which made up for the inability of either to speak the other's language, and eventually Henry egged Brandon on to propose to the duchess, which he did one evening, taking as a pledge one of the rings from her fingers. Margaret responded by calling him *un larron* (a thief), but he got the point only when one of the ladies in waiting offered the Flemish equivalent, *ein dief.* To finish the story, Brandon refused to return the ring and made such a fuss of his conquest that Margaret had to redeem the ring with another and issue vigorous denials of any agreement to marry.[25]

The probability that Anne Boleyn had been useful at the Lille and Tournai meetings is reinforced by what happened in the summer of the following year. On 14 August, Sir Thomas Boleyn wrote to the Archduchess Margaret from the court at Greenwich to ask her to release Anne and to return her in the care of the escort he had sent. The reason for this sudden withdrawal, which to judge from his letter caused Sir Thomas acute embarrassment – as well it might – was a sudden turn-about by Henry, who had abandoned the marriage between his 18-year-old sister Mary and the Archduke Charles, which had been reconfirmed only the previous autumn at Lille. Instead she was to marry Louis XII of France, a very decrepit 52. The affianced bride would need attendants who could speak French, and had not Sir Thomas a daughter who did? She must be sent for. And, as Sir Thomas wrote to his 'most redoubted lady', 'to this request I could not, nor did I know how to refuse.'[26]

In August 1514, therefore, Anne was on the list for France, but what happened then is not clear. Her sister Mary was also to go, and a list in the French archives shows that Mary Boleyn was one of the ladies in the household of the new queen of France, but it makes no mention of Anne.[27] The English sources concur. Mary Tudor left for France with a large escort and, after an appalling Channel crossing, arrived at Abbeville for the wedding, which took place on 9 October.[28] The expectation was that the main party would then return to England, leaving a selected group to remain with Mary Tudor. This included one, and only one, Mistress Boleyn. In the event Louis XII refused to put up with the interference of some of the older women and sent them packing the day after the wedding, but among those retained was yet again a single 'Madmoyselle Boleyne'.[29] The new queen stigmatized the survivors as 'such as never had experience nor knowledge how to advertise or give me counsel in any time of need', but these inexperienced young attendants evidently did not include Anne.[30]

Where then was Anne? Did she go to France at all in 1514? Some scholars have certainly suggested that she went to France some years later, at a date so far unknown. The objection to this is the unambiguous statement in 1536 by Lancelot de Carles, the French diplomat who reported her execution: 'My lord, I am well aware that you know and have known for a long time that Anne Boullant first came from this country when Mary [Tudor] left to go to join the king [Louis XII] in France to bring about the alliance of the two sovereigns.'[31] It could, of course, be argued that after such a time the two Boleyn sisters were being confused, but the French seem to have been well aware of their separate identities.[32] If, then, both sisters were in Mary Tudor's entourage, why was Anne not named? One hypothesis is that she was one of her sister's attendants and so does not figure on the establishment lists; perhaps she was too young to count. This seems unlikely in the light of the specific request to Sir Thomas to bring Anne back from Flanders to join Mary Tudor's party. On the other hand, if Anne was recruited as an interpreter, it would be common Tudor practice to pay and list such a person, or at least to list them, even if the pay was omitted. It is hard to resist the conclusion that Anne did not cross to France with the king's sister in the autumn of 1514. Again, where was she? The likely answer would seem to be 'somewhere in the Low Countries'. From the date of

Sir Thomas's letter to the departure of the wedding party from England was exactly seven weeks, to the wedding a further seven days.[33] It would have been possible for Anne to make it, provided there was not a hitch. One possible delay was that Margaret of Austria left Mechelen on 21 August to visit the islands of Zeeland, and the message from London dated 14 August may not have arrived in time to detach Anne from that expedition, or to allow her to say her goodbyes.[34] Another possible source of delay was that Margaret was personally affronted by the jilting of her nephew Charles and politically endangered by the *rapprochement* between England and her sworn enemy, France. She actually attempted to obstruct Henry's volte-face and might well have taken her time before giving permission for Anne to leave to assist in a marriage she so detested.[35] Whatever the reason, we must imagine Anne Boleyn catching up with Mary Tudor in Paris, where she was crowned on 5 November, and after the establishment lists which now survive had been drawn up; no doubt Anne would have appeared in later lists, but there were none. Louis lasted for eighty-two days with his young bride, and on 1 January 1515 Mary was a widow.

The situation of Mary and her attendants in a Paris where she was no longer queen was not enviable . The new king, Francis I, probably did not force his attentions on the young widow, as A. F. Pollard believed, but he was determined to exploit his temporary prize, at least to prevent her marrying a prince hostile to himself.[36] Henry sent over Charles Brandon to negotiate relations with the new monarch and to arrange Mary's return, with as much of her dower and jewellery as was possible. Suffolk, already in love with the beautiful *reine blanche*, as the French called a queen in mourning, had neither the stamina to resist Mary's Tudor determination nor the wit to see that Francis was playing him like a fish. Before he knew what was happening, he woke up in Mary's bed, secretly married to his sovereign's sister. Several abject weeks of grovelling and a series of humili-ating bribes to Henry VIII were necessary before Wolsey could secure the king's forgiveness, and permission for the pair to return to England. The match with Brandon was resented by his rivals for Henry's favour, but it was also a flagrant instance of a princess marrying beneath her. Although we have no details, there was certainly talk among Mary's attendants at Brandon's undue familiarity, and one might guess that somewhere here is the root of the dislike Mary Tudor had in later life for Anne Boleyn; the pert contempt of a 14-year-old product of the Habsburg nursery, well aware of Brandon's earlier and foolish behaviour with Margaret of Austria, might be hard to forgive and forget.[37]

Whatever the truth of this supposition, Anne Boleyn did not come back to England with Suffolk and Mary in April 1515, although her sister probably did. Neither, however, did Anne return to Mechelen and the Archduchess Margaret, but she entered instead the household of Francis I's wife, Queen Claude. Precisely how this was arranged is a mystery. Claude herself was only 15 years old and had been married to Francis for less than a year, and there are no known links between the Boleyns and either. Claude, however, was the daughter of Louis XII, and it could be that she had taken a particular liking to Anne when she joined the entourage of her young stepmother, Mary Tudor. If so, it might be natural, when Mary's brief time as queen of France came to an end, for her successor Claude to offer Anne a place in her household. Something of the kind was certainly the understanding of Lancelot de Carles, writing in 1536: 'After Mary had returned to this country, Anne was kept back by Claude, who later became queen.'[38] Once again the common-sense explanation is Anne's command of the language. Claude, whose appearance bordered on deformity, had a warm and gentle nature but could only have talked to her stepmother and to the magnificent English visitors she had to entertain at the time of the coronation by means of some interpreter: Anne perhaps?

Anne Boleyn was to stay with Claude for nearly seven years, a period for which we have no direct evidence. No doubt she visited her father when he became ambassador to the French court, and tradition has it that she had some sort of base at Briare on the Loire above Orléans.[39] This is by no means impossible, for the town was well placed in relation to the movements of the court of Queen Claude, where Anne's duties kept her much of the time. Although only of an age with Anne, Claude's short life (she was to die in 1524) was a succession of almost annual pregnancies spent very largely in the Upper Loire at Amboise and at Blois which, although it was the queen's own palace, was the site of the first major building scheme of her husband, Francis I.[40] Waiting on the queen of France could not have been markedly different from waiting on the regent of the Low Countries, and it is clear that Anne continued to soak in the sophisticated atmosphere around her. De Carles particularly emphasized her musical ability – 'she knew perfectly how to sing and dance . . . to play the lute and other instruments' – and her skill was such as to be remembered even in hostile reminiscences.[41] Nicholas Sander, the Elizabethan recusant exile, said that Anne could play 'on the lute and was a good dancer', while another and possibly earlier Roman Catholic source referred to her 'plausible qualities, for such as one to delight in, for she could play upon instruments, dance &c.'[42] Some confirmation, if not of her skill in performance, at least of her developing musical taste in France, is to be found in the Royal College of Music manuscript mentioned earlier.[43]

It was, of course, at Cloux, just outside Amboise, that Leonardo da Vinci came to settle in 1516 as a pensioner of the French king.[44] That Anne saw him seems probable; whether it meant anything to her we cannot know. One area of painting where we can show a response on Anne's part is book illumination. Claude of France was a noteworthy patroness of the miniature, a taste inherited from her mother, Anne of Brittany, who undoubtedly commissioned for her daughter the primer now in the Fitzwilliam Museum, Cambridge.[45] The Kraus Collection in New York includes two later works made for Claude, a book of prayers which was in the queen's hands before Anne Boleyn arrived in France (it probably dates from 1511–14) and a Book of Hours which Anne may well have seen arrive from the studio in 1517.[46] What was unusual about the latter (and so effective that Claude had five illuminations of a similar style inserted in the book of prayers) was the introduction of borders in Renaissance style, a fashion which had entered France ten years earlier.[47] Two types of border are known, pilasters or columns and candelabra (though there are combinations of the two), and the effect is quite different from the *trompe-l'oeil* decoration that Anne had experienced at Mechelen. When Anne, a queen herself, had her own illuminated treasures, these would include books decorated in the new fashion, with Renaissance-style borders.[48]

Experience at the court of Queen Claude thus built on the brief time that Anne Boleyn had spent with Margaret of Austria, but there was one obvious difference: life with Claude was much less public. Commentators who have been tempted to picture Anne in regular contact with the blatant sexuality of Francis I's household and his 'privy band of ladies' exaggerate. Political power, and all the concomitants of decision-making, rivalry and faction, travelled with the king who, although not an unaffectionate or absentee husband, certainly did not believe in companionate marriage.[49] One possibility is that Anne accompanied Claude and Louise of Savoy on their ceremonial journey in October 1515 to welcome back Francis I after his victory at Marignano.[50] This took them to Lyons with a pilgrimage detour to the supposed tomb of Mary Magdalene at Saint-Maximin-la-Sainte-Baume, and then to Marseilles, where the king and queen each made a ceremonial entry to the city. Another event which Anne probably took part in was the queen's personal triumph in May 1516, when she was crowned at St Denis and then made her state entry into Paris, a magnificent affair which the English government saw fit to ignore.[51] It seems very likely, too, that Anne was in attendance when Claude made her solemn entry into Cognac in 1520.[52]

Claude and her ladies also made appearances on two great occasions which involved the English, when Anne would certainly have been in demand as an interpreter. The first began on 22 December 1518, when a state banquet was given at the Bastille in honour of an English mission, which had come to negotiate for a marriage between Henry VIII's daughter Mary and the dauphin, born to Claude and Francis the previous February.[53] The courtyard of the fortress was covered with an awning of waxed blue canvas painted with the heavenly bodies, the floor was carpeted with white and orange cloth, and the whole was lit from sconces and chandeliers everywhere, reflecting on the mass of gold and silver plate on tables and cupboards. The English and French delegations were seated alternately with the ladies of the court who, after some hours of dancing later in the evening, served supper at midnight, dressed in the latest Italian costumes, all under the eyes of the queen and her mother-in-law, Louise of Savoy. No sooner had the guests gone than the setting was reconstructed to allow a tournament to take place, apparently a mêlée on foot, twenty-four a side with Francis leading one of the teams. That over, the set was reconstructed yet again for another evening of dancing and feasting.

The second great occasion was the Field of Cloth of Gold, the famous meeting between Henry VIII and Francis I outside Calais from 7 to 23 June 1520. This was something of a family affair for the Boleyns, with both Sir Thomas and Lady Elizabeth there, possibly the newly wedded Mary Carey and, one must assume, brother George among his father's allocation of eleven attendants (or one of the three gentlemen allowed his mother).[54] Called in the name of peace and friendship, the Field of Cloth of Gold was an occasion for international one-upmanship on a vast scale, no less deadly in intent for being (usually) polite. Richard Wingfield, who had taken over from Thomas Boleyn as ambassador to France four months previously, had written to Henry soon after his arrival to warn that the French royal ladies were as intent on gaining the day as their menfolk:

> Your Grace shall also understand that the Queen here, with the King's mother [Louise of Savoy], make all the search possible to bring at the assembly the fairest ladies and demoiselles that may be found. The daughters of Navarre be sent for; the Duke of Lorraine's daughters or sisters in like manner. I hope at the least, Sir, that the Queen's Grace shall bring such in her band, that the visage of England, which hath always had the praise, shall not at this time lose the same.[55]

Claude and her attendants made their first appearance at the Field of Cloth of Gold on Sunday, 10 June, when the royal ladies of both nations made their début at separate banquets, although Claude, being thirty-one weeks pregnant as well as naturally retiring, did leave the more active parts of the ensuing fortnight of festivity to Louise, the queen mother, and Marguerite d'Angoulême, the king's sister.[56] Queen Claude was, however, the star of the French contingent when the ladies made their first appearance in public at the joust on the following Monday.[57] She wore cloth of silver over an underskirt of cloth of gold, and rode in her coronation litter of cloth of silver decorated with friars' knots in gold, a device which she had taken over from her mother.[58] Her ladies rode in three carriages similarly draped in silver and, no doubt, were dressed to match the queen. Claude was also the hostess on the French side when, on several evenings, the kings, attended by ladies and gentlemen of their respective courts (usually in masque costume), changed places. Where Anne was in all this we do not know. Beside Queen Claude, one would assume. What seems unthinkable is that she was not present at all or that she did not meet Henry VIII there for a second time.[59]

The later sixteenth century interpreted Anne Boleyn's long service at the French court to mean that she must have had close relations with Marguerite d'Angoulême as well as Queen Claude.[60] Since Marguerite became a noted – if somewhat eclectic – supporter of religious reform, the assumption was easy to make. Soon even careful scholars like Herbert of Cherbury took it as a fact that Anne served in the household of 'the Duchess of Alençon, sister to Francis'.[61] That, however, is highly unlikely; when reporting Francis I's complaint in January 1522 about Anne leaving France, the imperial ambassadors described her quite unequivocally as one of his wife's ladies, just as she had been in 1515.[62]

On the other hand, Anne does seem to have known Marguerite. The duchess clearly must have met Thomas Boleyn in June 1519 at the christening of Claude's second child, the future Henri II, where he represented Henry VIII, and it is hard to believe that he did not introduce his daughter.[63] True, Marguerite may well have dismissed Anne as merely one of her sister-in-law's waiting-women. Something to that effect can be read into the efforts which the English made to get Marguerite (by then queen of Navarre) to accompany her brother to Calais in 1532 to meet Henry and Anne.[64] Francis came alone, and the conclusion Pierre Jourda drew from this was that imperial diplomats at the time were right in saying that Marguerite was bitterly hostile to the projected marriage.[65] Yet the French refusal to nominate ladies to the official Calais delegation could have a different explanation. Francis was just then angling for a match between his son Henry and the pope's niece Catherine de Medici – hardly the moment to appear to give public endorsement to Anne's position.[66]

Anne Boleyn's later behaviour certainly took her intimacy with Marguerite for granted. A message from her to the princess in September 1535 was 'that her greatest wish, next to having a son, was to see you again', while in the previous year Anne had assured her that although at the 1532 meeting there had been 'everything proceeding between both kings to the queen's grace's singular comfort, there was no one thing which her grace so much desired...as the want of the said queen of Navarre's company, with whom to have conference, for more causes than were meet to be expressed, her grace is most desirous.'[67] These could be the remarks of someone trying to turn mere acquaintance into a bosom friendship, but there are other indications that Marguerite was at least by this time favourable to England, and to Anne. The duke of Norfolk had two five-hour consultations with her in 1533, which convinced him that she was 'as affectionate to your highness as if she were your own sister, and likewise to the queen...My opinion is that she is your good and assured friend.'[68] In July 1534 Anne's intimacy with Francis's sister was exploited to conceal Henry's wish to withdraw from an agreed meeting with Francis. She was, Anne confided to Marguerite, expecting a child and so prevented from travelling, but she was very anxious to come to any meeting and, what was more, she needed Henry with her at the time of her confinement – so could the meeting be postponed until April 1535?[69] The true reason seems to have been Henry's fear of trouble at home, but why he should have felt the need for this roundabout way of postponing something as notoriously chancy as a royal summit meeting is not obvious. Whatever the motive, Anne's brother, who took the message to Marguerite, was told to insist that Henry was so determined to meet Francis as arranged that:

> Her Grace is now driven to her sheet anchor in this behalf, that is, to the only help of the said Queen of Navarre, and the goodness of the good King her brother, for Her Grace's sake, and at this Her Grace's suit and contemplation, to stay the King's Highness her husband, and to prorogue their interview till a more commodious and convenient time for all parties.

Nor was this the only occasion when the English used Marguerite as a stepping-stone to Francis; they did the same in November 1535, though without the 'woman to woman' touch.[70]

Anne Boleyn's career at the French court came to an abrupt halt towards the end of 1521 when she was summoned back to England.[71] Francis took this as one more sign of the growing *rapprochement* between his alleged friend Henry and his perpetual enemy, Charles V, although war between England and France did not break out until the following May. But, as Wolsey explained, Anne had been recalled for an entirely different reason. For this we have to go back to 1515 and the death in his nineties of Anne's grandfather, Thomas Butler, earl of Ormonde, leaving no legitimate offspring but the Boleyns and the St Legers as joint heirs-general. Given Sir Thomas's closeness to the king, it is no surprise that livery of his mother's new estates was granted in four months, but to be granted and to occupy were two very different things, at least in Ireland, where the rights of the heirs-general were obstructed by the late earl's cousin and heir-male, Piers Butler, who had been acting for years as the representative of the absentee earl.[72] Ireland was rarely high on the early Tudor agenda, but the rights of the Boleyns were the one topic there in ten years in which Henry VIII did show an interest, no doubt prompted by Sir Thomas. Letters to the Irish lord deputy, the earl of Kildare, produced a hearing on 18 November 1516 at which the Boleyns and St Legers were able to prove their case, but as the archbishop of Dublin explained to Wolsey three weeks later, legal right was not enough.[73] Piers Butler, styling himself 'earl of Ormonde', had mustered the support of the most powerful Irish lords, including Kildare himself, and was calling for trial before a common-law jury where, of course, Sir Thomas Boleyn would have had no chance. What was more, the English interest in Ireland needed Butler. No settlement was reached, and when in the spring of 1520 a second burst of royal interest selected the earl of Surrey, Thomas Howard, to go to Ireland as lord lieutenant, Surrey suggested to Wolsey that James Butler, Sir Piers' son, should marry Anne Boleyn and unite the warring claims.

Where Surrey got the idea is not clear. It was certainly from neither Wolsey nor Henry. Since Surrey was Boleyn's brother-in-law one might be inclined to suspect Boleyn (appearing reasonable might well suit the book of a man only recently restored to Wolsey's favour), were it not for the absence of any subsequent Boleyn enthusiasm for the scheme. It may rather be that we have here another example of Thomas Howard's skill in taking care of Thomas Howard. He loathed Ireland and knew that the king would soon tire of a problem which he did not have the resources or interest to solve. James Butler was available: he was being brought up – or kept as a hostage – in Wolsey's household. Surrey's niece Anne was of an age to marry and could easily be recalled from France. What better escape for Surrey than a scheme which would make respectable the abandonment of Ireland to Piers Butler as earl of Ormonde, with Anne and James Butler sealing his loyalty to and dependence on Henry (as long as Henry was looking)?[74] No sooner had Howard arrived in Ireland than Piers was his right-hand man, his title as earl taken for granted, his sterling virtues and commitment to the English cause trumpeted in letter after letter.[75] By early September 1520 the earl had got the Irish council to propose the match to Henry VIII, and a letter of 6 October jogging Wolsey's memory about the proposal crossed with a reply giving the king's reactions:

> And like as ye desire us to endeavour ourself that a marriage may be had and made betwixt the earl of Ormonde's son and the daughter of Sir Thomas Boleyn Kt., controller of our household; so we will ye be [a] mean[s] to the said earl for his agreeable consent and mind thereunto, and to advertise us, by your next letters, of what towardness ye shall find the said earl in that behalf. Signifying unto you, that in the mean time, we shall advance the said matter with our controller, and certify you how we shall find him inclined thereunto accordingly.[76]

Surrey kept up the campaign, sending over in December the draft of an Act for the Irish parliament, recognizing Butler as head of his family.[77] And then, nine months' silence.

The Boleyn–Butler marriage resurfaced in October 1521 after Surrey, already pressing for a recall, had fallen seriously ill. He appealed for approval of the Act in Butler's favour, asked for the return of James to help his father and sent a personal messenger to press his own problems.[78] Butler, meanwhile, sensed victory and started to haggle for the return of his son and the completion of the marriage with Anne.[79] Wolsey, who all this while was tied up in a European peace conference at Calais, advised Henry in mid-November that James Butler was too valuable a hostage to be surrendered, but

> I shall, at my return to your presence, devise with Your Grace how the marriage betwixt him and Sir Thomas Boleyn['s] daughter may be brought to pass, which shall be a reasonable cause to tract [delay] the time for sending his said son over to him; for the perfecting of which marriage I shall endeavour myself at my return, with all effect.[80]

Wolsey left Calais on 28 November, and soon after that Anne must have received her recall to England.[81]

Yet Wolsey, for the first but not for the last time, did not 'perfect' marriage for Anne Boleyn. Why is not clear. Butler's arch-rival in Ireland, the earl of Kildare, reported that by May 1523 Sir Piers had decided that he would have to defend his claim by force.[82] According to Kildare's new wife, formerly Elizabeth Grey, a woman with court experience reaching back as far as her attendance on the king's sister in France in 1514, Butler was trying to bind nobles to support him against the Boleyn claim, and the Kildares, fresh from England, knew that Henry would not approve.[83] If we are to take seriously these straws in the wind, then it was Butler who gave up hope of a settlement by marriage, presumably because Boleyn made difficulties – and the man who in 1521 had been promoted treasurer of the household was in a position to be obstructive. On this construction, what Anne's father was standing out for was the earldom of Ormonde, and her marriage was a lever to that end. However, it took until February 1528 to make progress by way of a compromise. This saw the Butlers taking the disputed lands on a long lease at very moderate rents, in return for surrendering the Ormonde title and receiving instead the earldom of Ossory.[84] Even then the last piece in the settlement, the earldom of Ormonde for Thomas Boleyn, slotted into place only in December 1529 after Wolsey had fallen from favour. It may well be that the cardinal was none too pleased at the way events had gone against him and once again delayed Boleyn to teach him who was in charge. But long before that, Henry's interest in Anne had become obvious, and Wolsey may well have rued the day when he had been unable to pack her off to Ireland.

Against this, it would seem curious that Wolsey should have taken it upon himself to 'perfect' Anne's marriage in 1521 without first consulting her father, for Sir Thomas was then at Calais with him. Perhaps Wolsey never intended the possibility of a match between James and Anne to be anything other than a long-term inducement to the Butlers to behave. If this alternative scenario is the correct one, we must see the period after Anne's return from France as a time of semi-engagement to James – and separation, for he returned to Ireland in the summer of 1526. Certainly he was not the only suitor she had.[85] Yet when he returned to England in the summer of 1528 it was to find even competition a thing of the past. The king had declared himself, and Anne was no longer on the marriage market.[86]

DÉBUT AT THE ENGLISH COURT

ANNE Boleyn a courtier's daughter, Anne Boleyn being educated abroad, Anne Boleyn a prospective bride. But the first direct glimpse we get of Anne on her return from France is at a court pageant in March 1522 – doing precisely what she had been trained for over all these years, and doing it before the eyes of experts from the Habsburg court at Brussels. A new chapter had just opened in the interminable saga of the Italian wars, and England, despite the protestations at the Field of Cloth of Gold, had decided to back Charles V rather than Francis I. Negotiations for a joint attack on France, a visit by the emperor to England and his betrothal to the Princess Mary were nearing completion, and the English court, to honour the ambassadors of the new ally, laid on specially magnificent pre-Lent festivities.

The theme of the opening tournament on 1 March was the cruelty of unrequited love, and this was continued when festivities reached a climax on the evening of Shrove Tuesday with a characteristically Burgundian pageant, the assault on 'the *Château Vert*'.[1] There were eight court ladies involved, each cast as one of the qualities of the perfect mistress of chivalric tradition – Beauty, Honour, Perseverance, Kindness, Constancy, Bounty, Mercy and Pity – with Anne playing Perseverance and her sister Mary, Kindness (roles of historic appropriateness). The king's sister Mary led as Beauty, with the countess of Devonshire as Honour – two women who would be among Anne's most implacable opponents – while of the other characters, Constancy was played by Jane Parker, soon to become Anne's sister-in-law. They wore white satin, each with her character or 'reason' picked out twenty-four times in yellow satin, and the head-dresses were cauls of Venetian gold set off by Milan bonnets. Opposite them were the eight male virtues of the ideal courtier – 'Amoress[ness]', Nobleness, Youth, Attendance, Loyalty, Pleasure, Gentleness and Liberty – with the king playing the lead. The men were dressed in caps and coats of cloth of gold and tinsel, with blue velvet buskins and 'great mantle cloaks of blue satin', each of which had forty-two scrolls of yellow damask on which were pasted, in blue letters, the name of the character and appropriate 'poems'. This was a wise precaution, as matters had got out of hand on a previous occasion when the character names had been made of actual gold, and the costumes had been stripped by spectators – one London seaman getting away with gold worth £3 14s. 8d., almost two ounces.[2]

The performance was put on at York Place, Wolsey's episcopal palace in Westminster which was later to become Whitehall Palace, with Anne the first queen to live there. It began after supper, with the audience being led into a large chamber, hung with arras and brilliantly lit, and at one end the glittering *Château Vert* itself. This was an elaborate wooden construction with three towers, painted green and with battlements covered in hundreds of pieces of green tinfoil. It contained hidden musicians, and standing on the towers were the eight ladies. Anne was probably in the main tower, which had a burning cresset and, like the other two, a banner – three hearts torn to pieces, a woman's hand gripping a man's heart and a woman's hand turning a man's heart upside down. The ladies were protected from assault by eight choristers of the royal chapel manning the lower walls and dressed as Indian women, each depicting one of the contrary feminine vices (or virtues) – Danger, Disdain, Jealousy, Unkindness, Scorn, 'Malebouche' (Sharp Tongue) and Strangeness (Off-handedness). The men entered, led by a spokesman, Ardent Desire, dressed in crimson satin embroidered with burning flames in gold, a role almost certainly played by William Cornish, master of the Children (choristers) of the Chapel Royal and very probably author, designer and producer of the whole affair.[3] Then Desire begged the ladies to come down, but when Scorn and Disdain announced that they would resist, he called on the courtiers to take the ladies by force. To a peal of cannon, synchronized from outside, Henry led the attack, bombarding the castle and its garrison with dates, oranges and 'other fruits made for pleasure' to which the 'ladies', genuine and choristers, replied with a barrage of sweetmeats and rosewater until Lady Scorn and the rest of the boys retreated, keeping up a defensive fire 'with bows and balls'. Female coldness having fled before masculine ardour, the warm and soft qualities were taken prisoner and brought out of the castle to dance. When the dancing was over, masks were removed and 'all were known'; they then went off with the audience to 'a costly banquet'. The whole performance had cost over £20, including three hats which the boys had lost in the course of their retreat.[4] Edward Hall tells us that the strangers were 'much pleased', at least by the dance, but Charles V's secretary apologized to his master: 'I have written very little about the reception accorded us by the king, the queen, and the cardinal, but Anthoine, your usher, saw most of the festivities and can recount them to you.' They were much more interested in the 6-year-old Princess Mary.[5]

Anne Boleyn thus made her début on an occasion which allowed her to show off all she had learned in her years abroad. But what was she like? Unfortunately, the first descriptions date from six years after the *Château Vert*, and already by then opinions were being coloured by the controversy surrounding her relationship with the king. By the time of her coronation in 1533, one hostile observer would be reporting to the court at Brussels that Anne's crown did not fit, that she was badly disfigured by a wart, and that she wore a violet velvet mantle with a high ruff to conceal a swelling in the neck, possibly a goitre.[6] Some writers have taken this seriously, although much of it is wilful misrepresentation. The crown was quickly taken off after the actual crowning, but this was because it weighed seven pounds. For the rest of the ceremonies Anne wore a crown specially made and weighing only three.[7] The practice was so sensible that it was followed for Edward VI, Mary and Elizabeth, each of whom wore a crown personally made for them (as did Elizabeth II at her coronation in 1953). As for the high collar, Anne wore the required coronation surcoat with a mantle of ermine, although the material seems to have been purple velvet and not white cloth of gold. If the style was the same as the surcoat and mantle her daughter wore at her coronation in 1559, then the neck was high.[8] The need to conceal a goitre is malevolent embroidery.

The most extreme exponent of this 'monster legend' was the Elizabethan recusant activist, Nicholas Sander. According to his account:

> Anne Boleyn was rather tall of stature, with black hair and an oval face of sallow complexion, as if troubled with jaundice. She had a projecting tooth under the upper lip, and on her right hand, six fingers. There was a large wen under her chin, and therefore to hide its ugliness, she wore a high dress covering her throat. In this she was followed by the ladies of the court, who also wore high dresses, having before been in the habit of leaving their necks and the upper portion of their persons uncovered. She was handsome to look at, with a pretty mouth.[9]

Apart from the evident self-contradiction of the last sentence, Sander, born in 1527 and in exile from 1561, was hardly a contemporary witness of the events of Anne's life or an expert on the vagaries of female attire in earlier generations – high necks came into fashion after Anne's death. The fact that he records well-established tradition, but tradition that was current among recusant exiles, also cuts both ways. Nevertheless, although we may dismiss the tooth, there might be some truth in the sixth finger and the wart. George Wyatt, writing at the end of the century to contradict Sander, and having access to some genuine family traditions of his own about Anne, was compelled not only to accept her 'beauty not so whitely as clear and fresh, above all we may esteem', but to admit that

> there was found, indeed, upon the side of her nail, upon one of her fingers, some little show of a nail, which yet was so small, by the report of those that have seen her, as the work master seemed to leave it an occasion of greater grace to her hand, which, with the tip of one of her other fingers might be, and was usually by her hidden without any blemish to it. Likewise there were said to be upon some parts of her body, certain small moles incident to the clearest complexions.[10]

A minor malformation of one fingertip thus seems very probable, and so too one or two moles, possibly on the chin, but never the disaster Sander imagined; one man's beauty-spot is hardly another man's 'wen'.

What makes the more horrific stories about Anne implausible is the undoubted impact that she made – not that she was ever a ravishing beauty. Lancelot de Carles did call her 'beautiful and with an elegant figure', and a Venetian reporting what was known of her in Paris in 1528 described her as 'very beautiful'.[11] Yet John Barlow, one of her favourite clerics, when asked to compare Anne to Elizabeth Blount, the duke of Richmond's mother, replied that Elizabeth 'was more beautiful', although Anne 'was very eloquent and gracious, and reasonably good looking [*competement belle*]'.[12] Simon Grynée, a professor of Greek at Basle whom Henry VIII employed to canvass Swiss opinion as to the validity of his marriage to Katherine, was similarly cautious (and also not entirely persuaded as to her morals): 'young and good-looking' was his verdict.[13] The Venetian diplomat, Francesco Sanuto, was even less certain, though he clearly knew of no goitres or 'large wens': 'Not one of the handsomest women in the world; she is of middling stature, swarthy complexion, long neck, wide mouth, a bosom not much raised and eyes which are black and beautiful.'[14] Henry, as we shall see, saw nothing wrong with Anne's breasts, but the overall evidence of these less prejudiced observers hardly suggests compelling physical attractiveness. All reports agree that Anne was dark. As well as Sanuto's 'swarthy', Thomas Wyatt gave her the poetic name, 'Brunet'.[15] Simon Grynée described her complexion as 'rather dark', while when her daughter Elizabeth was born it was remarked how fair she was, taking after her father rather than her mother.[16] A feature of which Anne herself was clearly proud was her hair. A good deal of comment was caused by her wearing her hair down for the coronation procession through London, but again this was simply in accordance with established etiquette. Anne, however, had also worn her hair down for the entirely unprecedented ceremony where she was created marchioness of Pembroke.[17]

Looks only tolerable, but a splendid head of dark hair and fine eyes – this was the impression that Anne Boleyn made on her contemporaries, but it would be good also to have some pictorial evidence. Here the past has not been kind. The painter coming into prominence at the English court was, of course, Hans Holbein the younger, but no painting of Anne by Holbein is known to have been made, and certainly none has survived.[18] Two of his drawings are alleged to be of her: one in the set of his drawings in the royal collection at Windsor (plate 6), and the other formerly at Weston Park and now in the British Museum (plate 5).[19] The Windsor drawing carries the legend 'Anna Bollein Queen', in eighteenth-century lettering; the Weston Park drawing, in a hand dating from the first half of the seventeenth century, has the Latin legend: 'Anne Bullen was beheaded, London 19 May, 1536.' The names on the Holbein drawings at Windsor are said to have derived originally from Sir John Cheke, Edward VI's tutor, and since Cheke had known Anne, the identification might appear to have authority.[20] However, the Cheke story is suspect – several of his supposed identifications are demonstrably incorrect – and there is evidence on the 'Anna Bollein' to link it with the Wyatt family.[21] More-over, the sitter is in evident *déshabillé*, and why should any such likeness of a queen be commissioned? It is also the case that when both Holbeins were in the collection of the earl of Arundel in the late 1630s, the Czech artist, Wenceslaus Hollar, chose to engrave the British Museum drawing in preference to the one now at Windsor.[22] Why Hollar selected that as a likeness of Anne it is impossible to say; either he had advice or the Windsor drawing had not yet been claimed as 'Anne'.[23]

The one firm contemporary likeness of Anne Boleyn is a single specimen of the portrait medal struck in 1534 (plate 8); it carries her motto, 'The Moost Happi' and the initials 'A.R.' – Anna Regina.[24] Such a piece can only have been prepared on royal authority. The common assumption is that the medal was struck to mark Anne's coronation, but the date makes that improbable.[25] Between Anne's coronation and a 25 March start to 1534 was ten months. The more likely occasion is the expected birth of

Anne's second child in the autumn of 1534, and her miscarrying would explain why multiple copies do not survive. Unfortunately the nose has been badly damaged, perhaps deliberately, so that its value as a likeness is impaired. Nevertheless the shape of the face is clear – long and oval with high cheek-bones, much the sort of face that her daughter Elizabeth was to have, according to some painters. Given the condition of the medal, it is impossible to go further than that, but it cannot be said to inspire confidence in the British Museum likeness endorsed by Hollar and still less the Windsor example. Judged by the medal, Anne sat for neither of the Holbein drawings.

A number of paintings from the later sixteenth century are claimed to be of Anne. They survive from sets of 'Kings and Queens of England' which Elizabethan and Jacobean gentry liked to have in their houses to demonstrate loyalty. There are two patterns which clearly represent separate traditions. The one best known at the time (thanks to the set it belonged to being engraved and published in 1618) depicts Anne in a gable hood with a single necklace of pearls with a cross decorated with rectangular stones. (plate 4).[26] In a painting in this pattern (now at Bradford), Anne wears a brooch in the form of a single drop pearl hanging from the monogram 'AB' in gold (plate 2).[27] The alternative pattern – and the one commonly reproduced today – has Anne in a French hood with a gold letter 'B' hanging from a pearl necklace.[28] Several examples survive. The painting in the best condition is in the National Portrait Gallery but the less glamorized versions, such as the one at Hever, show a women with a sharper face and a sallow complexion (plate 1). Neither pattern, however, can be regarded as authoritative since neither is earlier than fifty or sixty years after Anne's death or linked to the portrait medal, either directly or via a common ancestor. The engraved image does have the same sort of head-dress, yet neither it nor the Hever/NPG pattern has the medal's striking lift of the head.

There is, however, a resolution of this pictorial game of 'find the lady'. The key is an Elizabethan ring belonging to the Trustees of Chequers, the prime minister's country residence. The ring itself is mother-of-pearl, the shank is set with rubies and the bezel carries the monogram 'E' in diamonds. It was previously in the possession of the Home family, having, it is said, been given from the English royal treasures by James I to the then Lord Home.[29] The head of the ring is hinged and opens to reveal two enamel portraits, one of Elizabeth *circa* 1575 and one of a woman in the costume of Henry VIII's reign, wearing a French hood (plate 7). The portrait is minute – the ring itself is only 175 millimetres across – but not only is Anne by far the most likely woman of the previous generation to be thus matched with

Elizabeth, the face mask is quite clearly that of the sitter in the Hever and National Portrait Gallery paintings. Two important conclusions follow. First, the late Elizabethan 'Kings and Queens' image of Anne is pushed back some twenty years. Even more significant, that image must have been accepted in Elizabeth's court as a likeness of the queen's mother. Elizabeth herself could obviously have had no clear recollection of Anne's face, but others around her had known Henry's second wife well.

How does the Chequers enamel compare with the 1534 medal? There is a forty-year interval between them and the head-dresses are different, but the sitter is evidently the same – long oval face, high cheek-bones, strong nose and a decided chin: a face of character, not beauty. There is thus an authenticated sequence for Anne Boleyn, comprising the medal, the Chequers enamel and the Hever/NPG pattern.

With such a tiny ring it is hard to be certain, but between it and particularly the National Portrait Gallery example there seems to have been a prettying up and a loss of spirit.[30] Fortunately, the sequence also has the effect of corroborating a seventeenth-century miniature in the collection of the Duke of Buccleuch and Queensberry. Charles I had this copied as 'Anne Boleyn' by John Hoskins the elder (*c.*1590–1664/5), and it is endorsed 'from an ancient original' (plate 3).[31] How 'ancient' it is impossible to say. Although the relationship to examples in the NPG pattern is evident, these were only thirty years old or perhaps less. It is more likely that Hoskins had access to an earlier image of the kind from which the NPG image originated. A full-length portrait of Anne was owned by Lord Lumley in 1590 and existed as late as 1773.[32] Could it even be that Hoskins' source was or was derived from a Holbein painting now lost?[33] Speculation apart, the Hoskins is important because it preserves what a highly talented seventeenth-century miniaturist made of the image, and though again further softened, it is the best depiction of Anne we are likely ever to have, failing the discovery of new material. Portrait medal – Chequers ring – Hever/NPG pattern – Hoskins miniature: the chain is complete. We have the real Anne Boleyn.

Of the other alleged likenesses opinion must be left to judge. There is little to reinstate either Holbein drawing, but the Bradford painting is not impossible to reconcile with the authoritative image, especially as the sitter appears somewhat older. Moreover, as we have seen, that was the likeness chosen for engraving and printing in 1618. What is ruled out is the latest candidate as a likeness of Anne Boleyn, a portrait miniature assigned to the Flemish artist Lucas Hornebolte and found in two versions, in the Royal Ontario Museum and in the Buccleuch collection. The sitter is quite unlike the subject of the Chequers ring. There is also a difficulty about the date, for the Toronto miniature gives the sitter's age as 'in the 25th year' and it seems likely that the earliest English examples of portrait miniatures were not produced until 1527. Furthermore, since early duplicate miniatures seem limited to royal persons, Anne would hardly seem yet to qualify.[34]

Establishing a reliable image for Anne Boleyn only accentuates the evidence of contemporaries that her attraction was not outstanding natural beauty. What, then, explains her power? In the first place she radiated sex. The heir of the earl of Northumberland would try to break a six-year-old engagement for her; Sir Thomas Wyatt would become passionately involved; and it was the inability of a Flemish musician to stand the heady atmosphere around her that would help to bring Anne to destruction. As for Henry, the king's own letters show how explicit was his desire:

> Mine own sweetheart, this shall be to advertise you of the great loneliness that I find here since your departing – for I assure you methinketh the time longer since your departing now last, than I was wont to do a whole fortnight. I think your kindness and my fervencies of love causeth it; for otherwise I would not have thought it possible that for so little a while it should have grieved me ... wishing myself (especially of an evening) in my sweet-heart's arms, whose pretty dugs I trust shortly to kiss.[35]

That Anne was aware of her attractiveness to men seems obvious. While in France her place beside the retiring French queen would have kept her away from most of the notorious licentiousness which flourished in Francis I's own household. Nevertheless, Anne cannot but have been made aware of her power during such visits as Claude did make to a court which was much more explicitly erotic than those at London or Brussels. William Forrest, writing in 1558, recalled that 'no tatches [guile] she lacked of loves allurement', while days after her death de Carles waxed lyrical about her expressive eyes:

> ... eyes always most attractive
> Which she knew well how to use with effect,
> Sometimes leaving them at rest,
> And at others, sending a message
> To carry the secret witness of the heart.
> And truth to tell, such was their power
> That many surrendered to their obedience.[36]

Yet sexuality was only part of Anne Boleyn's attraction. What made her stand out was sophistication, elegance and independence, in fact the continental experience and upbringing which we have explored. De Carles wrote:

> To France, which brought her such fortune,
> Ah! what honour, What a debt
> She owed to the skill
> Of those from whom she had learned such accomplishments,
> Which have since made her queen of her own people.
> She was happy, but how more happy
> If she had trodden the way of virtue,
> And had kept to the direction of the way
> Which her honourable mistress had shown her.[37]

France and Queen Claude, and, one might add, Margaret of Austria: these had made the difference. There were other foreign ladies at the English court. Some, now ageing, had come over with Katherine of Aragon, but among the English there was nobody with a tithe of the continental polish of Anne Boleyn. One of Wolsey's servants who had known her remembered how she stood out among the other women at court 'for her excellent grace and behaviour'.[38] A less than enthusiastic Protestant writer of the next generation told how 'albeit in beauty she was to many inferior, but for behaviour, manners, attire and tongue she excelled them all, for she had been brought up in France.'[39] A Catholic account of the same period stressed that 'she was in the prime of her youth', and as well as her musical abilities 'had her Latin and French tongue'.[40] True, one of her chaplains recalled that she used to lament her ignorance of Latin, but the two memories are not incompatible; it was polite convention to plead inadequacy – her daughter did, and she was an excellent Latinist.[41] Even the recusant tradition remembered her elegance and gave her credit for it, if for nothing else: 'She was the model and the mirror of those who were at court, for she was always well dressed, and every day made some change in the fashion of her garments. But as to the disposition of her mind . . .'[42]

Anne Boleyn had style, and continental style at that. George Wyatt might look back and write of 'the graces of nature graced by gracious education', but Carles declared at the time: 'no one would ever have taken her to be English by her manners, but a native-born Frenchwoman.'[43] And she took the English court by storm.

4

SOURCES

ANNE Boleyn is the most controversial woman ever to have been queen consort of England. Disagreement among historians in more recent times only continues a controversy which began as soon as she was seriously linked with Henry VIII, was then subsumed in the adulation or vituperation which surrounded her daughter and finally became a crux in the confrontation between Protestant and Catholic controversialists. The consequence, as we have already seen, is that from the first there have been partisan disagreement even on simple points of fact.

To Roman Catholics, it was not just that in order to satisfy his lust Henry had displaced his rightful wife in favour of Anne Boleyn, and broken with the true Church. Anne herself was soon being blamed for what had happened. Reginald Pole claimed that she had never loved Henry and described her as 'the cause of all evil' and 'the person who caused all this'.[1] George Cavendish, in the confidence that God, through the accession of Mary, had restored right rule to England, produced a series of *Metrical Visions* in which over forty victims of political disaster, from Wolsey onwards, lament their ill fortune; Anne declares:

> I may be compared in every circumstance
> To Athalia who destroyed David's line,
> Spared not the blood by cruel vengeance
> Of God's prophets, but brought them to ruin:
> Murder asketh murder, by murder she did find,
> So in like wise resisting my quarrel
> How many have died and ended pareil [the same].[2]

By the accession of James I, an analysis preserved in the papers of those incorrigible recusants, the Treshams of Rushton, could attribute all the sufferings of Roman Catholics under Elizabeth's penal laws to the fact that Anne 'did beget a settled hatred of them against her and hers':

> Anne Boleyn, the bane of that virtuous and religious Queen Katherine, the ruin of many pious, worthy and famous men who favoured not that unlawful marriage, the first giver of entrance to the Protestant religion and the principal cause of her husband's dissolving of religious houses and slaughtering multitudes of religious people as not favouring her marriage with Henry VIII in the lifetime of his first wife.

Anne had been 'of bad parentage, of bad fame afore her marriage, and afterwards executed for adultery'.[3]

Very understandably, the descendants of Thomas More had a particularly nice line in insult. Sir Thomas, so we are told, dismissed worldly status as vanity, but we cannot assume that his family was as sanctified; one blow of the axe had put an end to their bright prospects and undone the patient social climbing of three generations.[4] William Roper, the chancellor's son-in-law, claimed that it was Anne's personal vendetta against More which encouraged Henry to demand that he conform.[5] It was More's nephew, William Rastell, religious exile and (briefly) judge of the court of Queen's Bench, who gave currency in his lost *Life* of his uncle to the lie that Henry VIII was Anne Boleyn's father.[6] He also alleged – with obvious echoes of Herodias, Salome and Herod – that Anne put on a great banquet for Henry at Hanworth, where she 'allured there the king with her dalliance and pastime to grant unto her this request, to put the bishop [Fisher] and Sir Thomas More to death'.[7] In his edition of More's English works, Rastell even edited out remarks by Sir Thomas which were favourable to the queen. What More had written in a letter to Thomas Cromwell in March 1534 was:

> So am I he that among other his Grace's faithful subjects, his Highness being in possession of his marriage and this noble woman really anointed queen, neither murmur at it nor dispute upon it, nor never did nor will, but without any other manner meddling of the matter among his other faithful subjects, faithfully pray to God for his Grace and hers both long to live and well, and their noble issue too, in such wise as may be to the pleasure of God, honour and surety to themselves, rest, peace, wealth and profit unto this noble realm.

As edited by Rastell this became:

> So am I he that among his Grace's faithful subjects, his Highness being in possession of his marriage, will most heartily pray for the prosperous estate of his Grace long to continue to the pleasure of God.[8]

That More should have recognized Anne as 'really anointed queen' was unthinkable; worse still, it must not be admitted that a saint had described a whore as 'noble'. To Catholics, the deaths of Anne and those accused with her and, later, of Cromwell, 'and most of all those who procured his death', were blood sacrifices to expiate More's murder, and the drops which fell from their bleeding corpses on to his grave at the door of the Tower chapel, 'peace offerings, or rather, confessions of the wrong they had done him'.[9]

Protestants told the opposite story. John Foxe staunchly defended both the queen's morals and her religious commitment. He hints at the involvement of the papists in her fall and cannot resist assigning responsibility to his *bête noire*, the conservative champion, Stephen Gardiner: 'neither is it unlike, but that Stephen bishop of Winchester, being then abroad in an embassy was not altogether asleep.'[10] And Foxe had clinching supernatural proof of Anne's virtue:

> to all other sinister judgements and opinions, whatsoever can be conceived of man against that virtuous queen, I object and oppose again (as instead of answer) the evident demonstration of God's favour, in maintaining, preserving, and advancing the offspring of her body, the lady Elizabeth, now queen.[11]

Bishop John Aylmer, replying in 1559 to Knox's *Monstrous Regiment of Women*, hailed Anne as 'the crop and root' of the Reformation whom 'God had endued with wisdom that she could, and given her the mind that she would, do it'; John Bridges, writing in 1573, elevated Anne to the status of 'a most holy martyr'.[12]

Protestant writers were not, however, always unanimous in praise of Anne Boleyn. William Thomas, that pseudo-intellectual hustler who was to be Northumberland's clerk of the privy council, and who was executed later for plotting Mary's assassination, firmly maintained the official version of Anne's guilt, even after Henry VIII's death:

> [Anne's] liberal life were so shameful to rehearse. Once she was as wise a woman endued with as many outward good qualities in playing on instruments, singing and such other courtly graces as few women of her time, with such a certain outward profession of gravity as was to be

marvelled at. But inward she was all another dame than she seemed to be; for in satisfying of her carnal appetite she fled not so much as the company of her own natural brother besides the company of three or four others of the gallantest gentlemen that were near about the king's proper person – drawn by her own devilish devices that it should seem she was always well occupied.[13]

A school of puritan opinion was prepared to imply that Henry's second marriage was as much a matter of lust as principle:

Whether he did it of an upright conscience or to serve his lusts I will not judge for in the burrows of man's heart be many secret corners and it cannot be denied but that he was a very fleshly man, and no marvel for albeit his father brought him up in good learning yet after...he fell into all riot and overmuch love of women.

As for Anne herself:

This gentlewoman in proportion of body might compare with the rest of the ladies and gentlewomen of the court, albeit in beauty she was to many inferior, but for behaviour, manners, attire and tongue she excelled them all...But howsoever she outwardly appeared, she was indeed a very wilful woman which perhaps might seem no fault because seldom women do lack it, but yet that and other things cost her after dear.[14]

It is indeed noticeable that a number of writers seem almost reluctant to write about Anne Boleyn in any detail. Thus Holinshed remarked:

Because I might rather say much than sufficiently enough in praise of this noble queen as well for her singular wit and other excellent qualities of mind as also for her favouring of learned men, zeal of religion and liberality in distributing alms in relief of the poor, I will refer the reader unto that which Mr. Foxe says.[15]

Foxe, however, had already himself referred to better-informed reports still to appear:

because touching the memorable virtues of this worthy queen, partly we have said something before, partly because more also is promised to be declared of her virtuous life (the Lord so permitting) by others who were then about her, I will cease in this matter further to proceed.[16]

No vindication of Anne Boleyn was ever published. Her chaplain, William Latymer, presented to her daughter an encomium on her religious activities, and the Scottish Lutheran, Alexander Ales, wrote an account of her fall, placing all the blame on the enemies of the Reformation, but both men evidently had patronage in mind. Ales, indeed, included an address for any financial contributions Elizabeth would like to send.[17] The reason for silence elsewhere is not far to seek. Few defences of Anne Boleyn have been entirely happy. Any vindication of the wife was an implicit criticism of the husband; if Anne was 'noble', 'virtuous' and 'worthy', Henry had been either a monster or a gull.

One of those who may have been concerned with a project for an official Elizabethan account of 'the mother of our blessed Queen' was George Wyatt of Boxley Abbey in Kent (1554–1624).[18] One of the most assiduous of Anne's defenders, Wyatt claimed that he had begun work at the request of an official biographer who had asked him to set down what he knew of Anne Boleyn's early years, and had continued it under the encouragement of the archbishop of Canterbury. With the accession of James, interest, so he implies, had waned, leaving him to carry on alone. George had a strong personal interest in vindicating the English Reformation in general and Anne Boleyn in particular; he was the youngest son (but also the heir) of Thomas Wyatt, the leader of the 1554 rebellion against Katherine of Aragon's daughter, Mary I, and grandson of Thomas Wyatt, the poet who had been imprisoned in the Tower in 1536 as one of those suspected of involvement with the queen.

George Wyatt devoted the latter part of his life not only to her biography but, as we have seen over the business of Anne's alleged deformity, to an effort to reply specifically to the Catholic propagandist, Nicholas Sander. Sander was no original authority, but his *Origins and Progress of the English Schism* (posthumously published in Cologne in 1585) had broadcast very effectively the scandalous stories about Anne which circulated in recusant circles.[19] A typical example is *La Vie de Anne Boulein ou de Boulogne mere de Elizabeth Royne Dangleterre*. Its *pièce de résistance* is the story that after her miscarriage in January 1536, Anne committed incest with her brother in order to beget a son and so set up the Boleyn dynasty.[20] In the end Wyatt was no more successful than others had been in publishing a defence of the queen, but more because of the grandiose nature of his plans than want of effort. Two, or possibly three, of his attempts have survived: the earliest a brief but completed 'Life of Queen Anne Boleigne', the second a vindication of the relations between Anne and Thomas Wyatt the elder, which may not be by, but is certainly after,

George Wyatt, and finally (and after 1603) the opening section of a massive 'History of the English Reformation'.[21]

The purpose of what George does have to say about Anne is naïvely obvious. 'Elect of God', 'heroical spirit', 'princely lady' – the adjectives abound. Henry VIII, so the 'Defence of Sir Thomas Wyatt' has it:

> joined himself unto her [Anne] as the oak to the vine, he sustaining her, she adoring him, both embracing and clasping one another with that most straight and sacred knot, that heaven and earth were consenting to knit not to be loosed ever without the impiety of those that envied so incomparable felicity, like to grow to this noble realm thereby... Thus they lived tokens of increasing love perpetually increasing. Her mind brought him forth the rich treasures of love of piety, love of truth, love of learning. Her body yielded him the fruit of marriage inestimable pledges of faithful and loyal love.

And what put a period to this idyll?

> She had a king, he not his like, ever liked and loved, and to be liked and loved of her, (alas), too much liked of others that were practised to draw his liking from her, thereby to have him not like himself, whereby they wrought her end.

Which, despite the attempted concealment of the play on words, is to say that the incomparable Henry was a dupe.[22]

The fact that writers have agendas according to their religious alignments does not, however, make them valueless to the historian. The test is, did they have access to real sources of information? The line from Sander back to William Rastell is direct, but if we are to believe Sir Thomas More, he never discussed Anne with Rastell or anyone else, and the personal recollections of the members of his family were confined to his life outside the council and the court. They certainly breathe no word of More's dangerous and sometimes highly secret encouragement of the opposition to the king's divorce.[23] On the other hand, even the author of a Catholic account as full of picaresque invention as the mid-century *Cronica del Rey Enrico Otavo de Inglaterra* had from time to time access to genuine recollections – for example, his report that Thomas Wyatt watched the execution of Anne's alleged lovers in 1536, which was only confirmed in 1959 when a manuscript containing hitherto unknown Wyatt material was identified in the library of Trinity College, Dublin.[24] As for George Wyatt, he had three particular sources to augment the material he collected about

Anne: 'some helps' left by his grandfather, the poet, the recollections of his mother Jane, who had married in 1537 and lived to the end of the century, and the memories of Anne Gainsford, later the wife of George Zouche, gentleman pensioner and a target for Catholic investigation in Mary's reign. Given such links, the volume of material Wyatt recorded is disappointing, but at least one important episode has independent warranty in other sources.[25]

The importance of persisting with material from partisan sources is well illustrated in the little which John Foxe does record about Anne. Undoubtedly Foxe wished to present Anne in a positive light, but he was equally aware that factual inaccuracy would lay him open to ridicule – and so too the Protestantism he espoused. In consequence, he regularly revised his account of the queen as his data improved.[26] In his first work, the *Rerum in ecclesia gestarum . . . Commentarii*, written while he was still abroad, he was little more than hagiographical:

> There was at this time in the king's court a young woman, not of ignoble family, but much more ennobled by beauty, as well as being the most beautiful of all in true piety and character, Anne Boleyn, whom the king greatly loved, as she well merited, and took as his wife and queen.

'The entire British nation' he went on, was indebted to Anne, not only for her own contribution to the commencement of the Reformation but as the mother of Queen Elizabeth, who has revived it.

> If only the freedom of the English Church, brought about this first time by Anne had lasted longer and she had been able to enjoy longer life.

Anne's fate he refused to discuss, but he did include her scaffold speech as evidence of her 'singular faith and complete modesty towards her king'. In 1563 Foxe, now back in England, was able to be more specific in the first edition of his great work, *The Acts and Monuments*, better known as *The Book of Martyrs*. He gave details of Anne's charitable activity, her support of named scholars, the discipline she kept in her household and her feeding of the reformist ideas of Simon Fish to the king. What is more, he cited sources, for example, Anne's silk woman, Joan Wilkinson. Seven years later, a second edition added other stories and identified the material about Fish as having come from his widow. Foxe also included a rebuttal of Anne's alleged offences, along with the barbed comment that Henry's immediate remarriage was 'to such as wisely can judge upon cases occurrant, a great clearing of her' – as near to the knuckle as he dared go. In the last edition (the fourth of 1583), he was able to tell of Anne's support for Thomas Patmore, the unorthodox parson of Much Hadham, almost certainly based on the text of a surviving petition. We also have an amount of material which Foxe assembled but did not use, or else abridged.[27] Foxe's overall purpose was to present Anne as a Protestant role model, but that is no reason *ex hypothesi* to discard material carefully collected, much of which can, in fact, be verified.

The problem of potential distortion is equally or more pressing with the one source that approaches anything like a regular commentary on English affairs. This is provided by the reports of resident foreign ambassadors, for, as well as regular domestic news reporting being unknown, Tudor monarchs were convinced that it was best for subjects to be told only what was good for them. The resident ambassador was a new breed in northern Europe. Only in the sixteenth century was it becoming generally recognized that a country needed to keep a representative at the court of an important neighbour, to watch over its own interests and to send back a steady flow of news. Older-style envoys continued to be sent to handle special negotiations, but there were now men stationed abroad and, according to the advice manuals, reporting back every few days, with monthly situation reports and, on their return, a *relation* or written debriefing. Theory did not turn out quite like that in practice, but a series of letters to the home government updating the situation every ten or twelve days – which is what survives from the best-organized embassies – is an outside commentary on affairs of unique value to the historian.[28]

The three principal embassies in England during Anne Boleyn's career were from Venice, from France and from the Holy Roman Empire. Venetian ambassadors were primarily concerned with trade questions and international relations. They tended to have short tours of duty (less than five years), and in 1535 representation lapsed to secretary level.[29] The French had a greater interest in English domestic affairs, and for much of the time they might hope for the chance to exploit Anne Boleyn in order to keep Henry VIII from allying with Charles V. Anne, indeed, was sometimes wholly identified with French interests, almost another ambassador in residence. Yet the reports of Francis I's representatives in London are frequently disappointing. Various reasons can be put forward for this. The French diplomatic service, if that term is not premature, was (like the English) still in its infancy, and it has not received the editorial attention from modern historians which its reports need and deserve. What is more, the relative ease and greater safety of communication between the French and the English courts may have encouraged the use of messengers for more difficult matters, rather than lengthy coded letters.[30]

Relations between London and Paris may, in any case, have been mainly at an official level, with the French ambassadors, representatives of the traditional enemy, finding it difficult to penetrate to non-government sources. In February 1535, when English suspicions of French treachery were running high, apparently even Anne Boleyn herself felt it unwise to talk freely with Francis's envoy, Gontier.[31] There was also a sense in which the French took Anne Boleyn for granted. She was there by Henry's will and they would use her, but policy was not determined by the need to support her position. Even more important, perhaps, was the brevity of French ambassadorial tours – the 1533 resident was complaining after six months![32] This did not impede the ambassador's representative duties, but it did limit his usefulness as a news-gatherer. Ambassadors tended to get better the longer they stayed. As a result in, for example, 1532, the year most critical for the English Reformation and for Anne herself, we have very little first-hand evidence from French sources. The ambassador, Giles de la Pommeraye, was new to the job but was gone within the year, and from 5 May to 17 June he was away in Brittany 'consulting with his government'.[33] He was a strong supporter of Henry's wish for a divorce; he worked hand in glove with the king and his ministers, even helping them to put out the official explanation for the anti-papal statute conditionally ending the payment of annates to Rome; above all, he was close to Anne. Yet none of this do we know from La Pommeraye himself.[34]

No contrast could be more marked than with the third of the principal foreign embassies resident in England. The Burgundian–Habsburg diplomatic service was the oldest in northern Europe and the best organized – essential in view of the far-flung territories which the Emperor Charles V had inherited and the issues he had to cope with. Furthermore, Charles was not simply interested in affairs in England because of their possible impact on his chronic rivalry with Francis I. He had a family interest in the treatment of his aunt, Katherine of Aragon, and the legitimacy of his cousin Mary. Thus, when it was suggested that the reports he received might contain too much about Henry's marital problems, the emperor requested even more information.[35] Not that Charles was allowing himself to be governed by sentiment; the traditional alliance with the Burgundian Low Countries would have powerful backing in England as long as Katherine could be supported as queen and Mary as the acknowledged heir.

This sophistication of diplomatic technique and depth of interest goes some way to explaining the fullness and utility to historians of reports from the imperial embassy in England. Yet what really makes the difference is the identity of the ambassador.[36] Eustace Chapuys, a lawyer from Annecy in Savoy, was not merely a highly efficient and assiduous envoy, writing between thirty and forty reports a year to the emperor, plus letters to his officers. Far more important was the length of time he spent in England; he arrived in 1529 and remained until almost the end of Henry VIII's life, retiring only in 1545 at the age of 56. This continuous residence enabled Chapuys to overcome many of the obstacles in the way of an ambassador seeking news.[37] In the first place, how was a stranger speaking no English to find informants? It took time to discover sensitively placed individuals who would supply information, or servants who could go out freely enough to be able to verify reports. Moreover, funds did not stretch to the employment of many agents and, in any case, the real secrets were at court. How was an ambassador to succeed there? The answer Chapuys adopted was the answer of the diplomatic manuals: speak French, make yourself *persona grata* with the elite, and news and contacts will come to you. And this is where his training and experience came in, and especially his standing as a humanist and a friend of Erasmus. A man of address, he was worth conversing with and very soon passed everywhere. Even in times of Anglo-imperial tension when another envoy might expect to be cold-shouldered, Chapuys continued to be welcomed as an individual. Henry VIII clearly enjoyed sparring with this shrewd, brilliant, cynical cosmopolitan. And Chapuys soon discovered something else as he worked tirelessly for the cause of Katherine and Mary. He became the focus for all those who disliked what was going on, who believed as he did. Here was a ready-made set of contacts as anxious to give him news as he was to collect it. His ear became almost the confessional for the king's critics, and Chapuys dabbled a good deal more deeply in English politics than the emperor either knew or would have sanctioned.[38]

The professionalism of Charles V's envoys, and especially the personality of Eustace Chapuys, come to us clearly over the centuries, and it is easy to succumb to their authority. Friedmann went as far as to write that: 'the agents of Charles V...spoke the truth, or what they believed to be the truth. Now and then they took a little too much credit for ability and energy; but they never gave an essentially false idea of the events they had to report.'[39] We must remember, however, that there were pitfalls awaiting even the ablest ambassador, and disadvantages as well as advantages in Chapuys' ready acceptance by English society, and especially by Anne's opponents. In the first place, his reporting on the court tends to derive from individuals who share a single point of view and, what is more, pass news on with the gloss which that view gave. Thus, when Chapuys reports bad feeling between Anne and Henry he is relying on informants who wanted to believe that Anne was falling out of royal favour and were ready to see hopeful signs in almost anything. What is more, many of those who spoke to him were out to serve their own agenda. That was certainly true of his official contacts. An instance of this which is specially relevant to Anne is the series of conversations Cromwell had with Chapuys during the crises of 1536. Of course, the envoy was well aware that Henry and his ministers would be trying to 'feed' him – and he reciprocated – but evaluating private individuals was more difficult. Courtiers might regularly express to him their loyalty to Mary, but this could reflect everything from genuine affection for her, through a desire to hedge bets or disguise true feelings, to a wish to stand well with a popular court figure or merely to be polite to his known prejudices. An ambassador could also let his own feelings mislead him. In the early 1530s certain conservatives sought to precipitate action by Charles V by claiming that the country was a powder-keg of resentment against Henry and Anne which awaited only the spark of an imperial invasion. Chapuys reported this enthusiastically because this was exactly what he himself wished to believe, and precisely how he wanted his home government to act. Ambassadors with Chapuys' level of commitment can easily find themselves in the business of self-fulfilling prophecy. It is also true that however long he remained in England, Chapuys continued to see things through Habsburg eyes – even when pink-spectacled. Thus his continual description of Anne Boleyn as 'the concubine' completely missed the point that to appreciate the situation in England as it actually was, it was vital to recognize that to Henry his marriage with Katherine had been, and would always be, a nullity. The ambassador's failure to see this cost Katherine's daughter dear in the summer of 1536.[40]

The inherent dangers in ambassadorial reports have led some scholars to play down their utility.[41] The difficulty with this is that, denied these reports, much early Tudor history becomes seriously, on occasion impossibly, opaque. The diplomatic reports of Eustace Chapuys, in particular, provide the only relatively continuous commentary on English politics and the royal court during the lifetime of Queen Anne; on particular episodes they are often the only evidence. Thus to dismiss them as inherently unreliable is to accept that we shall never know. An example is the agreement among ambassadors that Anne was involved in the attack on Wolsey. They could, of course, have all been misled by court gossip, but giving up on them leaves us in ignorance. It certainly does not allow us to assume that if their evidence is rejected, this establishes that she was not involved! The sources determine the limits of history – what can be explored, what cannot be explored. Hypothesis and speculation must not take the place of carefully evaluated evidence. The professionalism of the historian lies in reading such partisan material critically.

The danger of distortion is much less acute with administrative records, always assuming these were not prepared for public consumption. They are, however, sadly uninformative. Anne only became important in her mid-twenties and until then such material tells us no more about her than about other women of her age and class; nor should we expect it to. Even when she did become prominent, even when she was queen, we continue to know almost as little of her day to day as we do of the other women in Henry VIII's life. There are two significant exceptions to this lack of official data. The first is the account of Henry's private expenses which survives for just over three years from November 1529 to December 1532.[42] This gives a lively picture of the king's disbursements on Anne's behalf in the crucial period during which she was moving from being a recognized rival to Queen Katherine to being queen herself in all but name. The loss of similar accounts for earlier years does deny us valuable confirmation as to the date when the king first began to pay marked attention to 'the lady Anne', but the absence of later accounts is less significant. From the autumn of 1532, Anne was in receipt of a regular direct income – first as lady marquis of Pembroke and then as queen – and many of the costs previously borne by Henry would have gone through her own accounts (now, unfortunately, also lost). The second important official source is, somewhat surprisingly, the inventory drawn up after Henry's death. Despite the decade and more since Anne's execution, and all the intervening consorts, it provides substantial evidence of her lifestyle, vivid details found nowhere else.[43]

Where significant information about Anne Boleyn is to be found, as so often for her contemporaries, is in judicial records. The most important is the material covering her trial and that of her alleged accomplices. This includes commissions, writs, lengthy indictments detailing the supposed offences, jury lists and verdicts. After the trials these were all put in the *Baga de Secretis* – the Tudor equivalent of the file marked 'Top Secret' – and they survive virtually intact.[44] Other judicial material of value is the evidence which the Crown assiduously collected with a view to possible prosecution of Anne's critics, evidence which provides a clear indication of her general lack of popularity and the gossip which circulated about her. Even post-mortem material can be of use. In the autumn of 1539 the reformer, George Constantine, was fighting off a potential prosecution under the Act of Six Articles, and in evidence to Thomas Cromwell he set down his first-hand memories of the execution of Anne's supposed lovers three years earlier.[45] As in all such evidence, it must be remembered that the deponent has an ulterior motive – in Constantine's case, to gloss a past conversation so as to remove all hint of criticism of the Crown – but as a confession was subject to factual checking, variation is likely to be more in spin than in content.

Another obvious resource for the biographer might appear to be correspondence. Anne's own letters are disappointing. Few have survived and most are strictly concerned with practicalities – for instance, announcing the birth of Elizabeth. There is, admittedly, the remarkable letter which she is supposed to have written to Henry VIII on 6 May 1536, after her committal to the Tower. It exists in many copies, but none is contemporary, and although the tradition is that it was originally discovered among the papers of Thomas Cromwell, its 'elegance' (to use Herbert of Cherbury's word) has always inspired suspicion. It would appear to be wholly improbable for Anne to write that her marriage was built on nothing but the king's fancy and that her incarceration was the consequence of Henry's affection for Jane. Equally it would have been totally counterproductive for a Tudor prisoner in the Tower to warn the king, as the letter does, that he is in imminent danger of the judgement of God![46] There are practical objections, too. The ladies who watched Anne night and day in the Tower were charged with reporting all she said and did, but they made no mention of any such missive and it certainly could not have been smuggled out.[47] Similar improbabilities must also rule Anne out as the author of the lament *O Death, O Death, rock me on sleep*, even though it existed at least by the start of Elizabeth's reign and contains such apt lines as:

> Defiled is my name full sore
> Through cruel spite and false report,
> That I may say for evermore
> Farewell my joy, Adieu comfort.
>
> For wrongfully ye judge of me
> Unto my fame a mortal wound
> Say what ye will, it will not be
> Ye seek for that cannot be found.[48]

The scarcity of genuine letters from Anne is nothing to wonder at. Except in diplomacy or matters of exceptional importance, people at this period did not normally keep copies of the letters they sent. Correspondence is generally known only if the original has survived in the papers of the recipient. Letters to the queen are, indeed, somewhat more plentiful and more revealing, in particular the seventeen love-letters from Henry himself, ten in French and the rest in English, which have ended up – of all places – in the Vatican.[49] These letters have no dates; although some belong to the summer and autumn of 1528 there is, as with Shakespeare's *Sonnets*, no firm agreement about the order in which they were written.[50] Letters between third parties are also valuable, particularly to and from correspondents within court circles such as Lord Lisle, the governor of Calais, and his wife, but with one proviso: communicating political information or gossip could get people into serious trouble, so that sensitive material was normally conveyed by word of mouth.[51]

On-the-spot reporting of news had no place in sixteenth-century life, but a number of eyewitness accounts have survived of several of the episodes in Anne Boleyn's career, including a number by foreigners. These are, of course, confined to the more public events, from her creation as marchioness of Pembroke in September 1532 to her execution in the Tower three years and nine months later. Furthermore, they are subject to the prejudices of the various eyewitnesses. Carping descriptions of, say, Anne's coronation procession contrast with the initial neutrality of Judge John Spelman, the warmer recollection of Thomas Cranmer, and the semi-official propaganda of Wynkyn de Worde's pamphlet, *The noble tryumphant coronacyon of quene Anne, wyfe unto the most noble kynge Henry the VIII*. And in such a range of reporting there lies safety for the historian.[52]

An additional complication arises when first-hand reports have been worked into consciously produced pieces of literature. One example we have already encountered is the poetry of George Cavendish.[53] From about 1522 until the cardinal's death in 1530, Cavendish was one of his gentlemen ushers and so splendidly placed to collect first-hand information about Wolsey and the court, but he wrote in Mary's reign, long after the event. What is more, his intention to display the mutability of Fortune makes for verse heavy on lamentation and light on information; there are some nuggets of value, but the 365 lines covering Anne and her alleged lovers, one after another, contain fewer than twenty points of substance. Cavendish's better-known 'Life and Death of Cardinal Wolsey' is far more informative, but this work was also written from the hindsight of the mid-century.[54] Furthermore, given that theme is again the fickleness of Fortune, it casts Anne Boleyn as the agent of 'Venus the insatiate goddess', called in by Fortune to 'abate' Wolsey's 'high port' and humble him to the dust.

Another important literary source is Edward Hall's *The Union of the Two Noble and Illustre Famelies of York and Lancaster.* Better known as Hall's *Chronicle*, this is the work of a Londoner who did see much of what he described and tried to investigate more. Yet his stated theme – 'The triumphant reign of King Henry the VIII' – expresses the standpoint he took, and the finished narrative (to 1532) has only three isolated sentences about Anne, and a short paragraph about her dancing with Francis I at Calais.[55] The rest of the book, worked up posthumously from Hall's notes and drafts, has two sentences about Anne's marriage, another about her pregnancy, a long description of her coronation (in which Hall was involved), details of the birth and christening of Elizabeth, terse reports of Anne's reaction to Katherine of Aragon's death and of her own subsequent miscarriage, six final sentences on her condemnation and a brief version of her speech on the scaffold. Perhaps if Hall had lived to write the material in final form himself we would have had more, but a hint in one passage suggests that he intended to gloss over Anne's marriage as something on which 'the king was not well counselled'.[56] Anything else would be quite out of character for Hall's hero king. A 'Chronicle' which is truer to the style of London chronicles in general is that of Charles Wriothesley, Windsor Herald (*c*.1508–62). It is immediate – items were recorded as or soon after they occurred – and also well-informed since the author was close to government and took part in some of the events he describes.[57]

The literary account which is closest in time to the events described is the *Histoire de Anne Boleyn Jadis Royne d'Angleterre*, the French metrical account of Anne's trial and execution by Lancelot de Carles which we have already encountered. It was completed on 2 June 1536, a bare fortnight after her death. Manuscript versions exist in London, in a number of repositories in France, and in Brussels; it reached print at Lyons in 1545, with the author described as *Charles aulmosnier de M. le Dauphin*.[58] Although de Carles did not himself witness the trial of Anne and her brother, he was in London at the time; he could have attended the trial of the commoners accused, and undoubtedly had contact with well-informed eyewitnesses.[59] Because of this and the immediacy of his writing, de Carles's account has been assumed to have original authority. Caution should, in fact, have warned otherwise. How could de Carles report events not accessible to the public, notably his long and unique account of the speech by an unnamed lord reporting Anne's misdeeds to Henry in absolute confidence? The true source of his information was made clear when research revealed that a presentation copy of his poem, sent to Henry VIII, was listed as a 'French book written in form of a tragedy by one Carle being attendant and near about the ambassador'.[60] In other words, de Carles wrote on the basis of what was known by the French embassy, and the principal source for this would have been the English government. It is therefore no surprise that de Carles's account agrees with the information Cromwell had sent to Henry's ambassadors in Paris on 14 May, setting out for foreign consumption the Crown's version of her arrest and indictment.[61] The *Histoire* is, in effect, the government line in translation. One must also note the description 'in form of a tragedy'. De Carles imaginatively elaborated the queen's response to being found guilty into fifty lines of verse. Her scaffold speech, too, is enhanced and distorted. She seems to have said, 'I am come hither to accuse no man of my death, neither my judges nor any other,' or something of the kind.[62] The *Histoire* makes her say: 'The judge of all the world, in whom abounds justice and truth knows all, and through his love I beseech that he will have compassion on those who have condemned me to this death.' This is clearly one more in the category of 'last words' which should have been uttered but were not.[63]

Paul Friedmann closed his magisterial two-volume study, *Anne Boleyn: A Chapter of English History, 1527–1536*, with the depressing comment: 'my object has been to show that very little is known of the events of those times, and that the history of Henry's first divorce and of the rise and fall of Anne Boleyn has still to be written.'[64] The sources available today for a biography of Anne Boleyn suggest that we no longer need to be quite as pessimistic. True, there have been no block discoveries since Friedmann's day, but during the century and more since he wrote, valuable new evidence has come to light piecemeal, and despite their distortions and irregularities, the bits and pieces do add up. What is even more important is that historical research has transformed our reading of the period; the context into which evidence, old and new, has to be placed is far better understood. Our knowledge of the court, in particular, and also of the nature and progress of Henry's matrimonial affairs and their relation to religious Reformation means that we can now see Anne as an active, three-dimensional, proactive participant.

Friedmann's comment, nevertheless, remains true in one respect. The sources for the life of Anne Boleyn stop short of that level of inner documentation which biography ideally requires. Only at a handful of points in the story do we know anything of what Anne thought. Only in

Henry's love-letters and in remarks scrawled on that Book of Hours do we know for certain what they said to each other. All the rest is of the order of what somebody said somebody else thought or said – and according to tradition it was Henry VIII who remarked, 'if I thought my cap knew my counsel, I would cast it into the fire and burn it.'[65] The limitations are galling, given the fascination Anne Boleyn and her story have continued to exercise over the intervening centuries, and many have concluded that only artistic imagination will bring us to the truth. That is a valid position. There is a place for Donizetti's *Anna Bolena*, for *Anna of the Thousand Days*, for the variant dramatizations by Rosemary Anne Sisson and Nick McCarthy in the television series *Six Wives of Henry VIII* and for the many literary attempts at biographical *actualité*, provided we recognize them for what they are: statements about ourselves. They explore our values, they tell us how we feel men and women would react, might react, should react in an imagined situation. What they can never quite tell us is how Henry VIII and Anne Boleyn did react.

PASSION AND COURTLY LOVE

SOURCE problems are particularly relevant to our pursuit of Anne Boleyn in the years between March 1522 and the end of 1527. At the first, she was newly come from France, the most glamorous of the ladies rescued from the *Château Vert*, although in reality on passage to exile in Ireland. By the second, her name was beginning to pass along the diplomatic grapevine as Henry VIII's inamorata. In England her stock was soaring and Anne could 'look very haughty and stout [self-confident], having all manner of jewels or rich apparel that might be gotten with money'.[1] The events of these five years see Anne involved first with Henry Percy, heir to the earldom of Northumberland, then with Thomas Wyatt the elder, and finally with Henry VIII and the problem of his childless marriage.

The principal source for the Percy story, and the only one which gives any detail, is Cavendish's biography of Cardinal Wolsey. According to Cavendish – and he writes as an eyewitness – Percy was a young man in Wolsey's household and Anne a maid of honour to Queen Katherine.[2] When accompanying his master to court, Percy gravitated to the queen's chamber: 'And there would fall in dalliance among the queen's maidens, being at the last more conversant with Mistress Anne Boleyn than with any other, so that there grew such a secret love between them that at length they were ensured together intending to marry.' Henry, however, was himself taken with Anne, who 'for her excellent gesture and behaviour did excel all other', and ordered the cardinal to intervene. So when Wolsey got back to York Place, he called Percy to the gallery and told him off in no uncertain terms:

> I marvel not a little of thy peevish folly that thou wouldest tangle and ensure thyself with a foolish girl yonder in the court. I mean Anne Boleyn. Dost

thou not consider the state that God hath called thee unto in this world, for after the death of thy noble father thou art most like to inherit and possess one of the most worthiest earldoms of this realm? Therefore it had been most meet and convenient for thee to have sued for the consent of thy father in that behalf, and to have also made the king's highness privy thereto, requiring then his princely favour.

The king would have found him a far better match and formed a much better impression of his worth, but now he had offended both father and monarch at once. Wolsey would send for the earl to discipline his son and the king would insist on the relationship ending because he had planned another match for Anne (unknown to her) and 'was almost at a point with the same person'.

This reduced Percy to tears, but he defended both his right to choose and Anne's suitability, beseeching the cardinal to intercede with the king 'on my behalf for his princely benevolence in this matter the which I cannot deny or forsake'.[3] At this Wolsey addressed bitter comments to Cavendish and others of his household about the wilfulness of youth, but Percy insisted: 'in this matter I have gone so far before so many worthy witnesses that I know not how to avoid myself nor to discharge my conscience.' The worldly-wise cardinal saw no problem, sent for the earl and, in the meantime, forbade Percy to see Anne.

When the father arrived, he and Wolsey planned what to do. Then, as Cavendish and his fellows were escorting Northumberland to his barge, Henry Percy was sent for and given a public dressing-down by his formidable parent: 'Son, thou hast always been a proud, presumptuous, disdainful, and very unthrifty waster, and even so hast thou now declared thyself.' Threats of the king's displeasure, the horrible prospect that he would be the last Percy, earl of Northumberland, unfavourable comparison with his brothers and a threat of disinheritance followed in quick succession, and the earl swept out with a dire prophecy to those around that they would see it all come true. At this Lord Percy crumbled, and 'after long debating and consultation' (presumably with the canon lawyers), a way was found to invalidate the young lord's commitment to Anne, who had, in the meantime, been sent to her father's country house. To make assurance sure, Percy was married off to a daughter of the earl of Shrewsbury (George Talbot), and Anne thereafter nursed an implacable hatred for Wolsey, uttering threats that 'if it lay ever in her power, she would work the cardinal as much [similar] displeasure.'

Such is the story Cavendish tells, and the final act in the romantic tragedy was the ruin of Henry Percy.[4] He did succeed his father as sixth earl of Northumberland in 1527, but his marriage to Mary Talbot disintegrated and his health and his personality collapsed. In February 1535, accepting that he had no chance of a legitimate son and rejecting the king's wish to see one of his hated brothers groomed to succeed him, he made Henry his heir.[5] When in 1536 his brothers earned glory and martyrdom as leaders of the Pilgrimage of Grace, the head of the Percys skulked in Wressle Castle, a broken reed to both king and rebels. By June 1537 he was dead.

How much are we to credit Cavendish's account? Was Percy engineered out to let Henry in? David Starkey has argued that this was the case, citing hitherto overlooked evidence that the Percy–Talbot marriage did not take place until between March and August 1525 and possibly later.[6] However, the legalities for the Percy–Talbot marriage (which had been under discussion since 1516) were in their final stages in the autumn of 1523, with the marriage intended for the new year of 1524. The hitch obviously occurred then and thus is too early to be royal interference. Henry was probably sleeping with Anne's sister. The earl of Northumberland made an unexpected journey to London in June 1523 and it is tempting to see that as the occasion of the confrontation of father and son.[7] Cavendish's interpretation of Anne's reaction is also improbable. To go about making threats against the cardinal in 1522 or 1523 was both unwise and childish, and Anne was neither. When we have some first-hand evidence of her relationship with Wolsey some six or seven years later, it is far more subtle than is explicable by a long-held grudge.

It also seems likely that it was not Henry VIII who was incensed by the young Percy's 'folly'. Wolsey was committed to 'perfect' the marriage between Anne and James Butler, and he was adept at threatening royal wrath when he was the one frustrated.[8] Given the probability that Boleyn was dragging his feet with the Butlers, it could even be that Anne's encouragement of Percy had her father's approval. And if Wolsey had made clear a determination to get his own way, this would also explain the panic-stricken reaction Cavendish saw in the earl of Northumberland, who had learned at great cost in 1516 the lengths to which the cardinal would go.[9] There must be doubts, too, about the conversations reported by Cavendish. His eyewitness irrelevancies confirm events in outline, but after thirty-five years he can have retained only an impression of what was said. Hindsight plays a further part in the dialogue he writes – noticeably the earl's prophecy that his son will be 'a wasteful prodigal' and 'the last earl of our house'.

We cannot, however, ignore Cavendish. Wolsey's mention of the alternative plans for Anne certainly fits the discussions on the Boleyn–Butler marriage. Equally, Cavendish's stress on the seriousness of Percy's commitment can be echoed later. Indeed, in 1532 Mary Percy claimed that her husband had admitted that before he had married her, he had promised himself to Anne.[10] The earl was a known supporter of the queen, and the pre-contract story was, Chapuys said, common knowledge.[11] And it would not go away. Chapuys picked it up again in 1536 and Charles Wriothesley, another contemporary, stated categorically that Anne was divorced because of a pre-contract with the earl.[12]

A relationship of some sort is thus certain, but we cannot be sure about the level of the commitment between Anne and Henry Percy. Each denied Mary Percy's story. Her estranged husband would later write that before the king married Anne, he had been not only:

> examined upon my oath before the archbishops of Canterbury and York, but also received the blessed sacrament upon the same before the duke of Norfolk and other the king's highness' counsel learned in the spiritual law...to my damnation if ever there were any contract or promise of marriage between her and me.[13]

At the time, Chapuys believed that the earl had been got at, or was impelled by fear, and he certainly was frightened at the time of Anne's fall. The later information reaching the ambassador was that the Percy–Boleyn marriage had even been consummated. This seems improbable. Such a relationship no one could have overturned, not even a combination of Henry VIII, Wolsey and the fifth earl of Northumberland. Given the Butler negotiations, it would also be surprising if so insuperable an obstacle had not already been discovered. Chapuys' sources were, in any case, less than reliable, for he dates the supposed marriage to 1527.

If a consummated marriage is the unlikely extreme possibility, the minimum would be an understanding. Perhaps Henry Percy ended up pledged to both women, or felt himself more deeply committed to Anne than she to him – hardly novel situations. That, however, makes too little of the evidence. The Boleyn–Butler marriage plan did founder, and an entanglement of Anne with Henry Percy could explain why Piers Butler lost patience in 1523.[14] Something similar might explain the delay between Northumberland discussing the marriage of his son with the earl of Shrewsbury and the chief baron of the exchequer in the autumn of 1523 with an expectation of a wedding in the New Year, and the ceremony actually taking place more than twelve months later.[15] Plainly there was a problem, and the most plausible explanation is that Lord Henry's commitment to Anne had introduced obstacles which the lawyers needed time to resolve. Evidence from Anne's side agrees. The dispensation which Henry VIII sought from the pope in 1527, allowing him to marry when he was free to do so, sought cover also for problems with the intended bride. It allowed him to marry any other woman and any other woman to marry him, even where she had 'already contracted marriage with some other person, provided she has not consummated it'.[16] Does that refer to abortive marriage proposals we know nothing about and which might explain why Anne was still unmarried in 1527? Or had she been contracted to Percy, or perhaps even betrothed to Butler and then contracted to Percy?[17] Of course, dispensations attempt to cover every conceivable contingency; they are not evidence of fact. But the one thing we can be sure of is that matters had gone far enough between Anne and Percy or Butler or both, or unknown third parties, for Henry VIII to seek cover against possible future objections.[18] And yet? Was it just legal caution? The decree annulling Anne's marriage to Henry in 1536 does refer to 'certain just true, and lawful impediments, unknown at the making' of the statute in support of the Boleyn marriage, and now 'confessed by the said Lady Anne before the . . . archbishop of Canterbury, sitting judicially'.[19]

How long Anne Boleyn was away from court after the Percy episode – if she was away at all – is not known. The next evidence we have concerns Thomas Wyatt. This, second to her relationship with Henry VIII, is the episode in Anne's life which has commanded the greatest attention from subsequent generations: Anne Boleyn and the first great Tudor poet.

The Wyatt home at Allington Castle, near Maidstone, was some twenty miles away from Hever and the family was not only a neighbour of the Boleyns but moved in the same court circles. Despite this, their tradition that Thomas met Anne only on her return from France is probably correct, for at the time she left for Brussels he was barely 10 years old. But when they did meet, he was bowled over. His grandson George has it thus:

> The knight, in the beginning, coming to behold the sudden appearance of this new beauty, came to be holden and surprised somewhat with the sight thereof; after much more with her witty and graceful speech, his ear also had him chained unto her, so as finally his heart seemed to say, *I could gladly yield to be tied for ever with the knot of her love,* as somewhere in his verses hath been thought his meaning was to express.[20]

What we cannot assume is the nature of the relationship between Anne and Thomas. Ever since the sixteenth century there has been disagreement over this, and even sedate modern scholars seem strangely committed in their attempts to demonstrate that Anne did or did not share Wyatt's bed. His verse provides the only first-hand evidence, but this raises the age-old question, 'how autobiographical is poetry?' Some of, particularly, Wyatt's later or supposed poems do arise from specific events: the executions of Anne Boleyn's alleged lovers and later of Cromwell, his own misfortunes and imprisonments. But verses which arise from relationships are much more difficult to pin down. One Wyatt poem does, however, combine event and relationship and can serve as a datum line. It was written in 1532 when Wyatt was in the entourage accompanying Henry VIII and Anne Boleyn to Calais:

> Sometime I fled the fire that me brent
> By sea, by land, by water and by wind;
> And now I follow the coals that be quent
> From Dover to Calais against my mind.
> Lo how desire is both sprung and spent!
> And he may see that whilom was so blind,
> And all his labour now he laugh to scorn
> Meshed in the briars that erst was all to-torn.[21]

Taken literally, this suggests that Wyatt had been in love with Anne, had had to struggle not to become more deeply involved, and now, cured of his passion, ruefully contemplated the fool he had been. But are we to take this literally? Wyatt was writing within the often complex and baffling convention of courtly love, whose nature resembles nothing so much as an onion, where to peel away one layer is only to reveal a further layer underneath.

Courtly love was an integral element in chivalry, the complex of attitudes and institutions which was central to the life of the Tudor court and elite. To modern eyes, this appears to be a tissue of artificialities which fails to disguise the ephemeral nature and conspicuous waste of tournaments, pageants, dances and masques. In fact, the idiom of chivalry enabled society to say many important things and regulate many important relationships. At a tournament, for example, the focus was always the king – even if someone else actually won. By participating, men drew attention to their personal prowess, but more so to their service to the sovereign; by attending as spectators, the rest of the court elite demonstrated that it too was loyal. The fancy dress and role-playing of tournaments and indoor festivities could also make a specific statement about the royal person, as when Henry VIII appeared at the Field of Cloth of Gold in the guise of Hercules. There was also international one-upmanship. The forms of display were common throughout Europe, and a country was judged by its spectacles. There was as nice and as subtle a gradation in chivalric ballyhoo as in the cordiality (or otherwise) of the welcome accorded by a modern government to a visiting statesman.

At a very basic level, chivalry was also a defence against boredom and vice. The mark of a gentleman was, in the well-known words of Thomas Smith, Elizabeth I's secretary of state, being able to 'live idly and without manual labour', but there were still twenty-four hours in the day to fill. Chivalric convention therefore created as busy a lifestyle as ever would be experienced by future generations worn out by the exigencies of the London Season. The serious pursuit of entertainment was the only alternative to demoralization, as *Pastime with good company*, Henry VIII's most famous song, makes clear:

> Youth must have some dalliance,
> Of good or ill some pastance.
> Company methinks then best
> All thoughts and fancies to digest.
>> For idleness
>> Is chief mistress
>> Of vices all;
>> Then who can say
>> But pass-the-day
>> Is best of all?[22]

Out of doors, when not engaged in war or training for the pseudo-war of the tournament, the gentleman was busy with its substitute, hunting. Indoors – dancing, music, poetry, good conversation and the game of courtly love.

The notion that courtly love was an antidote to boredom when the weather was bad or hunting out of season is hardly romantic. Nor is the idea that another of its functions was to constrain gender relationships within an accepted convention. Among the Tudor elite, property consider-ations were accorded more importance than emotional satisfaction when it came to making a marriage. When Anne Boleyn was proposed as the bride of James Butler, personal feelings were not consulted, and when they did surface, as in the case of Henry Percy, material considerations allowed them short shrift. In some, perhaps in many, cases a relationship begun in property could grow into passion, but others were left to seek emotional or personal fulfilment with someone other than their spouse, not to mention those who were not yet economically free to marry, or might never be. The problem was at its most acute at the court, overwhelmingly masculine but not monastic, and with a queen and her attendant ladies at its centre. Courtly love was the safety device which prevented this critical mass from exploding.

The fictions of courtly love were based on the same ideal which disposed men to attend the king: service. The courtier, the 'perfect knight', was supposed to sublimate his relations with the ladies of the court by choosing a 'mistress' and serving her faithfully and exclusively. He formed part of her circle, wooed her with poems, songs and gifts, and if she was gracious enough to recognize the link he might wear her favour and joust in her honour. He might have a wife at home, but that was a separate life. In return the suitor must look for one thing only, 'kindness' – understanding and platonic friendship. A lady might, in fact, be older than her 'lover', and she would then act as his patroness and launch him into court society. At a deeper level too, courtly love could be important psychologically, meeting the need for emotional ties. To twenty-first-century eyes conditioned to see normal relationships between men and women as active sexually, such a convention appears repressive, but it worked well enough to regulate gender relations acceptably.

Some recent writers have, however, questioned whether courtly love was ever 'an actual social phenomenon'.[23] Others would 'deconstruct' it and see courtly love in terms of a literary device. Such scepticism flies in the face of the evidence. The court of Philip the Good of Burgundy, Margaret of Austria's great-grandfather, developed an elaborate code of chivalry in which versions of earlier romances were not only commissioned and read widely, but 'their contents inspired actual events at court.'[24] Nor was this a ducal fad. It set the standard for Europe. Even Pierre Sala, a modest French court official whom Anne could have met, procured an illuminated *Emblesmes de devises d'amour* for his 'mistress' Marguerite, the wife of the royal treasurer.[25] The English court followed suit. Henry VIII himself appeared in numerous guises, most famously in the great Westminster entertainment of 1511, when as *Cuer Loyall* (Loyal Heart) he led a tilting team comprising *Bon Voloire* (Good Will), *Bon Espoir* (Good Hope) and *Valiaunt Desire* assisted by *Bone Foy* (Good Faith) and *Amoure*

Loyall (Loyal Love). At the Shrovetide tilt in 1526 (which Anne would have attended) the recently remarried marquis of Exeter announced that his amours were now over by displaying the device of a burning heart being sprayed from a watering can held in the hand of a woman.[26] And, of course, unless the European fashion for courtly posturing had really existed, *Don Quixote* makes no sense.

We also need to be less solemn. To most participants the convention of courtly love was a game, 'pass the day', an etiquette of flirting. After all, unless courtly love was artificial, poets such as Wyatt lived in perpetual misery.

> Though I cannot your cruelty constrain
> For my good will to favour me again,
> Though my true and faithful love
> Have no power your heart to move,
>   Yet rue upon my pain.
>
> Though I your thrall must evermore remain
> And for your sake my liberty restrain,
> The greatest grace that I do crave
> Is that ye would vouchsafe
>   To rue upon my pain.
>
> Though I have not deserved to obtain
> So high reward but this to serve in vain,
> Though I shall have no redress,
> Yet of right ye can no less
>   But rue upon my pain.
>
> But I see well that your high disdain
> Will nowise grant that I shall that attain;
> Yet ye must grant at the least
> This my poor and small request
>   Rejoice not at my pain.[27]

The familiar tropes of courtly dalliance are all there – the disdainful mistress, the suitor whose love nevertheless remains true, the binding exclusivity of commitment, service as the highest of ideals, even when unrewarded.

We must, on the other hand, recognize that convention can be ambiguous. Most players of the game of courtly love may not have taken it too seriously, but the game was inherently sexual. At the fall of the

Château Vert Anne Boleyn did yield at least her hand in the dance to 'Amoressness', 'Nobleness' or whoever had captured 'Perseverance'. A lady was expected not to give sexual favours, but they were there to gain, and the lover who offered service also threatened possession. Hence Margaret of Austria warning her ladies to keep men at a distance and treat their advances with a light touch.[28] Cavendish's comment on Henry Percy is too apposite not to merit repetition: 'the Lord Percy would resort for his pastime into the queen's chamber and there would fall in dalliance among the queen's maidens, being at the last more conversant with Mistress Anne Boleyn than with any other, so that there grew a secret love between them.'[29]

Courtly love thus had an inner tension. In most cases stylized flirtation, in others it could also be a conduit for real passion; the love lyric may be artful or autobiographical, the 'mistress' may become the mistress. And this ambivalence is the problem with Anne and Wyatt's poetry. After 500 years, how is the historian to be certain? The difficulty is well illustrated by the so-called 'Devonshire Manuscript', once at Chatsworth and now in the British Library. For almost a hundred years this has been claimed as direct evidence linking Wyatt with Anne Boleyn.[30] The manuscript is a volume of poems associated with Anne's cousin, the Mary Howard who in 1534 married the king's illegitimate son Henry Fitzroy, duke of Richmond; her initials are on the original binding. Another person involved was Anne's waiting-woman, Madge Shelton, and a third, the king's niece Margaret Douglas (on one page there is a joint inscription to her and Mary Fitzroy). The manuscript was apparently lent quite widely at court, and borrowers repaid the loan by inscribing a poem they had access to; it now includes almost 200 items in a variety of hands. Some of these are undoubtedly biographical, for example, those related to the secret marriage between Margaret Douglas and Lord Thomas Howard, for which he was imprisoned in the Tower from 1536. About a dozen of the items are, indeed, by Thomas or Margaret themselves. Wyatt is certainly present – some 125 items attributed or assigned by scholars. If he had a relationship with Anne, she should be here too.

Evidence of Anne has been seen on a number of folios: a signature ('an'), an expression of good wishes ('amer ann i'), and a riddle:

am el men
an em e
as I haue dese
I ama yowrs an,

which is supposedly solved by the transposition of the second and fourth letters of the first three lines:

> a lemmen
> amene
> ah I saue dese
> I ama yowrs an.[31]

One of Wyatt's stanzas seems to complete the circle:

> That time that mirth did steer my ship
> Which now is fraught with heaviness,
> And fortune bit not then the lip
> But was defence of my distress,
> Then in my book wrote my mistress:
> 'I am yours, you may well be sure,
> And shall be while my life doth dure.'[32]

The poem goes on to lament that now his erstwhile mistress is 'mine extreme enemy' – Wyatt rejected by Anne.

Unfortunately for romance, very little of this stands up to close scrutiny. There is no evidence that Wyatt ever handled the Devonshire Manuscript; its Wyatt poems represent the taste of Mary Fitzroy and her circle. Nor is the evidence for Anne at all convincing. *That time that mirth did steer my ship* is assigned to Wyatt by only some modern editors. The 'signature' is a couple of letters written to test a pen. The expression of goodwill is a mere doodle and is certainly not in Anne's hand. As for the riddle, not only is it hardly intelligible in solution, on the page the lines are randomly scattered, probably not written at one time and possibly by different writers. They are better understood as casual exercises, the last two, clearly part-versions of phrases such as 'as I have deserved' and 'I am yours and ever will be' – expressions of courtly love as stock as the greetings on any Valentine card.[33]

If a text as closely associated with Anne Boleyn's entourage as the Devonshire Manuscript tells us nothing of Anne and Wyatt, it is small wonder that many attempts to interpret isolated poems by (or perhaps by) Sir Thomas carry little conviction.[34] Apart from the conventionality of courtly love and deciding whether a poem is autobiographical, Wyatt's active sexuality presents a problem; as he said himself, 'I grant I do not profess chastity.'[35] Thus only with the clearest corroboration can we assume that if any of his poems of desire, rivalry, possession, rejection or retreat are autobiographical, the woman they refer to is Anne Boleyn. And corroboration does not include supposed allusions to Wyatt losing Anne to a higher bidder. Even in a private poem (and poems were rarely entirely private) it was ill advised to write

> I quit the enterprise of that that I have lost
> To whomsoever lust [likes] for to proffer most

if that higher 'bidder' were Henry VIII.[36]

George Wyatt's suggestion that Anne is the subject of *I could gladly yield to be tied for ever with the knot of her love*, is ruled out by the reference to hair of 'crisped gold'. One of the pseudo-Wyatts could be a defence of the defiant motto which Anne adopted for a brief period in 1530 – *Ainsi sera groigne qui groigne* ('Let them grumble; that is how it is going to be') – but even if by Wyatt, that would only suggest that in 1530 he was one of the future queen's circle, which we might guess anyway.[37] Proper historical scepticism, indeed, leaves only four Wyatt poems where there can be reasonable confidence that he is referring to Anne Boleyn. The revealing 1532 poem about the journey to Calais we have already noted. Much less informative is an earlier poem (again genuine) in the form of a riddle to which the solution is 'Anna':

> What word is that, that changeth not?
> Though it be turned and made in twain?
> It is mine answer, God it wot,
> And eke the causer of my pain.
> A love rewardeth with disdain,
> Yet it is loved. What would ye more?
> It is my health eke and my sore.[38]

Even here, of course, it is a question of probability – the poem would fit any 'Anna' – but Anne Boleyn is an obvious possibility. At a surface level this is a courtly conceit, a teasing trifle ornamented with conventional emotions, but is there more behind the poem than that?

We are on better ground with the sonnet which mentions 'Brunet'. Again definitely by Wyatt, *If waker care, if sudden pale colour* tells of the poet falling in love again. The closing lines do not, in the final version, necessarily suggest Anne:

> If thou ask whom, sure since I did refrain
> Brunet that set my wealth in such a roar
> The unfeigned cheer of Phyllis hath the place

> That Brunet had: she hath and ever shall.
> She from myself now hath me in her grace:
> She hath in hand my wit, my will, and all.
> My heart alone well worthy she doth stay
> Without whose help scant do I live a day.[39]

That Brunet is Anne, however, is made clear by what Wyatt wrote initially:

> ...since I did refrain
> Her that did set our country in a roar
> The unfeigned cheer of Phyllis hath the place
> That Brunet had...[40]

Wyatt had the sense to suppress the indiscretion, but it indicates that at least he had enjoyed the permitted courtly relationship with Anne of servant and mistress. It could also mean more if we interpret literally 'Phyllis hath the place that Brunet had'. But poetic form is against that reading. The final quatrain has to present a contrast, in this case setting the depth and stability of his relationship with Phyllis (his mistress, Elizabeth Darell) against the turbulence of Brunet.[41]

Caution is equally called for by the final poem linking Wyatt and Anne, and the only one which makes a clear allusion to the king. It is, admittedly, inspired by a poem of Petrarch (and perhaps by other Italian sources), but as usual Wyatt twists 'Petrarch's meaning to suit his own more urgent and worldly interest'.[42]

> Whoso list to hunt: I know where is a hind.
> But as for me, alas I may no more:
> The vain travail hath wearied me so sore,
> I am of them that farthest cometh behind.
> Yet may I by no means my wearied mind
> Draw from the deer, but as she fleeth afore
> Fainting I follow. I leave off therefore,
> Sithens in a net I seek to hold the wind.
> Who list to hunt, I put him out of doubt,
> As well as I may spend his time in vain,
> And graven with diamonds in letters plain
> There is written her fair neck round about:
> '*Noli me tangere*, for Caesar's I am,
> And wild for to hold, though I seem tame.'[43]

What Wyatt appears to be admitting is being powerfully attracted to Anne, 'the hind', and having to break this by drawing back from her crowd of admirers, a sentiment close to the Calais poem. This time, however, he says that he had been only one of the hunt followers and by no means near the prey – 'I am of them that farthest cometh behind' – and that his 'travail' had been 'vain'. The final sestet is a warning: 'Anne belongs to Henry.' Though 'tame' (that is, approachable), she will shy away from any attempt at possession by another; the collar, which in Petrarch tells of Laura's devotion to God, has become a slave collar.

No doubt the search for autobiographical allusions in Wyatt's poetry will continue, but the few demonstrable references to Anne Boleyn add up to much less than some have claimed. If we discount the 'Anna' riddle as a mere triviality, the remaining three pieces each point to personal commitment on Wyatt's part. However, in the Calais poem Anne did not respond. *Noli me tangere* portrays her as remote, and only the poem written to his mistress after Anne's death can be read to suggest that she fully reciprocated his affection – and then only by defying the requirements of poetic form. Wyatt's poems alone are not enough to support the hypothesis that Anne and Thomas were lovers. They merely suggest that Wyatt became one of a number of Anne's acknowledged courtly suitors, found himself emotionally involved but drew only a limited response.

Against this conclusion is the fact that a poet is as capable of glossing over the past as anyone else. The testimony of Wyatt's grandson is not the only reason to believe that Sir Thomas was more taken with Anne than he later admitted. In 1530 Chapuys reported that the duke of Suffolk had revived stories about a courtier who had earlier been rusticated on suspicion of too great an interest in Anne, and this could very well have been the poet.[44] Admittedly there is no evidence that Wyatt was formally rusticated during Anne's lifetime, but he did make a spur of the moment decision to join Sir John Russell on a diplomatic mission to Italy, which can be dated to early January 1527.[45] Russell, George Wyatt tells us, had already set out by boat down the Thames when, obviously calling at Greenwich for last-minute instructions, he encountered Thomas.[46] Hearing of his journey, Thomas had announced then and there, 'I, if you please, will ask leave, get money and go with you' – and promptly did just that. Since it was about this time that Wyatt must have realized that the king was now seriously in pursuit of Anne, he could well have been taking the chance (and Henry gave him permission) for a visit abroad to extract himself tactfully.

What of Anne's feeling for Wyatt? Were they as cool as the poems suggest? That Anne was fond of Wyatt seems very probable. In 1533 Chapuys described the poet as one 'whom she loves very much', and particularly in her early years at court his attentions cannot have been unwelcome. Percy's was the greater scalp, but even at 19 Wyatt's enviable combination of physique and good looks, intelligence, an articulate personality, spontaneity and good humour made him very attractive. Yet there was one absolute block to the relationship going further than friendship. Separated from his wife because of her adultery, Wyatt was in no position to offer Anne anything but a place as his mistress. We can guess that Mary Boleyn might have counted 'all well lost for love', but as Anne's conduct with the king was to show, the younger sister thought otherwise. Any feelings she had for Thomas certainly did not prevent a characteristically robust response to Suffolk's scandalmongering in 1530.[47] Anne immediately asked Henry to send Wyatt away. The king obliged, but clearly with reluctance. Soon he was interceding for Wyatt and persuading Anne to allow him back into favour. Whereas in 1527 Henry may have been happy to see Wyatt out of the way, he evidently did not see him later as a skeleton in Anne's cupboard. 1536 confirms this. Wyatt's arrest in May shows that he could be linked with Anne; his release suggests strongly that the link was known to be innocent.

Anne's friendship with Wyatt is further illuminated by a bizarre tale in the *Cronica del Rey Enrico*.[48] This tells how, when Henry became interested in Anne, he angrily refused to hear evidence from Wyatt that she was 'a bad woman' and no fit wife. Instead Thomas was rusticated for two years, only to be arrested in 1536, though thanks to Cromwell's favour and his earlier attempt to warn the king, he escaped execution. He thereupon wrote to Henry, setting out the evidence that he had not been allowed to present. He had arrived at (presumably) Hever on a night when her parents were away, and gone up to Anne Boleyn's chamber, where she was already in bed.[49] 'Lord, Master Wyatt,' she said, 'What are you doing here at such a late hour?' Thomas – one is tempted to say Sir Jasper – explained that he had come for 'consolation': 'And I went up to her as she lay in bed and kissed her, and she lay still and said nothing. I touched her breasts, and she lay still, and even when I took liberties lower down she likewise said nothing.' Nothing discouraged, Wyatt began to undress, but then a great stamping was heard in the room above. Anne got up, put on a skirt and disappeared upstairs for an hour. When she came down she refused to let Wyatt come near her, although within a week he did have intercourse with her. And Wyatt's explanation for Anne's curious disappearance? She obviously had a lover waiting in the room above!

Of itself, this alleged visit to Hever is a farrago of rubbish, a reworking of a well-known novella from the *Decameron*. However, setting aside the Boccaccio embroidery, the story is built on friction between Henry and Wyatt over Anne, and a rustication which parallels Chapuys' reports. If, as is frequently the case with the *Cronica*, the source of the story is the Spanish merchant community in London, it would appear that the existence of some link between Anne and Thomas was not unknown in the City. Of course, the story could well be a retrospective attempt to explain the contradiction in Wyatt's treatment in 1536, something which the poet himself used to joke about grimly – 'God's blood! was not that a pretty sending of me ambassador to the emperor, first to put me into the Tower, and then forthwith to send me hither?'[50] But why should merchants, interested in Wyatt because of his subsequent career as the English ambassador in Spain, bother with his previous behaviour unless the poet's interest in Anne Boleyn had been common knowledge, well beyond what his verse suggests, and that Wyatt left court because of it?[51]

Catholic voices had no doubt. Wyatt and Anne had an illicit sexual liaison. The earliest report is that of Nicholas Harpsfield, archdeacon of Canterbury and a former religious exile, writing in the reign of Mary. Commenting on the bull allowing Henry to marry Anne despite any unconsummated pre-contract, Harpsfield added that the king was so bewitched that he would even 'marry her whom himself credibly understood to have lived loosely and incontinently before'.[52] The lover in question was Wyatt who, on hearing that Anne was to marry Henry, had gone to the king and said:

> Sir, I am credibly informed that your grace intendeth to take to your wife the Lady Anne Boleyn, wherein I beseech your grace to be well advised what you do, for she is not meet to be coupled with your grace, her conversation [way of life] hath been so loose and base; which thing I know not so much by hearsay as by my own experience as one that have had my carnal pleasure with her.

At this, Harpsfield says, the king was 'for a while something astonied' – one might imagine he would be – but then he said, 'Wyatt, thou hast done like an honest man, yet I charge thee to make no more words of this matter to any man living.' And of course, the marriage went ahead.

Harpsfield tells us that he had this tale from 'the right worshipful merchant Mr. Anthony Bonvise...which thing he heard of them that were men very likely to know the truth thereof'. What he says of Bonvisi's connections is true.[53] He was a banker from Lucca with close and friendly ties with English ministers, both traditionalists and innovators, and through Stephen Gardiner's chaplain, he knew Wyatt himself. This might suggest that Bonvisi had the sources and also the neutrality expected of an international banker. As Harpsfield himself wrote, 'This worthy merchant would oft talk of [More] and also of Sir Thomas Cromwell, with whom he was many years familiarly acquainted, and would report many notable and as yet commonly unknown things, and of their far [much] squaring, unlike and disagreeable natures, dispositions, sayings and doings, whereof there is now no place to talk.'[54]

That's as may be, but Bonvisi was not neutral. He had supported Thomas More in the Tower and the ex-chancellor called him 'the apple of his eye'.[55] In September 1549 he left England for Louvain without permission, accompanied or soon followed by Harpsfield, More's nephew, William Rastell, More's adopted daughter, Margaret Clement, and her husband, John.[56] Indeed, the survival of More's circle apparently owed a good deal to Bonvisi; Nicholas Sander is specific that it was Antonio who supported these catholic exiles at Louvain.[57] Therefore, not only was Bonvisi anything but disinterested, he was telling his stories among the same coterie which produced the claim that Anne Boleyn had been fathered by Henry VIII! There is also inherent improbability in the story. With Wyatt sworn to secrecy by the king, how did Bonvisi's informants get their knowledge? The answer could be 'after Wyatt's involvement in Anne's exposure in 1536', but the accusation that she was an adulterous wife would have collapsed at any suggestion of a known premarital reputation. Furthermore, the notion that Henry would overlook Anne's sleeping with Wyatt at the very time she was holding him at arm's length is ludicrous.

By the time the next generation of recusants told the story, it had become modified and embellished under the influence of the Katherine Howard episode. Sander has Wyatt initially tell the council, and when Henry is informed, his reaction is to dismiss the stories and affirm his belief in Anne's virtue.[58] Having his word doubted, says Sander, made Wyatt angry and he offered to give the king visible proof of Anne's affection for him. The king's response was 'that he had no wish to see anything of the kind – Wyatt was a bold villain, not to be trusted.'[59]

Refuting Sander took many lines of George Wyatt's heavy prose, and all to labour the obvious implausibilities and the improbability of a character such as Henry responding to Wyatt's warning in the way suggested.[60] George was, however, clearly unaware of an alternative Catholic eyewitness tradition which directly discredits all these recusant stories of misbehaviour between Wyatt and Anne. It is found in the writings of George Cavendish, not that he was other than hostile to Anne. *The Life and Death of Cardinal Wolsey* makes her pride very clear; his *Metrical Visions* accept entirely the story of her adultery:

> My epitaph shall be: – 'The vicious queen
> Lieth here, of late that justly lost her head,
> Because that she did spot the king's bed.'[61]

Yet despite his prejudices, Cavendish goes out of his way to make the point that Anne was still a virgin when she married:

> The noblest prince that reigned on the ground
> I had to my husband, he took me to his wife;
> At home with my father a maiden he me found,
> And for my sake, of princely prerogative,
> To an earl he advanced my father in his life,
> And preferred all them that were of my blood;
> The most willingest prince to do them all good.[62]

It is a conclusion which commands respect. After all, it is difficult to traduce Anne Boleyn both for promiscuity before and promiscuity after marriage; if she had always been as lecherous as some conservatives wanted to believe, Henry was more stupid than wronged.

A ROYAL SUITOR

AN abortive arranged marriage with Butler, a failed romance with Henry Percy and a flirtation with Thomas Wyatt hardly made the early 1520s a success for Anne. She was certainly interested in an 'advantageous marriage', but had she been too choosy, or had other suitors, despite her evident fascination, been put off by her independence?[1] However, to a man interested in a temporary liaison, independence might be an attraction, and the person who had no doubt that he could make Anne his mistress was the king. Having by or before 1526 discarded Mary Carey, Henry turned his interest on the younger sister.

Anne's former attendant, Anne Zouche (née Gainsford), told George Wyatt how this began, or how she remembered it beginning:[2]

> [Thomas Wyatt] entertaining talk with [Anne Boleyn] as she was earnest at work, in sporting wise caught from her a certain small jewel hanging by a lace out of her pocket, or otherwise loose, which he thrust into his bosom, neither with any earnest request could she obtain it of him again. He kept it, therefore, and wore it after about his neck, under his cassock, promising himself either to have it with her favour or as an occasion to have talk with her, wherein he had singular delight, and she after seemed not to make much reckoning of it, either the thing not being much worth, or not worth much striving for.

Thus far the story is typical of courtly dalliance.[3] The theft of the jewel and its subsequent exploitation is exactly parallel to Charles Brandon's theft of Margaret of Austria's ring, and Anne's reaction is very much that of Margaret, refusing to take such a male display routine with any seriousness.

Thomas Wyatt's attentions, so the story goes on, had the effect of whetting the king's interest. Henry first tested Anne's 'regard of her honour' by 'those things his kingly majesty and means could bring to the battery', and then set out 'to win her by treaty of marriage',

> and in this talk took from her a ring, and that wore upon his little finger; and yet all this with such secrecy was carried, and on her part so wisely, as none or very few esteemed this other than an ordinary course of dalliance.

A few days after this, the king made an occasion to warn Wyatt off. Playing bowls with Thomas and some other courtiers, Henry claimed that his wood held shot when it clearly did not; pointing with his little finger with the ring on it, 'he said, "Wyatt, I tell thee it is mine", smiling upon him withal.' The point was taken, but Wyatt, 'pausing a little, and finding the king bent to pleasure', decided on a bold response. He produced Anne's jewel and proceeded to use the ribbon to measure the distances, remarking, 'If it may like your majesty to give me leave to measure it, I hope it will be mine.' The king's good humour vanished – 'It may be so, but then am I deceived' – and he stalked off to see Anne. She, discovering what was wrong, explained the business of the jewel to Henry, and sunlight was restored.

George Wyatt probably wrote this account in the later 1590s, in which case he was retelling a conversation from ten or twenty years before, in which a woman in her eighties recalled events in her youth.[4] It is not surprising, therefore, to find inconsistencies. He suggests that the king's interest in Anne was secret, whereas the story needs Wyatt to perceive instantly both the identity and the significance of Anne's ring; Thomas then recognizes that the king was 'bent on pleasure' – engaging in courtly competition – only for the story to require the king to be immediately in earnest; Anne's response, however, is still in the language of courtly love, explaining to one favoured gallant that a rival has not also been given a token by her. These inconsistencies all disappear if the story in placed earlier in time, with Henry, Wyatt and, probably, other courtiers vying with one another for Anne's attention. We may also note on this reading that while the king's reaction might suggest that he was getting more deeply involved, Wyatt's implies that he has already decided that he is not going to succeed with Anne. And he said that in such circumstances he favoured what might today be called a laid-back style.[5]

How exact Anne Zouche's story was we do not know, but it does establish what the court remembered: Henry arriving on the scene as a competitor in the game of courtly flirtation. Furthermore, although Wyatt says that Henry was testing Anne's virtue 'by those things his kingly majesty and means could bring to the battery', the simple construction is that his initial intention was to sleep with her. Two developments were, in fact, at work concurrently – the move to divorce Katherine of Aragon, and Henry's growing involvement with Anne – and initially and for a long time they were quite separate. The rejection of Katherine had begun in 1524 when Henry gave up sleeping with her, although he had clearly been drifting away for some years.[6] She was 39 and had not conceived in seven years. Moreover, time had cruelly destroyed both her petite beauty and her gentle good spirits – she was thick of body and dull of appearance, and apart from passionate concern for Mary, her one child, only duty drew Katherine from religious observances to the frivolities of court life. With no hope of children if he slept with her, nothing made Henry wish to.[7] The situation was, of course, hardly novel, and although there is reason to doubt the king's famed sexual prowess, from time to time he had solaced himself in the manner of monarchs of his day by taking a mistress – most recently Mary Carey. But with the final recognition that he would have no son by Katherine, Henry's position changed. Occasional illicit pleasure was now no longer enough; if Henry – and the country – were to have a son to succeed him, he had to marry again. Already he was over 30.

When it was that Henry VIII reached the conclusion that Katherine must go, we do not know.[8] There are stories that he was thinking of a divorce as early as 1522, but the actual date was probably after June 1525, when he brought his one illegitimate child, Henry Fitzroy, out of obscurity and created him duke of Richmond (a title resonant of his own father, Henry VII), and gave the boy precedence over everyone except any legitimate son the king might have.[9] This was widely recognized as a portent for the future, and the Venetian ambassador – who reported that Richmond had actually been legitimized – was quick to observe that Queen Katherine had been deeply offended and that three of her ladies had been dismissed from the court for supporting her.[10]

Any thought of ousting the legitimate Mary in favour of the illegitimate Richmond involved extreme risk, and within the next eighteen months Henry turned to a more conventional answer, a decree of nullity. Popes were always sensitive to the special matrimonial problems of monarchs, assuming plausible rationalization could be offered, and Henry had discovered what he thought was irrefutable proof that his marriage with Katherine was defective and invalid in canon law. This conviction depended for its compelling force on the clear application to his position of a threat in the Bible: 'If a man shall take his brother's wife, it is an unclean thing . . . he shall be without children' [Leviticus 20: 21]. Henry *had* married the wife of his brother Arthur and Henry and Katherine *were* childless. They had had sons, but all of them had died.[11] The appropriateness of the text was psychologically overwhelming, and never thereafter did conviction desert the king. God had spoken directly to his condition; as a devout Christian Henry had no option but to obey, contract a legal (indeed, a first) marriage, and a son would be the reward. Post-Freudian scepticism may smile, but the vital point is that Henry believed. Armed with his certainty, by April 1527 he was consulting his advisers, and on 17 May took the first formal (and secret) steps to divorce his wife.[12]

Where did Anne Boleyn fit in? The one certain date we have is the end of August 1527, when the king applied to the pope for the dispensation to allow him to marry again. Anne is not identified by name, but as well as raising the case we have noted of a woman previously contracted in marriage, the draft dispensation also covered a woman who was related to the king in the 'first degree of affinity...from...forbidden wedlock' (that is, the sister of a previous mistress, in this case Mary Carey).[13]

The development of the relationship between Anne and Henry is chronicled in the unique series of seventeen love letters which the king wrote to her.[14] They fall into four groups. The first three letters belong to the period when Henry was trying to turn the conventions of courtly romance into something more serious. The earliest accompanied the gift of a buck which the king had killed the evening before, and chides his 'mistress' for neither keeping her promise to write nor replying to his earlier letter; it concludes: 'Written with the hand of your servant, who oft and again wishes you [were here] instead of your brother – H.R.'[15] The next letter is more serious:

> Although it doth not appertain to a gentleman to take his lady in place of a servant, nevertheless, in compliance with your desires, I willingly grant it to you, if thereby you can find yourself less unthankfully bestowed in the place by you chosen than you have been in the place given by me. Thanking you right heartily for that it pleaseth you still to hold me in some remembrance.
> Henry R.[16]

Clearly, Anne was being chary of the king's attentions. It was her place to be the servant, and the king had to capitulate in the hope that the relationship could continue at least on that basis.

The next letter was written after an interval, and is the most important of the three.[17] It shows a Henry who is confused by his continued feelings and by the signals he was receiving from Anne:

Debating with myself the contents of your letter, I have put myself in great distress, not knowing how to interpret them, whether to my disadvantage, as in some places is shown, or to advantage, as in others I understand them; praying you with all my heart that you will expressly certify me of your whole mind concerning the love between us two. For of necessity I must ensure me of this answer having been now above one whole year struck with the dart of love, not being assured either of failure or of finding place in your heart and grounded affection. Which last point has kept me for some little time from calling you my mistress, since if you do not love me in a way which is beyond common affection that name in no wise belongs to you, for it denotes a singular love, far removed from the common.

After more than a year, Henry now insisted on a straight answer:

If it shall please you to do me the office of a true, loyal mistress and friend and to give yourself up, body and soul, to me who will be and have been your loyal servant (if by your severity you do not forbid me), I promise you that not only shall the name be given you, but that also I will take you for my only mistress, rejecting from thought and affection all others save yourself, to serve you only.

What was Henry asking and offering? Clearly more than a conventional courtly love pose but certainly not marriage. He appears to be offering a recognized permanent liaison, perhaps like the French *maîtresse en titre*. Francis I, after all, had had Françoise de Foix and was even at that moment (though Henry probably had yet to hear of it) fixing his interest with the woman who was to be his companion for the rest of his life, Anne d'Heilly, later duchesse d'Etampes.[18] Why should Henry VIII not have his Anne Boleyn?

In the next four letters the relationship has moved on, yet not quite in the direction Henry proposed. He had asked for an answer to his offer either in writing or in person, but when they met something in Anne's response caused him to rush matters and deeply offend her. How he 'committed fault' – whether by becoming too ardent or by demanding unconditional acceptance of a place in his bed – is not clear. Anne, we are told,

fell down upon her knees saying, 'I think your majesty, most noble and worthy king, speaketh these words in mirth to prove me, without intent of defiling your princely self, who I find thinks nothing less than of such wickedness which would justly procure the hatred of God and of your good queen against us...I have already given my maidenhead into my husband's hands.

Such a story seems at first sight too proper to be true, but it is told by writers hostile to Anne who are forced to turn it to her discredit by suggesting that she, 'having had crafty counsel, did thus overreach the king with show of modesty.' Given that and George Wyatt's hints of something similar, we may well suspect a basis in fact.[19] Yet whatever the detail, Henry thought he had patched matters up before Anne retired to her parents' home, but a subsequent silence drove the king to write again:

> Since I parted with you I have been advised that the opinion in which I left you is now altogether changed, and that you will not come to court, neither with my lady your mother, and if you could, nor yet by any other way [the proprieties have suddenly begun to matter] the which report being true I cannot enough marvel at, seeing that I am well assured I have never since that time committed fault.

And if he knew Anne was, in fact, staying away deliberately: 'I could do none other than lament me of my ill fortune, abating by little and little my so great folly.'[20]

'My so great folly' is a highly perceptive remark from a man not given to much self-analysis. Moralists have frowned on such letters from a man already married (and on Anne for entertaining them), even implying something gross in middle age so obviously losing its head. But charity demands that we recognize the genuineness of the king's passion; from a person who hated writing as much as Henry did, such letters are in themselves a remarkable testimony. For the first time in his life he was having to build a relationship with a woman who had not been provided by the diplomatic marriage agency or whistled up by the *droit de seigneur*. What is less easy to interpret is Anne's position. Not only did she play at courtly love with Henry, she was undoubtedly attracted to him. It was a heady experience to have at your feet someone as magnificent as Henry VIII, but there was more than that: we must not forget that she kept his letters. Yet despite this, it seems certain that she did refuse to sleep with Henry and instead kept away from court, precisely what morality demanded. Surely the relationship should then have withered. Only one thing can explain why it did not: the king's realization that he could not live without Anne, and therefore she, rather than some foreign princess, would have to be the wife to replace Katherine.

The prospect of marriage transformed Anne's hitherto distinctly muted response to Henry's ardour. She signified her surrender by sending a gift – the word the king used for it was '*une étrenne*'. It was one of those trinkets concealing a meaning that Tudor people loved – a ship with a woman on board and with a (presumably) pendant diamond. The message was transparent. For centuries the ship had been a symbol of protection – the ark which rescued Noah from the destroying deluge; the diamond – as the *Roman de la Rose* had said – spoke of a 'heart as hard as diamond, steadfast and nothing pliant'.[21] Anne was saying 'yes'.

Henry reacted with delight:

> For so beautiful a gift, and so exceeding (taking it in all), I thank you right cordially; not alone for the fair diamond and the ship in which the solitary damsel is tossed about, but chiefly for the good intent and too-humble submission vouchsafed in this by your kindness; considering well that by occasion to merit it would not a little perplex me, if I were not aided therein by your great benevolence and goodwill, for the which I have sought, do seek, and shall always seek by all services to me possible there to remain, in the which my hope hath set up his everlasting rest, saying *aut illic aut nullibi* [either here or nowhere].
>
> The proofs of your affection are such, the fine poesies of the letters so warmly couched, that they constrain me ever truly to honour, love and serve you, praying that you will continue in this same firm and constant purpose, ensuring you, for my part, that I will the rather go beyond than make *reciproque* [equivalent response], if loyalty or heart, the desire to do you pleasure, even with my whole heart root, may serve to advance it.

And the king makes clear, for the first time, the basis of this new relationship between them. He wants Anne no longer as a mistress, but as a wife:

> Praying you also that if ever before I have in any way done you offence, that you will give me the same absolution that you ask [no doubt for appearing cold], ensuring you that henceforth my heart shall be dedicate to you alone, greatly desirous that so my body could be as well, as God can bring to pass if it pleaseth Him, whom I entreat once each day for the accomplishment thereof, trusting that at length my prayer will be heard, wishing the time brief, and thinking it but long until we shall see each other again.
>
> Written with the hand of that secretary who in heart, body and will is
> Your loyal and most ensured servant
> H. aultre (A B)ne cherse R.[22]

His next letter starts, 'My Mistress and Friend', and laments the prospect of more and more time spent apart (as propriety now dictated); it included a trinket for Anne to remind her of him, 'my picture set in a bracelet, with the whole device which you already know' – unfortunately a secret not revealed to us.[23] Then we find Henry telling Anne to urge her father to bring her back to court earlier than planned, and the inscription is again 'H. *aultre ne cherse* R.', with a heart surrounding the initials 'A.B.'[24] Henry was engaged!

Thus far the sequence of Anne's emotional journey with Henry. The chronology is more problematic. How soon before the application to Rome in August 1527 did Anne agree to marry? The likely answer is 'not long'. Henry's subsequent letters to Anne are concentrated in the ten months between December 1527 and October 1528, and it is hard to believe that the earlier ones form a detached series from months before.[25] Psychology too points in the same direction. It would be quite out of character for Henry not to act immediately Anne had yielded. It would be equally aberrant if Anne, who had resisted Henry for months, committed herself in advance of the king telling Katherine in June that he was seeking a decree of nullity. Circumstantial evidence also points in that direction. When Wolsey left for France on 22 July he knew of the plan to reject Katherine but nothing of any serious liaison with Anne, despite his own careful monitoring of the court and the vigilance of his agents in the privy chamber.[26] Nor were others more prescient. No hint of Anne's involvement with the king has been found in any records earlier than the summer of 1527 – an unlikely thing if the betrothal was already a fait accompli; the imperial ambassador only identified Anne in August.[27] Earlier that year her public position was what it had always been, that of a court lady with valuable links with France. When, in May, the French envoys who had successfully negotiated a marriage between Henry VIII's daughter Mary and Francis I himself, or his second son the duc d'Orléans, were guests of honour at a splendid evening at Greenwich, they merely reported: 'we were in the queen's apartments where there was dancing and M. de Turaine, on the king's command, danced with Madame the Princess, and the king with Mistress Boulan who was brought up in France with the late queen.'[28] The normally hawk-eyed Venetians did not become aware of Anne until February 1528.[29]

Not all scholars would agree with this reconstruction. Influenced by the Cavendish story, J. J. Scarisbrick decided that Henry's interest in Anne became serious in 1525–6, David Starkey likewise suggesting the later part of 1525, but with a measure of infatuation detectable by the start of that year.[30] He dates Anne's surrender to January because one meaning of the word *étrenne* is a new year's gift, and to 1527 because the equivalent in the preceding year does not fit with the king's claim to have been in love for more than a twelve-month.[31] Such early dating carries serious implications for both Anne's importance and her character. They make her the catalyst for the rejection of Katherine. Passion triggered Henry's wish-fulfilment. What had begun as a courtly flirtation so subverted the king that he seized on the monstrous notion that his devoted wife of sixteen years was nothing but an accomplice in fornication. By the same token, Anne's resistance to Henry becomes cold opportunism, 'the other woman' seeing the chance to prise husband and wife apart. That was Reginald Pole's contention at the time. He told Henry in 1536: 'At your age in life and with all your experience of the world, you were enslaved by your passion for a girl. But she would not give you your will unless you rejected your wife, whose place she longed to take.'[32]

We cannot, of course, know whether Anne did suspect that the Aragon marriage was vulnerable. Had Henry shared with her his concern about a son to succeed him? We cannot say either that had the divorce not materialized, Anne might not, in the end, have become the king's mistress, perhaps in desperation – suitors for her hand disappear after James Butler, almost certainly warned off by royal interest. Thus the sympathetic can see Anne's resistance as standing out for costly principle, the cynical gloss it as a calculated gamble, while the realistic can point to the discouraging prospects of a dumped royal mistress.

We have, however, seen that the circumstantial evidence is all against Anne's abandoning her resistance before marriage became a possibility in June 1527, and here the word *étrenne* deserves closer inspection. If Henry did not mean 'new year's gift' did he use the word only in its basic sense of 'gift'? Perhaps. Given that the word was acquiring an implication of 'novelty' or 'special occasion', it was quite *un mot juste* for Anne's message of surrender. Yet *étrenne* was also developing a second meaning – 'virginity'. In other words, by describing the gift as *une étrenne* Henry could be picking up on Anne's assertion that her maidenhead was reserved for her future husband. The jewel said that she had yielded totally and completely; Anne and her virginity now belonged to Henry.[33] The king's parenthesis shows that he understood her perfectly – 'For so beautiful a gift and so exceeding (taking it in all)' – and he responded in kind: 'my heart shall be dedicate to you alone, greatly desirous that so my body could be as well, as God can bring to pass.'

If, prior to Anne's promise, Henry had been 'above one whole year struck with the dart of love', and that promise was given shortly before the August appeal to Rome, it follows that the king began to be attracted to Anne in the first part of 1526. That being the case, since it is clear that

Henry's emotion grew out of a courtly-love pose, we may tentatively identify his first sign of interest in Anne with the Shrovetide joust in February when he appeared displaying the device of 'a man's heart in a press, with flames about it', and the motto 'Declare I dare not.'[34] His first letter accompanying the gift of the buck he had killed would then belong to the autumn of 1526.[35] Another significant conclusion would also follow. 'Above one whole year' from February 1526 would date Henry's offer to Anne of the position of *maîtresse en titre* to about Easter 1527, an offer made despite the fact that he was then beginning moves to divorce Katherine and marry again. Only in high summer did the king realize that Anne could solve both his sexual and his matrimonial frustrations, and hence the sudden moves in August to appeal to the pope behind Wolsey's back. As for the business with Wyatt, this could possibly have occurred before the court went on progress in July 1526 or more likely after it returned to Greenwich in October, and certainly before Wyatt's sudden decision to make himself scarce by accompanying Russell to Italy.[36]

If we put all these indications together with the dates of Henry's disintegrating marriage with Katherine, the following chronology emerges:

1524	Henry and Katherine cease to have sexual relations.
1525 (summer)	Attempt to build up Richmond as the alternative heir.
1526 (Shrovetide)	Henry begins the courtly pursuit of Anne.
1526 (autumn)	Henry's first letter to Anne.
1526 (post October)	Friction between Henry and Wyatt over Anne.
1526 (December)	Katherine isolated at court.
1527 (January)	Wyatt leaves for Italy.
1527 (April)	Henry consults about annulment.
1527 (Easter)	Henry presses Anne to become *maîtresse en titre*.
1527 (May)	Preliminary annulment hearing in secret.
1527 (June)	Henry tells Katherine of his annulment plans.
1527 (summer)	Henry and Anne agree to marry.
1527 (August)	Decision to ask the pope for a dispensation to free Henry and Anne to marry.

The difficulty in charting any emotional history, and the inadequacies of the sources, make this timetable necessarily speculative. Nevertheless it does fit the context as we understand it, and it is psychologically credible. There is also independent corroboration. Among the papers in the Public Record Office is a statement of jewels and other costly items delivered to the king in a period described as 'since 1 August in the year aforesaid' until the following May.[37] Obviously part of a larger list, it includes items for the king himself, such as three walking staves equipped with one- or two-foot measures, compasses and dividers, but many of the pieces are 'for Mistress Anne'. What was 'the year aforesaid'? The latest possible period must be August 1531 to May 1532, for by May 1533 Mistress Anne was queen. The list, however, includes the gift to Anne of an emerald ring at Beaulieu on 3 August and the only year between 1525 and 1531 when Henry was at Beaulieu in early August was 1527.[38] What we have here, therefore, is a record of the torrent of gifts which the king had begun to shower on Anne by the summer of that year: rings, bracelets, brooches, diamonds for a head-dress, diamonds set in true-lover's-knots, diamonds and rubies set in roses and hearts, gilt and silver bindings for books, velvet bindings, repairs to a book 'garnished in France' – the list goes on for page after page. Such a torrent can mean only one thing: Henry and Anne had an understanding – they were betrothed.

The timetable suggested brings to the fore an obvious, frequently overlooked but critical reality in the relationship of Anne Boleyn and Henry VIII: they were expecting to marry within months.[39] The delay in cohabiting would certainly be longer than the king had hoped when he had sought her for his mistress – the requirement for papal dispensation saw to that. Yet the couple were certainly thinking in terms of the existing norm where, after the possible marriage settlement had been hammered out, a quick decision was taken one way or the other, and any wedding followed promptly. English society was not equipped to handle a long engagement between betrothed adults. In canon law, if not in Church discipline, only sexual intercourse was lacking to make that relationship a lawful marriage – provided there was no impediment. Indeed, if (as Henry asserted) his union with Katherine was invalid, he was perfectly entitled to marry immediately and get the legal obsequies of the link with Katherine sorted out subsequently. He was, after all, still a bachelor. Suffolk, his brother-in-law, had solved his matrimonial problems by doing exactly that.[40] What blocked this option was not only that Henry would have to have the courage of his convictions, but that Katherine's imperial nephew was in a position to prevent the pope disposing of her marriage retrospectively, and that would have imperilled the legitimacy of any child the king might have by Anne. He had to wait on Rome, and this imposed a highly unnatural situation for a betrothed couple, a situation exacerbated by sexual passion and by Henry and Anne frequently living cheek by jowl. The strain is evident in the king's letters.[41] With hindsight, we know that legal technicalities in Rome and manoeuvres in England were initial moves in what would be a long-drawn-out and ultimately abortive attempt to secure an annulment. To Henry and Anne they were frustrating delays to a wedding which was imminent.[42]

PART II

A DIFFICULT ENGAGEMENT

A MARRIAGE ARRANGED

THE story of the struggle over Henry VIII's divorce has been told many times and in great detail, and here is not the place to rehearse it at length.[1] The king's conviction that his marriage with Katherine had brought down the wrath of God was one thing, but satisfying the proper Church authorities was another, and that, despite six years of continuous effort, a massive expenditure of funds and mobilizing all the resources of the English hierarchy plus the brains of a good part of Europe too, the king was never able to do – with momentous consequences for England, and for Anne Boleyn.

The first steps taken in May 1527 towards a divorce would have revealed to a less egocentric man than Henry that he did not have an open and shut case. On the face of it those steps were routine – Wolsey called Henry to answer the charge that he was living in sin with his brother's widow – but because Katherine was carefully kept in the dark it was suspected at the time, and has often been suggested since, that Wolsey and the king were trying to achieve a divorce by stealth. Yet nothing could have extinguished Katherine's right to appeal to the pope, so it is more likely that the water was being tested to see if support could be mustered for the king's case. If so, the water was very cold indeed; the lawyers shrank from deciding without advice from the senior bishops, and at least some of the latter felt that canon law was not in the king's favour.[2] At that date, all Western Europe accepted that marriage between a man and his former sister-in-law was incest, and Henry and Katherine had only been able to marry in the first place because a dispensation from the pope had allowed them to ignore that objection. Thus, if Henry's divine revelation was genuine, the pope had exceeded his powers and must now eat his words.

The international situation, too, was anything but favourable. For over thirty years the French and a succession of enemies (most recently the

Habsburgs) had been fighting for the mastery of Italy. In May 1527 this had reached a climax when troops loyal to the Emperor Charles V sacked the city of Rome. For some months Pope Clement VII was a prisoner in his own citadel and then a pauper refugee – a situation made far worse for him by a concurrent uprising in Florence which expelled his family, the Medici. In the first instance Clement looked for help to the French (backed by Henry VIII), but he never forgot that if they failed he would ultimately have to deal with the emperor. Fail the French did. By September 1528 they were pinned back to a few garrisons in Milan, and a final effort ended in defeat in June 1529 at the Battle of Landriano. It was only in the immediate aftermath of the Sack, when he was desperate for friends, that the pope had any incentive to accommodate Henry's wish to free himself from Katherine. Otherwise, although French gains always made Clement VII more amenable, he never committed himself to anything – such as annulling the marriage of the emperor's aunt – which would prevent an accommodation with Charles and the recovery of Florence, should the emperor triumph.

Divorce from Katherine, therefore, was difficult in law and impossible politically. Rome's answer was to make a series of deceptive concessions to Henry's demand that the case should be settled in England by Wolsey and a visiting papal legate, acting with full authority delegated from the pope. Even when the legate, Cardinal Campeggio, did arrive in the autumn of 1528, his powers were not complete, necessitating further wearisome and unsatisfactory negotiation with the papal Curia, while Katherine exacerbated the frustration by producing a new and different dispensation which meant that all progress thus far was threatened. Campeggio, who knew that the pope expected him to stall as much as possible, was eventually forced to start proceedings on 31 May 1529, but it was not until 21 June that the famous public confrontation between Katherine and Henry took place in the parliament chamber at Blackfriars, with the queen's plea to her husband which has re-echoed ever since on the Shakespearean stage.[3] When Henry sat in embarrassed silence, Katherine appealed from the partiality of Blackfriars to the justice of God, turned her back on husband and legates alike and walked out, never to return. Her counsel, however, continued, tying the trial up in technicalities, and Campeggio announced that, in conformity with the practices of the Curia, a summer recess would start on 31 July. By that time, in far-away Italy, the pope had bowed to imperial pressure and issued orders recalling the case to Rome and, by the Treaty of Barcelona, announced that, as Clement himself put it, he 'had made up his mind to become an imperialist, and live and die as such'.

In all this Anne Boleyn had no place – or not officially. The public line was always that the king's conscience was troubled. With the prospect of Campeggio's imminent arrival, in September 1528 Henry had sent Anne to Hever to stay with her mother, and he ostentatiously continued to live with Katherine.[4] In November 1528 he became seriously concerned about the rising level of popular support for the queen, and on Sunday the 8th called a meeting of his courtiers and counsellors and the leading citizens of London to insist that there was no result he would like better from the suit than the confirmation that Katherine was his wife.[5] And on the principle that a lie might as well be a good one, he said (so Edward Hall recollected):

> I assure you all, that beside her noble parentage of the which she is descended (as you all know), she is a woman of most gentleness, of most humility and buxomness, yea and of all good qualities appertaining to nobility, she is without comparison, as I this twenty years almost have had true experiment, so that if I were to marry again, if the marriage might be good, I would surely choose her above all other women.

Of course, in Henry's mind there was no 'if' about the marriage being valid. When Campeggio arrived he found the king impervious to reason: 'I believe that an angel descending from Heaven would be unable to persuade him otherwise.'[6]

But if Anne was out of sight – at least when convenient – she was not out of mind. The king's letters in 1528 show how significant was the pressure she exerted towards a divorce. When in February Stephen Gardiner, the up-and-coming man in the Church, and Edward Fox, who was beginning to make a name as an expert on the king's 'great matter', were sent to Rome with the latest bright new proposal, they were ordered to call in at Hever first, to report to Anne. 'Darling,' the king wrote, 'these [words] shall be only to advertise you that this bearer and his fellow be dispatched with as many things to compass our matter and to bring it to pass as our wits could imagine or devise.' He warned her that it would take time, 'yet I will ensure you there shall be no time lost that may be won, and further can not be done; for *ultra posse non est esse* [anything more is quite impossible]. Keep him not too long with you, but desire him, for your sake, to make the more speed.'[7] In a later letter, full of the misery of absence, Henry is careful to tell Anne that he has given himself a headache after four hours' work on the divorce; in another he sends her brother to break bad news tactfully.[8] When Campeggio at last reached Paris, he writes with the good news; when the legate, having at last arrived, failed to visit Anne, thus driving her into an outburst of fear and suspicion, he manages to calm her, and then writes to welcome her promise to behave sensibly in future:

> what joy it is to me to understand of your conformableness to reason, and of the suppressing of your inutile and vain thoughts and fantasies with the bridle of reason. Wherefore, good sweet-heart, continue the same, not only in this, but in all your doings hereafter; for thereby shall come, both to you and me, the greatest quietness that may be in this world.

And he very tactfully went on to mention wedding preparations![9]

The importance of Anne as a spur in the divorce is well illustrated in Edward Fox's letter to Stephen Gardiner, reporting his reception when, in May 1528, he returned to England. The ambassadors had written ahead to announce that the pope had conceded almost everything Henry had asked for, and when Fox arrived at Greenwich at five in the afternoon, only to find that Wolsey had already departed, Henry seized the chance to surprise Anne.[10] The envoy was told not to come to the king, but to go at once to Anne's chamber in the Tiltyard Gallery and break the news to her first. She was overcome with joy – so delighted, in fact, that she forgot Fox's name and insisted on calling him 'Master Stevens' (that is, Stephen Gardiner). Then the king came in to enjoy his little surprise and, after Anne had left, got down to detailed discussion with Fox. But Henry could not be without her at such a moment and he called her back for an intense barrage of questions to Fox – was the pope favourable, what had the lawyers said, what about the items that had not been conceded? Whereupon Henry sent Fox, then and there, on to London to see Wolsey. The poor man, who had not reached Sandwich until eleven the night before and had already that day ridden fifty-five miles, with several brushes with inquisitive local officials to delay him and then this excited interview, eventually got the cardinal out of bed at his London residence, well past ten o'clock.

Six months later the story was no longer of Henry wanting to demonstrate to Anne his success with the pope, but of Anne standing between the king and a total loss of nerve. The support for Katherine and the poor reception by the notables of his speech on 8 November so shook him that he rushed off to see Anne (despite his intention to keep his distance from her while the divorce was going through).[11] The imperial ambassador, believing Anne to be already Henry's mistress, interpreted this as a decision to pursue the amour with more privacy.[12] But it is more likely, one may hazard, that Henry was in despair at the difficulties, and making a frantic plea that Anne face the realities and accept the position of *maîtresse en titre* after all. Instead of that she stiffened his nerve and insisted that he return to London at once to press the divorce.[13] She seems to have insisted also on being allowed back to court herself; if Henry's resolve could crack like this, she needed to be on the spot. Given the need to preserve the dictates of modesty, and the presence of Katherine at court, this was not easy, but Henry was soon able to write to Anne that Wolsey had come up with the answer: 'As touching a lodging for you, we have gotten one by my lord cardinal's means, the like whereof could not have been found hereabouts for all causes, as this bearer shall more show you.'[14] Du Bellay, the French ambassador, was quick to notice, and to report on 9 December, that Anne was at last back at court and lodged grandly near to the king.[15] Where that was is not clear. One tradition suggests Durham House, where Wolsey had been staying while his palace, York Place, was being rebuilt, or the nearby Suffolk Place, but the most likely reading of Henry's letter suggests a suite at the king's palace at Bridewell, secured by Wolsey sweeping out the existing occupants.[16] Certainly when the court moved to Greenwich for Christmas, Anne had her own separate suite in the palace.

As the French ambassador pointed out, there was some delicacy in the king housing his current wife and her intended successor under the same roof, and he may have been right to suggest that Anne took care to meet Katherine as little as possible. Or perhaps he had it backwards.[17] Hall's account of Christmas 1528 does not suggest much enthusiastic participation by the queen:

> The more to quicken his spirits and for recreation, the king kept his Christmas at Greenwich, with much solemnity and great plenty of viands, and thither came the two legates, who were received by two dukes, and divers earls, barons and gentlemen, to whom the king showed great pleasures, both of jousts, tourney, banquets, masques and disguisings, and on the Twelfth Day he made the lawful son of Cardinal Campeius [Campeggio] born in wedlock, a knight, and gave him a collar of esses of gold. But the queen showed to them no matter of countenance, and made no joy of nothing, her mind was so troubled.[18]

Almost nothing has survived to reveal the personal relations of Anne and Katherine once the king's intentions were out in the open, or, indeed, before that. Cavendish would have it that Katherine behaved impeccably and 'shewed ([neither] to Mistress Anne, ne to the king) any spark or kind of grudge or displeasure'; indeed, she 'dissembled the same, having

Mistress Anne in more estimation for the king's sake'.[19] This, Cavendish says, showed her to be a true patient Griselda, as in the Boccaccio/ Chaucer story, and other writers made the same identification.[20] One may suggest, however, that Katherine was keeping her nerve. Kings had mistresses, Henry had had mistresses. So long as the wife tolerated the other woman she should present no danger; the only error was to treat her as a real threat and so elevate her to the status of queen in waiting. Katherine's mistake – and though she would have been a saint not to make it, a mistake that was fatal for her handling of Henry – was not to recognize the depth of Henry's self-deception. As for Anne, George Wyatt (and he is supported by some Catholic sources) claims that she was loyal to the queen and that Katherine tried to help her to resist the king's advances, which could be true at the stage of his 'courtly love' attack.[21] He spoils the story, however, by suggesting that Katherine did this by en-gaging Anne in frequent games of cards, which were intended to make it impossible for her to keep her deformed finger out of sight; this makes sense only if the games were intended to disgust the king rather than giving Anne an excuse to keep away from him. The muddle is probably Wyatt's, embroidering a family story about one card game (unidentified) in which Anne frequently turned up a king, and Katherine remarked, 'My lady Anne, you have good hap to stop at a king, but you are not like others, you will have all or none.' Whether, as is often suggested, Katherine was delivering a warning and a prophecy 'under game', or whether a chance remark in gaming subsequently assumed an unintended significance, it is impossible to say.[22]

As 'the other woman' in a difficult, public and unpopular divorce case, Anne Boleyn was in no enviable position. Despite Henry's promise to marry, she had nothing but his affection to rely on. For the moment that was a powerful resource, and all the evidence is of the king's increasing commitment. Du Bellay, the French ambassador, wondered whether the relationship would survive a sudden separation in June 1528, when one of Anne's ladies went down with an attack of the sweating sickness, a highly contagious and frequently fatal disease (probably a virus infection akin to the Spanish flu of 1918).[23] Henry took off on a flight from safe house to safe house at a speed which demonstrated his paranoia about infection.[24] Accompanied by Katherine, he began a most meticulous round of reli-gious observances. Yet the king still wrote to Anne, in quarantine at Hever, to tell her he was safe and to reassure her that 'few women or none have this malady.'[25] When this proved a false hope and Anne did go down with the sweat, Henry reacted with real anxiety. Off went William Butts, his second-best doctor – 'the physician in whom I put most trust is now at this time absent when he could most do me pleasure' – carrying a letter of sympathy and support from Henry, once more signed with the initials 'H' and 'R' flanking a heart and 'AB'.[26] Care and sympathy worked, and by 23 June Anne had recovered, while Henry was wallowing in the excitement of danger at a safe distance, averted by his own prompt response. Brian Tuke, one of the counsellors in attendance, was treated to a lecture on the subject. Wolsey had sent advice on precautions to take as the epidemic ran its course. Not to be outdone, the king, Tuke reported:

> thanked your grace: and showing me, first, a great process of the manner of that infection; how folks were taken; how little danger was in it, if good order be observed; how few were dead of it; how Mistress Anne, and my lord of Rochford, both have had it; what jeopardy they have been in, by returning in of the sweat before the time; of the endeavour of Mr. Butts, who hath been with them, and is returned; with many other things touching those matters, and, finally, of their perfect recovery.[27]

Perhaps a month later Anne was able to return to court and du Bellay noted that separation had made no difference: 'the king is in so deeply that God alone can get him out of it.'[28]

Despite this, Anne faced powerful opposition. Katherine of Aragon had much support in England; apart from her wider popularity, many powerful courtiers and nobles held her in real affection. Beyond them was the Emperor Charles V, and the traditional English sentiment in favour of an alliance with the Low Countries rather than the old enemy, France. Even among those recognizing the need for a divorce, some looked for a more suitable second queen: most probably a foreign princess who could do what royal brides were expected to do – cement international alliances, not satisfy royal passions. A different woman might have responded by ignoring the critics and trusting to her own attractions and her ability to nag or persuade the king into marriage, but not Anne Boleyn. Instead, she entered politics.

The first sign of this is her increasing readiness to exploit an influence over Henry. Given the realities of personal monarchy, the evidence that a person enjoyed royal favour was the ability to secure benefits, and since the hot money of courtly support flowed to where the rate of return was highest, securing benefits attracted clients. George Cavendish remarked of Anne that it was 'judged by and by, through all the court, of every man, that she, being in such favour with the king, might work mysteries [wonders] with the king and obtain any suit of him for her friend.'[29]

How near he was to the truth was made apparent when, in April 1528, Cecily Willoughby, abbess of Wilton, died.

The nunnery of St Edith at Wilton was a large Benedictine house with a number of aristocratic connections, which were not always conducive to the life of prayer and domestic duty.[30] To be blunt, it was the sort of community where a well-born woman who could not be found a suitable husband could retire to live the genteel life to which she was accustomed, without too irksome a religious routine. The obvious successor to Cecily was the second-in-command, Prioress Isabel Jordayn, whose sister was head of the even more prestigious nunnery at Syon. However, among the Wilton nuns were two sisters of William Carey of the privy chamber, husband to Mary Boleyn and thus brother-in-law to Anne, and William was determined to see the younger one, Eleanor, promoted and to block the elder and anyone else.[31] He secured Wolsey's support and then went for the bigger prize of the king's approval, which was given as a favour to Anne. Everything was going well, but at this point Eleanor Carey's past caught up with her. She had been the mistress of and had children by two priests, and more recently had lived with one of the entourage of the Willoughby family. It is not known whether this was before becoming a nun, in which case the late abbess had probably been helping to resolve a family scandal, or whether it was afterwards, in which case one might suspect some aiding and abetting, but the fact was clear enough.[32] When faced with it, Henry wrote to Anne that Eleanor Carey was quite impossible as a candidate and asked her to drop her support. However, he added that 'to do you pleasure' he had ordered that neither Isabel Jordayn nor the elder Carey sister should be appointed, 'but that some other good and well-disposed woman shall have it'.[33] In the event, Wolsey slipped up and nominated Isabel Jordayn, which precipitated one of those rare and terrifying letters in the king's own hand, and a display of grovelling submission by Wolsey. It was clearly a bad thing to cross Lady Anne, even if you were the king's chief minister and had right on your side.

Anne Boleyn's hand thus begins to be seen in the key political area of patronage, control of which was essential if a minister was to maintain his prestige and command the support of the court. Cavendish also tells us that she began to play a part in that other key activity, faction. The passage is crucial to an understanding of Tudor politics:

> The king waxed so far in amours with this gentlewoman that he knew not how much he might advance her. This perceiving, the great lords of the council,

bearing a secret grudge against the cardinal because that they could not rule in the commonweal (for [because of] him) as they would, who kept them low and ruled them as well as other mean subjects, whereat they caught an occasion to invent a mean[s] to bring him out of the king's high favour and them into more authority of rule and civil governance, after long and secret consultation among themselves how to bring their malice to effect against the cardinal. They knew right well that it was very difficult for them to do anything directly of themselves, wherefore they perceiving the great affection that the king bare lovingly unto Mistress Anne Boleyn, fantasying in their heads that she should be for them a sufficient and an apt instrument to bring their malicious purpose to pass; with whom they often consulted in this matter. And she having both a very good wit, and also an inward desire to be revenged of the cardinal, was agreeable to their requests as they were themselves, wherefore there was no more to do but only to imagine some pretended circumstance to induce their malicious accusation, in so much that there was imagined and invented among them divers imaginations and subtle devices how this matter should be brought about.[34]

Belling the cat was, however, difficult so long as Henry kept his confidence in Wolsey, and Wolsey his 'wonder wit'.

Faction in Tudor England is a phenomenon frequently misunderstood, but it was crucial in Tudor politics and vital to an understanding of the career of Anne Boleyn in particular.[35] It is easy to dismiss it as mere backbiting and self-advantage, but generically, faction is the form politics habitually takes when its focus is the will of one man – whether in Byzantium, medieval Japan, Stalinist Moscow, Tudor England or else-where. Direct opposition to that individual will is impossible. Only the rebel attempts to force policies on the ruler; only the conspirator attempts to force himself into place and profit. The loyal way to compete for benefit and for authority over policy is to seek to gain the ruler's goodwill, to achieve what men recognized Anne Boleyn had achieved with Henry VIII – royal favour. That opens the way to advance particular policies which, if accepted, the ruler will make his own and give the authority to execute. Necessarily, only a very few people reach a position to compete directly for royal favour, but because in sixteenth-century England a monarch's decision was relevant to so much, that minority was pressed to solicit favour for third parties, which they were willing to do, partly in return for material rewards and partly for status and prestige. Third parties could lead to fourth and fourth to fifth until the resulting pattern of clientage resembled nothing so much as a multilayered root system. By the nature of things, too, those who were in direct contact with the king were not of equal importance, and thus also had their own pattern of connection. The result was that these wider systems came together at court into a limited number of groups for mutual support and advantage, the test of sufficiency being the ability to persuade the king.

But why was Henry persuadable? A monarch should have been able to exploit competition for his favour on the divide and rule principle; Henry's daughter Elizabeth would turn this into an art. Some scholars have argued that the father too was adept at this, others that he was so dominant that factions simply followed his lead. But the story of his relationship with Anne Boleyn says otherwise. Henry was always in authority; he was nobody's fool; at times he did lead and he could not be taken for granted. But he was also significantly dependent on those around him, for reassurance and very often for ideas as well. He was also vulnerable to pressure. This does not mean that he was a puppet. His will remained dominant; when he decided, that was final. But the crucial question was, 'Who had he been listening to?' Factions did not always get their way, but on the right issues and in the right emotional circumstances he was vulnerable and men calculated accordingly. So did Anne Boleyn.

The ties in Tudor faction were organic, not ideological. They emerged from the realities of family relationships (good and bad), friendship and antagonism, locality, sponsorship, upbringing. Such relationships were not exclusive, so that factional alignments intersected like sets in mathematics, with an individual having principal loyalties to one group and ancillary (but not contradictory) links elsewhere. Furthermore, depending on context, links could exist in three dimensions, with superiors, with inferiors and with equals. Factions also varied in durability. Some groupings, some antagonisms, lasted for years, yet because the ultimate concern was to promote objectives in and through individuals, calculations could alter as circumstances changed. As we shall see, Anne Boleyn's fall was a consequence of precisely such a recalculation among some of her supporters.

Issues of principle and policy did, of course, impinge on faction, but they were not, as in a modern party, expressed in open political alignment and debate. Rather, they were personalized. Thus, since Wolsey's policies had been endorsed by the king, opposition to them took the form of efforts to undermine the royal favour the cardinal enjoyed, and, contrariwise, the desire to replace him in that royal favour encouraged the promotion of alternative policies. Similarly, as Henry's pursuit of a divorce produced increasing tension between Church and State in England and between England and Rome, support for traditional religion came to be expressed as support for Katherine and Mary, and again vice versa.

Likewise, acceptance of Anne meant hostility to Rome and (eventually) acceptance of royal supremacy over the Church.[36]

In 1527 Katherine of Aragon enjoyed the support of one of the most enduring factions of the time. Its origins went back to the reign of Henry VII, and although it is sometimes referred to as 'the Aragonese faction' it is better described as 'the Stafford–Neville', later 'the Neville–Courtenay' connection, after the principal families involved. In the early years of Henry VIII's reign its members were among the most prominent court-iers, with Edward Stafford, duke of Buckingham, Henry Stafford, his brother (later earl of Wiltshire), George Neville, Lord Burgavenny, and his brother Sir Edward Neville, always around the king and his young wife.[37] Towards the end of the second decade of the century, George Neville married Buckingham's daughter Mary, a former waiting-woman to the queen, and at the same time both families contracted alliances with another important group, the Pole family. The matriarch of that family, Margaret Pole, countess of Salisbury, was a close friend to Kather-ine of Aragon; her second son, Reginald, was being groomed at the king's expense for high office in the English Church; her cousin, Henry Courtenay, earl of Devon, was one of the king's intimates, having 'been brought up of a child with his grace in his chamber', and his second wife, Gertrude (also one of Katherine's ladies), was daughter to William Blount, Lord Mountjoy, chamberlain to the queen, by his wife Inez, one of the attendants who had come with her from Spain.[38] The faction had lost ground to Wolsey after 1514 and in 1521 had suffered a massive blow when Buckingham was executed and Burgavenny, Edward Neville, the countess of Salisbury and her eldest son, Henry, Lord Montagu, all fell into disfavour. But the faction survived and recovered somewhat as the 1520s progressed; the countess became governess to Princess Mary, while Henry Courtenay was raised to the rank of marquis of Exeter and appointed as one of the two noblemen serving in the privy chamber.[39] As Queen Katherine came under threat, the Neville–Courtenay connection was in a position to give her very powerful support, and Exeter and Montagu would live to be among the peers who condemned Anne to death.

What had Anne Boleyn to set against the queen, backed by the weight of canon law, popular sentiment and the support of a powerful faction at court? At first sight, perhaps, less than she would have had two years earlier. In June 1525 Sir Thomas Boleyn had at last achieved his peerage, but this had meant giving up the vital court post of treasurer of the household. Seven months later, Anne's brother George lost his formal position in the privy chamber as a result of the Eltham reorganization.[40] Both men, however, remained part of the king's intimate circle, and although the earl of Northumberland carried little weight and was, in any case, usually on duty in the north, another former admirer, Wyatt, had returned from Italy and was in high favour with the king.[41] Yet three men, however much in the king's graces, were not enough, and Anne set out to gain more. She did everything she could to secure the support of her brother-in-law, William Carey – hence the business of the appointment to Wilton. Another of the gentlemen of the privy chamber was Sir Thomas Cheney, whom Anne may already have encountered as a fellow resident in Kent. She first intervened on his behalf in March 1528, when he was in disgrace with Wolsey.[42]

A more serious problem over Cheney arose some months later, when the sweat carried off the stepson of another privy chamber gentleman, Sir John Russell. The young man, John Broughton, had been in service to Wolsey and had left £700 in chattels and substantial lands in Bedfordshire, so that his two sisters were considerable heiresses.[43] The younger, Katherine, was under age, and already her wardship had been granted to Wolsey, but Russell's wife was frantic to keep her daughter, and Sir John went to work at once to get Wolsey to sell the wardship to the family. He had good hopes – he was very much a Wolsey man and the cardinal had liked Broughton – but Cheney and another gentleman of the privy chamber, Sir John Wallop, were pressing the king and Anne Boleyn for support in securing both girls. Russell, therefore, mobilized Wolsey's contact man in the privy chamber, Thomas Heneage, and Thomas Arundel, one of the minister's closest aides, to intercede on his behalf and so secure from the cardinal the wardship of Katherine Broughton, as well as confirmation that her elder sister, Anne, was now of age. Cheney and Wallop, however, carried the day (after, apparently, insinuating that both girls were under age and in the king's gift), and Henry promised Anne Broughton to Sir Thomas and Katherine to Sir John. This put Wolsey in great difficulty – he was already in the king's bad books over the Wilton affair – but fortunately for him a blazing row broke out between Cheney and Russell and the king decided that his candidate had gone too far.[44] Richard Page, another of the gentlemen of the privy chamber, wrote to Wolsey:

> His grace answered that he [Cheney] was proud and full of opprobrious words, little esteeming his friends that did most for him, and did the best he could to put them to dishonesty that were most glad to do him pleasure and in such wise handled himself that he should never come in his Chamber until he had humbled himself and confessed his fault and were agreed with Mr. Russell.[45]

What part Anne played in all this is not known, but she was active on Cheney's behalf when the matter erupted again in January 1529 in a confrontation between him and Wolsey. No doubt insisting that the king's promise of Anne Broughton should be honoured, Cheney offended the minister and was rusticated, only to be brought to court by Anne, with many harsh words against the cardinal.[46] In May Wolsey gave up his effort to direct Anne Broughton's marriage, and she apparently passed into Cheney's control, eventually becoming his wife.[47] The cardinal did retain the wardship of the younger sister Katherine, and the king paid Wallop £400 in compensation.[48] Yet if this was the compromise it appears to be, it did not last long. On Wolsey's fall, Katherine's wardship was granted to Anne Boleyn's grandmother, and not long afterwards the girl was married to Anne's uncle, Lord William Howard.[49] Anne and her protégés now had everything, and Russell, who seems only to have wanted the happiness of his wife and stepdaughters, had nothing. A long feud with Cheney ensued, and it is no surprise, either, to find Russell less than enthusiastic for Anne Boleyn.[50]

Anne was beginning to collect allies among existing members of the king's immediate entourage, and it may be that she also had some influence on admission to the privy chamber.[51] This can hardly have been so as early as June 1527, when a post as gentleman of the privy chamber was given to Richard Page, who was later to be one of her loyal supporters and barely to escape with his life in 1536. In January 1528 Nicholas Carewe was recruited; a long-term boon companion of the king, he would be one of Anne's bitterest enemies. On the other hand, Wallop was appointed at the same time, and we have seen how he turned to Anne over Katherine Broughton. Thomas Heneage, whom Wolsey had insinuated into the department some weeks after Carewe and Wallop, was clearly *persona grata* with Anne, and this was probably a factor in his selection. Then there is the case of Francis Bryan, whom the king 'took into his privy chamber' on 25 June. As brother-in-law both to Carewe (and like him a victim both of the 1519 expulsions and the Eltham redundancies) and to Henry Guildford, the controller of the household, Bryan had every credential for court office already, and Anne was away from court when he was appointed. Yet one must note that Bryan was a replacement for Anne's brother-in-law, William Carey, who had died of the sweat, and he was soon on the way to France to escort (and accelerate) the impatiently awaited Campeggio.[52] That this was not uncongenial is clear from his letters later in the year, when he was sent to get further concessions from the pope. These reveal a strong supporter of Anne, confidently presuming on his family relationship with her.[53] Bryan may not have needed Anne's help to become a gentleman of the privy chamber again, but there is at least good reason to suspect that Henry knew that Anne would be pleased at the appointment of a man who would later write to him:

> I pray God my fortune may be so good to come with the tidings. Sir, I would have written to my mistress that shall be, but I will not write unto her, till I may write that shall please her most in this world. I pray God to send your grace and her long life and merry, or else me a short end.[54]

There is no similar insight into Anne Boleyn's relations in the 1520s with other powerful groups and individuals at court, such as the king's sister, Mary, and her husband, Charles Brandon, duke of Suffolk. The possible exception is her uncle, now duke of Norfolk. He had, after all, wanted to exploit Anne in 1520–1 to extricate himself from his job in Ireland, and it would have been obvious for a man like Thomas Howard to see what he could gain from the king's interest in her.[55] He was already finding it less easy to accept Wolsey's frustrating dominance than had his father, the old duke, who had died in 1524, and in 1525, when royal taxation had provoked unrest in Suffolk, he and Brandon had made joint, if half-hearted, attempts to bypass the cardinal and get their instructions directly from Henry.[56] Anne Boleyn might, as *The Life and Death of Cardinal Wolsey* suggests, appear a lever ready to hand.

George Cavendish is, however, somewhat premature in his dating of Anne's arrival on the factional secene. He claims that an attempt to use her against the cardinal was made some time before the rebellion of the duke of Bourbon against Francis I became public (in September 1523). That is far too early for any noble grumblings there may have been to have involved Anne. The next opportunity, according to Cavendish, was in the summer of 1527, when the international situation made it important to send an embassy to France.

> You have heard heretofore how divers of the great estates and lords of the council lay in wait with my lady Anne to espy a convenient time and occasion to take the cardinal in a brake [thicket]. [They] thought it then that now is the time come that we have expected, supposing it best to cause him to take upon him the king's commission and to travel beyond the sea in this matter...Their intents and purpose was only but to get him out of the realm that they might have convenient leisure and opportunity to adventure their long desired enterprise. And by the aid of their chief mistress (my lady Anne) to deprave him so unto the king in his absence that he should be

rather in his high displeasure than in his accustomed favour, or at least to be in less estimation with his majesty.[57]

That is far more probable. If we are to believe the new imperial ambassador who arrived in March, there was much feeling against the French alliance that Wolsey was pushing, and in May he was able to name Norfolk as one of those principally involved.[58] During the cardinal's absence, as we have seen, Anne did agree to marry Henry, and Wolsey had hardly been gone a month before he learned that the king was quite unexpectedly hosting an enormous house-party at Beaulieu in Essex, with both the dukes, Exeter, several other peers (including Rochford) and their wives – all the aristocratic heavy mob the cardinal feared most.[59] Even worse, he found the king listening to them. Henry's regular supper companions were Norfolk, Suffolk, Exeter and Rochford; and Dr William Knight, whom Wolsey was expecting to hold the fort for him, reported: 'This is to advertise your good grace that my lords of Norfolk, Suffolk, and Rochford, and Mr. Treasurer [Fitzwilliam] be privy unto the other letter that I do send unto your grace at this time, with these [i.e. this one], after the open reading whereof the king' – and Wolsey must have breathed a sigh of relief at this point – 'delivered unto me your letter, concerning the secrets.'[60] There were, then, still some secrets between the two!

The minister nevertheless felt he had to begin a counter-bombardment of flattery. The grossness of this demonstrates how scared he was – 'there was never lover more desirous of the sight of his lady than I am of your most noble and royal person.'[61] And when Wolsey returned to court on 30 September he had a worse shock. The long-standing custom had been to warn the king that he had arrived, and to ask for a private appointment in the privy chamber to report on his mission. When the cardinal's man arrived it was to find, as the imperial ambassador reported, that 'the king had with him in his chamber a certain lady called Anna de Bolaine who appears to have little good will towards the cardinal, and before the king could respond to the message she said, "where else should he come, except where the king is?"'[62] Henry indulgently agreed, and Wolsey found himself playing gooseberry to a courting couple and trying to talk diplomacy at the same time. He also realized how wrong he had been. He had gone to France ignoring Anne as a flirtation, and confident that a divorce would free Henry to marry a French princess; he now knew things were serious, for him, perhaps deadly serious.

ANNE BOLEYN AND THE
FALL OF WOLSEY

I T is tempting to draw a straight line – and a short one – from the events of July–September 1527 to Wolsey's fall in 1529. The battle had been arrayed: Wolsey against Anne and her allies, the cardinal between the Scylla of Anne Boleyn as queen, and the Charybdis of a king furious at being baulked of his divorce. That was how Cavendish saw it in retrospect, and others had thought that at the time. In October 1527, in language much as Cavendish would use, the imperial ambassador reported that Norfolk, Rochford and their friends had made a league against the cardinal and had been trying to ruin him in his absence.[1] Inigo de Mendoza was equally clear what a threat to Wolsey's power Anne would be as Henry's wife, unlike the present queen 'who can do him little harm'. The French ambassador reached a similar assessment, and some months later reported that the cardinal was planning to retire, knowing that his influence would not survive the marriage.[2] Mendoza suggested two reasons for Anne's hostility: Wolsey's assumption that the next queen would be French, and an earlier move by him which had deprived her father of 'a high official post'. This latter could refer to the pressure put on Boleyn in 1519 over the post of controller of the household, but more probably to Boleyn having, in effect, to pay for his peerage by giving up the treasurership without an equivalent post in compensation.[3] Mendoza was sure that Wolsey was doing his best to sabotage the divorce and was proposing to call a conference of experts in the hope that they would convince the king that the law was against him.

Mendoza, however, also reported that several courtiers thought differently. They believed that once Wolsey became convinced that Henry was adamant, he would execute a volte-face and support Anne rather than lose royal favour. This was the more perceptive analysis. Had not Wolsey risen to power on the principle (as Cavendish put it) that 'to satisfy the king's mind . . . was the very vein and right course to bring him to high promotion'?[4] Opposition in the spring and summer of 1527 thus turned out to be yet another brief testing of the cardinal's place in royal favour, the sort he faced periodically during his period in power. It certainly did not commit Anne against him. There was much to be said for her (and Henry) deciding, as they did, to stick with a man who knew his way about the international scene and who exuded the confidence that, so long as they trusted him, all would be well. Wolsey had quickly re-established his psychological dominance on his return from France in a number of grand set pieces, culminating in the splendid ceremony of 1 November 1527 in which a French delegation invested Henry as knight of the Order of S. Michel, and as news filtered back to England of the failure of the king's go-it-alone attempt to get papal support, the cardinal seemed even more the man to turn to.[5]

Anne Boleyn certainly thought so. Like her father before her, she decided that the greater percentage was in becoming a client of the cardinal. Despite her increased role in affairs, all through the first half of 1528 her effort was to stand well with the man who would give her what she wanted. The brunt of this fell on Thomas Heneage, newly arrived in the privy chamber from Wolsey's own household.[6] At dinner on Tuesday, 3 March, Anne complained to him that the cardinal was neglecting her, and when at supper Heneage was sent from Henry with a special dish for Anne's meal, she prevailed on him to join her at table – an act of the greatest condescension which Heneage well knew was not aimed at him. As the meal progressed, Anne's overtures became even plainer. How pleasant it would be during Lent, she mused, to have some carp or shrimps from Wolsey's famous fishponds. Heneage offered a wry masculine apology when passing on the request: 'I beseech your grace, pardon me that I am so bold to write unto your grace hereof, it is the conceit and mind of a woman.' However, not for nothing had the cardinal put one of his best men to 'mind' Anne, and a fortnight later Heneage was writing again to thank Wolsey for his 'kind and favourable writing unto her' – whether accompanied by a parcel of fish is not stated – and to pass on her 'humble' request for Cheney to be forgiven.[7] In June Heneage reported on the news of Anne's health after some ailment: 'Mistress Anne is very well amended, and commendeth her humbly unto your grace, and thinketh it long till she speak with you.'[8]

Wolsey marked Anne's recovery from the much more serious sweating sickness by 'a kind letter' and a 'rich and goodly present', which she acknowledged directly along with her indebtedness to Wolsey for his help:

of the which I have hitherto had so great plenty, that all the days of my life I am most bound of all creatures, next the king's grace, to love and serve your grace: of the which I beseech you never to doubt that never I shall vary from this thought as long as any breath is in my body. And as touching your grace's trouble with the sweat [in his household], I thank our Lord that them that I desired and prayed for are scaped, and that is the king and you.

The letter ends with a promise of what she will do for Wolsey when, as she puts it, 'this matter' is at 'a good end', a promise she repeated in another letter soon afterwards.[9] Most striking of all is a third letter at the start of August, when the ending of the epidemic allowed Anne to rejoin Henry.[10] In the first part she sent good wishes to the cardinal, expressed her debt to him 'never like to be recompensed on my part', and mentioned the anxious waiting for Campeggio. Then she handed the letter to Henry and nagged him to complete it: 'The writer of this letter would not cease till she had caused me likewise to set my hand; desiring you, though it be short, to take it in good part.' The king also made clear why the couple was writing – they were in a state because no news had reached England about Campeggio arriving in France. Very probably 'your loving sovereign and friend, Henry K' and 'your humble servant Anne Boleyn' got the reassurance they wanted by return of post.[11] Wolsey had an excellent professional manner.

Not everyone has read the correspondence of 1528 in this way. Some have seen evidence of Anne's volatile moods. Others, convinced by Cavendish that she bore a settled resentment following the Percy episode, have accused Anne of blatant insincerity. But Wolsey was suspected of that too. The imperial ambassador suggested in September 1528 that the more difficult the divorce could be made, the more Henry would need the cardinal, and the longer the suit could be strung out, the longer it would be before Anne could destroy his influence.[12] Wolsey was certainly keen to ingratiate himself with Anne. Cavendish remembered how he 'ordered himself to please as well the king as her, dissimulating the matter that lay hid in his breast, and prepared great banquets and solemn feasts to entertain them both at his own house'.[13] We may note too that Heneage's letter following his supper with Anne was written at eleven o'clock the same night, despite an exhausting day when the privy chamber had been exceedingly short-staffed; fish or no fish, Heneage clearly understood the priority Wolsey placed on news of Anne. By November the imperial ambassador was reporting that Wolsey had done a deal with Anne and her father, and stating as his own opinion that Wolsey would, in the end, go the way the king wanted – exactly what the more acute courtiers had told him a year earlier.[14]

There was, indeed, no reason not to trust Wolsey. The year 1528 did bring progress: first the commission brought back by Fox in May, and then the progressive news of Campeggio's preparations and eventual departure for England. What frayed the couple's nerves was the time it all took. Wolsey's nerves, though, were frayed by something different: not as ambassadors thought, fear for his own future once a divorce was achieved – he was sanguine enough to believe that he could cope with that, however much he affected a desire to retire. His fear was that he would not be able to secure a divorce on the terms Henry demanded. It was perfectly clear that the divine revelation to Henry about the meaning of Leviticus 20 would get nowhere. Campeggio would arrive fully and firmly convinced that the king was wrong in law, and Wolsey could share this with no one.[15] As early as July 1527 he had been accused by the king of being lukewarm on the divorce because he suggested an alternative line of approach; in June 1528 the king lost his temper when Wolsey again tried to explain the problem.[16] All this forced the minister to concentrate on two outside chances, either to try to bring about a French hegemony in Italy which would then make the pope the prisoner of an ally of England, or to deafen him with pleas to grant the divorce somehow and horror stories of what would happen if he did not. So long as that policy seemed to produce results, as it appeared to do in 1528, so long Wolsey seemed to justify the trust Henry and Anne had in him. The question was, how long would the impossibility of success by that route remain a secret?

It would be satisfying to be able to point to a single event, a precise occasion that broke the illusion of progress behind which Wolsey sheltered for so many months, but the realization was slow to dawn, especially on Henry. Campeggio wrote a very revealing report on 9 January 1529, showing that despite what he had tried to explain, the king had supreme confidence that 'his merits and the urgency he uses therein' could not fail; assurance of divine revelation is not always an advantage.[17] Wolsey, by contrast, was brutally pragmatic. 'I speak freely with his lordship to know his mind, and he generally ends by shrugging his shoulders and has nothing else to say but that the only remedy is to satisfy the king's wish in some way or other, and let it stand for what it is worth.'

Perhaps it was Anne who got to the truth first, possibly at the time when she insisted on being brought back to court, where Henry was soon, in the words of Campeggio, 'kissing her and treating her in public as though she were his wife'.[18] She had been frustrated by the legate's slow journey;

she had been suspicious at being kept out of Campeggio's way and ignored by him; she had been expecting rapid progress once he did arrive on 8 October, and a month later all that had been achieved was the ruin of Henry's self-confidence. Already on 1 November, Wolsey had warned the pope that 'many people were again and again insinuating to the king' the necessity of adopting policies which would inevitably threaten the authority of Rome. Nor was he bluffing. At the end of the month the king did send Anne's cousin, Francis Bryan, to Clement VII, along with Peter Vannes, his Latin secretary, with instructions personally approved by Henry to force the Holy Father into submission, if necessary with the threat that otherwise England would withdraw its allegiance to the see of Rome.[19] About the same time there was the first sign of another policy that would also be very definitely associated with the Boleyns – the preparation of a monster petition to the pope from the English political elite, urging him to grant the divorce in the national interest.[20]

It may, of course, be premature to see in all this the evidence of a serious rift between Anne Boleyn and Wolsey in November 1528, but if so it is premature by only a month or so. It was about the third week of the following January that Anne had her second brush with the cardinal over Cheney, and when the French ambassador reported her victory in this, he also noted that Norfolk and his faction (*'le duc de Nortfoch et sa bande'*) were already 'talking big'.[21] A few days later Mendoza had picked up the news. Anne had decided that Wolsey was trying to frustrate, not assist, the divorce, and had formed an alliance with Rochford and with both Norfolk and Suffolk.[22] The naming of Suffolk for the first time as one of the group attacking Wolsey is significant, and so too is the mention of Anne as an equal party, indeed, an instigator – in the brief 1527 skirmish, Mendoza had treated her as an adjunct of her father. The confidence of the group increased as letter followed letter from Rome. Sending Bryan, a man committed to Anne and Henry, and renowned for his plain talking to the king as much as to lesser mortals, had placed in Rome a source of information quite independent of Wolsey.[23] And it was not only Henry who now received the unvarnished truth; Bryan wrote direct to Anne, although when the news was particularly grim he asked her to consult the king:

> I dare not write unto my cousin Anne the truth of this matter, because I do not know your grace's pleasure, whether I shall do or no; wherefore, if she be angry with me, I must humbly desire your grace to make mine excuse. I have referred to her in her letter all the news to your grace, so your grace may use her in this as you shall think best.[24]

From the start the news was bleak. Bryan had arrived on 14 January, but because of the pope's ill health he had not even presented his credentials before Gardiner arrived a month later to strengthen the team, and it was a further month before they achieved their first substantive session with Clement.[25] Their reports were full of despair. On 20 March Henry read to Tuke, the treasurer of the chamber, the letters which had just arrived from Rome, and Tuke warned Wolsey:

> Mr. Bryan's letter, for as many clauses as the king showed me, which was here and there, as his grace read it, was totally of desperation, affirming plainly that he could not believe the pope would do anything for his grace, with these words added: 'It might well be in his paternoster, but it was nothing in his creed' [i.e. the pope might well pray that Henry would have his problem solved, but he would not commit himself to doing anything about it].[26]

Bryan also communicated from time to time with 'my masters and fellows of your grace's chamber', and although he was no doubt discreet, his failure to announce the great breakthrough could be interpreted by everyone, partisan of Anne or not.[27] Very soon, too, we find that one of the most brilliant of the king's advisers, Stephen Gardiner, had swung to Anne's support. A protégé of Wolsey and noted in August 1527 as a supporter of Katherine, the future bishop of Winchester had decided, with that acute political 'nose' which would desert him on only a couple of occasions in his life, that Anne was going to win.[28] He wrote in March assuring her of his devotion, and she replied in phrases typical of the patron to the client: 'I pray God to send you well to speed...so that you would put me to the study, how to reward your high service. I do trust in God you shall not repent it.' Anne took the chance, at the same time, to tie up the rest of the embassy by sending cramp-rings for Gardiner and the two other envoys (Bryan excepted): 'And have me kindly recommended to them both, as she that, you may assure them, will be glad to do them any pleasure which shall be in my power.'[29]

Ironically, the one person whom Anne found difficult to motivate against the cardinal was Henry. Whether this was scepticism about Norfolk's ability to succeed if Wolsey failed (in the event well justified), or a dependence engendered over fifteen years, or the minister's unrivalled ability and his proven record of success, Henry was anxious to cling to his right-hand man. There was a rumour in January that he was beginning to distrust Wolsey's promises, and he did keep Norfolk, Suffolk and

Rochford more in the picture.[30] Yet throughout the spring of 1529, Henry and Wolsey made common cause in an effort to force concessions from the pope. The king clung to the illusion that the pope was genuinely anxious to help and that he only needed encouragement, and the minister kept his doubts to himself. On 6 April they wrote in parallel to the English envoys to reject the 'desperation' in the reports from Rome, implying lack of zeal and urging greater efforts, although when Bryan's even gloomier next letter could not resist a suitably expressed 'I told you so,' it was Wolsey who had to make apologies on behalf of the king.[31] Every piece of correspondence from Rome, every word, was scrutinized for evidence of papal good intentions.[32] Clement would yield.

All this was based on nothing. In January the resident English ambassador at Rome had sent an envoy to explain that the pope would budge no further, and Campeggio had tried again and again to convince both Henry and Wolsey that the pope could not bend the law in their favour, that the Holy Father was adamant.[33] Clement would not quash the dispensation for Katherine's second marriage. The very idea that the English should expect this offended him deeply, as did their relentless pressure – what Bryan had described as 'first by fair means and afterward by foul'.[34] When eventually letters from Rome did carry conviction, Henry and Wolsey attributed failure entirely to imperial obstruction; and they turned on Campeggio, or rather, since they still needed him, on his senior staff, with a joint display of criticism which was only partly engineered by Wolsey to put the blame for his own public over-confidence on the pope's deceit.[35] Already, however, they had decided on a new tack: to go for a rapid decision on the suit in England. 'The king's highness,' wrote Wolsey, 'is minded for the time to dissemble the matter, and taking as much as may be had and attained there to the benefit of his cause, to proceed in the decision of the same here, by virtue of the commission already granted unto me and my lord legate Campeggio.'[36]

How proud Henry VIII was of his ability to 'dissemble'. Securing a favourable judgement in England would outflank the emperor's pressure and give the pope just the excuse he was supposedly looking for to help Henry. Confidence was maintained even when news arrived that imperial envoys were pressing Clement to revoke the case to Rome. Henry and Wolsey were sure the pope would never do that, any more than Francis I, who up to that time had stood solidly with them against Charles V, would make peace with the Empire at the international conference then being planned for Cambrai, and leave England in the cold. Suddenly Campeggio found himself rushed into action. A decision was wanted, now![37]

The opening of the legatine court at Blackfriars on 31 May 1529 was, therefore, the latest in a succession of manoeuvres that king and cardinal were confident would give them what they wanted and vindicate Henry's faith in his minister. Few other people were as sure. Campeggio knew he was under papal orders to avoid a decision at all costs.[38] Anne and her allies went on with their preparations against the cardinal, confident that only the miracle of a legatine decision could now save him. The letters from her supporters in Italy kept up an insidious denigration of Wolsey. Ostensibly Campeggio was the target, but there is little doubt who Bryan had in mind when he wrote: 'Whosoever made your grace believe that he [Clement] will do for you in this cause hath not, as I think, done your grace the best service.'[39] Already, when on his way to Italy in December, Bryan had passed on a warning from Francis I that Henry had quislings among his advisers.[40] In May, when Wolsey's ally, Sir John Russell, was ordered to France as the cardinal's representative and to stiffen the war effort there, he was recalled in the actual process of embarking his horses at Sandwich. Anne Boleyn had reminded the king of Bryan's warning, and Suffolk was dispatched to France instead, with secret orders to probe the matter.[41] The duke did so in a transparent attempt to implicate Wolsey, and although Francis spoke well of the minister's loyalty and his warning had actually been against Campeggio, under pressure he did (or so Suffolk reported) add the innuendo that Wolsey had:

> marvellous intelligence with the pope, and in Rome and also with Cardinal Campeggio. Wherefore, seeing that he hath such intelligence with them which have not minded to advance your matter, he [Francis] thinketh it shall be the more need for your grace to have better regard to your said affair.[42]

There was a second motive too behind the sending of Suffolk: to have an anti-Wolsey partisan to represent England at the peace conference which was beginning to assemble in Flanders, to put him in a position 'to do "a cardinal of York at Amiens" '.[43] Wolsey had intended to go himself, if the king had been in favour, but he had to content himself with hamstringing Suffolk's instructions and precipitating his early return.

When Brandon got back in the first week of July, he found that Anne's faction was ready for the showdown.[44] His wife's humanist schoolmaster, John Palsgrave, who also had links with the duke of Richmond and his mentor, the duke of Norfolk, had been called up to prepare a propaganda pamphlet mocking Wolsey's period in office as a time of pride, waste, autocratic repression and ineffective tinkering.[45] Lord Darcy, one of the principal supports of the previous reign who considered that he had been very badly treated by the cardinal, had drawn up a plan of action – an immediate arrest of Wolsey and his agents, the impounding of their papers and a thorough investigation of his administration: precisely the sort of coup that had destroyed Empson and Dudley in 1509.[46] The topics to be scrutinized were listed in detail, the texts drafted of proclamations inviting complaints, all with the obvious end of securing a parliamentary Act of attainder. The only refinement Suffolk needed to add when he got back was to have his own men keep watch on the posts going across the Channel. All that was lacking was the occasion for Anne to 'prove' to Henry that the suspicions about Wolsey that had been fed to him were justified. Deprived of royal favour, the cardinal would then be 'naked to his enemies'.[47]

The fiasco at Blackfriars appeared exactly the opportunity which was wanted. Anne herself was close enough to Henry during the hearings to deliver the *coup de grâce*, so close, indeed, that du Bellay, the French ambassador, confidently expected to hear that she was pregnant.[48] Katherine of Aragon had no doubt that a failure of the legatine hearing would provide the opportunity to break the bond between king and cardinal, and Edward Hall certainly states that it was the failure there which convinced Henry of Wolsey's double dealing.[49] This allowed the attack prepared by Anne and the rest to go in. A 'book' detailing thirty-four charges against the minister was presented to the king before he left for his summer progress, that is, between 31 July and 4 August, probably alleging that Wolsey was guilty of *praemunire*, the offence of introducing an illegal foreign authority into England, in other words, acting on the alien authority of the pope.

To the chagrin of the conspirators, Henry took no action. The only part of their scheme which was put in hand was the issue of writs to summon parliament.[50] The reason why the attack stalled was that Wolsey had pre-empted it. He had moved the very next day after the closure of the Blackfriars court to conciliate Rochford and the king with what each appreciated most, money. The previous February the cardinal had exchanged the bishopric of Durham (which he held in addition to the archbishopric of York) for the richest English see, Winchester. This had left the revenues of Durham at the king's disposal, and in the last week of July he had granted them to Anne's father. Wolsey thereupon threw in the four months' income due to him for the period October 1528 to February 1529, saying that he had always regarded that as belonging to the king and offering to expedite payment to Rochford.[51] Following the success of the bribe, Wolsey's indispensability rapidly reasserted itself, not only in the management of the divorce, where he was still the key man in relations with Rome, but also in diplomacy. All the evidence suggests that the summer vacation of 1529 began and promised to continue in the normal way, with the king and minister pursuing their own ways until Michaelmas but keeping up an active communication by letter and occasional meetings. The story that Henry refused to visit Wolsey is incorrect.[52] The king did call off an intended visit to his country home at the More near Rickmansworth, during which the cardinal would have stayed ten miles away at his abbey of St Albans. However, the reason was fear of the sweat – a motive which one may well credit, given the royal terror of the previous year – and Henry went instead to another Wolsey house, Tittenhanger, which had kept him safe in the 1528 epidemic. This was only three miles from St Albans and the king expected to 'take such cheer of your Grace [Wolsey] there as he should have had at the More'.[53] When drafting his plans Darcy had noted that, if Wolsey were pushed to answer the complaints against him, 'he clearly doubts not, as he and his affirms, but that he hath the guile and understanding to discharge him of all this light flea-biting or flies-stinging, and yet so to handle all matters that he shall reign still in more authority than ever he did, and all to quake and repent that hath meddled against him.'[54] It began to look as if he was right.

However, when Henry and Wolsey separated for the summer progress of 1529 there was one crucial difference from the year before: Anne Boleyn. There would be no more of the courteous communications and elegant gifts of 1528. Instead, as Wolsey well knew, Anne would have the field to herself and her supporters, who were dedicated to bringing him down and who now had a ready welcome at court – Norfolk, Suffolk, and particularly Rochford, whose duties as chaperon made him almost 'counsellor in residence'. Yet progresses end, and Wolsey could know that if he sat tight, the autumn would come and with it the chance to work his magic with the king once again; he could still prove himself too strong for them. August proceeded and the cardinal continued to handle English affairs as usual. Then, with a month or six weeks of the progress still to go, the cardinal began to make mistakes, mistakes which handed his enemies the issue that they had been looking for, not merely to curb his authority but to destroy him completely. His own errors did what the carefully planned coup in July had failed to do, and incredibly, these were in the two areas of his greatest competence – his understanding of the king and his handling of diplomacy. Cardinal Wolsey was not deprived of royal favour following the abortive divorce hearing at Blackfriars, or even after the aristocratic attack on his position which followed that fiasco. He lost Henry's confidence from late August onwards by miscalculating the king's mood and by mishandling the Treaty of Cambrai, in which Francis I totally deceived him and caused him, in turn, to mislead his master.

Exploring the diplomatic maze of 1529 would take us too far from Anne Boleyn herself, but a brief account will reveal how it enabled her and her faction to bring him down. Wolsey had for months recognized the probability of peace between Francis I and Charles V, and as early as March 1529 had begun to behave again as the doyen of European summit diplomacy, his favourite role, and one which opened up the possibility that Anglo-French co-operation might force the emperor to abandon Katherine of Aragon as part of the price for peace.[55] Wolsey and Henry were agreed on this approach, but the decision in early May to go for a legatine trial in England posed the question of priorities, and the cardinal found to his horror that the king believed that the hearing took precedence over international trouble-shooting.[56] Wolsey knew the odds against a decision at Blackfriars and that the only hope was to keep up diplomatic and military pressure to persuade the pope to oblige Henry, but he had to acquiesce.

The consequence was, first, that Russell had to be sent to France instead of Wolsey, only to be recalled, as we have seen, at the insistence of Anne, in favour of Suffolk. Then, when Wolsey had managed to neutralize that embassy, he found to his horror that his requests to have the peace conference delayed until after the Blackfriars verdict were being ignored by the French, thanks in part (though he was not aware of this) to the obstructive tactics of the French ambassador in London, du Bellay, whom he imagined was his firm ally.[57] Even then, with the negotiations at Cambrai due to begin on 5 July, Henry still refused to let Wolsey go, sending instead Bishop Tunstall and Thomas More, and the cardinal had to waste his time at Blackfriars while 175 miles away Europe's future was being settled between France and the Empire, with the English envoys (once they had arrived) kept in ignorance and on the sidelines.[58] Something of Wolsey's frustration became evident in an attempt he made in July to embarrass Suffolk (and Anne). The duke's probing of Francis I on the cardinal's loyalty had been under a strict pledge of secrecy, but Francis told du Bellay and the ambassador let something of this slip to Wolsey, who promptly complained to Henry that Suffolk had maligned him to the French king.[59] The king, unable to admit publicly his own complicity, had to side with the minister until a fortunate (or perhaps wise) indisposition kept Suffolk away from court and, with the simultaneous absence of du Bellay, made it difficult for Wolsey to make more of the affair.

The Treaty of Cambrai was signed on 3 August 1529, but this did not mean the end of Wolsey's nightmare. He had been forced to stand by powerless as the French had duped him.[60] Henry now faced the situation that he had most feared: a pope who was the emperor's man; the ending of the French pressure to force Charles out of Italy; the revocation of the divorce suit by Clement and the prospect of being cited to appear before a hostile tribunal in Rome. How could Wolsey now rescue his king and his own credit? He did manage to stall the citation but it was equally vital that the *rapprochement* between the Empire and France should not put an end to Francis I's support for the divorce. The only available lever was that Cambrai had to be ratified by England. This was because Henry had loaned money to Charles V and particularly to Francis I to pay for his ransom after being captured at Pavia. His two sons were hostages in imperial hands and, without the rescheduling of these debts, Francis I stood no chance of raising the ransom money. If Wolsey were to cause difficulties, it might be possible to push France into giving England greater support, and in particular to do more for the king's divorce – and, no doubt, for Wolsey.[61] It was not a policy without risk. The cardinal recognized the danger that the French and the imperialists might ratify the Cambrai peace bilaterally, leaving Henry to face Katherine's nephew unsupported.[62] Nevertheless, with Henry's concurrence, he set out to try.

Wolsey's notion of keeping Francis under pressure enjoyed considerable support during August because of the dubious behaviour of the French ambassador. He badgered Henry to implement the treaty but again and again failed to provide a full text of it.[63] Francis was also making demands based on the earlier Treaty of Madrid, and on 28 August the king asked the minister for private advice before he discussed this with the council and the ambassador.[64] An interim meeting with du Bellay the next day only increased Henry's suspicion.[65] In reply, Wolsey emphasized England's potential exposure to a claim by the French for military support and implied bad faith on their part in omitting a caveat he himself had negoti- ated at Amiens in 1527. Henry read his letter late on Monday, 30 August, when he came in from a good day's hunting, and his suspicions of the French were confirmed: he was 'much kindled and waxed warm and thought himself not well handled by them'.[66] However, he called for Wolsey's detailed points to be checked overnight against both the text of the Treaty of Madrid (to which the Cambrai accords frequently alluded) and the Amiens agreement.[67] Rochford and Gardiner were in attendance, and they were charged with the task. The following day sentiment changed. Further discussion convinced Henry that Wolsey had it wrong and that his recommendations should be ignored. The cardinal was told that full concessions would be made to France, and that he was allowing resentment at the Cambrai débâcle to cloud his judgement.[68]

What we cannot know is whether Wolsey was truly at fault, or whether Rochford set him up while Gardiner looked the other way. He had been appointed Henry's secretary on 28 July, and made it clear that he would not favour his former employer. Anne's father was an expert on foreign affairs and might easily have seen an opportunity to represent coolness towards France as imperilling progress towards the divorce. If Henry was to get free from Katherine, he needed Francis, and that should take priority above everything. Wolsey hit back, challenging Gardiner on the change in direction and making his resentment plain.[69] His erstwhile protégé protested his good faith and told the minister that he was suspected of an ulterior motive – wanting to stir Henry against the French. He also read back to the cardinal his own recipe for success with Henry: 'If your grace had been here and seen how the king's highness took it [you] would rather have studied how by some benign interpretation to have made the best of that which is past remedy than to have persisted in the blaming of not observation of covenants on the French part.'[70] Wolsey excused himself to Gardiner by return, but the damage had been done.[71] Du Bellay was able to report on 1 September that he and his brother had fully satisfied most English doubts, that Norfolk, Suffolk and Rochford were in high favour, and that Wolsey was now clearly on the way out.[72]

Only one thing could have saved Wolsey, and that was access to Henry in person, but while he was trying to work through the unreliable Gardiner, Norfolk, Suffolk and Rochford as the courtiers in favour and on the spot simply took over the execution of policy, while Anne conducted an open campaign of character assassination.[73] All Wolsey's anxiety to go to Cambrai in June and July was now represented as an attempt to delay the Boleyn marriage. He was also accused of having been for years in the pocket of Francis I's mother and mentor, Louise of Savoy; even Suffolk's ignominious retreat when only fifty miles from capturing Paris in 1523 was now attributed to Wolsey withholding the necessary cash at her behest.[74] Sometime in the second week of September Wolsey took the plunge and asked directly for an interview with Henry in order to impart information too sensitive for a letter, normally an infallible way to touch the suspicious Henry. However, on 12 September he was told that on this occasion he was to indicate in writing the subjects he wished to raise.[75] Henry was not going to trust blindly again – or was it Anne and her allies determined not to be caught out?

What happened when king and minister met is the subject of a famous passage in Cavendish, but with some contemporary support from the newly arrived Chapuys.[76] According to this, Wolsey was refused access to court until Campeggio insisted that he should accompany him when he came to take his leave of the king, but even then the two legates were told to come without pomp and ceremony. The date chosen was Sunday, 19 September, and the place, the king's hunting lodge at Grafton, near what is now Milton Keynes, a house so small that half the court had to sleep at Richard Empson's old house at Easton Neston three miles away.[77] Concerned that the cardinal's magic might still work on the king, Suffolk arranged for Campeggio alone to be given lodgings at Grafton. However, the emollient Norris, groom of the stool, lent Wolsey his room to change in, and the cardinal's supporters flocked to welcome him and warn of the latest situation. Then the two legates were called to the presence chamber, packed with every courtier who could find a place, with polite greetings all the way, sincere and insincere. Henry entered, and the old magic did begin to work. Raising the kneeling Wolsey, the king took him to one of the great window embrasures, made him put his hat on and engaged in a long and earnest conversation. The climax came when Henry produced against Wolsey one of his own letters, saying 'how can that be? Is this not your own hand?' only to be given a full and, as far as observers could tell, entirely satisfactory explanation.

Dinner followed, with Anne and her supporters more than worried. Norfolk dined with Wolsey and tried to make him angry. Anne entertained Henry to dinner in her chamber, and tried to make *him* angry:

> 'Sir', quoth she, 'Is it not a marvellous thing to consider what debt and danger the cardinal hath brought you in, with all your subjects?' 'How so, sweetheart?' quoth the king. 'Forsooth, Sir', quoth she, 'There is not a man within all your realm worth £5 but he hath indebted you unto him by his means' (meaning by a loan that the king had but late of his subjects). 'Well, well', quoth the king, 'As for that there is in him no blame, for I know that matter better than you or any other'.

Even this did not discourage Anne, or so observers retailed:

> 'Nay, Sir', quoth she, 'Besides all that what things hath he wrought within this realm to your great slander and dishonour. There is never a nobleman

within this realm that if he had done but half so much as he hath done but he were well worthy to lose his head. If my lord of Norfolk, my lord of Suffolk, my lord my father, or any other noble person within your realms had done much less than he but they should have lost their heads [bef]ore this'. 'Why then I perceive', quoth the king, 'Ye are not the cardinal's friend'. 'Forsooth, Sir', then quoth she, 'I have no cause nor any other man that loveth your grace. No more have your grace if ye consider well his doings'.

Despite this barrage, Henry went back to the presence chamber and had another long, private conversation with Wolsey, followed by an even more secret tête-à-tête with him in the privy chamber until bedtime, when the king told him to return early next day to continue their discussion. So Wolsey set out for Easton, and there he was joined by Gardiner, either to find out what he could for Anne, or else to mend his relationship with his old master. However, when Wolsey arrived back at Grafton the next morning, he found the plan changed. Anne was going riding with Henry to a new park three miles away, and had quickly arranged a picnic to ensure that the cardinals would be gone before the king returned.

It is a good story. It is psychologically right; it illustrates to perfection the importance of access to the monarch – and the ability to deny access; it ought to be true. Unfortunately, it does not square with other evidence about the meeting. Gardiner's letter of 12 September agreeing to a meeting does not suggest that Wolsey reached the king by hanging on to Campeggio's coat-tails – it looks more as if the Italian accompanied Wolsey. As well as Cavendish, Thomas Alward was at Grafton with Wolsey.[78] He had certainly heard the rumour that his master's days of power were numbered, but said that he had seen nothing out of the ordinary in the regular exchange of letters and messages between the cardinal and the court that vacation, and he seems to suggest that Wolsey attended court as much as would be expected. In particular, Alward noticed nothing unusual in his master's reception at Grafton, either by the king or by the courtiers, and nothing strange in lodgings being provided at Easton for, he says, both cardinals. His letter confirms Wolsey's lengthy sessions with Henry on the Sunday, but gives no support to the story of a change of plan for Monday. According to him, Wolsey sat in council with Henry all morning, and the king did not go hunting until after dinner; even then Wolsey did not leave until after dark. As for Suffolk, Rochford, Brian Tuke and Gardiner, Alward had heard stories but had noted 'as much observance and humility to my lord's grace as I ever saw them do', although he did add, 'What they bear in their hearts I know not.' Clearly not the most sensitive of men, and one also wanting to believe that things were as usual, but unlike Cavendish, Alward was writing five days, not almost thirty years, after the event. Regretfully we must discard the brilliantly opportunistic ride and picnic, and assume that if Henry did go out riding with Anne that day, it was after he had completed business with the two legates.

On this reading, Grafton was not the victory tradition has given to Anne. Nevertheless, as a counter-attack by Wolsey, success was short-lived. The day before, du Bellay had noted that the cardinal was counting on the support at court of certain people 'made by him' who had already turned their coats – undoubtedly Gardiner, and possibly Heneage and Tuke.[79] They would defer to his face and observe the proprieties, but they were unwilling to support the minister otherwise. Meanwhile, at court Anne was ever closer to Henry. Now the king even needed her to start the hunt, almost like the goddess Diana![80]

Wolsey retained office and chaired council meetings in the normal way as late as 6 October, but on the first day of the law term, 9 October, he found himself deserted in his own court and charged in King's Bench with *praemunire*.[81] A week or so later he was dismissed as chancellor, and on 22 October he pleaded guilty to the charge, surrendered all his property to Henry and threw himself on the king's mercy.[82] As du Bellay (who was still in touch with Wolsey) explained to Montmorency, the constable of France, he had been offered his chance with either king or parliament and had no doubt which threatened less. And that was despite Anne trying to block all hope of access to Henry by making the king promise never to receive his old friend; there would be no more Graftons.[83] How wise she was is clear from the evidence that Henry continued for many months to feel that Wolsey had value, and even to communicate with him in secret. Meanwhile the lovers went to inspect his Westminster house, York Place, to gloat over its treasures and decide that there they would build the palace of their dreams.[84]

The anti-Wolsey faction rejoiced, and began to argue about the spoils. Chapuys, quite rightly, congratulated Norfolk as the man who would be the king's new chief counsellor.[85] Yet the fall of Wolsey was first and foremost Anne's success. Without her they would not have made it. Wolsey himself explained his decision not to fight the *praemunire* on the grounds that it was impossible to challenge 'a continual serpentine enemy about the king'.[86] Anne had made the difference; Anne now had the triumph. Du Bellay reported: 'The duke of Norfolk is made chief of the council and in his absence the duke of Suffolk, and above everyone Mademoiselle Anne.'[87] He made it clear, indeed, that Anne and her father were determined to be recognized as enjoying and deserving the king's highest favour. Even before Wolsey's fall, Thomas Boleyn was seeking to impress his value on the French by deliberately frustrating the agreement du Bellay was trying to negotiate: 'at least he is the one who is keeping the dance going, expressly against the dukes and the cardinal of York whom I had so convinced that I thought I had gained my objective.'[88] What was needed was a letter from Louise of Savoy acknowledging Boleyn's new standing. With still no such letter of greeting to hand, du Bellay wrote again a week later. Anne Boleyn and her father were continuing their obstruction in order to demonstrate that they were as zealous in the king's affairs as Wolsey had been, and because they saw that Henry himself was already inclined against the ambassador's proposal. They were well aware, he noted, 'that one of the principal devices which the cardinal of York had to maintain his influence (given the nature of his master) was to heap praise on his opinions.'[89]

Du Bellay was now even more pointed about the relative importance of Anne and Thomas. During the discussions,

> [Boleyn] allowed everything to be said, and then came and suggested the complete opposite, defending his position without budging, as though he wanted to show me that he was not pleased that anyone should have failed to pay court to the lady [Anne], and also to make me accept that what he had said before is true, that is, that all the rest have no influence except what it pleases the lady to allow them, and that is gospel truth. And because of this he wanted with words and deeds to beat down their opinions before my eyes.[90]

The ambassador's firm advice to Paris was to flatter Boleyn pretensions and in particular to lionize the family's *petit prince*, George, who was just going on his first diplomatic mission. The arrival at the French court of such a young man as ambassador would probably provide a few laughs, but the new realities of power had to be recognized.[91]

STALEMATE, 1529—1532

WHAT puzzled European contemporaries most was that Henry VIII went about divorce the hard way. Wanting Anne as a wife instead of a mistress was eccentric enough, but his determination to bludgeon the pope into guaranteeing in advance, not only the outcome, but also his own distinctive interpretation of canon law, was unprecedented. Pressure on the pope – that was expected; but 'the urgency used' by Henry was a principal cause of his humiliation at Blackfriars.[1] Even then the king would not resign himself to having to wait for Rome to adjudicate, and swallow the ruling if he did not like it. The struggle began again. True, Henry had good reason to distrust Clement VII, but there was more than suspicion behind his enormous effort to force the pope to admit that in allowing him to marry Katherine, his predecessor Julius II had exceeded his powers.

Part of the explanation is that Henry was passionately in love. This was anything but a secret. Chapuys, hardly arrived and yet to go to court, could still report: 'The king's affection for La Bolaing increases daily. It is so great just now that it can hardly be greater; such is the intimacy and familiarity in which they live at present.'[2] On 8 December, seven weeks after Wolsey's dismissal, Henry publicly demonstrated his favour by elevating Anne's father not only to the coveted title 'earl of Ormonde' but to a senior English earldom as well: Wiltshire. George thereby became Viscount Rochford and was soon made a nobleman of the privy chamber.[3] Along with Wiltshire, two more of the anti-Wolsey nobles were promoted, becoming earls of Sussex and Huntingdon. The next day there was a grand celebration to which, if we believe Chapuys, the king's sister Mary and both the dowager duchess and the current duchess of Norfolk (the highest-ranking noblewomen in the land) were summoned to watch Anne taking the place of the queen at Henry's side.[4] To cap it all, early in the new year Boleyn replaced the bishop of Durham as lord privy seal, the third ranking officer of state.

There was, too, the tension the couple had to face. Katherine of Aragon still lived at court, formally recognized as queen by the king no less than the rest of the royal household, a permanent reproach to Henry and an irritant to Anne.[5] On the whole Anne coped better, allowing Katherine's mixture of martyrdom and complaint to drive Henry into her company. Thus on St Andrew's Day, a week before Rochford's promotion, Katherine had turned on Henry after dining with him, taxing him with unkindness and private neglect.[6] Defending himself, he boasted that the opinions on his case which were being collected were so weighty that the decision must go in his favour, and if it did not he would 'denounce the pope as a heretic and marry whom he pleased'. Katherine poured scorn on his arguments and Henry walked out in a huff. Anne took full advantage:

> Did I not tell you that whenever you disputed with the queen she was sure to have the upper hand? I see that some fine morning you will succumb to her reasoning and that you will cast me off. I have been waiting long and might in the meanwhile have contracted some advantageous marriage, out of which I might have had issue, which is the greatest consolation in this world. But, alas! Farewell to my time and youth spent to no purpose at all.

Even though Henry hoped to pacify her by placing her at his side at the 9 December banquet, it seems that Anne declined to appear at the Christmas festivities at Greenwich, which Henry celebrated with Katherine 'in great triumph'.[7] The tactic worked. On 31 December Henry sent Walter Walsh, groom of the privy chamber, to Anne with a gift of £110, while the imperial ambassador noted early in February 1530 that Henry was spending all his time at York Place with Anne, leaving Katherine alone at Richmond for their longest separation yet.[8]

The story of the St Andrew's Day outburst is recorded in one of Eustace Chapuys' early letters, and as we have seen, anyone studying Anne faces the problem that the immediacy and commitment of his reports can impose a particular view of events and motives. He was, however, wrong to see Henry as the besotted victim of a shrewd and calculating harpy whom Wolsey would stigmatize as 'the midnight crow'.[9] Irrespective of his desire for Anne, the obstruction he was experiencing was challenging something much deeper, the very core of his self-identity. He was discovering that he was less than the king God had made him. The drive to marry Anne was not only to satisfy emotion and desire; it became a campaign to vindicate his kingship.

As early as 1515, the Church–State crisis known to history as 'the Hunne affair' had seen Henry publicly back a judicial ruling that 'the positive laws [i.e. institutional decrees] of the church only bind those who receive them'; hence papal canons were admissible in England only with royal approval.[10] He did not deny the Church's traditional liberties or the Crown's exclusion from spiritual matters, but 'by order and sufferance of God we are king of England and kings of England in time past have never had any superior but God only. . . . Therefore we will not agree to your desire now any more than our forebears have in time past.'[11] As the frustration of the divorce suit dragged on, his mind increasingly debated the extent to which the pope could tell a king, a man appointed directly by God, what he could or could not do. Henry continued to press for papal approval, but casual remarks and private conversations showed that more and more he was beginning to question the pope's role in his 'great matter'. The threats that England would withdraw allegiance from Rome, or appeal over the pope's head to a general council of the Church, were far more serious than the huffing and puffing which Clement VII and, it seems, Henry's own men took them for. All orthodox Western Christians knew that, as Thomas More put it, authority over the Church rightfully belonged to the bishop of Rome, 'a spiritual preeminence by the mouth of our Saviour himself, personally present upon the earth, only to St Peter and his successors, bishops of the same see, by special prerogative granted'.[12] That papal authority was not thus divinely ordained was inconceivable, yet increasingly not so to Henry VIII of England. His determination to marry Anne Boleyn expressed something deep in the king's psychology.

Since this intense concern with what it meant to be a king antedates Henry's interest in Anne Boleyn by many years, it gives the lie to Eustace Chapuys and other writers (at the time and since) that the whole was driven by lust. Sex certainly provided them a ready and discreditable explanation for the change in a king who in 1521 wrote the apparently pro-papal *Assertio Septem Sacramentorum*, but later became ready, even eager, to butcher anyone upholding the thousand-year-old Christian conviction that the pope of Rome was head of the Church. But it was not Henry's loins which caused him to think radical thoughts. The Reformation changes were less unprecedented novelties than the consequence of long-held royal convictions breaking through traditional limits. The result was revolution, but a revolution produced more by extinguishing the independence of the Church than by inflating royal authority. This is not to say that in 1529 Henry VIII had grasped the 1532 principle that he was

'Supreme Head of the Church of England'. It is to say that many of the constituents of that concept were already present in the king's mind, and that in the heat of adversity they were beginning to fuse.

In all this, the regime which replaced Wolsey had nothing to contribute. The object of the new men had been to topple Wolsey, not to resolve the king's matrimonial dilemma. Possibly there was some feeling that a parliament might offer a route forward, but if so, nobody knew what that was, and in the thinking of Norfolk and the others, the principal need for the session was to attaint Wolsey.[13] That, indeed, was the one cause which held them together, and they grew terrified when it became clear at the beginning of December that the king would not permit a parliamentary bill of attainder, and was exhibiting every sign that he would bring the cardinal back into government.[14] Norfolk did his best to keep Henry and the former minister apart, but he had to give ground to the king and to the cardinal's friends at court, and accept Wolsey being pardoned and restored to royal favour on 12 February. The terms for this saw the cardinal retain the archbishopric of York plus a pension of 1000 marks from the see of Winchester, plus over £6000 in chattels returned by the king, which made him at least as wealthy as the duke.[15] Wolsey did everything possible to recruit support, and by May the council was known to be discussing the need to bring him back to run things. Norfolk alternated between vindictive fright and sycophantic self-preservation, and by the autumn the king was making ominous comments on the incapacity of his new advisers.[16]

The one person who kept her nerve was Anne. It was thanks to her that Wolsey's 'hinderers and enemies' retained the initiative and were able always to count on having 'time with the king before his friends'.[17] The former minister had recognized this from the start. He wrote to his agent, Thomas Cromwell, soon after his surrender: 'If the displeasure of my lady Anne be somewhat assuaged as I pray God the same may be, then it should [be devised] that by some convenient mean she be further laboured, [for] this is the only help and remedy. All possible means [must be attempted for the] attaining of her favour.'[18] When he fell ill in January 1530, he played on the king's genuine concern to extract a message of sympathy from Anne (plate 53).[19] She was, however, only superficially won over and, according to Chapuys, was more interested in whether Wolsey was genuinely ill, or merely milking the king's good nature.[20] Her response to the news that he had been pardoned was to lash out at Norfolk for caving in so abjectly; she cold-shouldered the cardinal's supporters at court, and a letter from him in May, even though brought by one of her own faction, was met with mere formality and the message that she 'will not promise to speak to the king for you'.[21] At the same time Anne was making it clear to the French, Wolsey's strongest supporters, that she could do more for them than he ever would.[22]

Perhaps failure to regain Anne's favour explains why Wolsey in the latter part of 1530 changed direction and began to work for a *rapprochement* with Katherine, Charles V and Rome. By October preparation was well advanced for a counter-coup, to be signalled by the arrival of a papal edict ordering Henry to leave Anne. Since Norfolk was for the moment away from court, Anne and her father had to move directly to forestall this disaster.[23] She whipped up the king's anger against such presumption on the part of Clement and treated Henry to a scene, or a series of scenes, which reduced him to tears. She brought out again her wasted youth and the reputation she had risked for Henry; she would leave him. In the end, Henry could only pacify her by agreeing to move against Wolsey. Of course, not even Anne could have urged Wolsey's arrest without colourable excuse. What this was is not known in detail – the cardinal died on 29 November 1530 on the way to interrogation – but it certainly included a revelation of Wolsey's recent dealings with Rome and, perhaps, with Francis I and the emperor also. The most likely source is a deliberate leak to Anne or her father by a French ambassador concerned to prevent England swinging back towards an imperial alliance.[24] Chapuys certainly interpreted the surprisingly dismissive reaction of the French at the news of Wolsey's death as an indication that they had earlier refused to go along with him and thus abandon support for a marriage with Anne 'on which alone depend the credit and favour the French now enjoy at this court'.[25]

Anne Boleyn's defeat of Wolsey's attempted comeback meant that those who had ridden to power behind her could sleep more peacefully, yet not too peacefully. 'The great matter' continued to defeat them in November 1530, as it had done from the start.[26] Suffolk was work-shy.[27] Thomas More, the new chancellor, had come in determined to defend the Church and stamp out heresy, but to have as little to do with the king's 'great matter' as possible.[28] Norfolk possibly felt the same, but the ineffectiveness of his public commitment to the divorce was not caused by lack of will but lack of ideas – Thomas Howard would have helped Henry to hell if he wanted to go there.[29] Even the brilliant Stephen Gardiner, imprisoned by his high view of the clerical office, came up with nothing.

The only support for Henry and the moving ferment of his ideas had come from Anne and her more committed backers. When the court arrived at Waltham in early August 1529, following the Blackfriars hearing, Stephen Gardiner and Edward Fox, the provost of King's

College, Cambridge, shared lodgings together as they had earlier in the year in Italy.[30] They were billeted on a certain Mr Cressey, only to discover that his sons were being tutored by a university acquaintance, the theologian, Dr Thomas Cranmer of Jesus College.[31] Cranmer had already some awareness of the king's predicament and when the subject came up over supper, he commented that canon law would get Henry nowhere; the problem was theological and theologians would give him the answer: 'whose sentence may be soon known and brought so to pass with little industry and charges . . . And then his highness in conscience quieted may determine with himself that which shall seem good before God, and let these tumultuary processes give place unto a certain truth.'[32] The suggestion had been made before, but when a couple of days later, Fox (also a theologian) reported Cranmer's opinion to the king, this time it struck an immediate chord. Was not his case precisely that canon law said one thing and divine revelation the other?[33] Let this perceptive scholar be sent for, not that the king waited until he could interview Cranmer. Within days the French ambassador was being badgered by Wolsey and Henry to find an excuse to return to France and consult the theologians there, a task he did not relish.[34]

Cranmer was eventually seen at Greenwich in October 1529.[35] His initial suggestion had now grown into a proposal that Europe's faculties of theology should be consulted, and Henry engaged him to write a thesis setting out the questions at issue. Who was backing this suggestion was made clear when Henry passed Cranmer over to Rochford to be cared for at Durham House while he got on with the writing.[36] Successfully completed, that task led to an appointment as royal agent to solicit the views of the Italian universities, and Cranmer left England in January 1530 in the entourage of (once more) Anne Boleyn's father. The earl was being sent to argue Henry's case yet again, this time to Charles V and Clement VII at Bologna.[37] A new and highly important member had been added to the Boleyn team.

Thomas Cranmer showed Henry a way to bypass the papal Curia and have doctors of the Church confirm that his private revelation was in very truth the age-old law of God. Some months earlier Anne had shown him something even more significant, a treatise which demonstrated the coherent political expression of his feelings about royal authority which Henry had been groping after. This was *The Obedience of the Christian Man and How Christian Rulers Ought to Govern*, published in October 1528 by the exiled William Tyndale, whose translation of the New Testament, with its Lutheran prologues, had been pouring illegally across the Channel since

1526. Anne acquired a copy of *The Obedience* soon after its publication and certainly before the following spring, when Wolsey instructed the dean of the Chapel Royal to undertake a purge of heretical books at court.[38] Having read it, Anne marked passages to show to Henry, but in the meantime lent the book to her gentlewoman, Anne Gainsford. However, the girl's suitor and future husband, George Zouche, 'plucked' it from her 'among other love-tricks' and, much taken with so shocking an author, refused to return the book, despite the entreaties of his beloved, fearful for both her mistress's property and the danger Tyndale presented. Predictably, the dean caught the young man reading it and the copy was passed to the cardinal. Hastily the girl owned up, giving Wolsey no time to smear her mistress (if, indeed, he planned to), and Anne Boleyn went to Henry, vowing 'it shall be the dearest book that ever dean or cardinal took away.' Henry listened, and sight of his ring caused the clerics to return the book. Anne, however, did not leave it there. She drew Henry's attention to the marked passages and suggested that he would find them well worth reading. The story certainly rings true, for Elizabethan Protestant hagiography would surely have credited Anne with promoting Tyndale's *New Testament* rather than a political text long forgotten. It is also doubly attested. John Lowthe, archdeacon of Nottingham, told it to John Foxe, and Lowthe had spent part of his earlier career in the Zouche household; George Wyatt learned of the episode directly from Anne Gainsford.[39]

The Obedience of the Christian Man set out to demonstrate 'the obedience of all degrees [in society] by God's word' and to show that 'all men without exception are under the temporal sword, whatsoever names they give themselves.'[40] The belief that the pope, the prelates and the clergy possessed separate power and authority was clean contrary to scripture. 'The king is in the person of God and his law in God's law.'[41] Hence the ruler is accountable to God alone and the obedience of the subject is an obedience required by God; indeed, when the subject obeys or disobeys the prince, he obeys or disobeys God. Papal claims are vacuous; there is no distinction in position between clergy and laity, Church affairs and temporal affairs: all is under the sole control of the monarch. For the Church to rule the princes of Europe – as it did – was not only 'a shame above all shames and a notorious thing', but an inversion of the divine order: 'One king, one law is God's ordinance in every realm.'[42] Here was a message which could not but resonate in Henry VIII's deepest inner convictions.

The arrival of *The Obedience* answers an obvious question – what did Anne and her more radical supporters have in mind when they began to move against Wolsey? Indeed, since Anne acquired her copy of the book about the time that she lost confidence in the cardinal, it could be that reading Tyndale influenced that decision. Until then, the only alternative to a papally sanctioned annulment had been the somewhat irresponsible French advice to marry at once and hope the pope would accept the *fait accompli*, a course which might have left Henry with no recognized second marriage and England open to the dreaded papal interdict.[43] Tyndale, however, now offered a realistic option: throw off Rome's judicial and administrative tyranny and restore the proper God-given status and power to the prince, who would then reform the Church and bring it back to true biblical purity. As Anne did not immediately alert Henry to the thesis, it seems probable that her initial intention had been to raise the possibility of unilateral action only if expectations from Blackfriars were disappointed. But though Henry may have received the text earlier than she had intended, he did not shy away. He declared, 'This book is for me and all kings to read.'[44] True, he did not surrender immediately. The assumptions of almost everyone around the king reinforced tradition, a divorce allowed by Rome was still preferable and Tyndale was tarred with the brush of heresy.[45] Nevertheless, Henry had been shown the radical alternative and was mightily attracted by what he saw. Indeed, he set about trying to recruit William Tyndale as a propaganda writer![46]

Anne also introduced Henry to more virulent anticlerical material. Simon Fish, a London lawyer, had fled to Tyndale after satirizing Wolsey in the Gray's Inn Christmas play of 1526 and then running contraband books.[47] From the comparative safety of the Low Countries Fish then flooded London with *The Supplication of Beggars*, a petition to Henry which made a searing attack on the blood-sucking avarice and shameless immorality of the English clergy, which was reducing the realm to penury. According to Fish's wife (who told Foxe the story), her husband sent Anne a copy of the pamphlet and she, after discussion with her brother, gave it to Henry. Once more the king found some of the ideas sympathetic. As Fish explained, clerical pretension made nonsense of the king's justice:

> So captive are your laws unto them that no man that they list to excommunicate may be admitted to sue any action in any of your courts. If any man in your sessions dare be so hardy to indict a priest of any such crime, he hath, ere the year go out, such a yoke of heresy laid in his neck, that it maketh him wish that he had not done it.[48]

The king immediately put in hand a pardon for Fish and a recall to England, and subsequently interviewed him.[49]

Anne was thus feeding the king with ideas. But though these confirmed his instincts, they stopped short of practical politics. The Boleyns, therefore, had also to move on the vital matter of implementation. The first tactic was the one they had mooted towards the end of 1528, a monster petition from the elite of England to the pope, begging for the divorce in the national interest. The draft presented at an initial meeting in June 1530, was too anti-papal to win immediate acceptance, but even when modified, the text was still full of menace. It warned Clement that, although refusing the divorce would make the condition of Henry's subjects 'more miserable…it will not be wholly desperate, since it is possible to find relief some other way'.[50] Months before, Wolsey had warned of the radical advice being poured into the royal ear; now this had helped shape a formal communication to the Holy See. The revision was carefully not put to a second full meeting, but touted round the country from individual to individual at a brisk canter. The man in charge was William Brereton, groom of the privy chamber, the first association with Anne's cause of a man who would die as her alleged 'lover' in 1536.[51] Assisting him was Thomas Wriothesley, a Gardiner man but one who may have owed his training at Cambridge to support from Thomas Boleyn.[52] All the adult peers accessible in the time available signed the petition, along with twenty-two abbots and the senior officers of the royal household, clerical and lay. Only six bishops did so – the remaining fourteen in England and three in Wales were not asked.

Few of those promoting this petition could have hoped much from any impact on Rome, but it had the great domestic advantage of whipping grumblers into line and isolating Katherine's more determined supporters. However, at the June meeting the king had also taken the opportunity to test the approach suggested by Cranmer.[53] Could he, armed with the opinion of the theologians of the Western Church, marry without obtaining papal approval? Stunned silence greeted the notion until 'one of the king's chief favourites' fell on his knees to warn Henry that this would provoke popular unrest and to beg him at least to wait until the cold and wet of winter would discourage troublemakers. Who this favourite was we do not know. Of the signatories, the one most likely to dare express such opinions was the marquis of Exeter, but irrespective of identity, that favourite had faced Henry with the unpleasant reality that radical policies might be politically impossible.

Some weeks after the June meeting, evidence of new and potentially even more radical thinking emerged from the Boleyn camp. Henry was handed a set of papers known as the *Collectanea satis copiosa*.[54] It was a product of research teams which had been working on the king's problems for many months and consisted of a data bank of scriptural, patristic and historical arguments which demonstrated – or claimed to demonstrate – that there was no warrant for the centuries-old assumption that the pope was supreme in spiritual matters. Henry would therefore be justified in taking into his own hands the solution of his matrimonial problem. The king greeted the document not so much as a drowning man greets a straw but as he might a rescue party from outer space.[55] Research was also in progress on the canon law and theology of marriage. Anne's father oversaw the publication of the opinions of the European universities in April 1531.[56] In November there followed an English translation and elaboration by Cranmer.[57] Its title, *The Determinations of the most famous and excellent Universities of Italy and France*, is somewhat misleading as the book developed the case put to the Blackfriars court and picked up a number of points from the *Collectanea*. It also achieved a new stage in menace by asserting in the vernacular that 'the duty of a loving and a devout bishop [was] to withstand the Pope openly to his face' for failing to enforce obedience to God in matrimonial cases such as Henry's.[58] Cranmer continued to enjoy Boleyn patronage and other researchers were similarly supported. One was the Hebraist Robert Wakefield who provided key advice that in the original, Leviticus 20: 21 specifically referred to sons.[59] The overall leader of research was Edward Fox, the king's future almoner. Involved from the start in the king's matrimonial affairs, in December 1529 Fox was granted a benefice in the bishopric of Durham, whose revenue was, pro tem, assigned to support the Boleyns, and he would soon begin filling the chapel of his Cambridge college with Boleyn iconography.[60]

The *Collectanea* material made possible two lines of argument on first principles. The first was that each province in the early Church had its own jurisdiction, independent of the pope. The proper body to settle Henry's divorce suit was therefore the English Church, and it alone. The second argument was even more drastic. It cut out the pope entirely, and established that in any kingdom, all authority, by divine institution, belonged to its king – exactly that God-authenticated right over Church and State alike that Henry hankered after. This, of course, was just what Tyndale and Anne Boleyn had told him, but there was a vital difference. Fox offered Henry the proof that he was already head of the Church – he had no need to vindicate his rights. The Church was the intruder, usurping authority which did not belong to it. Tyndale had called on Henry to invade previously sacrosanct territory against all accepted law and public opinion;

Fox made this superfluous. Henry was already in possession, an emperor answerable only to God for the conduct of every aspect of life in his realm, a conservative standing for traditionalist rights, innate in himself 'and all kings'. He had only to flex his muscles.

By June 1530 observers could tell that Anne Boleyn and her supporters felt themselves on the brink of a major advance, and when the *Collectanea* reached the king, the impact on the tone and content of royal pronouncements both in Rome and in England was immediate.[61] Henry went further in October, as a new parliamentary session approached, and proposed to a gathering of clerics and lawyers that the archbishop of Canterbury should be empowered by statute to decide the divorce suit, notwithstanding papal prohibition. When told that parliament could not act in this way, he reacted angrily, postponing the session until the new year and belabouring the papal nuncio with both *Collectanea* arguments, asserting that except over doctrine, the pope's power was 'usurpation and tyranny'.[62] Anne Boleyn and her father kept up the momentum with anti-papal tirades so violent as to shock the unshockable Chapuys and drive him from court, uttering dire warnings that together they would alienate England from the Holy See.[63] Wiltshire pressed the same line in council, as Henry informed the ambassador, and the king himself was similarly violent, especially on one occasion when Chapuys noticed Anne Boleyn listening at a nearby open window.[64] When Charles V's man seized the chance to respond with some home truths of his own, Henry quickly took the conversation out of earshot and the danger of an outburst from Anne. In London, royal printers were busy with propaganda. As well as the items derived in part from the trawl of European universities, 1531 saw *The Glass of Truth* (to which Henry made some contribution), the Latin text of *A Disputation between a cleric and a knight* (with an English version following in 1533) and Christopher German's *New Additions*.[65] Nor was diplomatic activity ignored. Anne in particular went out of her way to entertain the French envoys over Christmas, while Henry gave the senior of them rooms in Bridewell Palace itself.[66]

The climax came when parliament, and the Church's equivalent, the convocation of the province of Canterbury, assembled in the second and third weeks of January 1531.[67] Since the summer the king had been planning to extort a substantial sum from the English clergy and had begun a number of exemplary prosecutions of likely opponents for their involvement in Wolsey's offences. Convocation took the hint and quickly offered £100,000, in return for a pardon for any such complicity. The Boleyn faction had not, however, relaxed. Chapuys reported Anne on

New Year's Day as being full of confidence and brave as a lion, declaring 'that she wished all Spaniards were at the bottom of the sea...that she cared not for the queen or any of her family, and that she would rather see her hanged than have to confess that she was her queen and mistress.'[68] Katherine and a number of the courtiers were sure that Henry was going to act unilaterally, while even Norfolk, who privately found the implications of the *Collectanea* too extreme for his taste, was found expounding the new orthodoxy to a bemused Eustace Chapuys.[69]

As a consequence, royal policy became ever more radical by the day. Initially the pardon to be sold to convocation was for complicity in Wolsey's specific offences. The king's council then changed ground and offered a pardon for the Church's general exercise of illegal spiritual jurisdiction. When convocation jibbed, the king became more specific and demanded on 7 February that it immediately recognize him as 'sole protector and supreme head of the English church and clergy'.[70] Boleyn influence was at work and Anne's reaction was to make 'such demonstrations of joy as if she had actually gained Paradise'.[71] The king at last was moving in the direction she wanted.

Some days of haggling followed, and any doubt about who was advising the king is dispelled by the prominent part played in this by Anne's brother, George. Henry himself wanted his title recognized without any qualification, and sent Rochford with a number of tracts to persuade convocation of the scriptural case for the supremacy. The clergy were well aware of the influence the Boleyns were having and attempted (unsuccessfully) to substitute direct communication to Henry. Eventually a suggestion was made, possibly by Thomas Cromwell, to qualify the headship with the words 'so far as the law of Christ allows', and Henry realized, or had it explained to him, that he would lose nothing by accepting. The Church might tell itself that the phrase neutralized the new title – indeed, protests at home and to Rome would make clear that the clergy did think that. But because Henry knew absolutely that the law of Christ did give him headship of the Church, the qualification strengthened his title by rebutting the criticism that he was trenching on the mystical headship of Christ over the Church militant and triumphant.[72] He was perfectly well aware that the clergy understood differently, but exploiting ambiguity was characteristic of Henrician sharp practice.[73] In a similarly dishonest way, Henry would insist to the papal nuncio that he had not usurped Rome's authority, even though Chapuys could see that Henry understood the supposed 'limitation' as nothing of the kind and that '*ceste nouvelle papalité*' almost made the king 'pope in England'. He noted too how Anne and her father had been the chief promoters of the measure, and Wiltshire told Katherine's champion, Bishop Fisher, to his face 'that when God departed from this world he left behind him no successor or vicar on earth'.[74]

The 'Pardon of the Clergy' in the opening months of 1531 was the second triumph for Anne Boleyn and her supporters – first Wolsey, now the pope. It was not, however, a conclusive victory. There was no divorce, and eighteen months would elapse before Henry would marry her. Instead of applying the logic of the new title, time and effort were devoted to blocking any hearing of the divorce suit at Rome and to securing papal approval for a trial elsewhere – policies which should never have bothered a king fully determined to trust in his God-given *imperium*. Such a king would have pushed on with a hearing before the authorities of the Church of which he was now head – but not Henry in 1531.

A number of reasons help to explain this strange backtracking in the story of Henry VIII and Anne Boleyn. One undoubted factor was Europe. Francis I was anxious, in the face of the all-conquering Charles V, to retain the friendship of the pope as well as of Henry, and in 1531 he began a series of diplomatic moves to bring England and Rome together, raising the possibility that Henry might, after all, secure the generally recognized papal divorce he had so long struggled for.[75] More important, perhaps, was the firm resistance the Church had offered to the headship and, in particular, the blunt refusal of Archbishop Warham to defy long-established papal authority. Early in the 1531 convocation he had been subjected to a private interview with Henry, and had not budged.[76] The Church might have accepted, more or less, Henry's own definition of his position, but the king had as yet no way to compel it to do what he wanted. And beyond the hierarchy there was, as Chapuys liked to point out, the menace of a conservative-minded political elite and the nation at large.[77]

This in particular gave Henry great and increasing pause. The faction which came to power in 1529 had united only on a negative, 'Wolsey must go'; Anne Boleyn and her pretensions, for many, had been no more than a convenient tool. The realization that she was the true inheritor of that ultimate royal favour which had been Wolsey's strength came, therefore, as an unpleasant surprise. Even worse was the radicalism being advanced by the Boleyn faction and the imminent possibility that Anne would become queen. To those Wolsey opponents who had always been loyal to Katherine and to tradition – men like More or the earl of Shrewsbury – this merely confirmed the rightness of their position and the size of the stakes being played for. The marquis of Exeter even found himself in trouble because his servants, prompted or not, were recruiting retainers, on the ground that 'if the king's grace marry my lady Anne, there will be need of such good fellows.'[78] As for nobles and courtiers who had kept their heads down so far, they increasingly felt that it might be wise to take sides, so that through 1530 and 1531 there was a steady growth of opinion at court and in the council which was hostile to the marriage. One of the earliest of Anne's presumed allies to declare in favour of Katherine, albeit privately, was the king's favourite of the tiltyard, Nicholas Carewe. Although a cousin of Anne, strongly Francophile and as late as June 1531 one of the few who accompanied Henry on his more intimate courting expeditions, in 1529, while ambassador at the imperial court, he had made it clear whose side he was really on, and on his return he immediately opened up communication with Katherine and with Chapuys.[79]

Another defector was Suffolk. Uncomfortably aware that the coup against Wolsey had left him in the cold, and with a wife who had seen her precedence as the king's sister and dowager queen of France rudely set aside in favour of Anne Boleyn, the duke made no secret of his hostility.[80] Indeed, as we have seen, a story reached Chapuys in May 1530 that the duke had been banned from court after raking up what appears to have been a story about Thomas Wyatt in order to convince Henry that Anne was a woman with a past – evidently in the hope of driving a wedge between them.[81] Chapuys admitted that this was only a rumour and gave no other details, but Suffolk certainly nurtured an 'immortal hate' against Sir Thomas, and would be responsible for his arrest along with Anne in 1536.[82]

The rustication of Suffolk (if it was that and not just the duke making himself scarce) did not teach him wisdom. In August or September, when the French, with the support of Wiltshire and Norfolk, pressed the council to go ahead with the marriage and trust the pope to regularize it *post facto*, it was Suffolk who led the remaining councillors to reject the scheme emphatically.[83] In the spring of 1531 he openly espoused a pro-imperial policy in the council, while in the summer he told Henry that the king was the third person Katherine would obey; when Henry asked who the first two were, expecting the reply, 'the pope' and 'the emperor', the duke answered that God was the first and her conscience the second. Some days after this well-placed barb, Suffolk allegedly discussed the divorce with Fitzwilliam, treasurer of the household, and agreed that the time had come to co-operate together 'to unseat the king from his folly'. An appropriate signal would be the papal decision in Katherine's favour – and the sooner the better.[84] It is small wonder that Anne exploited Suffolk's colourful private life to hit back with the allegation that he had an incestuous relationship with his son's fiancée, and the accusation was the sweeter since the girl was the daughter of one of Katherine of Aragon's Spanish attendants.[85]

Another surprising defector from the ranks of Anne's supporters was her aunt, the duchess of Norfolk – surprising, until the background and circumstances of Elizabeth Howard are recalled. A daughter of the attainted duke of Buckingham and with many years of service as a lady-in-waiting at court, the duchess had had no cause to love Wolsey but plenty to revere Katherine. She also had a most powerful motive for returning to this earlier allegiance – a desire to strike at her husband who for three or four years had been quite blatantly keeping a mistress, Elizabeth Holland.[86] Dislike of Anne also played a part, and not only because Bessie Holland was one of Anne's ladies.[87] The duchess was hypersensitive about her status and had earlier clashed with Queen Katherine by claiming that she took precedence over the duke's step-mother, the dowager duchess. Now her niece Anne went ahead of both of them![88] She also resented Boleyn interference in the marriages of her children, especially Anne's insistence that her daughter should marry the duke of Richmond. Sharp words between them on this subject were soon followed by Elizabeth Howard sending Katherine a secret message hidden in an orange, and thereafter a series of reports about *la partie adverse* (some highly informative).[89] By Christmas 1530 the duchess's Stafford blood could not resist some acid comments on the upstart Boleyns – not for the first time, either – and her strident support for Katherine led to her being banned from court in the following spring.[90]

Chapuys is, of course, the only source for all this, and one must continue to test the characterization of Anne that he offers, but it is hard to imagine her assertive personality not becoming waspish under the strain of the situation.[91] As Christmas 1530 approached, she proclaimed her defiance by having the livery coats of her servants embroidered with a version of the arrogant motto she had learned from Margaret of Austria: *Ainsi sera, groigne qui groigne* – 'Let them grumble, that is how it is going to be!'[92] Anne seems even to have inspired a carol by her gesture – equally defiant, though more subtle:

> Grudge on who list, this is my lot:
> Nothing to want if it were not.
>
> My years be young, even as ye see;
> All things thereto doth well agree;

In faith, in face, in each degree,
Nothing doth want, as seemeth me,
   If it were not.

Some men doth say that friends be scarce,
But I have found, as in this case,
A friend which giveth to no man place
But makes me happiest that ever was,
   If it were not.

A heart I have, besides all this,
That hath my heart, and I have his.
If he doth will, it is my bliss,
And when we meet no lack there is,
   If it were not.

If he can find that can me please,
A-thinks he does his own heart's ease,
And likewise I could well appease
The chiefest cause of his mis-ease,
   If it were not.

A master eke God hath me sent
To whom my will is wholly lent
To serve and love for that intent
That both we might be well content,
   If it were not.

And here an end: it doth suffice
To speak few words among the wise;
Yet take this note before your eyes:
My mirth should double once or twice,
   If it were not.[93]

The piece is anonymous, but even if not by Anne or for Anne, it is certainly expressive of her position. Indeed, a bold hypothesis would seize on the personal allusions and suggest Anne as the performer of the song. 'If it were not' – the marriage of Katherine was now a publicly derided obstacle to Anne's happiness, and Henry's.

The device lasted only a few weeks. Chapuys' snide explanation was that Anne had discovered the original imperialist version, *Groigne qui groigne et vive Bourgoigne*, but he had forgotten – and perhaps did not know of – her time in Mechelen and Brussels years before.[94] The likely reason is that a blatant perversion of an imperialist motto was hardly the way to encourage English men and women to accept Anne in place of a highly respected Habsburg queen they had known for twenty years. Anne's attitude could certainly be counterproductive – witness the shock when she publicly declared that she wished all Spaniards at the bottom of the sea, clearly including Katherine in her ill wishes.[95] She was overfond of threatening to have members of the royal household dismissed, and several went the way of the duchess of Norfolk.[96] One unfortunate in the privy chamber caught the full force of her wrath when she discovered him one day taking fabric to Katherine to make into shirts for Henry, and this despite his excuse (which the king confirmed) that he was doing so on instructions.[97] One may sympathize with Anne, but it was no fault of the hapless courtier that Henry saw no implication in a wife he was claiming to have rejected being expected to continue caring for his linen![98]

On occasion, even Anne's father got the rough edge of her tongue for his timidity – the new earl, after all, now had much more to lose – while the duke of Norfolk found his position increasingly unenviable.[99] More and more he was called upon to present a radical Boleyn line he disliked, and (as his wife gleefully told Katherine) he had been heard to mutter that Anne would be the ruin of the Howards.[100] Stephen Gardiner, on the other hand, was careful to give her no opening to test her growing suspicion of him, and she met her match in Henry Guildford, controller of the household.[101] Although he signed the petition to the pope in June 1530, he had spoken out in council in favour of Katherine and, after accompanying an abortive delegation in May 1531 to persuade the queen to 'be sensible', had been heard to wish that all the lawyers and theologians arguing for the king could be put in a cart and shipped to Rome, there to be exposed for the charlatans they were. Anne was furious and warned Guildford that as soon as she was queen she would have him out. In that case, Sir Henry retorted, he would save her the trouble, and marched off to the king to resign then and there. Henry tried to smooth his old friend down with excuses about 'woman's talk', and Guildford did eventually take back the white stave of office, but he registered his displeasure by retiring to his home in Kent.

The opposition also began to argue back. Bishop Fisher and others had already written effective pieces in defence of Katherine, and in the spring of 1531 court preachers began to speak openly against Henry's claims.[102] At the same time, the handlers of the Canterbury mystic, Elizabeth Barton, 'the Nun of Kent', were busy broadcasting her anti-Boleyn 'prophecies'.[103] Reginald Pole, the king's cousin and a man with a fair prospect of ending up as cardinal-archbishop of Canterbury, abandoned his lukewarm assistance to the divorce suit and wrote a critique of the king's position so effective as to make Cranmer afraid that it would get into general circulation.[104] Particularly powerful were the pragmatic dangers Pole adduced: a disputed succession reviving the disasters of Lancaster and York, and economic damage should Charles V decide to block the two vital trade routes to Flanders and Spain. The points were shrewdly made and struck home.[105] Increasingly it began to look as though Henry might face a choice between a new wife and losing, or at least risking, his very crown.

At this time Anne must often have felt that her only firm allies were her brother, Thomas Cranmer and Edward Fox, none of whom had political weight or belonged to the council. She had influence, as in ambassadorial appointments or the readiness of Anthony Browne of the privy chamber to surrender to the Boleyns his Crown office in Rayleigh, Essex.[106] Nevertheless, no leading politician was ready to commit himself to exploiting the radical victory over the Church. Anne had helped Henry conceptualize his instinctive feelings about kingship; the researchers she patronized had shown him that he had rights over the Church, and she had stood behind the king as he had made his claim. Yet what good was this without, if not the support, at least the acquiescence of the people who mattered? Or were Katherine's supporters right: unilateral action was impossible? Francis Bryan no longer wrote hopefully to Anne or indeed mentioned her in the despatches he sent to Henry from the French court.[107] She was even deprived of Fox, whom Chapuys called 'a sophisticated negotiator and a fire-brand on the divorce issue'. He was abroad from May 1531 until the end of the year, when he and Bryan came back together.[108]

One success alone gave Anne hope as midsummer came and went. Henry split with Katherine. The curious *ménage à trois* inaugurated at the end of 1528 had become more and more a matter of comment, and most European observers drew the obvious conclusion that Anne was the king's mistress. If, as seems certain, this was not the case, it was not because they maintained a decorous separation: quite the contrary. Anne's mother might usually be somewhere about, but the couple were always together and Henry's privy purse expenses show how intertwined their lives were.[109] Anne would lay out money if Henry had no ready cash; far more often it was Henry who paid. When spring approached in 1530 he had set her up for travelling with him, with three saddles and a large quantity of tack, splendidly decorated in black and gold, and a set of harnesses for the mules which carried her litter.[110] It was perhaps in celebration of this present that Henry made an exhibition of himself on a journey from Windsor, by taking Anne up on his horse to ride pillion – and two observers who were ill-advised enough to comment found themselves in trouble.[111] Anne was also active in field sports, Henry's great passion. The same month in which she received the harness for her mules, she was supplied with a full set of archery equipment – bows, broad-head arrows, bracer, shooting glove – with a further four bows to follow.[112] On one autumn hunt, one of her greyhounds got out of control and with another, belonging to Urian Brereton of the privy chamber (William's brother), savaged a wretched cow.[113]

This is not to say – and here is the key to the relationship between Henry and Anne – that all was pastoral bliss, nymphs and shepherds, hearts and flowers. Anne was where she was because of her own character and merits, a self-made woman who saw no percentage in bloodless simpering. Submissiveness had not won the king; Anne's attraction was challenge. When a poison-pen drawing came into her hands, showing a male figure labelled 'H', and two female figures 'K' and 'A', and with 'A' having no head, she called to Anne Gainsford: 'Come hither Nan, see here a book of prophecy; this he saith is the king, this the queen, and this is myself with my head off.' The girl said sensibly, 'If I thought it true, though he were an emperor, I would not myself marry him with that condition.' Anne responded: 'Yes, Nan, I think the book a bauble, yet for the hope I have that the realm may be happy by my issue, I am resolved to have him whatsoever might become of me.' The patriotic desire for pregnancy has the ring of an Elizabethan accretion, but not the resolution.[114] Henry found himself facing a person prepared to stand up to him. When, in the summer of 1530, he dared to remind Anne how much she owed him and how many enemies she had made him, her reply was reported as: 'That matters not, for it is foretold in ancient prophecies that at this time a queen shall be burnt. [Were they, by chance, discussing the poison-pen drawing?] But even if I were to suffer a thousand deaths, my love for you will not abate one jot.'[115]

Henry, we must suppose, generally found this exciting – he certainly became more and more committed. But he could grizzle and he could grumble. At the start of 1531 Paris and Rome were laughing at the story that, having quarrelled with Anne, Henry had been reduced to begging her relations 'with tears in his eyes' to mediate between them.[116] In April, when the two fell out over Princess Mary, Henry complained to Norfolk about her arrogance and her domineering attitude, saying plaintively that she was not like Katherine, who had never in her life spoken harshly to him.[117] From Katherine's point of view it might have been better if she had. Observers noted, however, that once Henry had made it up with Anne, as 'happens generally in such cases, their love will be greater than before'.[118]

Through all this, Katherine had kept her hollow status, presided at court and, remarkably, continued the custom she and Henry had followed all their married life of communicating, if not in person at least by messages, every three days. Henry sometimes made half-hearted gestures towards a greater separation. After a formal state dinner on 3 May, Holy Rood Day, had turned out very well, Katherine ventured the next morning to suggest that Mary should pay them both a visit.[119] Henry, however, once more mindful of Anne, replied brutally that Katherine could go and visit her if she wanted to, and stay there too, whereupon the queen replied that neither for her daughter nor anyone in the world would she dream of leaving him; her proper place was at his side.[120] Anne Boleyn's one refuge was Wolsey's former palace of York Place, soon to be known as Whitehall. It had no separate 'queen's side' for Katherine and her suite to occupy, but Anne and her mother could lodge in the chamber under the cardinal's library, and her father and brother also had their own rooms elsewhere.[121] It was, thus, very much to her taste when Henry began the extensions at York Place in the spring of 1531, necessitating frequent visits to supervise the building which went on round the clock.[122]

The one disappointment was that there were none of Anne's leopard badges in the window-glass and on the striking new gate (later misnamed 'the Holbein Gate'), nor 'HA' monograms. But there were no Aragonese pomegranates either, and with Anne and Henry having a common project and a shared refuge in York Place, the queen's situation deteriorated. At the end of May the king was threatened with the supreme insult of having to appear before the pope at Rome; there could, Clement informed him, be no more delay. After intense discussion it was decided to make one last appeal to Katherine, and she was visited at Greenwich on the evening of the 31st by the most powerful delegation possible – some thirty nobles, courtiers and clerics.[123] For the sake of the country, they told her, she must save Henry from this indignity and consent to having the case settled in England. Katherine was impervious and they went away empty-handed. A few days later Henry began an almost continuous series of hunting trips, circulating restlessly between Hampton Court and Windsor and local hunting boxes, where he and Anne were accompanied only by Nicholas Carewe and two other attendants.[124] Early in July, the court and both the

women in the king's life moved to Windsor for the start of the summer
progress, but Henry's irresolution continued. Then on Friday, 14 July,
after he had dealt with an important despatch to Bryan and Fox, he left
with Anne for Chertsey Abbey and further hunting, saying no goodbye to
Katherine but sending her a message to stay where she was.[125] It was only
a few weeks past their twenty-second wedding anniversary, and this treatment hurt the queen as nothing before.[126] Her next regular message to
Henry, authenticated by the countersign they had used for so long, made
this hurt obvious, and the king exploded in anger. Katherine, he returned,
had brought the indignity of a personal citation to Rome on him, the
king of England; she had ignored the pleas of the wisest and most noble
of his counsellors; he wanted no more messages. Katherine answered
nevertheless, but her self-righteous tone, however justified, might have
been calculated to make matters worse. Henry sulked for four days and
then sent a bitter and formal reply, advising her to attend to her own
business.[127]

Predictably, Eustace Chapuys attributed even this to the malevolence of
Anne Boleyn, and we may imagine that Anne had time and again urged
Henry to pluck up his courage, leave Katherine and join her. Yet this
was not what he had done; egotistically he had chosen to suit himself.
Katherine's exclusion certainly left Anne supreme at court and so with an
enormous advantage in the battle to control the king's mind. But it did
not mean that Henry had taken a final decision. He had whipped himself
into a sense of grievance against a woman who had rubbed raw his kingly
pride, and what he had done in irritation he could undo as easily; as late as
November 1531, Henry and Katherine were attending state occasions
together, though apparently they did not meet.[128] Anne's own marriage
was no nearer – indeed, as the months went by the obstacles must have
seemed ever more formidable. The Venetian, Mario Savorgnano, visiting
England soon after the separation, had no doubt about the odds:

> There is now living with him a young woman of noble birth, though many
> say of bad character, whose will is law to him, and he is expected to marry
> her, should the divorce take place, which it is supposed will not be effected,
> as the peers of the realm, both spiritual and temporal, and the people are
> opposed to it.[129]

He noted too, that though the king's pressure had somewhat reduced
visitors to her court, Katherine still had thirty maids of honour and a
household of 200.

THE TURNING-POINT, 1532—1533

C HRISTMAS 1531 was the most miserable anyone at court could remember. Henry VIII made a great show, but 'there was no mirth because the queen and the ladies were absent.'[1] Anne Boleyn herself was in no position to replace Katherine. She might occupy the consort's lodgings at Greenwich and have a flock of attendants, but the increasing polarization of opinion made her more and more isolated.[2] She continued to extend her influence and her word began to command attention as far away as Calais.[3] Yet the continuation of that influence was wholly precarious; this, indeed, may explain her reported anxiety to see Princess Mary lodged as many miles away as possible.[4] At Rome the divorce suit was going from bad to worse; in December Henry had been reduced to bribing cardinals to achieve a six-month hold-up.[5] That in turn reflected the situation in the king's council, where the majority continued to resist the radical alternative, but could only suggest further appeals to Katherine's good nature.[6]

The events of New Year's Day 1532 certainly made clear who held the moral initiative.[7] Tradition dictated that on that day the members of the royal family and the court exchanged gifts. Anne duly gave Henry an exotic set of richly decorated Pyrenean boar spears and, in contrast to New Year 1531, he seems not to have had to pay for his present in advance. His gift to her was a matching set of hangings for her room and bed, in cloth of gold, cloth of silver and richly embroidered crimson satin.[8] As for Katherine, the king had decided for the first time not to give presents to her or to her ladies and, rather meanly, had ordered the courtiers to follow suit.[9] He had not, however, forbidden Katherine, who recognized a splendid opportunity to circumvent the prohibition on sending messages to Henry. Nothing had been said about gifts. Carefully choosing a gold cup of a highly distinctive design and of obvious expense, the queen sent it to be presented to her husband. The unfortunate gentleman of the privy chamber on duty could not refuse it, but when he came to present the cup to Henry, he found himself the target of predictable fury. Two hours or so later the king realized his error and sent to get the cup back, frantic that it might already have been returned to Katherine. If so, it could have been re-presented during a court function when Henry would have found it impossible not to accept and thereby recognize publicly his relationship with Katherine. Fortunately the privy chamber still had the cup, and orders were given not to return it until the evening, when it would be too late for Katherine to try that ploy. Christmas was not happy for either Henry or Anne.

Behind the scenes, however, movements were already in train which would break the political impasse and transform stalemate into victory. The first sign was a breakthrough on the vital question, 'By what mechanism could a lay monarch assert his God-given authority over the Church if the clergy refused to obey?' This was triumphantly answered in 1531, in the 'new additions' which a septuagenarian lawyer, Christopher St German, made to a work already in print, known to later generations as *Doctor and Student*.[10] In the main text St German had argued that only the sacramental functions of the Church were outside the concern of human, that is secular, law. In practice, however, ancient prescription allowed the Church a great deal more, and in the 'new additions' St German faced head-on the question: what was 'the power of the parliament concerning the spiritualty and the spiritual jurisdiction'?[11] Traditionalists such as Thomas More believed that no local legislature could prevail against the universally recognized liberties of the Church. St German showed otherwise. A statute binds all men because all have assented to it, the Lords directly and the Commons through their representatives. It can, therefore, properly regulate all the actions of the Church which belong to the temporal sphere, prescription or no. In effect, whenever the Church wanted to do more than exhort, it needed statutory authority. 'The king in parliament' is 'the high sovereign over the people which hath not only charge on the bodies but also on the souls of his subjects'.[12]

Felicitous plotting would bring Christopher St German on the scene as a protégé of Anne Boleyn. Alas, history is not so neat. He was, however, directly in touch with Henry VIII and working as a parliamentary draftsman.[13] In other words, however he had come to royal attention, St German was not just another theorist. He was actively drafting legislation to give statutory effect to the supreme headship with, as the ultimate prize, the achieving of the king's divorce by parliamentary authority.

The second development that promised hope to Anne Boleyn in 1531 was the arrival not of a book, but of a man: Thomas Cromwell. Since Cromwell would bring Anne to the throne at last – and himself, in the process, to high favour with the king – and since he would, within three years of that, destroy her as he manoeuvred to become supreme in government, a good dramatist would have scripted a memorable first encounter. Yet this too would be false, and not merely because life is not art or, more prosaically, because our first evidence is of Anne sending him a verbal message in March 1529. Cromwell at first meeting would have seemed nothing remarkable.[14] About 45, fourteen years a business agent and solicitor for Thomas Wolsey, he had saved himself from the wreck of the cardinal's enterprises by neat footwork, which had left him in charge of salvage operations on behalf of the king. Cromwell had also worked for the duke of Norfolk, particularly on parliamentary matters, but by the opening of 1531 he had risen to be a sworn royal counsellor. Opinions about him were fiercely discrepant while he was alive, and historians today are no more in agreement. For some he was a fixer, a hit-man firing bullets others made to bring down men better than himself. Alternatively he was the bureaucrat, the agent, the archetypal staff officer. Or, yet again, he was a perceptive statesman, the original mind which reallocated the atomic weights in the periodic table of English politics.

What, then, did the arrival of Thomas Cromwell in 1530–1 mean for Anne Boleyn? The difficulty with this question is separating the man then from the man we know later. It is all too easy to see the ferment in royal ideas and policies in 1532 and afterwards, and to argue that he was the new yeast. What we need to ask is what our assessment would be if Cromwell had died in 1532. The working papers he left show him already active in a myriad matters, but there is no reason to believe that if the papers processed by other busy counsellors had survived, we would not have material of much the same character. Certainly, by Wolsey's standards, his archive suggests an executive and not yet a policy-maker. And we have no need of a policy-maker. Tyndale's unitary sovereign state, Fox's supreme headship, St German's king in parliament – here already is the philosophy, the proclamation and the mechanism of the Henrician Reformation. Not that Cromwell had nothing to contribute. He was quickly associated with the new thinking, the offer to convocation in February 1531 of the Trojan Horse formula 'as far as the law of Christ allows', and he was perhaps already toying with the implications of 'empire'.[15] Yet in ideas Cromwell was a latecomer, and to load him with responsibility for the innovative thinking behind the Reformation is to distract from his real originality in the Boleyn camp. At last Anne was backed by a first-rate politician.

Henry VIII had initially planned to recall parliament for October 1531, but the lack of clear policies among the counsellors put back the meeting twice, eventually until 15 January 1532.[16] Hard though it is to follow the arguments of these preliminary weeks, it is clear that several options were being canvassed. Anne spoke defiantly of achieving the divorce irrespective of Charles V, and her alliance with the French (who themselves exuded confidence in a rapid divorce) was demonstrated to all at a banquet in late October, when she sat at the head of the table between Henry and the senior French envoy, Jean du Bellay, while his colleague sat with Norfolk and her parents and, less comfortably, Gardiner and Fitzwilliam.[17] Cranmer's *Determinations* appeared in November, and Cromwell and his ally, Thomas Audley, Speaker of the Commons and from November a king's serjeant-at-law (a senior legal adviser to the Crown), produced drafts for legislation to enable the divorce to be granted by the English Church and papal countermeasures to be ignored.[18]

On the other hand, Cromwell and Audley were also busy drafting bills for a quite different scenario – the continuation of the struggle for a divorce at Rome. Very probably this was on instructions from Henry or Norfolk or both. One draft made it treason to bring into England any sentence by Clement against Henry; another attempted to curb the activities of English clerics abroad, possibly to bind Reginald Pole before his departure to Avignon and Padua was permitted in January 1532. A related scheme was an attempt to hit the pope financially by cutting off annates from England (payments made by new appointees to major benefices). This may have begun as a radical plan based on the *Collectanea*, and it did include clauses to ensure that the English Church would function irrespective of any papal censures, but it was drafted using language about the pope which it is mild to describe as sycophantic.[19] Norfolk certainly presented the annates bill to the Lords only as a device to put more pressure on Clement VII, and never seriously believed that it threatened the link with Rome.[20] Even so, it ran into vigorous opposition in both houses, which was quelled only by Henry's personal intervention and that more than once, and even then only after significant concessions.

The reception which the annates bill received did not augur well for parliament's willingness to adopt the full gospel of St German. In any case, opposition at court and in the council could no longer be ignored.[21] Early in the new year, Anne's uncle – desperate to find the least traumatic way to make progress – tried, with the assistance of her father, to persuade Archbishop Warham to defy the pope. Having failed at that, Norfolk called his supporters together, and putting as strongly as he could the lesser *Collectanea* argument about English privilege (topped off with the St German-like argument that matrimonial causes belonged to the temporal sphere and so to the Crown), he asked for their commitment to defend these royal rights. The faction broke, then and there. Thomas, Lord Darcy, who had been with Norfolk all the way since the attack on Wolsey, spoke bluntly and for the majority. His life and his property were at the king's disposal, but matrimonial cases belonged without question to the Church courts. And, he added ominously, king and council knew perfectly well what to do 'without wishing to put a cat betwixt other people's legs' or dragging in outsiders.[22] If the king heeded the advice and the implied warning, there was no future for Anne.

After this episode, Cromwell could have had little hope that legislation to secure Henry's divorce was politically possible. However, the odds are that he had merely gone along with Henry and Norfolk to allow their exertions on the annates bill to prove they were up against an impenetrable wall of opposition. The Boleyn option was the only way forward. Cromwell also realized what was needed to achieve this. That was to bounce the king into a whole-hearted acceptance of the radical gospel – all doubts, all caution, all the warning voices swept aside by the rush of events and the force of the king's emotion. He could also see an opportunity in an issue which had been rumbling round the Commons since 1529, 'the crueltie of the ordinaries [church judges]' towards people accused of heresy. It is a fashion of some historians to discount this because the pre-Reformation English Church was clearly popular and played a valued part in the life of individuals and parishes. Yet this is to misunderstand anticlericalism. Orthodox belief and support for the existing Church did not rule out criticism of the way the clergy abused its privileged position; take, for example, the 'catch 22' rule by which innocent people were burned for refusing to abjure heresies which they did not hold. In the first session of parliament, a sizeable number of voices had been able to carry some reforms, particularly of abuses in Church courts. Since then, however, and largely by More's enthusiastic use of the chancellor's office to encourage persecution, heresy had become the issue – with the first burnings for more than fifteen years. In the notorious case of Thomas Bilney, there was real doubt whether he was in any way a heretic, and although More had not been directly involved, immediately he had realized that the Bilney case would be aired in parliament he set to work on a massive cover-up.[23]

All this Cromwell could see. He had memories of the 1529 agitation, probably some of the anticlerical material prepared at that time, and he may even have noted that Bilney (and other alleged heretics) had attempted to appeal from the Church courts to Henry himself as 'supreme head', and had been ignored. Here was the point where the Church was vulnerable.

Complaints in the Commons about the prosecution of heresy became louder – fuelled, no doubt, by signs in convocation that the Church was determined to increase the pressure against unorthodox opinions but, no doubt, also discreetly encouraged by Cromwell himself. Then at an opportune moment we find the House debating a petition against the Church courts drafted by Cromwell and his assistants, the so-called 'Supplication against the Ordinaries', and this was submitted to the king on 18 March. Henry seems not to have recognized any special significance in this, and neither did convocation when it was asked to comment on 12 April, but the Supplication was a brilliantly conceived booby trap. It invited the king as 'the only sovereign lord, protector and defender' of both clergy and laity to legislate in parliament to 'establish not only those things which to your jurisdiction and prerogative royal justly appertaineth, but also reconcile and bring into perpetual unity your said subjects, spiritual and temporal.'[24] The overtones clearly echo St German and the *Collectanea*, and when the Church was called on to reply it was at once on the spot. It had either to abandon its traditional independence or tell Henry to his face what had been said so far only privately or unofficially – that the title 'supreme head' meant nothing.

Here chance took a hand. Convocation gave to Stephen Gardiner the job of preparing an immediate response to the first and most dangerous clause of the Supplication, which queried the independent jurisdiction of the Church. An obvious choice – brilliant, the king's secretary, the odds-on favourite to succeed Warham at Canterbury – Gardiner had two fatal disabilities. First, he was an uncompromising advocate of the clerical privilege that had raised the son of a Suffolk cloth-maker to the richest bishopric in England, and to be, in Henry's own words, the king's 'right hand'. In the second place, Gardiner had been abroad for ten weeks and had returned only in time to see the difficulty the Crown had had in securing the annates measure, in a modified form.[25] The conservatives had fought. Warham had had a violent altercation with Henry across the House of Lords and now faced a *praemunire* charge; More had organized an almost subversive opposition in the council and in the Commons; on Easter Sunday, William Peto, head of the Observants, the court's favourite order of friars, had preached a sermon telling Henry to his face that he would end up like the Old Testament tyrant Ahab (though he left unspoken the implication that Anne Boleyn was Jezebel). When, the following Sunday, a royal chaplain was put up to reply, he was barracked by another of the friars and, for good measure, hauled before convocation for breaching ecclesiastical discipline – a convocation which already had its claws into Hugh Latimer, one of Henry's favourite clerics.[26] And when parliament reassembled after Easter and Henry asked the Commons to vote him money, members sympathetic to Katherine told him that the best way to guarantee national security was to take her back. Anti-Boleyn opinion, clerical as well as lay, was everywhere standing up to be counted, and it would have required a man much less self-assured than the bishop of Winchester not to feel that now he had returned, a counter-attack must be successful. His earlier support of Anne Boleyn was dead; the independence of the Church was too great a price to pay for the king's happiness.

Gardiner's reply to the Supplication was, therefore, an unequivocal assertion of the ancient privilege of the Church: 'We your most humble subjects may not submit the execution of our charges and duty, certainly prescribed by God, to your highness's assent.'[27] Henry reacted as Cromwell knew he would. If churchmen believed this, the title 'supreme head' was empty of meaning and their concession in 1531 had been a dishonest attempt to deceive. Gardiner's reply reached the king about 27 April, and Henry reacted with stunning force to this impugning of his God-given position. He unmanned Gardiner by his fury, and called up Thomas Audley to invite the Commons to renew agitation against the Church; then on 10 May he sent Edward Fox to convocation to demand unequivocal surrender. When the clergy showed signs of fight, Henry stepped up pressure in parliament and Cromwell produced a bill to strip the Church of its powers. Thomas More, realizing that the crisis had come, threw his weight openly against the king, most probably by mobilizing again the conservative lobby in the Lords which had emasculated the annates bill, and he too received the full blast of Henry's wrath.

With Gardiner and More both in disgrace the Church offered a compromise, but the king promptly prorogued parliament, so blocking the ability of the bishops, abbots and lay peers of a conservative turn of mind to support from the Lords the sort of rearguard action that had won the day in 1531. Instead, convocation itself was ordered on 15 May to adjourn that same day – having first, of course, given the king what he wanted – and to make the point clear, a party of leading courtiers and counsellors made a quite unprecedented descent on the upper house (the bishops and abbots). Significantly, this was made up of Norfolk, Anne's uncle, Wiltshire and Rochford, her father and brother, Oxford, father-in-law to Norfolk's son and on close terms with Cromwell, Sandes, the lord chamberlain and an archetypal sycophant, and Katherine's ally, the marquis of Exeter, in yet another exhibition (or test) of his loyalty to Henry rather than to principle.[28] Their ultimatum given, they took the Church's answer back to the king, only to return later in the day with Henry's final terms. Warham knew he was beaten. Resistance would invite a series of disastrous *praemunire* prosecutions, and anticlerical statutes in the next session of parliament. It would also infuriate the king. Better to save what could be saved. Sending home the hot-headed lower house of convocation, he gathered varying degrees of support from six other bishops and perhaps a further half-dozen abbots, and gave in to the king's demands. The following day, when the king's anger had sufficiently cooled, Norfolk was able to arrange a relatively harmonious audience for Sir Thomas More to surrender the great seal.

There is no contemporary evidence of Anne Boleyn's reception of the news of the submission of the clergy, but it revolutionized her position. Thomas Audley replaced More, and Thomas Cromwell became undeniably the key man in government.[29] Within the royal household where, in May 1532, death had conveniently removed Anne's old critic, Henry Guildford, his place as controller was taken by another of Cromwell's allies, William Paulet.[30] With her brother already one of the two noblemen of the privy chamber, and her father lord privy seal, Anne Boleyn now had supporters in many of the vital positions in government and court. As always, of course, her uncle, the duke of Norfolk, had survived, despite growing disquiet at Anne's independence of mind and hatred of the religious radicalism with which she was associated, and despite the defeat of the policy he had been advocating of even more pressure on Rome. But whatever his doubts and however substantial the lead that Cromwell now had in royal favour, the duke, with his willingness to 'suffer anything for the sake of ruling', had predictably finished up on the winning side and remained, if somewhat shaken, still a piece on the political board for Cromwell and Anne to reckon with.[31]

Among those who had overtly resisted the radicalism of Anne and her supporters, the rush was on to make amends.[32] None moved more rapidly than Stephen Gardiner. In 1530 he had marked his successful beginning as the king's secretary by buying out Sir Richard Weston's interest in the royal estate at Hanworth in Middlesex. Henry VIII and his father before him had created a fine country property there, with a moated manor-house connected by bridges to the gardens (which were noted for their strawberries), an aviary, ponds, an orchard and a park beyond – and very convenient for Hampton Court and the River Thames. All this the bishop now surrendered to Anne in an effort to retrieve his monumental blunder.[33] Henry moved in workmen, fitted out the house with specially made furniture and instructed his Italian experts to provide the latest fashion in Renaissance ornament, some of which was taken from Greenwich (see plate 48).[34] Not that the king was wholly mollified. Gardiner was never entirely comfortable as secretary thereafter, and his formal replacement by Cromwell in the spring of 1534 only recognized the realities. Even his brilliant exposition of the royal supremacy in his 1535 best-seller, *De Vera Obedientia*, never quite persuaded Henry to trust him as he once had.

We may also detect signs that realists were recognizing where the future lay. Honor, the wife of Arthur Plantagenet, Viscount Lisle, made strenuous efforts in the summer of 1532 to secure Anne's attention, sending first a present of peewits and then a bow, a gift which fell somewhat flat when it proved too heavy for Anne to draw. What Lady Lisle wanted was some concessions for a trading venture, and although Anne replied that the time was not opportune 'for certain causes' – no doubt the unhappy state of the royal coffers following parliament's failure to vote adequate taxes in May – she did promise 'to do you good in some other way'.[35]

Court gossip also blamed Anne's influence for the shocking spectacle of a young priest being drawn and hanged without first being degraded from his orders, and this for a coining offence which was naïve rather than treasonable. When her own father had asked her to intercede for the prisoner, she was supposed to have replied that there were too many priests in the country already.[36]

It was clear too that the relationship between Henry and Anne had moved to a different level: the signs were that marriage was an imminent possibility. As well as the gift and furnishing of Hanworth, the king talked openly of marrying again.[37] There was also a distinct jump in the amount of money Henry spent on Anne. In both 1530 and 1531 he had paid out from his privy purse about £220 on or for Anne. In 1532 the figure jumped to £330, although that did include nearly £50 lost to her in ten days playing 'Pope Julius', an early version of the card game 'Commerce'. Much of the expenditure went on clothes, and while it is anachronistic to talk of a 'trousseau', Anne was certainly being fitted out for the role of queen. Two garments are described in particular detail. One was an open-sleeved cloak of black satin, lined throughout in the same material and with three and three-quarter yards of matching velvet at the collar and hem. The other was a black satin nightgown (dressing-gown), lined with black taffeta and edged with velvet. And lest we forget how striking this must have been with Anne's dark hair, there was an equally calculated gown in green damask.[38]

Preparations necessary for a coronation were put in hand, with building workers being impressed in every part of the land to assist in the renovation of the royal lodgings in the Tower of London, an important venue for part of the ritual.[39] Cromwell too was busy drafting legislation to protect the king's new powers from opponents at home and abroad. Archbishop Warham – a longed-for bonus, this – died after forty years serving the Crown and two defending the Church, and the Boleyns were able to secure the immediate selection of Cranmer to succeed him, a remarkable demonstration of influence, since a bishopric was usually left vacant for a year in order to milk the income for the Crown.[40] And the imperial ambassador became aware that something else was afoot that summer. The English were, in great secrecy, feeling their way towards a meeting between Henry VIII and Francis I.[41]

The basic plan was for Henry to spend some time on French soil at Boulogne, and for Francis to visit Calais in return, but the detail proved difficult. Henry and Anne wanted as public a triumph as possible, to confer the European recognition she needed, and they angled for the attendance of Marguerite d'Angoulême and an impressive array of French noblewomen (Francis's second wife, Eleanor, was a niece of Katherine of Aragon and quite out of the question).[42] This was agreed, but later Marguerite withdrew, pleading ill-health – a polite way, it was said, of showing her disapproval of Henry's intended marriage.[43] More likely, she was responding to second thoughts by Francis, who was anxious to avoid anything that could hinder the alliance he was hoping to make with the pope.[44] The French did suggest the duchesse de Vendôme instead, but she was too closely associated with the livelier side of Francis I's court to please Henry, who was intent on the utmost propriety. In the end it was agreed that no ladies would be officially present on either side, but that as Anne would go to Calais with Henry, Francis would meet her when he arrived there.

The proposal was kept secret for as long as possible. Any hint of a summit meeting with the French was guaranteed to rouse English hostility. In the event, much of the credit for achieving the less grandiose final scheme belonged to Anne herself. Giles de la Pommeraye, the French ambassador, was invited on the royal progress that summer. Hunting was the great entertainment and La Pommeraye was often asked to escort Anne, sharing a butt as they shot the deer with crossbows or going with her to watch coursing, and she presented him with a huntsman's coat and hat, a horn and a greyhound.[45] When the arrangements for the Calais meeting were complete, Anne had La Pommeraye as a guest at the dinner she gave for Henry at Hanworth.[46] The ambassador claimed in his despatches that Anne was doing all this at the behest of the king to honour Francis I, but he admitted privately to Chapuys that her services to France were more than could ever be repaid.[47]

This is not to say that Henry did not join in with enthusiasm. He was determined to make a good show, and called up almost all the English nobles who were fit and could be spared from duties at home.[48] An agreement was made to limit display by both sides, especially the wearing of cloth of gold or silver, but even so, Henry's own expenditure on the spot may have exceeded £6000, and the limitation on attire did not, of course, apply either to the king or to Anne.[49] Henry also seems to have seized the opportunity to reset much of the royal jewellery, setting aside many of the best stones for Anne, as in the case of four bracelets, which yielded her no fewer than eighteen tabled rubies.[50] On top of this, Henry stripped Katherine of her jewels. The indirect message, that he wished her to give them to him – the customary way in which the king expressed requests that could not be refused – elicited the response that ever since the new year she had been forbidden to give Henry anything, and the rare barbed comment that it would be a sin to allow her jewels to adorn 'the scandal of Christendom'. This riposte forced a typically self-righteous reply from the king, and the vulgarity of a direct order.[51]

Jewels were not, however, all that Anne needed to be fitted for the European stage. When Francis I had last seen her she had been a lady-in-waiting to his wife. If she was to meet him now as England's intended queen, she needed status. This she was given at an impressive ceremony in Windsor Castle on the morning of Sunday, 1 September.[52] There, her hair about her shoulders and her ermine-trimmed crimson velvet hardly visible under the jewels, Anne was conducted into the king's presence by Garter King-at-Arms, with the countesses of Rutland and Derby, and her cousin Mary Howard, the duke of Richmond's prospective wife, carrying the crimson velvet mantle and gold coronet of a marquis. Henry was flanked by the dukes of Norfolk and Suffolk and surrounded by the court, with the officers at arms in their tabards and La Pommeraye as a guest of honour. Anne kneeled to the king, while Stephen Gardiner read out a patent conferring on her in her own right and on her offspring the title of marquis of Pembroke.[53] Henry placed on her the mantle and the coronet and handed her the patent of nobility, plus another granting lands worth £1000 a year. Anne thanked him and withdrew, after which the king proceeded to St George's Chapel and a solemn high mass sung by Gardiner. Henry and Francis (represented by La Pommeraye) swore to the terms of a treaty between England and France; Edward Fox preached a sermon extolling their intention to co-operate against the Turkish infidel, and announced the plan for the two to meet at Calais. The service ended with a magnificent *Te Deum*, with trumpets and orchestration, after which everyone returned to the castle for a great banquet.

For several weeks afterwards diplomatic Europe buzzed with rumour and counter-rumour about the prospective meeting – would it even take place? Speculation was ended on Friday, 11 October, when before dawn Anne took ship with Henry at Dover, on *The Swallow*, and found herself at ten in the morning, and after almost twenty years, landing once more at Calais. But this time she was at the side of her intended husband and being greeted by the thunder of a royal salute, the attentions of the mayor and lord deputy of Calais, and a parade of the garrison. Not that her own party was very prominent. Among the 2000 or so nobles, knights and lesser men escorting Henry, Anne's twenty or thirty ladies must have been almost lost, and despite his best efforts they were only from the Boleyn faction, or else they were time-servers.[54] Many of the more important Englishwomen were missing – most noticeably his sister Mary.

Anne had ten days in Calais with Henry, living like a queen, escorted by him everywhere and lodging with him at the Exchequer, the only interruption being the surprise arrival of a delegation of welcoming notables from Francis I on the 15th.[55] Then, on the 21st, the king left to meet 'his beloved brother' and to spend four days at the French court at Boulogne for what has been described as a 'stag party' – 'the great cheer that was there, no man can express it.' Then it was England's turn, and Henry arrived back at Calais with Francis on Friday, 25 October.

We hear nothing of Anne Boleyn during Francis's magnificent reception in Calais – all told, 3000 guns were fired in his honour – and his lodgings at Staple Hall on Calais's main square were some distance from the Exchequer. One of his first actions on arrival was to send the provost of Paris to her with the present of a diamond worth £3500, but still she made no appearance. Anne had a sense of theatre, and was reserving her entry as the climax of the great banquet Henry was to give on the Sunday night. The room for this was magnificently prepared, with hangings of cloth of tissue and cloth of silver, ornamented with gold wreaths encrusted with precious stones and pearls, lit by twenty candelabra of silver and silver-gilt carrying 100 wax candles.

It was after the dinner and its 170 different dishes prepared alternately in French style and English style that Anne made her entry, leading a masque of six ladies 'gorgeously apparelled'.[56] There was her sister Mary Carey, her aunt Dorothy, countess of Derby (one of her supporters at Windsor), another aunt, Elizabeth Lady Fitzwalter, her sister-in-law, Lady Rochford, her client (or dependant) Lady Lisle and lastly Lady Wallop, wife of the ambassador to France and at least a former client.[57] They wore costumes 'of strange fashion' – loose, gold-laced overdresses of cloth of gold, with sashes of crimson satin ornamented with a wavy pattern in cloth of silver. All were masked, and they were escorted by four maids of honour in crimson satin and tabards of cypress lawn. Each chose a Frenchman to dance with: the countess of Derby led out Marguerite d'Angoulême's husband, the king of Navarre, and the other ladies their partners, but Francis himself was, of course, claimed by Anne. After a couple of dances, Henry could no longer restrain his childlike excitement and removed the masks 'so that there the ladies' beauties were showed'. Dancing then went on for another hour, but Francis and Anne spent much of this in private conversation before Henry escorted his guests back to Staple Hall.

The last full day of the Calais visit, 28 October, soon passed with a chapter of the Order of the Garter and a wrestling match, which saw Henry's specially imported Cornish wrestlers restore the national honour lost at the Field of Cloth of Gold, though very wisely the king did not again take on Francis in person as he had in 1520 (when he lost).[58] Thus amity persisted to the final day, Tuesday, 29 October, when Henry accompanied the French king to the border-crossing into France. Farewells over, there was a rush to get back to England, but the brilliant weather which had so far graced proceedings now broke in a furious north-westerly gale which, coupled with a spring tide, drove the lucky ones back to Calais and the unlucky on to the inundated shores of Flanders.[59] Someone, however, must have got over to set in motion the propaganda that Henry saw as one major purpose of the meeting with Francis. Wynkyn de Worde had *The manner of the triumph at Calais and Boulogne* on the streets of London within the week.[60] He may, indeed, have been fed a deliberate piece of disinformation. He lists Anne Boleyn first among the ladies dancing on Sunday night, followed by 'my lady Mary', that is, her sister. Next come the countess of Derby and Lady Fitzwalter, but in no way could Mary Carey have actually taken precedence over either of them. Moreover, 'my lady Mary' would normally indicate Princess Mary. The suspicion, there-fore, must be that the news sent to England was 'spun' to suggest that Henry's daughter had been present and had countenanced the priority given to Anne Boleyn.[61]

Henry and Anne had intended to stay at Calais until the 8th, so they missed the dangers and the shipwrecks, but the storm, which only began to slacken on Monday, 4 November, must have kept them confined to the Exchequer. Not that that was a hardship. It was a large house with extensions including a tennis court, with a gallery to walk in, a king's garden and a queen's garden and, if Anne occupied the accommodation designated for her on a planned later visit, she had a suite of seven main rooms (including a chamber overlooking the garden), and her bedroom backed onto Henry's own, with interconnecting doors.[62] All the while the wind remained foul for the crossing, and when the intended departure day arrived it rose to a new violence which cleared pedestrians from the Calais streets. The return of fine weather on Sunday, 10 November, encouraged Henry to have his bed and baggage sent aboard, but a Channel fog put an end to any immediate departure. They got away eventually at midnight on Tuesday, 12 November, and reached Dover early on Thursday morning after a painfully slow crossing of twenty-nine hours. The counsellors at Westminster breathed a sigh of profound relief at the king's safe return, and rapidly organized a *Te Deum* at St Paul's Cathedral. Henry, however, took his time; he had only reached Eltham by the 24th.[63] And the explan-ation we can guess. Somewhere, sometime, perhaps as the wind tore through the Calais streets or in a manor-house in Kent, Anne at last slept with Henry.[64]

WEDDING NERVES

W ITH Anne Boleyn and Henry VIII living together, albeit discreetly, it might be expected that the time of doubt and irresolution would be over. To many historians, the crucial decision to cohabit was made possible by September's Anglo-French treaty and whatever was finally agreed at Calais. Armed with French guarantees, Henry must at last have felt secure enough to consummate his relationship with Anne – and she, for her part, must have been convinced at last that it was safe for her to respond. Alternatively, what freed Henry and Anne was the recall of Thomas Cranmer from Germany on or before 1 October. The next metropolitan could be relied on to give Henry justice.

If we see the decision to cohabit as a response to such external events, the next few months can be presented as a natural sequence, leading to Anne's public recognition. In the new year she and Henry went through a wedding ceremony, probably on 25 January.[1] About this time Anne may have begun to suspect that she might be pregnant. For some weeks the marriage was kept secret, even from Francis. Montmorency, the *grand maître* of the French royal household, was still addressing Anne in March as *Madame la marquise*, unaware that her brother was then on the way to tell his master that she was now both wife and expectant mother.[2] Chapuys was kept entirely in the dark. He did report in February that Henry had been formally betrothed, but on 31 March he could still only pass on strong rumours that the marriage would take place after Easter. Carlo Capello from Venice was the earliest ambassador to report (on 12 April) that Henry had already been married for several months.[3]

The news was hardly much quicker to circulate in England, and the slowness of observers to tumble to what was going on again shows how deep-rooted was the conviction that Henry simply could not remarry without the pope's consent. However, for eyes that avoided this

conditioning, the signs had been clear.[4] During December Henry transferred to Anne over three hundredweight of gilt and partly gilt plate, and
in the second week of the month he had gone with Anne to view the new
building in the Tower and, most exceptionally, shown her the royal
treasure room. When the French ambassador arrived with an important
message, Anne apparently persuaded Henry to open the room again and
show the ambassador as well, a gesture Henry had specifically avoided
some days previously. Once Henry began to reveal financial secrets
a relationship had gone deep indeed.

On 24 January the news that a Boleyn protégé would be the next
archbishop of Canterbury became common knowledge. Cranmer had
got back to England earlier in the month, having been collected by a
special messenger sent by Henry to hasten his return.[5] Thomas Audley
was promoted to the rank of chancellor on 26 January, and a few days
later Chapuys reported what seems to have been a meeting to discuss
Cromwell's penultimate draft of the Act of Appeals, which would put on
the statute book a statement of the royal supremacy and break the judicial
links with Rome.[6] Meanwhile Henry and Anne were beginning to talk
even more freely about marriage, and applicants for places in her household were told that they would not have long to wait.[7] Her father, the earl
of Wiltshire, told the earl of Rutland on 7 February that the king was
determined to marry Anne at once, and sounded him out on his reaction
to the forthcoming Appeals bill. When Rutland (even though a Boleyn
supporter) said that parliament had no competence in spiritual matters,
Boleyn flew into a rage and browbeat him into agreeing to vote for the
king; other peers were probably handled similarly.[8]

Although the fact of the wedding remained a secret, Anne's pregnancy
became generally known within the court, if only from proud hints she
dropped herself.[9] Chapuys reported that on 15 February she had said
quite openly to the duke of Norfolk that if she was not pregnant by Easter
she would undertake a pilgrimage to pray to the Virgin Mary. A week later
she said to one of her favourites, probably Wyatt, and again in the hearing
of many courtiers, that she had developed a craving for apples, which the
king said was a sign that she was pregnant but which she had denied –
clearly in jest, for she went back into her room laughing loudly. On
St Mathias' Day, 24 February, Anne held a sumptuous banquet for the
king in her own rooms, which were hung for the occasion with the best
tapestries, and the tables were set with a mass of gold plate. Henry was
in fine form. He spent the whole meal bantering and flirting with Anne
and her ladies and ignoring the duke of Suffolk, the chancellor and his

other guests, although he was heard to ask the dowager duchess of Norfolk, Anne's step-grandmother, whether she did not think that 'madame la marquise' had made a good marriage and had a great dowry, since all the furnishings and all the plate belonged to her.[10]

By the second week of March Henry was confident enough to put up preachers at court who proclaimed the immorality of his marriage with Katherine and (by implication) 'the virtues and secret merits' of Anne, while on the 14th Cromwell introduced the Appeals bill in the Commons. With the arrival of the necessary papal bulls, Cranmer too could at last be brought into play, and on the 26th convocation was asked to pronounce on the validity of a dispensation to marry a brother's widow.[11] The following Sunday, 30 March, the new archbishop was consecrated under the traditional forms, a few days before the Appeals bill cleared both Houses of Parliament and convocation gave its decision in Henry's favour. There was now nothing to stop Anne's public recognition.[12] By the end of March her household had at last been formed.[13] On the Wednesday of Holy Week, Katherine was told that she had to reduce her title and lifestyle to that of a dowager princess of Wales; Bishop Fisher, the lone voice speaking up for her, had already been silenced by detention.[14] And the following Saturday, the eve of Easter Day 1533, Anne went to mass as queen, at last.[15] Glittering with jewellery, wearing a pleated gown of cloth of gold, her train borne by her cousin, the future duchess of Richmond, and with sixty maids of honour in attendance, Queen Anne was prayed for by name and given full regal honours.[16]

Told in this way, the months before Easter 1533 marched with an ever-increasing tempo towards the inevitable climax of the long years of courtship. The submission of the clergy had been the decisive break-through; mass on Easter eve, the victory parade. Yet there are problems. Despite the coherence and pace of the story, despite its romantic convic-tion, disturbing pieces of evidence do not fit in. They, suggest, rather, that the courtship of Henry VIII and Anne Boleyn remained difficult to the end. In the first place, why had Henry not married earlier, as soon as death had silenced Warham's intransigent refusal to defy the pope. Surely, with no archbishop to answer to, whoever conducted the January marriage would have been equally willing to officiate? Another oddity is the indeci-sion behind the postponement of parliament until the new year, despite the guarantee of French protection against Charles V, and even though the drafting of legislation on the relation between England and the papacy may have been well advanced.[17]

There are signs, too, that the king's advisers were still not happy with the radical option, despite the submission. Norfolk claimed that he, and particularly Anne's father, had blocked a wedding in May 1532; he even told Chapuys that Wiltshire had *contrefit le frenetique* ('pretended insanity') on that occasion and that both had earned black looks from Anne as a result.[18] Be that as it may (and Chapuys had detected no hint of this performance at the time), the duke may well have been more than a little involved on the conservative side over the submission. He certainly made a curious trip to Dover in March 1532, which allowed him to meet Stephen Gardiner on his return from France and to escort him back to London.[19] In June too he quarrelled with the French ambassador, and Anne had to move in to save the Calais meeting.[20] As late as the end of May 1533, Chapuys was still reporting tension between Anne and Norfolk and Wiltshire, and he passed on the story that when the latter saw his pregnant daughter enlarging her gowns and had remarked that she should not try to hide the baby but thank God for the condition she was in, he had been publicly crushed by Anne's reply that she was in a better state than he had wished her to be.[21]

Popular discontent rumbled. The progress towards Nottingham, which had begun in July 1532, was cut short to expedite negotiations with France, but, according to Chapuys, Anne had been hooted and hissed in a number of places.[22] Outright opposition persisted as well, and from a very difficult quarter: Henry's sister Mary and her husband, Charles Brandon, duke of Suffolk. During the Easter break between the two parliamentary sessions in 1532, Mary made opprobrious remarks about her brother's choice of Anne, and these set off an affray in the Sanctuary at Westminster which, quite in the style of Capulet and Montague, had left one of the Brandons' principal gentlemen dead and the court in an uproar. The duke had to promise to control his men; the killers were then in June allowed to purchase a pardon, and the duke and duchess apparently made themselves scarce in their house in Oxfordshire. The matter, however, did not end there. A group of Suffolk's servants swore to take revenge, and Cromwell promptly told the king.[23] We may note that it was a week after this that Henry paid an apparently unscheduled visit to his sister and brother-in-law, very probably to insist that they accept Anne. According to Chapuys, Henry had to repeat the lesson a month later, before Charles Brandon would at least do his duty and appear at Boulogne, although he was deliberately absent at Shrovetide 1533, when Anne presided at a great feast in honour of the French ambassadors.[24] His wife, Mary – the only person in England in a position to do so – seems adamantly to have refused to accept her brother's choice. Her absence from Calais was widely interpreted as a direct snub.[25]

In the summer of 1532 some of Anne's enemies were also able to threaten her with a ghost from the past, Henry Percy. We have seen how his marriage to Mary Talbot quickly became a disaster, and by 1530 the earl had effectively separated from his wife. When, in the course of yet one more marital altercation, Mary charged her husband with neglecting her, he replied that they were not married, because he had previously been legally contracted to Anne Boleyn. Seeing a way out of her own troubles, the countess reported the matter to her father, a staunch supporter of Queen Katherine. He, however, chose not to send the news to Anne's more obvious opponents, but to the duke of Norfolk; Howard, in his turn, took a similarly cautious line and showed the letter to Anne. Each peer was clearly afraid of alienating both the favourite and the king if the matter did not stand up to examination. Anne's characteristic response was to take the letter to Henry himself and insist that it be investigated. So during July 1532 Northumberland was interrogated on oath by the two archbishops and then, in the presence of the duke of Norfolk and the king's canon lawyers, he swore on the Blessed Sacrament that there had been no pre-contract with Anne.[26]

Another sign that progress from the defeat of the Church to pregnancy and marriage was less than straightforward is the probability that Henry had at one time considered marrying Anne at Calais, even perhaps in the presence of Francis I. Gossip in England warned that this was the plan; both the imperial and the Venetian ambassadors reported to this effect. Charles V, although horrified, also expected the marriage to go through.[27] Observers of the conference itself believed the story right to the last. One even suggested that Sunday, 27 October, was the appointed day and that the officiating priest would be Jean du Bellay, bishop of Paris, formerly the ambassador to England and a favourite with Anne.[28] When no marriage took place, this was put down to fear of the emperor or, more likely, advice from Francis.[29] Geoffrey Pole confessed in 1538 that he had gone to Calais in disguise and then had been sent by his brother, Lord Montague, to tell Katherine that, although Henry had pressed his case to the limit, Francis would not approve of the marriage.[30] In fact, Anne had announced in late September that 'now, if the king wished to marry she would not consent,' as her desire was to be married at Westminster, but that remark nevertheless confirms that marrying at Calais had been under consideration.[31] Indeed, if we are to trust reports, during August she was dropping palpable hints in her correspondence that she would marry there.[32] Other indications, however, suggest that consideration was given to the alternative of marrying before going to France. When Henry's

Vatican agent, Gregory Casale, arrived at Calais, Anne rounded on him, accusing him of managing the divorce incompetently, and, we are told, was all the more angry because she had hoped to be married in mid-September.[33] Evidently the marriage plans of Henry VIII and Anne Boleyn were anything but settled.

Perhaps the most significant evidence of continuing uncertainty is the strange wording of Anne's patent as lady marquis of Pembroke. This allowed the extraordinary possibility that the title would descend to her son even if he was born outside lawful marriage.[34] This was achieved by the simple omission of two words – 'lawfully begotten' – and it is doubtful whether anyone noticed as the Latin patent was proclaimed at Anne's investiture.[35] Perhaps the very unusual creation of a woman as a peer in her own right had posed problems in drafting, but omitting such a standard form by accident seems highly unlikely. If, then, the wording was deliberate, what was its significance? Friedmann argued (and others have read the grant in the same way) that with Warham's death removing the last major obstacle to their marriage, Anne began to live with Henry, but that the grant of the title and the wealth to support it was an insurance against any last-minute disaster for herself and any children she might have by the king.[36] That argument, however, requires Anne, who had stood out for marriage for six years, to change her mind and gamble on a divorce still in the uncertain future; she could have got equivalent terms for at least several months, if not years. Equally, it is strange that Henry, desperate for a legitimate heir, should at this late stage have chosen to contemplate the possibility of a bastard child. Perhaps we should turn Friedmann's argument on its head and see the patent insuring Henry against the continuing anxiety that despite all his efforts, when at last he and Anne married, it might not be possible to vindicate the legality of the relationship. The patent thus becomes not an announcement by Anne to the world that she was going to sleep with Henry, nor an admission that she had lowered her price. It is evidence that Henry is still not certain that he is going to succeed.

We may point, finally, to the clear indications that, whatever Cromwell's legislative drafts were telling him, Henry had still not been completely liberated from psychological dependence on the papacy. The failure to go ahead with annulment proceedings, despite a demoralized convocation, and the wait instead for Cranmer to arrive in the new year, are only explicable by a conviction that papal endorsement was vital for a valid appointment to Canterbury and that nothing must be done to prejudice this.[37] In the same way, Henry's interpretation of what was agreed at Calais shows that he still hankered after papal approval. Negotiations with Rome continued – partly, no doubt, to stave off Clement VII's judgement in favour of Katherine, and to ensure that Cranmer could be appointed in the traditional way.[38] However, signs of a compromise did begin to appear. It is hard to say who took the initiative or how serious it all was, but a softer tone from Henry after the Calais meeting, plus a tactful suppression by his Vatican agents of earlier more aggressive instructions, had coincided with increased willingness at Rome to find a way out of the impasse. Even when he had married Anne, Henry boasted that Clement was beginning to yield, and only a day or two later, news was received from Francis I that his cardinals had reached the pope and were making good progress.[39] The papal nuncio was soon heavily involved in secret negotiations with the king and his council, much to the concern of Chapuys, who feared the pope would desert Katherine.[40] Of course these talks, like the strict secrecy surrounding the marriage, may have been primarily intended to pull the wool over Clement's eyes, but they were, at least in part, an attempt to create the impression for home consumption that at last the pope had given Henry what he wanted. On 8 February the papal nuncio was invited to attend the king to the House of Lords, where he was placed at the right of the throne. Since the French ambassador was put at the left, the tableau was clearly intended to suggest that Henry enjoyed full support from both Francis I and Clement VII.[41]

All this makes a good deal more plausible the recusant tradition that Henry deliberately misled the priest who conducted his marriage to Anne in January by claiming that he had papal approval. Sander reports the story, apparently from Harpsfield, and it occurs in an anonymous attack on Henry that is independent of but related to the Harpsfield text.[42] According to this tradition, the wedding took place in the upper chamber over the Holbein Gate of Whitehall, before dawn and with very few witnesses. When the celebrant asked if the king had the pope's permission, he was given a somewhat ambiguous assurance that this had been received. Not happy with this, he asked again and suggested that the document should be read out; the king, with a smile, effectively challenged the priest to call him a liar and declared that the licence was among his private papers, but 'if I should, now that it waxeth towards day, fetch it, and be seen so early abroad, there would rise a rumour and talk thereof other than were convenient. Go forth in God's name and do that which appertaineth to you.'[43]

Some details in the story are independently vouched for – for instance, the tiny number of witnesses and the extreme secrecy.[44] Others are very plausible, such as the attendance of Henry Norris and Thomas Heneage of the privy chamber, the two men one would expect to be in the king's confidence. Anne's attendant was supposedly Lady Berkeley, and this again is credible. Anne Savage, as she then was, had been a gentlewoman at court for some years and was a dependant of William Brereton, groom of the privy chamber; one account states that a groom was also present, and if so this was most probably William.[45] Admittedly, not every detail in the story is reliable. The celebrant was remembered in recusant circles as Rowland Lee, later bishop of Lichfield, but evidence from Chapuys – though admittedly from 1535 – identifies the priest as George Brown, the prior of the Augustinian Friars of London and later archbishop of Dublin.[46] But that aside, the story does carry a ring of truth. The words credited to Henry are typical of his penchant for qualified honesty: ' "I trust you have the pope's licence..." ' "What else", quoth the king.' Or again, 'Think you me a man of so small and slender foresight and consideration of my affairs that unless all things were safe and sure I would enterprise this matter? I have truly a licence...which if it were seen, should discharge us all.' Elizabethan recusants were intent on suggesting that Henry uttered a blatant lie, but of course he did have a papal licence to marry Anne. True, this was conditional upon a declaration that his marriage with Katherine was void, but it did not specify who would make that declaration of nullity.[47] Assume that Henry was certain that either the pope would, after all, oblige, or if not Cranmer would, and the assertion becomes at least a half-truth. Little can be certain about that pre-dawn gathering over the Whitehall gate; but the probability is that even then Henry felt he had to imply papal consent to his marriage.[48]

If we put together all this evidence of uncertainty despite the dramatic collapse of convocation in May 1532, that victory begins to look somewhat less decisive. The move towards Anne's marriage and the breach with Rome was achieved only by continuing struggle. Here we have to make a fundamental choice in interpretation. Which of the couple was making the running, Henry or Anne? The crux is the November 1532 decision to sleep together. Did Henry decide that he was now certain of victory? Did Anne agree to intercourse now that the prize was in sight? Each view has had its advocates, but neither is entirely satisfactory. Is it likely, given the obstacles still in the way of any marriage, that Henry would abandon five years of heroic chastity and chance a son by Anne being born illegitimate? Suppose the pope refused to accept Cranmer? And why should Anne agree, even if Henry did now want to take the risk? What had changed the situation? The provision for illegitimate offspring in the recent Pembroke grant was hardly encouraging. Could the real answer be that the decision to cohabit was a calculated initiative by Anne? Since the submission and the death of Warham, the radical solution to the 'great matter' had been there for the taking. All that stood in the way was Henry's indecision. Throughout their relationship it had been Anne who had stiffened the king's resolve. Did she, even at the last, have to precipitate the decisive crisis, sure that if she became pregnant Henry would have to act?

The circumstances of Elizabeth's birth on 7 September 1533 could certainly suggest this. Protocol and custom dictated that a queen would go into purdah a month or six weeks before the expected date of her confinement. It was called 'taking her chamber'. Anne, however, entered the maternity rooms specially prepared for her only ten days before Elizabeth arrived.[49] Possibly Anne and the midwives miscalculated, but the other explanation is that Elizabeth was somewhat premature. If so, this would indicate that it was probably only in mid-January that Anne could have begun to suspect that she had conceived. And if that was so, then the sudden flurry of that month falls into place: the rapid appointment of Cranmer, the promotion of Audley, the burst of parliamentary drafting and, most of all, the hurried ceremony on the 25th. If there was a possibility that Anne was pregnant, Henry had to secure the sanction of the Church, pope or no pope. In other words, the hugger-mugger of that pre-dawn ceremony in the Whitehall gatehouse and the king's attempts to keep it quiet are a measure of the psychological block which Anne had forced Henry to overcome.

There is an alternative scenario, suggested by something Edward Hall says. 'The king, after his return [from Calais] married privily the Lady Anne Bulleyn on Saint Erkenwald's Day, which marriage was kept so secret, that very few knew it, till she was great with child, at Easter after.'[50] St Erkenwald's Day was the day the couple returned to Dover. Later Protestants canvassed that date to protect Elizabeth's reputation; even at full term she could not have been conceived earlier than the start of December. Hall, however, had no such motive and his date does coincide with the approximate start of cohabitation (which must have been known in court circles). Significantly, too, Nicholas Sander dates the marriage as 14 November although he had every reason to slander Elizabeth's legitimacy.[51] It could be, therefore, that Thursday, 14 November 1532, was when Henry and Anne made some sort of formal commitment. Given the regular ceremony in January before a priest, it is unlikely that November 14 saw a formal marriage. But for Anne and Henry to abandon years of self-denial, their commitment must have been sufficiently robust to stand up in canon law – probably espousals *de praesenti* before witnesses which, if sealed by intercourse, would have been canonically valid, always assuming that the union with Katherine would subsequently be struck down.[52] If Hall was referring to something of this kind, it is again clear that the initiative can only have come from Anne. By marrying, Henry effectively threw away the agreement with Francis I he had sought for over a year and had specially travelled to Calais to secure only days earlier.[53] Anne, on the other hand, secured the formal commitment she had always stood out for. She had also ensured, crucially, that she would be the wife in possession whenever the divorce came through. Ending Henry's marriage to Katherine would not now create a vacancy which her enemies could try to exploit.

Some observers of the behaviour of Henry and Anne, and many more commentators at second hand, would have found this discussion quite unnecessary. All over Europe the assumption was that Henry had married his mistress. There was even gossip that they had already had a child or children.[54] Yet the grounds for believing that Anne remained a virgin until the last months of 1532 are strong. Sander might claim that she was promiscuous at a very early age, but as we have seen, the equally Catholic George Cavendish, who had known her, was unequivocal:

> The noblest prince that reigned on the ground
>   I had to my husband, he took me to his wife;
> At home with my father a maiden he found me.[55]

There is no evidence that Anne bore any children before 1533, neither in the comments of informed observers nor – and this is more significant – in any administrative or financial records. No process was ever made at Rome on the ground of her immorality, and Katherine's case suffered by its eagerness to assume the worst without proof.[56] Evidence of adultery would have decisively weakened Henry's claim to be acting on grounds of conscience, but it was never forthcoming. Anne's determination to be a wife and not a mistress meant that self-interest lay in morality. Henry's need for a legitimate heir made for the same – and the argument is the stronger if we should see the king doubtful about the success of his divorce almost to the last. Neither could afford the risks of incautious passion. That the relationship had a physical element – at least on Henry's side – is well attested, and how this could be expressed yet controlled over six years may intrigue the curiosity and challenge the belief of a generation brought up to different norms of behaviour. We may even wonder how strong that physical element was. But controlled it was; when full sexual relations began, they were initiated by calculation – and the calculation was very possibly Anne's.

A CORONATION
AND A CHRISTENING

L ONDON was all a-bustle as the Easter season of 1533 came to an
end. Anne Boleyn, now the king's 'most dear and well-beloved wife',
was to be crowned on Whit Sunday, 1 June, and orders had arrived for the
full panoply of a royal coronation.[1] The city had to 'make preparation as
well to fetch her grace from Greenwich to the Tower by water, as to see the
city ordered and garnished with pageants in places accustomed, for the
honour of her grace when she should be conveyed from the
Tower to Westminster', and with only two and a half weeks to get ready
for what was to be the first major exhibition of civic pageantry since 1522
– indeed, only the second of its kind in the whole reign.[2]

Now scores of participants were mobilized – nobles and others who
claimed the right to serve in particular capacities, those selected to be
knighted in honour of the occasion and those who were to take part in the
processions.[3] Lady Cobham found herself allocated the role of attendant
horsewoman and required to find white palfreys for herself and her own
ladies, and although her own robes and the long cloth of gold (or perhaps
red velvet) trapper for her horse were provided, she was expected to equip
her attendants herself, 'as unto your honour and that solemnity appertaineth'.[4] And the lesser folk were busy on the decoration, the railing and the
gritting of the streets to give footing to the horses – all the preparations,
large and small, inseparable from the great occasion.

The pageantry of a coronation spread over four days.[5] On the first, the
monarch would be escorted by river to the Tower; the next was devoted to
court rituals, and on the afternoon of the third a road procession took
place from the Tower, through the city to Westminster; on the final day
came the coronation itself and a great banquet in Westminster Hall. There
were some half-dozen 'places accustomed' for pageants on the route
through the city, and all were decorated on the occasion of Anne's

coronation, plus three more, making the show as big as that for Charles V in 1522 and larger than Katherine of Aragon's in 1501. The water pageant, too, was outstanding.

It was about one o'clock on Thursday, 29 May, that, escorted by numerous smaller vessels, the fifty great barges of the London livery companies set out from the rendezvous at Billingsgate. The term 'barge' is now somewhat misleading.[6] Company barges were sixty or seventy feet long with a beam of ten feet or so, shallow draft and a large covered cabin for passengers. They were powered by four to eight oars a side up forrard and were highly decorated. On that Thursday they were more elaborately dressed than even for the lord mayor's procession, with flags and bunting overall, hung with gold foil that glistened in the sun and with little bells that tinkled; the vessels were packed with musicians of every kind, and more cannon than seems safe on such a crowded waterway. The fleet was led by a light wherry in which had been constructed a mechanical dragon that could be made to move and belch out flames, and with it were other models of monsters and huge wild men, who threw blazing fireworks and uttered hideous cries. A very safe distance behind came the mayor's barge, with the aldermen in scarlet and the common councillors. To the starboard of the mayor's craft came the famous bachelors' barge, provided by the Haberdashers, the company of the then mayor. Hangings of cloth of gold and cloth of silver concealed 'trumpets and divers other melodious instruments', flags carried the arms of the company and of the Merchant Adventurers, the rigging was decorated with streamers which had little bells at the end, two great banners (one fore, one aft) were blazoned with the arms of Henry and Anne, and the starboard gunwale was covered with thirty-six shields showing the two coats of arms impaled. On the opposite side of the mayor's barge was another wherry, this time carrying an outsize representation of Anne's principal badge, a white falcon crowned, perching on red and white roses which burst out of a golden tree-stump growing on a green hill surrounded by 'virgins singing and playing sweetly'.

Rowing against the tide, it took the procession two hours to reach Greenwich, reverse its order and come to anchor off the palace steps. In mid-afternoon Anne entered her own 'sumptuously' decorated barge, along with the principal ladies of the court. A second barge carried the rest of her women, then came the king's barge full of his guard 'in their best array', with the royal trumpets and minstrels, followed by the barges of the courtiers – totalling, with the livery company vessels, some 120 large craft and 200 small ones. Observers rhapsodized about:

the banners and pennants of arms of their crafts, the which were beaten of fine gold, illustring [reflecting] so goodly against the sun, and also the standards, streamers of the cognisances and devices, ventalling with [waving in] the wind, also the trumpets blowing, shawms and minstrels playing, the which were a right sumptuous and a triumphant sight to see and to hear all the way as they past upon the water, to hear the said marvellous sweet harmony of the said instruments, the which sounds to be a thing of another world.[7]

Now rowing with the tide, the flotilla was making better than seven knots. All sea-going vessels had been ordered out of the fairway, but they joined in with gun salutes as Anne passed, almost as though officially lining the route. When the main anchorage of the Pool of London was reached, the salvoes became so many, drowning the continuous ripple of the cannon-fire among the barges, that observers lost count. But the best was yet to come. As the procession rounded the bend of the river at Wapping and came in sight of the Tower, the gunners there received the order they had been waiting for and 'loosed their ordinance', four pieces at a time. While the rest of the fleet 'hovered' – backed water – off Tower Wharf, to one final crescendo of noise the barges carrying Anne and the lord mayor pulled in to the landing steps. They were greeted by a party of the Tower officers and the heralds; then Anne and the London notables proceeded through the crowd to a second reception party, the officers of the royal households, and then on to be greeted by the great officers of state; finally through the postern gate into the fortress and to the king himself who, that day, as throughout the coronation festivities, had been compelled by ancient tradition to observe in secret. Henry embraced his wife, who turned to thank the citizens 'with many goodly words', and so too the king. London had done him proud.

Henry too had achieved something more than magnificence by mobilizing city and court to do honour to his new wife. What the feeling of observers and participants was we do not know, but even if we discount as wishful thinking many of the assertions that, whenever they appeared in public, Katherine of Aragon and her daughter Mary were greeted with enthusiasm, there must still have been many in both the court and the city who had mixed feelings about this new marriage. But just as it was intended to do, this magnificent river pageant had drawn thousands of excited spectators, and what they had seen was the city oligarchy and the elite of the realm uniting to honour the king's second wife. As one herald put it, 'all the lords that might come, but especially temporal peers of all the realm in their barges', while another seems to imply that before the queen and her entourage embarked there had been some formal acclamation of Anne 'as queen of England by all the lords of England'.[8] Who could blame the populace for concluding that those who knew agreed with what Henry had done? And who could expect critics such as the duke of Suffolk not to look at the banks as they passed by and decide that Henry had popular support for his actions? The pageant had been engineered as a piece of corporate idolatry. All had apostatized before the king's command; all had bowed the knee to the new goddess. And even for those with harder heads and less imagination, there was an equally significant lesson. Henry had had his way; the king's will was irresistible.

The first public ceremony over, the royal couple spent the next forty-eight hours in the Tower, enjoying the reconstructed apartments which had been readied for the occasion at Cromwell's personal direction. Virtually nothing of them remains, but they were in the south-east corner, in the innermost ward, between the White Tower and the main curtain wall. As well as lesser rooms, Anne had available a rebuilt great chamber and a rebuilt dining-room, while a new bridge across the moat gave access from her private garden into the city. The plans for a private gallery for the queen had been dropped, but there was the restored great gallery to do double duty. And within the privacy of the Tower, the court rituals of the coronation continued to proclaim the lessons of the day, particularly this time to the nobility and gentry. Eighteen Knights of the Bath were created, in ceremonies which lasted from dinner on Friday to Saturday morning, and involved a special overnight vigil in chambers fitted up for each candidate in the White Tower. These included up-and-coming courtiers such as Francis Weston, the king's former page, and William Windsor, the son of Lord Windsor, keeper of the great wardrobe, but many were connected with Anne Boleyn or her Howard relations. Henry Parker, George Boleyn's brother-in-law; the earl of Derby, whose wife was Anne's aunt; Thomas Arundel, who had recently married Anne's cousin; Henry Saville of Thornhill in Yorkshire, who was already identified as the man to block the pretensions of her open enemy, Thomas, Lord Darcy; possibly Lord Berkeley, whose wife had been Anne's bridesmaid back in January – all these and others were object lessons that the new way to honour was support for the new queen.[9] Then on the Saturday Henry dubbed nearly fifty knights bachelor.[10] Since the honour was in some ways a burden that could only be avoided by paying a fine, some men were probably there under compulsion, but we can again pick out the names of protégés of such Boleyn supporters as Cromwell, Henry Norris, William

Brereton and the earl of Derby. There could be little doubt who it was 'the king delighteth to honour'.[11]

The weather on Saturday, 31 May 1533, was perfect for the procession to Westminster. By about midday the mayor had made one last check on the arrangements, riding back to the Tower from the spot allocated to the aldermen near the Cross in Cheapside, past the craft guilds and the merchants lined up behind railings on one side of the street, and on the other, the general populace, held back by a line of constables. In addition to the special pageants, the houses of Cheapside had been hung with cloth of gold, velvet and tissue, while Cornhill and Gracechurch Street were decorated in scarlet and crimson, with arras, tapestry and carpets on display.[12] There had been some difficulty in getting the procession organized, and instead of starting from the Tower at two o'clock it did not leave until five, but now, as it began to make its way through the crowds, the message of the river procession was again reflected bright and clear.

Anne herself chose to dress in the French fashion, and the procession was headed by twelve servants of the new French ambassador, Jean de Dinteville, Francis I's *maître d'hôtel*. They wore blue velvet with yellow and blue sleeves, and had white plumes in their hats, while their horses had trappers of blue sarcenet, powdered with white crosses. In December, Francis would reimburse the ambassador for his outlay with a gift of 500 gold *écus* (£100).[13]

Then came the gentlemen of the royal households, marching two by two, each man by tradition the eyes and ears of the king he served. They were followed by the nine judges, riding in their scarlet gowns and hoods and wearing their collars of SS; each one had been summoned individually, so that the law would be seen to warrant the coronation. They had been unable to get into the Tower in time to form up, and had had to slip into place as the procession passed Tower Hill. Next came the new Knights of the Bath, followed by the full weight of government and social status – the royal council, the ecclesiastical magnates and the peers of the realm. Individuals could then be seen, making their gesture of support: the chancellor; both the archbishops; the ambassador of France emphasizing again his monarch's personal backing; the ambassador of Venice, implying European recognition; the lord mayor; the deputy earl marshal and beside him the constable of England, Charles Brandon, the king's brother-in-law, keeping his thoughts to himself but showing all outward acquiescence. As the 200 or 300 filed slowly past the waiting crowds, this massive demonstration of solidarity with the king and his new marriage could not have failed to make its point.[14]

At last, behind the courtiers and magnates, came the queen in her litter. She was dressed in filmy white, with a coronet of gold. The litter was of white satin, with 'white cloth of gold' inside and out, and its two palfreys were clothed to the ground in white damask. In ravishing contrast was the queen's dark hair, flowing loose, down to her waist. Over her was a canopy of cloth of gold held up by the barons of the Cinque Ports. Then came her own palfrey, also trapped in white. Twelve ladies in crimson velvet rode behind, then two carriages decked in red cloth of gold. Next, seven more riders, two more carriages – one white, one red – and thirty gentlewomen on horseback, this time in black velvet. These were followed by the king's guard in two files, one on each side of the street, 'in their rich coats . . . of goldsmiths' work', and last all the servants in the livery of their masters or mistresses. It was, said the published report, a 'most noble company'. Anne might not be universally popular, but she was magnificent.

Knowledgeable observers would, admittedly, have noticed significant absences. Neither the king's sister Mary nor her daughter Frances was there, nor was the premier English duchess, the duchess of Norfolk. The first carriage had, therefore, to be occupied by the dowager duchess, Anne's step-grandmother, along with (and reports vary) either Anne's mother or the dowager marchioness of Dorset. But Henry's sister was near to death and her daughter hardly out of childhood, and the absence of the duchess of Norfolk could easily be discounted, given her notorious quarrel with her husband. The earl of Shrewsbury, another doubter, was also missing, but he had taken care to claim his traditional coronation role and to send his son to represent him. The wisdom of showing at least acquiescence was illustrated by the fate of Thomas More, who did deliberately refuse to attend. Sent £20 to buy a suitable gown for the occasion by Tunstall, Gardiner and John Clerk, bishop of Bath and Wells, in the hope that he might be able to recover at least some royal favour, More took the money but declined to join his former conservative allies in a procession which, he was quite explicit, must undermine their integrity. As far as we know he never saw Tunstall again, and within a year of this declaration of intransigence More was in the Tower.[15]

It is, however, hard to assess wider reaction to the coronation procession. Hostile accounts delighted in disparaging everything. The report that reached Brussels, the one containing the story that Anne concealed a goitre behind her high collar, says quite uncompromisingly that the crowds did not cheer or even take their hats off when Anne passed.[16] When challenged on this, the mayor said that he could not command the hearts of the people, and it was left to Anne's fool to retort that they were keeping their caps on to cover their scurvy heads. The 'HA' monogram of the king and his new queen was maliciously read as 'Ha, Ha!' and the French presence was greeted with the cry, 'Whoreson knave, French dog.' A similar story is told in the *Cronica del Rey Enrico*, which has Anne replying to a question from Henry about the decorations in London, 'Sir, I liked the city well enough, but I saw a great many caps on heads, and heard but few tongues.'[17] On the other hand, we must remember that the *Cronica* is a compote of truth, half-truth, rumour and nonsense, while the overstatement in the Brussels account invites suspicion. It is extremely unlikely that so disciplined an assembly as the livery companies, and their journeymen and apprentices, denied the minimum courtesies. The most objective eyewitness, the Venetian ambassador, stresses 'the very great pomp' and the enormous crowds, and remarked on 'the utmost order and tranquillity' of the occasion.[18] 'Dumb insolence' is, however, hard to estimate, and as he made no comment on any positive show of enthusiasm, perhaps the safest conclusion is that the Londoners crowding the streets that day were more curious than either welcoming or hostile. And in any case, in contemporary thinking what mattered more than crowd reaction was what we might call the psychological impact of the procession and the careful observance of all the right ritual. As Edward Baynton, Anne's worldly-wise chamberlain, wrote to George Boleyn on 9 June, the coronation had been performed 'honourably' and 'as ever was, if all old and ancient men say true'.[19]

This was undoubtedly true of the actual coronation at Westminster Abbey on Whit Sunday, despite the fact that Anne was almost six months pregnant. The advantages of a crown for his new wife must have been considerable for Henry to accept the risk of such an ordeal. The great procession began to assemble in Westminster Hall from seven in the morning, but it was just before nine that Anne herself entered. They then set out along a railed route carpeted with cloth of blue ray all along the 700 yards between the dais of the hall and the high altar of the abbey.[20] For this occasion, the court and the peers in their parliament robes were joined by the lord mayor, aldermen and judges, each in scarlet; the monks of Westminster and the staff of the Chapel Royal, all in their best copes; four bishops, two archbishops and twelve mitred abbots in full pontificals; and the abbot of Westminster with his complete regalia. Anne was resplendent in coronation robes of purple velvet, furred with ermine, with the gold coronet on her head which she had worn the day before, though it is not clear that she followed tradition by walking barefoot. Over her was carried the gold canopy of the Cinque Ports, and she was preceded by the sceptre of gold and the rod of ivory topped with the dove, and by the lord great chamberlain, the earl of Oxford, bearing the crown of St Edward, which had previously been used to crown only a reigning monarch. Anne was supported, again as tradition dictated, by the bishops of London and Winchester; the dowager duchess of Norfolk carried the train – a very long one – and she was followed by a host of ladies and gentlewomen dressed in scarlet, with appropriate distinctions of rank.

Special stands had been erected in the abbey, and in particular one from which the king could watch proceedings incognito from behind a lattice-work screen. In the choir stood St Edward's Chair, draped in cloth of gold, on a tapestry-covered dais two steps high, which was itself set on a raised platform carpeted in red. Here Anne rested for a moment before resuming her endurance test. As tradition dictated, the coronation was set in the context of a solemn high mass, sung, apparently, by the abbot of Westminster. It was, however, Cranmer who prayed over Anne as she prostrated herself before the altar. Then he anointed her, before she returned to St Edward's Chair, where he crowned her and delivered the sceptre and the rod of ivory. After the *Te Deum*, St Edward's crown was exchanged for a lighter one and the service continued for Anne to take the sacrament and to make the customary offering at the shrine of the saint. Then a break for some brief refreshment, and the procession back, past the clock tower in New Palace Yard and its five cisterns running with wine, and into Westminster Hall beneath the splendidly redecorated north front. If More had seen taking part in the procession on the Saturday as an assault on his integrity, how much more was the actual coronation. The elite of the land had taken Anne as queen in the sight of God, and under the most solemn and hallowed sanctions of Holy Church. Shakespeare would declare a generation later:

> Not all the water in the rough rude sea
> Can wash the balm from an anointed king.

This mystique of monarchy now belonged to Anne Boleyn. Only death could take it away.

Even with the procession over, Anne had several hours more to face, and on her return she withdrew to her room while the guests were settled in the hall for the coronation banquet.[21] The judges had been turned out days before, their courts dismantled, the windows reglazed, the seating and statuary gilded, and the hall hung with arras for the occasion. Two tables had been set lengthwise on the south of the central blue carpet and two on the north, and the diners sat in order of precedence (see plate 21). At the upper and more honourable end, on the southern table nearest the wall, sat the barons of the Cinque Ports and the masters in chancery; the parallel table had the peers on one side and the bishops on the other, and below them the judges and the royal council. On the opposite side of the great blue carpet, but on the north side of the table only, sat the duchesses and great ladies and the gentlewomen. This allowed them each to be served formally and directly from the centre aisle – as befitted a day of triumph for women. The remaining table, against the north wall, held the mayor and aldermen of London and the senior freemen.

Then, when all was set, Anne herself entered. She sat at the long marble table across the hall, on the king's great marble chair mounted on the dais twelve steps up, under a cloth of estate. Only the archbishop of Canterbury shared the table with her, and he was a good way to her right. Nothing and nobody must be allowed to blur the focus of the occasion. Beside the queen stood the dowager countess of Oxford and the countess of Worcester, who held a cloth up to conceal her from time to time, whenever Anne wished 'to spit or do otherwise', and two gentlewomen sat at her feet, under the table, to do her bidding. To ease her during the lengthy proceedings, a comfortable inner chair had been purpose-made to fit inside the marble one. Henry, meanwhile, occupied a box specially built for him overlooking the high table, from which he would watch events in privacy, along with the ambassadors of France and Venice.

Given the enormous numbers of important folk on duty that day, it seems hardly credible that 800 people remained to sit down. One list of attendants names almost 100 gentlemen and higher ranks, as well as scores of lesser mortals. Only the eight nobles appointed to serve the queen were allowed on the holy ground surrounding her, but there were about 120 more support staff for the top table alone. Overall responsibility lay with the duke of Suffolk as high steward, a function that he discharged in a doublet and jacket dripping with pearls, and from the saddle of a horse magnificently trapped in crimson velvet. Also on horseback, and all in crimson, was Lord William Howard, who was in charge of serving the banquet; his horse's purple velvet trapper was embroidered with the Howard white lion and slashed to show the white satin lining. He was deputizing for his brother, the earl marshal, who had been sent with George Boleyn on an embassy to France. Suffolk and Howard now escorted in the first course, twenty-eight dishes for the queen and the archbishop, which were carried by the new Knights of the Bath. Twenty-four dishes followed for the second course and thirty for the third – each heralded with as much noise as the king's trumpets and minstrels could make – and even though the lower tables had fewer dishes, according to a carefully graded scale, the lord mayor and his companions were very satisfied with their two courses of thirty-two. The king had exacted tribute from far and wide, and the lavishness and magnificence of the food (provided from specially enlarged kitchens) was set off by a profusion of 'subtleties', those curious devices so beloved of the Burgundian tradition of royal feasting.[22] The wax ships were singled out for particular praise. It was 'the most honorable feast that hath been seen'. And even when the banquet was over, there were still the closing ceremonies to get through before the queen was able to retire. It was nearly six o'clock. She had been 'on parade', almost continuously, for nine hours.

How much all this cost we do not know, still less the expense for the whole four days. The Milanese ambassador guessed that it cost the City an incredible £46,000 (200,000 ducats) and the king half that amount, but whatever the figure, it was clearly huge. Equally clearly, Henry found it all worthwhile.[23] Chapuys' description of the events as 'cold, meagre and uncomfortable' is sour grapes; the 'concubine' had been accorded the fullest possible inauguration as queen.[24] No doubt the elaboration, the attention to detail, the evident overkill does indicate a measure of insecurity, and we must remember that all the participants knew that the king was watching, just as he had watched the court's original acceptance of Anne the previous Easter. Nevertheless, in the same way that the popular and the religious liturgies had been performed, so had the banquet. It had been a test, a sacrament of loyalty. The great of the land had dined to honour Anne Boleyn, their queen; they had drunk to their sovereign's new consort; whatever their inner doubts, they had identified with her. In More's simile, they had been 'deflowered' – raped. The seductiveness of the old magic is seen in the reactions of those hard-headed judges for whom Westminster Hall was the normal workaday environment. When summoned to the coronation, they had felt it necessary to meet to discuss how to respond. There is even, in Justice Spelman's account, a hint of minimal acquiescence, of the tradition of avoiding as far as possible taking political sides. But by Sunday they were scrambling for places on the stands in the abbey and flattered by the honourable positions accorded them at the feast. Spelman noted with pride that, as they kneeled to Anne as she left the hall, she smiled and said, 'I thank you all for the honour ye have done to me this day.' And even though we may suspect that this was a general thank-you to the company, the judges clearly thought it was just for them.

The coronation banquet marked the end of the official ceremonies, but custom dictated that a court celebration should follow. Monday, 2 June, therefore, was devoted to jousting, balls and a 'goodly banquet in the queen's chamber', though it is only the first that we know much about. The original plan had been to have the jousters, challengers and answerers, ride in the coronation procession with all the elaborate costumes and devices that had been prepared for the tilting, but when Lord William Howard, who was to lead the challengers, had been obliged to deputize as earl marshal elsewhere in the procession, the idea was dropped.[25] These 'great jousts' were perhaps the first to be held in the new tiltyard that had been built opposite the gate of the new palace of Whitehall, and as usual, there were plenty of guests as well as the general public.

The entertainment, however, was not a success. The eight jousters in each of the two teams ran six courses apiece, but there were not, as the published account pretended, 'broken many spears valiantly'.[26] Very many of the horses veered away from the central barrier, or tilt, so that the riders found it difficult to secure flush hits on their opponents. The likely explanation for the poor sport is some unexpected problem presented by the new arena, although since Anne's enemy, Nicholas Carewe, was leading the answerers, one might in other circumstances suspect lack of enthusiasm. However, one can hardly imagine that Sir Nicholas would publicly invite the suspicion of the king or risk his own standing in jousting circles. Whatever his private emotions, he knew very well that refusing to accept Anne would destroy his career. Carewe, along with everyone else, except for More and a few stiff-backed men like him, was busy doing his best to impress the royal couple with his enthusiasm to honour them. That was certainly the atmosphere remembered by a somewhat effusive French tradition:

> The initiatives of the gentlemen and lords were notable as the English sought, unceasingly, to honour their new princess. Not, I believe, because they wanted to, but in order to comply with the wishes of their king. The lords and ladies set to dances, sports of various kinds, hunting expeditions, and pleasures without parallel. Numerous tournaments were held in her honour – each man put his lance under his thigh or fought to the death with the sword – and everything a success. And as well as magnificent and joyful celebrations, everyone strove to be as attentive and solicitous as possible to serve their new mistress.[27]

The psychological dominance that had been established over the court was very real.

The end of the celebrations did not mark any end to the high spirits at court. Anne's chamberlain, writing to her brother in France, reported that 'pastime in the queen's chamber was never more. If any of you that be now departed have any ladies that they thought favoured you, and somewhat would mourn at parting of their servants, I can no whit perceive the same by their dancing and pastime they do use here.'[28] The death of the king's sister Mary on 24 June seems to have made little difference. Any mourning was brief. What mattered was the delivery at Greenwich on the 28th of Anne's wedding gift from Francis I, a magnificent litter with three mules specially purchased from the dauphin, and originally presented to George Boleyn in Paris. She immediately took it on a three-mile trial.[29]

Henry did find time to issue a proclamation warning of the penalties of according royal honours to anyone but Anne.[30] The authority for this was the Act of Appeals, though it is doubtful how many of the members of parliament or peers who passed the bill had expected it to be used to outlaw a lifetime of respect to Katherine and Mary, a habit which even the duke of Norfolk found it embarrassingly hard to break.[31] Neither mother nor daughter had been willing to accept relegation to the status of 'princess dowager' and 'Lady Mary', while their household servants backed them in every way they could – with shows of dumb stupidity or feminine tantrums to the limits of caution and beyond. There was, after all, remarkably little that Henry could do when Katherine put her people into new liveries embroidered, as for the last twenty-four years, with 'H' and 'K' – remarkably little, that is, unless Chapuys' wilder fantasies about poison and treason trials were turned into fact.[32] Efforts to deprive Mary of plate and jewels now thought excessive were defeated by the disappearance of the inventory, while Katherine, who was willing to surrender like a dutiful wife everything Henry had ever given her, refused point-blank to let Anne have the splendid christening robe she herself had brought from Spain:[33] 'God forbid that I should ever be so badly advised as to give help, assistance, or favour, directly or indirectly in a case so horrible as this.' And for once Henry had to acquiesce.

More and more, indeed, attention began to focus on Anne's fast-approaching confinement. For some time after the coronation, reports of her health continued to be good, but there is reason to believe that the advanced stages of the pregnancy were, in fact, difficult. Henry, it was later said, had been at his wits' end, even hoping for a miscarriage if it would save Anne's life.[34] Certainly, he declined to go on the usual summer progress because of his wife's condition, and the couple retired to Windsor, where he could hunt in the forests thereabouts, while she waited until it was time for her 'to take her chamber'.[35] This curious custom, part religious, part medical, part feminine mystery, would keep her secluded through the last weeks of pregnancy until she was 'churched', or purified, a month or more after delivery.[36] 'Chamber' must be understood in the usual court sense of a suite of rooms, duplicating the normal privy chamber suite but specially prepared, with an oratory (prayer was often the only obstetric help available), 'the rich font of Canterbury' (in case a weak baby needed instant baptism), and heavy, draught-proof hangings. Outside, her presence chamber was divided by a curtain, beyond which the queen stayed for the whole time; a special 'bed of state' was built there for her to preside on, instead of the usual chair. The male officers of her household were never openly allowed further than the outer or great chamber, where they had to kick their heels in attendance while their duties were taken over by the ladies of the court. Details of the arrangements were handed on from one royal confinement to the next, so that in late July Katherine of Aragon's former chamberlain had sent the necessary papers to Cromwell to be passed to the new incumbent, and in early August the carpenters and joiners moved into Greenwich, where the confinement was to take place.[37]

On Thursday the 21st Anne and Henry together left Windsor for Whitehall. After spending the weekend there they went on to Greenwich, where Anne took formal leave of the masculine world on the Tuesday following.[38] With his wife in her chamber, Henry took his mind off his anxieties by planning a splendid joust to mark what he hoped would be the safe delivery of a son to be called Henry or Edward, but he was not left in suspense for long. His daughter was born at three in the afternoon on Sunday, 7 September.[39]

The sex of the baby was some disappointment to Anne and Henry. The pundits (all but one) had been predicting a son, and Chapuys made the most of this. There is, however, no evidence of the crushing psychological blow that some have supposed. After all the alarms, Anne had had an easy labour; the child was perfect and took after her father.[40] Henry's predominant emotion was relief. The jousts, of course were abandoned; as with the arrival of Mary in 1516, public celebrations for the birth of a princess were low-key, but a herald immediately proclaimed this first of Henry's 'legitimate' children, while the choristers of the Chapel Royal sang the *Te Deum*.[41] Letters announcing the news were sent out far and wide, a second and public *Te Deum* was sung at St Paul's, and preparations were at once put in hand for a magnificent christening on Wednesday, 10 September, to be followed by bonfires and free wine in London.[42] Edward Hall waxed eloquent over the ceremony: the procession from the Great Hall at Greenwich, along a carpet of green rushes and between hangings of arras, to the church of the Observant Friars; the lavish arrangements in the church, and the splendour of those taking part. Elizabeth was brought back from the ceremony that autumn afternoon, escorted by over 500 lighted torches. Henry had, as the French noted (again their ambassador was a guest of honour), ensured that once more 'the whole occasion was so perfect that nothing was lacking.'[43]

The occasion was also used to humiliate Anne's critics even further. The friary itself had been the centre for the most vehement and public opposition to the divorce. The name Elizabeth was given to the child, rather than the name of one of the godmothers, deliberately to identify her with the royal dynasty, especially Henry VIII's mother. The marquis of Exeter was called on to carry 'the taper of virgin wax'; the duke of Suffolk escorted the child; John, Lord Hussey, 'Lady Mary's' chamberlain, helped to carry the canopy. Most striking of all, Katherine's friend, the marchioness of Exeter, was one of the godmothers, and it was common knowledge that 'she really wanted to have nothing to do with this,' but took part 'so as not to displease the king'; the need for her to give an impressive christening present as well – three engraved silver-gilt bowls with covers – can only have rubbed salt into the wound.[44] Humiliation for the conservatives was accentuated by the triumphant role played by the Boleyns and the Howards and their allies. Among the twenty-one participants listed by Hall, there were Anne's father and brother and eight Howard connections, Thomas Cranmer (as godfather), one person who was linked to William Brereton and another to Thomas Cromwell.[45] We also know that Cromwell himself was among the observers; he had been largely responsible for the success of the coronation and it seems probable that he organized the christening as well.[46] Those who had backed the Boleyn marriage might well triumph. Anne and Henry had won.

Or had they? Hindsight suggests that there is another and more disturbing conclusion that should have been drawn from this impressive end to a climactic twelve months – twelve months that had made Anne, still only the younger daughter of a newly elevated earl, first lady marquis of Pembroke, then the king's wife, next the queen crowned and finally mother of the heir to the throne. The birth of Elizabeth may have cemented the relationship between the parents, but it undeniably weakened Anne's position in the eyes of the world. Before the marriage she had seemed to embody the hope of a son for England; in pregnancy she could be presented as the promise that that hope would be fulfilled. But with a daughter in the cradle, Anne had still to establish her claim to the throne. The birth of Elizabeth undid much of what the coronation had set out to achieve; Anne Boleyn remained a pretender. If she had had a son in September 1533, her position would have been beyond challenge. All but the most intransigent of Katherine's friends would have seen the wisdom and advantage of accepting the new heir and his mother; the Boleyn marriage would have become the accepted reality in political life, and court faction would have realigned accordingly. Charles V would have recognized that the restoration of Katherine and Mary was a lost cause. Even Mary herself would have been hard put to resist the prior claims of a boy. Katherine of Aragon was able to resist demotion of herself and her daughter because she had powerful Habsburg connections. Anne Boleyn had no such protection. The birth of a son would have given her precisely the objective endorsement she lacked; passion would have been under-pinned by parenthood. As it was, the birth of a daughter ensured that Anne would continue under pressure from both enemies at court and hostility abroad. It also kept Mary's claim alive; even if she were of doubtful legitimacy, so was Elizabeth, and age and the imperial connection made her much the stronger candidate as heir presumptive. Thus instead of faction being stabilized by the marriage, the coronation and the birth of a prince, the arrival of Elizabeth revived and perpetuated instability. Security would come only if Anne could have a son.

PART III

ANNE THE QUEEN

A ROYAL MARRIAGE

A MONG the relics of Henry VIII's daughter Mary is a book of prayers where the page devoted to intercessions for women with child is said to be stained with tears.[1] In the later twentieth century the problem of childlessness attracts considerable attention in the Western world, but no pressure on the would-be mother today can match the peculiar strain on a sixteenth-century queen. Her essential function was to bear sons; otherwise she was a failure. Princesses of the blood were brought up to see this as their destiny. Anne Boleyn had won her way by education, personality and courage, but now she had to accept that success as an individual was unimportant against biological success or failure. Only one thing was now expected of her. Her stepdaughter Mary fiercely resented Anne and rejoiced at her discomfiture, but she too would come to know the private physiological hell of the childless Tudor wife. Anne had described children as 'the greatest consolation in the world', but the Spanish ambassador had the right of it when he wrote of Mary years later that 'the queen's lying-in is the foundation of everything.'[2]

To have a son, one son – that was all that was necessary. Surely that was not too difficult in an age of large families; surely that could not be difficult with a husband like Henry, who at the time (and since) was recognized as a 'fleshly' man, fond of women, and a sexual predator.[3] All that might seem necessary was a healthy wife, and sons would arrive; Anne had only to lie back and do her duty for England. And when healthy sons did not arrive – as they had not arrived to Katherine before her – it was obvious where to place the blame. Yet this is wide of the mark. The popular idea that our ancestors reproduced themselves with the efficiency of some populations today is a fallacy. Even among the nobility, where birth rates and child survival rates were higher than among the general population, large families were by no means the rule, and there were many instances of childlessness or of couples that produced only daughters. Guaranteeing a male heir was no more possible than it has ever been. Nor was Henry as the popular image would have him. As well as the difficulties and hazards of conception and pregnancy in an age when medical knowledge and practice were more of a danger than a help, Anne had to contend with a husband who was anything but a good prospect for paternity.

The evidence that Henry VIII had sexual problems is, first of all, circumstantial. Between 1509 and 1547 he is known, or can be presumed, to have had sexual relations over some months or years with eight women – that is, his six wives and his two known mistresses, Elizabeth Blount and Mary Boleyn. Only four of the eight conceived, and we may note that the last time was at New Year 1537, when Henry was only 45.[4] As well as the poor record of conceptions, Henry's partners had a poor record of maternal success. Setting aside Jane Seymour, who died after the birth of her one child, only three pregnancies produced a healthy infant, one each for Katherine of Aragon, Elizabeth Blount and Anne Boleyn. There were other pregnancies that ended in miscarriage, stillbirth or neonatal death. Anne herself had two miscarriages – that is, in two of her three known pregnancies. Katherine, her predecessor, had an even poorer record – five failures in six, and over a much longer period.[5]

This case history raises the possibility that it was Henry and not his wives who was responsible for silence in the royal nursery. At a distance of some 500 years, deficiencies in fertility or genetic defects can be nothing more than suspicions, and the one thing which seems clear is that venereal disease was not to blame (as is sometimes suggested). The king's medical history and the record of the medicines he was prescribed show quite clearly that he was never treated for syphilis, unlike, for instance, Francis I, who was heavily infected. The leg ulcer which periodically darkened Henry's life from 1528, and is often assumed to be venereal, has been convincingly argued to be caused by osteomyelitis resulting from falls in the tiltyard.[6] We have, of course, to take into account the health and fertility of the women concerned. There is the evidence about the difficulty of Anne's first pregnancy, and the five years' delay between her agreement to marry Henry and the commencement of sexual relations in 1532, when she was over thirty, must have lessened her chances of successfully having children. But all the women could not have been bad risks. There is nothing in the history of Katherine of Aragon's sisters to suggest a tendency to impaired childbearing; Mary Boleyn became pregnant as soon as she left Henry for her husband, William Carey; the same was true of Katherine Parr, when she married Thomas Seymour after the king's death in 1547.

Whether or not Henry suffered from any congenital impairment, there is direct evidence to support the suggestion that he was, or became, partially impotent. In 1540 his divorce from Anne of Cleves was secured on the ground of the king's sexual incapacity. Henry's own deposition admitted his lack 'of the will and power to consummate the same', though he slept regularly with his fourth wife for several months.[7] But the blame was placed on his German bride's lack of attractiveness (and allegedly suspect virginity), while concern for the obvious reflection on Henry led his doctors to pass on to the court (with some details decently veiled in Latin) the king's assurance that he 'thought himself able to do the act with other but not with her'.[8] The same problem had bedevilled the relationship with Anne Boleyn. At his trial in May 1536, George Boleyn was asked whether Anne had told his wife that the king was incapable of sexual intercourse, implying that he was unable to attain or sustain an erection (*le Roy n'estoit habile en cas de soy copuler avec femme et qu'il n'avoit ne vertu ne puissance*). Such a delicate question was handed to Rochford in writing, and the story was that it was reading the allegation out aloud which sealed his fate.[9] That is improbable, but the asking of such an amazing question is proof enough that doubts about the king's vigour did circulate.

We can, indeed, take the matter a little further.[10] No hint of impotence had prevented Anne rapidly becoming pregnant in December 1532, and she was pregnant again just over a year later, three or four months after the birth of Elizabeth. But we have a most revealing insight into the way Henry's mind worked in an interview with Chapuys in April 1533.[11] When the ambassador pointed out that a new wife to replace Katherine by no means guaranteed children, Henry asked excitedly, 'Am I not a man like other men? Am I not? Am I not?' The ambassador had, he declared, no reason at all to deny this – he was not privy to all the royal secrets (that is, that Anne was then four months pregnant). Quite obviously, Henry associated virility and sexual potency with having children. The birth of Elizabeth reassured him, as did the second pregnancy, and Chapuys noted in February 1534 that Henry was quite happy that he would have a son this time.[12] By April the queen's condition was obvious, and Henry's confidence is seen in the highly elaborate silver cradle which was ordered from his goldsmith, Cornelius Hayes, with Tudor roses, precious stones, gold-embroidered bedding and cloth-of-gold baby clothes.[13] All was well as late as July, and then tragedy struck.[14] Anne miscarried.[15]

The secret of the disaster was so well kept that it was only on 23 September that Chapuys reported that the queen – or 'the lady', as he insisted on calling her – was not, after all, to have a child.[16] We have to remember that the ambassador had been out of touch with the court while it was on summer progress. Away from the public eye, with a smaller number of attendants than at other times and with both Anne and Henry desperate to conceal it, total discretion was achieved. But the damage had been done. The ominous reminder of Katherine's history brought all Henry's doubts flooding back. It is notorious that anxiety about virility can lead to a loss of sexual potency, and this is what seems to have happened with Henry. Perhaps, after all, he was not 'like other men'. The confidence and stimulation of the new marriage was shattered, and it would be more than a year before Henry could make Anne pregnant again.

It is, perhaps, significant that it was after the miscarriage in the summer of 1534 that the first hints appear of a rift between Henry and Anne. Tradition regularly backdates these by a year, to the last weeks before Elizabeth was born. On 13 August 1533 Chapuys had reported that he saw signs of hope for Katherine in Henry's long absence from Anne.[17] Even more dramatic, the imperial ambassador at Rome passed on to Charles V the story that the king's loss of affection in the face of Anne Boleyn's arrogance had led him to switch his attentions to someone else.[18] On 3 September Chapuys had remarked on how lucky Anne was to have received her magnificent state bed (for her presence chamber) two months previously, since:

> Full of jealousy – and not without reason – she used words to the king which he did not like, and he told her that she must shut her eyes and endure, just like others who were worthier than she, and that she ought to know that he could humiliate her in only a moment longer that it had taken to exalt her!

After this, Henry refused to speak to her for two or three days.[19]

The case looks ominous. Yet under scrutiny the story evaporates. The report from Rome of the alleged mistress is an error in dating by a modern editor: it belongs to the late autumn of 1534.[20] Several letters from different sources reported independently that in July and August 1533 the royal couple were in good health and enjoying life; Henry was in tearing high spirits at the thought of the baby.[21] As for Chapuys, he was reporting gossip. He was in London in August, so how could he know that Henry was neglecting Anne at Windsor? Furthermore, the ambassador himself tells us that when Henry specially summoned him to meet the king and his council, the meeting was away from the court, at

Guildford, and was disguised as a hunting trip precisely to avoid causing Anne anxiety.[22] In any case, a second letter from Chapuys admitted that he had got things wrong.[23] His September report of Henry's bitter remarks to Anne is also suspect. By that time Anne had 'taken her chamber', so the most the ambassador could have had to work on was a story about what had allegedly been overheard by an attendant during one of the king's private visits. For a husband who, a few weeks before, had invented a hunting trip to protect his wife from anxiety, the speech as recorded seems inconsistent, to say the least. Perhaps in the discomfort of her late pregnancy Anne did make a scene, perhaps Henry's own worry caused him to bite back – such an episode would be neither surprising nor significant. Or perhaps the whole was exaggerated by the wishful thinking of Katherine's ally, the marchioness of Exeter, who was probably the ambassador's informant.[24] Whatever occurred or did not occur, we need to note that Chapuys himself dismissed it as 'a lovers quarrel'. So should we.

The rumours reaching the Low Countries via the Hanse merchants painted quite a different picture – not of a besotted king coming to his senses but of one who was more besotted than ever, constantly at his wife's side and letting court discipline go to the dogs.[25] And that may be much nearer the truth. In late October 1533 Anne's maids of honour were repeating Henry's brazen remark that he loved the queen so much that he would beg alms from door to door rather than give her up. The two are still described as 'merry'. Henry kept Anne, as always, in selective touch with diplomatic affairs, visited Elizabeth after the baby was given her own special establishment in December 1533, and gave the general impression of remaining firmly under his wife's thumb. As the session of parliament due in January 1534 approached, Anne helped her husband to whip opinion into line, and Henry warned the marquis of Exeter that the least signs of disloyalty would cost him (and anyone else) his head.[26]

So much for the 1533 rumours. The story that trouble arose between Henry VIII and Anne a year later is based, as are almost all the specific stories of friction between them, on Chapuys.[27] It was his report that the imperial ambassador at Rome was echoing, and the first notice of the affair is in the despatches sent to Brussels in late September. What Chapuys reported was that with the ending of his hope for a child, Henry had 'renewed and increased the love that he had had previously towards another very beautiful maid of honour [*demoiselle de court*]'. Anne had responded by wanting to dismiss the girl, but Henry had been most upset and had informed her that 'she had good reason to be content with what he had done for her, which he would not do again, if he were starting afresh, that she should remember where she had come from, and many other things.'[28] A fortnight later Chapuys had more to tell. George Boleyn's wife had been forbidden the court because she had plotted with Anne to pick a quarrel with Henry's new fancy and force her to withdraw.[29] Anne's influence was wilting daily, and the rival was sending encouraging messages to Mary that her trials were nearly over. Many of the courtiers were encouraging Henry's new interest, with the intention of separating him from Anne. The affair was still going on in December, when the king was again annoyed at Anne's complaints, but by the end of February it was finished. In her place was Anne's own cousin, Margaret Shelton, the daughter of the governess in charge of Elizabeth and Mary.[30]

What should be made of all this? The conventional interpretation is that the marriage of Henry VIII and Anne Boleyn was breaking or had broken up. Descriptions of Anne after her fall are projected back to present Henry as a king whose life was made 'hell' by a 'barren, old and ill-natured baggage'. 'Importunity' (nagging) and 'cursedness' had destroyed every vestige of the king's great passion. Henry, the great lover, was looking elsewhere.[31] Yet the facts do not justify such a picture. We have to remember the tainted sources of so much of Chapuys' information – the story of the king's annoyance at Anne's complaints in December 1534 came from her enemy Carewe.[32] The ambassador could also get things wrong, as he himself recognized. His pleasure on New Year's Day 1535 that even such a Boleyn partisan as the earl of Northumberland was turning against the regime had changed to doubt within the month.[33] His earliest mention of the alleged 1534 romance carried the warning not to attach too much importance to it, since Henry was so fickle and Anne knew how to manage him. Even in the last weeks of her life, when she faced the threat of Jane Seymour, Chapuys would still be sceptical.

There are also reasons why we should be sceptical. Who was this new flame in 1534? Some have supposed that she was Jane Seymour, but there is nothing to support this, and when Jane does appear on the scene there is no reference to any earlier affair with Henry. How are we to understand the arrival of Margaret Shelton? This has been variously interpreted as a deliberate piece of procuring by Anne in order to supplant her anonymous rival, or by Norfolk to supplant Anne, from whom he was now estranged. And why does Margaret Shelton suddenly drop out of the limelight? Another problem is the role of Lady Rochford, who is otherwise known as Anne's enemy. As to the reference that the king was renewing a *previous* relationship, that too becomes mysterious with the redating of the supposed 1533 Rome despatch, unless we see a connection with Chapuys' cryptic remark in 1533 that Anne's jealousy was 'not without reason'.

A far more likely explanation for the evidence than the 'irretrievable breakdown of marriage' is, in fact, suggested by Chapuys' own description. The relationship between Henry and this new lady was first of all a limited one; it would be significant, he said, only if it lasted and if it became warmer than it had been. And what that limitation was he indicated by describing the girl as 'the damsel whom the king has been accustomed to serve'. 'Accustomed to serve' – this is the language of chivalry. What Henry had done was to offer his knightly service to a new 'mistress' for the game of courtly love. As in the case of Anne Boleyn herself, this could sometimes lead to a genuine relationship, but Chapuys is clear that in this case it did not do so, nor when the king's interest turned to Madge Shelton. Indeed, it is easy to see why an amour which remained superficial should attract a man anxious to appear a terror with the women, but deeply uncertain of his capacities.

Henry was probably doing no more than substitute 'a lady to serve' while his wife was recovering from the miscarriage, but it is nevertheless obvious why Anne would object to Henry's gallantry. She had for six years been Henry's 'sovereign lady'; she had been the adored mistress. How could she accept the new situation and see Henry become the 'servant' of another woman? And she must have suspected, as we do, that Henry would not have relegated her to conventional treatment as queen if she had had a son. It was not, however, a mere matter of pride or hurt feelings, or of failure to adjust to her new position. Henry might well get annoyed at such over-sensitiveness: he was behaving as the rules said a king should behave, so why could not she? There had never been any rivalry between Katherine and the ladies whose praises Henry had sung over the years, who had danced with him, who had played the game of flirtation with him; she was the queen and her place at the head of the court and of society was hers by incontestable right. Anne, however, knew that her right to that title was contested. She could not take for granted the protection of recognized status; she still had to compete for and win the king's favour. She was in the contradictory position of being expected to behave as a queen, but having to continue to challenge as a mistress.

The place that Anne occupied was flawed in another way. She was now a wife and mother. Convention – and Henry was nothing if not conventional – dictated that she should now take a subservient role, neither disputing with nor presuming to criticize her husband. Once the honeymoon period was over, the husband was expected to find his concerns in the masculine world; he was certainly not expected to live in his wife's pocket. One of the worst things that Flemish rumour could say about Henry was that he did just this and let the court go to the devil. Anne, however, as we have seen, was that Tudor rarity, the self-made woman. She was where she was by virtue of her own abilities and what she had made of herself, not by virtue of wealth or family.[34] It was asking a great deal of her, after so many years, to abandon the formula that had brought her the most amazing success.

There was one thing more. However complicated the motivation, however we gloss the phrase, Henry and Anne were lovers. In an outburst against the new regime, a Colchester monk had declared with contempt that when the two had been at Calais in 1532, Anne had followed Henry round like a dog.[35] Certainly they quarrelled, and not simply on Chapuys' evidence. The Venetian ambassador reported in June 1535 that Henry had had more than enough of his new queen.[36] The alleged remark of 1534 that he could reduce Anne as rapidly as he had raised her makes sense only if Henry was blazingly angry at the time, for at the very same moment he had Cromwell hard at work drafting the statute which would vest the succession to the Crown in the children of the Boleyn marriage. If he said it, he certainly did not mean it. As Chapuys had said of the friction between Henry and Anne over the new 'mistress', these were lovers' quarrels and not much notice should be taken of them. If some of them were provoked by Anne's natural resentment at the king's shallow gallantries to other ladies, at other times the queen could laugh about such flirtations. She nearly caused an international incident at a banquet on 1 December 1533 by bursting into laughter when she was talking to the French ambassador. Offended, he had asked, 'How now, Madam! Are you amusing yourself at my expense or what?' Trying to mollify him, Anne explained that Henry had gone to bring another guest for her to entertain, and an important one, but on the way he had met a lady and the errand had gone completely out of his head.[37]

In the relationship between Henry and his second wife, storm followed sunshine, sunshine followed storm. A fortnight after the Venetian report that Henry was satiated with her, the returning French ambassador told Paris that she was very much in charge.[38] In an ultimate sense, the problems of Henry and Anne arose from the fact that there was emotion in the relationship. Occasionally even Chapuys' hostile spin cannot disguise the intimacy. On St John's Eve 1535, Henry went to see a pageant and so enjoyed it that he sent Anne a message suggesting that she must see the next performance on St Peter's Eve, five days later.[39] The conventions of the day, of courtly love, of sovereign and consort, were simply not capable of accommodating the fierce passions which united Anne Boleyn and Henry Tudor.[40]

The tensions within the marriage were undoubtedly made worse by external problems. The most immediate was Katherine's daughter, Mary. Aged 17 at the time of the second marriage, she was adamant in refusing to recognize Anne and her child, despite her father's determination that she should do so. Though Katherine helped to inspire Mary, Henry could largely ignore his ex-wife. Relegation to a modest establishment away from court was a proper fate for a princess dowager, and Katherine was not one who would, so he believed, ever plot against him. Mary, on the other hand, was undeniably part of the royal family. Intelligent, gifted, not unattractive and of a winning disposition, popularity made her adherence more important and her opposition more dangerous. Disloyalty to Henry did not seem like disloyalty when it was thought to be support for the rightful heir, and increasingly Mary became the focus for all dislike of Anne and everything she appeared to represent.

Henry saw Mary's behaviour as a straightforward case of disobedience and, despite his obvious affection for her, put increasing pressure on his daughter to conform.[41] She lost her royal style and her household; she was forced as 'a bastard' to join the household of the 'legitimate' Elizabeth and give her half-sister precedence at all times, under the oversight of Elizabeth's governess, Anne Shelton, who was Anne's aunt. Mary was kept away from her mother, isolated from her former friends and servants, and deliberately slighted and ignored by Henry. The result was a head-on clash with a Tudor obstinacy as great as his own, but at the cost of permanent damage to Mary. The story is not pleasant to modern reading, although what was questioned at the time – and not only by her committed supporters – was not so much the treatment meted out for her disobedience as the unfairness of it. According to Chapuys, when Norfolk and Rochford rebuked Anne Shelton for being too lenient with Mary – the family must not fail the king – Anne's aunt replied that even if Mary was the bastard daughter of a poor gentleman she would deserve respect and kindness because of the girl she was.[42] Henry disagreed. He was determined to break his daughter's will. It was Anne Boleyn, however, who got the blame. To believe it was her fault made it much easier for Charles V to keep up some civil relationship with Henry, much easier for Mary (and Katherine) to resist pressure. Her father could not really know; he was not to blame; it was the harpy who had her claws in him. When Anne was dead

Mary discovered the truth, and the abasement which Henry exacted scarred her for life.

This is not to say that Anne was guiltless. Chapuys' letters are full of her railing against Mary and of her lurid threats to curb 'her proud Spanish blood'.[43] But much though the ambassador warned of poison and worse, Anne was ranting, not thinking. There is an obvious ring of truth in his story that, assuming she would be regent if, as expected, Henry went to Calais to meet Francis I again, Anne swore to seize that chance to put Mary to death. When her brother pointed out, very simply, that this would anger the king, she retorted that she did not care, even if she was burned for doing it.[44] So Anne's language was violent and threatening, but this sprang not from malevolence but from self-defence. For Henry, Mary was a disobedient child. For Anne, she was much more. Her obstinacy was an insult, a denial of Anne's own identity and integrity. If Katherine's marriage was valid, then she, Anne, was a whore. And there was an added twist. In canon law – and this fact was widely appreciated at court – a child born to a couple who at the time were apparently lawfully married, remained legitimate even if it was subsequently found that the union had been invalid.[45] If anyone had, as the lawyers put it, been conceived 'in good faith', that person was Mary, and by refusing to recognize the priority of Elizabeth she was in effect asserting her own claim to be the heir to the throne.[46] For Anne, therefore, the negative policy of disciplining Mary and excluding her from court was a defeat; every day that she withheld the positive endorsement of Anne's title made the queen's weakness more obvious. Active conformity alone would do. Anne knew that the stakes could not be higher: 'She is my death, and I am hers.'[47]

Mary was certainly frustrating to deal with, and this is a further reason for Anne's outbursts and her support for harsh treatment. On three distinct occasions Anne put out feelers for a better relationship. In February or March 1534, when on a visit to Elizabeth, she offered to welcome Mary if she would accept her as queen, and to reconcile her with her father.[48] Mary's response was that she knew no queen but her mother, but that if the king's mistress would intercede with her father she would be grateful. Even after this offensiveness Anne tried again, before leaving the house in high dudgeon, vowing to repress such impudence. It was perhaps a few months later, when the two half-sisters were at Eltham, that Anne and Mary found themselves in the palace chapel together.[49] An attendant, either out of kindness or in order to see the fun, or as part of a deliberate plot to set Anne up, told her that Mary had acknowledged her before leaving. The queen immediately sent a message to the princess apologizing for not noticing, saying that 'she desires that this may be an entrance of friendly correspondence, which your grace shall find completely to be embraced on her part.' Mary's reply could not have been ruder. From the publicity of her dinner table she declared that the queen could not possibly have sent the message; she was 'so far from this place'. The messenger should have said 'the Lady Anne Boleyn, for I can acknowledge no other queen but my mother, nor esteem them my friends who are not hers.' Her curtsey, she explained piously, had been made to the altar, 'to her maker and mine'. The story has a good pedigree, but it is a late one, and we may doubt whether even Mary dared to be that offensive. But even allowing considerable discount, Anne would still have been justified in being offended.

It is not surprising to find after this that Anne left Mary to reflect for eighteen months before trying again, but with Katherine on her deathbed and Anne certain that she was pregnant again, Lady Shelton was instructed to press once more the queen's desire to be kind.[50] This was followed, after the old queen had died, by a message that if Mary would obey the king she would find Anne a second mother, and be asked for minimal courtesies only. When Mary replied discouragingly that she would obey her father as far as honour and conscience allowed, Anne tried to frighten and warn her at the same time. She wrote a letter to Anne Shelton, which was left 'by accident' in Mary's oratory where she read it, as clearly she was expected to do. Efforts to persuade Mary were, Anne wrote, to cease; they had been an attempt to save the girl from her own folly, not because Anne needed her acquiescence. One may think that only partly true, but there is no doubt of the chilling realism of Anne's warning of what would happen to Mary if, as she expected, the child she was carrying was a son: 'I have daily experience that the king's wisdom is such as not to esteem her repentance of her rudeness and unnatural obstinacy when she has no choice.' This was only literal truth, as anyone knew who was familiar with Henry's behaviour towards those who had offended him but sought mercy too late.[51] Mary took a copy of the letter for Chapuys, restored the original to its place and ignored the warning.

Mary's failure to accept Anne was one problem, but it was linked to another: an increasing opposition to the queen among the nation at large and among the elite. There is no doubt that a good deal of Anne's unpopularity was on account of Mary and the repudiation of Katherine. The sentiment was frequently found among women, for obvious reasons.[52] Margaret Chanseler, from Bradfield St Clare in Suffolk, demonstrated a particularly personal line in invective when she said that Anne was a 'goggle-eyed whore . . . God save Queen Katherine.'[53] Feelings were usually more circumspect among the elite, but no less real. Anne could not but notice the readiness of courtiers who accompanied her to see Elizabeth, to slink off at the same time to pay their respects to Mary.[54]

Much of the hostility to Anne was, however, also associated with a dislike of Henry's recent policies: in the first place taxation, but even more, interference with the Church. The abbot of Whitby declared comprehensively that 'the king's grace was ruled by one common stewed [professional] whore, Anne Bullan, who made all the spirituality to be beggared and the temporalty also.'[55] The less educated could be just as direct, in their own way. On Monday, 4 May 1534, a certain Henry Kylbie was attending to his master's horse in the stables of the White Horse in Cambridge. Perhaps the horse was lame; we do not know. At any rate, Kylbie had arrived with his Mr Pachett the Saturday before on the way from London to Leicester, and he was heartily sick of waiting. The ostler of the inn strolled over and the two got into conversation. Did he know, the ostler asked, that there was no longer a pope, only a bishop of Rome? As a man who may well have stabled the horses of the Cambridge Reformers when they met in the inn for their evenings of convivial but risky debate, the ostler evidently was well up in religious gossip. Not so Henry Kylbie. There was a pope, he insisted, and anyone who said contrary was 'a strong heretic'. When the ostler, playing his ace, said that 'the king's grace held of his part,' Henry lost his common sense and his temper. Both ostler and king were heretics, and 'this business had never been if the king had not married Anne Bullen.' Angry words became blows, and ended with Henry breaking the ostler's head.[56]

Those at court in the forefront of the battle for the papal headship did their best to exploit such plebeian sentiments. When two of the Observant Friars on the run from Greenwich were asked whether Elizabeth had been christened in cold water or in hot they replied, 'hot water, but it was not hot enough.'[57] When the Blessed Richard Reynolds, 'the most learned monk in England', went to the scaffold with the Carthusian martyrs in May 1535, he took with him John Hale, a Cambridge Fellow and vicar of Isleworth in Middlesex, who was part of a cell which Reynolds had been feeding with gossip about the morals of the Boleyn family and the falseness of Henry's claim to be supreme head.[58] It was Hale that confessed that Mary Boleyn's son by William Carey had been pointed out to him as the king's son. The group also dabbled in the cryptic prophecies that circulated widely in moments of crisis – that a queen (Anne) would be burned, that Henry was the cursed Mouldwarp prophesied by Merlin, and so forth.

We know of all these cases, and more, because of the tireless efforts of Thomas Cromwell to monitor every possible source of discontent. He also put together an armoury of statutory weapons for use if necessary.[59] The Succession Act required every person to take an oath to support the Boleyn marriage, and a massive attempt was made to swear all adult males in the country.[60] The Act also made it a treasonable offence to write or act against the marriage with Anne, with lesser penalties for gossip or for refusing to take the oath specified, while the clergy and Church institutions were also forced, in a variety of ways, to abjure the power of the pope. Another Act, passed later in the year, extended the definition of treason to cover anything spoken, written or done which deprived the king of his title or seriously defamed him.[61] And as the Acts came into force the popular voice was clear – Anne was responsible. When George Cavendish wrote his *Verses* in Mary's reign he has Anne saying:

> I was the author why laws were made
> For speaking against me, to endanger the innocent;
> And with great oaths I found out the trade [method]
> To burden men's conscience: thus I did invent
> My seed to advance; it was my full intent
> Lineally to succeed in this Imperial crown:
> But how soon hath God brought my purpose down![62]

She was assumed to be encouraging her husband's brutality, particularly the deaths of the Carthusians and of Fisher and More.[63] 'The people, horrified to see such unprecedented and brutal atrocities, muttered in whispers about these events and often blamed Queen Anne.'[64] Since Sir Thomas More himself had, according to a report circulating on the continent within weeks of his death, said at his trial that the real reason for condemning him was his refusal to assent to the Boleyn marriage, it was all too plausible to present Anne as a latter-day Salome demanding the head of a new saint.[65]

More dangerous than popular gossip was opposition was within the political establishment. How much Anne, or for that matter Henry, knew of this, it is impossible to say. Henry was aware of the possibility. He said of Katherine: 'The lady Katherine is a proud, stubborn woman of very high courage. If she took it into her head to take her daughter's part, she could quite easily take the field, muster a great array, and wage against me a war as fierce as any her mother Isabella ever waged in Spain.'[66] Such evidence as we have is hidden deep in the correspondence of Chapuys. If we are to believe him, a majority of the magnates – in importance, if not in numbers – were critical of the way matters were going. Many were even talking of actual revolt against Henry. But as with most magnate conspiracy, it was only talk. Apart from the initial psychological effort needed to break free from the chain of loyalty to the king, the odds against a successful concerted rising were high, and dissatisfaction with affairs had to compete with the very real desire not to come into the open before success was assured. Much of the conversation and messages reaching Chapuys were, indeed, attempts to avoid that decision by having Charles V take the first step.[67]

The duke of Norfolk's increasing dissatisfaction was of a different kind. Anne and her supporters were leaving him behind. He had been prepared for her to be a Boleyn when taking risks, but he fully expected her to be a Howard when enjoying success. The queen, however, had a good memory. Despite the fact that his mistress was one of her ladies-in-waiting, the duke found himself in much less favour than he felt was his due. Perhaps Anne felt that she had paid her debts to the Howards by persuading Henry to marry his illegitimate son, the duke of Richmond, to her cousin Mary without the large payment the king would normally have expected for disposing of so valuable a match.[68] Norfolk, however, was soon complaining that the sweets were going elsewhere.[69] Perhaps even more than by Anne, Thomas Howard was put out by Cromwell, who was now in effective and obvious charge. The secretary's usefulness and record of success were, in fact, taking him out of the Boleyn clientage and making him an independent political figure in his own right, but he maintained his links with the queen and to outward appearances was still her man – perhaps Anne herself did not recognize the change.[70] Yet Norfolk, though sometimes goaded into grumbling in public, remained loyal to Henry and acquiescent towards the Boleyn marriage. And this was not only because his only known principle was self-advantage ensured by spaniel-like sycophancy to the king, or because there was still some advantage in having a niece on the throne. The point was that Anne had only a daughter and a miscarriage to her credit; for Norfolk to have the king's only living son as a son-in-law was too good a hand to throw away. And it was one which made Anne and her brother increasingly suspicious.[71]

The problems facing Anne – the lack of a son, the intransigence of Mary, increasing unpopularity – were compounded by the international situation. As always, the controlling reality was the hostility between Francis I and Charles V. It was one of the periods of 'cold' rather than 'hot' war, with the antagonists each regarding Henry and his quarrel with the pope as one extra circumstance to be exploited or contained, as appropriate. Henry's principal reliance continued to be on his 'good brother Francis', but he was never confident that England's interests were wholly safe there. Thus, in a relationship which has rightly been described as 'ambiguous', Henry and Francis each tried to exploit their alliance in a thoroughly selfish fashion.[72] The result was a great deal of suspicion, one of the other, and with Anne personifying to the English the French connection, the opprobrium fell on her.

Anne had been fully involved in the attempt to postpone the meeting between Henry and Francis proposed for the summer of 1534, and the expected arrival of a French embassy in the following November was prepared for with care and enthusiasm.[73] The admiral of France was, however, bringing an imperial suggestion for a settlement between Charles and Francis which involved the marriage of Mary to the dauphin. This shocked Anne because it implied that her patron, Francis, considered that Mary had a better claim to the English throne than her own daughter, and matters were made even worse when the French were lukewarm at Henry's counter-proposal for a marriage between Elizabeth and Francis's third son. The result was a perceptible coolness on the side both of the French envoy and the queen. Anne nevertheless did her best to improve matters towards the end of the mission, and we hear of her entertaining the admiral at the final great banquet, while Henry sought out Gontier, the ambassador's secretary and a man of considerable influence, to come to talk with his wife. It was a different story two months later, when she saw Gontier on his return with the answer to the proposal about Elizabeth.[74] Anne upbraided him for the time he had taken, which had aroused all Henry's suspicions. If the French did not allay them at once, her own position would become impossible, for she felt herself more precarious than even before she was married; she could say no more, with everyone watching, including Henry, and she could not write to the envoy or see him again. She then withdrew, and Henry went off dancing.

We have to remember that in sixteenth-century diplomacy – if not in diplomacy generally – what is said often had an ulterior motive, and in February 1535 the intention of the English was certainly to frighten the French.[75] However, on this occasion Anne's concern convinced Gontier: 'I assure you, my lord, by what I can make out, she is not at her ease.'[76] And there is no doubt that she had good cause to fear the loss of French support, as their hard bargaining caused Henry to press Francis for more and more public commitment to his cause.[77] Nor were matters improved by a banquet given by the resident French ambassador, where many of Anne's critics were present to hear gruesome tales of the persecution of unorthodox religious opinions then in full swing in Paris.[78] Eventually a meeting of representatives was arranged for Calais in May 1535. Cromwell was at first to go himself, but he fell ill, and the Boleyn interest was represented instead by Rochford – characteristically, Chapuys suggested that Cromwell was evading the responsibility for any failure.[79] And fail the negotiations did, despite a rapid return to England by Rochford in search of further instructions.[80] When he arrived, it was significant that he first had a long discussion with his sister before reporting to the king himself; and it was noted that Anne's conversation had suddenly become bitterly anti-French. Nor did she stop at talk. Within a fortnight she had put on a notable entertainment at Hanworth, with a guest list both large and select, but she pointedly omitted the French resident, who was duly and satisfactorily incensed.[81] Soon after, Bishop Fisher and Thomas More were executed, and Francis I's reaction to the news, laced with comments about Anne's morals, lowered the temperature of Anglo-French relations still further.[82] Anne might be 'wholly French', but by the summer of 1535 this threatened to become yet another liability, and a serious one.

Plate 1 *Anne Boleyn*, by an anonymous painter. Hever Castle, Kent.

Plate 2 *Anne Boleyn*, by an anonymous painter. Private collection. Courtesy Bradford Art Galleries and Museums.

Plate 3 *Anne Boleyn*, attributed to John Hoskins. Duke of Buccleuch and Queensberry.

Plate 4 *Anna Boloenia Henrici VIII Coniunx*, by Reynold Elsrack. Henry Holland, *Bazilowlogia* (1618).

Plate 5 *Unknown Lady*, by Hans Holbein the younger, inscribed *Anne Bullen decollata fuit Londini 19 May 1536.* © The British Museum.

Plate 6 *Unknown Lady*, by Hans Holbein the younger, inscribed *Anna Bollein Queen.* The Royal Collection © 2004, Her Majesty Queen Elizabeth II.

Plate 7a Detail of 7 showing the image of Anne.

Plate 7 (left) Queen Elizabeth's ring. The Chequers Trust.

Plate 8 A portrait medal of *Anne Boleyn*, inscribed *A.R. THE MOOST HAPPI ANNO 1534.* © The British Museum.

Plate 9 (left) *Henry VIII*, attributed to Lucas Hornebolte. The Royal Collection © 2004, Her Majesty Queen Elizabeth II.

Plate 10 (right) *Katherine of Aragon*, attributed to Lucas Hornebolte. National Portrait Gallery, London.

Plate 11 *Margaret of Austria*, by Bernard van Orley. Musées Royaux des Beaux-Arts Brussels.

Plate 12 *Charles V*, attributed to Lucas Homebolte. V&A Picture Library.

Plate 13 Mechelen, the palace of Margaret of Austria: the southern range from the courtyard.

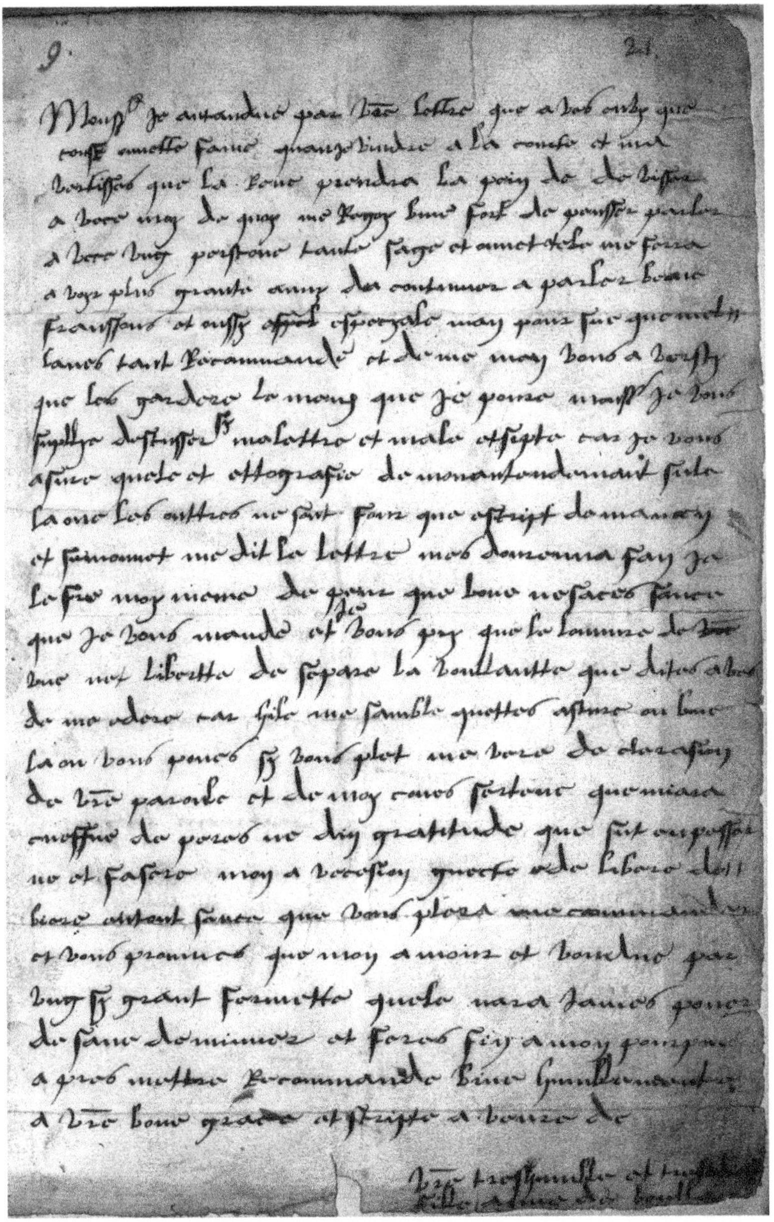

9.

21

Plate 14 Letter from Anne Boleyn to her father from Terveuren, Belgium, 1513–14. By permission of the Master and Fellows of Corpus Christi College, Cambridge.

Plate 15 *Claude of France*, by Jean Clouet.

Plate 16 *Francis I* circa 1514, by an
anonymous painter. The State
Hermitage Museum, St Petersburg.

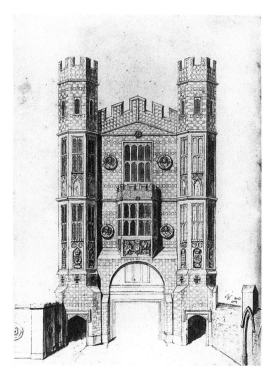

Plate 17 *Whitehall: Holbein Gate*, by George Vertue. The Society of Antiquaries of London.

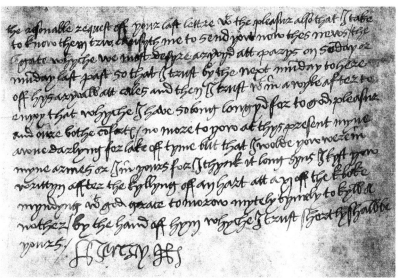

Plate 18 A letter from Henry VIII to Anne Boleyn, September 1528: 'the reasonable request off your last lettre with the pleasure also that I take to know them trw, causyth me to send yow now thes news. The legate whyche we most desyre aryvyd att Parys on Sonday or Munday last past, so that I trust by the next Munday to here off hys aryvall att Cales, and then I trust within a wyle after to enyoy that whyche I have so long longyd for, to God's pleasur and owre bothe comfortes. No more to yow at thys present, myne owne darlyng, for lake off tyme, but that I wolde you were in myne armes or I in yours, for I thynk it long syns I kyst yow. Writtyn affter the kyllyng off an hart at xj off the kloke, myndyng with God's grace tomorow mytely tymely to kyll a nother. By the hand off hym whyche I trust shortly shallbe yours. Henry R.'
© Biblioteca Apostolica Vaticana, Vat. Lat. 3731A.

Plate 19 *The Annunciation*, from an illuminated Book of Hours (King's MS 9, fol. 66v). British Library, London. Anne's signature has been cut from below the couplet she wrote to Henry:

Be daly prove you shalle me fynde,
To be to you bothe loving and kynde.

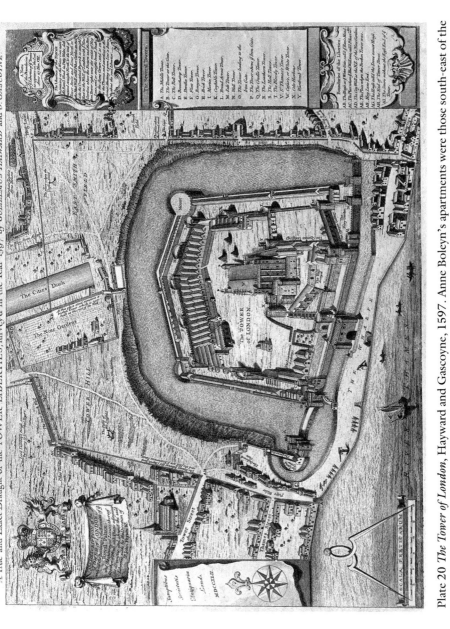

Plate 20 *The Tower of London*, Hayward and Gascoyne, 1597. Anne Boleyn's apartments were those south-east of the White Tower, labelled 'The Queen's Lodgings'; the structure north of 'The Lieuten.ᵗˢ Lodgings' is not the scaffold; that was erected as needed, probably north of the White Tower, fifty yards to the east of the chapel of St Peter ad Vincula. The Society of Antiquaries of London.

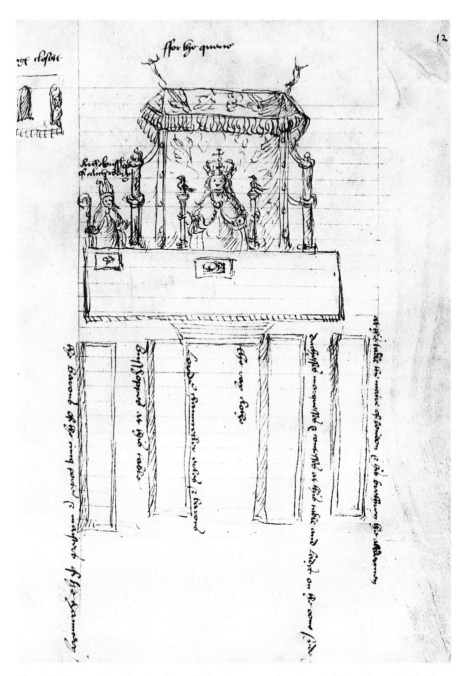

Plate 21 The seating plan for Anne Boleyn's coronation feast in Westminster Hall. Top left – 'kinges closett'; top centre – 'ffor the quene'; next to Anne – 'Archebusshop of canterbury'. The legends by the tables read, from the right: 'at this table the maire of london & his brethren the alldermen'; 'duchesses marquesses & contesses at this table and ladys on the oone side &c'; 'the ray clothe'; 'lorde chauncellor erles & barons'; 'busshoppes at this table'; 'the barons of the cincq portes & maisters of the chauncery'. MS Harley 41, f. 12r. British Library, London.

Plate 22 A printed Book of Hours (Paris *c.*1528 [*sic*]), Hever Castle, Kent.

Plate 23 A Psalter (Paris or Rouen 1529–1532), showing Anne Boleyn's monograms and the black lion of Rochford. Sotheby's.

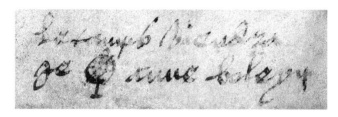

Plate 24 Anne Boleyn's inscription, astrolabe and signature (detail from plate 25): *le temps viendra / Je* [device] *anne boleyn*. Hever Castle, Kent.

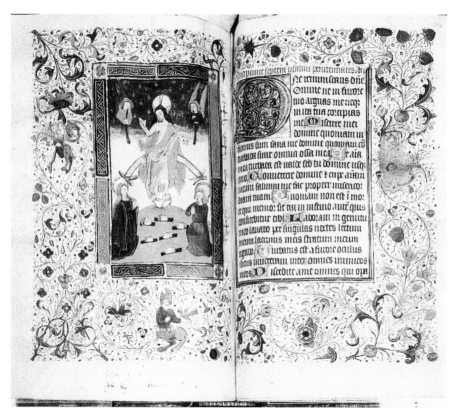

Plate 25 A Book of Hours (Bruges *c.*1450) owned by Anne Boleyn. Hever Castle, Kent.

Plate 26 Page 4 of 'Motets and Chansons', a music book at the Royal College of Music (MS 1070), possibly showing a falcon pecking a pomegranate. Royal College of Music.

Plate 27 Lower right corner of the front of 'The Ecclesiaste', Percy MS 465 showing the clasp (possibly after Holbein) and the corner guard decorated with the falcon badge. Duke of Northumberland, Alnwick Castle.

Plate 28 New Testament (Antwerp, 1534) owned by Anne Boleyn. The translation is by William Tyndale. British Library, London.

Plate 29 The back cover of the second volume of *La Saincte Bible en Francoys* (Antwerp, 1534) owned by Anne Boleyn. The translation is by Lefèvre d'Etaples. The binding is partly original. The text reads 'LA GRACE ET LA VERITE EST FAICTE PAR JESV CHRIST'. British Library, London.

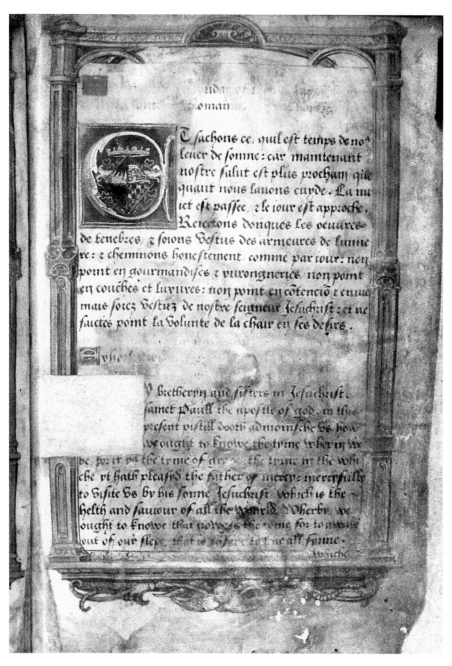

Plate 30 Jacques Lefèvre d'Etaples, 'The Pistellis and Gospelles for the LII Sondayes in the Yere', translated for Anne Boleyn by her brother George. MS Hartley 6561, f. 4r. British Library, London.

Plate 31 (top) The falcon badge: a historiated letter T from 'The Ecclesiaste', Percy MS 465, f. 23r. Duke of Northumberland, Alnwick Castle.

Plate 32 (bottom left) A symbolic design: a historiated letter E from 'The Ecclesiaste', Percy MS 465, f. 34r. Duke of Northumberland, Alnwick Castle.

Plate 33 (bottom right) A symbolic design: a historiated letter I from 'The Ecclesiaste', Percy MS 465, f. 54r. Duke of Northumberland, Alnwick Castle.

Plate 34 Coffer of the organ screen in the chapel of King's College, Cambridge: detail showing falcon badges and 'HAmat' monogram. King's College, Cambridge.

Plate 35 Detail from the southernmost bay of the organ screen in King's College Chapel.

Plate 36 The Boleyn Cup, 1535–6, St. John the Baptist's Church, Cirencester. The knop is a falcon on the roses. Photo © Woodmansterne.

Plate 37 Clock (partly sixteenth-century). The weights are engraved 'H' and 'A', with lovers' knots and the mottoes 'Dieu et Mon Droit' and 'The Most Happy'. The Royal Collection © 2004, Her Majesty Queen Elizabeth II.

Plate 38 (above) *Mount Parnassus*, by Hans Holbein the younger. BPK Berlin / Kupferstichkabinett.

Plate 39 (left) *Nude Spraying Liquid from her Right Breast*, by Hans Holbein the younger. Oeffentliche Kunstsammlung Basel, Kupferstichkabinett.

Plate 40 *Design for a Standing Cup*, by Hans Holbein the younger. Anne's falcon badge is visible between the left and centre satyrs. Oeffentliche Kunstsammlung Basel, Kupferstichkabinett.

Plate 41 *Design for a Table Fountain*, by Hans Holbein the younger. Oeffentliche Kunstsammlung Basel, Kupferstichkabinett.

Plate 42 *Solomon and the Queen of Sheba*, by Hans Holbein the younger. The Royal Collection © 2004, Her Majesty Queen Elizabeth II.

Plate 43 *Solomon and the Queen of Sheba*, attributed to Gallion Hone. King's College Chapel, window 4D. Originally, in the top corner above the queen, was a putto holding a shield with the monogram 'HR' (now misplaced). King's College, Cambridge.

Plate 44 *'The Ambassadors', Jean de Dinteville and George de Selve* by Hans Holbein the younger. National Gallery, London.

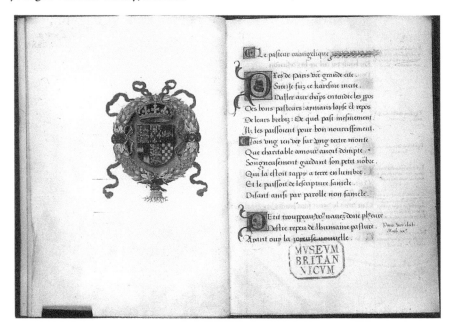

Plate 45 Frontispiece and title-page of *Le Pasteur évangélique*, Royal MS 16E. British Library, London. Anne Boleyn's falcon badge hangs from the wreath below her arms. The silver (white) is oxidized.

Plate 46 A detail of the valance from the hangings of a bed, decorated with the monogram 'HA' and a design of honeysuckle and acorns (white satin and black velvet appliqué). Burrell Collection, Glasgow Museums.

Plate 47 A carving of Anne Boleyn's shield of arms in the Beauchamp Tower, Tower of London. The adjacent carvings were made by later prisoners in the sixteenth century. Crown Copyright: Historic Royal Palaces.

Plate 48 (above) 'Antique' terracotta plaque by Giovanni da Maiano at Hanworth Park, formerly at Anne's house at Hanworth. Reproduced by permission of English Heritage, NMR.

Plate 49 (right) A brass of Thomas Boleyn from Hever Church. V&A Picture Library.

Plate 50 *Princess Mary*, attributed to Lucas Hornebolte. Private collection.

Plate 51 *Jane Seymour*, attributed to Lucas Hornebolte. Sudeley Castle.

Plate 52 *Thomas Wolsey*, by an anonymous painter. National Portrait Gallery, London.

Plate 53 '*Mistress Anne sends her tablet of gold*' by Dr Butts to the sick Wolsey: an Elizabethan illustration for *Thomas Wolsey late Cardinall, his lyffe and deathe*, by George Cavendish. The Bodleian Library, Oxford, MS Douce 363, fol. 76r. The messenger is Dr Butts; Wolsey is shown in bed on the right.

Plate 54 *Thomas Howard, duke of Norfolk*, by Hans Holbein the younger. The Royal Collection © 2004, Her Majesty Queen Elizabeth II.

Plate 55 *Thomas Cromwell*, by Hans Holbein the younger. Copyright The Frick Collection, New York.

Plate 56 *William Warham*, by Hans Holbein the younger. The Royal Collection © 2004, Her Majesty Queen Elizabeth II.

Plate 57 *Thomas Cranmer*, by Gerlach Flicke. National Portrait Gallery, London.

Plate 58 (top left) *Henry Percy, earl of Northumberland* (detail from the Black Book of the Garter). The wall medallion at Alnwick is a latecopy. By permission of the Dean and Canons of Windsor.

Plate 59 (top right) *James Butler, earl of Ormonde*, by Hans Holbein the younger. The Royal Collection © 2004, Her Majesty Queen Elizabeth II.

Plate 60 (bottom left) *Thomas Wyatt*, by Hans Holbein the younger. The Royal Collection © 2004, Her Majesty Queen Elizabeth II.

Plate 61 (bottom right) *Nicolas Bourbon*, by Hans Holbein the younger. The Royal Collection © 2004, Her Majesty Queen Elizabeth II.

Plate 62 *Mary Tudor, Queen of France, and Charles Brandon, duke of Suffolk*, by an anonymous painter. By kind permission of the Duke of Bedford and the Trustees of the Bedford Estates. Copyright is assigned to the Duke of Bedford and the Trustees of the Bedford Estates.

Plate 63 *Nicholas Carewe*, by Hans Holbein the younger. Oeffentliche Kunstsammlung Basel, Kupferstichkabinett.

Plate 64 *Princess Elizabeth* aged about thirteen by an anonymous painter. The Royal Collection © 2004, Her Majesty Queen Elizabeth II.

INFLUENCE, POWER AND WEALTH

IT is a reflection on the essential maleness of history, of those who made most of it and those who have written most of it, that we still do not know enough about the position of the queen consort in England. Of her place beside the king in public appearances, yes; of her success or failure as a mother, yes; but very little about the queen in her own right, and this despite the fact that in the royal household 'the king's side' was always matched by a smaller but parallel 'queen's side'. Some studies are appearing, principally of individual consorts, but much of the necessary record material no longer exists or is almost inextricably mixed up with the king's archive.

This partial submerging of a queen in the overall royal entourage is one explanation for there being less notice of Anne Boleyn's active participation in public affairs after 1533. Her influence on Henry could now be exercised in private. She also attracted less attention from observers because marriage had settled the issues in which she had been personally a combatant. There are nevertheless sufficient signs that her influence remained, even though exercised behind the scenes. Indeed, for many, Anne mattered precisely because of her closeness to Henry. A petition to the king in 1535 describes her as having 'the name to be a mediatrix betwixt your grace and high justice'.[1] Anne's remarkable achievement in securing the grant to her uncle, the duke of Norfolk, of the wardship and marriage of the king's own son, the duke of Richmond, free, gratis and for nothing, demonstrates how effective she could be.[2] She saw influence as something to be used with circumspection, as her refusal to seek a customs exemption for Lady Lisle in 1532 had demonstrated, but it was there.[3]

The queen was, however, more than a seductive voice on a pillow. As early as 1531 the duke of Milan was advised that he should treat her as a force in her own right, and equip his ambassador with some novel and flashy Italian knick-knacks for her, worth 1200 crowns or so.[4] We have already seen her involvement in diplomatic contacts with France, and it is notable how English envoys seem anxious to keep in with her.[5] Then again, when Lord Leonard Grey returned to Ireland in the autumn of 1535 with considerable forces and substantial rewards from the king, Anne was present at the final briefing session; she gave Grey the chain round her waist, worth 100 marks, and a purse of twenty golden sovereigns.[6] Above all, Anne was very active in religious matters, as will appear.[7]

Following marriage, Anne's potential as a patron grew too. One of Lord Lisle's correspondents assured him that, 'I have moved a friend of mine about the queen concerning Master Howard's matter, and I mistrust not but that I shall obtain your desire in that behalf.'[8] On another occasion she wrote, apparently to Cromwell, asking him to assist the career of a young man deserted by his family and saying that he could not 'do a better deed for the increase of your eternal reward in the world to come'.[9] She would also act directly. The dean and chapter of Exeter, expecting soon to have a farm to rent out on the expiry of a lease, found themselves invited by Anne to grant a new sixty-year term to a nominee of hers at the existing rent; a letter from Anne was reckoned in 1531 to smooth matters at Calais for her uncle Lord Edmund Howard, the controller there; when she became aware of an excessive delay in one chancery suit, she thought nothing of writing to the chancellor, requesting speedier action.[10] A dispute between rival claimants to a vacancy in the Calais garrison, in which Cromwell and everybody who mattered at court seem to have had one special interest or another, found Anne too initially supporting one of the candidates. Then she changed her mind and issued letters in favour of George Gainsford, a relative of her receiver-general, George Taylor, which were described 'as a stay' if 'the worst fall' – in effect, a veto.[11] In all this too, Anne presumably received her share of the gratuities which custom dictated that suppliants should offer. The vicar of Halifax, in contention with Sir Richard Tempest and his own parishioners, allegedly declared that he has 'cast such a flower' into the queen's lap that he would be listened to as readily as Sir Richard.[12]

Anne was, of course, no isolated figure. She still had behind her the supporters who had brought her to power and were now intent on reaping the fruits of that power. Not enough is yet known of the ramifications of the Boleyn faction – its presence and policy can be principally demonstrated in religious matters – but its dominance in affairs generally is beyond doubt. The archbishop of Canterbury was Thomas Cranmer. The lord privy seal was Anne's father, the king's secretary was Thomas Cromwell. The lord chancellor was Thomas Audley, to whom Anne lent a house at Havering in 1535 to escape the plague in London.[13] Of these posts, all but the privy seal had, at the start of 1532, been in the hands of men loyal to Katherine of Aragon and her daughter Mary. In the privy chamber, Anne's brother was one of the two noblemen, and Henry Norris was groom of the stool and the king's right-hand man, while lesser men like Brereton occupied a number of the other places there. Potential rivals were in eclipse. Stephen Gardiner kept a low profile, intent on regaining royal favour; thanks to his expertise he was soon back at work for the king, but the seriousness of his rift with Henry (which never really healed) was known as far afield as Padua.[14] The dukes of Norfolk and Suffolk continued to attend court from time to time, but Suffolk in particular counted for little. Not only was he now only the king's ex-brother-in-law, but by 1535 he was being stripped of his assets to pay outstanding debts to the Crown.[15] Chapuys' letters show how often the ambassador now had to deal with Cromwell, instead of either Brandon or Howard. This is not to say that all supporters of Katherine and Mary were in eclipse. Several of the privy chamber were still in the king's good books – Carewe, Neville, Browne and Russell – while even Exeter kept his place as a counter to Rochford. There can, however, be no doubt where the weight of royal favour lay. Chapuys told the emperor's adviser, Granvelle, in November 1535 that Cromwell, the king's secretary, stood above everybody except 'the Lady'.[16]

In all of this, particular interest inevitably concentrates on this last, the relationship between Anne and Cromwell. Although he would eventually grow to become a cuckoo in the Boleyn nest, until then there is nothing to suggest that Anne ever saw the secretary as other than her loyal dependant, and to all outward appearances he remained 'her man'. She appointed him her high steward at £20 a year.[17] Cromwell sent the warrant for the delivery to Anne of her letters patent creating her lady marquis of Pembroke, and Cromwell probably directed the survey of her Welsh pro-perties; the file copy of the survey instructions remained with him, along with a copy of the order to local royal officers to assist and an estimate of the value of the properties inspected.[18] The success of the coronation was largely attributed to him. And this close relationship continued. Its tone is very clear in a letter Anne sent to the minister when his ally, Christopher Hales, the attorney-general, began to meddle with a wardship which had been granted to her:

Master Secretary, I pray you despatch with speed this matter, for mine honour lies much on it, and what should the king's attorney do with Pointz's obligation, since I have the child by the king's grace's gift, but only to trouble him hereafter, which by no means I will suffer, and thus fare you well as I would ye did. Your loving mistress, Anne the Queen.[19]

Privately Chapuys bracketed together 'the king, the concubine, Cromwell and their adherents', and Anne and Cromwell were linked together as far away as Lübeck.[20] In 1535 we even find Cromwell having a book of physick sought out and sent to Anne.[21]

On occasion we see queen and minister working together. In 1531 Sir Thomas Wharton tried to forestall their anticipated opposition by securing a supporting letter from the king and sending individual copies to both Cromwell and Anne.[22] In September 1535, Hugh Latimer wrote to Cromwell:

I trust you have not forgotten my last suit, with which I was minded to have gone to the king; but the queen, remembering at what end my lord of Salisbury was, said it would be enough to leave it to you.[23]

The closeness of Anne and Cromwell is also evident in the way petitioners would approach the queen through Cromwell. Soon after Anne's recognition, Edmund Bonner wrote to Cromwell from Rome, sending:

a letter of congratulation to the queen's highness, to be delivered unto her by your hands; not doubting but like wise, as of your goodness without any my merit it hath pleased you to set me forward, so it may like you with her grace so to set forth my service and good will to her grace.[24]

Audley secured his refuge from the plague by asking the minister to approach the queen.[25] Christopher Hales even expected Cromwell to pass letters on to her.[26]

Anne, in her turn, was known to be an effective influence on Cromwell. In 1532 Richard Lyst, a Franciscan lay brother at Greenwich, sent her news of the misdeeds of his superior, John Forrest, in the clear expectation that she would pass it on.[27] When the earl of Oxford despaired of securing certain hereditary offices by direct application to the king, he approached Anne and, armed with her support, then wrote to Cromwell.[28] A drive against river obstructions late in 1535 threatened the weir which Lady

Lisle's family owned at Umberleigh in Devon. Direct applications to Cromwell and the king were found useless, but it was thought worth considering an alternative application via the queen.[29] When the lord deputy of Ireland died on the last day of 1535, his widow, Anne Skeffington, petitioned Cromwell to secure payment of his overdue fees, plus free passage from Ireland where the new lord deputy, Leonard Grey again, was trying to hang on to as many as possible of the assets of his predecessor. Yet at the same time Lady Skeffington wrote directly to Anne, imploring her to secure the king's backing for her petition to the minister.[30] We may see something of the same sort in the efforts of Elizabeth Staynings to secure access to the queen.[31] Her husband, Walter, was in prison for debt, but despite the king's instructions to Cromwell to sort the matter out, as well as the reminders of Norris and other men of standing, the minister always pleaded pressure of other work. This has been interpreted as Cromwell frustrating the intervention of the privy chamber, but it reads more like an attempt to use administrative delay to assist Staynings' creditors, or in order to exact the price for Cromwell's own services too.[32] Mrs Staynings, knowing that she would soon have to leave London to have the child she was carrying, wrote to her aunt, the Viscountess Lisle, then in Calais: 'Good madam, if there be any lady of your acquaintance in the court that you think that is familiar or great with the queen, that it please you to write unto her that I may resort unto her sometime, for I feel me that trouble is not yet at an end.'[33]

There is some evidence to suggest that Anne was seen as particularly receptive to female petitioners. We have already had instances concerning Lady Skeffington and Elizabeth Staynings. The latter's husband too, when desperately looking for protection in April 1533, sought the help of his wife's aunt, who was in attendance on the newly proclaimed Anne: 'I judge in my mind the queen will be good and gracious lady unto me upon your special request, to see me have the laws executed indifferently between me and my adversaries that keeps me in prison.'[34] Over the winter of 1535–6 Katherine Howard, Anne's aunt, was trying to secure a separation from her second husband, Henry, Lord Daubeney. She told Cromwell that the only assistance she was receiving was from the queen herself, and this despite the strenuous efforts which were being made to destroy her standing with Anne.[35] The help may have been very practical indeed; Lord Daubeney, who was certainly pleading financial hardship at one stage, reached an amicable agreement with his wife after Anne's father had made available £400.

Anne's elevation to the throne also had repercussions within her family, of which she seems to have become the accepted head. When the son of Sir William Courteney of Powderham died, the father was approached to assist in a match between his widowed daughter-in-law and Cromwell's nephew, Richard Cromwell.[36] Courteney, however, replied that the girl was a near relative of the queen and he would not move unless Cromwell could send him a request from the king that he should promote the match, to guarantee him against 'her grace's displeasure'. This puts into a somewhat different light the rustication from court of Anne's sister Mary. In 1534 she had secretly married 'young Stafford', one of the hangers-on at court, the second son of minor Midlands gentry, and the marriage had been discovered only when it became obvious she was pregnant. The reason for Anne's rigorous attitude was not pique or pride. It was that Mary had failed to recognize her position, both by making what was an obvious *mésalliance* for a queen's sister, and by failing to accept the directing role which Anne now possessed within the Boleyn family.[37] Mary should have been under no illusions. As early as November 1530 the king had given Anne £20 to redeem a jewel Mary possessed, presumably one he had given her. Anne, the wife, wanted no one to remember Mary, the mistress.[38]

At a less intimate level, Anne could also exercise influence through her household. There were the jobs it could offer. Stephen Vaughan, a merchant adventurer and an old friend of Cromwell, tried very hard to get his wife accepted as the new queen's silk woman, even to the extent of her submitting unsolicited – and in the event unnoticed – samples of her work.[39] Nor was this the only instance of competition for places in the queen's household, although few were as direct as David ap Powell, who applied to Cromwell for a post either as yeoman purveyor to the queen or yeoman of her carriage, because he had not the capital to trade any longer.[40] Anne's service was evidently lucrative – her uncle, Edmund Howard, saw it as much more profitable than his position as controller at Calais.[41] Men who entered her service would also have hoped eventually to qualify for a bonus in the form of a royal grant of some kind, though in the event few had achieved this by 1536. A number of questionable characters even made a living by claiming to belong to the queen's staff. A priest called James Billingford, alias Kettilbye, had a good thing going in the Midlands in 1534–5, where he conducted visitations of a number of abbeys, styling himself variously as Anne's chaplain, her (or her father's) kinsman, her scholar, the nephew of the duke of Norfolk and servant to Thomas Cromwell – just the sort of person whom it would be wise to 'sweeten'; after all, Lady Lisle thought it an investment to send venison to the queen's genuine servants.[42]

Given this, it is very strange that only a few of Anne Boleyn's staff appear to have had personal ties with their mistress. George Taylor, her receiver-general, we have already met. He had been in Anne's service for several years before the coronation and may have begun as a lawyer, but although his was a post of importance, carrying a fee of £50 a year, he has correctly, if unkindly, been described as 'part of the background'.[43] That can certainly not be said of Cromwell, her high steward, but as we have seen he appears to have been involved in major policy issues for Anne, not day-to-day affairs. Her chancellor was her uncle, James Boleyn, with whom, as with Cromwell, she shared some sympathies, but her aunt by marriage was not among her favourite attendants.[44] Her other ladies included her sister-in-law and a cousin, Madge Shelton.[45] However, these names apart, Anne's staff appears not to have come from her existing contacts. The chamberlain at the head of her household was an insignificant peer elevated in 1529, Thomas, Lord Burgh of Gainsborough. His first achievement for Anne was to vandalize Katherine of Aragon's barge and his last to assist in her trial, while his subsequent performance in the Lincolnshire Rising of 1536 would be loyal but lacklustre.[46] Her master of the horse was William Coffin, a professional household administrator, actively concerned with the staffing of his department; he was later to serve Jane Seymour in the same capacity.[47] Lord Burgh's deputy was Sir Edward Baynton. He, as we shall see, shared some of Anne's religious opinions, but he was a long-term career courtier and went on to serve as vice-chamberlain to all Henry VIII's later wives.[48] John Uvedale (or Udall), her secretary, had even longer in royal service, beginning as an exchequer clerk under Henry VII and ending as treasurer for the northern garrisons under Edward VI. He also combined what was obviously a part-time post for Anne with that of secretary to the duke of Richmond.[49] Her surveyor, John Smith, was a professional auditor who, on Anne's death, simply transferred to Jane Seymour.[50] Judging by her predecessor, the council running Anne's affairs (which met in a specific 'council chamber' with a designated keeper) would have consisted at least of her chancellor (Boleyn), receiver-general (Taylor) and surveyor (Smith), plus an auditor, attorney-general, solicitor-general and a clerk, all yet to be identified.[51] The queen would also have retained six lawyers 'of counsel' and three court attorneys.

The senior men of the household, according to later stories, were
forced to keep a wary eye out for their mistress, who would intervene in
person if things went awry. William Latymer, one of her chaplains, recalled
that, as soon as she had set up her household, she called her 'council and
other officers' to a formal meeting, where she lectured them on their
duties. Her first requirements, he remembered, were honour, equity and
justice, and value for money: 'such mediocrity [balance] that neither
sparely pinching, nor prodigally consuming, may restrain you from
the golden mean of frugal expending.' Since we would have expected
Latymer to see true religion as the first priority, we may take his story as
genuine. Virtue, however, was not to be neglected, especially among
the lower members of the court, who were to attend chapel daily,
behave with propriety, and keep away from 'infamous places' and 'evil,
lewd and ungodly disposed brothels'. Persistent offenders were to
be sacked and barred from the court for life, 'to their utter shame'.[52]
Nor was Anne's direction merely verbal. We know of an actual case
where she intervened to get the bill of her supplier of cheese and
butter paid.[53]

Remarkably, we have for the whole period of Anne Boleyn's marriage a
continuous record of the relationship with this court of one couple –
Arthur, Viscount Lisle, and his wife, Honor – and of their attempt to
build up and exploit a relationship with the queen in every possible way.
To the good fortune of the historian, Lord Lisle's posting to Calais as lord
deputy necessarily meant not only that many things which in England
might have been left to word of mouth had to be put down on paper, but
that there was a positive demand for a steady flow of news and gossip to
keep starved exiles in the swim. By then Lady Lisle had been close to Anne
for some time, and it was in her entourage that she got her first sight of
Calais in October 1532.[54] Her last engagement before returning there in
June 1533 was undoubtedly to take part in the queen's coronation procession.[55] Once in Calais, Honor Lisle became meticulous in ensuring that
she was recommended whenever possible to the queen and to the ladies of
the court – out of sight was certainly not going to be out of mind if she
could help it. A series of luxuries and elegant presents crossed the channel
at suitable intervals, such as a dozen and a half dotterels (a special treat,
and taken live to Dover so as to arrive fresh) accompanied with a linnet in a
cage.[56] Lady Lisle's favourite dog had to go the same way to obtain one
favour, with some of the kudos going to Francis Bryan, the intermediary.[57]
Anne became very fond of the animal, as Margery Horsman explained
to Lady Lisle almost a year later: 'The queen's grace setteth much store by

a pretty dog, and her grace delighted so much in little Purkoy that after he was dead of a fall there durst nobody tell her grace of it, till it pleased the king's highness to tell her grace of it.'[58] Evidently the suggestion was that Purquoy should be replaced – with a dog, not a bitch, Mrs Horsman insisted – but subsequent advice was that the queen did not want another.[59] The proposal some months later of a monkey was firmly turned down. Anne could not abide the sight of them.[60]

The Lisle correspondence preserves an informative vignette of the business of new year's gifts, seen from the point of view of the Lisle agent, John Hussey:

> On New Year's even, by the advice of Mr. Taylor the queen's receiver, I delivered your gift unto her grace by the hands of Mr Receiver. And I then being in [the] place where her grace's New Year gifts were appointing, her grace came in, and asked me how your ladyship did, and how you liked Calais. To which I answered that your ladyship did like it well, and that you humbly recommended you unto her grace, praying God to send her grace many good New Years.[61]

From all points of view this was a perfect occasion – a gift and its accompanying sentiments graciously received, and the attention of the recipient to the giver caught, if only for a moment. And Anne confirmed the renewed bond by a gift to Honor Lisle of a pair of gold beads, with tassels, weighing three ounces, and that value even greater since they were 'of her grace's own wearing'.[62]

It was soon after this that Lady Lisle decided that she must secure from the queen a livery kirtle to demonstrate that, though on detached duty with her husband, she was properly part of Anne's household.[63] A present of cloth, specially chosen and then submitted for approval beforehand to Taylor, the receiver-general, reminded Anne of Lady Lisle, and the promise was graciously given. It was, however, a year before the kirtle was actually supplied, partly because the queen had to select a suitable one, but more because Taylor saw delay as a means to further with the Lisles the interests of his relative, George Gainsford. Although Lady Lisle was always careful to keep in with the queen's attendants with periodic messages and tokens, in this case Taylor forbade any inducement to the wardrobe staff to expedite the gift, so that Hussey found himself 'driven off' five times in six days. Even when Hussey, it seems, slipped the staff a bolt of cambric behind the receiver's back, everything had to wait for Taylor's elegant note of apology – he had, he said, been away – and even then it would be two months before the livery was actually handed over on 18 March to another of the Lisle servants, Thomas Warley:

> This day in the morning I had a token of Mistress Margery that the kirtle should be delivered to me in the queen's grace wardrobe, where upon sight of the said token I received the said kirtle, which is of cloth of gold paned...After I had received the kirtle I returned to the queen's chamber to give thanks to Mistress Margery, and to know if she would anything to your ladyship, which as [she] then was returned into the privy chamber, so that since, I could not speak to her. But, God willing, I intend to be at the court tomorrow...And if it may please your ladyship to send a letter to Mistress Margery and another to Mr. George Taylor, giving them thanks for their pains, as your ladyship knows better what is to be done than my simpleness can advise you...Also that it may please your ladyship to remember them of the queen's wardrobe, as shall be your pleasure.[64]

'Royal patronage' was definitely not a simple business of asking and receiving. It is sad that after such endeavours to secure so magnificent a garment, Lady Lisle could only have worn it for a matter of weeks; after May Day 1536, there was no value in the livery of a disgraced queen.

To the influence that Anne exercised personally must be added her importance as a rich woman. This gave her not only economic power but social authority. One glimpse of this is revealed in a mix-up of instructions about settling a local dispute in Worcestershire; her attorney-general was issuing contrary orders to those her council had already issued, so that her officers on the spot were being 'dishonested'.[65] Her estate began with the grant in the summer of 1532 of the manors of Hanworth and Cold Kennington, and this was followed up in October by additional lands to support her new status as lady marquis of Pembroke.[66] On 1 January 1533 came the gift of almost a hundredweight of silver plate, mostly gilt.[67] Three months later, further grants transferred lands and revenues that had, till then, been held by Katherine of Aragon as part of her jointure, and in the following year parliament confirmed these to Anne as her dower and jointure.[68] Taken together, the grants accumulated in 1532 and 1533 made Anne wealthier than Katherine had been or any of Henry's future wives would be.[69] A good deal of her income came in fee farms charged on particular properties, but a proportion arose from estates which Anne was given to administer and exploit.[70] The statute which vested this extra property in the new queen also cancelled all existing offices and leases except where these were straight economic contracts, in which case titleholders were given until the autumn to establish that they were exempt from this resumption. The measure (which had the immediate effect of negating all the favours granted by Katherine) raised a number of eyebrows, but we would be wrong to see it primarily as a political move.[71] Even someone as obviously committed to Katherine as Sir Edward Neville of the privy chamber was confirmed by Anne in the tenancy he had had from her predecessor.[72]

The resumption seems, in fact, to have had a primarily economic intention – squeezing more money from the tenants – and a number of papers have survived from what was obviously a serious attempt at tighter management. There was a detailed settlement of accounts to March 1533 with Katherine's receiver, and a careful note of outstanding liabilities. A complete list of annuitants was prepared as well.[73] That Anne herself was directly involved in what was going on is clear from a memorandum evidently drawn up for a discussion with her.[74] It brought the queen up to date with the activities of her council, which directed and supervised the commissioners actually involved in the resettlement of the tenancies, and it listed major policy issues which required her decision. Thus she was asked what she wanted done with former tenants of Katherine who were offering good terms for the renewal of title, what the policy should be towards applicants for replacement leases who missed the Michaelmas deadline, and what the position was of those who had offered an increased rent instead of a lump sum cash down. All this makes it very much more likely that Anne herself had been similarly involved in the ripple of activity which had followed the grant to her of the lands to support her new dignity as marquis of Pembroke in September 1532.[75] A commission of her men had taken immediate possession of the properties and set to work on a detailed survey of the estates, which was completed by the following March.

Unfortunately, the only complete summary of Anne's finances to survive is for the year 1534–5, without the detailed accounts from which it was compiled.[76] Nevertheless it does provide a general outline of her expenditure. It shows that Taylor, her receiver-general, had to account in that year for £6381 8s. 9¾d. Of this, £4423 3s. 1¾d. came from her English estates, and £633 13s. 10d. from Wales, a total of £5056 16s. 11¾d. from lands overall. Taylor received the remainder, £1324 11s., from the queen's 'coffers', clearly to fund expenditure at seasons when the flow of rents proved inadequate for day-to-day expenses. This shows that already, after only two and a half years of marriage, Anne's reserves were at least equivalent to 25 per cent of her annual income. In fact they were evidently more, for at the end of the 1534–5 account Taylor returned

£2508 13s. 1½ d. to the coffers, a net surplus of £1184, or over 20 per cent, on this one year. As this implies, Anne was as yet not saddled with many bad debts or arrears; Taylor had to carry forward a net liability for a mere £32.

On the expenditure side, both the 'Wardrobe of the Robes' and the 'Wardrobe of the Beds' cost surprisingly little. The Robes, which is where Honor Lisle's livery kirtle would eventually have been charged, expended only some £69, the Beds even less, £44. These amounts might suggest that 1534–5 was a freak year, but it is much more probable that these two departments paid bills only after considerable delay. At the time of Anne's death, eight months into the next financial year, the Robes owed over £500 and the Beds £166. The Stables, by contrast, owed only £157 whereas its 1534–5 costs had been nearly £600. Clearly it was only one quarter in arrears – fodder merchants had to be paid.[77]

Almost £1000 went on Wages and Annuities, with nearly £200 on Gifts and Rewards – a further useful reminder of the patronage at the queen's disposal, which, as we have noted, meant for her, as well as for lesser lords, income as well as the exercise of favour. Even Thomas Cromwell had had to pay £99 15s. for his post as high steward.[78] Also in the category of patronage and good lordship must be put the 'rewards for New Year's gifts' which amounted to more than £250 in all, although once again there was some quid pro quo in the form of gifts received. It may be, however, that although the custom was that the king gave and very often received plate at the new year, plate was less the rule in the queen's household. The Manners family, for instance, continued to give Anne elaborately embroidered clothing – frontlets and sleeves – as they had before her marriage, and the gifts of the queen's ladies to Henry were certainly of the same personal sort.[79] In 1534 Anne's mother gave him a velvet case embroidered with the royal arms, containing six collars, three worked with gold and three with silver; her sister-in-law, Lady Rochford, presented a shirt with a collar of silver work.[80] Anne's first gifts to her ladies as queen were palfreys and saddles. In that case too, Anne's choice seem to have been agreed in advance with Henry himself.[81]

By far the largest expenditure in the accounts – no less than £1525 9s. 9¼ d. – fell in the rag-bag category, 'Divers Necessary Emptions'. Some insight into this is given by the list of suppliers to whom Anne owed money in May 1536.[82] This casts a revealing light on the often forgotten economic significance of a royal court, with its contingent of suppliers (mercers, drapers and clothiers) and the army of craft workers – tailors, embroiderers, fustian-maker, silk women, pinner, coffer-maker, gold-wire drawer, skinner, furrier, painter, farrier and a dozen more besides. One of the itemized supporting accounts has survived, presented by William Lok, the mercer most employed by the queen.[83] A leading Londoner, Lok travelled abroad for Anne and at new year 1536 had given her (or possibly Henry) a mother-of-pearl frankincense box mounted on the heads of four silver and gilt dolphins.[84] By a macabre irony, he would also be called on to assist in clearing the Tower of foreigners on the occasion of her execution.[85] His bill covered the three months from late January to late April 1536, and shows Anne spending £40 a month, mainly on clothes for herself and Elizabeth. On top of this, the general haberdashery bill for approximately the same period was £68 4s. 1½d.[86]

What remains something of a mystery is how Anne had financed herself before the Pembroke grant and the gift of a thousand pounds, which accompanied it.[87] She may have had some income from a court post, but the jewel she sent to Henry to indicate that she would marry him must have cost a good deal.[88] Certainly it marked the point when Anne decided that the prospect of a wedding ring was worth real money. Perhaps she turned to her father – she was, after all, now an excellent investment. The subsequent expense of being the king's unacknowledged fiancée would have been even more costly, but here her principal resource seems to have been Henry. That he made her a regular allowance is unlikely. In the two years from November 1529, the earliest for which we have his privy purse accounts, the king met individual bills on Anne's behalf totalling nearly £750.[89] As we have seen, in December 1530 he even paid for his own new year's gift.[90] Her basic living expenses at court were presumably charged on the royal household, but there is a most intriguing privy purse entry for February 1531: £66 13s. 4d. paid to her servant, George Taylor, for purchasing 'the farm at Greenwich to the use of my lady Anne Rochford'.[91] Perhaps this was a 'love nest', perhaps not.[92] Henry also lost a great deal of money to her, playing cards. In ten days in November 1532 he paid out over £50 to Anne, Francis Bryan and Francis Weston.[93] Having a partner outside marriage did not come cheap.

IMAGE

T HE ways in which temperament and personality as well as physique
descend – or fail to descend – from generation to generation are a
never-ending cause of discussion. With Anne Boleyn and her daughter
Elizabeth, we can be sure of the facial resemblance, less sure whether
the daughter's taste for things scholarly and musical was inherited or
was the product of careful education and the atmosphere at the Tudor
court. The parallels, however, are there. It is clear that in dress sense and
wardrobe Anne Boleyn anticipated Elizabeth I's acute awareness of the
politics of ostentation. Each had more than a love of mere finery, rather a
recognition that in order to play the part one must dress the part. The
mother also anticipated the daughter in another way: the exploitation of
the cult of monarchy, which was to reach its height in England in the reign
of 'Gloriana'. The Bible, chivalry, art and – most original in 1533 – the
language of humanism, all were mobilized to present Anne as a divine
ruler. It was not, of course, an approach peculiar to England. There was
an international technique to image-building. Yet between Anne and
Elizabeth there was an uncanny similarity of attitude towards the projec-
tion of monarchy, and of themselves as chosen by God to rule.

The most extensive demonstration of Anne's position and role as queen is
in the elaborate pageants prepared for her coronation procession through
the City of London on 31 May 1533. We have followed the event, but we
have not yet looked closely at the devices that set the scene – and very
revealing they are. They have been criticized as lacking imagination and
technical novelty, but time was largely to blame; machinery could not be
built at a moment's notice. In 1522 there had been ten weeks to arrange
the reception of the Emperor Charles V, while the welcome in 1501 for
Katherine of Aragon had been the climax of two years' work, not the 400
hours allowed in 1533.[1] In spite of this, a hugely impressive display was

mounted which projected exactly the image Henry (and Anne) intended. Edward Hall could say, 'he that saw it not, would not believe it.'[2]

That the initiative in planning came ultimately from Henry VIII is clear. In the case of the intended but abortive coronation of Anne's successor, the actual commission has survived.[3] Clearly based on, but intended to eclipse the celebrations for Anne, it laid down the themes and even the mottoes to be used for twelve main displays, but then left fourteen 'other subtleties to be at the pleasure of the maker'. Apart from the absence of instructions about materials and colours, the order is very similar to contemporary contracts for a painting or a piece of sculpture. Nothing like this survives for Anne, but the sequence of events tells the same tale.[4] The royal order to prepare a water procession from Greenwich and pageants on the route from the Tower to Westminster was received by the mayor on Tuesday, 13 May. The aldermen met the next day and decided on a minimum initial response. Organization of the water pageant was passed to the mayor's livery company (the Haberdashers) which could provide two suitably impressive barges. As for the route to Westminster, the Standard in Cheapside and three of the principal conduits would be 'goodly hanged and garnished' and their fountains supplied with wine, 'with minstrelsy and children singing at every of the said conduits'. However, on such occasions joint discussion with the Crown was the rule, and the City sent four representatives (including the chronicler Edward Hall) to present their plans to 'the king's most honorable counsel to know their minds'.

The meanness of the City's initial plan was, in all probability, a negotiating ploy. If so, the delegates came away from the meeting with all they wanted. The duke of Norfolk and Thomas Cromwell, the counsellors in charge, agreed to lean on the Hanse, the resident community of North German merchants, to fund one of the pageants, royal musicians would be available, the King's Works would find painters and other craftsmen, and the ships in the river would be moved to line the banks and fire salutes. In return, the City asked Norfolk whether he wanted any other 'devices'. The duke certainly did – although clearly he would now have to finance them and find the necessary labour. The result was the river procession of fifty barges, not two, and twelve pageants instead of three, indeed, a greater number of tableaux than in any previous entry. Hundreds of people were involved. The line of merchants of the Steelyard and the London guilds along the route stretched as far as St Paul's – 1300 yards; children were prominent, as performers and in two large groups – in one case 200 strong. Norfolk probably also proposed John Leland and Nicholas Udall to 'make' the six principal devices (that is, to design and script them).

Leland was the king's antiquary and had been taught by William Lily, who had written the Latin verse for Charles V's entry into London in 1522.[5] He shared Anne's religious perspective, as did his younger friend Udall, who was responsible for 80 per cent of the actual script.[6] While at Oxford, Udall had got into trouble over the sale of prohibited books, but the year after the procession he became head of Eton, possibly as a reward for his successful work for Anne on that occasion.

What was expected from Leland and Udall is very different from the insipid predictability of modern British street decoration. The closest parallel is with the didactic displays of twentieth-century totalitarian regimes. Leland and Udall too had messages to deliver. Their starting-point was the well-established Western European formula that the first entry of a queen consort into a major city should reflect 'the Assumption of the Blessed Virgin Mary'.[7] She, so the Church taught, had been taken up ('assumed') in bodily form into heaven ('the Heavenly City') and been crowned 'as Queen of Heaven and the glory of all the saints'.[8] Entries therefore 'sought to display the city as a type of the Celestial Jerusalem' and the queen as 'a type of the Blessed Virgin'.[9] The first Leland–Udall tableaux to apply this Marian syllabus to Anne did so by means of the one mechanical device that there had been time to make. It was built backing on the Leaden Hall in Gracechurch Street at the junction with Cornhill, a location chosen not just as one of London's principal buildings but because it conveniently housed the City's pageant staff and their work-shops. Open to the front, the castle-like structure was roofed with a cupola painted inside with clouds and the heavenly bodies. The floor was green, representing a field, and out of it rose a hill surmounted by a tree-stump. On the hill sat St Anne and her supposed descendants. On one side of the saint were her daughters – the 'Three Marys' – the Blessed Virgin with the Christ child, Mary Salome with her husband and their two sons (St James and St John), and Mary Cleopas, with her husband; on the other side were the four Cleopas children. One of these greeted Anne as 'Most excellent Queen and bounteous Lady' and explained that the tableau expressed the hope of London that the pregnant Anne Boleyn would go on to rival the maternal success of her patron saint.

> For like as from this devout Saint Anne
> Issued this holy generation,
> First Christ, to redeem the soul of man;
> Then James th'apostle, and th'evangelist John;
> With these others, which in such fashion
> By teaching and good life, our faith confirmed,
> That from that time yet to, it hath not failed.

Right so, dear Lady! our Queen most excellent!
Highly endued with all gifts of grace,
As by your living is well apparent;
We the Citizens, by you in short space
Hope such issue and descent to purchase;
Wherein the same faith shall be defended,
And this City from all dangers preserved.[10]

Very tactfully, no one remarked that St Anne had produced only daughters!

Immediately the boy had finished, the machinery started. The stump on the hill began to pour out a mass of red and white roses. A cloud painted on the roof opened and a white falcon swooped to settle on the flowers. Finally an angel descended from the cloud and placed an imperial crown on the falcon's head. Another of the children then declaimed:

Honour and grace be to our Queen Anne,
For whose cause an Angel Celestial
Descendeth, the falcon (as white as [the] swan)
To crown with a diadem imperial!
In her honour rejoice we all,
For it cometh from God, and not of man.
Honour and grace be to our Queen Anne![11]

The identification of Anne as 'the white falcon' ultimately derived from the heraldic crest of the Butlers, earls of Ormonde. Anne's father had been recognized in 1529 as the Butler heir and the bird 'displayed' appears as a crest on his magnificent brass in Hever church (plate 49). Anne's response to her father's new status had been to use a shield of arms showing her mother's descent from Edward I and from the earls of Surrey, her father's earldom of Ormonde and his earlier barony of Rochford, but she continued with the Rochford badge of the black lion rampant. When she became marquis of Pembroke a coronet was added to this achievement and the monogram 'AP' adopted, but again no bird.[12] What appears then to have happened is that on her marriage, or in anticipation of its announcement, Anne had been granted or had adopted a badge of her own, a white falcon but this time alighting, and alighting on roses.[13]

The immediate message of the badge is hardly subtle. With the advent of Anne, already pregnant, life would once more burst forth from the apparent barrenness of the Tudor stock. There were less obvious allusions too. The tree-stump (or 'woodstock') was a centuries-old royal badge so, as well as speaking of his previous barrenness, it expressed Henry's right as heir to the medieval Plantagenets. That point was elaborated by the flowers which burst from the stump. These were not Tudor roses combining red and white petals, but separate red and white blossoms: Henry as the son of Henry of Richmond and Elizabeth of York, entitled to claim by both the Lancastrian and the Yorkist line.[14] The crown on Anne's falcon also made a special point. It not only referred to her impending coronation but, as Udall's verses were careful to point out, it was specifically a 'close', that is an 'imperial' crown, not a 'kingly' coronet. This was a deliberate allusion to the claims Henry had recently emphasized that he had the powers of an emperor in his own kingdom and so was entitled to reject papal authority.[15] Finally the bird holds a sceptre not only as a routine symbol of regality but as a sign of authority given by God.

What, one may ask, did all this have to do with St Anne? To modern readers the apology offered by one child in the tableau for 'our simpleness . . . the brief time considering' may appear inadequate to excuse this incongrous *mélange* of religion and heraldry. In fact, Leland and Udall were cleverly linking the conception of Anne's child and the conception of Christ. The New Testament tells how an angel came to the Virgin Mary to announce that the Holy Ghost would descend on her and that she would conceive the Son of God.[16] In Western art this descent was regularly pictured as a white dove coming down to Mary. To transmute the white dove who descended on Mary into the white falcon (Anne) descending on the tree-stump (Henry) was, therefore, to assert that the child whom the couple expected was a divine gift. Moreover, the crowning of the falcon associated Anne's own coronation with Mary's coronation by God in the city of heaven. All in all, therefore, the Leaden Hall tableau welcomed Anne as the source of a revived Tudor family, a mother sent by God, whose pregnancy was according to the will of God's Spirit, and one on whose head the crown would soon be placed as a sign of divine grace and acceptance. Nor was the message left to the eye or only to the speeches made by the children. Udall wrote additional Latin verses for the educated – on the St Anne theme, on the falcon and the roses, and on the coronation of the bird (that is, Anne), while a Leland stanza summed up. Finally, the queen left to the strains of a ballad about the white falcon. Perhaps Udall may have had Anne's physique in mind when he wrote:

> Of body small,
> Of power regal
>   She is, and sharp of sight;
> Of courage hault,

No manner fault
Is in this falcon white.

What, however, is without doubt is that the final verses refer to papal obstructiveness and spell out that justice had at last been done and the country could now relax.

> And where by wrong
> She hath flown long,
>   Uncertain where to [a]light;
> Herself repose
> Upon the Rose
>   Now may this falcon white.
> Whereon to rest
> And build her nest,
>   God grant her most of might!
> That England may
> Rejoice alway,
>   In this same falcon white.[17]

Analogies between Anne Boleyn and St Anne and between Anne and the Blessed Virgin contributed to the coronation's immediate purpose, investing the new queen with a sacred identity. There are, however, interesting continental parallels. Indeed, the notion that Leland and Udall should exploit the descent of the Holy Spirit and the crowning of the Virgin may well have come from Anne herself. At Queen Claude's entry to Paris in 1517, in which Anne almost certainly took part, a mechanical dove (the Holy Spirit) descended to place a crown on the queen's head.[18] Early sixteenth-century attitudes saw no embarrassment in subsuming the Virgin Mary in the personality of an earthly woman. The Marian motet *O salve genetrix Virgo* may very possibly have been adapted for use at Anne's coronation, while other Marian pieces could be sung unchanged because of the implication of a promised son to be born.[19]

The theme of Anne's 'assumption' was continued in one of the pageants which were not designed by Leland and Udall. Located at the gate into the precinct of St Paul's, it consisted of a throne set high and awaiting its new occupant.[20] Below sat three splendidly dressed women, unidentified but clearly representing either holy virgins or more probably the Sibyls of antiquity who prophesied the advent of Christ. Those on either side held silver placards with suitable general-purpose texts from the Bible written in blue, but the central figure held a gold placard with the inscription (also in blue), *Veni amica coronaberis* ('Come, my love, thou shalt be crowned'), a deliberate appropriation of the Marian hymn, *Veni corona-beris*.[21] And to make a double point, two angels sat at the base of the tableau holding up a crown, an imperial crown.

The climax of the Marian series came at the Conduit in Fleet Street, 500 yards from the limit of the City's jurisdiction at Temple Bar.[22] The images on the Conduit itself had been gilded and its coats of arms new painted, but a special tower with four turrets had also been erected on the top. This was intended to represent the Heavenly City itself. Indeed, Hall commented that inside the tower were 'such several solemn instruments that it seemed to be a heavenly noise'. To make the identification even more obvious, the exterior was apparently painted the jasper green mentioned twice in the *Revelation of St John*.[23] In each turret stood a speaker representing one of the Cardinal Virtues, without which no one could enter the Holy City. They, however, promised never to leave the queen 'but to be aiding and comforting her'. Anne's 'Assumption to Heaven' was complete. She could now proceed to her coronation.

The pageants at the Leaden Hall, St Paul's Gate and the Fleet Street Conduit thus developed and elaborated a traditional religious syllabus. Four other sites, however, deliberately broke with tradition in favour of classical themes. At the turn from Fenchurch Street into Gracechurch Street a likeness of Mount Parnassus (in classical legend the abode of Apollo and the nine Muses) had been constructed with its sacred fountain of Helicon, all carefully following Virgil.[24] The 'fountain' was made of white marble – or pseudo-marble – and consisted of a large antique-style basin with a classical column rising from the middle to support a smaller bowl a metre and more above. The basin was filled with 'racked' (filtered) Rhenish wine and from its rim four nozzles jetted wine into the upper bowl, the whole being driven by pressure. On Mount Parnassus, above and behind the fountain, Apollo, the god of music and poetry, sat enthroned, with his eagle perching above, and Calliope, the Muse of epic poetry, at his feet, with the other Muses of art and learning grouped on either side. Latin verses by Leland and Udall drew Anne into the scene as one whom the gods had come expressly to honour, and each of the deities in turn praised Henry's new queen. According to Edward Hall, the Muses did not actually speak their lines but had them displayed in letters of gold, while the goddesses themselves played on a variety of musical instruments; whether Apollo was similarly treated is not clear. The advantage of this was not just that it spared Anne lengthy Latin speeches, which she possibly would not have understood, but that she could have the verses pointed out and translated without embarrassment. Furthermore, it was probably asking a good deal of London's musical and dramatic talent to assemble at short notice a large consort, each of whose members could also declaim Latin verse effectively.

Beauty, chastity, virtue, noble descent, these were the qualities that the Muses proclaimed, along with the assurance that she was now to give Henry the companionship and consolation he had lacked for too long – and children, above all children, and male children at that. There was no diffidence about drawing glad attention to Anne's pregnancy. It was her supreme achievement and her greatest merit. Anne Boleyn was flaunting in front of critics and public opinion her divine right to the king's bed and to the throne. As the words given to Clio, the Muse of history, declared in the sophistication of Latin:

> Anna comes, the most famous woman in all the world;
> Anna comes, the shining incarnation of chastity.
> In snow-white litter, just like the goddesses,
> Anna the Queen is here, the preservation of your future.[25]

To support this paean of praise to Anne, and to defy the world, Udall plundered the full repertoire of classical myth and allusion. Here were the roses of Paestum; the festival of Ceres; Cybele. Henry was Nestor, Anne one of the Sibyls; he was to love her as Titus Sempronius Gracchus the elder loved his wife Cornelia; Anne was purer than the rigid morality of the Sabines; her love for Henry was the love of Portia for Brutus.[26] This classical metaphor is in marked contrast to previous processions. Here we find humanism in the service of monarchy, whereas in 1501 the medieval pageant tradition had been dominant, and so too even in 1522 (despite Lily).[27] Admittedly the classicism only overlays traditional forms and ideas, and that somewhat thinly – as when the Muse Thalia based her speech on Anne's heraldic badge, the falcon – but this is more a comment on Tudor humanism generally.[28] The significant point for our purpose is that Anne Boleyn should have committed herself so firmly to the new humanist style.

The Gracechurch Street tableau is also important for another connection. It was the 'device' which the council had persuaded the Hanse merchants of the Steelyard to pay for, and it was designed by Hans Holbein the younger, who had returned to England for his second and lasting stay in 1532. With the exception that, as executed, the triumphal arch was omitted and the Muses were all seated and grouped slightly differently, the drawing now in the Staatliche Museen in Berlin closely matches Hall's description and also fits Udall's verse (plate 38). Scholars have normally accounted for Holbein's design by his connection with the Hanse, but given the short time available and the government imprint on the celebrations, it seems certain that the role of the merchants was simply to pay, and that Holbein executed a design to a detailed English specification.

Holbein's presentation of Parnassus gave rise to one of the hostile canards which so bedevil the story of Anne Boleyn. A month after Chapuys had dismissed the coronation as 'a cold, meagre and uncomfortable thing', he got hold of the story that the eagle hovering over Apollo had been deliberately placed there by the German merchants as a reference to the emperor, Charles V.[29] His symbol thereby towered over the arms of Henry VIII and Anne which, the drawing suggests, were on antique pillars, framing the nine Muses. Three weeks later he repeats the tale, and others have repeated it ever since. It is first of all quite implausible that foreign merchants who 'made' the tableau as a favour to the English Crown should negate their subservience with a deliberately offensive gesture, even assuming they chose the theme. Second, it is clear that the eagle in Holbein's drawing is not the two-headed bird of the Habsburgs. Third, the iconography of the tableau demands that the eagle be the one associated with Apollo; to have incorporated the imperial bird associated with Zeus, and without any justification in the Virgilian text, would have been illiteracy of the first order. We may note, too, that according to the classical story the eagle was blinded by Apollo's brilliance – hardly a compliment to Charles V! Indeed, if we are at all to credit Chapuys' story of Anne being annoyed, it was probably irritation at the ignorance of *hoi polloi*.[30]

The second of the classical pageants was at the Conduit in Cornhill, where the Three Graces of Roman mythology waited to greet the queen. Although framed by a Latin prologue and epilogue, the display was again somewhat incongruous because the deities announced themselves by English equivalents typical of chivalric disguising – Heart Gladness (Aglaia), Stable Honour (Thalia) and Continual Success (Euphrosyne).[31] A similar *mélange* was also prepared at the Great Conduit and the Standard in Cheapside, where static displays of heraldic devices and coats of arms were coupled with Latin speeches and music. Reality interrupted just beyond the next landmark, the newly decorated Eleanor Cross, with the aldermen presenting a gold purse containing a thousand marks (£666.66), but classicism took over again at the Little Conduit, much more convincingly this time, though still largely in English.[32] The tableau depicted 'The Judgement of Paris' in which Mercury, the messenger of Jupiter, gives Paris a golden apple to present to the fairest of three goddesses, the wealthy

Juno, the wise Pallas Athene and the beautiful Venus.[33] Each tries to outbid the others before Paris awards the prize to Venus. Thus far the script was in line with the classical story, but Paris then came up to date:

> Yet to be plain
> Here is the fourth lady now in our presence,
> Most worthy to have it, of due congruence,
> As peerless in riches, wit and beauty,
> Which are but sundry qualities in you three.
> But for her worthiness, this apple of gold
> Is too simple a reward, a thousandfold.[34]

A child then capped what Paris had said by announcing that there was another reward prepared for Anne, the crown imperial, and hailing the queen as a demonstration of divine providence. The parting song to Anne concluded with the stanza:

> The golden ball
> Of price but small,
> Have Venus shall,
>   The fair goddess,
> Because it was
> Too low and bare
> For your good grace
>   And worthiness.[35]

This is the way the script ends, but at the last minute there may have been an addition. Both Hall and *The noble triumphant Coronation* tell of a golden ball being presented to Anne; Hall says it was presented by Mercury and was divided into three sections, signifying gifts which each of the goddesses gave – riches, wisdom and happiness.[36]

In dividing the pageants prepared for Anne into religious and classical, it is important not to overdo the contrast; the categories overlap. This was very much the case with the recurring humanist motif that Anne was the harbinger of a new age. Each of the classical pageants deliberately cited the prophecy in Virgil's fourth *Eclogue* of the return of the Just Virgin who will usher in the reign of Saturn, that is, innocence and plenty. At the Gracechurch Street tableau, Apollo hailed Anne as the inspiration of the Golden Age, and the verses with which the Muses greeted Anne repeat the theme and announce her arrival as the start of eternal spring. At the Conduit in Cornhill, the third of the Graces, Euphrosyne, promised:

Long fruition with daily increasement
Of Joy and honour, without diminishment.
Never to decay, but always to arise![37]

So far the theme appears classical, but the relevant Vergil passage had been understood ever since the fourth century to refer to the advent of the Blessed Virgin, the mother of the Messiah, whose victory has ushered in the new heaven and the new earth. Hence, above the three Sybils at St Paul's Gate with their Marian reference was the legend *Regina Anna! Prospere, procede et regna!* ('Queen Anne! Prosper, go forward and reign!'), and at their feet a long scroll with the inscription (again in Latin), 'Queen Anne, when thou shalt bear a new son of the King's blood, there shall be a golden world unto thy people.' And the religious symbiosis of Mary and Anne was reinforced by the three ladies having supplies of wafers to throw to the crowds, wafers which carried not religious images but the message of the long scroll in letters of gold.

The most impressive demonstration of an interest in the new fashion for antiquity was, unfortunately, not part of the work of Udall and Leland, and thus is known only by descriptions and not by the text. This was the bringing together of the 200 children on specially built staging at the western front of St Paul's School, overlooking the churchyard. They declaimed a series of translations from the Latin poets, praising both Anne and Henry. It is also the one episode to which we know Anne's spontaneous reaction on the day. She 'said "Amen" with a joyful smiling countenance'.[38]

Comparison with subsequent royal pageants, real and abortive, demonstrate how distinctive the set pieces for Anne's coronation procession were and endorse the conclusion that they reflected her personal taste. The syllabus which survives for the abortive coronation of her successor, Jane Seymour, describes twelve of the intended pageants in detail. One was a display of caged singing birds in a meadow, one a maiden with a unicorn by a fountain, and a third the new queen's badge and motto. All the rest used traditional religious themes – the Vision of St John, the Coronation of the Virgin, the Transfiguration and so on – with not a classical allusion in sight.[39] Edward VI's coronation procession was largely cobbled up from the programme devised for Henry VI in 1432, though one Latin speech was scripted and the rear of one stage featured the Golden Fleece.[40] Where Edward's did copy Anne was in the descent of a heraldic bird, this time the Seymour phoenix.[41] Much less is known of Mary's coronation procession, where the three 'mightiest' pageants (and the only sign of classicism) were provided by foreign merchants – the Genoese, the Hanse and the

Florentines.[42] Her husband's entry in 1554 was more Latinate – not sur-prisingly, since Philip had limited English – but only one of the four principal pageants was on a classical theme.[43] Elizabeth's coronation procession in 1559 exploited no classical motifs, though plenty of material in Latin.[44]

The distinctive classicism of Anne Boleyn's entry in 1533 should almost certainly be traced to her time in France, where this newer style was beginning to evolve. At first the fashion was for chivalric myth and religious analogy, as in Queen Claude's 'annunciation', and where classicism did appear it was anything but pure. The entry of Mary Tudor into Paris in 1514 had had Bacchus facing Ceres inside a ship (the city's badge), while a display of heraldry had the morality play characters 'Justice', 'Truth' and 'Unanimity' in discussion with Minerva, Diana and Apollo.[45] However, at Lyons in 1515, Francis I was depicted as Hercules gathering fruit in the garden of the Hesperides, and at Rouen in 1517 there was a depiction of the battle between the gods and the Titans.[46] Then in 1520 came the entry into Cognac of Queen Claude, with Anne Boleyn almost certainly in attendance. Claude was met by Mercury, who declared that the gods had come down to greet her, and her cavalcade encountered first Diana and her nymphs, and then Apollo, before being arrested by flames issuing from the forge of Vulcan. Next Venus arrived, followed by Saturn, Jupiter and Mars. At the city's river bridge, Neptune appeared, escorted by dolphins, and when dusk fell, Pluto, Cerberus, Charon and the Furies.[47] It is true that the mythological continuity was twice interrupted by knightly feats of arms, but the classical entry had arrived.[48]

Anne's procession reflected her French background in another way. The very first of the tableaux (not by Udall and Leland) was built against the east wall of St Gabriel's in Fenchurch, where the procession had to split either side of the church. It was peopled entirely with children dressed as merchants and they 'welcomed her to the City with two proper prepositions both in French and English'.[49] Even more flattered was Anne's interest in music. Apart from the playing of the Muses in Gracechurch Street, the ballad of the falcon, the singing at the Judgement of Paris and the instrumental music at the Fleet Street Conduit (augmented by a carillon and a children's choir), 'great melody with speeches' was also provided at the Great Conduit.[50] An ensemble of voices and instruments was grouped on top of the Standard in Cheapside and a choir of men and boys on the roof of St Martin's, Ludgate, sang 'new ballads made in praise of her'.[51] Finally, at Temple Bar a choir of men and boys stood ready to serenade Anne's departure.

In the twenty-first century a little symbolism goes a long way. Thus, what the modern mind would ask of the iconography and symbols mobilized for Anne Boleyn's coronation procession is what the contemporary observer made of it all. Would the ordinary Londoner have known enough to catch these esoteric significances? The answer is probably no. Though undoubtedly more aware of symbols than later generations desensitized by literacy, all that the Tudor generality was expected to absorb was the overall magnificence of the occasion. The detail and complexity was an 'in-language' intended for the social groups that mattered, the leading citizens and the attendant gentry, and they were expected to be able to deconstruct all or at least part of what was being said. Comparison with Anne's daughter, Elizabeth, is helpful here. Her well-known pose as 'Gloriana' was not simply what today would be called 'media hyperbole'. It was underpinned by a language of ideas, metaphor and symbol even more elaborate and complex than her mother's presentation in 1533.

Iconography and symbolism was a form of communication found across Europe, but the seeds of some of Elizabeth's images can clearly be traced to her mother. Sometimes the identity is exact. Elizabeth continued to use the falcon and roses badge, a message of life from the dead which her own early dangers had now made doubly poignant.[52] A famous painting of Elizabeth by the monogrammist HE (dated 1569) takes as its theme 'The Judgement of Paris', and depicts the queen confronting the three goddesses, just as Anne had done in Cheapside thirty-three years earlier.[53] The classicism is now better integrated with the compliment; Elizabeth has absorbed the role of Paris and, instead of the apple going to Venus and the crown to Anne, the apple is now the orb of England and is retained by the queen against all divine competition. Nonetheless, the essential exploitation of the myth is the same. Another parallel is the identification of both daughter and mother with the nymph Astraea and the new golden age.[54] The lord mayor's pageant in 1591 would say:

> Lo, the Olympus' king, the thundering Jove,
> > Raught hence this gracious nymph, Astraea fair:
> Now once again he sends her from above,
> > Descended through the sweet transparent air;
> And here she sits in beauty fresh and sheen,
> Shadowing the person of a peerless queen.[55]

Perhaps most striking of all – in view of the intervening hardening of religious identities – is that Elizabeth, like Anne, was identified with the Virgin Mary.[56] Gloriana was the offspring of 'the falcon white' – or as assiduous a follower of the European cult of majesty as her mother had been.

ART AND TASTE

T HE twenty-first century draws a clear distinction between normal living and occasions for spectacle. Royal pomp, ceremony at an installation, or even private display at a wedding is one thing, day-to-day ostentation another. Sixteenth-century Europe believed otherwise. Society was hierarchical and lifestyle exemplified rank and value. The exterior revealed the interior – does not Christ say 'by their fruits you shall know them?'[1] Kings and queens had to live the part and hence magnificence was a regal virtue, an external proof of the right to rule. This was the lesson Anne had learned from Margaret of Austria and Queen Claude, and she was a prize pupil.

Her gold and silver plate provides the first indication. In Tudor society that was always the most visible demonstration of wealth and status. The *pièce de résistance* at the 1532 Calais banquet to launch Anne in Europe was a display of seven shelves of gold plate – not a single piece of silver or silver-gilt – plate which Henry either took over with him specially or else borrowed from the town. However, as we have seen, by February 1533 Henry was bragging about the amount of plate Anne owned personally, and this included a cup-board display of gold that Chapuys described as the best ever seen.[2] Indeed, in the inventories of Henry's property which were drawn up in his son's reign, over 120 items of plate apparently associated with his second wife can still be traced.[3] This is remarkable, given that a deliberate attempt had been made to obliterate Anne's memory, but either the king was not embarrassed by or was protected by his household from reminders of his second wife. In some cases pieces were evidently saved from the smelting pot by the value of the workmanship. Despite being 'stricken' with Anne's arms, one silver-gilt chandelier was even remade some three years after her death, evidently because it belonged to a set of three with the sockets for the candles made 'like drones'.[4] True, in a few cases where the inventories mention 'Queen Anne' there may be a confusion with Anne of Cleves, but not many items are likely to have been produced for her in a marriage to Henry which lasted only 185 days.[5]

Despite the banquets of 1532 and 1533, by the time the inventories were taken most plate in the king's possession was no longer gold but silver-gilt. However, of the gold spoons Henry owned at his death, three can certainly be linked to Anne. Two were a pair, one decorated with a (no doubt Tudor) rose and the other with a crowned falcon.[6] One large gold item which appears to have been melted down before the king's death was a bowl with a cover, weighing 40 troy ounces (0.91 kilograms), with Queen Anne's cipher on it, supplied to Henry by the Flemish goldsmith, Thomas Trappers, for £90.[7] Where gold was lavishly used was as decoration. One item which escaped the inventory of pieces to be sold by James I in 1620 was:

> one basin and layer [small jug] of mother of pearl garnished with gold, the backside only of the basin silver gilt, enamelled with scriptures and devices of cosmography, the layer having a falcon in the top, being in a case of black velvet, garnished with a parsivent lace [a fret] of Venice silver, with four joints and one handle of white silver, weight, the basin and layer only, one hundred and four score and five ounces scant.[8]

Among the silver-gilt items in the inventory, one of the most magnificent was:

> a pair of [silver-]gilt bottles, the feet and body chased in panes, with branches of two sundry works having the king's arms in a plate on the one side, and on the other the king's arms and the arms of Queen Anne in a plate together, having on either side an angel with a great chain and a small [one] on either bottle, their necks graven with branches, the knobs or 'stopples' having double roses and thereupon crowns imperial.

Made by the king's jeweller, Morgan Wolf, they were a present to either Henry or Anne on New Year's Day 1536 and weighed together 6.35 kilograms.[9] Another craftsman working for Anne was Cornelius Hayes, the king's Flemish goldsmith. It was he who, as we have seen, made the highly elaborate but unused silver cradle ordered in 1534.[10] Several pieces of the plate associated with Anne were in the antique, that is, Renaissance style – a standing cup 'wrought with antique work'; a little standing cup 'having a naked boy in the top holding a staff in the one hand and a plain shield in the other'; 'three gilt bowls chased with long bullions having antique heads in the bottom'.[11] By miraculous chance, one piece which Anne owned has survived. It is a silver cup and cover (314 millimetres high) made in 1535 (plate 36), now among the treasures of Cirencester parish church. The cover is topped by the falcon on the tree-stump, but its chief interest is the design, which picks up once again the interest in humanist fashion. It attempts to achieve in silver a form characteristic of contemporary Venetian glass.[12] At least two other cups 'glass fashion' and associated with Anne were in the royal collection in 1547. One of them was also decorated in classical style:

> one Cup glass fashion, gilt, chased with H A, upon the top of the cover a woman holding in the one hand a ball and in the other hand a shield.[13]

How much actual glass Anne had owned it is impossible to say, given its fragility. One item which did survive until 1547 was 'a cup of glass with two ears' mounted in silver-gilt and with her cipher on the silver-gilt cover.[14] Another was a glass of beryl garnished with gold and carrying her arms.[15] At a more mundane level there was a considerable quantity of silver plate, most of it not gilded, carrying both the royal and the Rochford arms. What is not clear is whether this was plate which Anne had owned and to which the king's arms had been added, or vice versa, or whether it was acquired for joint use. Perhaps some of it should be identified as part of the considerable quantity of plate which was re-marked in late 1532.[16]

The artist and designer of most interest who was working in England in these years is Hans Holbein the younger. Did he work for Queen Anne?[17] Holbein's earliest demonstrable commission from Henry was to paint Jane Seymour, and his first known regular Crown employment dates from 1538.[18] Given this and his surviving *œuvre*, many writers have concluded that in the earlier 1530s he worked for London immigrant merchants and increasingly for lesser figures at court.[19] However, we have seen that the only role of the Hanse merchants in the *Mount Parnassus* commission was to pay, and that the work was not only undertaken in response to government initiative but also reflected Anne's personal interest in the antique. Holbein's first royal engagement was thus aimed at Anne and, as will appear, he certainly undertook subsequent commissions for her. That she continued his patron is confirmed by the experience of the French poet and reformer Nicolas Bourbon. Early in 1535 he came to England under the queen's protection, and it was as part of her circle that he met and became an admirer of the artist (plate 61).[20] True, it can be objected that

Bourbon subsequently described Holbein as 'the king's painter', but when he made that comment Anne was already dead.

Can Holbein commissions other than *Mount Parnassus* be linked to Anne? The most remarkable candidate is *The Ambassadors*, the double portrait of Jean de Dinteville, Francis I's *maître d'hôtel*, and George de Selve, bishop of Lavaur, standing full-length each side of a cup-board laden with various items (plate 44).[21] The first reason to connect Holbein's greatest surviving masterpiece with Anne is its date. Dinteville, on the left, arrived as the French ambassador to England shortly before 15 February 1533.[22] The bishop came on a special visit to see Dinteville but had left by 4 June and possibly by 23 May.[23] The painting, in other words, was conceived exactly in the weeks when Anne Boleyn was recognized as queen and her coronation prepared, at the very time when Holbein was working on *Mount Parnassus*. The next connection depends on the purpose of Selve's visit. It could simply have been private, but not only would that be somewhat unusual, there is no previous evidence that the two men knew each other well. A more convincing explanation is that Dinteville's diplomatic instructions had been overtaken by Anne's public recognition as queen and that the bishop came to bring confidential directions for the ambassador (and possibly a private message to Anne). This construction would certainly explain why Dinteville was insistent that news of de Selve's visit should be kept from Francis I's strongly imperialist principal minister, the duc de Montmorency.[24] It would also explain why the ambassador was ready to accept a prominent part in the coronation when his original instruction had been concerned with Francis I's plans to meet Clement VII, and the prospect that the pope would offer an accommodation over the Aragon marriage.[25] If de Selve did come with such a briefing, then given that Anne was accepted as queen from 11 April, we are able to say that de Selve sat to Holbein between late April and the end of May 1533.

Thus far the evidence would only indicate that ambassadors involved in Anne's recognition and coronation sat to an artist who was at the same time engaged on a project for Anne's coronation. However, two elements in the painting itself make specific reference to the queen. As the ambassador rests his left arm on the cup-board he almost touches a small upright wooden cylinder. This is a 'shepherd's' or pillar dial, a device to determine dates by the sun. The settings on the instrument are clear to read and they indicate the date 11 April, in other words, the precise day on which the royal court (and no doubt Dinteville) was told that Anne was henceforward to be accorded royal honours.[26] That the date on this dial is no accident is shown by the second reference, this time to Anne's actual coronation. This was made by choosing to place the figures not, as one would expect, on a Turkey carpet, but on a highly distinctive *cosmati* pavement. The only example of such *cosmati* work in England was the floor of the sanctuary in Westminster Abbey, and the reason why Holbein made this a major feature in *The Ambassadors* has long been a puzzle. However, that pavement was the precise spot where Anne Boleyn was anointed queen, that most solemn moment in the coronation ritual which was the distinctive spiritual mark of English monarchy, a ritual which Dinteville witnessed by special invitation of the king. The choice of the *cosmati* floor thus made the painting a permanent reminder of the high point of the ambassador's career. With this allusion, it is also hard not to suppose that Holbein depicted Dinteville in the costume he appeared in for the coronation and which he was so worried about being paid for.[27]

We can also be sure that Anne would have endorsed much of the syllabus of *The Ambassadors*. As is well known, many of the objects Holbein depicted appear to refer to the contemporary state of the Church. Most immediate to the eye is the lute with one string broken. Next to it is another symbol of harmony, a case of flutes, but with one instrument missing. Beneath the lute is a pair of dividers and on the left an arithmetic book half-open at a page on division. However, Dinteville was strongly influenced by evangelical reform in France, which was not schismatic – particularly the writings of Jacques Lefèvre d'Etaples. The painting, there-fore, also offers hope. The green curtain behind the sitters is drawn back to reveal sufficient of a silver crucifix. The arithmetic book is prevented from closing on the division page by a set-square. In front of the lute is a hymnal with on one page the *Veni Creator Spiritus* ('*Come Creator Spirit*'), and on the other the Ten Commandments. Although these were basic anthems of the Latin Church, Holbein shows them in a vernacular Lutheran ver-sion.[28] Crucifix, set-square, Lutheran vernacular and texts known to all Christians together express the conviction of evangelicals that the way to unity in the Church was a response to Christ by the Holy Spirit, leading to a life of everyday obedience to the commandments. As we shall see, Anne Boleyn (who had almost certainly met Dinteville in 1531 if not earlier), shared his evangelicalism and would work with him two years later to rescue the like-minded Nicolas Bourbon from religious difficulties in France.[29] Given that Holbein was also of a reformist turn of mind, the religious message of *The Ambassadors* was common to sitter, artist and artist's patron alike.[30]

As well as an association with the largest of Holbein's surviving works, Anne is linked to the most beautiful of his miniatures, *Solomon and the*

Queen of Sheba (plate 42).[31] The intended recipient was quite obviously Henry VIII himself, and the gift appears distinctly personal. It is very unlikely to have been a new year's gift since extant lists of these rule out a date before January 1535 and the stylistic links are with the artist's two murals, *The Triumph of Riches* and *The Triumph of Poverty*, which are conjecturally dated 1532–3.[32] Internal evidence also suggests a date soon after the submission of the clergy in May 1532.[33] At that time the only person likely to be able to make a private gift to the king of such an intimate piece is Anne herself, and strong internal evidence points in that direction.

Superficially, the subject is the Old Testament story of King Solomon receiving a visit from the Queen of Sheba (*Regina Saba*). The inscriptions in gold to the left and right of the throne are taken from the Vulgate account of the visit found in the Second Book of Chronicles, chapter 9. Holbein, however, very deliberately depicts Solomon as Henry VIII, so equating the king with the wisest man in the world. That is only the first layer of meaning. The Solomon and Sheba episode had for many centuries been interpreted by the Church as a foreshadowing of the homage of the Church to Christ – 'one greater than Solomon'.[34] But if the Queen equals the Church, Solomon equals Christ and Henry equals Solomon, then the homage of the Church Universal to Christ must be equated with the submission of the Church in England to the king as its head under Christ. And to make sure that this reference to the 1532 victory was understood, the Biblical quotation above Solomon's head (a conflation of II Chronicles 9, verse 8, and I Kings 10, verse 9), was deliberately distorted. The Vulgate original states that God made Solomon king in order 'to do justice'; the miniature says 'to be king (appointed) for the Lord your God'.[35] In other words, Henry is 'the supreme head of this his realm of England immediately under God'.[36] There is possibly a third layer of meaning too. New Testament symbolism pictures Christ as 'the Bridegroom' and the Church as 'his Bride'. But if Solomon stands for Christ, he must also be the Bridegroom, and if the Queen of Sheba is a symbol of the Church, then she must also be equivalent to the Bride of Christ. Must she not, therefore, also be the Bride of Solomon? Italian painters certainly made the connection, and if Holbein did likewise, then the figure of the Queen of Sheba stands for Anne herself. In this way, the Queen of Sheba's gesture, presenting the homage of her escort to Solomon, becomes a gesture by Anne to the Church in England, which in part she had brought to submit to Henry. If the Queen of Sheba is Anne, then the miniature is a memento of the victory of 1532.

To twenty-first-century minds all this may appear convoluted in the extreme! Nevertheless, other indications suggest that the significance of the miniature was meant to be peeled away in this fashion. Tradition saw the Queen of Sheba as also a 'type' of the 'Virgin Mary Crowned', and we have seen how Anne's coronation cast her in the same role. The Vulgate texts each side of Solomon's throne directly echo Anne's motto, 'the most happy'.[37] What is more, after her marriage to Henry, not only was the organ screen in King's College Chapel, Cambridge, ornamented with a riot of references to Anne, the stained glass which was installed nearby to tell the Sheba story depicts a Henry/Solomon and a Queen who are very clearly derived from the Holbein miniature.(plate 43).[38] It could even be that the inscription 'REGINA SABA' on the miniature, unnecessary as it is and out of place, could be one of the acronyms Tudors loved, possibly '**R**egina **S**alomonem **A**nna **B**oleyn **A**mat,' Anne Boleyn the queen loves Solomon.

Although no drawing or painting of the queen by Holbein has survived, this substantial connection strongly reinforces the probability that she did sit to him and that her portrait was one of those lost in the course of time.[39] Holbein also produced for her designs for jewellery and silver-work.[40] The most impressive is his drawing of a standing cup and cover, now in Basle (plate 40).[41] This can confidently be identified as a piece designed to Anne's order or else for her, because it is engraved with a crowned falcon on the roses. Evidently the artist's famous British Museum design for Jane Seymour's cup was not the first he had prepared for an English queen. Jane's was, however, an improvement on Anne's, for the Basle drawing cannot be described as a happily integrated design. The imperial crown, which forms the knop on the cover, and the engraved heraldic falcon are decidedly incongruous in a piece which is otherwise wholly 'antique': three semi-nudes in Renaissance style supporting the stem, four satyrs holding up the rim and four classical heads decorating a band round the bowl of the cup.

The oft-repeated story that Holbein had a hand in the 1534 cradle is disproved by the original itemized bill.[42] However, a piece he was almost certainly responsible for was the silver-gilt table-fountain which Anne gave to Henry at New Year 1534, a pumped device which circulated rosewater into a basin so that diners could rinse their hands. The New Year Gift list describes it as

A goodly gilt bason, having a rail or board of gold in the midst of the brim, garnished with rubies and pearls, wherein standeth a fountain, also having a rail of gold about it garnished with diamonds, out whereof issueth water at the teats of three naked women standing about the foot of the same fountain.[43]

Many writers have identified this with the Basle cup and cover, but this is unquestionably wrong.[44] First, the Basle drawing is not a water device. There is nothing to suggest that it could ever be described as a basin, or even be in a basin, apart from a faint horizontal line and some imagination.[45] Next the Gift List description makes no mention of the major feature of the Basle cup, the four satyrs, nor do they figure in any of five later references to a piece which was disposed of only in 1620.[46] Conclusively, these later descriptions indicate that instead of a crown, the fountain had a 'plate of gold in the top of the cover with the Queen's arms and Queen Anne's'. The 1534 fountain and the Basle cup and cover are clearly not related, and since the latter does not appear in later lists, it was presumably among the items melted down in the aftermath of Anne's fall.

The evidence that the 1534 fountain was, nevertheless, designed by Holbein is provided by two other drawings in the Basle collection. The first is a rough sketch of a naked woman spraying liquid from her right breast (plate 39).[47] If this was not a preliminary sketch for the women of the 1534 fountain, it was a sketch for something very similar. Equally striking is the second Basle drawing.[48] This shows a table fountain in a shallow basin with 'naked women standing about the foot' possibly with water issuing from the breast (plate 41). The drawing is not a final design for Anne's fountain since it is surmounted by an image of Jove with a thunderbolt, not a plate carrying Anne's arms. But the parallel is beyond doubt, and the link may be closer still. At the bottom right is the rough sketch of a nude female torso with obvious similarities to the first drawing.

In recent years a case has been made to credit Anne with the patronage of another artist, or, rather, a family of artists, the Horneboltes from Ghent: Gerard the father, Margaret of Austria's court painter, and his children Lucas and Susanna, each of whom had followed in the family profession.[49] Anne, however, was certainly not involved in their decision to try their fortune on this side of the Channel, for Lucas was in England at the latest by September 1525. What is possible is that he had a letter of introduction to Thomas Boleyn – even, perhaps, from the archduchess herself – for one of Lucas's first commissions was a portrait of Boleyn's son-in-law, William Carey.[50] The Horneboltes may have been discreetly absenting themselves from the Low Countries, where an outburst of religious persecution was under way. Yet even if they were heterodox, the date of their arrival rules out any protective connection with Anne of the kind she offered after 1533.

On the other hand, once she was in a position to do so, Anne might have employed a reformist refugee like Lucas Hornebolte just as she did the slightly suspect Holbein. The patent appointing Lucas as king's painter for life in June 1534 certainly suggests some personal recommendation to the king: 'For a long time I have been acquainted not only by reports from others but also from personal knowledge with the science and experience in the pictorial art of Lucas Hornebolte.'[51] The year 1534 was a high point in Boleyn influence and it is tempting to see Anne as Hornebolte's sponsor. Against this, Lucas had been in England long enough to acquire contacts with the circles around Katherine, and many pieces attributed to him link him with Anne's enemies.[52] The jury is out, but the omens for a close link between the Horneboltes and Anne Boleyn are not promising.

Even if Anne did not employ the Horneboltes personally, she must have known one aspect of their work where they were unsurpassed: manuscript illumination. In the thinking of the day, such objects were more akin to jewels than to books, and Anne had an obvious enthusiasm for them as well as decided tastes of her own. Only a small number have survived or can now be identified as hers, but the proof that she was an enthusiast is the trouble that was taken to prepare for her a presentation copy of the exemplification of the royal patents that she had been granted between June 1532 and her jointure on 21/22 March 1533.[53] The first item, the patent creating her lady marquis of Pembroke, begins with a massive letter 'H', 114 by 107 millimetres, illuminated in gold and blue and incorporating the crowned falcon on the roses. The whole impressive document may well be 'the jointure of Queen Anne' for which the chancery provided four skins of vellum along with silk and gold, at a cost of 18 shillings in the year 1533–4.[54]

The oldest illuminated manuscript so far identified with Anne is a Book of Hours now at Hever Castle, which dates from the mid-fifteenth century (plate 25). Produced at Bruges specifically for an English client (unidentified), it is lavishly decorated with thirty-three large illuminations plus twenty-two small and one historiated initial, within fine foliage borders enriched with flowers, fruit and grotesques.[55] Anne certainly owned it before 1529, although when it was obtained or how is not clear.[56] Since the liturgical content is specifically English, Anne is unlikely to have acquired the book abroad, making the alternatives a second-hand purchase in this country or a family connection. At the time it was produced, her grandfather Geoffrey could certainly have afforded the book, but there is no positive evidence to support the conjecture that he was the original owner.[57]

Anne's taste in illumination was not confined to an appreciation of things Flemish. The first instance of this is a Book of Hours printed in Paris and now also at Hever Castle (plate 22).[58] It qualifies as illuminated only by courtesy, for it is an example of a late fifteenth-century publishing initiative to make devotional books cheaper and more readily available, by supplying a printed text and woodcut illustrations which could then be coloured by hand. Anne's copy was, however, printed on vellum, making it a more up-market product than one on paper; the cuts have been coloured, the initials also, and the pages have been given gilt borders in an architectural style. Once again the circumstances of acquisition are unknown, but the relative cheapness of the book suggests that it is more likely to have been acquired by her as a teenager in France rather than specially imported.

Each of the Books of Hours at Hever contains an inscription by Anne. In the printed book she wrote:

> Remember me when you do pray,
> That hope doth lead from day to day.
> Anne Boleyn

Presciently she wrote this opposite a depiction of the coronation of the Virgin.[59] In the older volume she chose to use French and wrote '*le temps viendra / je anne boleyn*' below a miniature of the Second Coming and the Resurrection of the Dead (plate 24).[60] Within this inscription, between '*je*' and '*anne*', Anne inserted a small drawing; on close examination this turns out to be an armillary sphere. Evidently this was a device Anne adopted before switching to the falcon on the roses.[61] Other manuscripts were specially produced for Anne in France. At least one clearly came from a top *atelier*. In italic script, delicately heightened with colour, it is a specially adapted text of Clément Marot's poem, *Le Pasteur Evangélique*, which Anne received after her marriage to Henry VIII.[62] What is not certain is whether the impressive frontispiece of Anne's arms surrounded by a wreath of oak leaves and Tudor roses, with the falcon badge almost as a pendant, came with the book or was added in England (plate 45).

The most splendid of the illuminated manuscripts produced for Anne combined Flemish-style illumination and a French text. Now in the collection of the duke of Northumberland at Alnwick, 'The Ecclesiaste' (plate 27) is in such good condition that Anne herself might almost have put it down a moment ago.[63] True, black has faded to grey, but otherwise we see exactly what those frequent payments to Hayes, the goldsmith, for fine velvet bindings were for. At the centre of the front cover is Anne Boleyn's shield of arms in enamel on a metal base, probably silver, surmounted by a crown. All four corners of the book, front and back, are guarded with brass, decorated with a roundel on which is engraved a royal badge – the crowned lion rampant regardant, the dragon, the crowned falcon on the roses, and the greyhound – and there are two decorated brass clasps. These last are very similar to known designs by Holbein and could well be attributed to him.[64]

The manuscript provides a text of the Old Testament book of Ecclesiastes plus a commentary. The title-page is almost an imitation of printing, but it does introduce the ground colours for the illuminations, pink and slate, a combination Anne seems to have favoured elsewhere.[65] The running title is in a bright blue, which is also used to number the twelve chapters and to divide the treatment of each page into *texte* sections in French, and *annotation* (commentary) in English. Each section of *texte* and *annotation* has an initial letter 20 millimetres square and illuminated alternately in sky-blue lit by white and in dusky pink, each on a slate-blue ground speckled with gold. These are impressive enough, but the initial letters of each chapter are treated in a truly magnificent fashion. Four times the size – 40 millimetres square – they comprise a series of eight designs, superbly executed. Even what appears to be just a flower-like letter 'J' in pink on a slate ground, with 'H' and 'A' in gold, turns out on closer examination to be lined with green and picked out in white, with a fine gold filigree over the slate and the whole shadowed and in perspective, as though the letter were in relief.[66] The first illumination of all, the combined shield of Henry and Anne, is in no fewer than seven colours and tones.[67]

The Alnwick 'Ecclesiaste' was produced for Anne during her three years as queen, although the exact date was subsequently disguised by a deliberate erasure of part of the colophon, leaving only M^{1}CCCC.[68] In style it clearly belongs to the school of illumination fashionable at the Habsburg court in Brussels, which she had first experienced twenty years before under Margaret of Austria. However, it is almost certainly not produced in the Low Countries but by Flemish-trained craftsmen working in England. It was, in fact, not the first manuscript that these experts had produced for Anne. Over the winter of 1532–3, between the time of Anne's becoming lady marquis of Pembroke and her recognition as queen, the same scribe and possibly the same illuminator had produced the somewhat less elaborate 'The Pistellis and Gospelles for the LII Sondayes in the Yere', now in the British Library (plate 30).[69] It too follows the distinctive format of a *texte* in French and an *exhortation* in English, with blue used for editorial matter. The preface is illuminated with a large representation of Anne's arms as marquis of Pembroke – Ormonde, Brotherton, Rochford and Warenne quartered on a lozenge surmounted by a coronet. The list of contents on folio 2 recto has architectural borders in gold, while on 2 verso is a third of the illuminated pages, a depiction of the Crucifixion, with Mary, St John and Mary Magdalen within an architectural border, which includes figures of St Peter and St Paul and medallions of the evangelists. Thereafter, however, there are only small decorated initials, including Anne's arms on a lozenge and the initials 'AP', 'Anne Pembroke'.

As well as these obvious links, 'The Pistellis and Gospelles' contain cryptic references to the Boleyns. The first is a cipher on folio 1 verso (upside down) which appears to contain letters making up 'George Boleyn'.[70] Then, spaced around her lozenge of arms are four examples in gold of a second cipher which combines the letters 'H', 'E', 'N' (this last backwards), 'R', 'E', 'X', 'S', and 'L'.[71] The cipher also occurs among the decorated initial letters. 'HENricus REX' is an obvious reading, but that leaves the last two letters, 'S' and 'L', to be accounted for. 'Sovereign Lord', 'Sovereign Liege', seem the likely interpretations. Perhaps the refrain of the court song, 'My Sovereign Lord', is relevant here, with its queen (or mistress) using that title to praise 'the eighth Harry' and his tiltyard exploits in her honour.[72]

This monogram recurs in another manuscript known to have been made for Anne.[73] A psalter, it dates from the period between her father's elevation to an earldom in December 1529 and Anne's own promotion in September 1532, and was specially ordered from one of the studios in Paris or Rouen which supplied the court and elite society of France. No surprises are presented by the two full borders in the book, one in French Gothic style and one of Renaissance candelabra. Nor are there any in the armorial achievement facing the first folio, a display of Anne's arms on a lozenge (held up by two somewhat muscular winged putti within an architectural frame), and the lozenge is repeated in a number of the historiated letters which occur at various points later in the text. Opposite the Renaissance candelabra, however, two wingless putti hold up a different lozenge at the centre of which is the 'HENREXSL' monogram in purple (plate 23). This lozenge (which also recurs in a smaller form elsewhere in the book) has two other devices a well, the black lion of Rochford at the bottom and a smaller cipher at the top, again in purple. This consists of a curiously formed letter 'A', with a stroke through the apex and the normal horizontal stroke written as a 'V'. That this is more than a fancy piece of penmanship is clear from the occurrence of exactly the same format in the sections of the coving of the organ screen of King's College, Cambridge, which, as we shall see, celebrates the marriage of Henry and Anne (see plate 34).[74] As Tudor monograms go, the interpretation is once more simple. Writing the letter 'A' in this way also creates the letters 'T' and 'M', so making the Latin 'amat' ('loves'). The whole therefore means either '[Henry] loves A[nne]' or 'A[nne] loves [Henry]', or both. It has been suggested that this psalter was a gift from Jean du Bellay, who, as Francis's ambassador in England, did become very friendly with Anne. However, the intimacy of the monograms makes this very unlikely. Given the foreign provenance of the psalter and yet the use of such personal symbols, it is plausible to surmise that the order for the book came from the king himself.[75]

Even more significances are to be found in the Alnwick 'L'Ecclesiaste'; indeed, each of the historiated initials has its meaning.[76] Some are unsurprising – chapter 1: the royal couple's shield as on the cover enamel (the arms of the husband impaling those of the wife); chapter 8: Anne's own shield, crowned; chapters 2, 7, 11: the initials 'H' and 'A'. The crowned falcon on the roses features twice (chapters 3 and 10, plate 31) as does Anne's motto 'the most happy' (chapters 5 and 9). The three remaining letters (chapters 4, 6 and 12) are different, riddles intended to be accessible only to those in the know. Chapter 6 begins with the pronoun '*Il*'.[77] The historiated 'I' is notably delicate (plate 33). Each side of the upright stroke, in a space no bigger than a normal postage stamp, is a curved stalk in gold with eleven oak leaves, seven acorn cups (four full and three empty) and a honeysuckle bloom with a tiny tendril in white and gold. The significance of this is that Anne and Henry had adopted honeysuckle and acorns, either separately or together, as a private motif. When this happened is not clear but, as we shall see, both featured regularly in palace furnishings.[78] The symbolism is hardly profound, but identifying it provides another of those rare glimpses into the intimacy between husband and wife. Chapter 12 is harder to elucidate.[79] The opening letter 'E' is in pink on a blue ground decorated with a gold foliage pattern above the horizontal stroke, which is repeated below in reverse. The stems and leaves are akin to those of chapter 6, but there are no acorns or honeysuckle blooms. Perhaps we have honeysuckle stems as a symbol of Anne alone. If so, the interpretation could be that the mirror image makes it possible to read the stems in the lower part as springing from a tree-stump and in the upper part as life culminating in a crown – new life and a future for the dynasty?

Even more challenging is the historiated 'E' at the start of chapter 4: '*Et me suis*' (plate 32).[80] This is in pink, picked out in white and lined with green, with a white scroll round the horizontal bearing the motto *Fiat voluntas tua* – 'Thy will be done.' Behind the letter is an anchor in blue with a gold stock, hanging from an armillary sphere, also in gold; beside the sphere is the abbreviation 'IHS' and, below the scroll, '6 H' – all these in gold too. Again the technique is superb; the shadow cast by the anchor on the background is lovingly indicated, and the effect of light and shade on the cage-work of the sphere is meticulous, inside and out. As for the meaning, once again it has to be unpeeled, layer by layer. The motto and the monogram for 'Jesus' suggest a possible link with the opening subject of the chapter, which deals with the reality of oppression in human experience. The celestial or armillary sphere appears in a number of Holbein's designs for medallions, though without its meaning becoming apparent. However, at the end of the century the device was customarily interpreted as a symbol of constancy.[81] This would make good sense of the anchor, another symbol of firm commitment, and relate nicely to the motto which is taken from the words of total obedience to God uttered by Christ in the Garden of Gethsemane.[82]

Beneath this surface religious interpretation, one would expect this illumination, as with the honeysuckle and the oak and all the other historiated letters, to have a meaning that referred directly to Anne or Henry, or both of them. The key to that is the interpretation of the '6 H'. If instead of '6', this is read as the Greek letter sigma, σ, we have the equivalent of 'S' in English, and 'S' in royal monograms means 'Sovereign'. In that case, the religious level of meaning is indicated by the monogram 'IHS' for Jesus above the central scroll, and the secular by 'σH' for 'Sovereign Henry' below it, the appropriate position for a supreme head 'under Christ'. 'Christ's will be done: Henry's will be done,' and the two are effectively congruent. What then is the private significance of the sphere and the anchor? The explanation here is that, as we have seen, Anne used the sphere as a personal symbol, so that in association with the anchor, it spells out her own reliance on Henry. Significantly, their daughter used the symbol of the armillary sphere throughout her reign and possibly while still a princess.[83] One wonders whether those who commissioned paintings of Elizabeth wearing a celestial sphere, or her successive champions, Sir Henry Lee and the earl of Cumberland, who displayed it, recognized in it a covert reference to her mother. That connection must surely have been in her mind when, possibly before 1559, Elizabeth wrote a poem in a psalter opposite the drawing of an armillary sphere, condemning 'the inward suspicious mind' as worse than any physical deformity.[84] Her father's perhaps?

Any survey of Anne Boleyn's interest in art and fine objects must leave one question in doubt. 'What significance did they have for her?' The personal references which can be uncovered in the material, even after an interval of 500 years, certainly suggest that the objects themselves were more than the expected adjuncts of monarchy. This, in turn, gives value to the teasing references in the sources to much which has been lost – payments for forty pieces of fine silver enamelled with Anne's arms as lady marquis, for garnishing books with silver and gilt, for mending a little book 'garnished (with gold) in France', for binding books in velvet.[85] Anne very clearly had interests akin to those of her first mentor, Margaret of Austria. Whether we should elevate this to a passion is a different question and impossible to answer. Nor do we, in our present state of scholarship, know how unusual Anne was among Henry's later wives. Indeed, that question is hardly realistic, for only Katherine Parr lasted more than eighteen months. She possessed plenty of jewellery but much less plate than Anne, and though she is noted as having over a dozen books, they seem distinguished by their bindings rather than their contents.[86] Thereafter the next queens consort were James I's wife, Anne of Denmark, and his son's wife, Henrietta Maria, each of whom did certainly exhibit considerable artistic interest, but, of course, in the quite different cultural milieu of the seventeenth century. Yet when all allowance is made for proper caution, the cultured reality which was Anne still comes through. Whatever else she might have been, she was a woman of a certain aesthetic commitment and discrimination. We must not distort her into a major Renaissance patron in the mould of her contemporary, Isabella d'Este, but we can allow Anne Boleyn a respectable and perhaps distinctive place in the cultural story of sixteenth-century England.

LIFE AT COURT

TO his subjects, Henry VIII's court was less a location than an ecosystem, an organism which sustained not just the king as ruler but the king as a person. Indeed, only theorists made much of the difference between the two, which they came to refer to as his two 'bodies'.[1] When the king moved, the court moved, and Henry and Anne moved often, on average thirty times a year.[2] During winter, spring and early summer they could be found in the larger royal houses, which were capable of taking their full entourage of perhaps 1000 or more people for several weeks at a time. These 'standing houses' were mostly to be found on the artery of the Thames, with Greenwich as a favourite. High summer and autumn saw the royal couple on progress, travelling with a reduced number of attendants within a hundred-mile radius of London, as dictated principally by a search for the best hunting.[3] While on progress they stayed at smaller Crown properties or houses owned by their subjects or by the Church. Thus, during the first six months of 1535, Anne interspersed various periods at Greenwich, at Whitehall and at Hampton Court, ending finally at Windsor. Then came a lengthy progress, a return to Windsor, and finally a move to Richmond in early December.[4]

Married life for Anne meant travelling. For much of the time it also meant living in a building site. From the start of his reign, Henry built. At first he worked at one remove via Cardinal Wolsey, but after 1529 he blossomed as an architect *manqué*. Although the flood-tide of his construction did not set in until 1535, Anne's coming into favour coincided with the acquisition of two major sites, the unfinished Hampton Court and York Place (later Whitehall). Even this was not enough for Henry, augmented though it was by continual large and small building projects in his then eighteen or so other properties. In 1531, before Whitehall was anywhere near finished, the king decided to build St James' – a mere half-mile away. Yet Anne was not a wife who simply put up with the builders; Simon Thurley has described her as Henry's 'enthusiastic partner in building campaigns'.[5] We have seen how the two of them gloated over York Place in the autumn of 1529, and Henry spent the ensuing Christmas designing additions there 'to please the lady who prefers that place for the King's residence to any other'.[6] Anne took over Wolsey's personal lodgings there, leaving Henry to wait for the builder. On one occasion at least she dealt directly with the Whitehall paymaster of works, and her enthusiasm and involvement certainly contributed to the frenzy of activity which overtook Wolsey's former house from 1531 onwards.[7] Impressment of labour, construction by artificial light, canvas screens to allow work to continue in all weathers – everything was done to finish in record time, and it was in the new gatehouse of Whitehall that Henry and Anne were married.[8] By the time she died the site of the former episcopal palace, already made magnificent by Wolsey, had been significantly enlarged, and the existing buildings swallowed up to create what was becoming the king's main residence in (or rather, on the edge of) the city of London.[9]

Because many of the relevant building accounts have been lost, it is difficult to say much more about the impact Anne had on the development of Whitehall. Not so at Hampton Court, where much of the documentation survives. Thus we know from a bill for broken windows that she had her own lodging there by June 1529 if not earlier.[10] While Katherine was still nominally queen Henry built there only for himself, pointedly leaving his first wife in the rooms Wolsey had provided for her in 1526. However, once living with Anne, he put a new queen's suite in hand immediately; indeed, since the foundations were being measured out in January 1533, planning must have begun very soon after the couple returned from Calais.[11] Henry and Anne kept a constant eye on progress, and in November bricklayers were on overtime to finish the walls before the next royal visit.[12] And the king kept on designing. When the couple were staying there in the following July, the payhouse provided papers for 'sundry platts drawn at the king's commandment'.[13]

Anne's new suite broke completely with the recent past. At Richmond, rebuilt after a 1497 fire, Henry's parents had rooms one above the other.[14] At Eltham, modernized between 1519 and 1522, Katherine and Henry had lodgings on opposite sides of the courtyard, though the king seems to have had a bedroom reserved in her suite; at Hampton Court the consort's rooms were on the floor above the king and at Bridewell on the floor below and across the inner courtyard. In sharp contrast, Anne's new apartments at Hampton Court were constructed on the same floor as the king's (the first) and with direct private access to his suite.[15] Although swept away in 1689 by Christopher Wren, it is known that they were erected on the east face of the palace, looking out on the park and backing on an internal gallery. The main entry was at the northern end of this gallery and led to the watching chamber, the presence chamber and the privy or withdrawing chamber and then to the more private rooms, ending with the queen's bedchamber and her jewel chamber. The connection with Henry's existing suite was achieved by extending his privy gallery to link with the southern end of Anne's corridor and to open into a magnificent bedroom for Henry, close to Anne's. At the same time a new privy stair was installed near the junction of the two corridors to give the couple access to the privy garden on the south. The ground floor below Anne's personal suite was a service area including her wardrobe, kitchen, larder and a nursery, all set behind an arcade fronting the park.

The decision to build Anne's rooms over an arcade raises the interesting possibility of French influence. An obvious inspiration could have been 'the façade of the loggias' at Blois which was constructed during Anne's residence there with Queen Claude. On the other hand, considerable caution needs to be exercised when claiming 'artistic influence', and the arcade may simply have echoed existing structures elsewhere in the palace.[16] Where we can rule out Anne's experience at the French court is in the decision to place the suites for king and queen contiguously on the same floor. The rooms Queen Claude occupied at Blois were above those of King Francis, who had access by a private circular stair.[17] As a source for the innovation at Hampton Court, an immediate possibility is the juxtaposed accommodation which Anne and Henry probably occupied during their 1532 visit to Calais.[18] This could well have taught them the advantages of greater intimacy. Alternatively, the Hampton Court plan could simply reflect that rarity in royal marriages, a love match.

As well as major building at Whitehall and Hampton Court, Anne's public recognition meant scores of minor changes in all the royal palaces, replacing heraldic glass and decorations which employed Katherine's arms and symbols, and at Greenwich the opportunity was taken to erect Anne's arms in place of Wolsey's on the great organ in the chapel.[19] In the gallery at Eltham, where the baby Elizabeth played in bad weather, ten of her mother's badges were inserted in the glass at a shilling each. Given the deal of new glass elsewhere in the palace, no doubt similarly decorated, Mary's celebrated rudeness to Anne in the Eltham chapel seems at least more understandable.[20] The royal beasts in the Hampton Court gardens had to make room for a newcomer, a leopard – Anne's secondary badge, derived from the Brothertons – and a leopard was also set up on the hall roof. Fortunately for economy, her successor's device would be a panther, so all that was necessary in 1536 was some anatomical modification.[21] No such modification proved possible to the roof of the Great Hall, which to this day continues to display Anne's arms, the falcon on the roses and the 'HA' monogram.[22] Of more accessible locations, at least one escaped the removal of every trace of Anne's existence which was attempted at her fall; her ciphers are still to be seen on the St James' gatehouse.[23]

From time to time we get glimpses of Anne's own taste. At Greenwich, the ceilings in her presence chamber and bedchamber were decorated with gilded bullions and buds on a lattice of white battens; the areas in front of the chimneys in the main rooms were protected by Seville tiles, and the other alcoves paved in yellow and green Flanders tiles costing a third of the price.[24] At Eltham in 1534, arrangements 'against the coming of the prince' (the child Anne was to lose in the summer) included an iron canopy over the cradle, special measures to exclude draughts, and the redecoration of the suite in yellow ochre.[25] Occasionally we even meet Anne herself. On the king's orders, three bird coops were built at Sir Henry Norris's house in Greenwich town in 1534, for 'the peacock and the pelican that were brought to the king out of the New Found Land'. Anne had complained bitterly to Henry that the birds must be got out of the garden because she 'could not take her rest in mornings for the noise of the same'. Anyone who has had to live in the vicinity of a peacock will sympathize – and feel equally sorry for Norris and his neighbours.[26]

Anne's taste for the antique continues to come through from all the evidence. When Henry had the house at Hanworth fitted up for her, parts of the exterior were decorated with antique work and he had the antique heads transferred there from Greenwich repainted by two Italian artists in his employ (plate 48).[27] Patterned grotesque work covered much of the interior of Whitehall, even the passage to the privy kitchen, and eventually the exterior as well, while *Solomon and the Queen of Sheba* shows very clearly how would-be classical columns and ceilings were used internally.[28] At Hampton Court, Anne's new lodgings were decorated by a German 'moulder of antique', clearly a specialist.[29] Another foreign expert, 'Philip the sculptor', was responsible, with local men working under him, for the one piece of interior design associated with Anne to have survived, the screen at King's College, Cambridge (plate 34), which we have already noticed.[30] The earliest major timber construction in the country entirely in Renaissance style, the screen is a paean of praise to Henry VIII and particularly to his marriage with Anne. The three bays of blind arcading on each side of the double doors have round heads, with carvings in high relief in each tympanum. These, with one exception, are shields displaying royal arms and symbols, two of which refer specifically to Anne. One, supported by cherubs, has the cipher 'RA', and the other the arms of Henry and Anne impaled. Below this latter is a stylized woman's profile (plate 35) and under that a bull's head, a punning reference to the queen's family.[31] The final carving is quite different. In a graphic Renaissance style which could owe something to the Sistine ceiling, it depicts God casting the devil's angels from heaven. At first sight this may seem to clash with the rest of the screen, but in reformist circles the fall of the angels was equated with the rejection of the pope. The carving therefore very probably expresses divine approval for the break with Rome.[32] Over the blind arcade is a continuous coving to accommodate the wider gallery above. In two of its eight sections, a central boss is flanked by the profile of a crowned falcon on the roses in relief, with a third falcon at the base, head-on and visible down to its wings as it displays towards the nave. In the corners of the first are 'HAmat' ciphers; in the other, the cipher 'RA/HEN REX S[overeign] L[ord]'. That monogram also appears in another section of the coving, balancing 'HR' for Henricus Rex. 'RA' opposite 'HR' can also be found on the inner face of the screen over the Provost's stall.

Antique taste can also be detected in Anne's furnishings. When her vice-chamberlain, Edward Baynton, visited Baynards Castle (in the city of London), which she had taken over from Katherine of Aragon, he selected for her from her predecessor's belongings 'a cup of horn with a cover, garnished with antique work, the knop of the cover and the foot of the cup [made of] ivory'; on an earlier occasion, the plate she received from the estate of Henry Guildford included six bowls with 'the feet wrought with antique work and faces'.[33] When Anne 'took her chamber' before Elizabeth was born, her rooms were equipped with two specially made folding tables, one 'for a breakfast table' and the other 'for her grace to play upon' – that is, at cards. Each of these was made 'with tiles entailed [patterned] with antique work'.[34] The one royal artefact which survives, possibly from Anne's actual rooms, is also 'antique work'. It is a gilt metal clock, Renaissance in form and ornamented with grotesque work, busts and pilasters (plate 37). The connection with Anne is evident from its weights which are engraved with 'H' and 'A', true lovers' knots and the mottoes *Dieu et mon droit* and 'The Most Happy'.[35]

What must not be forgotten, however, is that personal taste always served the greater purpose: magnificence. Bills due in the last five months of Anne's life provide a vivid glimpse of the deliberate ostentation royalty was expected to show.[36] For the hunt or the progress, a set of elaborate decorations for the queen's own saddle cost almost £4 10s., four tassels of gold, silver and black silk a further 53s. 4d. Anne's closest attendants had to complement their mistress too, and the provision of a saddle and harness decorations for Lady Margaret Douglas, the king's niece, cost £4 13s. 7½d. Interiors had to be similarly impressive. There were payments for chair decorations in crimson silk, in green silk, and in Venice gold with crimson fringes; for a red sarcenet 'great bed' with a matching sparver, or canopy, lined with blue buckram; for crimson and orange curtains; for a 'little bed' of green satin; for fringes, ribbon, buttons and tassels, often in gold. Even things hidden had to be to a standard. Thirty-two and three-quarter yards of green buckram were purchased just to line the presses or cupboards in the queen's apartments, not that such care was extravagant, given the fine materials Anne had to store. In 1535 Henry gave her more than twenty yards of green satin and over thirteen yards of green cloth of gold and she died owing £8 for forty yards of Venice gold 'wrought with chain work' and £61 5s. for forty-nine pounds of 'sleeved' silk from Spain.[37]

Where accounts mislead is in being effectively silent about tapestry. This was magnificence exemplified. Henry's inventories list hundreds of tapestries, a third of them top quality, but there is nothing to say which ones had belonged to Anne. This is not surprising since the borders where cognizances were usually displayed could be easily removed. Tapestries Anne certainly had. As well as the set of hangings for her room, of cloth of gold and silver and richly embroidered crimson satin, which Henry gave her at new year 1532, in May a further gift of gold arras followed, thirty-two Flemish ells costing £74 13s. 4d.; enquiries after her death also reported 'most goodly hangings' in her house at Hanworth.[38] What we do know more about is jewellery. Henry had lavished this on Anne, even before the pieces he had wrested from Katherine. In the year to May 1532 Cornelius Hayes' bill included three dozen items of jewellery for 'Mistress Anne', costing almost £100. The largest item is a girdle of crown gold billed at £18 10s. 4d., but the most intriguing is a Catherine wheel of gold set with thirteen diamonds at just under £4.[39] The items which Holbein designed for Anne included a pendant with a central stone and the initials 'H' and 'A' intertwined, and a shield with the same cipher.[40] Some time after her death a wooden desk was inventoried, full of pieces, including one diamond ring with the 'HA' cipher, another with the cipher and the text (in Latin), 'O Lord make haste to help me', while a third had a broken part of her motto, 'Moste . . .' Among a quantity of jewellery in boxes were items with 'HA' and a brooch with 'RA' – 'Regina Anna' – in diamonds.[41] One pictorial tradition always shows her with three strands of pearls across the bodice, a necklace of rubies and pearls, a choker with pendant to match, and a brooch made up of the letters 'AB' in gold and a drop pearl.[42] Another tradition depicts her with a pearl choker supporting a letter 'B' in gold with three drop pearls, a second strand of pearls and a golden chain.[43] Except for the 'B' pendant, these pearls are so like those worn in the earliest portrait of Elizabeth as to suggest that the daughter may have been allowed some of her mother's finery (plate 64).[44] Of this personal jewellery, none has survived to be identified. Items remaining from the hundreds of pieces made and remade for the Tudor sovereigns are extremely rare – the taste of one generation is raw material to the next – and in Anne's case many of the items specific to her must have been immediately broken up. Even so, Henry apparently repurchased from Thomas Trappers a gold bowl 'having Queen Anne's sapphire upon the top of the cover' and his post-mortem inventories included a dust bowl of gold (for blotting ink) with a crown on the lid and 'H' and 'A' in enamel.[45] The king also kept a tablet of gold bearing the monogram 'HA'. Set with small emeralds, pearls and one diamond, it suggests vividly what has been lost.[46]

On costume the record is detailed, thanks to William Lok's bill for January to April 1536.[47] This tells of Anne buying gowns in tawny velvet with black lambs' fur, in velvet without fur, in damask, and in satin furred with miniver; a russet gown in caffa (heavy silk), two in black velvet, one in black damask, one in white satin and a second with crimson sleeves; a gown in purple cloth of gold lined with silver, and new carnation satin from Bruges to insert into the sleeves of a gown of tissue. There were eight nightgowns, two embroidered and another in russet trimmed with miniver; and three cloaks – of black Bruges satin, of embroidered tawny satin and of black cloth lined with black sarcenet – while Arnold the shoemaker had eight lots of black velvet to make shoes and slippers. Thirteen kirtles included white satin and white damask, black velvet embroidered and crimson satin 'printed', with matching sleeves. These elaborate detachable sleeves were an important part of female costume; among the scores of 'sleeves for women' in Henry's inventory are at least two pairs which honeysuckle embroidery identifies as belonging to Anne, one 'of white satin embroidered over with purled gold acorns and honeysuckles tied with ten pairs of aiguilettes of gold' and the other 'of cloth of gold embroidered with a great trail of purled gold with honeysuckles tied with ten pairs of aiguilettes of gold'.[48] Sleeves like this did not come cheap. Hayes charged nearly

£5 for the jewelled borders for one pair – gold set with ten diamonds and eight pearls.[49] Many of Anne's costumes would also be enhanced with jewels, such as the nineteen diamonds set in trueloves of gold which Hayes supplied in January 1532, along with twenty-one rubies and twenty-one diamonds set in gold roses and hearts. Anne's liking for French hoods was costly too, at £9 for the jewelled billament.[50] Nicholas Sander's story that 'every day Anne made some change in the fashion of her garments' is entirely credible.[51] Had she lived, her wardrobe might well have rivalled the 2000 costumes which tradition assigns to that most fashion-conscious of monarchs, her daughter Elizabeth. Anne certainly started her child on that route. In that three-month period Lok supplied the two-year-old with a gown of orange velvet, kirtles of russet velvet, of yellow satin, of white damask and of green satin, embroidered purple satin sleeves, a black muffler, white ribbon, Venice ribbon, a russet damask bedspread, a taffeta cap covered with a caul of gold. Anne, apparently, was especially fussy about her daughter's caps: one made of purple satin required at least three journeys to Greenwich to get it right.

These bills take us very much into the domestic life of a Tudor queen. Sewing, tapestry, embroidery: the expected activity of the great lady, her maidens and their humbler assistants. Silks – black, white, orange, tawny, red, green, bought by the ounce and half ounce; ribbon – red, tawny, black, purple, carnation; needle ribbon to roll the queen's hair; fringes, tassels, Venice gold with chain work for a nightgown. Again Henry VIII's inventories show us how right George Wyatt was to say that Hampton Court was sumptuous with 'the rich and exquisite works for the greater part wrought by [Anne's] own hand and needle, and also of her ladies'.[52] At the palace in 1548 was a

carpet of gold, silver, and silk needlework with roses of red and white, and Queen Anne's ciphers with a border about the same of honeysuckles, acorns, 'H' and 'A' of like needlework, fringed at both ends with a deep fringe and at both sides with a narrow fringe of Venice gold silver and silk and lined with green damask being in length three yards and in breadth two scant [nearly].[53]

There was also a cushion embroidered with honeysuckle, acorns, Anne's motto and the letters 'H' and 'A', and another with honeysuckle and the letter 'H'.[54] Anne and her women were very productive. Two 'low chairs of cloth of gold' embroidered with Anne's cipher were still at Hampton Court in 1550.[55] There was also a chair of iron covered all over with needlework, all over wrought with silk and gold with the late Queen Anne's cipher, the post and back fringed with Venice gold with four pommels of silver and gilt, with the king's and the said Queen Anne's arms in them, the seat covered with cloth of gold.[56]

Much of the less elaborately embroidered furniture can likewise be assigned to Anne's initiative. For example, 'a woman's chair with HA crowned in it' appears to have been one of a matching set of nine 'covered with cloth of gold raised with crimson velvet, fringed with Venice gold and crimson silk'.[57]

The most magnificent evocation of the work of Anne and her entourage is a description in Henry VIII's inventories of the hangings made for the gilt and painted bedstead at Oatlands 'called Queen Anne's bed'. These comprised a

'celure' [i.e. canopy], tester [covering for the bed-head], six valances and three bases of crimson cloth of gold with works paned with white cloth of silver, with works richly embroidered with borders of purple velvet upon the seams, and with 108 badges of the king's and Queen Anne's with crowns over the badges, and two great arms of the king's and Queen Anne's joined together in a garland with a crown imperial, the one arm [shield of arms] being in the celure, the other in the tester; the tester and bases being fringed with a narrow fringe of Venice gold and silver, and the valances fringed with a double deep fringe, the one side of red silk and white and the other of Venice gold and silver, and the ends of the said valances being fringed with a narrow fringe of the said gold and silver.

The bed had a counterpane to match, made

of crimson and white damask paned together embroidered about with a border of cloth of gold, with the badges of the king's and Queen Anne's in the four corners and a like arms in the midst (as was in the celure and tester), lozenged all over with cording of Venice gold [i.e. cords making a diamond pattern], fringed with a narrow fringe of Venice gold lined with russet sarcenet.

There were also five matching curtains, though the panes of white silk had been replaced.[58]

By a remarkable coincidence a piece of valance embroidered by Anne has survived. It is in the Burrell collection and is made of white satin with appliqué motifs in black velvet and the decoration includes both the letters 'HA' and acorns and honeysuckle (plate 46).[59] The set of hangings it belonged to cannot be found in Henry's inventories so it was presumably disposed of in his lifetime, but five other beds with furnishings associated with Anne's team can be identified. At Hampton Court the bedstead itself was 'curiously wrought and carved with the late Queen Anne's ciphers and cognisances, painted walnut colour and parcel gilt', with hangings embroidered with Henry and Anne's arms and her cipher.[60] The Greenwich bed, somewhat incongruously, had a counterpane and hangings embroidered with Henry's arms and Anne's monogram, matched with a headboard painted with the king's arms and Jane Seymour's cipher.[61]

Embroidering the hangings and coverings for a bedstead was a major undertaking, as the seventeen feet (5.2 metres), of the surviving fragment of the Burrell valance shows.[62] The counterpane which fitted the Greenwich bed was nine feet and nine inches (3 metres) long and nine feet, two and a quarter inches (2.8 metres) wide. As for the bed at Oatlands, we can only guess how long Anne and her helpers spent on the 108 small and four large royal badges and four great shields of arms, to say nothing of the other embroidery. And there were smaller projects too. The most interesting is listed among the 'sundry parcels' – the miscellanea – at Westminster. It is

one lily pot wrought with the needle and a branch of roses white and red with a white falcon crowned upon the top of the same branch likewise wrought with the needle.[63]

Containers for lilies are regularly seen in Flemish representations of the Annunciation, but these are generally in brass or pottery, not, as here, concealed beneath a cover.[64]

Building, decoration, furnishing, jewels, tapestries, clothing for herself and her daughter, embroidery, all the magnificence of daily royal living. But to twenty-first-century eyes one activity is glaringly omitted: personal attention to her daughter Elizabeth. Although we can almost riffle at will through Anne Boleyn's finery, when we ask about Elizabeth there is no answer. Of course, a great lady of the day did not take daily care of her child. At the age of three months Elizabeth was sent to be fostered at Hertford, although in the first quarter of 1535 she was at court for five weeks.[65] We have seen Anne's concern to see the child turned out in the style to which her status entitled her.[66] We may, if we wish, see something maternal in her providing a fringed crimson satin cover for the head of the child's cradle, or sending 'a pair of pyrwykes', apparently a device to straighten the fingers, about which Elizabeth would later be very proud.[67] Anne also visited Elizabeth, both alone and with Henry, and she was clearly in regular touch with Margaret, Lady Bryan (the mother of Sir Francis), who had actual charge of the child.[68] Indeed, she took a financial bond from Lady Bryan.[69] Yet as the mother of a princess, Anne could have only a partial say in the major decisions about her child; Henry and his council had the last word.[70] When instructions were given to have Elizabeth weaned, at the age of twenty-five months, they were given 'by his grace, with the assent of the queen's grace'.[71] Anne did send a private letter to Lady Bryan, possibly full of maternal instructions about weaning, and she may have felt a special affinity with the woman looking after Elizabeth for she was her mother's half-sister.[72] But that was accidental; Lady Bryan had not been chosen for that relationship, but because she had previously watched over the infancy of the Princess Mary.[73] The choice was clearly Henry's.

There are only a few vignettes of Anne with Elizabeth, or with Elizabeth and Henry. One, two days before her arrest, shows Anne attempting to appeal to Henry through the child and hints at powerful emotions of which we know no more.[74] Already by then Anne had begun to think about Elizabeth's future. A day or two earlier, she had had a conversation on the subject with her chaplain, Matthew Parker. To his dying day he believed that Anne had in some way commended Elizabeth to his spiritual care, though whether this was more than a significance he read into the discussion because it turned out to be the last he ever had with Anne, we cannot know.[75] But even if she was only sharing with him her hopes for Elizabeth's education, the fact that she chose to talk to a man of the kind we shall find Parker to be is a significant pointer to the intellectual and religious upbringing she wanted for the child.[76] It was the upbringing she had had, but managed not with the facilities her father had provided as a rising courtier, but as for a princess. In the event others would train Elizabeth, but she would turn out to be very much her mother's daughter.

It is, of course, quite possible that the surviving sources underplay Anne's involvement with her daughter. Sparse evidence always brings the risk of distortion, and not only in such a private context as mother and child. How different would our appreciation of Anne's life at court be if Henry VIII's inventories had not survived but several sets of firedogs had? The problem is particularly severe in respect of the social life of the court. Its banquets, celebrations and entertainments were the *mise en scène* for Anne's splendid wardrobe, but the chroniclers and letter-writers pass over them in virtual silence once she has become queen. Only the accident of her trial lets us see her dancing with her ladies and the gentlemen of the court in her bedchamber.[77] The one glimpse we do have, and this through a glass darkly, is of Anne and her music. Her skill in performance is commented on by everyone. She also listened. Sir John Harrington's father passed on a verse which he said was written by the king and sung to Anne.[78] Anne's debts included payment for the decoration of a pair of clavichords – perhaps the ones that her 'lover' Mark Smeton was to play on.[79] There is even an outside chance that the Victoria and Albert Museum has a case of virginals played by Anne. Known as 'Queen Elizabeth's Virginals', it has been dated to the first part of that queen's reign, but the decoration is a royal coat of arms and a falcon on the tree-stump.[80] Was Elizabeth only repeating Anne's badge or was something of her mother's being reused?

The principal evidence of Anne's interest in music is the Royal College of Music Manuscript 1070 (plate 26).[81] It is not dated, but the contents of the book would appear to be particularly relevant to Anne's situation in 1533. A majority of the works are in praise of the Virgin Mary or prayers to female saints, and so are fully congruent with the persona Anne presented at her coronation.[82] Indeed, the opening motet (otherwise unknown) is a quasi-secular piece which mixes humanism, classical allusion and Christian symbol very much in the style of that occasion. Other pieces place a strong emphasis on child-bearing, most strikingly two by the French court composer, Jean Mouton. One quotes the Old Testament prayer of rejoicing uttered by Hannah (Anna) when her son was born.[83] The second, a petition for children, specifically mentions the name 'Anne'. This is because it had originally been written for the marriage of Anne, duchess of Brittany, the mother of Anne's patroness, Claude of France. With the typical readiness of a Renaissance prince to pirate a good thing when he heard it, Henry had previously plagiarized the prayer, substituting Katherine for Anne, which gives added point to Anne's return to the original text.[84]

On the other hand the manuscript, as we have seen, is endorsed in a contemporary hand, 'Mistress A Bolleyne nowe thus'.[85] This use of the family name not only makes a 1533 date impossible, but indicates a text in existence prior to Thomas Boleyn's promotion to an earldom in December 1529.[86] The apparent discrepancy with the contents is, however, resolved by a close scrutiny of the inscription 'Mistress A Bolleyne'. The letter 'A' is the 'A' of the 'amat' monogram we have already found in Anne's psalter and in King's College Chapel. Much follows from this. First, the collection must belong to the period from 1527 when Henry and Anne were confidently looking forward to early marriage and the arrival of children, precisely the themes of many of the compositions. Likewise, the ending of that hopeful time would explain why the book was not finished and the manuscript put straight into use instead. Second, it gives immediate relevance to the fourth piece in the collection, a setting of the Gospel in the nuptial mass. Its closing words, 'whom God has joined together let no man put asunder', become a triumphant proclamation of the rightness of Henry's action in repudiating Katherine, whom God had not joined to him, and of heaven's endorsement of the marriage to Anne. Similarly the words 'nowe thus' below 'Mistress A Bolleyne' become an assertion of her confidence in Henry's current affection and in the promise of future change or, alternatively, a boast that her situation as plain Mistress Boleyn was only temporary. We can even speculate on the curious musical notation which follows: three minims and a longa.[87] Self-evidently the notes refer to time, so the three minims could be a code for the interval Anne and Henry knew was unavoidable before the longa of a happy conclusion.[88]

Date, however, is not the only issue to be resolved – there is quality: paper rather than vellum, frequent corrections, and omissions in both text and score. Four illustrations per folio were intended, but only twenty sheets were completed (one in seven) and with a decidedly old-fashioned collection of fruit, foliage, grotesques and monsters, not by the best of illustrators. The mediocre quality led Lowinsky to rule out the idea of a gift from the French court or of a gift commissioned by any courtier of standing. Searching for a donor of lower rank with musical skill, court connections, and an acquaintance with Anne's tastes in music, he came up with the name of Mark Smeton, the musician with whom she was accused in 1536. Unfortunately for the conjecture, in and before 1529 Smeton appears to have belonged to Wolsey's household.[89] The alternative suggestion, that Anne acquired the manuscript in France, or even during her stay with Margaret of Austria, seems unlikely, given the marital reference of the contents. A more mundane possibility is that the manuscript is a draft destined eventually to go to a professional, and that the illuminations were either rough indications of what was wanted or the work of an amateur once further development had been abandoned when marriage seemed to recede into the distance.

The date and contents of Manuscript 1070 raise difficulties, but the substantive evidence it provides must not be overlooked. We have already noticed the link between the contents of the book and what Anne had experienced abroad.[90] Four items are by composers whom Archduchess Margaret recruited during her brief time as duchess of Savoy, and nine are by Margaret's favourite, Josquin des Prés, whom Anne would at least have seen, if not met, during her months in the duchess's service.[91] From the French court, Josquin's pupil, Jean Mouton, is the most represented. We can be sure that Anne would have met him; not only was he at the height of his career during her years in France, but he was indebted to Claude, whose mother had launched him at court.[92] All this repertoire calls for professional singers, so Anne Boleyn would not have taken part herself. It is however, not unreasonable to see her influencing the musical life of the court by favouring the choral style she had come to know in her formative years abroad.

Although most of the compositions in the book are for church use, six are secular. One by an anonymous composer is a neo-Latin poem linking the New Testament story of Lazarus with Olympus and the Greek gods. Two are Italian humanist poems set by Josquin. The remaining three are, in many ways, the most interesting. They are examples of the new style of Parisian *chanson*, which had become especially fashionable at the French court during Anne's stay with Claude. With an evident lyrical melodic line, the *chanson* strove for lightness and for music married to the rhythm of words chosen for grace and wit, often bordering on the risqué. Amateur ensembles could perform these. One of the *chansons* in Anne's book is a setting by Claude de Sermisy of a poem by Clément Marot. During Anne's time in France Marot was at the start of his court career, and she would later offer him refuge from persecution.[93] Sermisy she must have encountered. He was one of Francis I's favourite musicians, and under the soubriquet of 'Claudin', his eventual output of 160 or so *chansons* included some of the most popular music of his day.[94] The Claudin/Marot piece is a dialogue with 'Joy':

> Jouyssance vous donneray,
> Mon amy, et vous meneray
> Là où pretend vostre esperance.
> [I will give you joy my friend and lead you where your hope lies]

and the impudent answer is:

> De vostre mort mary seray
> [I would be very sad at your death]

For the other two chansons in the book, we have only a title, but these too give a flavour of the new form: *Venes regres venes tous* ('Come repining, come whatever') and *Gentilz galans compaignons* ('My gentle, gallant fellows'). We can have little doubt that Henry joined Anne to sing these and others like them.

THE ADVENT OF REFORM

THE most haunting description of Anne Boleyn is 'Anna of the Thousand Days'. The brevity of her marriage, the gradient of catastrophe from the coronation to Tower Green, her final total vulnerability, it is all there, above all the transience – gone, almost as though she had never been. The image is arresting, but the Protestant leaders in her daughter's reign would have rejected it decisively. John Foxe declared of Anne: 'What a zealous defender she was of Christ's gospel all the world doth know, and her acts do and will declare to the world's end.'[1] Of course, remarks like this are what we would expect of Foxe and the rest. From 1558, although Elizabeth, the new queen, was committed to restoring and defending her father's supremacy over the English Church, she needed (the reformers believed) every possible stiffening to persuade her to adhere to a clearly Protestant position. Yet the evidence is on their side; Anne Boleyn was not a catalyst in the English Reformation; she was a key element in the equation.[2]

We have seen how Anne played a major part in pushing Henry into asserting his headship of the Church. That headship was not just a constitutional rejection of the primacy of Rome. It was, as Thomas More and others at the time were well aware, a change with profound implications, revolutionizing the ethos of Christianity in England. Yet over and beyond this, Anne was a strong supporter of religious reform – defined as we shall see later – and she was the first to demonstrate the potential there was in the royal supremacy for that distinctive element in the English Reformation, the monarch's freedom to take the initiative in religious change. Whatever the chances were of any grass-roots movement for reform on this side of the Channel, it made all the difference when the impetus towards change came from the highest level in the land. Brief though Anne's influence was, it was a thousand days of support for reform from the throne itself. And hindsight can say more. The breach in the dyke of tradition which she encouraged and protected made the flood first of reformed, and later of more specifically Protestant Christianity, unstoppable. Catholic hatred of Anne damned her for the break with Rome and for the entrance of heresy into England. It was right on both counts.

The most striking evidence of Anne Boleyn's influence in the Church is what Alexander Ales described to Elizabeth as 'the evangelical bishops whom your most holy mother had appointed from among those scholars who favoured the purer doctrine of the gospel'.[3] William Latymer listed them as Cranmer, Hugh Latimer, Nicholas Shaxton, Thomas Goodrich and her almoner John Skip, although the latter was not elected a bishop until three years after Anne's death. The actual list is somewhat longer. Chapuys noted the partisan appointment of John Salcot, alias Capon, to Bangor, while William Barlow, elected to St Asaph's and St David's in quick succession in 1536, was a staunch Boleyn supporter.[4] Indeed, of the ten elections to the episcopate between 1532 and Anne's death in 1536, seven were reformers who were her clients. Another, Edward Fox, was clearly being rewarded for his sterling support for Anne during the divorce, and the list also included John Hilsey who, though not directly linked to Anne, was a protégé of Cranmer.[5] Alexander Ales was, of course, exaggerating when he wrote of Anne 'appointing' these men – William Latymer was more correct to talk of her 'continual mediations' with the king 'for their preferment' – but the point is clear. And the influence of this spate of appointments was crucial to the future of the Reformation. At the end of the reign, the reforming bishops in office were still predominantly those patronized by Anne Boleyn.[6]

Anne's religious patronage extended to lesser positions in the Church as well. When Henry Gold, Archbishop Warham's former chaplain, was executed for complicity with the Nun of Kent, Anne secured his benefice of St Mary Aldermanbury for Dr Edward Crome, only to find that fashionable London cleric somewhat slow in responding to his royal patron. The result was a stinging rebuke, linking the neglect of his own best interests with neglect for the advancement of godly doctrine.[7] This was in 1534, but Anne had been exercising an influence on appointments long before this. In the summer of 1528 she was pressing Wolsey to change his mistaken nomination of William Barlow to the living of Tonbridge into the living of Sundridge, which was what her father had originally asked for.[8] Nor, as the letter to Crome shows, was her interest just in securing rewards for favourite clerics, but in using them to promote reform. It was no accident that when she wanted to place a 'friend' in the hospital of St John Redcliffe, she couched her letter to the corporation of Bristol as a request to grant the next appointment to two reformers in her entourage, Baynton and Shaxton, and David Hutton, a local reformist leader.[9]

We know, indeed, a little of the way in which William Barlow exploited the promotion Anne secured for him to the priory of Haverfordwest in Pembrokeshire, a year or so before his appointment as a bishop in North Wales.[10] Cromwell also wanted the bishop of St David's to accept Barlow as suffragan, but Bishop Rawlins would have nothing to do with this incomer and his contentious preaching of 'God's Word'. Considerable friction arose in the monastery between the conservatives and the new prior, who was supported by his brother John, another Boleyn protégé, who knew Anne well and was reckoned to owe to her his position as dean of Westbury. The infighting grew so bad that at one point William was forced to leave Pembroke. The correspondence between London and West Wales that the quarrel produced gives tantalizing glimpses of the network of conservative resistance to reform at the centre and in the provinces, at one point even touching Dr John Incent of St Paul's, who was to be accused of the murder in 1536 of the anticlerical London member of parliament, Robert Pakington.[11] Be that as it may, Anne was certainly engaged against Incent in another battle – to wrest control of the St Paul's chapter from him and his fellow conservatives.[12] When Anne was arrested, John Barlow's commitment to her nearly led him to disaster. Apparently deciding that the first news of this was a malicious conservative rumour, he descended on Pembrokeshire, only to have the informant, who was, as he suspected, one of the leading anti-reformers, threaten him and declare that one as close to Anne as Barlow must have been privy to her treason and should be arrested in case he made an escape by sea from Milford Haven. Fortunately for the dean, he kept his head and arrested the informant instead, making dark threats about papist sympathizers.

As the involvement of Thomas Cromwell in the Pembroke quarrels demonstrates, Anne Boleyn was not alone in her support for reform. She was one of a group of powerfully placed individuals whose loss was lamented in the early 1540s by Richard Hilles, a London merchant of reformist leanings who after the death of the queen found England increasingly hot for him: he listed Anne herself, Rochford, Cromwell (all dead), Latimer (resigned), and he could have included Shaxton too.[13] Other names were added by John Foxe in a later remark: 'So long as Queen Anne, Thomas Cromwell, Archbishop Cranmer, Master Denny, Doctor Butts, with such like were about [Henry VIII], and could prevail with him, what organ of Christ's glory did more good in the church than he?'[14] Rochford's support for reform had been particularly open; Chapuys hated being entertained by him because of his insistence on starting religious debates.[15] Anne's brother referred to this love in his speech on the scaffold, which was widely reported in England and abroad:

> I was a great reader and a mighty debater of the word of God, and one of those who most favoured the gospel of Jesus Christ. Wherefore, lest the word of God should be brought into reproach on my account, I now tell you all, Sirs, that if I had, in very deed, kept his holy word, even as I read and reasoned about it with all the strength of my wit, certain am I that I should not be in the piteous condition wherein I now stand. Truly and diligently did I read the gospel of Christ Jesus, but I turned not to profit that which I did read; the which, had I done, of a surety I had not fallen into so great errors. Wherefore I do beseech you all, for the love of our Lord God, that ye do at all seasons, hold by the truth, and speak it, and embrace it; for beyond all peradventure, better profiteth he who readeth not and yet doeth well, than he who readeth much and yet liveth in sin.

The final sentence has lost its freshness and part of its point in the course of translation. Constantine remembered Rochford's words 'to the effect' that 'I had rather had a good liver according to the gospel than ten babblers.'[16]

There is even a possibility that the Boleyns sought, or maintained, private links with reformers abroad. In 1535 and 1536 Master Thomas Tebold, later known as one of Cromwell's continental agents, was travelling in Europe, supported by the earl of Wiltshire with some assistance from Cranmer.[17] Very few of the regular letters he sent home have survived, but in July 1535 he was in Antwerp, reporting to Cranmer on his enquiries into the arrest of William Tyndale. We may note here that the appeals for Henry VIII to intervene to save the translator passed from Thomas Poinz, his landlord in Antwerp, to Poinz's brother John, who was one of Anne's receivers, and from him to Cromwell.[18] Tebold meanwhile had intended to go into Germany, but no doubt the Tyndale furore decided him on a detour to Orléans, unless, that is, he went there with the intention of reporting to the Boleyns, as he did on 9 January, on the current state of religious persecution in France, where an impudent reformist propaganda campaign – the Affair of the Placards – had created a massive conservative backlash. His cover, if that is not too strong a term, was scholarship and a desire to study languages, and by the spring of 1536 he was travelling in southern and central Germany, including Wittenberg, meeting everyone who was anyone – among them, it seems, the Strassburg reformer, Martin Bucer – spreading the idea that Thomas Boleyn was a promising patron of works, theological and other, keeping up a flow of diplomatic news, and enlivening his hosts by explaining the advantages of dissolving monastic houses. He was also in touch with French reformers in flight from the Placards persecution, and was able to send back to Anne's father a piece published by Clément Marot.

The reforming group was thus more numerous than Anne alone, but it is clear that the queen was a key figure. After her death, Nicholas Shaxton wrote personally to Cromwell, begging him to be as diligent in promoting 'the honour of God and his Holy Word than when the late queen was alive and often incited you thereto'.[19] Ales went so far as to say to Elizabeth I, 'True religion in England had its commencement and its end with your mother.'[20] This explains why Cranmer, no less than Shaxton, was terrified in 1536 that she would bring down the cause of reform with her.[21] Already in 1532, Dr John London, one of the secretary's unlovelier clerical agents, was showing great anxiety to stand in her good books; in 1534 Cranmer asked an unknown correspondent to accelerate an appointment as a personal favour, but carefully hinted that he could provide letters from Henry and from Anne if forced to do so; when the archbishop wrote to Cromwell in 1535 of the need to plant reform in Calais, he reported that he had already written to Anne to secure the next two benefices that became vacant in the town.[22]

The queen's concern for religion is especially well documented in the case of monastic houses. Soon after her coronation, one of the rival factions in the abbey at Burton-on-Trent was apparently expecting that Cromwell, under pressure from Henry and Anne, would countermand the orders he had already given for the election of a new abbot.[23] In 1533 she took action to get Cromwell to investigate conditions at Thetford Priory, and later that summer she was communicating with him about the abbey of Vale Royal in Cheshire.[24] All this certainly gives credibility to the stories told by her chaplain, William Latymer. If we accept his testimony, Anne was fully behind the campaign to impose new injunctions on the monastic houses, which Cromwell began in the summer of 1535.[25] One of these injunctions prohibited the display of 'relics or feigned miracles'. When, in the third week in July, Anne and Henry arrived on progress at Winchcombe in Gloucestershire, close to the famous pilgrim centre of Hailes Abbey, she sent a posse of her chaplains to the monastery to 'view, search and examine by all possible means' the bona fides of the house's greatest attraction, 'the blood of Hailes', which was supposed never to have congealed since Christ's crucifixion. They reported that it was duck's blood or wax, whereupon Anne went to the king, and the relic was removed – to the comfort, Latymer says, of ignorant and weak Christians, but one might rather suppose their bewilderment at a raid by such exalted sceptics. Unfortunately for Latymer's story, the relic was still there in 1538, when a more thorough inspection removed the contents and decided it was some kind of resin, but it may still be true that Anne did intervene at Hailes Abbey in 1535.[26] A visit to the house by Henry and Anne was undoubtedly intended, and that may have led to the abbot being interviewed by Cromwell; certainly the secretary was involved with the community. There is even support for the possibility that Anne did achieve some temporary removal of the relic. When preaching about the deception in 1538 and announcing the latest findings, John Hilsey apologized for spreading the story that the material was duck's blood, which clearly implies an earlier questioning of the relic, and agrees exactly with one of the explanations William Latymer gives of what Anne was told.

One episode for which Latymer is the sole authority is the visit that Anne Boleyn paid to the nuns of Syon, that remarkable flower of English monasticism which combined aristocratic exclusiveness with genuine piety and serious learning.[27] The detail Latymer gives does allow us to date the visit to early December 1535, when the queen was at nearby Richmond, and so to establish the authenticity of the story, since at that time a major effort was being made to compel this prestigious community to accept the new order.[28] As well as lesser agents, Cromwell himself went down; and a day or so later, on Tuesday, 14 December, John Skip and Dr William Butts, the king's physician (of whom more anon), formed the first wave of a concentrated assault. The next day the king himself sent four high-powered academics, and Lord Windsor, whose sister was a nun at Syon, also did what he could; on the Thursday the bishop of London arrived. Come Saturday and a full report to the king, and it seems likely that Anne's visit was the outcome. Perhaps a woman, the queen herself, would have more success. She arrived when the nuns were in choir, to be refused entry on the ground that she was married and so excluded by the rule of the order. Anne declined to accept the answer and waited, with her attendants. Eventually the choir doors were opened and her party came in, only to discover all sixty or so nuns prostrate, with their faces fixedly 'downward to the ground'. Thereupon, if we are to believe Latymer, Anne addressed this unpromising audience with 'a brief exhortation' about the moral decline of the congregation – all sorts of slanders were being reported back to the court – and she also rebuked them for persisting with Latin primers which they could not understand, offering them English primers instead which, after some resistance, the nuns accepted. Throughout his memoir Latymer makes Anne appear painfully stilted, and the absurd pomposity of this speech invites disbelief; it is hardly effective to admonish the backs of an audience's heads, and Anne, of all people, must have known that these daughters of the best families and of the most scholarly religious house in England were better Latinists than she. But whatever really happened, Anne's visit did not effect the desired conversion. We do not know that the nuns ever promised to accept the king's headship of the Church.

The particular agents of Anne's religious influence were her chaplains, whom she chose with care from the most promising young reformist scholars, particularly from Cambridge.[29] Her talent-spotter was Dr William Butts, who combined a privileged position as a medical man with an interest in reform and a concern for his former university, especially his old college, Gonville Hall. It was Butts who brought Latimer to court, where he became a chaplain to Anne and was on very good terms with her vice-chamberlain, Edward Baynton. Shaxton and Skip were Gonville men and so was Crome, whom we have already noticed. Sometimes Butts went direct to the king, as he did when he recommended John Cheke, Prince Edward's future tutor, for promotion, but when Cheke sought support for the up-and-coming William Bill, later Elizabeth's almoner, Anne was the person he approached, via another of her chaplains, Matthew Parker.[30]

The queen's pursuit of Parker, who would end his career as her daughter's first archbishop of Canterbury, is particularly well documented. William Betts, another Gonville Hall man, had moved to Corpus Christi college and later became Anne's chaplain. Parker, also a Corpus man, was evidently commended to Anne by Betts, and on the latter's death she decided that Parker should succeed him. No time was lost. Her almoner, John Skip, wrote two letters on the same day, urging him to come at once without bothering to collect much baggage – a long gown would do.[31] Six months demonstrated how well she had chosen. The king sent Parker, 'chaplain to our dearest wife', a doe to enjoy; and Anne gave him something more permanent, the post of dean of the collegiate church of Stoke by Clare in Suffolk.[32] He preached to the household of the Princess Elizabeth, and then before Henry on the third Sunday in Lent 1536.[33] Whether Cranmer gave him the advice about preaching that he gave to Latimer is not known – don't grind axes, don't get at individuals, and don't go on too long: 'an hour, or an hour and a half at the most, for by long expense of time the king and the queen shall peradventure wax so weary at the beginning [of the series of sermons] that they shall have small delight to continue throughout with you to the end.'[34] Probably Parker had sense enough to tell how much Anne could stand, for their relationship of patron and client, laywoman and Christian pastor, was evidently sympathetic. As we have seen, less than six days before her arrest, Anne seems to have laid a particular responsibility on him to watch over her daughter. That charge, and the debt he felt he owed to Anne, stayed with him for the rest of his life.[35]

Cranmer's advice to be cautious in sermons was wise, for Anne's clerical favourites were very much marked men. Several, indeed, were men with a past. William Betts had been associated with the scandal at Wolsey's college in Oxford in 1528 over the circulation of prohibited books; at the time Anne herself had interceded with Wolsey for one of the others involved, possibly the Thomas Garret who was burned at the stake in 1540.[36] A number of these men were also associated with the martyr Thomas Bilney, notably Hugh Latimer and Parker, who saw Bilney die.[37] Yet it would be wrong to picture Anne as a patron of a tight and unified caucus. The clergy she supported differed among themselves – Edward Fox, Hilsey and possibly Cranmer found Latimer far too extreme at times – and although some would end their lives as martyrs for 'Protestantism', others such as Shaxton would find their place among the upholders of 'Catholic' ways.[38]

Applying confessional labels in the 1520s and 1530s is, in fact, wholly inappropriate. In was, in Lucien Febvre's telling phrase, a period of 'magnificent religious anarchy'.[39] When Anne first began to patronize the more innovative clergy of the day, Luther's ninety-five theses were hardly more than a decade old; the events which gave rise to the very name 'Protestant' occurred only two months before the opening of the legatine court at Blackfriars. Even on the continent, lines were in the course of being drawn – among reformers, as well as between reformers and conservatives. Indeed, within nine months of the Protestant 'protestation', reform had been disrupted by a disagreement about the nature of the eucharist, which would produce permanent division. There would henceforth be Catholics, Lutherans and sacramentaries, as well as 'anabaptists', that inchoate religious self-help minority which added withdrawal from established society and its obligations to the sacramentarian belief that the bread and wine at the eucharist were a symbol of Christ's death and not, in some real sense, Christ's own body and blood. But with

London being 450 miles and two languages away from this turmoil of definition, to say nothing of an admittedly imperfect but nevertheless highly active English censorship, it is appropriate during Anne's lifetime to see only two general positions in England – that the Church needed to be supported as it was, and that the Church as it was needed to be reformed – around which and between which most individuals ranged with varying levels of commitment.

What then did reform mean to Anne Boleyn? Chapuys damned her, her father and her brother as Lutherans, but he was probably not implying any direct link, merely an equality in error. There is no hint, either, that Anne had links with previous English heresy, although Latimer was accused of being a Lollard, and there were congruences between the new critics of the Church and the persecuted underground which looked back to John Wyclif. The absolute conviction which drove Anne was the importance of the Bible. For that reason, if her brand of reform needs to be given a label, that label must be 'evangelical' – 'pertaining to the *euangelion*, the gospel, and especially to the written gospel'.

First of all, Anne talked about the Bible, just as her brother did. William Latymer describes her habit of discussing some scriptural problem whenever she dined with Henry, and said that this was copied at the tables of her chamberlain and vice-chamberlain.[40] From time to time Henry would join in, and Latymer had himself seen the correspondence which arose out of one debate between the king and Sir James Boleyn on one side and Hugh Latimer and Nicholas Shaxton on the other. Scriptural debate at table is hardly in favour today, but it was certainly the thing among sixteenth-century evangelical hostesses. Katherine Parr, Henry's last wife, also encouraged the king's taste for this latest in intellectual stimulus.

Anne also studied the Bible. Her private preference, as Latymer says quite correctly, was for the French text:

> Her highness was very expert in the French tongue, exercising herself continually in reading the French Bible and other French books of like effect and conceived great pleasure in the same, wherefore her highness charged her chaplains to be furnished of all kind of French books that reverently treated of the holy scripture.[41]

A vivid picture of this was drawn by Louis de Brun, author of 'Vng Petit Traicte en Francoys', a treatise on letter-writing, which he dedicated to Anne at new year 1531:

When I consider the great affection and real passion which you have for the French tongue, I am not surprised that you are never found, if circumstances permit, without your having some book in French in your hand which is of use and value in pointing out and finding the true and narrow way to all virtues, as, for example, translations of the Holy Scriptures, reliable and full of all sound doctrines, or, equally, of other good books by learned men who give healthy advice for this mortal life and consolation for the immortal soul. And most of all, last Lent and the Lent before [i.e. 1530 and 1529], when I was attending this magnificent, excellent and triumphant court, I have seen you continually reading those helpful letters of St. Paul which contain all the fashion and rule to live righteously, in every good manner of behaviour, which you know well and practise, thanks to your continual reading of them.[42]

While Anne read for herself in French, she was eager to disseminate the Bible in the vernacular. According to Latymer, she kept an English version on a lectern in her suite for anyone to read who wished.[43] If strictly true, this must refer to the final months of her life, since Coverdale's Bible did not appear until 1535 in Zurich. The exiled Bible translators were certainly keen to secure royal patronage; George Joye, a former associate of Tyndale, printed a sample sheet from Genesis and sent a copy to Henry and one to Anne.[44] Anne's copy of Tyndale's 1534 edition of the New Testament is still extant (plate 28).[45] Printed on vellum, with the capital letters hand-coloured in red, many of the woodcuts in full colour, and the edges gilded, it looks very like a presentation copy. The significant point about the Tyndale is that it was a banned book in England; one conservative cleric had declared soon after the first edition that no one who received it could be a true son of the Church.[46] Coverdale's work, too, would be banned when it appeared, despite the unofficial dedication to Henry.

Anne also defied established ecclesiastical authority by protecting the illegal trade in Bibles. It was probably as early as the end of 1530 that a Thomas Alwaye prepared to approach her in the hope that she would get the bishops off his back, following his arrest and imprisonment for possessing an English Testament and other prohibited books.[47] A year after she became queen she put in hand the restoration of the Antwerp merchant, Richard Herman, to membership of the English society of merchants there, from which he had been expelled in Wolsey's time, 'only for that that he [still like a good Christian man] did both with his goods and policy, to his great hurt and hinderance in this world, help the setting forth of the New Testament in English'.[48] It has also been suggested that Anne may have been behind the licensing of a Southwark printer from the Low Countries to produce the Coverdale text in England, and therefore free of the dangerous glosses which foreign books so often carried. Add to that the possibility that so long as she was alive, the drafts of the injunctions to the clergy being prepared in 1536 included a clause requiring every parish to set up a Latin and an English Bible in its church, 'for every man that will to look and read thereon'.[49]

To recognize the dominant place in life which Anne Boleyn gave to the Bible is to locate her faith firmly in the world of Christian humanism. For a man like Erasmus, the premier Christian humanist of all, the Bible, in as reliable a form as scholarship could produce, was central to all good living:

> If you approach the scriptures in all humility and with regulated caution, you will perceive that you have been breathed upon by the Holy Will of God. It will bring about a transformation that is impossible to describe... Man may lie and make mistakes; the truth of God neither deceives nor is deceived.[50]

Erasmus, indeed, was aware of Anne. Already he had translated the Twenty-second Psalm for her father, but when in 1533 he wrote two more pieces dedicated to the earl, *A Preparation to Death* and *A Plain and Godly Exposition or Declaration of the Common Creed*, he began the latter:

> To the right excellent and most honourable lord, Thomas earl of Wiltshire and of Ormonde, father to the most gracious and virtuous Queen Anne, wife to the most gracious sovereign lord, King Henry the VIIIth, Erasmus of Rotterdam, Greeting![51]

Yet Anne's particular religious affinity was not with Erasmus but with the Christian humanists of France. We have already noted her manuscript French psalter with its muscular *putti* and monograms. It employs a translation from Hebrew credited to the Picquard scholar, Louis de Berquin, who was burned as a heretic in 1528. The French Bible which Anne used was a 1534 Antwerp edition of the 1525 translation by Jacques Lefèvre d'Etaples, the first great evangelical figure in France, a text which the Paris Faculty of Theology was equally anxious to consign to the fire. Lefèvre had to flee to Strassburg.[52] Anne's Bible is now part of the collection of the British Library. It is in two volumes and retains much of the binding put on when it was received in England (see plate 29). There are 'HA' ciphers and Tudor roses, and a decidedly evangelical choice of texts for the front and back of each volume:

AINSI + QUE + TOVS + MEVRENT + PAR + ADAM:
AVSSY + TOVS + SERONT + VIVIFIES + PAR + CHRIST.
LA + LOY + A + ESTE + DONNEE + PAR + MOYSSE:
LA + GRACE + ET + LA + VERITE + PAR + IESV + CHRIST.[53]

The full-page frontispiece of the creation is coloured.

Two more of Lefèvre's works which Anne owned we have already met as illuminated manuscripts. 'The Pistellis and Gospelles for the LII Sondayes in the Yere' is part copy, part English translation of his *Epistres et Evangiles des cinquante et deux semaines de l'an*, printed by Simon du Bois at Alençon, 1530–2.[54] The actual copy the scribe worked from has also survived; manuscript annotations establish that it is now in the British Library (shelf-mark 1016.a.9). 'The Ecclesiaste' is a similarly hybrid version of a Lefèvre publication, his translation of a commentary by Johannes Brenz. This was printed *circa* 1531 as *L'Ecclesiaste*, also by du Bois at Alençon.[55] What must be the copy text of this also survives in the British Library (1016.a.5).

Why would anyone go to the labour and expense of turning printed French texts which Anne could read perfectly well into such mixed and elaborate manuscripts? For more than a century the translator of 'The Pistellis and Gospelles' was thought to have been Henry Parker, Lord Morley, George Boleyn's father-in-law, but in 1998 James Carley managed to read a damaged inscription and establish that the person responsible was none other than George himself.[56] His dedication is worth recording as a demonstration under the guise of courtly gallantry of the closeness of brother and sister, but even more for the evidence that George was writing at Anne's request:

> To the right honourable lady, the Lady Marchioness of Pembroke, her most loving and friendly brother sends greetings.

> Our friendly dealings, with so divers and sundry benefits, besides the perpetual bond of blood, have so often bound me, Madam, inwardly to love you, daily to praise you, and continually to serve you, that in every of them I must perforce become your debtor for want of power, but nothing of my good will. And were it not that by experience your gentleness is daily proved, your meek fashion often times put in use, I might well despair in myself, studying to acquit your deserts towards me, or embolden myself with so poor a thing to present you. But, knowing these perfectly to reign in you with more, I have been so bold to send unto you, not jewels or gold, whereof you have plenty, not pearl or rich stones, whereof you have enough,

but a rude translation of a well-willer, a good matter meanly handled, most humbly desiring you with favour to weigh the weakness of my dull wit, and patiently to pardon where any fault is, always considering that by your commandment I have adventured to do this, without the which it had not been in me to have performed it. But that hath had power to make me pass my wit, which like as in this I have been ready to fulfil, so in all other things at all times I shall be ready to obey, praying him on whom this book treats, to grant you many good years to his pleasure and shortly to increase in heart's ease with honour.[57]

Two important conclusions arise from this dedication. First it nails once and for all the canard that Anne saw illuminated religious books primarily as fine art. If a fine manuscript was all that was wanted, why ask George to translate this particular text? Secondly, the affinity between 'The Pistellis and Gospelles' and 'The Ecclesiaste' effectively makes it certain that George was also responsible for the latter. That in turn authenticates a passage in George Boleyn's scaffold speech which was uniquely recorded by a Calais soldier, Elis Gruffudd – probably passed on by the executioner:

Truly so that the Word should be among the people of the realm I took upon myself great labour to urge the king to permit the printing of the Scriptures to go unimpeded among the commons of the realm in their own language. And truly to God I was one of those who did most to procure the matter to place the Word of God among the people because of the love and affection which I bear for the Gospel and the truth of Christ's words.[58]

Promoting the vernacular Bible was clearly a Boleyn family enterprise.

Why Anne should ask her brother for part translations can only be guessed at. The comments of Latymer demonstrate that she was anxious for others to hear the evangelical message, but the elite quality of 'The Ecclesiaste' and 'The Pistellis' shows that these particular manuscripts were not for general use. Perhaps it was that even if Anne, as we have seen, was herself ready to ignore the episcopal ban on English Bibles, professional scribes and illuminators were reluctant to do so. Alternatively, retaining the Bible passages in French may simply illustrate the fact that individuals dislike changes to scripture versions they are familiar with.[59]

It is also possible to follow up Latymer's reference to Anne's chaplains being 'furnished of all kind of French books that reverently treated of the holy scripture', and du Brun's mention of her having 'other good books by learned men who give healthy advice for this mortal life and consolation for the immortal soul'. We have seen Thomas Tebold sending home books, and the queen used other agents as well. William Lok, her mercer, ran errands for her on his trips to the Low Countries, and his daughter remembered in her eighties how 'Queen Anne Boleyn that was mother to our late Queen Elizabeth caused him to get her the gospels and epistles written in parchment in French, together with the psalms.'[60] William Latymer himself was on a book-buying trip for Anne when she was arrested.[61] A clue to what they bought is given by the existence of shelf-marks in the copy of *L'Ecclesiaste* which George Boleyn used to prepare his translation. These demonstrate that the book ended up in the royal library at Westminster, no doubt when his (and his sister's) property was confiscated by the Crown in 1536. But that library also contained a substantial number of other French evangelical books, also published by du Bois and all issued between 1527 and 1534, but not later. The conclusion seems irresistible. They too had been owned by Anne and her brother. Indeed, this was probably the case with other evangelical works published abroad in these key years and which are known to have been subsequently in the Westminster library, notably the nine items (including Anne's French Bible) which were printed by Martin Lempereur, who also produced the copy Anne owned of Tyndale's New Testament. In all, the Boleyn confiscations might have yielded as many as forty evangelical books in French or by French printers.

Anne's link with French reform also accounts for her presentation manuscript of 'Le Pasteur Evangélique'.[62] This is an anonymous poetic discourse on the tenth chapter of the Gospel of John where Christ contrasts the good and the bad shepherds, hence the title under which it was published at Antwerp in 1541: *Le Sermon du bon pasteur et du mauvais*.[63] The Antwerp title-page gives the author as Clément Marot, one of the enduring lights of French reform, but this has been questioned, and the theory propounded that the poem was specifically written for Anne during a visit to England by Almanque Papillon, a valet of Francis I.[64] The earliest known text of the poem is certainly the copy presented to Anne, and it concludes with twenty-five lines which eulogize Henry VIII as Francis I's constant friend and a monarch endowed with the virtue of true riches, one of the great Christian rulers of the day, and a veritable Hezekiah reforming the Church. The final sestet addresses Anne directly with a prophecy that the Good Shepherd [Christ] would give her a son in Henry's image, whom the couple would live to see grow into manhood:[65]

> Oh Anne my lady, Oh incomparable queen
> This Good Shepherd who favours you

will give you a son who will be the living image
of the king his father, and he will live and flourish
until the two of you can see him reach the age
when a man is mature.

Unfortunately for the theory that the poem was specially written for Anne, three other endings are known. These suggest that even if Anne was the first recipient, *Le Sermon* was conceived as a piece of reformist humanism which could be adapted as required. As for authorship, the Sorbonne as well as the printer had no doubt that Marot was responsible. Who the donor of the manuscript was we do not know. The evident expense argues that this was not the poet himself, and the most plausible candidate must be Anne's favourite, Jean de Dinteville. Indeed it could be his gift on the occasion of, or in commemoration of, the coronation, since the lines about Anne must date from after her marriage and before late 1534, when Marot fled from France, pursued by name as a leading 'Lutheran', the pejorative label the conservatives gave to reform.[66] Be that conjecture as it may, the poem remains another most persuasive demonstration of Anne's link with French reform.

Anne Boleyn, however, was not content with book-collecting. Latymer tells of Anne coming to the immediate rescue of a French refugee, 'Mistress Mary', who had fled to England to escape persecution, and of her efforts to get John Sturm, the future Strassburg educator, out of Paris on a safe-conduct.[67] We know most, however, about her efforts on behalf of the poet Nicolas Bourbon. Borbonius, as he called himself in suitable humanist fashion, was the son of an ironmaster from Champagne, a noted neo-Latin author and schoolmaster, and a man prominent among that first generation of French evangelical reformers who from the 1520s had as their patroness the king's sister, Marguerite of Navarre.[68] He was in touch with Erasmus, enjoyed an old acquaintance with Guillaume Budé, the premier Greek scholar in France, knew Clément Marot intimately, and also Gérard Roussel, one of the original members of that early evangelical preaching team, the Cercle de Meaux, and later Marguerite's almoner. Bourbon himself entered the duchess's service in 1529 as tutor to her infant daughter, Jeanne d'Albret, the future mother of Henry IV.

Despite, or rather because of, the protection of the king's sister, this group lived dangerously, watched for every false move by the die-hard conservatives of the Sorbonne and its ally, the *parlement* of Paris; and while the Affair of the Placards saw Marot scamper abroad, Bourbon was slower or less lucky. His first book of epigrams, the *Nugae* (*Trifles*), published in Paris in 1533, had contained a scathing attack on the enemies of the humanist 'new learning', and this was quite enough to get him arrested and gaoled – during which time he lost all his possessions, including his pet nightingale.[69] According to Latymer, Bourbon got a letter out of prison to William Butts, conveyed, one guesses, by Jean de Dinteville, who had been at school with the poet.[70] Bourbon may even have sent an appeal for transmission to Anne:

> A poor man, I lie shut up in this dark prison: There is no one who would be able or who would dare to bring help: You alone, Oh Queen: you, Oh noble nymph, both can and dare, as one whom the king and whom God himself loves.[71]

Butts informed Anne, and Henry intervened in France on Bourbon's behalf. The poet then found himself having to travel to England, an experience which he did not enjoy, but once here, he lodged with Butts at Anne's expense and later with Henry's goldsmith, Cornelius Hayes.[72] The nearly fifty verses he wrote in England or on English subjects show that he rapidly became part of the evangelical scene: two epigrams addressed to Cromwell, 'aflame with the love of Christ', three to Cranmer, a gift from God, 'a head to his people', and one to the two of them together.[73] William Butts appears as 'my Maecenas and my father', Holbein as 'the incomparable painter', Latimer as 'the Eternal Father's trumpet', and above all, Anne.[74]

> For no crime, but through a false charge brought by certain individuals and their hatred, I was shut up in prison. I was praying for all good fortune for those who afflicted me. Why? I kept unshaken hope and faith.
> Then your pity lighted upon me from the ends of the earth, snatching me in my affliction, Anna, away from all my troubles. If this had not happened, I should be chained in that darkness, unhappily languishing, still under restraint.
> How can I express my thanks, still less, Oh Queen, repay you? I confess I have not the resources. But the Spirit of Jesus which enflames you wholly with his fire, He has the wherewithal to give you your due.[75]

In all Anne figures in six of Bourbon's 'trifles', far more than anyone else, and shares a seventh with Henry.[76]

Trifles is an appropriate name for Bourbon's elegancies, but in one he offers a perspective on Anne which would otherwise pass us by.[77] The epigram in question ends as others do with a reference to what he owed

the queen for rescuing him and to the importance of the queen's commitment to Christ. Its unique opening, however, acclaims Anne as a figure of
international significance.

> Just as the golden sun dispels the gloomy shadows of night and at day-break
> makes all things bright: so you, O queen, restored as a new light to your
> French and enlightening everything, bring back the Golden Age.

At one level 'your French' is an elegant reference to Anne's status as
almost an honorary Frenchwoman – the kind of sentiment we have
already see in de Carles. Her service to Claude had clearly left an impression. Bourbon, however, seems to mean something more, hailing Anne
not simply as one who has learned from France but who is a beacon to
France. And that promises a 'Golden Age' as her royal leadership revivifies
reform on the continent. Was this anything more than a client's conceit?
Or was there really a possibility that had Anne survived to hold Henry to a
course of moderate reform, she could have been a formative influence on
the religious shape of Europe, just as her daughter would be?

PERSONAL RELIGION

THE habit of scribbling in books is much to be deplored, except where the offender is a person of historic interest. Anne's signature in the older of the Hever Books of Hours certainly guaranteed value when it reached the sale-room, and the tiny drawing she added of an armillary sphere has, we have seen, considerable interest. Even more importance, however, attaches to the rest of the inscription: *le temps viendra* – 'the time will come.'[1] The phrase is an abbreviation of a proverb of which the full version is 'a day will come that shall pay for all' and of itself may seem hardly remarkable for someone of an evangelical persuasion to write below an illumination of the Last Judgement.[2] Effectively it is a précis of the comment in *L'Ecclesiaste* that 'the judgment of God shall be general and universal where as all things shall be discovered and nothing shall abide hidden, whether it be good or evil.'[3] Nevertheless, that Anne should write this, and write it when comparatively young, does provoke a deeper question about the faith she espoused. What did it mean for her personally?

That would not be an easy question to answer, even given the best documentation. As George Wyatt said, 'in the burrows of man's heart be many secret corners.'[4] Self-interest and ambition – which Anne had in plenty – each pointed to reform as the cause that would serve her best after the pope revoked Henry's annulment suit to Rome. Yet Anne's evident interest in French reform cannot be dismissed as a posture taken up for the occasion. She had had no direct contact with France since 1521. Her only visit thereafter would be the month she spent with Henry in Calais in October 1532. Her brother George is, of course, a possible link. He made regular diplomatic visits to France, but his first was late in 1529, months after du Brun had seen Anne already deep in St. Paul.[5] By then Anne's reformist allegiance was well established and the certainty is, therefore, that she was 'infected' during her years in France.

Earlier writers assumed that the person responsible was the king's sister, Marguerite of Angoulême. To someone like Nicholas Sander, it seemed blatantly obvious. Infection passed from Marguerite to Anne, and from Anne into England. That now seems improbable, given that (as we have seen) Anne was never a member of the duchess's household and, in her letters, appears more a suitor than a disciple.[6] Recent research, however, has shown, that in France sympathy with non-schismatic reform was far from an eccentricity of Marguerite's.[7] Widely shared among the upper members of French society, the evangelical position would be openly embraced by the queen's sister Renée, and Claude herself was certainly not hostile.[8] Thus in the ordinary course of Anne's duties around the queen, she would have worked with and become familiar with many aristocratic women seeking spiritual fulfilment. Almost certainly, too, she would have listened to court sermons from reformist clerics. She could hardly have missed, for example the evangelistic preaching of Michel d'Arande in the autumn of 1521 about which Marguerite wrote: 'The spirit which Our Lord caused to speak through his mouth will have struck the souls of those open to receive his word and to hear the truth.'[9] Perhaps, indeed, we should go further and speculate that, while in France, Anne was one of those who did go through a spiritual awakening. She had a good brain; the burning issue of the day was the nature of religious experience; later she would respond to the most winning of spiritual directors, such as Latimer and Parker; she was close to her brother, who 'spoke the language of Zion' on the scaffold; only her two oldest religious books were traditional Latin works of devotion.[10] Why should we not allow her genuine religious experience? Where, perhaps, we should then place Marguerite is not as a direct mentor to Anne in France, but as a role model once she had herself achieved royal status.[11] That would certainly account for the tone of Anne's letters and for the fact that many of the books she collected came from authors and printers encouraged by the queen of Navarre.[12] There are, too, parallels between Anne expressing her faith in fine illuminated manuscripts and Marguerite doing the same.[13] We could even speculate that Anne would have possessed a copy of Marguerite's own *Le Miroir de l'âme pécheresse*, published in 1531, and that this was the copy which her daughter Elizabeth would use in 1545 when translating the work for Katherine Parr.[14]

One objection which is raised to a genuinely devout Anne Boleyn is her life as a great court lady.[15] Bourbon saw her as 'a divine helper' whom God used to feed the afflicted, but how does that Anne relate to Anne the cynosure of the court, or the 'haughty' Anne of the 1520s, described by

Cavendish? If we are to believe Latymer, Madge Shelton got into the hottest of hot water with Anne when it was discovered that her prayer book had 'idle poesies' written in it, and yet this scandalized queen had exchanged love notes with the king on the pages of her (or his) Book of Hours.[16] Circumstances do, of course, alter cases, and so do advancing years. We must recognize also that William Latymer was committed to portraying Anne as the archetypal 'godly matron' and so very ready to air-brush out anything worldly. But more fundamentally, the sixteenth century saw no contradiction between religious commitment and human glory. As Latymer reports Anne saying to her chaplains:

> the royal estate of princes, for the excellency thereof doth far pass and excel all other estates and degrees of life, which doth represent and outwardly shadow unto us the glorious and celestial monarchy which God, the governor of all things, doth exercise in the firmament.[17]

The monarch who upheld his status glorified God, and never more than when he of all people bowed in worship. Besides this, again as *L'Ecclesiaste* put it, 'worldly goods, honour, puissance, joy, voluptuousness, health and all the other things . . . be good and gifts of God.'[18] Certainly to abandon oneself 'unto all voluptuousness and delights' is 'to be out of the wit [crazy]', but the world of ascetic renunciation is far away:

> Should I say for all this that it is prohibited for to be merry and that Jesuchrist hath only chosen sturdy people: seeing that he himself hath helped at feasts: specially that in the law was promised the rejoicing under the fig tree? No surely. But at such joys we may not bring forth Adam but Jesuchrist that is to say we should rejoice in the Lord which we find merciful and from whose hand we receiveth his gifts and blessings.[19]

Hair shirts, Thomas More's included, tell us more about psychology than spirituality.

It is, indeed, hard to deny Anne a personal faith. Apart from the Bible in which, significantly, we know she had an interest in Paul's epistles, the works she read and collected are certainly redolent of a Christianity of commitment and not of routine observance. The *Ecclesiaste* ends with the injunction 'Fear God and keep his commandments for this is the whole duty of man,' and George Boleyn's translation of Lefèvre's accompanying *annotation* is worth quoting at length.[20] What is crucial, it says, is to follow the sequence in the text; the fear of God is the necessary precondition for all obedience:

For faith which giveth the true fear of God, is it that doth prepare us for to keep the commandments well, and maketh us good workmen, for to make good works; and maketh us good trees for to bear good fruit. Then if we be not first well prepared, made good workmen, and made good trees we may not look to do the least of the commandments. Therefore Moses giving the commandments for the beginning said: 'Hearken Israel, thy God is one god', which is as much as to say as, believe, have faith, for without faith God doth not profit us, nor we can accomplish nothing: but the faith in God, and in our Lord Jesuchrist is it which chiefly doth relieve us from the transgressions that be passed of the sentence of the law, and yieldeth us innocents, and in such manner that none can demand of us anything, for because that faith hath gotten us Jesuchrist, and maketh him our own, he having accomplished the law, and satisfied unto all transgressions. Then faith having reconciled us unto the Father, doth get us also the Holy Ghost. Which yieldeth witness in our hearts that we be the sons of God. Whereby engendereth in us true childerly fear, and putteth away all servile and hired fear. And then it sheddeth in our hearts the fire of love and dilection, by the means whereof we be well prepared for to keep the law of God, which is but love: and without the which it is aswell possible for us to keep the said commandments, as unto the ice to abide warming and burning in the fire. For our hearts (without this fire of the Holy Ghost) be over hard frozen and cooled, and overmuch founded and rooted in the love of ourselves. (fols 147–8)

For a man who would avoid eternal damnation, 'there is nothing better than by true faith to take Jesuchrist of our side for pledge, mediator, advocate and intercessor. For who that believeth in him and doth come with him to this judgment, shall not be confused.'[21] If this was Anne Boleyn's experience of faith, then she was an evangelical by conviction and not just by policy. Compare this with the assertion in *The Ten Articles* (endorsed by Henry within weeks of Anne's execution) that penance was 'so necessary for salvation that no man . . . can, without the same, be saved or attain everlasting life'.[22] When it came to personal religion, husband and wife were miles apart.

For a writer to be able to turn the book of Ecclesiastes, with its refrain 'Vanity, vanity, all is vanity', into a paean to faith is a remarkable testimony to evangelical determination. The other great concerns of Christian humanism are to be found here also. First, concern for the Bible and its proper scholarly interpretation: 'We have been too long without all the Holy Scripture' so that the 'doctrines of men' have been embraced.[23] Before 'the books of men' are read, one 'must have read the true rule of the great architector or master workman', that is, the Bible.[24] Too many books by the unwise have led to 'pernicious sermons'.[25] God gives true wisdom irrespective of age, status or wealth: 'Say not then: "he is a pope, he is an emperor, he is a king, he is ancient, wilt not thou believe and follow him?" '[26] 'The Pistellis and Gospelles' carry the same message. As M. A. Screech put it, 'Not a father of the church, not a holy exegete, not a doctor [of the church] is mentioned. [Lefèvre] makes an absolute distinction between the bible and tradition.'[27] The homily on the gospel for the feast of the Nativity of Our Lady says quite bluntly 'Scripture says nothing of the human birth of Mary and so one cannot preach about it.'[28] The sidelining of scripture, as *The Ecclesiaste* makes clear, has been the fault of rulers:

If it had been so in times past, the holy Word of God should not have been so long hid, nor out of use and in the stead of the same so many superfluous and unprofitable books and curious vain questions brought forth which serve not only to lose time but they be clean contrary from the true and pure truth.

Kings and princes have a responsibility to govern their realms not only by 'iron and sword' (which on their own produce 'subjects like bondmen'), but by 'good doctrine'.[29]

We also find the Christian humanist concern to exploit rhetoric for effective communication; classical allusions as illustrations; popular sayings; homely illustrations like the parallel between the endless thirst of the diabetic and the vain pursuit of worldly reason ('there is no means for to have the perfectness and certainty in all things but by true faith'); even an attempt to translate Solomon's revenue into contemporary coinage.[30] Practical application is there too – an application which Anne could accept for herself. She might well have reflected after her coronation on the rightness of this exposition of Ecclesiastes chapter 3, verses 1–8:

Then it is unto God that we must lift up our eyes when one goeth about to be married. If it be ordained that thou shalt have her, she shall be thine without thy care; if it be not ordained thou losest thy pain. And this place here is to put aside the foolish love with all the hard anguish and cares thereof. When it is time for to seek, truly without doubt thou shalt find, or else thou losest thy pain. Wherefore we may attribute nothing unto ourselves but we must put all into the hands of God.[31]

Whether she would have felt the same about an earlier section on the subject, if it had arrived during her long courtship, one cannot know:

'When God joineth then it is time to embrace and to use the fruit of marriage; and if he do not join, neither care nor labour shall not prevail.'[32] Or after marriage, about the arrival of children: 'Sara with great desire did as much as to her was possible for to have children, but she lost her time for that time was determined by God. In like wise Rachel was frustrate of her desire unto the time determined by God.'[33]

In all this there is no word of the role of the Church, of the priest, of the whole structure of sacraments, which command our attention when we look at established Christianity at the time. This does not mean that a woman who entertained such writings, as Anne did, rejected all established religion. It was a question of priorities. Sometimes, it is true, a passage may have critical implications, as in the commentary in 'The Pistellis and Gospelles' on Hebrews, chapter 9, which deals with the sacrificial death of Christ. Orthodoxy held that during mass, Christ's death was re-presented to God as consecration by the priest transformed bread and wine into the 'host', that is, the body and blood of Christ (*hostia*, victim for sacrifice). However, the commentary says: 'the true host is Jesu Christ which hath suffered death and passion for to save us, the which in shedding his precious blood upon us all, hath given unto us life and hath wholly purged us of sin.'[34] What is being implied here is not a challenge to belief in the bodily presence of Christ in the consecrated host. The target is the late medieval focus on the miraculous mechanism of the mass rather than its significance. Anne herself continued to revere Christ's bodily presence in the consecrated bread and wine. As a condemned prisoner in the Tower she took her oath on it, received communion at least once and spent her last night praying before it.[35]

A valuable insight into the nature of the non-schismatic reform Anne promoted is given by passages in a sermon which, as we shall see when considering Anne's fall, had the queen's wholehearted support.[36] It was preached at court by her almoner, John Skip, on Passion Sunday, 2 April 1536, and in the course of it he defended the value of 'the little ceremonies' of the Church, such as holy water, holy bread, holy ashes, palms 'and such other'. No one 'of learning and good judgement' would want them abandoned. They had no objective sacred power – that was certain – but they were aids to memory and 'very good and profitable if they be used for the purpose and intent that they were first ordained and instituted':

> holy water ... to put us in remembrance that our sins be washed away by the sprinkling and shedding of Christ's blood; holy bread [to remind us] that all

we that have professed Christ's faith be one body mystical and ought to be one in mind in spirit in Christ our head, even as these many pieces of holy bread which we receive be cut or divided out of one loaf; holy ashes [to remind us] that we be but ashes and dust... and palms [to remind us] that our Saviour Christ hath gotten the victory and overcome the devil and sin.[37]

The question, therefore, was proper use or abuse, and there responsibility lay with the king. 'The king's office is to see the abuses taken away and not the good things themselves except it so be that the abuses cannot be taken away, as Hezekiah took away the brazen serpent when he could not take away the abuse of it.'[38] In other words, if superstition could not be eradicated, even useful customs must be sacrificed.

In these years, evangelicals in England saw the task as winning the Church back to the inwardness of true religion and to the spiritual realities which underlay its fossilized formality; their call was to breathe life into dead bones, not bury them. Hence Anne apparently was happy to own copies of translations into French by the renegade friar, François Lambert of Avignon (including Luther's *Prophetie de Iesaie*), but when Tristram Revell, early in 1536, tried to dedicate to the queen his English translation of Lambert's own *Farrago Rerum Theologicarum*, which denied the sacrifice of the mass, Anne refused the request.[39] Her attitude would be characteristic of all shades of English evangelical reform for at least a decade more: real spiritual experience, yes; the priority of faith, yes; access to the Bible, yes; reform of abuses and superstition, yes; but heretical views on the miracle of the altar, no.[40] In contrast to Revell, whom she rejected, she patronized Richard Tracy, whose father's body had been exhumed and burned in 1531 because his will had implied disbelief in the Church's ability to serve the needs of departed souls – a 'superstition' which was increasingly coming under reformist questioning.[41] In the same way she was thought to be willing to intervene for Thomas Patmore, who had been imprisoned following his recantation of heresies, principally about that other issue of contemporary debate, clerical marriage.[42]

Another of the concerns of Christian humanists which the *Ecclesiaste* particularly emphasized was the responsibility of the elite to the poor:

The court of kings, princes, chancellors, judging places and audiences be the places where one ought to find equity and justice. But, oh good Lord, where is there more injustice, more exactions, more oppressions of poor widows and orphans, where is there more disorder in all manners and more greater company of unjust men than there, whereas should be but all good order and just people of good and holy example of life.[43]

For future generations of Protestants, Anne Boleyn provided the model response. Again it is Latymer who provides the detail, with corroboration from elsewhere.[44] He tells of Anne giving standing orders for the relief of the deserving poor – needy and impotent householders with large families – and for the prompt handling of petitioners, under threat of her personal intervention. The purses at the royal maundy were substantially increased. The ladies of her household spent considerable amounts of time sewing clothes which were taken on progress and distributed to the poor at each stopping place, with a shilling a head, by arrangement with the local priest and two parishioners; pregnant women received a pair of sheets and two shillings. Individual cases of misfortune might be reported by a chaplain, especially if the person concerned was of the right religious emphasis. One specific story concerns a parishioner of Hugh Latimer who was brought to Anne's attention after the death of most of his cattle. When the queen arrived at Sir Edward Baynton's house nearby – which dates the episode to about the end of August in the progress of 1535 – she interviewed the man's wife and gave an initial gift of twenty pounds.[45]

John Foxe appears to be responsible for elaborating this charity into a fantastic suggestion that in three-quarters of a year Anne distributed £14,000 or £15,000 in poor relief.[46] Such a sum is twelve times larger than the annual surplus on Anne's expenditure. George Wyatt repeated the figure twenty years later, but also said that her regular charity amounted to £1500 a year which, though still an exaggeration, is just about credible.[47] Perhaps we have here a single reported amount to which Foxe or his printer added an extra zero. Anne may also have played a part in the government's decision to propose radical and far-reaching action on poverty to the 1536 parliament.[48] The importance of action had been drawn to her attention the year before, when William Marshall had dedicated to her *The Form and manner of subvention or helping for poor people, devised and practised in the city of Ypres*, a practical account of recent policies introduced by the city fathers. Marshall was already a Boleyn protégé, but he had a very specific object in making this dedication:[49]

> My very mind, intent and meaning is (by putting of this honourable and charitable provision in mind) to occasion your grace (which at all times is ready to further all goodness) to be a mediatrix and mean unto our most dread sovereign lord ... for the stablishing and practising of the same (if it shall seem so worthy) or of some other, as good or better, such as by his majesty or his most honourable council shall be devised.[50]

Not only was Marshall apparently enlisted by Cromwell to draft the necessary legislation, the king came down to the Commons in person on 11 March 1536 to introduce the measure and promised to contribute to the costs of the public works the bill envisaged.[51] Perhaps it is a memory of Anne's encouragement of this 1536 legislation which lies behind Foxe's further story that she was involved in a scheme to establish stocks of materials in various places to enable the poor to be given work. Alternatively, perhaps Anne took private action in anticipation of the bill.[52]

Poor relief was not the only practical cause Anne espoused. If there was one hope that buoyed up all Christian humanists, swept along as they were by events towards the rocks of the establishment and the reefs of worldly realities which would eventually break them, it was that education and scholarship would rescue them and society together. Comparatively few literary dedications to Anne are so far known, other than those already noted, which, rather than anything else, probably reflects the shortness of her period as lady marquis and queen.[53] She was, however, the subject of adulatory Latin poems by Robert Whittington, one of the older generation of humanists, and tutor to the king's henchmen.[54] Anne also appears under her father's name at the head of a work by another senior scholar, Robert Wakefield. The *Kotser Codicis R. Wakfeldi* was an impressive demolition of the validity of Henry's first marriage by a scholar of some reputation, who as early as 1519 had been professor of Hebrew at Busleiden's College at Louvain. The dedication makes clear Wakefield's move from earlier conservative patronage to reliance on the whole Boleyn family: Thomas, his wife, 'the daughter of each of you, our Queen Anne in whose happiness I rejoice exceedingly', and her uncle James, and there are dark references to a former benefactor, 'ungrateful, harsh, inhuman and unfair', who owed nearly £100 in lost payments of an annuity, a sum which he hints the Boleyns might enforce.[55] Perhaps the earliest author who gambled on Anne in her own right was Louis de Brun, whose treatise on letter-writing is dedicated to 'Madame Anne de Rochfort', Anne's title after her father became an earl in December 1529. The manuscript was prepared for the illuminator but never begun, which is strange, considering how long it remained in Anne's hands. Why it should have been left incomplete is not known. Apart from the religious appeal we have seen already, the book stresses its practical utility, explaining how various individuals should be addressed, depending on the status of the writer. It is a neat compliment that the examples of addressing a superior range from the Holy Father the pope, to the king, the bishop of London and Monsieur de Rochfort.[56]

If the weight of literary dedications to Anne Boleyn is comparatively light, the evidence of her involvement elsewhere in the world of learning is quite the opposite. She was remembered for years as a generous patron of students, and several cases can be cited to warrant the tradition. As early as 1530, when John Eldmer lost the contest to become abbot of St Mary's, York, Anne persuaded the successful candidate to permit and support his return to Cambridge to study. After some years the new abbot called him back to the community and ruined his chance to study by loading him with administrative chores – clearly, fellow monks resented his prolonged skiving – only to have Anne intervene again to secure Eldmer's return to the university.[57] Not only did William Barker benefit from being one of those Anne maintained at Cambridge – which opened the way to quite a literary output – but he was able to use the connection to secure favour from Elizabeth in 1559, and mercy in 1571, following his involvement in the treason of the duke of Norfolk whose secretary he had become.[58] Anne also backed scholars studying abroad. One such was John Beckynsaw, whom she supported with £40 a year to learn and eventually teach Greek at Paris.[59] When Wolsey's bastard son, Thomas Winter, found the money running out and returned from Padua to make what he could of Cromwell's affection for his father, the secretary pointed him in the direction of Henry and Anne. The king was too busy shooting to give him the attention he (and possibly the king) felt he deserved, but all was well the next day when Anne assured him that 'I am aware, my dear Winter, that you are beloved by the king and have many friends who wish you well. Reckon me among the number.' Whether the Latin periods represent Anne's actual words hardly matters, or mattered to Winter; it was her assurance to do what she could for him that counted.[60]

Anne also supported learned institutions, perhaps with annual subventions to Oxford and Cambridge (over and above the poor scholars) of as much as £80 each. More enduring, she interceded with the king to secure the exemption of both universities from the new clerical tax, the tenth, and from clerical subsidies.[61] At a humbler level, there is her interest in Matthew Parker's reform of the collegiate church of Stoke by Clare near Sudbury, to which Anne had appointed him.[62] The reforms included, as well as regular preaching, the appointment of a lecturer on the Bible to teach four days a week in English and Latin, a new grammar school with a well-paid master and facilities for fee-paying as well as free pupils, and finally eight or ten choral scholarships, which could lead to a six-year bursary at Cambridge. Anne Boleyn was designated the new founder of the college. Here was the model of what the redeployment of Church endowments might have achieved. Circumstantial evidence indicates that she intervened in the headship of Eton, and when Nicolas Bourbon arrived, he too was put to work at his profession of teaching, but this time the sons of courtiers, particularly those from a reformist background – Thomas, the son of Sir Nicholas Harvey, Anne's old friend and fellow evangelical; Henry Norris, the eldest son of the groom of the stool; Henry Dudley, the son of the future duke of Northumberland, and her own nephew, Henry Carey:

> You, Oh queen, gave me the boys to educate,
> I try to keep each one faithful to his duty.
> May Christ grant that I may be equal to the task,
> Shaping vessels worthy of a heavenly house.[63]

It is fitting, perhaps, that a discussion of Anne Boleyn's religious life should end with a French humanist evangelical. That was her milieu, and in it she mattered. Bourbon wrote the dedication to Book Seven of the *Nugarum*, which was to appear in 1538, soon after his arrival in London – the date is the Ides of May, 1535. Addressing 'the benevolent reader', he remarked that he had two great patrons, 'the Most Christian King, our Francis' and 'the brilliant Henry VIII, king of the Britons'. Between them they exhibited the greatest piety and encouragement of the arts in that age.[64] Every good humanist had to be a flatterer and a beggar. Bourbon was, perhaps, nearer the truth in the dedication of Book Six, which he apparently added when he was back in France; the reference there is to 'the liberality of Henry VIII that most humane of princes and of his wife the queen' – a remarkable piece of honesty, for by that time Anne was disgraced and dead.[65]

PART IV

A Marriage Destroyed

THE RIVAL, 1535–1536

T HE story of the events which led to the disgrace and death of Anne Boleyn needs to begin almost a year before the tragedy itself. Henry VIII spent the summer of 1535 on a progress to the Severn and then across to Hampshire for most of September and October. The sport was good, particularly the hawking. The king had not hunted the area for some years, and after a few weeks away from the stress and blood of recent events, he was in tremendous form. So was Anne, who accompanied him throughout, and when the couple returned to Windsor in late October she was pregnant, though she could not yet know it.[1] The common people gave Henry and Anne a good reception, and the public highlight had been the consecration of three favoured clerics as bishops at Winchester on 19 September, apparently in the presence of the king; given that the three were Edward Fox, Hugh Latimer and John Hilsey, Anne's presence can be taken for granted.[2] Henry had been so enjoying himself that he had signed very few documents during the progress, and there was something of a panic to get the formalities for the new bishops completed in time, with Anne herself advising Latimer to leave it to Cromwell.[3]

In the end, several documents were signed at Wolf Hall near Marlborough, where the king stopped for a week in early September on his way to the New Forest, a visit which hindsight has endowed with enormous significance.[4] Wolf Hall was the home of Sir John Seymour and his large family – among them his eldest daughter Jane, who nine months later would become Henry's third queen. At the time, however, it is very unlikely that anyone, including Anne and Henry, saw anything momentous about the visit. Jane may or may not have been present, Anne must have been, and myth and legend are all that suggest that this was the start of the king's pursuit of the woman who, as the mother of Edward VI, would in Henry's terms be his only truly successful wife.[5] Jane Seymour had, in fact, a long association with the court, where she had been one of Katherine of Aragon's ladies.[6] If she left court at all when the latter's household was reduced in the summer of 1533, she was back in Anne Boleyn's entourage by the new year, when she received a gift from the king along with others of the queen's ladies such as Anne Zouche, Madge Shelton and Bessie Holland.[7]

The real significance of the royal visit to Wolf Hall was that it marked one further stage in the rise of Jane's eldest brother, Edward. A protégé of Wolsey, with some genuine military talent (he had been knighted on the 1522 campaign while still in his teens), Edward reached the court rank of esquire of the body in 1530, and had accompanied Henry and Anne to Calais in 1532.[8] Now, after helping to host a successful royal visit, he went up a notch in his master's esteem – and we know that the week was successful because in October Henry toyed with the idea of staying at Edward Seymour's own Hampshire house, Elvetham, although in the end he changed his mind.[9] Seymour's position – and his father, too, was of good standing in court circles – would alone make nonsense of the legend that it was by catching Henry's eye at Wolf Hall that Jane secured a place in Anne's household; the family had quite enough weight to place a daughter at court, if she had not been there already.

An alternative tale comes via one of Mary I's later attendants, Jane Dormer, who married a Spanish nobleman and became the revered patroness of Elizabethan Catholic exiles.[10] This was that Jane Seymour's uncle, Sir Francis Bryan, took her to court and placed her with Anne, following the refusal of the Dormers to accept her as a bride for William, the heir of the family. Bryan, however, was certainly not Jane's uncle, merely a distant relative, and the marriage of William to Mary Sidney, supposedly made in haste in order to frustrate Bryan's plans, did not take place until January 1535.[11] The most that any memory could be based on is a recommendation from Bryan, back in 1533, that Anne should take Jane over from Katherine, but there is no corroborating evidence for this and no such sponsorship would be needed for a lady already established in the royal entourage. One has to remember that Jane Dormer was born two years after Anne's death and that the story was first recorded in Spain by her steward, thirty years after Jane herself had died in 1612. The likeliest explanation of the Dormer legend is that it is an attempt to illustrate the family sanctity of Jane Dormer's grandmother, who had turned her back on a glittering match for her son with a relative of the wicked Francis Bryan, Henry VIII's 'vicar of hell'.

Far from Henry and Jane having their first romantic meeting at Wolf Hall, it is a reasonable certainty that the king's interest in her became marked only in January 1536. True, in the first days of October 1535 the French ambassador, the bishop of Tarbes, did inform Francis I that Henry's feelings for Anne were cooling steadily because he had 'new amours', but his opinion is contradicted by reports from various English correspondents in attendance at court, dated 2, 6 and 9 October, that Henry and Anne Boleyn were 'merry'.[12] The earliest mention that Jane Seymour had been singled out for the king's attentions is a Chapuys letter of 10 February 1536.[13] In his previous letter of 29 January, the ambassador had reported the rumour of a third marriage, but as he then had no name and dismissed the tale even though from 'a good authority', the natural conclusion is that the matter was of fairly recent origin – indeed, he termed it *une nouvelle amour*.[14]

There is, thus, no reason to suspect a rift in the royal marriage when the couple left the Seymours. Indeed, as the 1535 progress came to an end, Anne began to hope that her ultimate challenge was about to be met – come the spring, there would be a prince. The other difficulties that she and Henry faced were, nevertheless, still there, and some as serious as ever. The French and imperial ambassadors commented independently on the prevailing mood of so far sullen resentment at the king, his wife and his policies.[15] Support for Mary was as strong as ever, or stronger. True, June had seen the death of George Neville, Lord Abergavenny, politically the most formidable of the princess's sympathizers, but while the small summer court was in Hampshire, there was a public demonstration at Greenwich in support of Mary by the wives of a number of London citizens, aided and abetted by some ladies of the royal household not on duty.[16] Among the ringleaders who ended in the Tower were Anne's aunt, Lady William Howard, and her sister-in-law Jane, Lady Rochford. Evidently Jane did not share her husband George's commitment to Anne's cause. The matter was hushed up, but the king, encouraged by Anne's condition, began to talk in a way that suggested that, if Mary persisted in her resistance, she would soon find herself in the Tower too.[17] Katherine, also, had at last decided that submission was not enough; unknown to Henry, in October she wrote to Charles V, inviting him to intervene.[18]

In the country at large fear of religious change was now widespread. Stories of heretical preaching abounded; royal commissioners were surveying the Church estates, down to the poorest parish; Cromwell's deputies were visiting the monasteries to enforce disturbing royal injunctions and confiscate many long-venerated relics; the recent impositions on the clergy were beginning to bite, with Wednesday, 1 December, set for payment of the new tax of 10 per cent per annum on all clerical incomes; some small religious houses were already giving up the struggle to survive. The London merchant community was full of rumours that war with the emperor was imminent, with the consequence of the loss of England's vital markets in the Low Countries and Germany. Friction between the king and the Hanse merchants already threatened the closure of the Baltic with its grain reserves, and this appeared all the more ominous as the vital weeks of fine harvest weather at home obstinately refused to arrive. Half the crops, it was said, had been lost, and the threat of famine after what turned out to be the worst season for eight years and the fourth worst since Henry's accession, made it impossible to levy the taxes granted by parliament. Plague, too, was rampant. And it was no use the king's preachers exploiting the text, 'whom the Lord loveth he chasteneth'; ordinary Englishmen knew that the king was to blame, and even more the woman whom he had done everything for and who egged him on in his godlessness.[19]

Abroad, the situation was more fluid even than it had been earlier in the year. First, Charles V's great victory at Tunis had freed him from Mediterranean distractions to intervene against Henry if he wished, while the pope had responded to the death of Fisher by excommunicating the king. The French, seeing increased danger to England, had upped the price of their support, making it clear also that it was marriage between the dauphin and Mary which really interested them. Then, on 1 November, the situation changed: the death without heirs of the duke of Milan threw open again the issue over which Francis and Charles had been quarrelling since 1515. That might appear to tip the balance of need in Henry's favour, but equally Francis might now call for the financial support which Henry had hinted at, so dragging England, if not into direct hostilities with Charles, at least into increasing difficulties in its relations with the Low Countries. The pope, however, was pressing an alternative, a coalition to punish Henry, so there was a good deal of talk about a negotiated settlement between the Empire and France and a joint descent on England.

From the distance of the twenty-first century, it is hard to believe that England was in any real danger of isolation and invasion, or that Henry would be unable to avoid the entanglements of Francis I. Yet at the time the confusions, and the readiness of each power to take opportunist advantage of every other, did produce real anxiety. Matters were made more opaque by the universal passion for disinformation and by the existence within each country of divided counsels. In France there was a war party and a peace party, and in England two policies competed – either to rely on France or to seek an accommodation with the emperor. Henry, with Anne's strong support, believed that he ought to be able to depend on French self-interest, though so long as Francis insisted on maintaining close relations with the pope and refused English advice to follow down the road of royal supremacy, the king never felt he could quite trust his 'brother' as he once had. This doubt about France explains why, in October, Anne was anxious to interest the French envoys in a match with Elizabeth, why Francis I's recovery from a severe illness in November was marked in London by an ostentatious show of relief, and why Anne's overture to Marguerite of Navarre in September was followed up in November and December by exploration from both sides.[20] Cromwell, by contrast, seems to have been much readier to consider doing a deal with the emperor, even though he was aware of imperial protests at the treatment of Katherine and Mary, and probably guessed at Charles' reluctance to come to terms so long as Anne Boleyn usurped his aunt's place as queen.[21] Henry, for the same reason, found it hard to discuss the emperor with Chapuys without losing his temper.[22]

The opening of the new year brought further dramatic developments. On 7 January, Katherine of Aragon died at Kimbolton Castle, on the edge of the Fens. She had suddenly and somewhat unexpectedly gone downhill at the end of December, and her death was greeted at court by an outburst of relief and enthusiasm for the Boleyn marriage, which gives the lie to later historians who suggest that Anne was already living on borrowed time. She gave the messenger who brought the news to Greenwich a handsome present. Her father and brother made it clear that only one more thing was needed – for Mary to go the way of her mother. Henry cried, 'God be praised that we are free from all suspicion of war!' He would now have the advantage over the French, who would have to toe his line or risk an English alliance with Charles, 'now that the real cause of our enmity no longer exists'. The next day, Sunday, the king and queen appeared in joyful yellow from top to toe, and Elizabeth was triumphantly paraded to church. After dinner Henry went down into the Great Hall, where the ladies of the court were dancing, with his sixteen-month-old daughter in his arms, showing her off to one and another. After several days of such paternal enthusiasm, he evidently decided that something more masculine was called for, and the tiltyard was soon busy with his favourite form of self-exhibition.[23] Even though, as is possible, he paid public court there to Jane Seymour, Anne could be sure that Elizabeth and her unborn child were the true centre of Henry's interest, while she was herself now, for the first time, sole queen of England.

Eustace Chapuys took all this as a personal insult. His grief for Katherine was genuine and his sympathy for Mary all the more real because instructions had recently arrived from Charles, dampening all prospects of imperial support for a rising against Henry and Anne.[24] In January Francis I had intervened in the duchy of Savoy, which had been quickly overrun in what was an obvious preliminary to renewed hostilities over Milan. For the foreseeable future, Italy would be the imperial priority and England even more of a sideshow than usual. The end of the month, however, brought the ambassador comfort. Rumours began to reach him of Anne exhibiting signs of distress, afraid that she might go the same way as Katherine.[25] Chapuys, however, was clearly right to express caution about a story that made sense only if Anne believed the nonsense that Henry would abandon not only her but the child in her womb.

The likeliest explanation for the tale is that once again Anne's pregnancy was proving difficult, and it was death, not divorce, that she feared. And death came very near. On 24 January the king's horse fell heavily in the tiltyard at Greenwich, knocking Henry unconscious for two hours.[26] For a big man wearing nearly a hundredweight of armour to be thrown from a moving horse of, perhaps, seventeen hands high was no laughing matter – still less if the horse, as it may have done, also rolled on him.

The king must still have been suffering the after-effects when death came for real. On 29 January Anne miscarried. The immediate details appear in Chapuys' despatch of 10 February.[27] He reported that the 'child had the appearance of a male about three months and a half old'. A note made privately by Charles Wriothesley, Windsor Herald, agreed that it had been 'a man child' but gave the date as 30 January and was very specific about the length of gestation, saying that Anne 'said that she had reckoned herself at that time but fifteen weeks gone with child'.[28] This we may well credit since Wriothesley's post gave him a ready entrée to the court, and his cousin Thomas was clerk of the signet and close to Cromwell. The sex of the baby, however, may have been guesswork; the gender of a foetus cannot, it seems, be determined much before seventeen weeks. In any case, even if Anne's calculations were wrong, how reliable would amateur diagnosis by the queen's normal attendants have been, especially since Tudor households did not enjoy the clinical conditions of modern medicine? Experienced midwives are unlikely to have been on hand so early in Anne's pregnancy.[29] In Elizabeth's reign, the story in Catholic circles was that Anne had miscarried of 'a shapeless mass of flesh', but the person who popularized the tale was the Catholic propagandist in exile, Nicholas Sander.[30] Of course, it is in theory possible that Sander was passing on knowledge long concealed by the recusant community, but there is not a shred of evidence direct or circumstantial to substantiate such heroic self-censorship. No deformed foetus was mentioned at the time or later in Henry's reign, despite Anne's disgrace. In Mary's reign, when there was every motive and opportunity to blacken Anne, the substantial anti-Boleyn material which appeared in England said nothing. Nor was any such report known to the more raffish European Catholic sources nor to William Thomas, a Protestant writer hostile to Anne. Lacking all corroboration, the appearance of the story forty years after the event must be dismissed as a Sander promotion designed to support his description of Anne as a misshapen monster. It is as little worthy of credence as his assertion that Henry VIII was Anne's father.

The deformed foetus story would not merit a moment's consideration apart from a mountain of fantasy that has been built on it. In particular, it has been conjectured that the true explanation for Anne's subsequent rejection lies in the sixteenth-century superstition that deformity in a baby was a sign of sexual misbehaviour by a parent.[31] Given a deformed foetus in January 1536, Henry's delicate conscience would need to be absolved from any such suspicion and a cover story provided to stop possible gossip. Therefore an alternative parentage for the lost child had to be invented and hence the accusation that Anne had committed adultery with five lovers. This is historical 'Newspeak'! Common sense would ask why, having gone to all that trouble to shift responsibility, no one ever mentioned the deformed foetus, either when moves against Anne were beginning, or after her arrest or at her trial or subsequently. A cover story which held for 450 years but had been unnecessary in the first place invites more than a raised eyebrow. In history, evidence matters, not invention, and no evidence whatsoever supports the alleged deformity. To claim otherwise is, in the words of Jennifer Loach, 'wishful thinking'.[32] In any case, far from protecting Henry's reputation, accusing Anne of adultery opened him up to contempt. The reaction of the parson of Freshwater was to say: 'Lo, whilst the king and his council were busy to put down abbeys and pull away the right of Holy Church, he was made a cuckold at home.'[33]

Some sixteenth-century moralists did associate witches with monstrous births, so fantasizing about a 'deformed foetus' has led to historians speculating about a link between Anne's fall and an accusation of witchcraft.[34] Here, at first sight, there does appear to be some evidence. According to Chapuys, the Exeters reported that Henry had said to a courtier (in absolute secrecy) that he had 'made this marriage seduced and constrained by sortileges and for this reason he held the said marriage void and that God had demonstrated this in not allowing them to have male heirs and that he considered that he could take another.'[35] What should we make of this? Quite conceivably Henry's remark may have been no more than bluster – after all, he would later weep and say that Anne had had intercourse with a hundred men and had planned to poison the duke of Richmond and the Princess Mary![36] More significant, Exeter did not at that time know the reason for Henry's remark, nor did he himself hear Henry's comment.[37] What we have is Chapuys' report in French of what he had understood of whatever a messenger had conveyed by word of mouth of a report from the Exeters of what the marquis and his wife said they had been told by 'ung des principaux de court' of what Henry had said to him, presumably in English.[38] Thus, did Henry use the term 'sortilege', or was the word provided *en route*? Even if Henry did use the noun, since its primary English meaning was 'divination' and since Henry spoke in the same breath of male heirs, the simple construction is that he was referring to the premarital predictions that union with Anne would produce sons. Less commonly, the word 'sortilege' could be used for occult practices, but in usual parlance 'bewitched' meant no more than 'deceived' – as in Tyndale's 1526 New Testament: 'Oh foolish Galatians, who has bewitched you?'[39] In any case, alleging witchcraft was a common-place excuse for foolish male behaviour. Chapuys himself had written of Anne and Henry in 1533 that, 'This accursed lady has so enchanted and bewitched him that he will not dare to do anything against her will.'[40] Fifty years earlier, Richard III had attributed Edward IV's unsuitable match with Elizabeth Woodville, a widow far his social inferior, to the sorcery and witchcraft of Elizabeth and her mother.[41] And once again, evidence – or rather, the lack of it – settles the matter. No accusation that she had dabbled in the black arts was ever levelled against Anne.

To less conspiracy-prone scholars, Anne's loss of a child in January 1536 has seemed the turning-point to tragedy. Persuaded by the fate she met in May that Henry had long tired of his second wife, they conclude that she 'had miscarried of her saviour'.[42] Setting hindsight aside, the evidence suggests something different. The loss – and above all the loss of a son – was a huge psychological blow to Henry. Childlessness had revealed the wrongfulness of his marriage to Katherine; was it now condemning his union with Anne? As reported, his immediate reaction rings all too true: by denying him sons, God had shown that the marriage with Anne must be void. Old fears were now out in force, and Henry's mind was full of them when, still shaken by his own recent brush with mortality, he saw Anne for the first time after her miscarriage.

Chapuys' despatches again provide the only contemporary insight into what took place. His letter of 10 February reported that Anne was blaming the miscarriage on Norfolk frightening her with the news of the king's accident, but that general opinion put the real cause down to either 'the concubine's' inability to bear children or a fear of her fate now that the king was paying so much attention to Jane Seymour.[43] Just over a fortnight later he amplified the story.[44] Henry had spoken to Anne only ten times in the last three months. His only remark to her about the miscarriage was to repeat, 'I see that God will not give me male children,' and when he left her he said, as if in spite, 'When you are up I will speak to you.' Anne, in turn, had hit back. She told Henry that she had miscarried partly because of the shock of his accident, but also because she was heartbroken whenever he paid attention to another woman; her feelings for him were much stronger than Katherine's had ever been. These remarks upset Henry for a long time and at Shrovetide he went to stay at Whitehall by himself instead of celebrating with Anne at Greenwich, whereas previously he could not leave her for an hour.

Not all of this is true. The point about Henry ignoring Anne for three months cannot be correct. Chapuys had forgotten his own report of the king's behaviour after Katherine's death. The significance he placed on their being apart at Shrovetide is equally contradictory. Either the separation was as ominous as he claimed, or the couple had been estranged for months – it is hard to believe both. The gloss the ambassador put on the king's departure to Whitehall can in any case be queried. Shrovetide 1536 coincided with the key stages of the final session of the Reformation Parliament. The bill to dissolve the monasteries was on the point of being put into the Lords and, even more important, five days before Shrovetide, the final dispositions had been made to achieve victory in the king's five-year campaign, fought against bitter resistance, to secure legislation restoring his feudal rights. Henry needed to be on the spot. If, as is likely, Anne was still convalescent, necessarily he had to go to Westminster alone.[45] We must remember, too, that Chapuys was equally ready to tell the absurd story (also spread by Francis I) that there had never been a pregnancy to miscarry.[46] It had simply been an attempt by Anne (with the help of her sister Mary) to deceive Henry into believing that she could conceive. Women prisoners did try to cheat the gallows by claiming to be *enceinte*, but Anne could only have hastened disaster by such a trick; it would have invited exactly the collapse of confidence the king had displayed in 1534, and had now experienced again. And why should Anne end the deception at fifteen weeks while the king was still interested in Jane Seymour?

So, as always, Chapuys tells a loaded tale, gleaned from a distance. But we may take the repeated remark, 'I see that God will not give me male children,' as genuine, and note that Henry emphasized the will of God rather than the failure of Anne. Yet it is also easy to believe that in the immediate aftermath of the miscarriage, Anne too would have been highly emotional. George Wyatt's tedious prose probably preserves for us the tradition from her ladies in waiting: 'Being thus a woman full of sorrow, it was reported that the king came to her, and bewailing and complaining unto her the loss of his boy, some words were heard to break out of the inward feeling of her heart's dolours, laying the fault upon unkindness.' To this Henry allegedly replied that 'he would have no more boys by *her*!'[47] Later recusant sources embroider the possibility that Henry, wrapped up in his own disappointment, guilty at his flirtations with Jane and making too little allowance for his wife's condition, did resent criticism. Sander has Henry answer Anne's complaints 'by saying, "Be of good cheer, sweetheart, you will have no reason to complain of me again", and [he] went away sorrowing.'[48] Jane Dormer has Anne 'betwitting' the king with his unkindness: 'who willed her to pardon him, and he would not displeasure her in that kind hereafter.'[49] As for Anne Boleyn's reply, Sander claims that Anne 'bewailing her mishap, and angry at the transference to another of the king's affections, cried out to him, "See, how well I must be since the day I caught that abandoned woman Jane sitting on your knees."' The Dormer version is that 'there was often much scratching and bye-blows between the queen and her maid,' and that 'anger and disdain' at finding Jane on Henry's lap produced the miscarriage.

What makes this late embroidery suspect is that Henry, as will appear, continued determined efforts to persuade Europe to accept Anne as his legitimate wife.[50] He clearly had not been poised to discard her should the pregnancy not end as he wanted. Anne, for her part, recovered her resilience, comforting her attendants with the assurance that she would conceive again, and that no one this time would be able to claim that her son was illegitimate.[51] The miscarriage of 29 January was neither Anne's last chance nor the point at which Jane Seymour replaced Anne in Henry's priorities. It did, nevertheless, make her vulnerable yet again. What Anne had lost was not only a longed-for child but the objective endorsement of her marriage which the birth of a son would have given. A queen from abroad could rely on family identity and the support of her European connections. With the hope of a prince gone, Anne was pitched back into being exclusively reliant on her relationship with Henry. She became exposed again, and to an even greater degree, to attack from the partisans of Mary, resentful at the dominance of the Boleyns and their heretical policies.

The position was, in some ways, a repetition of the autumn of 1534 following her first miscarriage, but with crucial differences. Mary, now motherless, was a much more formidable opponent than Katherine had been. Anne and her daughter were no longer protected by the dilemma that to assert Mary's legitimacy meant challenging the king's conviction that the Aragon marriage had been invalid. Now that Katherine was dead, all that was needed was for the girls' father to accept, as was undoubtedly true, that the elder sister was the child of good faith – 'bona fide parentum gotten, conceived and born' – and Mary became legitimate in law and would displace Elizabeth as heir presumptive.[52] This way round the obstacle of the first marriage offered conservative critics of Henry and Anne a far more realistic agenda than the treason which had been discussed with Chapuys, and one which could be pursued by all the familiar methods of court intrigue. And the omens were good. With the end to all immediate hope of a son, Henry's intention to exact the succession oath from Mary evaporated, and a relieved princess found her treatment somewhat improved. Ironically, the solution of accepting both daughters by seniority was one towards which Henry himself would move eight years later.

Not only was support for Mary a more promising option than support for her mother had been; for the first time since 1533 it became realistic to hope to unseat Anne herself. No longer was the alternative to the Boleyn match the reinstatement of an aged and barren Katherine, a return to a female heir presumptive and, by implication, submission to papal authority. The possibility that God had condemned his marriage to Anne had already entered the king's mind, if only briefly. He might now be susceptible to the suggestion that getting rid of Anne would make possible a third and wholly uncontested match, and offspring recognized at home and abroad. Anne's opponents took heart. Their leader seems to have been Nicholas Carewe, but he was backed by the rest of the privy chamber staff opposed to Anne.[53] Exeter, Rochford's opposite number as 'nobleman of the privy chamber', continued as the link with Chapuys, and other courtiers involved included Lord Montagu and his brother Geoffrey, Sir Thomas Elyot, and the king's cousin, the dowager countess of Kildare.[54] The shock of the executions of Fisher, More and the Carthusians had also hardened opinion, and there was an increased willingness to risk the queen's anger. At court, Nicholas Carewe made no bones about sheltering the king's fool from Henry's wrath after he had unwisely praised Katherine and Mary and denigrated Anne and Elizabeth.[55] From Rome Richard Pate, archdeacon of Lincoln and a career diplomat though he was, wrote in agonized support of Mary, well aware, even at that distance, of the risk that he was taking.[56]

Where did Jane Seymour fit in to all this? It is clear, first of all, that Henry's interest in her began as mere courtly gallantry. As late as 1 April, Chapuys was still describing her by the significant label 'the lady whom he serves'.[57] Effectively, she took the place of the pregnant Anne as Henry's courtly 'mistress'. The danger in this was, of course, that convention might again develop a real human content. Jane is generally supposed to have attracted Henry on the strength of a contrast to Anne: fair, not dark; younger by seven or eight years; gentle rather than abrasive; of no great wit, against a mistress of repartee; a model of female self-effacement, against a self-made woman. Chapuys was very under-impressed. 'She is of middle height, and nobody thinks that she has much beauty. Her complexion is so whitish that she may be called rather pale. She is a little over twenty-five ... The said Semel is not very intelligent, and is said to be rather haughty.'[58] Much to her advantage, of course, was the recent rise of her brother in royal favour. Despite Edward Seymour's later self-projection as 'the good duke of Somerset', no man showed 'himself more greedy of wealth or ruthless to others than [he] when he built up his fortune during Henry VIII's lifetime'.[59] He needed no reminding of the value of a sister who caught the king's eye. As Thomas Wyatt explained to aspiring courtiers:

> In this also see you be not idle:
> Thy niece, thy cousin, thy sister or thy daughter,
> If she be fair, if handsome by her middle,
> If thy better hath her love besought her,
> Advance his cause, and he shall help thy need;
> It is but love, turn it to a laughter.
> But 'ware, I say, so gold thee help and speed,
> That in this case thou be not so unwise
> As Pandar was in such a like deed:
> For he, the fool, of conscience was so nice
> That he no gain would have for all his pain.[60]

In the event, Edward Seymour received something even better than gold, appointment at the beginning of March to the staff of the privy chamber, an even more promising place from which to act as his sister's ponce.[61]

According to contemporary mores, Anne should have shut her eyes to Henry's pursuit of Jane Seymour. Queens were expected not to notice husbandly diversions. George Wyatt commented that 'wise men in those days judged' that if, like Katherine, Anne had been more tolerant of peccadilloes she would have risked less; however, 'her too great love' prevented what 'she might the rather have done respecting the general liberty and custom then that way'.[62] Wyatt's prose is heavy-footed, but it does point to an easily overlooked but drastic weakness in Anne's position.[63] Royal marriages, both before, during and after the sixteenth century, were expected to be business affairs, related to international diplomacy and the continuation of a dynasty. Spouses were suggested to, not chosen by, a monarch. Romance featured only accidentally; its expected place was the affaire. Henry VIII, almost uniquely, defied this expectation and both chose and married Anne for romantic reasons. The only other English or British monarch since the Conquest to do the equivalent was his grandfather, Edward IV. In marrying for love, Henry in effect confused the role of the wife and the mistress, with the result that personal emotion was the basis of his relationship with Anne and hers with him. Anne was therefore right to say that her feelings were more exposed than those of Katherine. The corollary was that, as well as being hurt by royal philandering, Anne was compelled to fight to protect this personal relationship with Henry. She could not distance herself as Katherine of Aragon had. She could not ignore it if her husband had become infatuated with Jane, even though the inevitable result was to make Jane more significant than she need have been. Though tolerating infidelity would have been the safer course, Anne was forced to put herself on a level with Jane and challenge Henry to choose between them.

The highly personal basis of Anne's marriage explains why she could not ignore the affair with Jane, but it does not explain how a royal flirt in January 1536 was in a position four months later to supplant a queen. That opportunity arose from a coming together of the Seymour dalliance and the sympathy for Mary. The princess's supporters, particularly among Edward Seymour's new colleagues in the privy chamber, realized that here was a heaven-sent opportunity to supplant Anne and bring Katherine's daughter back to her rightful place. As for Seymour, he had already made gains from encouraging Jane's responses to Henry so far; for his sister to become more than the king's latest amour promised the jackpot. The alliance between the Seymours and the conservatives was made and Jane was coached to behave accordingly.[64] She was instructed to poison Henry's mind against Anne whenever possible, stressing particularly the illegitimacy of his second marriage – in effect presenting herself as an implicit alternative. However, she was to pick her moments and express such views especially when others of the faction were in attendance to chorus their agreement. The Exeters approached Chapuys to add his voice when opportunity offered. He agreed with alacrity and, with Mary's approval, also set about active lobbying of Cromwell and others 'most fit for the purpose'.[65] Indeed, the thought of the merit in thereby serving the princess's interests, striking a blow against heresy and helping to save Henry from mortal sin, quite made him forget to mention the advantage it would bring to Charles V. And above all the schemes to bad-mouth Anne, one thing was firmly impressed on Jane. Her price now was marriage, nothing less.

Henry discovered the new Jane at the end of March. He was in London and she at Greenwich, and Chapuys described how:

> [the king] sent her a purse full of sovereigns and a letter. The young lady, having kissed the letter returned it to the messenger unopened and falling on her knees besought him to ask the king on her behalf, to consider carefully that she was a gentlewoman, born of good and honourable parents and with an unsullied reputation. She had no greater treasure in the world than her honour which she would rather die a thousand times than tarnish, and if he wanted to give her money she begged that he would do so once God had sent her a good match.[66]

Setting aside for a moment Jane's theatrical exhibition of virtue, why did she not open the king's letter? The obvious reason is that she knew what was in it – a summons to the royal bed – and that provided she had not read it, she would not need to reply. Henry had propositioned Anne face to face; he thought that with Jane matters were far enough advanced that a letter would be enough. According to the marchioness of Exeter, the effect of Jane's response was to increase Henry's interest '*merveilleuse-ment*' and he announced that he would 'henceforth (*desormais*)' only speak with Jane in the company of her relations. '*Desormais*' certainly invites a raised eyebrow and supports the late tradition that the king's affection was stolen when Anne was well into her pregnancy. The Protestants describe her 'as not so fit for dalliance' while the Catholics have Anne saying bluntly: 'I saw this harlot Jane sitting on your knees while my belly was doing its duty!'[67] What is more, the king's newly announced concern for respectability only amounted to evicting Thomas Cromwell from his room at Greenwich, which had a private passage to the king's apartment, and putting in Jane's brother Edward and his wife as the nominal occupants. Chapuys was decidely unconvinced of Jane's modest unavailability.

As we have seen, a somewhat similar story is told about Anne playing hard to get, and it may appear a kind of justice that Jane's refusal to sleep with Henry should now help to destroy her predecessor.[68] Historians have, however, been somewhat taken in by the Seymour 'image of virtue and quiet virginity' which was to a degree a deliberate pose. Jane was willing to be used to oust Anne; Henry's first marriage was dead before Anne came on the scene; Anne's sexuality challenged Henry, but Jane dangled her virtue as a bait. Anne offered Henry marriage or nothing, Jane upped her price once the chance of a bigger prize appeared; Anne was no man's creature, Jane was a willing tool whose personality it is more than kind to describe as 'pliable'. Agnes Strickland went as far as to declare that the picture of Jane preparing for marriage to Henry while Anne was under sentence of death in the Tower 'is repulsive enough, but it becomes tenfold more abhorrent when the woman who caused the whole tragedy is loaded with panegyric.'[69] That, however, is an over-harsh Victorian judgement. Chapuys considered that the guilt was primarily Henry's. Londoners watching at the time blamed Henry and Jane, both. The king had to warn his new inamorata accordingly:

> there is a ballad made lately of great derision against us, which if it go abroad and is seen by you, I pray you to pay no manner of regard to it. I am not at present informed who is the setter forth of this malignant writing; but if he is found, he shall be straitly punished for it.

There is some satisfaction in the fact that Henry never did find him.[70]

The Response,
January—April 1536

ABOUT the time that Henry discovered that Jane Seymour now had a new price-tag, several of her backers were dining with Eustace Chapuys – the subject of discussion, a new bride for Henry. By the end of April they were seeking ecclesiastical opinion on the validity of any divorce.[1] If hostile tales are to be believed, they may even have succeeded in encouraging the king to speculate with Jane about the possibility of marriage, and certainly an atmosphere of doubt about the long-term future of the Boleyn marriage was encouraged.[2]

The response of Anne Boleyn and her supporters was to fight. Chapuys reported only that Anne was raging against Jane, but the signs of more serious resistance are plain. George Boleyn maintained a high profile. He was much in evidence at court, and when the king had to choose a peer to cast the proxy vote of Lord Delaware for the session of parliament which began on 4 February, it was to George that it went.[3] The Boleyns continued to enjoy noted royal favour. Early in March they secured letters patent reconstructing Thomas's lease of the Crown honour of Rayleigh in Essex, with the term extended, George brought in as joint tenant and a 20 per cent rebate on the rent.[4] One of the Acts of parliament which received the royal assent on 14 April stripped the bishopric of Norwich of the town of Lynn and other properties; a week later, Chapuys had discovered that the beneficiary was to be the earl of Wiltshire, and that a couple of abbeys were earmarked for him as well.[5] Other Acts assured property to Anne, including Colly Weston which Henry had transferred from the duke of Richmond.[6] It is true that on St George's Day, Sir Nicholas Carewe was elected to fill up a vacancy among the Knights of the Garter, and that Chapuys interpreted this as a defeat for Rochford and a sign of Anne's weakened influence, but the choice was at least in part dictated by the king's earlier half-promise to Francis that Carewe was next in line.[7] Anne retained her influence almost to the last, and may, indeed, have been exploiting her position to disarm the opposition. Certainly she was exerting herself at the request of the earl of Westmorland to secure favours for his brother-in-law, Henry, Lord Stafford – an unlikely association, for Stafford was the son of Katherine's favourite, the last duke of Buckingham, and his wife was sister to Lord Montagu, who even then was plotting against the queen.[8] Anne did not lightly surrender her husband to Jane Seymour.

One development in the early spring of 1536 was full of ill omen. Anne and Thomas Cromwell quarrelled. Chapuys learned of this fatal split towards the end of March and confirmed it to his own satisfaction at a meeting with Cromwell on 1 April.[9] Next day, by the end of mass, everyone in the royal chapel knew. As we have seen, the preacher appointed for that Passion Sunday was Anne's almoner, John Skip, who made very clear his own (and the queen's) support for moderate reform.[10] In contrast, the remainder of his discourse was anything but moderate. The text he had chosen was John, chapter 8, verse 46, 'Which of you can convict me of sin?' and the sermon almost caused a riot. Skip was accused of malice, slander, presumption, lack of charity, sedition, treason, disobedience to the gospel, attacking 'the great posts, pillars and columns sustaining and holding up the common wealth' and inviting anarchy.[11] The reason for this furore was the way he had developed his text. Skip identified the congregation as 'you', and in particular the royal counsellors, whom he accused of gross sycophancy – a king's 'counsel nowadays will move him no otherwise unto any things but as they see him disposed and inclined to the same'.[12] The 'me' Skip applied to the English clergy collectively, so making his sermon a no-holds-barred rebuttal of the generalized attacks on the clergy which, he said, were rife 'nowadays'. He readily accepted that particular clerics might be fallible, but criticism of the entire clerical estate was totally unjustified. What was more, it was hypocritical. 'He wished that men would therein use a more temperance and first amend their own lives before they taxed other men's.'[13] And Skip was blunt about lay motives: 'nowadays many men . . . rebuke the clergy . . . because they would have from the clergy their possessions.'[14]

No cleric in Anne's household would have dared say such things without her specific approval. Early in the sermon Skip even risked a coded swipe at Henry's interest in Jane Seymour and the Crown's preoccupation with money.[15] King Solomon, he reminded his hearers:

in the latter end of his reign he became very un-noble and defamed himself sore by sensual and carnal appetite in taking of many wives and concubines and also by avaricious mind in laying too great or sore burdens and yokes upon his subjects, over-pressing them too sore thereby.

The chapel took the point. How, Skip's critics would ask later, could the preacher have intended this otherwise than:

> to touch the king's grace with the said similitude. Albeit he showed not his mind in plain and express words [the congregation] conceived right well the malice of his mind as well by that general example as if he had coined the similitude particularly.[15]

Later the preacher went further and made Anne's endorsement explicit – and so too her split with Cromwell. This followed from his assertion that a king needed:

> to be well wary what he does after the counsel of his counsellors for some time for the malice that they bear toward many men or toward one man as of a multitude they would have the whole multitude destroyed.[16]

To illustrate this Skip took the example of Esther, the Jewish wife of the Persian ruler Ahasuerus. As he recounted the Old Testament story, Ahasuerus had been deceived by his adviser, Haman, into ordering a massacre of his Jewish subjects on the ground that they were disregarding his laws. But,

> there was a good woman (which this gentle king Ahasuerus loved very well and put his trust in because he knew that she was ever his friend) and she gave unto the king contrary counsel.[17]

The Jews were saved and Haman was hanged. The Esther story was very familiar to a Tudor congregation, and Skip's allusions were impossible to miss. The clergy overall were the Jews, Henry VIII was Ahasuerus and Cromwell was Haman. And the good woman? Everybody in the chapel that day knew that it was Ahasuerus's wife Esther – Henry's wife Anne.

The occasion for Skip's diatribe, and the cause of the breach between Anne and Cromwell, was the legislation to confiscate the wealth of the smaller monasteries, which at that moment was awaiting the royal assent. Indeed, the sermon's bitter attack on laymen exploiting tales about clerical vices in order to justify the pillage of Church wealth gave the lie direct to the minister. Less than a month before, Cromwell had released the *Compendium compertorum*, a carefully edited catalogue of gross monastic indecencies, in order to sway parliamentary opinion in favour of confiscation.[18] Hugh Latimer's recollection was that 'when their enormities were first read in the Parliament house, they were so great and abominable, that there was nothing but "down with them".'[19]

Skip, of course, was not suggesting that Anne supported the monastic status quo. Indeed, at court, in government, in parliament and among the higher clergy many felt that reform of the monasteries was needed and some redirection of Church assets 'to better uses'.[20] However, what were 'better uses'? Anne – along with most other prominent reformers – had counted on endowments being allocated to education or other charitable causes; after all, they represented the charitable donations of past generations. The refounded college at Stoke by Nayland was the model of what she wanted to achieve.[21] There was firm precedent for such repositioning of assets; the most recent major example was Wolsey's transfer of the endowments of several semi-defunct monasteries to new educational foundations in Oxford and Ipswich. Skip urged a similar course, emphasizing 'the great decay of the universities in this realm and how necessary the maintenance of them is for the continuance of Christ's faith and his religion'.[22] Cromwell thought otherwise. For some years the government had been toying with the possibility of confiscating ecclesiastical land and thereby solving the king's deep-rooted financial problem. Here was the minister's opportunity to make Henry 'the richest prince in Christendom' and provide funds to modernize the country's antiquated defences. It would also dramatically increase royal (and ministerial) influence by multiplying the fund of royal patronage. The policy had Henry's enthusiastic concurrence and it carried the day in parliament – possibly after the king had come down to the Commons in successive weeks to ensure that the bill got through.[23]

Preached in the interval between the Dissolution Bill being passed by parliament and the royal assent being given, Skip's sermon was Anne's call to courtiers and counsellors alike to change the advice they were giving the king and to reject the lure of personal gain. Indeed Skip publicly and deliberately endorsed the popular suspicion that in proposing secularization, the real motive of Cromwell and his henchmen was to feather their own nests.[24] To make that point clear beyond all doubt, he deliberately reversed a detail in the Esther story. According to the Vulgate text of the Bible, Haman, the minister, offered to *pay* the king 10,000 talents to cover the cost of the archers required to destroy the Jews, although the king refused to accept the money. Skip, however, said that Haman promised that the pogrom would *raise* 10,000 talents for the Crown, and Ahasuerus

responded that the minister could take the money for himself.[25] In consequence Haman was 'much more crueller upon them [the Jews] because he
perceived that he should have the x^M talents himself'.[26] In effect, Anne's
almoner was publicly attacking Cromwell's motives and integrity.

Possibly Skip's sermon was as direct and belligerent as it was because
Anne had been duped. The material issued by Cromwell's office had been
clearly disingenuous. It had claimed that the object of the dissolution was
'the maintenance of certain notable persons of learning and good qualities
about his Highness' and the bill referred to the use of the confiscated assets
'to the pleasure of Almighty God and to the honour and profit of this realm'
and specifically included bodies politic and corporate among those who
would benefit.[27] The queen, indeed, may only have discovered that total
secularization was intended following the shady deal by which the king had
effectively sold Sawley Abbey in Yorkshire to the courtier Sir Arthur Darcy,
before the Dissolution Bill was even on the statute book.[28] Whatever the
surprise, Anne rapidly became the leader of the opposition.[29]

The agenda was no longer a need to convince the generality of the
appropriateness of dissolution, something which still concerned one of her
chaplains, Robert Singleton, when preaching at Paul's Cross only the day
after Skip's sermon.[30] Anne now called on reform-minded preachers 'to be
very curious [careful] how they should minister occasion in any of their
sermons touching the subverting of any houses of religion, but rather to
make continual and earnest petition for the stay of the same.'[31] Skip was
not the only cleric she sent into battle. William Latymer reported that she
summoned Hugh Latimer, the country's premier preacher, and instructed
him to suggest in his next sermon before the king that houses should not
be dissolved but converted to better uses.[32] The bishop chose to preach
on the parable of the vineyard in Luke, chapter 20, in which unsatisfactory
tenants deny rent to an owner. The point he drew out from the Gospel
story was that once the bad tenants had been evicted, the vineyard was not
destroyed but handed over to worthier occupants. Monasteries, therefore,
should be converted 'to places of study and good letters'.

Anne's opposition was not confined to the pulpit. Earlier in Lent,
Archbishop Cranmer had preached a sermon on the old agenda, supporting the secularization of abbey land and arguing that money spent on
masses for the dead would be better spent on the poor.[33] Suddenly, on 22
April, he wrote urgently to Cromwell, saying:

> I was ever hitherto cold, but now am in a heat with the cause of religion
> [that is, the religious orders] , which goeth all contrary to mine expectation,

if it be as the fame goeth; wherein I would wonder[fully] fain break my mind unto you.[34]

Had Anne got to the archbishop and convinced him that the dissolution Cromwell was implementing would bring the poor nothing? Latymer also tells of a delegation of abbots and priors calling on the queen once her opposition to secularization was known, and asking for her protection.[35] The queen, he claimed, read the group a stern lecture on their notorious corruptions and attacked them for their connections with Rome, for their refusal to admit the preachers of 'God's Word' and for the inadequate support they gave to scholars at the universities.[36]

> My opinion is the dissolution of your houses to fall upon you for your just demerits as a deserved plague from Almighty God, who abhorring your lewdness, derideth your blind ignorance.

But her final menace before she walked out also offered a glimpse of hope:

> Until such time as you shall cleanse and purify your corrupt life and doctrine, God will not cease to send his plagues upon you to your utter subversion.[37]

The abbots responded to the hint by offering the queen substantial cash sums to support preachers and scholars, and also the right to present to many of the best livings in their gift, and Anne appointed 'certain trusty men' to manage matters. Precisely when this visit took place is not clear. Latymer implies that it was an attempt to block the passage of the Dissolution Bill, but since he says that what was agreed was aborted by Anne's death, the episode most probably postdated the passage of the legislation through parliament in March.[38]

Securing the Dissolution Bill did not, however, mean that Cromwell was now safe. The Crown had probably always envisaged saving certain religious houses, so the Act had included a provision for Henry to reprieve any he wished. Given Anne's opposition, that clause now became a real hostage to fortune. The minister could never count on being in a position always to block the queen's persuasions, and the horrendous possibility threatened that Anne would urge Henry to make substantial exemptions for educational purposes.[39] What was worse, Cromwell's relationship with Anne had been fatally damaged. If we are to believe Chapuys, he may actually have tried to moderate the dissolution somewhat, no doubt in an attempt to preserve his links with the queen, but secularization had the king's active support and Henry gave him short shrift.[40] Now Cromwell could not possibly withdraw. Yet if he persisted, he would be in Wolsey's predicament – facing a hostile Anne with a unique hold over Henry. He had seen her lead a putsch against the cardinal. Would he be next?

Anne, indeed, may already have begun trying to subvert secularization. If the abbots' visit did take place after the Bill had passed both houses of parliament, then their real object was to conciliate Anne in the hope of future support for exemptions.[41] If so, Anne was colluding in illegality since for heads of houses to convert assets in the way Latymer describes was directly contrary to the statute. Certainly, as soon as the Act was passed, Anne was asked to secure the continuation of the Yorkshire convent of Nun Monkton.[42] It is also possible that it was Anne who offered Henry 2000 marks to reprieve the convent at Catesby.[43] That these were probably not the only examples is suggested by a subsequent exchange between Henry and Jane Seymour, which was retailed to Jean du Bellay by an English correspondent. When his new queen pleaded for the preservation of religious houses, the king responded brusquely that she should 'attend to other things, reminding her that the last Queen had died in consequence of meddling too much in state affairs'.[44]

Cromwell's estrangement from Anne Boleyn was exacerbated by problems in foreign policy. An imminent French threat to the imperial position in Italy had created a powerful incentive for Charles V to compose differences with England. With his aunt Katherine no longer in the way, Anne was less of an offence to the Habsburg family, and the emperor intervened early in the year to block publication of the papal sentence depriving Henry of his throne. Charles's policy was now to tie England to the Empire by establishing the claim of his cousin Mary to be heir presumptive to the English crown. This meant that he had somehow to deal with the obstacle of Elizabeth, who by statute stood in the way. Assuming, as he always had, that Anne was the king's mistress, Charles decided to behave accordingly and buy her out. Instructions were sent to Chapuys to do a deal with 'the concubine' and, if necessary, to use Cromwell as an intermediary to get the best possible terms, with either Mary recognized as the heir or the succession left in suspense.[45] It might even be in Charles's interest to see Anne and Henry stay together, because that would prevent a subsequent French marriage. Thus at Rome in March 1536 the emperor offered the English ambassador, in return for the legitimation of Mary, imperial support for 'the continuance of this last matrimony or otherwise' as Henry wished.[46]

In England too, opinion was swinging towards a *rapprochement* with the emperor, and Anne and her supporters made common cause with it.[47] It would do no harm for the queen to adopt a more pro-imperial stance and so neutralize the damaging assumption that she was in Francis I's pocket, and so too the fear that her presence spelled danger to the vital economic links with the Habsburg Low Countries. Other factions supporting the same line had different motives. Carewe, though also a Francophile, saw a change to an imperial alliance as a first step towards reversing the policies and removing the personalities of recent years. Yet whatever the motives, the approach was generally supported, and after a series of detailed discussions between Cromwell and Chapuys, negotiations reached their climax at a meeting at Greenwich between the ambassador and the king himself on 18 April, the Tuesday after Easter.[48]

On arrival at court that day, Chapuys was effusively welcomed by George Boleyn, and Cromwell brought a message from Henry, inviting him to visit Anne and kiss her hand. The ambassador excused himself – that was going too far, too fast – but Rochford conducted him to mass and to a far more public encounter with the queen. Anne accompanied Henry from the royal pew down to the chapel to make her offering, and knowing that Chapuys was placed behind the door through which she entered, she stopped, turned and bowed to this representative of the Empire, and necessarily he responded likewise. After mass, Chapuys was careful not to go with the king and the other ambassadors to dine with Anne, but again it was her brother who entertained him in the presence chamber, while Anne, having enquired for Chapuys, gave deliberate vent to a series of remarks that were highly critical of France. These were duly carried back to the envoy. After dinner, Henry took Chapuys for a lengthy personal conversation in the privacy of a window embrasure in his own room, observed from a distance only by Cromwell and Audley.

At this stage, however, the ambassador sensed that something was wrong. His negotiations with Cromwell had been on an imperial proposal which envisaged the possibility of a restoration of some relations between England and Rome, the inclusion of Mary in the line of succession, and military support for Charles V in the expected war with France over Milan. The king, however, now showed himself distinctly cool to the package. Why this was is nowhere recorded, but the invitation earlier in the day to kiss Anne's hand suggests that Henry was expecting unconditional recognition of his marriage, and certainly nothing about recognition for Mary. Although Cromwell had been willing to discuss that with Chapuys and for months had been treating the princess with increasing respect and courtesy,

Henry's refusal to countenance the slightest recognition of his first marriage was absolute. Chapuys' suspicion that the ministers were out of step with Henry became stronger when he withdrew and watched the king in deep debate with Cromwell and Audley. By now Edward Seymour was in the room, and as the ambassador made polite conversation with him, he saw Henry and Cromwell beginning to dispute angrily, to the point where Cromwell had to excuse himself, claiming he needed a drink, and sat on a chest out of the king's sight in order to recover his temper. Henry then moved out into the room to see what had become of Cromwell and to tell Chapuys that he had to have everything in writing. When, in accordance with his instructions, the envoy demurred at this, the king turned on him and started to mimic an adult calling to a child, declaring that he was not an infant to be alternately whipped then petted; it was for the emperor first to apologize to him for his past ill-treatment. Henry then began to rake up grievances against Charles which were ten years old and more, until he talked himself to a standstill. In the end, all the king would agree to was to look at the texts of existing treaties between England and the Empire, and Chapuys left the court to compare wounds with Cromwell who, like Audley, had listened to the king's tirade in silence.

Cromwell professed himself completely baffled by the king's behaviour, but one thing stands out clearly.[49] Despite the agreement between all factions to back an imperial alliance, Henry remained prepared to haggle. Cromwell told Chapuys that at a council meeting the day after this exhibition of royal obstinacy, every councillor went on his knees to persuade him to continue negotiations.[50] Yet neither minister nor ambassador should really have been surprised. Already at Christmas the king had expressed to Chapuys his reservations about a *rapprochement* with Charles.[51] Astute as he was in foreign affairs, Henry was clearly interested in a deal with the Empire and knew very well that he would not, in the end, get even a diplomatic apology for past wrongs. But by being difficult he hoped to use the fear of a renewed Anglo-French axis to compel Charles to accept an alliance without domestic conditions, and so tacitly accept that Henry had the right to settle his own affairs himself – religious, matrimonial and parental. And to achieve this Anne had to remain his wife, and his daughter Mary a bastard. Hence the king's offer, late in 1535, of an imperial marriage for Elizabeth, and when feelers put out by Cromwell brought no response, Henry broached the matter to the ambassador himself.[52] Likewise, Chapuys' visit to court on 18 April was clearly stage-managed to compel the ambassador to recognize Anne, and his bow to her did cause great annoyance and apprehension among Mary's supporters.[53]

The treatment of Francis I was all of a piece with this. He was urged into war with Charles, but at the same time maximum concessions were demanded for guarantees of English support. This, in turn, allowed Henry to up the price to Charles for England remaining neutral.[54] Francis I, however, was hard to handle. The English learned that he had in his possession a copy of the papal decree depriving Henry of the throne, something which Charles was obstructing, but which it might suit the French to publish in order to secure the support of the pope for their interests in Italy.[55] By the last week of April the council was sitting every day to decide what to do – whether to call the French bluff and hold out for complete victory over Charles, or whether to clinch the imperial alliance on somewhat looser terms.[56] Far from the issue of April 1536 being 'When will Anne go and how?', Henry was exploiting his second marriage to force Europe to accept that he had been right all along. As late as 30 April he was briefing his ambassadors in France in order to increase the pressure on the emperor.[57]

According to Chapuys, Cromwell was hard hit by the king's obstinacy and took to his bed, and there is no denying the spot the minister was in.[58] As early as June 1535 he had suggested to the ambassador that if Anne knew how close their relations were, she would have his head.[59] At the end of that year Henry had cautioned Chapuys that Cromwell was exceeding his authority, a point which Cromwell himself admitted later (although subsequently he retracted and did try to claim that his overtures had the king's approval). On the other hand, the minister was clear that England had to switch to an imperial alliance. He had invested a great deal in the negotiations with Chapuys, and there can be no doubt what his position was in the council debates on the value which might or might not remain in a French alliance. As yet Cromwell was unaware of Charles's new readiness to change tack, and the imperial climb-down over Anne Boleyn which the king was demanding must have seemed an impossibility. And, so he told Chapuys, his negotiations for an imperial alliance were again raising suspicions in Henry's mind.[60] Cromwell would even lose the chance of building credit with those who wanted that alliance as much as he did, if he had to cool discussions in an attempt to force from Charles the concessions the king sought.

By the middle of April, therefore, Anne Boleyn had become a major threat to Thomas Cromwell. If his only problem had been the disagreement over foreign affairs, the minister could, perhaps, have remained sanguine. His customary neat footwork might well have distanced him from Chapuys, and he certainly absorbed the lesson that

Mary's illegitimacy was non-negotiable. But following Anne's public attack on monastic secularization, this diplomatic difficulty was the last straw.

There were political consequences too. With Anne alienated, he would have few allies to fall back on. No longer would he be able to rely on the rest of the Boleyn faction and their vital role in the privy chamber. No minister under threat could expect staff there to risk their own careers for him – as Cromwell himself was to prove when he fell from royal favour in 1540. Furthermore, despite his current mastery of government policy and administration, the minister was in the second division when compared with the personal favour and private influence wielded by a man like Henry Norris. To Norris, Rochford and the senior members of the privy chamber circle, Cromwell was a functionary – someone who might from time to time be awkward and drag his feet, someone it was important to cultivate because of his mastery of the bureaucratic machine, but in the end a man who in their world of patronage, intrigue and profit would do whatever they could persuade the king to command, if necessary by enlisting Anne. Thus, although the Boleyn group in the privy chamber had been an asset to him, as long as they were there, Cromwell would always be constrained. Ambition as well as self-preservation therefore argued that he might be better off if the queen was out of the way, and that option, in the person of Jane Seymour, now appeared a realistic possibility for the first time since Anne's marriage.[61]

A switch to supporting Jane Seymour was, nevertheless, replete with risk. Jane's backers were all talk, and the odds were very much on the queen. Then, too, Cromwell had much in common with Anne – beliefs, ideals, even religious experience. He had achieved great things with and for her, and she had helped to make his career. Moreover, if Anne were rejected in favour of Jane, the victorious conservative faction would look to reverse the very policies Cromwell himself had put in place. How could he expect to remain in office or even, perhaps, keep his head on his shoulders? Anne or Jane – Cromwell was between the devil and the deep blue sea. How long the minister deliberated we do not know, but as he later told Chapuys, he concluded that he must act.[62] A hostile Anne threatened both his standing with the king and his key financial achievement, as well as encouraging the king in demanding diplomatic impossibilities. Henry must be brought to want someone else. Despite the risk, despite all his past debts, Cromwell's very survival no longer coincided with the survival of the queen. She must go.

Thomas Cromwell set out to plan the removal of Anne Boleyn with the caution the exercise demanded; the risk involved was a measure of his desperation. Simply to remove the queen would be to invite his own ruin. He had to come to terms with the conservatives first. But even should the respect he had recently shown to Mary and the kindnesses he had done her, such as returning a cross which her mother had left her, secure his safety, there was no profit in a mere exchange of masters.[63] Moreover, the policies he had devoted the past four years to promoting would be at risk. Somehow, therefore, he must achieve the gymnastic feat of a double reversed twist, ridding himself of Anne first, with the support of Mary and her allies, and then ditching them too.

The secretary's first step was to gain the confidence of Carewe, Seymour and the others supporting Jane and Mary. How he achieved this, and achieved it within a matter of days, we do not know. Chapuys was probably the broker, for the ambassador certainly secured the guarded approval of Mary.[64] Cromwell's switch also tells us much about his convincing personality, for it would be two months before these new allies realized that Cromwell did not share their view that the destruction of Anne and the restoration of Mary were two sides of the same coin. Knowing his monarch's constitutional convictions in a way his intimate attendants did not, possessed of a wider, more analytical experience than minds formed by the ideals of *The Courtier* and the *Roman de la Rose*, being a statesman and politician where they were bred in the court and conspiracy, Cromwell understood and shared – as they did not – Henry's commitment to the royal supremacy. Already the king had been warned that to divorce Anne could imply acceptance of the papal decision in favour of Katherine of Aragon, and, without precautions, the same implication could be drawn from the restoration of Mary.[65] Thus, the minister could be sure that the king's *amour propre* would demand a show of obedience and contrition before the princess was restored to favour, and that this would include acceptance of Henry's title as supreme head and the invalidity of her mother's marriage. The princess, in effect, could be compelled to offer an equivalent of the loyalty oath she appeared to have escaped. That would cut the ground from under her supporters and force them to acquiesce, at least in public, in the policies that Cromwell had carried through since 1532. The victory of that year would be confirmed, and there would now be only one victor, Thomas Cromwell. What is more, in the euphoria at Anne's fall, indiscreet advocacy of Mary might well draw the conservatives within the provisions of the new treason law. If they were given enough rope they could hang themselves – or at least allow Cromwell to truss them up.

What to do about Anne was more difficult. Until Cromwell joined them, the opponents of the queen seem to have thought in naive terms of Henry being persuaded to repudiate her – that is, to admit what they had believed all along, that Anne was only 'an *affaire*' – and this despite the time, effort and, most significantly, money that the king had expended over almost a decade to convince everyone, at home and abroad, that the opposite was the case.[66] Alternatively their talk was of 'divorce', yet with Henry publicly endorsing Anne's position on the Tuesday after Easter, how could any separation be achieved, still less one convincing enough to quiet English and European opinion?[67] Above all, would Anne go quietly and could Henry be relied on not to return to his 'so great folly'?

In any case, the problem was not simply Anne. Cromwell might wish to disengage himself, but the Boleyn faction would not go away. Norris, Rochford and their associates had rallied to the queen and would undoubtedly seek to keep her in power. After all, if Jane replaced Anne, the Seymour faction would become the 'ins' and they would be the 'outs', forced to smile at promotions and policies they did not like, just as Carewe and the others had done for nearly a decade. But if the Seymours were successful and the Boleyn faction remained, Cromwell would have no chance of 'dishing' the conservatives and coming out on top. Removing Anne from Henry's bed was no answer by itself. Her supporters had to be neutralized at the same time. Any change which left Thomas and George Boleyn in place, Norris as groom of the stool, Anne as marquis of Pembroke and Elizabeth begotten in as 'good faith' as Mary ever was, would be no more safe or final than the defeat of Wolsey had been in the autumn of 1529. When, late in Easter Week 1536, Cromwell put his mind, as he said, to 'think up and plan' the coup against Anne, he faced the biggest challenge of his life.[68]

THE COUP, APRIL—MAY 1536

IF we are to believe Thomas Cromwell – and there is no good reason not to – he moved against Anne Boleyn only when the king's behaviour on Easter Tuesday 1536 had finally convinced him that so long as she was queen, Henry would obstruct what was safest both for his kingdom and for his secretary. From that point twelve days turned decision into action, and on Sunday, 30 April, the first suspect was under arrest. Less than three weeks later Anne was dead. A month and a day – from Chapuys' acknowledging her in the Chapel Royal at Greenwich on Tuesday, 18 April, to her burial in the Tower on Friday, 19 May – this is all the time it took for the most romantic, the most scandalous tragedy in English history. It was a tragedy which took the life of a queen, her brother George, Henry Norris – the closest to a friend Henry VIII had – Francis Weston, William Brereton and Mark Smeton (all of the privy chamber), and left yet another of the privy chamber staff, Sir Richard Page, in prison in the Tower, along with Sir Thomas Wyatt. It was Wyatt who wrote the epitaph to it all:

> These bloody days have broken my heart:
> My lust, my youth did them depart,
> And blind desire of estate.
> Who hastes to climb seeks to revert:
>   Of truth, *circa Regna tonat.*[1]

'About the throne the thunder rolls' – a sentiment from the classics which has shaped discussion after discussion of Henry VIII's repudiation of Anne Boleyn. The decision to charge her with high treason was made, so the story goes, by 24 April, when the king approved the setting up of a commission of oyer and terminer to investigate and dispose of a catch-all selection of treasons and other offences in Middlesex and Kent.[2] On the 27th, writs went out to summon a parliament. This was an emergency measure – the Reformation Parliament had been dissolved only a fortnight before – and, when Lords and Commons met on 8 June, the summons was explained by the need to settle the succession and to repeal statutes favouring Anne.[3]

Mark Smeton, the first suspect, was detained at Cromwell's house in Stepney on Sunday, 30 April, accused of adultery with the queen. Despite this, the May Day jousts at Greenwich went ahead. Anne's brother, Rochford, led the challengers and Henry Norris the answerers, and nothing untoward was noticed by the spectators. Indeed, if we may trust the French verse account of 2 June 1536, the king was very affable and offered his own mount when Sir Henry's renowned charger began to play up.[4] But suddenly, at the end of the joust, Henry left for Whitehall, travelling on horseback instead of by river and with only six attendants, one of them Norris whom, throughout the journey, he had 'in examination and promised him his pardon in case he would utter the truth'.[5] Norris insisted on his innocence, but was sent to the Tower at dawn on Tuesday, 2 May.[6] Later that morning the queen was accused of adultery apparently with three men, and told that she would be taken to the Tower.[7]

Thus much is fact and traditional interpretation, but tradition bristles with difficulties. Why, if the court to try Anne was set up on 24 April, was she not arrested until 2 May? The Tudor rule was arrest first, interrogate later; no need to wait to collect evidence; delay spelled danger, particularly for Thomas Cromwell. Why did the arrests take place piecemeal? Suspects were still being discovered a week later. Why did the king, so careful of his majesty, invite gossip by walking out of a tournament being held in public? In Hall's words, 'many men mused' at Henry's behaviour.[8] The state of the tide may have dictated a journey to London by road, but why with the chief suspect?[9] The standard procedure was to isolate immediately anyone accused, precisely to prevent access to the king. Above all, there is the contradiction of a scrambling and drawn-out climax to a coup which had supposedly been lined up for a week, and by someone who had even foreseen the need to call parliament. The resolution to these questions is often said to be that Henry willed the end but kept aloof from advance knowledge of the means. Yet to suppose this is to suppose that Cromwell chose a remarkably risky course. Norris was renowned for his influence with Henry. Supposing he had been able to convince the king of his innocence during that fateful hour-long ride?

Where traditional assessment has gone wrong is in failing to recognize that it was hugely difficult to separate Henry and Anne. The king, in spite

of the inducements of the Seymours and their allies, had openly committed himself to Anne during the Easter celebrations, and he was unlikely
to reverse this within days, merely because Cromwell added his voice to
the chorus against the queen. Only one way offered any hope: the technique which the minister had used so brilliantly in 1532. Bounce the king
into decision! Henry must be tipped by a crisis into rejecting Anne. Yet
what crisis was on offer? By the end of the month, all that Chapuys' usual
'good authorities' could come up with was annulling the Boleyn marriage
on the grounds that the queen had married the earl of Northumberland
'nine years before' – whatever that meant – and had consummated the
match.[10] That was hardly a spectre to frighten Henry into the arms of Jane
Seymour. He knew all about the 1532 investigation and it is hard to have
much faith in the witnesses which Chapuys said had now become available.
Given such vague notions among his new conservative allies, Cromwell
was certainly in difficulties. Indeed, it is tempting to see that as explaining
Chapuys' report (in a private letter of Saturday, 29 April) that Cromwell
had just spent four days closeted with Richard Sampson, the dean of the
chapel, the royal adviser on canon law who would represent Henry when
he came to divorce Anne.

   Chapuys, however, did not connect those discussions with Anne – the
rumour was that Sampson was to go on an embassy – and the ambassador
commented that he had nothing of importance to report. Certainly, too,
he exaggerated whatever time the minister spent with the lawyer.[11] The
dominant issue of that last week in April was deciding between an imperial
and a French alliance, and despite his council, Henry continued to insist
on vindicating the Boleyn marriage. This was made crystal clear, on
Tuesday, 25 April, in a letter to Richard Pate, the ambassador at Rome.
The king rehearsed very fairly the altercation with the imperial envoy, and
instructed Pate to press the line of policy taken on that occasion when he
came to negotiate with the emperor (then in Italy). His letter also referred
to 'the likelihood and appearance that God will send us heirs male', and
described Anne as 'our most dear and most entirely beloved wife, the
queen'. Parallel instructions were sent the same day to Gardiner and
Wallop in Paris.[12] As well as the wording of these letters, the fact that
they were sent once again says that Henry had no intention of rejecting
Anne. If tradition were correct and he had already begun to move against
his wife, why did he instruct Pate to implement a course of action predi-
cated on the continuance of the Boleyn marriage? Similarly, if he was not
still committed to Anne, why, on Sunday the 30th, the day before the first
arrests, did he sign with his own hand conditions for an Anglo-French

alliance which required Francis I to end his alliance with the pope unless the Curia annulled all actions against England?[13] Anne's death would void all existing positions. Henry VIII was capable of considerable self-deception, but self-deception which issued instructions he knew were out of date before they were sent seems decidedly improbable.[14]

What then of the patent of oyer and terminer of 24 April? Had the king forgotten his signature of the day before? Not at all, because despite what is universally assumed, he had signed nothing; such commissions appear to have been authenticated by the chancellor and issued of course.[15] On the other hand, the 24 April commission to investigate and try treason was highly unusual in one key respect – timing. During Henry's reign there were seventeen politically sensitive treason trials where the crown's procedural material was deposited in the *Baga de Secretis*, the Tudor equivalent of the top-secret file. In fifteen of these, formal legal moves were begun against the accused only *after* arrest and interrogation.[16] The two exceptions are the trials of Anne and her 'lovers', where the commission was issued six days *before* the first arrest.

How then to explain this aberration? At first sight it might appear to support the story given to de Carles that investigation of Anne's conduct took some time, during which Henry 'treated her as if he had no cause for displeasures and showed her in every way that she was more than ever dear to him', and even when he was convinced 'he gave no indication of this [and] enjoyed all pleasures together with her.'[17] However, that conjecture collapses because, as the seventeen examples in the *Baga* establish, a commission of oyer and terminer had nothing at all to do with *investigation*.[18] It set up a special court to *try* the accused. The king needed no commission in advance to authorize enquiries or arrests, or to empower him should he want to play a suspect like a fish. Thomas More was interrogated for eight weeks before the oyer was issued against him on Saturday 26 June. He was tried the following Thursday – six days from start to finish. At the end of the reign the earl of Surrey (a commoner) was held for four weeks, then indicted on 7 January, an oyer was issued on the 10th and he was tried on the 11th. If the accused was a peer, a commission appointing a high steward took the place of the oyer and terminer, but the result was the same. In 1521, the duke of Buckingham was held for two weeks before a steward was appointed and tried and condemned eleven days later.[19]

As Henry would subsequently make clear to Cranmer, once a suspect was in custody, machinery took over – hence the chancellor's power to issue trial commissions ex officio.[20] Thus, even if by 24 April the king was intent on disposing of Anne, he could have relied on the appropriate commission appearing in due course.[21] Issuing an oyer and terminer in advance served no purpose. It was not the habit of the Tudor state to hang about once it had decided to dispose of a victim judicially.

If Henry is absolved from responsibility for the patent, the only other suspect is Thomas Cromwell. He was well placed to secure a secret commission – Lord Chancellor Audley was a close ally – and the twenty peers, judges and officials to whom it was addressed (any four of whom could act) would not know they had been nominated until called upon to begin work. But was a commission even needed for an attack on Anne? As peers of the realm, the queen and her brother would have to be tried before the high steward (as was Buckingham), not before commissioners of oyer and terminer. A possible reason for deciding to act by commission was that it could receive indictments and forward them to the high steward. However, that seems not to have been necessary in the duke's case. A more sinister motivation could be that an oyer commission would be required if commoners were to be dealt with as well as the queen. Does that imply that Cromwell already had Norris in his sights? And there is still the problem of dates. Why did Cromwell need an oyer and terminer on 24 April before there was anyone to try? The likeliest explanation is speed. Delay between issuing an oyer and the consequent trial averaged eleven days, but if the king had to be bounced into action, delay spelled danger, particularly in respect of someone so essential to Henry's personal comfort as Henry Norris. The plan, therefore, seems to have been to go from arrest directly to prosecution. With a commission to hand process could start at once, allowing no possibility of second thoughts while examinations were conducted. Condemnation could be achieved in as little as four days. Hence too, there was no serious interrogation of either Anne or Rochford.[22] In the event, of course, it would be eleven days from arrest to the first trial, but that is readily explained by Anne's psychological collapse. After her first night in the Tower, Cromwell knew that the queen had fatally incriminated herself – and others.[23]

One matter in the week which must have required Henry's sanction was the summoning of parliament, and it may be that we should see this as the earliest identifiable move against Anne. On the other hand, for that to be the case, something must have happened to cause the king to act on Thursday, the 27th, against his 'entirely beloved wife' of Tuesday, the 25th. Indeed, since discussions must have preceded the order to start work on the parliamentary writs, we could even have Henry making contradictory decisions within twenty-four hours. Equally difficult is explaining what was gained by calling parliament in advance of Anne's arrest, if repudiating her was the only issue. When parliament did meet it had to wait three weeks for the relevant bill to be ready.

An alternative is that Cromwell explained the need for a parliament on grounds which Henry and his advisers could accept, keeping to himself the possibility of using it against the queen. If that were so, the legislation which was so imperative must have been 'the act extinguishing the authority of the bishop of Rome', a measure usually assumed to be a tidying-up operation, but which reached the statute book only after some difficulty.[24] It closed a loophole in earlier statutes which had omitted to criminalize defending papal authority. Thereafter any murmur of even respect for the traditional head of the Western Church was a *praemunire* offence. Henry might well have agreed on the necessity for such a bill, assailed as he was at home by the conservatives and abroad by the efforts of Charles V to persuade him to put the royal supremacy on the negotiating table in an effort to reach a settlement with the pope. A law to strike at the 'imps of the said bishop of Rome and his see, and in heart members of his pretended monarchy', which also imposed an oath on everyone who mattered and which it was treason to refuse (no second Sir Thomas More), went a long way towards satisfying the king's obsession about the inward thoughts of his people. Even more necessary would such an Act seem to Cromwell, now faced with the need to disavow in due course the supporters of Mary, who clearly fell into the impish category. One may note that in mid-June, even as the bill was being readied for the Commons, Mary was forced 'for the perfect declaration of the bottom of her heart and stomach' to repudiate 'the bishop of Rome's pretended authority'.[25] The issue of parliamentary writs on 27 April could mark the king's first move against his wife, but that seems decidedly improbable.

So as the end of April 1536 approached, Cromwell had not yet found his crisis. He had the oyer and terminer ready and a parliament summoned, but no occasion to use them. And then, suddenly, the opportunity presented itself. Henry had planned to go with the queen and the court to Calais that spring, and preparations had been in hand for some time.[26] May Day was to be celebrated at Greenwich, and then the journey would begin, with the first night, Tuesday, 2 May, being spent at Rochester. At eleven o'clock on the Sunday night, 30 April, without warning, these arrangements were cancelled and instructions given that the king would be travelling a week later.[27] It is rare in Tudor history to be able to date an episode so exactly, but evidently something had happened that was serious enough to cause the king to change his plans at the last minute and remain in England to sort matters out.[28]

What had happened was a major dispute between the queen and Henry Norris, either on Saturday, 29 April, or early the following day. In a furious altercation, Anne had made personal accusations about Norris's feelings for her and had been too angry to notice an audience.[29] Soon the story was all over the court.[30] When sanity returned the queen tried to forestall gossip by instructing Henry Norris to go to her almoner on the Sunday morning and volunteer to take his oath that the queen 'was a good woman'. This incredible step – and we have Anne's word for it – almost certainly explains a second confrontation, nearly as public, but this time between Anne and Henry. The Scottish Lutheran divine, Alexander Ales, sent an account of this to Anne's daughter in September 1559.[31] He had, he said, been at court that Sunday, seeking from Cromwell the payment of a gift Henry had promised him:

> Never shall I forget the sorrow which I felt when I saw the most serene queen, your most religious mother, carrying you, still a little baby, in her arms and entreating the most serene king your father, in Greenwich Palace, from the open window of which he was looking into the courtyard, when she brought you to him. I did not perfectly understand what had been going on, but the faces and gestures of the speakers plainly showed that the king was angry, although he could conceal his anger wonderfully well. Yet from the protracted conference of the council (for whom the crowd was waiting until it was quite dark, expecting that they would return to London), it was most obvious to everyone that some deep and difficult question was being discussed.

Although the dispute between Anne and Norris will explain Sunday, 30 April – the involvement of Anne's almoner, Henry's anger and Anne's desperate defence even to the point of appealing to him through Elizabeth – it was clearly insufficient to provide the jolt Cromwell was looking for. Somehow the two must have quieted the king's mind, for Sir Henry remained in attendance and the May Day celebrations went ahead as planned.[32] But sufficient tension remained for the king to postpone the move to Rochester, and if anything more emerged, the attempts of Anne and Norris to pacify the king would then seem like a conspiracy to deceive. That fatal catalyst would be Mark Smeton.[33]

Smeton is variously described as a musician, a player of the virginals or the spinet, or an organist; he was possibly not much over 20 years old. According to Cavendish, he was the son of a carpenter, but perhaps better evidence suggests that he was a Fleming, as others of the king's leading musicians were. Initially on Wolsey's staff, he had been recruited by the king and nurtured alongside Francis Weston.[34] But unlike Weston, he was not a gentleman. His court upbringing thus made him *déclassé*, and he belonged nowhere. Highly vulnerable, Smeton had, on the crucial Saturday, made a moody exhibition of himself in Anne's apartments. The story reached Cromwell, who had him taken the next day to his house at Stepney and interrogated. The young man seems to have held out for nearly twenty-four hours, but in the end he confessed to adultery with the queen and was committed to the Tower, arriving about six o'clock on the Monday afternoon.[35] As soon as he had the confession, Cromwell must have informed Henry, who thereupon left Greenwich and, with his previous day's suspicions of Anne and Norris seemingly confirmed, proceeded to challenge his groom of the stool. There is, in fact, a hint that the initial accusation was of concealing Smeton's offence, and that only when Norris denied that he knew anything of the musician's adultery was the conclusion drawn that the groom of the stool must have been involved as well.[36] Smeton's confession turned the denials of Anne, Norris, and later Rochford into evidence of guilt. Sir Edward Baynton wrote on the Wednesday or Thursday morning to William Fitzwilliam, one of those who had interviewed Anne on the Tuesday:

> here is much communication that no man will confess anything against her, but all-only Mark of any actual thing. Where of (in my foolish conceit) it should much touch the king's honour if it should no farther appear. And I cannot believe but that the other two [Norris and Rochford] be as fully culpable as ever was he. And I think assuredly the one keepeth the other's counsel . . . I hear farther that the queen standeth stiffly in her opinion . . . which I think is in the trust that she [hath of the] other two.[37]

How Smeton's confession was obtained is not known. George Constantine, one of Norris's servants, reported some years later that 'the saying was that he was first grievously racked, which I never could know of a truth.'[38] His caution is in contrast to the *Cronica del Rey Enrico*, which tells a story of Cromwell enticing Smeton to his house, where he was seized by six men while the secretary forced him to confess by tightening a knotted rope around his head.[39] Such a course would have been illegal, and in any case is at variance with the racking in the Tower which Constantine suspected. By the time Smeton had arrived there, the king had already received the information which drove him from Greenwich.[40] What undoubtedly was used against the musician was psychological pressure. Possibly Smeton, like Norris, was promised pardon if he confessed, although he may only have been promised royal favour, which might mean life or, failing that, at least a quick and decent death – not the agony of being dragged through the streets on a hurdle, half-strangled, castrated and then disembowelled while still conscious. Cromwell kept up the pressure too by holding the musician in irons (the only one of those arrested so treated), an earnest of what worse might befall if he changed his story.[41]

Read in this way, the coup against Anne Boleyn was a piece of inspired improvisation. But there was more to it than grabbing a chance to remove the queen at the cost of a few unfortunates who had given grounds which might be represented as suspicious. Cromwell may well have rationalized his actions as duty in the face of what he had learned, yet the fact that Norris had become vulnerable meant that the most influential man in the Boleyn faction could be neutralized at the same time as the queen. As we have seen, this would mean that Cromwell could henceforth expect to exercise greater control over the privy chamber, but it is doubtful whether that was yet his prime concern.[42] The immediate gain was that the minister had by a single pre-emptive strike taken out both the queen and the groom of the stool. It remained to be seen whether the Boleyn faction possessed a second-strike capacity.

Cromwell, therefore, could not relax. He left Henry to Carewe, the Seymours, and the seductive promise of Jane, and to the king's own capacity for self-pity. A maudlin readiness to feel sorry for himself was one of the least endearing features of Henry VIII's unappealing personality and he now indulged it to the full.[43] He claimed that Anne had had more than a hundred lovers and, if Chapuys had the story right, he even poured his sense of ill-usage into a tragedy which he carried in his pocket and tried to get people to read. On the very night of Anne's arrest, when the duke of Richmond had come to say goodnight to his father, Henry had begun 'to weep and say that he and his sister [Mary] owed God a great debt for having escaped the hands of that cursed and poisoning whore who had planned to poison them.' This exchange with Richmond also allows us to see how quickly the Seymour alliance had got to work. The story that Anne intended to poison Mary and actually had poisoned Katherine had been a fixation with them for months. As for Jane, she was removed to Sir Nicholas Carewe's house at Beddington, near Croydon, ostensibly for propriety but actually to inflame royal ardour. The result was a series of romantic night-time assignations and river trips which actually began to win popular sympathy for Anne. No man, Chapuys reported, ever paraded with such regularity the fact that his wife had cuckolded him, and with so little sign that he minded![44]

Cromwell, meanwhile, had more serious things to attend to. The Boleyn faction must not to allowed to recover its balance. That alone necessitated the arrest of Rochford, and it may be that George did attempt to intervene. He was detained at Whitehall on Tuesday and transferred to the Tower at two o'clock. Since he could perfectly well have been held and interrogated at Greenwich, as Anne was, it is reasonable to suspect that George had gone to London with the intention of reaching Henry.[45] That he failed was probably due to Cromwell's block on access to the king. Boleyn supporters were simply unable to get through; Henry remained incommunicado, venturing out only 'in the garden and in his boat at night, at which times it may become no man to prevent him'.[46]

Obstruction certainly killed Cranmer's attempt to speak up for Anne. As soon as she was in the Tower, he was summoned to return to Lambeth but instructed not to attempt to see the king. This left the archbishop having to write the most difficult letter of his life, pleading for Anne without impugning either the king's actions or motives, while at the same time (since he did not know the strength of the evidence) trying to distance Anne from the reformed cause she had favoured.[47] That some writers have stigmatized his efforts as sycophantic or cowardly is a measure of their failure to appreciate Cranmer's dilemma. He was then called across the river to the Star Chamber, where the council presented the accusations against Anne as fact. This produced a postscript to his letter, expressing one final vibration of doubt before the inevitable loyal coda: 'I am exceedingly sorry that such faults can be proved by the queen, as I heard of their relation. But I am, and ever shall be, your faithful subject.'

Francis Bryan was similarly treated. He was away from court but was 'sent for in all haste on his allegiance', and only admitted to the king's presence after an interview with Cromwell.[48] A man with either a greater loyalty or perhaps a less well-developed sense of self-preservation was Sir Richard Page. He, like Bryan, was away from court at the time and, no doubt, called back by another 'marvellous peremptory commandment', but on Monday, 8 May, he was in the Tower.[49] Sir Thomas Wyatt was another taken there earlier that day, though we have no details.[50] It would be all of a piece with his character for Wyatt to have shown open contempt for the servile rush to vilify Anne and the other unfortunates; even the Tower would only keep him quiet briefly. Other Boleyn men seemed lucky to have escaped. Harry Webbe, sewer of the chamber, was suspected by some; George Taylor, Anne's receiver-general, was reported to be showing visible signs of relief after the executions were over.[51]

The arrest of Rochford and the others and the blocking of access to the king drew the teeth of the remaining Boleyn supporters. The earl of Wiltshire bought safety by a willingness to condemn his daughter's alleged lovers, while others, like Bryan, began to think more about adapting to the new situation and coming away with a share of the inevitable spoils. Yet, as Edward Baynton stressed on 3 May, Cromwell still had to demonstrate that 'such faults can be proved'. What sources, then, were available to the secretary as he built the case against the queen and the five men?

Rumour there was in plenty. Alexander Ales would have it that Anne had persuaded Henry to ally with the German Protestants, and that to frustrate this, Stephen Gardiner, that *bête noire* of the reformers, sent reports from France, where he was ambassador, to the effect that stories were circulating at the court there (based on certain letters) that Anne was guilty of adultery. This was disclosed to Henry by Cromwell and his allies. He told them to investigate, and spying, bribery and invention did the rest.[52]

An anonymous French poem told of a plot by Rochford, Anne Boleyn and their supporters to poison the king, who intended to abandon Anne and return to Katherine (*sic*), a plan that is overtaken by two counsellors who strike at Anne by accusing her of adultery with Brereton, Weston, Smeton, Norris and Rochford himself.[53] The Spanish *Cronica del Rey Enrico* has Anne fall for Smeton and use an elderly female attendant named Margaret to hide the boy naked in the sweetmeat closet in the anteroom to the queen's bedchamber, and produce him when she calls for marmalade. The queen has also to sleep with her former lovers to assuage their jealousy, and the dénouement comes via a Thomas Percy, who envies the material prosperity that has followed Mark's nightly services and informs Cromwell of the musician's activities.[54] Margaret is then racked, confesses all and is burned by night in the Tower.

These and later stories, such as Sander's tale of Henry being finally convinced of the queen's guilt when she threw one of her lovers a handkerchief to mop his face after the exertions of the May Day tilt, have enlivened many accounts of Anne Boleyn's fall, but they preserve what was essentially popular gossip.[55] In stark contrast to their speculations is the note made by John Spelman, a judge who took part in Anne's trial:

> Note that this matter was disclosed by a woman called the Lady Wingfield who was a servant of the said queen and shared the same tendencies. And suddenly the said Wingfield became ill and a little time before her death she showed the matter to one of her etc.[56]

Despite what has sometimes been assumed, the final 'etc.' is not a sign that something is missing, but a lawyer's abbreviation for self-evident matter, in this case, 'who reported the story'. Bridget, Lady Wingfield, was the daughter of Sir John Wiltshire, of Stone Castle in Kent. She had married Richard, one of the twelve Wingfield brothers and a knight of the Garter prominent in diplomatic circles until his death in 1525. Her second husband was Sir Nicholas Harvey, an ambassador to Charles V and a strong supporter of Anne Boleyn. He died in 1532 and Bridget then married another courtier, Robert Tyrwhitt.[57]

Chapuys reported Lady Wingfield's arrival at court in 1530, no doubt interested in the wife of the ambassador to his own home government, but she was in no way a newcomer. She was in Katherine's retinue as far back as the Field of Cloth of Gold.[58] That she was subsequently close to Anne is clear from a tantalizing letter which Anne wrote to her between 1529 and her elevation as marquis of Pembroke:

> I pray you as you love me, to give credence to my servant this bearer, touching your removing and any thing else that he shall tell you on my behalf; for I will desire you to do nothing but that shall be for your wealth. And, madam, though at all time I have not showed the love that I bear you as much as it was in deed, yet now I trust that you shall well prove that I loved you a great deal more than I fair for. And assuredly, next mine own mother I know no woman alive that I love better, and at length, with God's grace, you shall prove that it is unfeigned. And I trust you do know me for such a one that I will write nothing to comfort you in your trouble but I will abide by it as long as I live. And therefore I pray you leave your indiscreet trouble, both for displeasing of God and also for displeasing of me, that doth love you so entirely. And trusting in God that you will thus do, I make an end. With the ill hand of
>
> Your own assured friend during my life,
> Anne Rochford[59]

The most plausible explanation of this letter is to presume that when Chapuys first noticed Lady Wingfield, she was responding to Anne's invitation and returning to court after an interval.[60] If so, the letter suggests that initially she had been reluctant, for two reasons: first, her sense that Anne, in her new-found prosperity, had been neglecting an old friend (something that Anne freely admits and promises to correct), and second, an 'indiscreet trouble'. Alternatively, since 'indiscreet' and 'displeasing to God' imply that it is Lady Wingfield's reaction to her trouble that is being questioned as excessive, an obvious though unlikely occasion would be Harvey's death in August 1532.[61]

These are by no means the only possible constructions – there may be far more in Lady Wingfield's grievance than they allow for – but what is more important is that the letter establishes her as a bona fide source for Anne's behaviour. Thus her deathbed revelations, if genuine, could have been very relevant. Nevertheless, their opportune appearance invites suspicion. To start with, how did whatever she said reach Cromwell? There are two possible routes, neither of them neutral. One is through the family of her third husband, the Tyrwhitts of Kettleby in Lincolnshire. The behaviour of her erstwhile father-in-law, Sir Robert, during the Lincolnshire Rising, plus his links with Lord Hussey and with Sir Robert Constable, a leader of the Pilgrimage of Grace in Yorkshire, suggest that Tyrwhitt might willingly have supplied evidence against Anne.[62] The other possible vector is the duke of Suffolk whom, as we have seen, Wyatt blamed for his arrest.[63] The duke's lack of sympathy with Anne is not in doubt and the Wingfields were his clients. They could readily have passed on reminiscences – say, of Anne's early passages with the poet. Any such stories would have been ten years old, in which case 'the deathbed' was embroidery to disguise the time lag. In Tudor society, safety lay in revealing dangerous knowledge as soon as possible.[64] Moreover, when did Lady Wingfield die? Her last certain mention is in January 1534.[65] Given the perennial watch kept by the queen's enemies for material to use against her, it is hard to believe that anything of substance would have been left to gather dust until Cromwell started to ask questions.

We know nothing of any response which Anne or George made to stories from Lady Wingfield's deathbed, but George did respond to the evidence of another court lady, his own wife Jane. It was she who had told the Crown of Anne's remarks about Henry's sexual capacities, and according to de Carles, Rochford said to his judges, 'On the evidence of only one woman you are willing to believe this great evil of me, and on the basis of her allegations you are deciding my judgement.'[66] A foreign visitor to London in May 1536 wrote of 'that person who more out of envy and jealousy than out of love towards the king did betray this accursed secret and together with it the names of those who had joined in the evil doings of the unchaste queen'.[67] The lost journal of Antony Antony also referred to the role of Lady Rochford, and probably included words to the effect that 'the wife of Lord Rochford was a particular instrument in the death of Queen Anne.'[68] Bishop Burnet was no contemporary, but access to sources no longer extant could explain his assertion that Jane Rochford 'carried many stories to the king or some about him', and in particular, damaging evidence, 'that there was a familiarity between the queen and her brother beyond what so near a relationship could justify.'[69]

Why Jane Boleyn provided information is another question. We can dismiss out of hand the nonsense that she felt insulted because George was a homosexual, a fiction for which there is not a scintilla of evidence, indeed, quite the reverse.[70] Burnet's suggestion that Jane was motivated by jealousy of Anne's closeness to her brother could be correct. Alternatively, she could have been influenced by her own family's long association with the Princess Mary.[71] Jane did, it is true, send to ask after her husband in the Tower and promised to intercede with the king, apparently to get him a hearing before the council. However we may, if we choose, smell malice, for the message was brought with Henry's express permission and by Carewe and Bryan in his newly turned coat.[72] It is also the case that Lady Rochford's interests as a widow were carefully looked after by Cromwell.[73]

Three other court ladies – Anne Cobham, 'my Lady Worcester' and 'one maid more' – were also believed to be sources of information against Anne. John Hussey listed them in a letter to his employer, Lord Lisle.[74] The significance of what Mrs Cobham said we do not know, but the anonymous lady was almost certainly Margery Horsman, who was well known and useful to Hussey, and whose identity he therefore had reason to keep close.[75] Edward Baynton, Anne's vice-chamberlain of the household, had already pointed to her in his letter of 3 May about the need to find more evidence: 'I have mused much at [the behaviour] of Mistress Margery which hath used her [self most] strangely toward me of late, being her friend as I have been. But no doubt it cannot be but that she must be of council therewith; there hath been great friendship between the queen and her of late.'[76] Margery Horsman's involvement may explain the 'Marguerite' or 'Marguerita' of the European accounts, but these clearly magnify and blacken her role out of all reason. Despite what Baynton says as to her obstinate support of her mistress, on Anne's death Margery Horsman passed smoothly into the service of her successor.[77]

What, then of Elizabeth, the countess of Worcester? She was the sister of Sir Anthony Browne of the privy chamber, a staunch supporter of Mary, and step-sister of Sir William Fitzwilliam, treasurer of the household and a person heavily involved in the Boleyn enquiries.[78] Elizabeth was certainly close to Anne, close enough, indeed, for the queen to lend her £100 secretly.[79] She had been married to Henry, earl of Worcester, for nine years, and the earl's sister was married to William Brereton. In the spring of 1536 Elizabeth was expecting a baby, and the queen was very concerned at the difficulties which the countess was experiencing. Even in the Tower,

Anne 'much lamented my lady of Worcester for because her child did not stir in her body, and [Lady Kingston] said, "What should be the cause?" She said, "For sorrow she took for me." '[80] What Anne meant is not altogether clear. She apparently made the remark on the day of her arrest, so she cannot have been referring to Lady Worcester's reaction to the shock of immediate events. Presumably the queen had in mind some earlier failure of the baby to quicken, so that 'sorrow she took for me' must refer to Anne's own miscarriage or to her recent struggle to preserve her marriage, or both. Certainly the remark indicated that Lady Worcester was a Boleyn supporter worth cross-examining.

Cromwell, indeed, constructed the official version of events round the countess, choosing to present her evidence rather than the events of 29 April as the first warning of Anne's offences. She is never directly named and Cromwell's own summary, which he sent to the English ambassadors in France (and later refused to elaborate), simply stated that the ladies of the privy chamber told certain counsellors about Anne's behaviour and an interrogation of some of the privy chamber and a number of the queen's staff followed.[81] However, the fuller version of the story supplied to the French ambassador in London and put into verse by his assistant, Lancelot de Carles, specifies a single woman as the source of the story, and describes her as the sister of one of the most strait-laced of the king's counsellors.[82] That we should identify the two as Antony Browne and Lady Worcester seems highly plausible, particularly because the name 'Antoine Brun' survives in an otherwise garbled French prose account of the crisis dating from Elizabeth's reign and now among the Lansdowne Manuscripts in the British Library.[83]

What is noticeable about these accounts is their distance from the actual events of that single violent weekend. Cromwell indicates a measured investigation and de Carles concurs, describing an enquiry over several days.[84] Smeton meanwhile is under investigation in prison, and his eventual confession satisfies Henry, only for the king to continue to conceal his suspicions until after the May Day tilt. The reality of the actual forty-eight-hour crisis sits ill with all this; de Carles even puts Rochford and Norris in the frame from the start. The lords who go to break the news to the king say that:

when at night you retire, she has her toy boys [*mignons*] already lined up. Her brother is by no means last in the queue. Norris and Mark would not deny that they have spent many nights with her without having to persuade her, for she herself urged them on and invited them with presents and caresses.[85]

This is moonshine, of a piece with the spin which would appear in the indictments.

Cromwell tried to cover up the inadequacy of the Crown's case by telling Gardiner that the story was 'so abominable' that a good part had not even been given in evidence at the trial.[86] One may doubt, indeed, that whatever Lady Worcester said gave him a great deal; Justice Spelman, who heard all the evidence presented at the trial, makes no mention of her. De Carles, however, does provide ground for a reasonable guess. He says that the countess was taken to task by her brother for loose behaviour, and hit back by saying that the queen was worse and had offended with both Mark Smeton and her own brother.[87] This sounds very much like exaggeration of an altercation in which Antony Browne criticized his sister's involvement in the lively society of the queen's chamber and she hit back that she was no more, or even less, of a flirt than the queen. That would certainly have fallen into Spelman's category that 'all the evidence was of bawdry and lechery.'

Of itself, knowledge of an altercation between Browne and his sister would have done little more than direct attention to the possibility of making something incriminating out of behaviour in the queen's household, but it was then that Thomas Cromwell found an unwitting ally in Anne herself.[88] She managed with dignity the ignominious daylight journey from Greenwich – not yet three years since her coronation triumph along the same stretch of river – with a hostile escort of men like Cromwell whom she had trusted, in through the Tower gates as far as the inner ward; and when the counsellors made to leave her at the Court Gate she was able to go on her knees to declare her innocence and ask them to intercede for her with the king. When, however, she realized that Kingston, the constable of the Tower, was taking her to the royal apartments, relief broke her. He reported to Cromwell what happened:

'Master Kingston, shall I go in to a dungeon?'
'No, Madam you shall go into your lodging that you lay in at your coronation'.
'It is too good for me. Jesu, have mercy on me!'
And she kneeled down weeping a great pace, and in the same sorrow fell into a great laughing, and she hath done so many times since.[89]

Put with four unsympathetic attendants, she began to babble incriminating material, and Kingston, whose instructions had been to discourage conversation with the queen, seized the chance to inform Cromwell of this flood of talk.[90] Unfortunately, his letters were damaged by fire in 1731, but a good deal can be reconstructed from the work of John Strype, who had used them earlier.[91] The first thing to come out from Anne's temporary nervous collapse was the full story of the quarrel with Norris. It had begun by Anne asking Norris, till then a close ally, why he was postponing his proposed marriage to her cousin, Margaret Shelton, the king's old flame. She obviously suspected that Norris was reluctant to complete the match in view of the current pressure on the Boleyns, so the noncommittal reply he made provoked Anne into a shocking imprudence. Flinging away the safety of courtly convention, she said, 'You look for dead men's shoes; for if ought came to the king but good you would look to have me.' Norris's horrified response to this totally unfair and improper shift in the basis of their relationship was to stammer that if he had any such thought, 'he would his head were off,' but the queen would not let him escape. She could, she said, undo him if she wanted to. A right royal quarrel about their relationship had then ensued.

Of itself, the pretence that Norris loved his sovereign's wife was the common currency of courtly dalliance. What made the Norris episode so dangerous was the current tension at court and the fact that the queen was the aggressor. The rules said that the courtier should proposition the great lady, but Anne had reversed the roles. At once that put Norris's reply on a different level. Anne was attempting to force a commitment far beyond convention. Even worse, 'if ought came to the king but good you would look to have me' could be interpreted as Anne having a personal interest in Norris, hence the oath offered to her almoner.

If admitting this encounter was not dangerous enough, Anne had also told her attendants that she was more afraid of what Francis Weston would say. More than a year before, she had taken him to task for neglecting his own wife and flirting with Madge Shelton, instead of leaving the field clear for Norris. He had replied that Norris came to the queen's chamber more for Anne than for his intended bride, and had capped that by saying that he himself loved someone in her household better than either his wife or Madge. Anne had, she said, asked, 'Who is that?' and when Weston replied, 'It is yourself,' she had 'defied him' – slapped him down. All this was evidently part of a cheeky game, but the revelation led to Weston's immediate arrest – a valuable bonus for the secretary, since Francis's affinities were with those hostile to Anne. She had clearly thought of the danger if he deposed that Norris had had a personal interest in her for more than a year. Cromwell, however, realized that Weston was more use as a victim; his arrest disproved the allegation that the whole affair was a sordid factional putsch.[92] That, however, is what it was, and about the same time as Weston, yet another of the Boleyn faction was taken to the Tower: William Brereton, groom of the privy chamber.[93]

The next Kingston letter furnished the secretary with further details about Mark Smeton's behaviour.[94] The scene was Anne's presence chamber at Greenwich on Saturday, 29 April. Smeton was standing in a window embrasure, and noticing that the young man appeared downcast, Anne had asked why. Smeton replied that it did not matter, at which the queen said, 'You may not look to have me speak to you as I should do to a noble man, because you be an inferior person.' 'No, no, Madam,' he answered. 'A look sufficed me, and thus fare you well.'

This interchange is revealing. It shows Anne not acting in the 'unfeminine' way she had to Norris (which commentator after commentator has censured as evidence of either guilt or immodesty), but exercising authority in a way which was kind and considerate. The exchange also suggests that, though he was a skilled and valued professional, Smeton resented being excluded as an 'inferior person' from the game of courtly love around the queen and her ladies. At the subsequent trials, a separate count in the indictment alleged friction and competition between Anne's alleged 'lovers', and most of the comments on the affair imply that Smeton was trying to compete above his station. The poem attributed to Wyatt clearly portrays him as an outsider:

> A time thou haddest above thy poor degree,
> The fall where of thy friends may well bemoan:
> A rotten twig upon so high a tree
> Hath slipped thy hold, and thou art dead and gone.[95]

Alternatively, Smeton may have genuinely failed to distinguish between being a servant in the menial sense, which he was, and being a servant in the chivalric sense, which he was not.[96] Most poignant of all is the possibility that the young man had failed to realize that courtly love and true love were different coin.

Kingston's original instructions to discourage conversation with Anne show that Cromwell had not expected to get anything incriminating out of the queen after her arrest. All we know of her initial questioning at Greenwich is that she was, so she said, 'cruelly handled', apparently by having accusations of misconduct with three (possibly unnamed) men hurled at her by Crown lawyers, unchecked by a bemused handful of counsellors.[97] Anne described how her uncle, the duke of Norfolk, 'said,

"Tut, tut, tut" ... shaking his head three or four times, and as for Master Treasurer [Fitzwilliam], he was in the Forest of Windsor [dreaming]', although she did allow 'Master Controller [William Paulet] to be a very gentleman'.[98] Rochford asked to appear before the council but apparently never did, and there is no evidence that he was ever formally interrogated.[99] Is it too cynical to suspect that Cromwell did not dare to give sister and brother a chance to answer until in the disadvantage of the court room? But, armed with Kingston's letters, Cromwell now had material to work on to whip into shape a case against Anne. How substantial he could make it was another question, and one which first would have to be decided by two grand juries and then by two trial juries, one for the four commoners and the other for the trials of Anne and her brother, comprised of peers and presided over by the lord steward of England. When the queen had been taken into custody by Sir William Kingston she had asked, 'Master Kingston, shall I die without justice?' and he had replied, 'The poorest subject the king hath, had justice,' whereupon she laughed.[100] It remained to be seen whether her laughter was justified.

JUDGEMENT

AFTER a week Cromwell had enough for his purpose. The judicial machine was then put to work with a despatch eloquent of the need to end matters speedily.[1] On Tuesday, 9 May, the sheriffs of London were ordered to assemble the next day a grand jury of 'discreet and sufficient persons' to decide prima facie on the offences alleged at Whitehall and Hampton Court. Despite the short notice the sheriffs produced a list of forty-eight men, three-quarters of whom, as instructed, turned up at Westminster before John Baldwin, chief justice of the common pleas, and six of his judicial colleagues.

Why Baldwin was there is a minor puzzle. John Fitzjames, chief justice of the king's bench, was the obvious choice, and Baldwin was Norris's brother-in-law. Whether he was selected to forestall later obstruction, or because Fitzjames had been less than decisive in the prosecution of Thomas More, it is impossible to say.[2] Practically speaking, the jury's only option was to send such serious allegations for trial, but to make doubly sure the foreman was none other than More's son-in-law, Giles Heron, while another grand juryman was a senior officer of the royal household. The next day, Thursday, Baldwin and three colleagues went to Deptford, where a Kent grand jury gave a positive verdict on the offences alleged at Greenwich. Meanwhile, in London there was frantic activity. As soon as the Middlesex return was in – or very possibly in anticipation – the constable of the Tower was ordered to have Weston, Norris, Brereton and Smeton at Westminster Hall the next Friday, 12 May. At the same time individual summonses must have gone to the trial jury; the orders from the sheriffs only went out on the actual day, by which time thirty-six knights and esquires were already on the way to do their duty.

Westminster Hall that day was a grim contrast to the scene three years before. The prisoners found themselves only feet away from where Queen

Anne had sat, but instead of the blue carpet, the golden tapestries and the laden tables, there were the timber scaffoldings of the law courts. Where the king's musicians had filled the air, there was the silence of his guard and the brooding presence of the great axe, the edge for the present turned away from the prisoners, but ready to swing towards them if judgement was given against them.[3] As the jurymen were called into the court, Norris and the others knew their fate was sealed. Cromwell had pre-selected as hostile a panel as could be imagined. The foreman was Edward Willoughby, who owed Brereton money. Next came William Askew, a welcome guest in Mary's household; then Walter Hungerford, a scape-grace dependant of Cromwell's and a homosexual; Giles Alington was married to More's stepdaughter; Sir John Hampden's daughter was sister-in-law to William Paulet, controller of the royal household; William Musgrave, the government witness who had failed to make treason charges stick against Lord Dacre, was desperate to cling to Cromwell's favour; Thomas Palmer was one of Henry's gambling cronies and a client of William Fitzwilliam. Robert Dormer was a known opponent of the breach with Rome; Richard Tempest was related to and an ally of another conser-vative, Lord Darcy (and also on good terms with Cromwell); William Drury was an esquire of the body and an associate of John Russell; Thomas Wharton was a leech clinging to the earl of Northumberland, who was desperately afraid that his earlier courtship of Anne would drag him down too.

Whether the defendants challenged any of the jury is not clear. Under normal rules the four could have refused twenty (or possibly thirty-five) each, so preventing the trial that day and for several days to come. But there was doubt whether such challenges applied in treason trials, and nobody before had tried the tactic. Possibly Norris or one of the others did refuse both the ex-lord mayor, John Champnes, who was probably going blind, and Antony Hungerford, who was related to Jane Seymour, but instead they only got William Sidney, an old colleague of Lord Darcy and close to the duke of Suffolk as well. And behind Sidney were many more of that same ilk.[4] In any case there was, to such lifelong courtiers, only one hope – that the king would relent. It was a faint hope, but it would be entirely extinguished by too much obstinacy and obstruction. And it was, of course, entirely in the king's hands to mitigate the full rigour of any sentence for treason – or to refuse to do so.

The trial ground through its established procedures. Smeton confessed to adultery, but pleaded not guilty to the rest of the charge; Norris, Weston and Brereton pleaded not guilty to all. Even where a jury was not loaded in advance, defendants in a Tudor criminal trial – even more, a state trial – were at an enormous disadvantage. They had no advance warning of the evidence to be put, and since defence counsel was not allowed, they were reduced to attempting to rebut a public interrogation by hostile and well-prepared Crown prosecutors determined not so much to present the government case as to secure a conviction by fair questions or foul. The expected verdict came – guilty. And the judgement – drawing, hanging and quartering in all its horror. The edge of the axe was turned to the prisoners, and they were returned to the Tower to await death.

Anne and her brother had the weekend to endure. They were tried on Monday, 15 May, in the King's Hall in the Tower, a matter of security, not privacy; the special stands erected to hold the 2000 who attended could still be seen in 1778.[5] They watched a scene of the utmost solemnity: the duke of Norfolk under a cloth of estate, sitting as lord steward, with his son at his feet deputizing as earl marshal, plus a jury of twenty-six peers assisted by the chancellor and the royal justices.[6] Anne was brought in by the constable and the lieutenant of the Tower to be tried first, accompanied by Lady Kingston and her aunt, Lady Boleyn. After formal courtesies on both sides, Anne sat in the chair provided, raised her right hand when called, and pleaded 'not guilty' to the indictment.

The queen was once more in command of herself and clearly of the situation. Her sparing and effective answers quietly dominated the court.[7] From the moment of her arrest, Anne had realized the difficulty of establishing her innocence. She had said to Kingston: 'I can say no more but "nay", without I should open my body'; and, 'If any man accuse me, I can say but "nay", and they can bring no witnesses.'[8] Yet when the time came, her manner did carry conviction. No, she had not been unfaithful; no, she had not promised to marry Norris; no, she had not hoped for the king's death; no, she had not given secret tokens to Norris; no, she had neither poisoned Katherine nor planned to poison Mary; yes, she had given money to Francis Weston, but she had done the same to many of the always penurious young courtiers; and so it went on. Charles Wriothesley, who was temperamentally inclined to Katherine and Mary, expressed the common view: 'She made so wise and discreet answers to all things laid against her, excusing herself with her words so clearly as though she had never been faulty to the same.'[9] If de Carles is correct and Anne was in some way formally deprived of her honours before sentence, even then she kept the sympathy of the onlookers, but not of the jury, as it deliberated under the watchful eye of the duke of Suffolk. The peers returned to their seats and in traditional form gave their verdicts one by one, starting with the most junior: 'Guilty, guilty, guilty...' Norfolk pronounced sentence, weeping as he did so – and is it cynical to wonder whether they were tears more of relief than sympathy?

> Because thou has offended our sovereign the king's grace in committing treason against his person and here attainted of the same, the law of the realm is this, that thou hast deserved death, and thy judgement is this: that thou shalt be burned here within the Tower of London, on the Green, else to have thy head smitten off, as the king's pleasure shall be further known of the same.[10]

Burning or beheading? An angry rustle went round the judges; such an either/or judgement was most improper![11] Anne, however, did not hesitate as she addressed the court. Speeches at such a moment are notoriously subject to later embellishment, and de Carles puts into the queen's mouth an eloquent defence plea which is the less credible because delivered after and not, as procedure dictated, before the verdict.[12] Parts do, however, agree with Chapuys' report that Anne said in mitigation that she was ready to die but regretful for those innocent and loyal men who were to die because of her. There may also be a ring of truth in the words:

> I do not say that I have always borne towards the king the humility which I owed him, considering his kindness and the great honour he showed me and the great respect he always paid me; I admit, too, that often I have taken it into my head to be jealous of him... But may God be my witness if I have done him any other wrong.[13]

She knew that she had not been the waxen wife of conventional expectation, to be moulded or impressed at her husband's will. What she did not say was that the king had pursued her precisely because of this; he had needed her steel and was only where he was because of it. Instead she asked for time, time to make her peace with God. And then she was gone.

A minor flurry caught the attention. The earl of Northumberland, who had given his verdict along with the rest against the woman he had once courted, collapsed and had to be helped out. Then the second trial began, as Rochford was brought to the bar of the court. Again the plea was not guilty, and again a Boleyn used intellect and wit to crumble the royal case to dust. The performance of Anne and George that day is a clear indication of their calibre and why they had to die; they were certainly not upstarts or pasteboard figures, enjoying favour only because and for as long as Henry lusted after Anne's body. The question about the king's sexual performance was asked, and Rochford showed his contempt by reading out what Cromwell wanted kept secret. Again the audience was with him – not even More had been so effective – and the odds, Chapuys said, ran ten to one for an acquittal. Again, not so among the peers. 'Guilty' . . . and the duke of Norfolk found himself again condemning one of his sister's children to death, the full butchery of the male sentence for treason. For the second time there was no collapse. Rochford made a conventional acceptance of death – was not every man a sinner and deserving of death every day? – but his main thought was for those he owed money, and who faced ruin if the king, who would now take all his property, chose not to pay them. According to Chapuys, he actually read out a list of his debts before leaving the court, and he certainly continued to be troubled about them in the little time that was left.

In Tudor thinking, judgement marked the point when the accused must cease to be concerned with mortal life and turn instead to consider eternity. Each of the men was warned by the constable of the Tower early on the day after Anne's trial that he was to die on the Wednesday morning, and they used that last twenty-four hours in trying to clear their consciences and their obligations.[14] Rochford continued to worry about the financial ruin his death would bring others – so much so that the hardened Kingston wrote to Cromwell, 'you must help my lord of Rochford's conscience'; he was also upset when his favourite priest failed to turn up to hear his confession. What, however, is clear is that conviction of innocence remained as strong as ever. Rochford asked for the exceptional privilege of access to the eucharist before he died.[15] Most impressive to modern minds ignorant of the reality of Hell must be Norris choosing death rather than admit to Anne's dishonour. He had quickly withdrawn whatever statement he had made at the persuasion of Fitzwilliam.[16] William Brereton, too, insisted on his innocence. Before he was arrested, his old school companion, George Constantine, 'did ask him and was bold upon him', and the answer Brereton gave was 'that there was no way but one with any matter [alleged against him].' His wife certainly believed him; in her will, nine years later, she bequeathed to her son 'one bracelet of gold, the which was the last token his father sent me'.[17]

On the scaffold the men's conduct was of a piece with this. Royal mercy had excused the ghastly preliminaries to the beheading, and they were to die on Tower Hill. The crowd which assembled knew the ritual. Men about to face imminent divine judgement should forgive and ask for forgiveness and prayers, and as those judged by due process of law it was proper to endorse the system which had condemned them. Railing against injustice was unacceptable. Thus Rochford began: 'I was born under the law, I am judged under the law and I must die under the law, for the law has condemned me.' He then went on to confess that he was a sinner whose sins had deserved death twenty (or a thousand) times. Then, declaring that his fate was a warning to his fellow courtiers not to trust in the vanity of fortune, he asked anyone whom he had offended to forgive him. But abandoning convention, he omitted to say that he deserved death for the crimes alleged against him. Only Smeton said that: 'Masters I pray you all pray for me for I have deserved the death.' Norris said almost nothing; Weston said that his fate was a warning to others not to presume on life, for 'I had thought to have lived in abomination yet this twenty or thirty years and then to have made amends.' Brereton came the nearest to asserting his innocence: 'I have deserved to die if it were a thousand deaths. But the cause whereof I die, judge not. But if ye judge, judge the best,' a phrase he repeated several times. Their remarks and general demeanour were sufficient to convince the average onlooker that they died 'charitably' – they confessed 'in a manner', so Constantine said.[18] Yet he picked up also the significance of what was not said, particularly in the case of Brereton: 'By my troth, if any of them were innocent it was he. For either he was innocent or else he died worst of all.' According to de Carles, Anne's only reaction to the executions was when told that Mark had persisted in admitting his guilt: 'Alas! I fear that his soul will suffer punishment for his false confession.' De Carles also noticed that Rochford avoided admitting any offence against the king.

Tudor criminal trials were more about securing condemnation by due process than evaluating evidence, but two grand juries, a petty jury, and a jury of peers sitting twice rejected the defence presented by Anne Boleyn and her alleged lovers. Surely this must indicate that whatever the government's motives, it had at least been able to present a plausible case. When the duke of Suffolk's 'Guilty' completed the Rochford verdict, ninety-five successive voices had spoken against them.[19]

The Crown case had consisted in large part of allegations of repeated adultery. In Middlesex, Anne was indicted of one dated offence of soliciting and one of illicit intercourse with each man, and similarly in Kent, twenty specific offences in all. The earliest alleged misconduct was with Henry Norris at Westminster on 6 and 12 October 1533, followed by Norris and William Brereton at Greenwich in November. May and June 1534 saw offences by Weston at Whitehall and Greenwich and by Smeton at Greenwich; the latter's Middlesex offence was at Whitehall in April 1535.

Rochford appears in November 1535 at Whitehall and in December at Eltham. These locations raise an immediate question. Why the near exclusive concentration of offences at Whitehall and Greenwich? Only Brereton 'obliged' the queen at Hampton Court, only Rochford at Eltham and nobody at all at Richmond. Unsullied morality reigned in all other shires visited by the court. Perhaps it was the air of Kent and Middlesex.

Investigation, furthermore, shows that even after nearly 500 years, three-quarters of these specific allegations can be disproved. In twelve cases Anne was elsewhere or else the man was. Accusing Anne of soliciting Norris at Westminster on 6 October, with intercourse following on 12 October, was particularly careless and medically improbable; she was at Greenwich recovering after childbirth, indeed possibly still in purdah pending being churched. Two more charges can be ruled out if we presume that Anne was with the king at the alleged time. Soliciting Smeton at Greenwich on 13 May 1535 can also be discounted, since it supposedly led to intercourse there on 19 May, by which time Anne was actually at Richmond. The only offences for which there are not alibis are those alleged at Greenwich in November 1533 and over Christmas 1535–6. Perhaps the Crown just hit lucky, but in the latter case there is a darker possibility. Everyone, prisoners included, would remember where they had spent their most recent Christmas. Carelessness about facts except where it might be noticed must bring the whole adultery allegation into question. The Crown, however, was wise to that and had added to each charge the catch-all phrase: 'and on divers other days and places, before and after'. Thus, even if a dated charge was challenged, the force of the indictment would remain.[20] Only a wife confined to a closed nunnery could hope to escape that trap.

The detailed particulars of Anne's adultery were thus fiction. What, however, reveals the depth of government cynicism is that they were also immaterial. To have intercourse with a queen who consented was no crime at common law – ill-advised, to be sure, but punishable only by the Church courts as an affront to morality.[21] The adultery charges were there to prejudice opinion by repeating the phrase 'treasonably violated the queen' five times. Not that there had been any violation. Given Anne's alleged consent, that too collapsed! The indictments, were, in fact, a device by the Crown to extend existing treason law in novel and oppressively retrospective ways. And there can be no doubt that this was deliberate, because the legal term for rape – *felonice rapuit* – was carefully avoided. In 1542 the Crown would effectively admit it had acted *ultra vires* by securing a statute making adultery with a queen high treason. Other accusations were also deliberate distortions. Anne was accused of corrupting the men's allegiance with gifts. She supposedly did this at Westminster on 27 November 1535, when she was actually at Windsor. The other occasion was at Eltham on 31 December, when the queen certainly had gifts to give. It was New Year's Eve! Her lovers were said to quarrel among themselves and vie for her favour – disputes made to seem worse by hints about sexual excess which, we have seen, derived from Smeton. The inference the prosecution intended should be drawn even reached France, where one rumour was that Henry was to be poisoned, after which one of the men would marry Anne and take the throne. The queen, in turn, was said to become incensed whenever any of them paid attention to another woman. The story that Anne had poisoned Katherine and intended to poison Mary was dragged in, even though it was not in the indictment.[22] The Crown also slipped in a statutory treason by alleging 'slander, danger, detriment and derogation of the heirs' of Henry and Anne. This was a virtual quotation from the 1534 Succession Act and the judges responded on cue by ruling that the offences would be treason under that statute.[23] Anne, in other words, was a traitor to her own daughter.

The determination of the Crown to secure convictions is also seen in the gossip that was shared with the court, what John Spelman meant by saying that 'all the evidence was of bawdry and lechery, so there was no such whore in the realm.' Its effect was deliberately enhanced by the decision not to try Anne first as the principal and the men only then as accessories. Instead, the four commoners were tried first on the basis of Anne's Tower revelations before she had had an opportunity to challenge the construction placed on them. John Hussey wrote the next day to Lady Lisle of the huge impact this produced, even taken with a pinch of salt:

Madam, I think verily, if all the books and chronicles were totally revolved [turned over], and to the uttermost persecuted [prosecuted] and tried, which against women hath been penned, contrived, and written since Adam and Eve, those same were, I think, verily nothing in comparison of that which hath been done and committed by Anne the Queen; which though I presume be not all thing as it is now rumoured, yet that which hath been by her confessed, and others, offenders with her, by her own alluring, procurement and instigation, is so abhominable and detestable that I am ashamed that any good woman should give ear thereunto. I pray God give her grace to repent while she now liveth. I think not the contrary but she and all they shall suffer.[24]

When Anne came into court two days later, her guilt had already been established in law; adulterers necessarily come in pairs.[25]

The charge that this farrago of bawdry and lechery was designed to embellish, and the one that mattered, came last in the indictment – treasonable conspiracy to procure the king's death. The specific allegation was that the plotters met at Westminster on 30 October 1535 and at Greenwich on 8 January 1536, although given the cover-all addition 'at divers other days and places' it hardly mattered that on the first the court was at Windsor and on the second at Eltham. But the really dangerous element in this charge was the assertion that the queen had many times promised to marry one of her lovers, once the king was dead, and had often said that the king never had her heart. The accusation was general, and Weston's behaviour could easily be inverted and presented as supporting it. Chapuys, however, makes it clear that Norris was the particular target and that gifts by Anne to him were interpreted as tokens of this contract. This was very evidently based on Anne's assertion on 29 April that Norris was waiting for dead men's shoes. On her own admission she had discussed with the groom of the stool what would happen 'if the king dies' – or was it 'when the king dies', or 'as soon as the king is dead', or even, 'if only the king were dead'? To speculate about and to wish for may be a wafer apart. Imagining the king's death was treason by the original treason law of 1352, but it had recently been clarified that this also included words said. For good measure, the indictment did in fact claim that the king's life had been endangered by the impact of the revelations; yet not only did the public pursuit of Jane Seymour show this supposedly enfeebled monarch decidedly in rut, the trial appears to have been silent on a construction which opened every adulterer to a charge of causing grievous bodily harm.

The point which is crucial in the argument about guilt or innocence is that the events on which this key conspiracy charge was based occurred on 29 and 30 April, and that the details were revealed by Anne's frenzied disclosures in the Tower on and after 2 May. Anne and the others were not arrested and charged on the basis of carefully collected information; they were arrested, and the facts (so-called) then came to light. The judicious sequence of suspicion, investigation, evidence and arrest which Cromwell reported is a lie. Indeed, in the case of one of the accused, William Brereton, there seems to have been no evidence at all. Anne showed little reaction to the news of his late arrest, and despite his efforts, George Constantine never managed to discover the grounds for the charge against his old schoolfellow. The appearance of Brereton among the queen's 'lovers' is indeed odd. He was not a prominent courtier; Wyatt described him as 'one that least I knew', and as the king's contemporary, he was an older man in the background of the Boleyn faction.[26] He was a dependant of Norris and, as we have seen, may well have been in on the secret of Anne's wedding. However, he had wider links at court, with the duke of Norfolk and especially with the latter's son-in-law, Richmond, so that when Norfolk and Anne fell out, Brereton was pulled two ways. All this might suggest that Brereton was unlucky to be singled out in May 1536 – a small fish caught up with the main catch. In fact, his arrest reveals the brutal pragmatism behind the choice of victims. He was picked on as an act of gratuitous malice (or perhaps rough justice), following an earlier and quite separate altercation with Cromwell.

Using his place at court, William Brereton had secured a virtual monopoly of royal appointments in Cheshire and North Wales. He exploited this authority to further Brereton interests, was a nuisance to Cromwell's local agent, Bishop Rowland Lee, and promised to be an obstacle to plans then in their infancy to settle the Welsh border.[27] However, what really marked Brereton was a notorious judicial murder. His victim was a Flintshire gentleman, a John ap Gryffith Eyton, whom he blamed for the death of a Brereton retainer. In 1534, William exploited his local muscle to arrest Eyton and send him under armed guard to London. Although Eyton was acquitted, Brereton had him rearrested, possibly with Anne Boleyn's help, returned him to Wales and, after a rigged trial, saw him hanged – and all this in defiance of Cromwell's efforts to save him.[28] In his *Metrical Visions* twenty years later, George Cavendish still echoed the feeling that Brereton's fate was a deserved retribution:

> Furnished with rooms I was by the king,
> The best I am sure he had in my country.
> Steward of the Holt, a room of great winning
> In the Marches of Wales, the which he gave to me,
> Where of tall men I had sure great plenty
> The king for to serve, both in town and field,
> Readily furnished with horse, spear and shield.
>
> God of his justice, foreseeing my malice,
> For my busy rigour would punish me of right,
> Ministered unto Eyton, by colour of justice –
> A shame to speak, more shame it is to write:
> A gentleman born, that through my might
> So shamefully was hanged upon a gallows tree,
> Only of old rancour that rooted was in me.

Lo, here is th'end of murder and tyranny!
Lo, here is th'end of envious affection!
Lo, here is th'end of false conspiracy!
Lo, here is th'end of false detection
Done to the innocent by cruel correction!
Although in office I thought myself strong,
Yet here is mine end for ministering wrong.[29]

The irony of Brereton hanging an enemy on a flimsy charge of felony, and then being himself executed on a flimsy charge of high treason, was a moral too good to forget.

Under analysis, the case presented by the Crown in May 1536 collapses. But one decisive argument for innocence remains – the evidence the Crown was unable to produce. In the Tudor court, privacy was a rare commodity. The queen would normally be attended, day and night. In no way could she pursue a liaison unaided. Any alteration in routine (for example insisting on sleeping alone or travelling away from court) would raise immediate comment. Even with Lady Rochford's help, Henry's fourth wife, Katherine Howard, had to entertain her suitor, Thomas Culpeper, in a privy! When Katherine did admit Thomas to her bedchamber, Jane Rochford had to be present, though she feigned sleep, and this conniving took her to the block along with the queen. But where was Anne Boleyn's accomplice? How could a queen live a nymphomaniac life without help? Here is 'the dog that did not bark'. Indeed, far from being accused or even smeared by association with their disgraced mistress, Anne's attendants switched their service to Jane Seymour. Anne could simply not have behaved as alleged.[30]

What seems to have come out from the interrogations of the women amounted to no more than 'pastime in the queen's chamber'. Thus it was said that she danced with her ladies and the king's gentlemen in her bedchamber (something that was perfectly usual), and much was made of her being handed from partner to partner in the course of the dance.[31] If such stories had any point beyond darkening the atmosphere, it was in order to make out the most difficult case of all, that against Rochford. He, in particular, was accused of leading Anne into the dance – and so of handing her to the next man in the set. Much was made of Anne and George exchanging a kiss in public – although English women were famed for this across Europe and anyway, George was her brother – but the Crown claimed that this had been 'deep kissing'.[32] Anne was accused of writing to tell George she was pregnant – a very sinister act. He was also asked about a suspiciously long stay alone with his sister in her room. Deliberately misrepresented, conventions of the court, courtly love and even family affection could be made damning.

One or two items among all the rest do, however, give pause. There was the accusation that the king had been held up to ridicule, that his clothes had been laughed at, and so too his attempts at writing verse.[33] Anne's ramblings about Weston show that the licence she tolerated sometimes went quite far, while her own probing of the private emotions of the courtiers suggests an inability to keep a safe regal distance. She could not break herself of that even in the Tower, wanting to know how the other accused were housed and who made their beds, and when told that nobody did, joked that if they could not make their pallets they might be able to make ballets (ballads). There was a good deal in the response of one of her attendants (the not very favourite aunt), that 'Such desire as you have had to such tales has brought you to this.'[34] Evidence of excessive high spirits never sounds good in a law court, and 'pastime in the queen's chamber' does seem to have got somewhat out of hand. The lack of a son compelled Anne to continue playing the mistress, but did she go over the top in response to the appearance of a rival in Jane Seymour?[35] Alternatively, was Anne instinctively demonstrating to Henry that other men still found her exciting, or was she even hoping to make Henry jealous? Or perhaps there always something febrile in the game of courtly love. It has, indeed, been suggested that 'unguarded speech and gossip' is alone sufficient to account for Anne's destruction. It triggered suspicion about the queen and the others and once an investigation began the consequence was inexorable.[36] This is unlikely, given the clear evidence of a political coup. But while loss of control within her household is not by itself sufficient to explain her destruction, it was where Anne was vulnerable and Cromwell ruthlessly exploited the weakness.

The most dangerous part of this courtly brinkmanship was, of course, tolerating the discussion of how good – or bad – the king was in bed. When Rochford was asked, as we have seen, whether Anne had talked about that to his wife, he neatly evaded the question as likely to impugn the royal issue. He was, however, silenced by a supplementary: 'Had he at any time spread the story that Elizabeth was not Henry's child?' Very clearly something of the kind had been said, and apparently more than once. We can imagine it as a joke – 'With his problems, it's hard to see how the king ever produced Elizabeth!' – but could anything be more foolish to joke about or for Anne to condone? Strange though it is – and we may put it down to ageing, to stress, to overconfidence, to what we will – Anne had allowed herself to relax at the point of her greatest strength, her court-craft. Perhaps she now remembered with bitter regret the advice of Margaret of Austria over twenty years before: 'Trust in those who offer you service, and in the end, my maidens, you will find yourselves in the ranks of those who have been deceived.'[37]

Folly was, nevertheless, not crime, nor was it justice to punish with death what at most deserved the rustication which Henry had imposed on Carewe, Bryan and other 'minions' who forgot their place years before. The ninety-five voices which had cried 'guilty' were lying, or deceived, or chose to be deceived. A case sufficient to quiet the general public and satisfy pliant consciences had been manufactured by innuendo and implication, but those in the know were aware how flimsy it was. Clearly informed by his friend Nicolas Bourbon, the French reformer Etienne Dolet published an epigram declaring Anne falsely condemned and beheaded for adultery.[38] Chapuys did not believe her guilt – 'condemned on presumption and not evidence, without any witnesses or valid confession' was his conclusion – and the reaction of Mary of Hungary, that niece of Margaret of Austria whom Anne had known as a 7-year-old in Mechelen, was completely cynical.[39] The king had

> paid considerable attention to [Jane] before her predecessor was dead which, along with the fact that none of those executed with her except for the organist admitted the deed, any more than she had, made people think he invented the ploy to get rid of her. Nevertheless the woman herself suffered no great injustice by this for she was well known to be a worthless character... I think that women will not be all that happy if such ways of going on become the custom – and with good reason. And although I do not intend to take the risk myself, yet for the sake of the female sex I will pray like the rest that God will protect us!

Thomas Cromwell made a more personal assessment in which we may detect at least a hint of posthumous amends. When discussing her with Chapuys early in June, he went out of his way to praise the intelligence, spirit and courage of the queen and her brother.[40]

Henry VIII, by contrast, had to face the fact that in permitting the arrest of his wife and friends, he had taken a step which he could not reverse, even if the rage and suspicion which had tipped him over the edge were to seem more questionable in the cold light of reflection. He admitted nearly ten years later that a victim in the Tower had no defence against false evidence.[41] In the case of Anne, the Jane Seymour faction kept up the enticement, while Cromwell fed Henry 'facts' about Anne's guilt which he could hide behind. The king responded by whipping up a prurient self-righteous-ness which anaesthetized all doubt. He declared that his wife had been unfaithful with more than a hundred men, and was morbidly concerned about the plans for the executions, even to the making of the scaffolds.[42] He was at his most judicious in refusing the very considerable persuasions and inducements he was offered to reprieve Francis Weston, so unhappily caught on the wrong side of the factional battle.[43] Since Francis's father was still alive, his death would bring the Crown little profit, and Henry would not normally have turned down the chance to trade blood for cash. But not so this time; justice must be done! The king was at his most nauseous in making arrangements – even perhaps in advance of the trial – to bring over the executioner of Calais to kill Anne.[44] He was an expert in the use of the heavy continental executioner's sword which could cut the head off a prisoner who was kneeling upright, in place of the clumsier English axe needing the prisoner's chin on the block. He charged £23 6s. 8d.[45] A death in the French style may have been requested by Anne herself; it was certainly intended as an act of grace towards her, to add to the kindness of a death by beheading, instead of the accustomed fire of the female traitor. The warrant for Anne's execution actually states that the king, moved by pity, was unwilling to commit her to the flames.[46] One can only wonder at a psychology which transmutes doubt about the guilt of a loved one into a loving concern about the way to kill her.

James Anthony Froude, that great nineteenth-century historian of Eng-lish nationalism, laboured mightily to exonerate Henry's ministers from the charge of judicial murder.

> Though we stretch our belief in the complacency of statesmen to the furthest limit of credulity, can we believe that Cromwell would have invented that dark indictment – Cromwell...the dearest friend of Latimer? Or...Norfolk...who had won his spurs at Flodden? Or...Suffolk and...Fitzwilliam, the Wellington and the Nelson of the sixteenth century? Scarcely among the picked scoundrels of Newgate could men be found for such work; and shall we believe it of men like these?

As for the king himself:

> I believe history will be ransacked vainly to find a parallel for conduct at once so dastardly, so audacious, and so foolishly wicked as that which the popular hypothesis attributes to Henry VIII.[47]

A. F. Pollard, too, found uxoricide hard to square with his vision of 'Henry the Lion':

it is not credible that the juries should have found her accomplices guilty, that twenty-six peers should have condemned Anne herself, without some colourable justification. If the charges were merely invented to ruin the queen, one culprit besides herself would have been enough. To assume that Henry sent four needless victims to the block is to accuse him of a lust for superfluous butchery, of which even he, in his most bloodthirsty moments, was not capable.[48]

In the very different atmosphere of recent years, the thought has been that Anne was justified in being unfaithful:

Anne, realising that her survival depended on her production of a son, may have hoped that other men would succeed where the king had failed. The king, moreover, was being unfaithful to her, and she may have tried to get her own back. Above all, perhaps, she was losing her beauty and was anxious to reassure herself by the admiration of others – an admiration which would always be forthcoming from an ambitious courtier.[49]

G. W. Bernard has gone further and argued 'that Anne and at least some of her friends were guilty of the charges brought against them'.[50] The evidence, however, justifies nothing of this. Two days before Anne appeared to plead 'not guilty' the Crown began breaking up her household and, according to Chapuys, Henry had told Jane on the morning of the trial that Anne would be condemned by three in the afternoon.[51] His wife was the victim of a struggle for power, and Henry at his rare moments of honesty admitted it. When he told Jane Seymour not to meddle in affairs of state, he pointedly advised her to take Anne as a warning.[52]

Innocent but a prisoner, guiltless but condemned, Anne awaited her fate. We need not believe that she was forced to watch the execution of her brother and the others, as Chapuys suggests.[53] This would have meant moving her across the Tower, to one of the few vantage points in the Bell Tower from which the Tower Hill scaffold could be seen 200 yards away. The prisoner who did watch from there was Thomas Wyatt:

> The Bell Tower showed me such a sight
> That in my head sticks day and night:
> There did I learn out of a grate,
> For all favour, glory or might,
>   That yet *circa Regna tonat*.[54]

Excused such horrors, and after the hysteria of the first few days, Anne showed some signs of adjustment, but all the time she was battered by the demoralization and fragmentation of the prisoner under constant and unsympathetic scrutiny. What we learn of her then is certainly revealing. Nothing has come down to us of anything Anne said about her daughter of 2 years and 8 months. From the start, her family was uppermost in her mind, not only her 'sweet brother' but her mother, and the father we think of as deserting her.[55] Perhaps he did, but Anne was evidently concerned that her whole family would be destroyed with her – as it very largely was. Thomas Boleyn would, in fact, end with little to show for his lifetime of service to Henry VIII except for his earldom.[56] Not that he gave up in May 1536. Despite losing his place in Henry's inner circle and its many benefits, he set himself with enthusiasm once more to climb the greasy pole. He helped to suppress and punish the rebels of 1536, paid his subsidy in full and promptly, buttered up and co-operated with ministers (even lending Cromwell his chain and 'best' Garter badge), was assiduous at the Order's functions, active in royal ceremonies and by January 1538 was back at court and 'well entertained'.[57] There was even talk of his marrying the king's niece, Margaret Douglas.[58] Thomas also promised Henry that he would settle the Ormonde lands on the illegitimate Elizabeth, although in the end he thought again and they went to his surviving daughter.[59] In the past Anne had easily eclipsed her sister, but now Mary was the only legitimate hope of the Boleyn line.

Deserted, cut off and disoriented in time, Anne became avid for news. She built great castles of imagination – that it would not rain until she was released, that the evangelical bishops would intervene on her behalf, that most English people were praying for her, that a disaster from heaven would follow her execution. She harked back to the happy time with Margaret of Austria.[60] Sometimes her hope ran high – the king was doing it all to test her, she would be sent to a nunnery; at others she would be determined to die, and would discuss the technical details with Kingston as if it was the most amusing subject in the world. There would, she said, be no difficulty in finding her a nickname: 'Queen Anne the Headless'. Then her mind would run over details of her treatment or she would recall a promising bet on the game of tennis she had been watching when first summoned before the commissioners – 'if it [the chase] had been laid she had won.' But, increasingly, preparation for death occupied her thoughts, hours spent with her almoner and before the blessed sacrament until her spirit reached the exaltation of the martyr. Kingston wrote towards the end: 'I have seen many men and also women executed and that they have been in great sorrow, and to my knowledge this lady hath much joy and pleasure in death.'[61]

Yet before Anne could be allowed to die there was to be one final twist in the story, and the nastiest. Her marriage to Henry was declared null and void and Elizabeth, the daughter whose legitimacy she was supposed to have defamed, was bastardized. The formal award was made by Cranmer at Lambeth on Wednesday, 17 May – the afternoon following the execution of the men – but no justification was published and, as the cause papers have disappeared, we do not know the grounds alleged.[62] It is clear that the notion of a divorce had been under consideration for some days. The previous Saturday (that is, before Anne was tried), the earl of Northumberland wrote to Thomas Cromwell because news had reached him that the old story of the supposed pre-contract had been resurrected. He reminded the secretary of his denials in 1532, and insisted that he would stick by that 'to his damnation'. As well as showing that to divorce Anne was not, as is often said, a last-minute idea, this letter disposes of one explanation which was circulating.[63] Chapuys picked up two others – that Elizabeth was the daughter of Norris and that Henry's relations with Anne's sister Mary had been summoned up again.[64]

Some writers see Henry's sending of Cranmer to hear Anne's confession on 16 May as a tactic to secure grounds for a divorce.[65] Did the archbishop hint at life in return for compliance? Did Anne confess to a consummated relationship with Percy or a third party, a quid pro quo, perhaps, for Henry not rejecting Elizabeth? There is no way of knowing what passed between the client, now archbishop, and his patron, now a condemned traitor.[66] In all probability the meeting was what it purported to be, pastoral. Now that the verdict had been given against Anne, it was safe to let Cranmer back on the scene to do what he excelled at. It asks a great deal to believe that the archbishop secured information on the Tuesday (volunteered or by deceit), and was then able to rush the legal processes through in time to pronounce sentence within twenty-four hours.[67] In any case there was no reason to rush; the court at Lambeth could as easily have sat on the Thursday. That it sat when it did implies that by the time of Cranmer's visit, annulment was well in hand.

Cranmer's decision, of course, could simply have been pragmatic – 'least said, soonest mended'; Anne was a condemned traitor and the sword would provide reason enough. Tudor minds, however, set great store on due process, and the Second Succession Act of July 1536 specifically states that the marriage with Anne was void because of 'certain just, true and lawful impediments unknown at the making' of the legislation protecting it 'and since that time confessed by the Lady Anne'.[68] The ground for this was almost certainly a retrospective construction of a little-noticed qualification in the Dispensations Act of 1534.[69] This had decreed that existing dispensations should remain valid but that dispensations should in future be issued in England, not Rome. There was, however, one specific exception: dispensations could not be issued for causes 'contrary or repugnant to the Holy Scriptures and laws of God'. Henry, of course, had argued for years that the papal dispensation to marry his deceased brother's wife was repugnant to scripture, but Clement VII had also provided a dispensation to cover Henry's affaire with Anne's sister. Supposing that too was 'repugnant'? As God had revealed to Henry, holy scriptures and the laws of God forbade marriage to a sibling's widow but might that prohibition not apply to sexual relations per se? If so, Henry had never been validly married to Anne either. The king had known from the first that intercourse with her sister was a barrier; what had been 'unknown' to him was that such a barrier was insurmountable. Chapuys was right. Mary was the impediment.

That this was the argument Cranmer relied on in annulling Anne's marriage is effectively confirmed by legislation put through two months later. The Second Succession Act includes an incongruous clause stating that:

> it is to be understood that if it chance any man to know carnally any woman, that then all and singular persons being in any degree of consanguinity or affinity... to any of the parties so carnally offending shall be deemed and adjudged to be within the cases and limits of the said prohibition of marriage.

This was divine law and could not be dispensed; marriages already made were declared invalid and their offspring illegitimate, exactly as Elizabeth was.

Whatever the ground, the decision to annul Anne's marriage immediately after accusing her of adultery was, of course, schizoid. If she had never been the king's wife, plans to marry Norris were perfectly proper. The point, so glaringly obvious to us, does not seem to have been made at the time, probably because (as Chapuys recognized) the divorce was not directed at Anne herself. She was doomed; the target was Elizabeth.[70] Henry was determined not to admit the legitimacy of his elder daughter Mary. Bastardizing the younger as well would leave him no legitimate children and a serious case could be made for the only boy, the duke of

Richmond, as the heir presumptive. Of course Henry hoped for a son by Jane Seymour, but he would not bank on it as he had with Anne. This line of thinking explains the provisions of the Succession Act of July 1536. This switched the legitimate line from Elizabeth to the offspring of Henry and Jane or any future wives, but it also provided that if Henry had no legitimate heirs, then he could by letters patent or his last will declare who the next ruler would be. Richmond, therefore, could be held in reserve should Jane fail to produce the heir, *sans reproche*.[71] In the end, however, all this went for nothing. Disease took its grip on the young duke, and four days after the Succession Act became law, he was dead.[72]

Anne Boleyn was not at Lambeth that Wednesday to watch the twists and turns of Cranmer and the lawyers in their attempt to give the king what he wanted. Instead she was facing what she expected to be the last night of her life, and by two o'clock the next morning the sleepless queen was closeted with her almoner. Her preparation for the sacrament complete, she called Kingston to hear mass with her soon after dawn on the Thursday. It was then that, at the damnation of her immortal soul, she swore on the sacrament that she had never been unfaithful to the king. She did so twice – before and after receiving the body of Christ – and the constable duly passed on her oath, as she knew he would.[73] At some stage she made arrangements to distribute the £20 which Henry had sent her to distribute in alms.[74] Then there was only the waiting. Later that morning Kingston was summoned again. Anne had heard that she was not to die until noon: 'Master Kingston, I hear say I shall not die afore noon, and I am very sorry there for, for I thought to be dead by this time and past my pain.'[75]

In fact, as Kingston knew, she had never been intended for the scaffold that day. He had just received a letter from Cromwell, instructing him to clear the Tower of foreigners, but the timing of Anne's execution was only notified early on Friday.[76] Where Anne got her mistaken expectation is not clear, and some have suspected deliberate malice.[77] More likely, she had jumped to the conclusion that she would follow her brother to death as soon as the divorce was through, and had not realized that it was Kingston's custom to give the victims warning early on the morning of the day they were to die. The constable avoided revealing his ignorance of the timetable by seizing on Anne's last remark. The execution, he explained, would not be painful; the blow was 'so subtle'. Anne replied: 'I heard say the executor was very good, and I have a little neck' – and she put her hands round her throat and burst out laughing.[78]

FINALE

I T was a short journey. Out of the Queen's Lodgings, past the Great Hall where she had dined on the night before the coronation, through the Cole Harbour Gate, along the west side of the White Tower and then the first sight of the scaffold.[1] It stood three or four feet high, draped in black, surrounded by perhaps a thousand spectators: the lord mayor and aldermen come to see the king's justice done, and behind them 'certain of the best crafts of London' – no foreigners – Englishmen and women come to see the first English queen executed.[2] And around the scaffold itself the faces she knew so well: Thomas Audley, the lord chancellor, whom she had last seen at her trial; Charles Brandon, duke of Suffolk, whose life had been so entwined with her own, ever since her journey to France as a 13-year-old attendant on the king's sister Mary, who had married Brandon, had hated her and was now dead; Henry Fitzroy, her 17-year-old stepson, who had only nine weeks to live; and Thomas Cromwell, who had climbed to power behind Anne, and now had to destroy her in order to retain that power.[3] How Anne and Thomas reacted at this last meeting we can only guess. Pride on her part, and on his, the formal last deference due even to a fallen queen, and the relief that it was Anne, and not himself, at the centre of the drama.

Escorted by Sir William Kingston, followed by the four 'wardresses' she had disliked, Anne walked the final fifty yards.[4] Over a grey damask gown lined with fur she wore an ermine mantle with an English gable hood.[5] The constable saw her safely up the steps (no Thomas More jokes this time), and following the etiquette of state executions, Anne moved to the edge of the scaffold to address the crowd.[6]

Good Christian people, I have not come here to preach a sermon; I have come here to die.

Did she know that she was echoing the words of her brother two days earlier?

> For according to the law and by the law I am judged to die, and therefore I will speak nothing against it. I am come hither to accuse no man, nor to speak of that whereof I am accused and condemned to die, but I pray God save the king and send him long to reign over you, for a gentler nor a more merciful prince was there never, and to me he was ever a good, a gentle, and sovereign lord. And if any person will meddle of my cause, I require them to judge the best [shades of William Brereton]. And thus I take my leave of the world and of you all, and I heartily desire you all to pray for me.

Again the submissiveness which the crowd expected, but which reveals the enormous gulf between the sixteenth-century mind and our own. Once more we feel compelled to ask, 'How could she not protest her innocence, how acquiesce in such injustice?' Convention demanded it; religion demanded it, and it would be Elizabeth who would suffer from the luxury of defying the king and his supposed justice. But the crowd, far more attuned to nuances than we are, could also see beyond the humility to the silent point Anne was making. There was no public admission of sin, even in general, still less any confession that she had wronged Henry. Anne spoke firmly, 'with a goodly smiling countenance', and soon the news would be all round London that she had died 'boldly', without the acceptance of the morality of the sentence which a truly penitent adulteress should show.[7]

The speech done, the ermine mantle was removed, revealing the proud neck Sanuto the Venetian had noted years before, and a low collar which would present no obstacle to the sword. Then Anne herself lifted off her head-dress, and the crowd saw for the last time the brief glory of her hair as she tucked it into a cap one attendant had ready. The only sign of nervousness was her trick of continually glancing behind her; like many similar victims, her fear was that the executioner would strike when she was not ready. She had no chaplain with her, no one to repeat a prayer, and no psalm was said, but we can guess what she tried desperately to hold in her mind. In the happy days of 1535 Erasmus of Rotterdam had written for her father *A Preparation to Death*: 'In peril of death, man's infirmity is overpowered unless instant by instant, unless with a pure affection, unless with an unvanquished trust he crieth for the help of him which only reviveth the dead.'[8]

A brief farewell to her weeping servants, a request for prayer, and Anne knelt down, saying all the while, 'Jesu receive my soul; O Lord God have pity on my soul.' Continentals were amazed that she was not bound or restrained in any way: only a blindfold, tied for her by one of the ladies. 'To Christ I commend my soul!' And while her lips were still moving, it was suddenly over.[9]

Almost, it seemed, in slow motion, the ladies-in-waiting covered Anne. Then one with the head in a white cloth, quickly red, and the other three with the body wrapped in a sheet, they carried the queen unaided the seventy yards or so into the chapel of St Peter, past the two newly filled graves, Norris with Weston, Brereton with Smeton. There the clothes were removed – the Tower claimed its perquisites even from a queen – and the corpse was placed in an elm chest which had contained bow-staves for Ireland, but was now to go no further than the chancel of the chapel.[10] There, near her brother, Anne Boleyn was buried, three years and thirty-seven days after she had 'first dined abroad as queen' on Easter Sunday 1533.

She had been a remarkable woman. She would remain a remarkable woman even in a century which produced many of great note. There were few others who rose from such beginnings to a crown, and none contributed to a revolution as far-reaching as the English Reformation. To use a description no longer in fashion, Anne Boleyn was one of the 'makers of history'. Yet historians see through a glass darkly; they know in part and they pronounce in part. What Anne really was, as distinct from what Anne did, comes over very much less clearly. To us she appears inconsistent – religious yet aggressive, calculating yet emotional, with the light touch of the courtier yet the strong grip of the politician – but is this what she was, or merely what we strain to see through the opacity of the evidence? As for her inner life, short of a miraculous cache of new material, we shall never really know. Yet what does come to us across the centuries is the impression of a person who is strangely appealing to the early twenty-first century. A woman in her own right – taken on her own terms in a man's world; a woman who mobilized her education, her style and her presence to outweigh the disadvantages of her sex; of only moderate good looks, but taking a court and a king by storm. Perhaps, in the end, it is Thomas Cromwell's assessment that comes nearest: intelligence, spirit and courage.

Life is cruel to the dead, the more so where guilt and fear together censor memory. Francis Bryan had taken the news of Anne's condemnation to Jane Seymour; and now, with equal alacrity, the rest of the court turned its back on the past.[11] For the first time since the execution of Buckingham in 1521, there was the chance of a bonanza in forfeited property, and competition started as soon as news of the first arrests was out. Rochford had two large annuities, but apart from the Cinque Ports he had only just over £100 a year gross in royal offices, farms and grants, and the Boleyn family lands remained in the hands of his father. Weston, too, was probably worth relatively little. Brereton, however, had over £1000 a year gross from the Crown, and Norris over £1200.[12] On 2 May, the very day of Anne's arrest, a Gray's Inn lawyer, Roland Bulkeley, had written to his brother, Sir Richard, in North Wales, sending news of the early victims and urging a swift journey to London to press his suits in person; Roland evidently saw this as an inside tip – 'when it is once known that they shall die, all will be too late.' His messenger talked too much and ended up in Shrewsbury town gaol, but Sir Richard, who had been Norris's deputy in North Wales, still got in quickly enough to secure and apparently advance his interests.[13] Stephen Gardiner, not for the last time, risked his credit with the king by expressing dissatisfation with his share; £200 was cancelled of the 300 pounds per annum he had previously paid to Rochford and Norris, but he still resented the remainder passing to Bryan.[14] Viscount Lisle came too late, and seems never to have found satisfactory replacements for the court contacts he had lost in 1536. When, after fifteen months of solicitation, his stepdaughter was admitted as maid of honour to the new queen, her first and last duty was to take part in Jane Seymour's funeral.[15]

Unaware of what the future held, the victorious faction exuded satisfaction at the destruction of Anne Boleyn. Sir John Russell wrote: 'The king hath come out of hell into heaven for the gentleness in this [Jane] and the cursedness and the unhappiness in the other.'[16] Even before Anne had faced her judges, Henry had sent Carewe to bring her successor to a house on the river a mile from Whitehall, and as soon as news of the execution reached him he set off to meet Jane.[17] The following day they were betrothed, and on Tuesday, 30 May, the marriage took place in the queen's closet at Whitehall.[18] A week later Edward Seymour was elevated to the peerage, and soon after Henry Seymour, probably his younger brother, took the privy chamber place made vacant by Smeton's death.[19] And always comparison was made to Anne's disadvantage, although we may not today draw quite the pejorative implication intended by another John Russell remark, made after attending the marriage, that 'the richer she [Jane] was in apparel, the fairer and goodly lady she was and appeared; and the other [Anne] he said was the contrary, for the richer she was apparelled, the worse she looked.'[20] Anyone familiar with Holbein's portrait of Jane Seymour might be forgiven for feeling that she needed all the help she could get.[21]

For Thomas Cromwell, intent on being free of these troublesome courtiers, the death of Anne, Rochford, Norris and the rest was only the end of Act One. The Seymour family had been paid off for the moment – and he would have to work with them anyway – but Carewe and the other supporters of Mary were in a high state of excitement, daily expecting her return to favour and a place in the succession.[22] London was buzzing. Cromwell appeared to countenance these expectations, but from the start he knew the price to be exacted from Mary: full acceptance of the supremacy and her own illegitimacy. There was to be no conservative reaction or return to the traditional powers and status of the Church, as the princess and her allies fondly expected. Poor Mary; it was so obvious to her that everything was the fault of Anne, 'nobody dared speak for me' – and we may add 'or the Church' – 'as long as that woman lived, which is now gone.'[23]

For a while the princess's comeback seemed a formality, but it was not long before the secretary revealed the terms.[24] Mary's moral fibre held, and Cromwell, who had clearly promised Henry to secure her submission, began (or so he said) to feel for the head on his own shoulders; there are signs indeed of Henry's own characteristic sledgehammer in the start of judicial moves against his daughter. By now, however, the secretary had enough on Mary's supporters to proceed against them; he convinced Henry that they were behind her obstinacy, thereby facing the princess with isolation and the loss of her friends. Fitzwilliam was excluded from the council, and his half-brother, Anthony Browne, interrogated. The seriousness of the situation is indicated by orders to list the treasurer's grants and offices, as was done when Rochford was arrested.[25] Exeter, too, was banned from the council, Lady Hussey was put in the Tower, and other court ladies found themselves being grilled by Cromwell and Audley, along with members of the privy chamber staff; and there was a burst of activity in the royal households, demanding that suspects should swear allegiance to the established succession.

At this point Mary succumbed both to the king's pressure and to the pleas of her friends to sign whatever her father wanted. She admitted all that was asked of her. Even so, Cromwell continued to press his enquiries, and despite denials to a man – and woman – of any disloyalty, and especially of any discussion of the bona fide argument about Mary's legitimacy, he soon had ample evidence for a charge of conspiracy far more convincing than that against Anne. Lady Hussey was still being held in the Tower under investigation as late as August.[26] This time, however, there was no need to press matters to the scaffold. The court, led by Mary, surrendered abjectly to the will of the king and his minister. Cromwell's triumph was complete. At the start of July Anne's father, Wiltshire, was required to hand over to him the office of lord privy seal, and a week later Cromwell was raised to the peerage.[27]

The relegation of Mary and her supporters to the periphery of power had a number of consequences. The fear Rochford had expressed on the scaffold, and which Cranmer had certainly shared, that Anne's destruction would mean the end of religious reform, would not now materialize. Instead, the clients she had promoted would remain to hold and consolidate a bridgehead for the Protestant religion in England. The defeated conservatives had nowhere to go and, although the rebellions which broke out in the autumn in Lincolnshire and the north were substantially popular and immediate in causation, one factor was undoubtedly the behaviour of Mary's discredited supporters.[28] Hussey and Darcy would die by the executioner's axe for their lukewarm loyalty, and although a number of Mary's friends chickened out of supporting the rebels in the field, an attitude of continued disaffection marked them out for suspicion. Several of Anne's conservative enemies thereby followed her to the scaffold – Exeter, Lord Montagu and Sir Edward Neville in December 1538, Carewe in the following March; Lady Exeter was in the Tower for eighteen months and her son for nearly fifteen years. Richard Tempest, one of the petty jury which condemned Norris and the other commoners, caught typhus and died in the Fleet Prison in August 1537; Giles Heron, foreman of the Middlesex grand jury which endorsed the original indictment, was drawn, hanged and quartered at Tyburn in August 1540.[29]

In the narrower confines of the royal court, the check to the Marian faction allowed some recovery among those associated with Anne. Richard Page was released from the Tower and restored to favour, but decided to give up being 'a daily courtier'.[30] Wyatt, who seems to have been protected by Cromwell himself, celebrated his release by telling the truth in circumspect but suggestive verse.[31] One poem attributed to him is an elegy on May 1536:

> In mourning wise since daily I increase,
> Thus should I cloak the cause of all my grief;
> So pensive mind with tongue to hold his peace
> My reason sayeth there can be no relief:
> Wherefore give ear, I humbly you require,

The affect to know that thus doth make me moan.
The cause is great of all my doleful cheer
For those that were, and now be dead and gone.

What though to death desert be now their call,
As by their faults it doth appear right plain?
Of force I must lament that such a fall
Should light on those so wealthily did reign,
Though some perchance will say, of cruel heart,
A traitor's death why should we thus bemoan?
But I alas, set this offence apart,
Must needs bewail the death of some be gone.

As for them all I do not thus lament,
But as of right my reason doth me bind;
But as the most doth all their deaths repent,
Even so do I by force of mourning mind.
Some say, 'Rochford, haddest thou been not so proud,
For thy great wit each man would thee bemoan,
Since as it is so, many cry aloud
It is great loss that thou art dead and gone'.

Ah! Norris, Norris, my tears begin to run
To think what hap did thee so lead or guide
Whereby thou hast both thee and thine undone
That is bewailed in court of every side;
In place also where thou hast never been
Both man and child doth piteously thee moan.
They say, 'Alas, thou art far overseen
By thine offences to be thus dead and gone'.

Ah! Weston, Weston, that pleasant was and young,
In active things who might with thee compare?
All words accept that thou diddest speak with tongue,
So well esteemed with each where thou diddest fare.
And we that now in court doth lead our life
Most part in mind doth thee lament and moan;
But that thy faults we daily hear so rife,
All we should weep that thou art dead and gone.

Brereton farewell, as one that least I knew.
Great was thy love with divers as I hear,
But common voice doth not so sore thee rue

As other twain that doth before appear;
But yet no doubt but thy friends thee lament
And other hear their piteous cry and moan.
So doth each heart for thee likewise relent
That thou givest cause thus to be dead and gone.

Ah! Mark, what moan should I for thee make more,
Since that thy death thou hast deserved best,
Save only that mine eye is forced sore
With piteous plaint to moan thee with the rest?
A time thou haddest above thy poor degree,
The fall whereof thy friends may well bemoan:
A rotten twig upon so high a tree
Hath slipped thy hold, and thou art dead and gone.

And thus farewell each one in hearty wise!
The axe is home, your heads be in the street;
The trickling tears doth fall so from my eyes
I scarce may write, my paper is so wet.
But what can hope when death hath played his part,
Though nature's course will thus lament and moan?
Leave sobs therefore, and every Christian heart
Pray for the souls of those be dead and gone.[32]

Of the victims, Wyatt misses only one – Anne herself. In the years to come few voices would be raised in her favour, though the king's rapid remarriage made suspicions about the official story widespread.[33] For her, the most poignant memorial was in the Tower of London, where it remains to this day on the wall of one of the cells in the Beauchamp Tower (plate 47). There crudely and hastily scratched by a man who knew he had little time, is Anne Boleyn's falcon.[34] Which of her 'lovers' made it we do not know, but the image is unmistakable. The tree-stump is there – the barren Henry – the Tudor rose-bush bursting into life, the perching bird whose touch wrought the miracle. But there is one change to the badge which Anne had proudly flourished in the face of the world. This falcon is no longer a royal bird. It has no crown, no sceptre; it stands bareheaded, as did Anne in those last moments on Tower Green.

EPILOGUE

F OR twenty years after May 1536, Anne Boleyn was a non-person. People who had known her said nothing, while the king, who knew most, grew old, obese and bad-tempered. When he had allowed Cromwell to strike Anne down, Henry had been at the height of his magnificence. By the time he allowed Cromwell himself to be struck down four years later, the physical deterioration was obvious. Four more attempts at marriage brought him little joy. Jane Seymour's death in childbirth left him with the son he had done so much evil to get, but his remaining wives were barren. Number four was divorced; number five, Katherine Howard, died by the axe on Tower Green and is buried in St Peter's, near her cousin Anne; but the luck of the sixth held out, despite the risks of mothering a sick and irascible old man. And all the while there was little said of Anne, and little left of her but her child, the young Elizabeth, who had been declared a bastard but who was nevertheless acknowledged as the king's daughter. Despite her youth and her mother's shame, she was a valuable card in the diplomatic marriage game and in 1544 she was restored to the succession. A 'very pretty', bright and intelligent girl, prematurely cautious. When her elder sister Mary came to the throne in 1553, the 20-year-old Elizabeth found she needed that caution as never before. On Palm Sunday 1554 Anne Boleyn's daughter was brought by river to the Tower of London, just as her mother had been almost eighteen years earlier. Suspected of plotting rebellion, she spent the next two months in the Bell Tower, followed by almost a year under house arrest in Oxfordshire.

In 1558, however, the miracle happened. On Monday, 28 November, to the cheers of the London crowd and the roar of the Tower artillery, Elizabeth came through the gates to take possession of the fortress as queen. The bastardized daughter of the disgraced Anne Boleyn, with her father's complexion but her mother's face, splendidly dressed in purple velvet: Elizabeth, by the grace of God, queen of England, France and Ireland, defender of the faith. Is it fanciful to feel that after twenty years, the mother in the nearby grave in the chapel of St Peter was at last vindicated?

NOTES

Chapter 1   A Courtier's Daughter

1   Parker, *Correspondence*, p. 400. In calling himself Anne's 'poor countryman', Parker is following sixteenth-century usage where 'country', applied within England, meant 'county' or district. For full information on all abbreviated titles, see Bibliographical Abbreviations, pp. 425–34.

2   For the Boleyn pedigree see J. C. Wedgwood and A. Holt, *History of Parliament: Biographies* (1936), pp. 90–1; *House of Commons*, i.456; G. E. C., *Peerage*, x.137–40.

3   Strickland, *Queens of England*, ii.273.

4   For William Boleyn see *Cal. Close Rolls, Henry VII* (1955–63), i.143; *Cal. Inquisitions Post Mortem, Henry VII* (1898–1955), i.322; Polydore Vergil, *Anglica Historia*, ed. D. Hay, Camden Society, 3rd series, 74 (1950), pp. 52, 94.

5   *LP*, xi.17.

6   The earl of Ormonde was chamberlain to Henry VII's wife, Elizabeth of York.

7   G. E. C., *Peerage*, x.137.

8   *LP*, i.20 (p. 13).

9   Sergeant, *Anne Boleyn*, p. 50.

10   Friedmann, *Anne Boleyn*, i.55.

11   *St. Pap.*, i.490 [*LP*, xi.842]. Cf. his treatment of Tunstal in 1530: Starkey, *Six Wives*, p. 367.

12   Brewer, *Henry VIII*, i.168 n.2.

13   *LP*, iii.3386.

14   For a classic discussion of the following see S. Anglo, 'The Courtier', in *The Courts of Europe*, ed. A. G. Dickens (1977), pp. 33–53.

15   BL, King's MS 9, ff. 66v, 231.

16   Quoted in Fletcher and MacCulloch, *Tudor Rebellions* (1997), p. 134.

17   Thomas More, *Utopia*, trans. Ralph Robinson (1556), ed. E. Arber (1869), p. 55.

18   Ibid., pp. 64–5.

19   For Wyatt see Thomson, *Sir Thomas Wyatt and his Background*; Muir, *The Life and Letters of Sir Thomas Wyatt*, and pp. 67–80 above.

20   Wyatt, *Poems*, CV, lines 56–64. Wyatt was reworking a recently published Provençal satire on court life. For this and Wyatt's modifications see *Collected Poems of Sir Thomas Wyatt*, ed. K. Muir and P. Thomson (Liverpool, 1969), pp. 347–50: 'colours of device' = deceptions; 'join the mean' etc. = accept outrageous behaviour as normal; 'as to purpose likewise' = and likewise as it shall be opportune.

21   Ibid., CV, lines 14–16. 'me list' etc. = I do not wish to criticize honour and seek it at the same time.

22   Ibid., CVII, lines 18–28.

23   For a discussion of this satire see David Starkey, 'The Court: Castiglione's ideal and Tudor reality', in *Journal of the*

Warburg and Courtauld Institutes, 45 (1982), 232–9.

24 Muir, *Life and Letters of Wyatt*, p. 216.

25 He probably had some legal training also: *LP*, i.438 (3 m.7). For his career generally see G. E. C., *Peerage* and *Dictionary of National Biography* (1885–1900), v.321. For Boleyn and Erasmus see below, p. 270. For his linguistic ability see *LP*, viii, p. 71.

26 G. E. C., *Peerage*, x.140–2; *Tottel's Miscellany*, ed. H. E. Rollins (Cambridge, Mass., 1965), ii.83. For George's translations see pp. 271–2.

27 *LP*, i.App.9; Anglo, *Great Tournament Roll*, p. 55.

28 On tournaments and court festivals generally see ibid., pp. 19–40; Anglo, *Spectacle*, pp. 108–23.

29 Anglo, *Great Tournament Roll*, p. 54.

30 Hall, *Chronicle*, p. 518.

31 *LP*, ii.1500–2; cf. ibid., ii.1490.

32 *Cal. S. P. Span., 1529–30*, p. 422.

33 *LP*, i.1448.

34 Ibid., i.1338.

35 J. A. Guy, *The Cardinal's Court* (Hassocks, Sussex, 1977), pp. 28, 99.

36 *LP*, ii.1475.

37 For the debt of the English court to Burgundy see Kipling, *Triumph of Honour*.

38 For this and the following paragraph see A. R. Myers, *The Household of Edward IV* (Manchester, 1959); Starkey, thesis, and 'Intimacy and Innovation' in *The English Court from the Wars of the Roses to the Civil War*, ed. David Starkey (1987), pp. 71–118

39 The ordinance promulgated at Eltham in 1526 was directed towards reform in the management of the royal household, but Wolsey used the opportunity to remove several courtiers from their privileged positions in the privy chamber: thesis, pp. 133–81. Dr Starkey has identified the importance of privy chamber office – it gave access to the king *ex officio* and promised predictability of contact with him; hence the constant and almost irresistible demand for places. Yet many privy chamber appointees made little mark, and in any discussion of privy chamber influence allowance has to be made for royal cronies without formal posts.

40 *LP*, ii.124, 125.

41 Ibid., iii.223.

42 Ibid., ii.2487, 2500; Giustinian, *Four Years at the Court of Henry VIII*, i.320, 326.

43 *LP*, ii.4409.

44 Ibid., iii.118.

45 Ibid., iii.223.

46 BL, Cotton MS Cal.D vii, f. 118 [*LP*, iii.246].

47 Hall, *Chronicle*, p. 598; Giustinian, *Four Years at the Court of Henry VIII*, ii.270–1.

48 *LP*, iii.447.

49 By Sept. 1520 (*St. Pap.*, ii.57).

50 *LP*, iii.1712, 2481, g.2587. He was succeeded by Sir Henry Guildford.

51 e.g. ibid., ii.3489; iii.491, 528.

52 Ibid., iii.p. 1539.

53 Herbert, *Henry VIII*, p. 399; Sander, *Schism*, p. 25; William Camden, *Annales* (1612), p. 2. The weight of argument favoured 1507, see J. H. Round, *The Early Life of Anne Boleyn* (1886), pp. 12–23; Brewer, *Henry VIII*, ii.170; J. Gairdner, 'Mary and Anne Boleyn', and 'The Age of Anne Boleyn', in *EHR*, 8 (1893), 53–60; 10 (1895), 104. Friedmann's conjecture of 1503 or 1504 [*Anne Boleyn*, ii.315] was based on a fallacious pictorial identification.

54 Corpus Christi College, Cambridge, MS 119, f. 21.

55 For the following see Paget, in *BIHR*, 54, 162–70 and pp. 19, 26–7 above.

56 Warnicke, *Rise and Fall*, pp. 9, 12–16. The attempted analogy with Anne Brandon [ibid. p. 12] is unhelpful as her date of birth is uncertain and so too her status at Brussels.

57 Clifford, *Dormer*, p. 80.

58 *LP*, viii.567.

59 Ibid., iv.546(2).

60   Cavendish, *Metrical Visions*, p. 21; *LP*, iv.1939(14).

61   See pp. 59–60.

62   *St. Pap.*, vii.219.

63   Du Bellay, *Correspondance*, i.105. George was married by the end of 1525 and so must have been born no later than 1511 [*LP*, iv.1939(14)]. His part in the Christmas revels of 1514–15 [*LP*, ii.1501] was obviously as a child.

64   Ibid., xii(2), 952. See also Friedmann, ii.325–6.

65   *LP*, vi.923; viii.565(2), 567, 862; cf. ix.1123.

66   Later Catholic writers got round this problem by alleging that Anne was conceived in 1509 during the absence of Thomas Boleyn on a supposed embassy to France lasting two years: e.g. Trumble MS 5 (Berkshire Record Office), 'La vie de Anne Boulein ou de Bouloigne', and Eyston MS vii g15 (private collection), 'The Character and Life of the Lady Anne Boulen'. I am indebted to Messrs T. M. and E. Eyston for access to the latter.

67   Gairdner, in *EHR*, 8, 58–9.

68   Most recently R. M. Warnicke, 'Anne Boleyn's childhood and adolescence', in *Historical Journal*, 28 (1985), 942–3, and *Rise and Fall*, pp. 9, 258.

69   Warnicke claims that Anne was the elder on the ground that priority is implied by her being appointed at Brussels [ibid. p. 9]. This is unconvincing since Mary, if the elder, would have been too old for appointment, to say nothing of her evident inferior potential. The description of Anne being brought up as a child in the royal nurseries of Burgundy and France [ibid, 12–13, 17–23] is entirely suppositious. Her alleged childhood companion, Renée, duchess of Ferrara, (b. 1510) remembered Anne as *a maid of honour*: ibid, p 41. Furthermore, Mary was no landed heiress, so a marriage in 1520, when she was not yet 12, would have been exceptional; *pace* Warnicke, *Rise and Fall*, pp. 34–5. This would also make her

Henry's mistress at the latest in her very early teens.

70   See p. 84.

71   Marriage would normally signal the end of a royal amour with a single woman. Elizabeth was Lady Tailbois at the latest by June 1522 but could have been married as early as the second half of 1519, following the birth of Richmond: Murphy, *Bastard Prince*, pp. 31–3. In that case any liaison with Mary prior to her marriage would have been a very brief fling, but cf. the date of the royal grants. My suggestion [*Anne Boleyn*, p. 20] that there is significance in *The Mary Boleyn* being part of the royal fleet in 1523 was mistaken; she was originally a Boleyn vessel. *LP*, iii.3358.

72   *LP*, x.450: 'per una grandissima ribalda et infame sopre butte'. But if Mary was younger than Anne, she could not have been more than 12 in 1514.

73   *House of Commons*, iii.419.

74   LP, iii.510; xii(i).822. Gardiner was in post by 1528: William Dugdale, *Monasticon* (1817–30), iii.307.

75   Her first child, Henry Carey, was born in March 1526. The story that he was the king's son was spread about by supporters of Katherine: *LP*, viii.567. For Henry's fertility see pp. 190–1.

76   See pp. 34–5.

77   *LP*, xi.17.

78   *Cal. Close Rolls, Henry VII* (1955–63), ii.179.

79   See the brasses at Hever and Penshurst: M. Stephenson, *List of Monumental Brasses* (1926), ii.236, 251.

Chapter 2   A European Education

1   De Boom, *Marguerite d'Autriche*, p. 118. For this chapter see also T. Kren, 'Flemish Manuscript Illumination', and Janet Backhouse, 'French Manuscript Illu-

mination' in *Renaissance Painting in Manuscript*, ed. T. Kren (1983), pp. 69–78, 147–92; de Iongh, *Margaret of Austria*; Otto Pächt, *The Master of Mary of Burgundy* (1948); Sterling, *Master of Claude*; *The New Grove Dictionary of Music* (1980), *passim*.

2 Warnicke argues that the queen in question was Henry's sister Mary: *Rise and Fall*, p.15. It is difficult to see why, if this was the case, Anne should need to learn French to converse with her: see below, n.5.

3 Neither the copy of Margaret's letter reporting the arrival of Anne, nor Anne's own letter, is dated. She could not have gone before Boleyn had established himself at the Burgundian court, where he arrived in May 1512, and the letter recalling her to England is dated 14 August 1514. The summer of 1513 looks the most likely date within this period, because Margaret's letter shows that Boleyn was then back in England, and he was in the Low Countries continuously from 26 June 1512 to early May 1513. Margaret was expecting Boleyn back, and thus earlier end-date is the arrival of new English ambassadors in February 1514: Paget, in *BIHR*, 54, 164–5; *LP*, i.2655.

4 Paget, in *BIHR*, 54, 164–5.

5 Ibid., 54, 166; Sergeant, *Anne Boleyn*, pp. 275–6.

6 See p. 148.

7 De Boom, *Marguerite d'Autriche*, pp. 126–7.

8 Anglo, *Spectacle*, pp. 102–3, 107, 116–19.

9 De Boom, *Marguerite d'Autriche*, pp. 43, 52.

10 Quoted in ibid., p. 123.

Fiez-vous y en vos servans
Dehure en avant, mes demoiselles,
Et vous vous trouverés de celles
Qui en ont eu des décepvans.
Ils son en leurs ditz, observans
Motz plus doulx que doulces pucelles,
Fiés-vous-y.

En leurs cueurs ils sont conservans,
Pour decepvoir, maintes cautelles,
Et puis que ils ont leurs fassons telles,
Touts ainsi comme abavantz
Fiés-vous-y.

11 Quoted in ibid., pp. 123–4.

Belles paroles en paiement,
A ces mignons présumptieux
Qui contrefont les amoureux,
Par beau samblant et aultrement,
Sans nul credo, mais promptement,
Donnés pour récompense a eulx
Belles paroles.
Mot pour mot, c'est fait justement,
Ung pour ung, aussi deulx pour deulx,
Se devis ils font gracieulx,
Respondés gracieusement
Belles paroles.

12 *Cal. S. P. Ven., 1509–19*, 1235.

13 For Margaret see Till-Holger Borchet, *The Age of Van Eyck* (Bruges, 2002), especially D. Eichberger, 'The Habsburgs and the cultural heritage of Burgundy', pp. 187–92.

14 Kipling, *Triumph of Honour*, pp. 3–10.

15 Ibid., pp. 61, 68–71.

16 Margaret owned two works by Bosch, one a *Temptation of St Antony*, and two by Jan van Eyck, *The Virgin and Child by a Fountain* (Koninklijk Museum, Antwerp) and *The Arnolfini Marriage* (National Gallery, London).

17 Margaret owned this by 1516. See Lorne Campbell, *The Fifteenth Century Netherlandish Schools* (National Gallery 1998), p. 174.

18 osterreichische Nationalbibliothek, Vienna. Cod. 1857, f. 43v.

19 See pp. 6–7.

20 See pp. 257–9.

21 Lowinsky, in *Florilegium*, fig. 13.

22 De Carles, in Ascoli, *L'Opinion*, lines 43–8.

23 Scarisbrick, *Henry VIII*, pp. 36–7; de Iongh, *Margaret of Austria*, pp. 148–9.

24 *LP*, i.2375.

25 De Iongh, *Margaret of Austria*, pp. 150–1; Brewer, *Henry VIII*, i.5; de Boom, *Marguerite d'Autriche*, pp. 118–19; *LP*, i.2941; *Chronicle of Calais*, pp. 71–6.

26 Paget, *BIHR*, 54, 167.

27 The list of Mary Tudor's ladies paid for the period Oct. to Dec. 1514 includes Marie Boulonne, but not Anne [Paris, BNF, MS fr.7853, f. 305b]. The list includes Anne de Boulogne and Magdaleine de Boulogne, but these had been paid from 1509 [ibid., ff. 311, 313]. I am indebted to R. J. Knecht for the references to this MS, which is of extracts from a lost original. The names agree with those in *LP*, i.3357, except for the payment to Mary Fiennes, which must argue for the reliability of the transcription.

28 *LP*, i.3348(3).

29 *LP*, i.3348(3), 3357.

30 Ibid., i.3355, 3356.

31 Carles, in Ascoli, *L'Opinion*, lines 37–42.

32 See p. 16.

33 A journey partly by post and without hitches took, in 1531, six days inclusive, Brussels to London: *Cal. S. P. Ven. 1527–33*, 682.

34 *LP*, i.3235.

35 Scarisbrick, *Henry VIII*, pp. 54–5.

36 Pollard, *Henry VIII* (1951), p. 51; Knecht, *Francis I*, p. 38 n.4.

37 *LP*, ii.80.

38 de Carles, in Ascoli, *L'Opinion*, lines 49–51; Herbert, *Henry VIII*, pp. 161, 218.

39 Jan. 1519 to Mar. 1520; see p. 10; Sander, *Schism*, p. 25; Friedmann, *Anne Boleyn*, ii.320. But cf. Gairdner, in *EHR*, 8, 56.

40 Knecht, *Renaissance Warrior and Patron*, pp. 114–16, 134–7.

41 de Carles, in Ascoli, *L'Opinion*, lines 55–8.

42 Sander, *Schism*, p. 25; BL, Sloane MS 2495, f. 2v. The author claimed to know eyewitnesses of Henry VIII's funeral.

43 Lowinsky, in *Florilegium*, pp. 206–17; see pp. 257–9.

44 Knecht, *Renaissance Warrior and Patron*, p. 140.

45 J. Harthan, *Books of Hours* (1977), pp. 134–7.

46 Sterling, *Master of Claude*, pp. 16–17.

47 Ibid., pp. 11–15.

48 See pp. 242–3.

49 Francis's sexual excesses were at their worst later in life: Knecht, *Francis I*, p. 428 n.7.

50 Anne Puaux, *La Huguenotte: Renée de France* (Paris, 1997), p. 27; Knecht, *Renaissance Warrior and Patron*, p. 83.

51 Knecht, *Renaissance Warrior and Patron*, pp. 114–16.

52 See p. 229.

53 *LP*, ii.4674, 4675. According to Hall, *Chronicle*, p. 596, her father was also present.

54 Russell, *Cloth of Gold*, pp. 195, 202, quoting Oxford, Bodleian, MS Ashmole 1116. This gives [p. 204]: 'Cary Lord Fitzwater's daughter', but *Rutland Papers*, ed. W. Jerdan, Camden Soc., 21 (1842), p. 38 divides this entry into two, and *Chronicle of Calais*, p. 25, lists 'mistres Carie' and later 'mistres Margery, Lord Fitzwaren's dowghter'.

55 *St. Pap.*, vi.56.

56 Russell, *Cloth of Gold*, pp. 159–61; Knecht, *Renaissance Warrior and Patron*, pp. 114–16.

57 Russell, *Cloth of Gold*, pp. 124–5.

58 Sterling, *Master of Claude*, pp. 8–9.

59 For language problems among the ladies see Russell, *Cloth of Gold*, p. 125.

60 Sander, *Schism*, p. 56; George Wyatt, *Papers*, p. 143; Dowling, in *JEH*, 35, 32, referring to *Extracts from the Life of the virtuous...Queen Anne Boleigne*, ed. R. Triphook (1817), pp. 14–15.

61 Herbert, *Henry VIII*, p. 399.

62 *Cal. S. P. Span., Suppl. 1513–42*, p. 30; *LP*, iii.1994. Anne does not appear in Marguerite's accounts: *Comptes de Louise de Savoie et de Marguerite d'Angoulême*, ed. A. Lefranc and J. Boulenger (Paris, 1905).

63 Jourda, *Marguerite d'Angoulême* (Paris, 1930), i.56

64 *Cal. S. P. Span., 1531–33*, pp. 257, 990; *LP*, v.1187.
65 Jourda, *Marguerite d'Angoulême*, i.172; *Cal. S. P. Span., 1531–33*, p. 588.
66 See p. 157.
67 *LP*, ix.378; *St. Pap.*, vii.566 [*LP*, vii.958].
68 *LP*, vi.692.
69 *St. Pap.*, vii.565–9 [*LP*, vii.958]; *Cal. S. P. Span., 1534–5*, p. 229; *Lisle Letters*, ii.240 [*LP*, vii.1014].
70 *LP*, ix.838.
71 *Cal. S. P. Span., Suppl. 1513–42*, p. 30, quoting a report which can be dated 12–14 Jan. 1522; *LP*, iii.1994, dated 11–23 Jan. 1522. But the ambassador with the original complaint had left France before 6 Jan. [*LP*, iii.1946], possibly before 26 Dec. 1521 [ibid., iii.1947], making it certain that Anne left France in 1521.
72 Ibid., ii.1277.
73 Ibid., ii.1230, 1269.
74 *St. Pap.*, ii.49 [*LP*, iii.1628]; D. B. Quinn, 'Henry VIII and Ireland, 1509–34', in *Irish Historical Studies*, 12 (1961), 331; the letter of 6 Oct. 1520 could be taken to hint that Butler favoured the scheme at an early stage, which would explain his support for Surrey: *St. Pap.*, ii.50–1 [*LP*, iii.1011].
75 Ibid., ii.35, 58 [*LP*, iii.924, 1034].
76 Ibid., ii.50–1 [*LP*, iii.1011].
77 Ibid., ii.63 [*LP*, iii.1099]; *LP*, iii.1926.
78 Ibid., i.69; ii.49, 84, 91 (*LP*, iii.1646, 1628, 1583, 1830].
79 Ibid., i.69–70, 72–3, 76–7, 81–2; ii.88–91 [*LP*, iii.1646, 1675, 1709, 1718]; *LP*, iii.1719.
80 *St. Pap.*, i.92 [*LP*, iii.1762].
81 *LP*, iii.1817.
82 *St. Pap.*, ii.100 [*LP*, iii.3048].
83 Ibid., ii.101 [*LP*, iii.3049]. Kildare had supported Boleyn and St Leger in 1516; see above, p. 34.
84 *LP*, iv.3937, 3950.
85 Quinn, in *Irish Historical Studies*, 12, 333. James was at court until at least 27

Aug. 1526 [*LP*, iii.1628; iv.1279, 2433]. For Anne's other suitors see chapter 3.
86 James Butler was in Ireland from at least 27 Dec. 1527 to 20 May 1528, at court on 26 June 1528 and in Ireland again by 18 Sept. 1528 [*LP*, iv.3698, 3922, 3952, 4283, 4422, 4748]. For a convincing identification of the Windsor Holbein 'Ormond' [Parker, *Drawings*, no. 23] as James Butler, see David Starkey, 'Holbein's Irish sitter?' in *Burlington Magazine*, 123 (1981), 300–3.

Chapter 3   Début at the English Court

1 *LP*, iii.1559; *Cal. S. P. Span., Suppl. 1513–42*, pp. 69–73; Hall, *Chronicle*, p. 631.
2 Ibid., p. 519.
3 Anglo, *Spectacle*, pp. 121, 179–80. It is clear from Hall's account that Henry was not Ardent Desire [*pace* Anglo, ibid., p. 121]. Since Ardent Desire was a speaking role in dialogue with the Children, he was probably not a courtier at all. Cornish had played similar roles in other entertainments [ibid., pp. 119–20].
4 *LP*, iii.1559.
5 *Cal. S. P. Span., Suppl. 1513–42*, p. 86.
6 RO, PRO 31/8f. 51 [*LP*, vi.485].
7 See the accounts cited, p. 392 n. 5. For Anne's and the other Tudor royal crowns and the ceremony, see J. Arnold, 'The coronation portrait of Queen Elizabeth I', in *Burlington Magazine*, 120 (1978), 731–2.
8 Ibid., 120, 727–41; NPG, no. 5175.
9 Sander, *Schism*, p. 25.
10 George Wyatt, in *Wolsey*, ed. Singer, p. 424.
11 Carles, in Ascoli, *L'Opinion*, line 61; *Cal. S. P. Ven., 1527–33*, 236.
12 *Cal. S. P. Span., 1531–33*, p. 473. Contradictory versions have been published of what Barlow said, muddling the terms used: '*ladite dame*' and '*ladite fille*'.

The context makes clear that the former is Anne, and the BL text reads in the original: '*Ledit doyen* [Barlow] *respondit qu'il avoit connaisance tant de ladite dame que de ladite fille, et que ladite fille estoit plus belle que ladite dame mais ladite dame estoit bien eloquente et gracieux et competement belle et de bonne maison*' [Add. MS 28585, f. 45].

13   *Original Letters*, ii.553.

14   *Cal. S. P. Ven., 1527–33*, 824.

15   See, pp. 74–5.

16   *Original Letters*, ii.553; *Cal. S. P. Ven., 1527–33*, 824; Carles, in Ascoli, *L'Opinion*, lines 170–1.

17   *Ordinances for the Household*, pp. 123–4. For the creation as lady marchioness, see pp. 158–9.

18   NPG, *Portraits*, i.7. Seventeenth-century inventories reveal that other portraits of Anne did exist, e.g. Historical Manuscripts Commission, *Manuscripts of the Marquess of Ormonde*, new series (1902–20), vii.507.

19   H. M. the Queen, Windsor [Parker, *Drawings*, no. 63]. BM, Dept. of Prints and Drawings, 'Portrait of a Lady', 1975-6-21-22.

20   For the vicissitudes of the Holbein drawings, see Parker, *Drawings*, pp. 7–20; J. Rowlands, 'A portrait drawing by Hans Holbein the younger', in *British Museum Yearbook*, 2 (1977), 231–7.

21   John Rowlands and David Starkey, 'An old tradition reasserted: Holbein's portrait of Queen Anne Boleyn', in *Burlington Magazine*, 125 (1983), 88–92, argue for the identification of the Windsor drawing as that of Anne, on the basis of Cheke's authority and on circumstantial grounds. However, the fact that Margaret Gigges, More's foster daughter, is called 'Mother Iak', i.e. Mrs Jackson, Edward VI's nurse, whom Cheke as the king's tutor must have known, must cast doubt on the story about the identifications being made by him. More's daughter-in-law Elizabeth Dauncey, called 'The Lady Barkley', is similarly worrying; Parker,

Drawings, p. 53 no. 63; Ives in *Apollo*, 140, 42.

22   Rowlands, in *British Museum Yearbook*, 2, 233–4.

23   The above summarizes E. W. Ives, 'The queen and the painters: Anne Boleyn, Holbein and Tudor royal portraits', in *Apollo*, 140 (1994), 40–4.

24   BM, Dept. of Coins and Medals. G. Hill, *Medals of the Renaissance*, rev. J. G. Pollard (1978), p. 145.

25   e.g. J. Rowlands, *The Age of Dürer and Holbein* (1988), p. 236.

26   Engraved by Richard Elstrack and published in Thomas Holland, *Baziliwlogia* (1618), the only queen consort to appear in this series of English monarchs.

27   NPG, *Portraits*, ii. plate 10.

28   NPG, no. 668.

29   P. Somerset Fry, *Chequers, the Country Home of Britain's Prime Ministers* (1977), p. 52; *Catalogue of the Principal Works of Art at Chequers* (HMSO, 1923), no. 507; *Princely Magnificence: Court Jewels of the Renaissance* (Victoria and Albert Museum, London, 1980–1), no. 37 and p. 26; *Elizabeth*, ed. Doran, pp. 12–13. A. G. Somers Cocks has suggested that the appearance of an enamel phoenix arising from a flaming crown beneath the bezel of the ring indicates a connection with Edward Seymour, earl of Hertford, who campaigned ceaselessly to get Elizabeth I to recognize his marriage with Jane Grey's sister, Katherine. The device, however, would serve a double reference for Elizabeth, who both used the phoenix symbol and had risen miraculously from the flames of the destruction of her mother, the only one of Henry VIII's later wives to wear a crown. The ring is not mentioned in the inventories of Elizabeth's jewels, but must have been made for her, or as an elaborate gesture of loyalty to her, and the association of the image is secure either way.

30   The apparently inferior version of the National Portrait Gallery pattern owned

(1969) by Mrs K. Radclyffe agrees with the version at Hever (plate 1): NPG, *Portraits*, ii. plate 9.

31   Duke of Buccleuch and Queensberry. H. A. Kennedy, *Early Portrait Miniatures in the Collection of the Duke of Buccleuch*, ed. C. Holmes (1917), no. C8: 'From an ancient original' is written on the back of the mounting.

32   NPG, *Portraits*, i.7.

33   Cf. the close similarity of pose with the *Portrait of a Lady* at Toledo, wrongly disseminated as *Catherine Howard*: NPG, *Portraits*, i.42–4; Rowlands, *Paintings*, cat. 69.

34   Strong, *Artists*, no. 14 and pp. 39–40; Strong, *Renaissance Miniature*, no. 22 and pp. 36, 189.

35   *Love Letters*, p. 47 [*LP*, iv.4597].

36   De Carles, in Ascoli, *L'Opinion*, lines 62–8; cf. William Forrest, *The History of Grisild the Second*, ed. M. D. Macray (1875), lines 52–3. *pace* Warnicke, *Rise and Fall*, p. 270, Forrest was not chaplain to Katherine of Aragon but to her daughter, Mary I.

37   De Carles, in Ascoli, *L'Opinion*, lines 75–84.

38   Cavendish, *Wolsey*, p. 29.

39   George Wyatt, *Papers*, p. 143.

40   BL, Sloane MS 2495, f. 2v.

41   Oxford, Bodleian MS C. Don. 42, f. 32.

42   Sander, *Schism*, p. 25.

43   George Wyatt, in *Wolsey*, ed. Singer, p. 423; de Carles, in Ascoli, *L'Opinion*, lines 53–4.

Chapter 4   Sources

1   *Correspondence of Reginald Pole*, ed. T. F. Mayer (2002), i. 101, 106, 108.

2   Cavendish, *Metrical Visions*, pp. 41–2.

3   Hist. Mss. Comm., *Various Collections* (1901–14), iii.131.

4   A substantial early 17th-century attack on Anne with elaborate late 17th-century annotations exists in the library of the descendants of John More the younger: Eyston MS vii g15.

5   William Roper, *The Life, Arraignement and Death of... Syr Thomas More*, ed. E. V. Hitchcock. Early English Text Society, 197 (1935), p. 74.

6   Sander, *Schism*, p. 23 n.2.

7   Harpsfield, *More*, p. 235.

8   *LP*, vii.289 at pp. 123–4.

9   BL, Sloane MS 2495, f. 27.

10   Foxe, *Acts and Monuments*, v. 136–7.

11   Ibid., v.137.

12   John Aylmer, *An harborowe for faithfull and trewe subiectes* (Strassburg, 1559), sig. B4v.; John Bridges, *The Supremacie of Christian Princes* (1573), p. 853.

13   William Thomas, *The Pilgrim*, ed. J. A. Froude (1861), p. 70.

14   George Wyatt, *Papers*, pp. 141, 143.

15   Raphael Holinshed, *Chronicles* (1577), 1565.

16   Foxe, *Acts and Monuments*, v. 136.

17   Oxford, Bodl. MS C. Don. 42, ff. 20–33; RO, SP70/7, ff. 1–11 [*Cal. S. P. For.*, 1558–9, 1303].

18   George Wyatt, *Papers*, pp. 20–1.

19   *Nicolai Sanderi, De origine ac progressu Schismatis Anglicani liber*, ed. Edward Rishton (Cologne, 1585); see pp. 39–40.

20   Dowling, Cronickille, p. 40.

21   'The Life' was edited in *The Life of Cardinal Wolsey by George Cavendish*, ed. S. W. Singer (2nd edn, 1827), pp. 417–49; 'The History' in George Wyatt, *Papers*, ed. D. M. Loades. Camden Soc., 4th series, 5 (1968), pp. 19–30; 'A Defence of Sir Thomas Wyatt the elder, etc.' in ibid., pp. 181–205.

22   Ibid., pp. 24, 29, 185–6.

23   J. A. Guy, *Thomas More* (2000), pp. 151–63; G. R. Elton, 'Sir Thomas More and the opposition to Henry VIII', in *Studies*, i.155–72.

24   *Cronica del Rey Enrico*, p. 88; *Chronicle*, ed. Hume, at p. 68; Muir, *Life and*

Letters of Wyatt, p. 221; Wyatt, *Poems*, CXLIII.

25 George Wyatt, *Papers*, p. 27; in *Wolsey*, ed. Singer, p. 422; see pp. 132–3.

26 For the following see Freeman, *Hist. Journ.* 38 (1995), 797–819.

27 See *Narratives of the Reformation*.

28 G. Mattingly, *Renaissance Diplomacy* (Boston, 1955).

29 *Cal. S. P. Ven., 1534–54*, 31, 242.

30 *LP*, vi.184.

31 Ibid., viii.174.

32 Ibid., vi.614.

33 He arrived 24 Dec. 1531 [ibid., v. 614] and was replaced Nov. 1532 [ibid., v.1531, 1579]; in Brittany: ibid., v.1013, 1110. Chapuys guessed he returned a week earlier: ibid., v.1109.

34 *Cal. S. P. Span., 1531–33*, pp. 378, 417, 463–4, 475–7, 525, 561; *LP*, v.614.

35 *Cal. S. P. Span., 1531–33*, p. 466 (*LP*, v.1109].

36 For this and the following see G. Mattingly, 'A humanist ambassador', in *Journal of Modern History*, 4 (1932), 175–85.

37 *Cal. S. P. Span., 1531–33*, p. xxvii; ibid., *1536–38*, p. xviii.

38 Ibid., *Suppl. 1513–42*, pp. xxxviii, 452.

39 Friedmann, *Anne Boleyn*, i. p. viii. To be fair to Friedmann, he was contrasting this with English duplicity, and he later made points qualifying this encomium: ibid., i. p. xiv.

40 See p. 361.

41 Warnicke, *Rise and Fall*, pp. 1–3 and passim.

42 *Privy Purse Expenses of King Henry the Eighth*, ed. N. H. Nicolas (1827), from BL, Add. MS 20030.

43 *The Inventory of King Henry VIII*, ed. David Starkey (1998).

44 Edited in Wriothesley, *Chronicle of England*, i.189–226.

45 T. Amyot (ed.), 'A memorial from George Constantine', in *Archaeologia*, 23 (1831), 50–78.

46 Burnet, *History*, iv.291–2; vii.239–40; *LP*, x.808; Herbert, *Henry VIII*, pp. 569–70. Cf. the genuine letter from Katherine of Aragon: Mattingly, *Catherine of Aragon*, p. 308.

47 Anne was not allowed to send letters: *Wolsey*, ed. Singer, p. 454.

48 BL, Add. MS 15117, 17492, etc. Quoted Shakespeare, *Henry IV, part 2*: II iv 191. Published in John Hawkins, *History of Music* (1776) as communicated to him 'by a very judicious antiquary, written either by or in the person of Anne Boleyn'.

49 How the letters reached Rome is not known. Most probably this was in Mary's reign. The failure to use them in the divorce suit disposes of the suggestion that the letters were purloined to assist Katherine's case: Warnicke, *Rise and Fall*, pp. 76–7; Starkey, *Six Wives*, p. 278.

50 *The Love Letters of Henry VIII*, ed. H. Savage (1949), pp. 27–48; *LP*, iv.3218–21, 3325–6, 3990, 4383, 4403, 4410, 4477, 4537, 4539, 4597, 4648, 4742, 4894. The Savage edition must take priority because it contains photographs of the letters, but readings below usually follow *The Private Lives of the Tudor Monarchs*, ed. C. Falkus (1974), whose translations are normally to be preferred.

51 *The Lisle Letters*, ed. M. St. Clare Byrne (1981).

52 See pp. 177–8, 181.

53 Cavendish, *Metrical Visions*, pp. 20–47.

54 *The Life and Death of Cardinal Wolsey by George Cavendish*, ed. R. S. Sylvester. Early English Text Society, 243 (1959). The completion date of the MS containing both the *Metrical Visions* and the *Life* was 24 June 1558.

55 The (revealing) full title of the *Chronicle* is *The Vnion of the two noble and illustre famelies of Lancastre and Yorke beeyng long in continual discension for the croune of this noble realme, with all the actes done... beginnyng at the tyme of Kyng Henry the Fowerth, the first aucthor of this deuision*

and so successiuely proceadyng to the reigne of the high and prudent prince Kyng Henry the Eight, the vndubitate flower and very heire of both the sayd linages.

56 Ibid., ed. H. Ellis (1809), pp. 789–90, 793–6, 798–806, 818–19.

57 Wriothesley, Chronicle, i. pp. ii–vi.

58 BL, Add. MS 40662; Brussels, Bibliothèque Royale Albert Ier, MS 19378, ff. 1–19v. For a collation of Paris, BNF f.fr. no. 12795 collated with six versions in France see G. Ascoli, *La Grande-Bretagne devant l'opinion française* (Paris, 1927). The poem, printed as *Epistre contenant le proces criminel faict a l'encontre de la royne Anne Boullant d'Angleterre*, by Carles, aulmosnier de Monsieur le Dauphin (Lyons, 1545), was reprinted in *Lettres de Henri VIII à Anne Boleyn*, ed. G. A. Crapelet (Paris, 1826), pp. 167–214. It is probably the Brussels MS '*Traictie pour feue dame Anne de Boulant, jadis Royne d'Angleterre, l'an Quinzecem trent trois*' that Meteren used for his account of Anne's fall, which was taken up by Burnet, *History*, iii. 222–5. A 'fantasy' by a French prothonotary 'touching the process of the late Marquis of Pembroke and of her complices' was sent to Henry by Paget in 1543: *St. Pap.* ix.346 [*LP*, xviii.381].

59 De Carles cannot have seen the trial in the Tower as he reverses the order, placing Rochford's first, but the Westminster Hall trial account shows a good acquaintance with English criminal procedure.

60 Bernard, in *EHR* 106, 596; Ives, in *EHR* 107, 657–9.

61 *LP*, x.873

62 Comparing Hall, *Chronicle*, p. 819; Wriothesley, *Chronicle*, i.41–2; Friedmann, *Anne Boleyn*, ii.295 n.2, with de Carles, in Ascoli, *L'Opinion*, lines 1235–9.

63 Another French MS poem tells the story of Rochford in the first person: in ibid., pp. 273–8.

64 Friedmann, *Anne Boleyn*, ii.312.

65 Smith, *Henry VIII, p. 36.*

Chapter 5 Passion and Courtly Love

1 Cavendish, *Wolsey*, p. 35.

2 Ibid., pp. 29–34.

3 Friedmann, *Anne Boleyn*, i.44 interpreted this as a request to break his earlier betrothal to Mary Talbot, but such a construction is clearly wrong.

4 J. M. W. Bean, *The Estates of the Percy Family, 1416–1537* (Oxford, 1958), pp. 144–57; cf. M. E. James, *Change and Continuity in the Tudor North* (York, 1965), pp. 13–15; R. W. Hoyle, 'Henry Percy, sixth earl of Northumberland and the fall of the house of Percy 1527–37', in *The Tudor Nobility*, ed. G. W. Bernard (1992), pp. 188–211.

5 *LP*, viii.166.

6 *Illustrations of British History*, ed. E. Lodge (1838), i.20–1; *LP*, ii.1893, 1935, 1969–70, 3819, 3820; E. B. de Fonblanque, *Annals of the House of Percy* (1887), i.385.

7 David Starkey's suggestion that the liaison lasted beyond 1523 does not allow time for the legalities needed to extricate Percy. See below, n.15.

8 The Boleyn–Butler match had not been initiated by the king and he was not committed to it unreservedly.

9 J. A. Guy, *The Cardinal's Court* (Hassocks, Sussex, 1977), pp. 27, 31, 122, 163.

10 See p. 166.

11 *Cal. S. P. Span., 1534–35*, p. 33 [*LP*, vii.171]: 'manifeste a plusieurs': Vienna, Haus-, Hof- und Staatsarchiv, England Korrespondenz, Karton 5, Konvolut 1532, ff. 1–2.

12 See p. 354. Wriothesley, *Chronicle*, i.41.

13 See Wolsey, ed. Singer, p. 645.

14 See p. 36.

15 *LP*, iii.3321, 3322, 3648.

16 *LP*, iv.3986; Pocock, *Records*, i.22; Herbert, *Henry VIII*, p. 394; Kelly, *Matrimonial Trials*, pp. 35–53.

17 Ibid., p. 53.

18 Setting aside Kelly's more extreme hypothesis of marriage to a person unknown.

19 28 Henry VIII, c.7; Kelly, *Matrimonial Trials*, pp. 245–59; see pp. 354–5.

20 George Wyatt, in *Wolsey*, ed. Singer, pp. 424–5.

21 Wyatt, *Poems*, LIX. 'quent' = quenched; 'erst' = erstwhile; lines 7–8 = 'And he who was once torn to pieces when he was entangled in the briars, can now laugh contemptuously at all the effort he expended.' Warnicke denies that this poem refers to Anne: *Rise and Fall*, p. 252.

22 John Stevens, *Music and Poetry in the Early Tudor Court* (Cambridge, 1979), pp. 344, 388–9. I have omitted the first and third stanzas and utilized readings from both the Ritson and the Henry VIII MSS.

23 e.g. R. M. Warnicke, 'The conventions of courtly love and Anne Boleyn', in *State, Sovereigns and Society*, ed. C. Carlton et al. (Stroud, Glos., 1998), pp. 103–18. This paper omits to consider that what matters is not the significance of medieval courtly literature but what the Tudors made of it subsequently.

24 R. Vaughan, *Valois Burgundy* (1975), p. 163.

25 *Renaissance Painting in Miniature*, ed. T. Kren (1983), pp. 169–74. Opposite Sala's portrait are the words '*Reguardez en pytye votre loyal amy qui na jour ne demy bien pour votre amytye*' ['Look with pity on your loyal friend, who for love of you enjoys not a day or even a half-day of happiness'].

26 Hall, *Chronicle*, p. 707. For the 1511 Westminster tournament and disguising see ibid., pp. 517–19; Anglo, *Great Tournament Roll*.

27 Wyatt, *Poems*, LVII.

28 See pp. 21–2. The fact that didactic texts warned of the dangers to female reputations is good evidence that women took risks.

29 See above, pp. 63–7.

30 For the following, see R. Southall, *The Courtly Maker* (Oxford, 1964); R. C. Harrier, *The Canon of Sir Thomas Wyatt's Poetry* (Cambridge, Mass., 1975), pp. 23–54; *Collected Poems of Sir Thomas Wyatt*, ed. K. Muir and P. Thomson (Liverpool, 1963), pp. xiii–xv.

31 BL, Add. MS 17492, ff. 56, 67v, 69. 'amer ann i' = (supposedly) 'love Ann'.

32 Wyatt, *Poems*, CXLII.

33 Harrier, *Canon*, pp. 31–2, 41–5; see also R. C. Harrier, 'Notes on Wyatt and Anne Boleyn', in *Journal of English and German Philology*, 53 (1954), 581–2. The hand that wrote the jottings and 'signature' occurs elsewhere in the MS [Harrier, *Canon*, pp. 28–9]; since the poem '*That time that mirth*' concludes by imagining the relationship of poet and mistress restored, it cannot be directed to the supposed loss of Anne to Henry VIII [Muir, *Life and Letters of Wyatt*, pp. 16–17; Thomson, *Wyatt and his Background*, p. 22]. The second line of the 'riddle' should read 'anem e' and the final 'an' in the last line is possibly also detached: BL, Add. MS 17492, f. 67v.

34 G. F. Nott, *The Works of . . . Surrey and of Sir Thomas Wyatt* (1815–16), suggested '*Alas poor man, what hap have I*', which Harrier and Muir agree not to assign to Wyatt; Strickland, *Queens of England*, ii.219, and M. A. S. Hume (ed.), in *Chronicle* p. 69, offer '*Forget not yet*', a Wyatt probable, but concerned with reminder rather than renunciation. S. W. Singer (ed.), *Wolsey*, p. 425, suggested '*A face that should content me*', but the addressee had blonde hair! A. K. Foxwell, *The Poems of Sir Thomas Wiat* (1913) proposed '*Now must I learn to live at rest*', but this con-

cerns hurt pride at being conned by a woman who pressed her attentions but then failed to deliver. Raymond Southall argues for '*Ye know my heart*' on the slim ground that the phrase 'I and mine' echoes a motto attributed to Anne, 'Me and Mine' [*Courtly Maker*, p. 174]. His argument [ibid., 174–5] for '*Lux, my fair falcon*' as referring to Anne's falcon badge cannot be accepted, since the imagery is of flight as freedom and there is nothing to associate it with any particular of the badge.

35   Muir, *Life and Letters of Wyatt*, p. 206; cf. Wyatt, *Poems*, CXXVI.

36   Ibid., V, and the editor's comment on line 24.

37   For the motto, see pp. 173–5. R. L. Greene, 'A Carol of Anne Boleyn by Wyatt', in *Review of English Studies*, NS 25 (1974), 437–9; but Harrier, *Canon*, p. 54, rejects Wyatt's authorship. For the text see pp. 141–2.

38   Wyatt, *Poems*, L. 'answer' = 'An'er' = Anna.

39   Ibid., XCVII.

40   Harrier, *Canon*, pp. 204–5. R. M. Warnicke denies that 'Brunet' refers to Anne: 'the brunette could have been his wife or anyone else from Kent': *Rise and Fall*, p. 253. It is hard to discover any other brunette who made a stir in Kent equal to Anne, or imagine why otherwise Wyatt would change the verse.

41   Muir, *Life and Letters of Wyatt*, pp. 37, 85. The relationship existed by at least 1536–7.

42   Thomson, *Wyatt and his Background*, pp. 194, 196–200.

43   Wyatt, *Poems*, VII; 'sithens' = seeing that; George Wyatt implies that Anne adopted the motto 'I am Caesar's all, let none else touch me', no doubt on the authority of this poem by his grandfather: George Wyatt, *Papers*, p. 185.

44   See pp. 77, 140; the courtier is never named but has been assumed to be Wyatt: Muir, *Life and Letters of Wyatt*, p. 22.

45   He was, however, rusticated later in life.

46   The court was at Greenwich.

47   *Cal. S. P. Span., 1529–30*, p. 535.

48   Muir, *Life and Letters of Wyatt*, pp. 22–3.

49   The text reads: 'the Lady Anne's father and mother were in the court eight miles from Greenwich, where as everybody knows, they had taken up residence.' This is possibly a confusion for 'in the court at Greenwich, eight miles from where …' although Hever is actually 28 miles from Greenwich. Alternatively, the author may suppose that the Boleyns resided at Greenwich and had gone to join the court at, say, Whitehall (8 miles by river).

50   Muir, *Life and Letters of Wyatt*, pp. 66, 200–2.

51   Alternatively the story could be an insertion by the anonymous author.

52   Harpsfield, *Pretended Divorce*, p. 253.

53   Harpsfield, *More*, p. 341.

54   Ibid., p. 138.

55   Ibid.

56   Harpsfield, *More*, pp. clxxvii, clxxx; Sander, *Schism*, p. 201.

57   Ibid.

58   Ibid., pp. 28–30.

59   The initial accusation against Katherine Howard was made to counsellors and Henry did dismiss the report as slander and assert his wife's innocence.

60   George Wyatt, in *Wolsey*, ed. Singer, pp. 430–1, claims that Sander's original was a story in which Francis Bryan told Henry of his own prior relationship with a lady the king was pursuing (not Anne); see also *Papers*, pp. 182–5.

61   Cavendish, *Metrical Visions*, p. 43; NB the pun: 'queen'/'quean'.

62   Ibid., p. 41

Chapter 6 A Royal Suitor

1   See p. 128.

2   George Wyatt, in *Wolsey*, ed. Singer, pp. 426–7. The courtly setting suggests Anne Zouche as the source rather than

Jane Wyatt, who was a girl at this date: *Narratives of the Reformation*, p. 52.

3   Wyatt, *Poems*, LVI.

4   She must have been born not later than *c*.1510; George Wyatt was born in 1554. He implies [in *Wolsey*, ed. Singer, p. 422] that his mother was dead, and she was probably alive in 1595 [George Wyatt, *Papers*, p. 10]. Wyatt's 'Life' certainly postdated Sander, *Schism* (1585).

5   Wyatt, *Poems*, CXXXIV.

6   Brewer, *Henry VIII*, ii. 162; Scarisbrick, *Henry VIII*, p. 152.

7   He occasionally shared her bed for appearance's sake.

8   Henry told different stories about the origin of his doubts [Scarisbrick, *Henry VIII*, pp. 152–4]. The two versions differ in detail, but the claim that the French raised the question of Mary's status during marriage negotiations was never denied. English attempts to keep the knowledge of French objections from the emperor strongly suggest that Paris had raised the matter. Charles was concerned lest a divorce would permit Henry to contract a menacing marriage with a French princess.

9   Scarisbrick, *Henry VIII*, p. 154.

10   *Cal. S. P. Ven., 1520–26*, 1037, 1053.

11   Henry believed that the original Hebrew read 'without sons': V. Murphy, in *Henry VIII*, ed. MacCulloch, p. 139.

12   See p. 96. Richard Fox was consulted in April: ibid. p. 135. Henry may have begun distancing himself from Katherine at the end of 1526. It took the imperial ambassador two months from late December to see the queen privately. However, the diplomatic situation could account for this: *Cal. S. P. Span., 1527–29*, 17, 110, 116.

13   J. Gairdner, 'New light on the divorce of Henry VIII', in *EHR*, 11 (1896), 685; Herbert, *Henry VIII*, p. 393.

14   See p. 59.

15   *Love Letters*, pp. 40–1 [*LP*, iv.3220].

16   Ibid., pp. 38–9 [*LP*, iv.3219]. The letter ends with a cryptogram which can be transcribed variously. For one hypothesis, see Starkey, *Six Wives*, p. 281.

17   Ibid., pp. 32–4 [*LP*, iv.3218].

18   Knecht, *Francis I*, p. 192.

19   BL, Sloane MS 2495, f. 3; George Wyatt, in *Wolsey*, ed. Singer, p. 426.

20   *Love Letters*, pp. 29–30 [*LP*, iv.3326].

21   Chaucer, *Roman de la Rose*, line 4385.

22   *Love Letters*, pp. 34–6 [*LP*, iv.3325]: last line = 'looks for no other'.

23   Ibid., pp. 27–8 [*LP*, iv.3221].

24   Ibid., pp. 41–3 [*LP*, iv.4537].

25   The later letters can be dated by internal evidence.

26   *Cal. S. P. Span., 1527–29*, p. 432.

27   Ibid., p. 327.

28   Quoted in J. Lingard, *History of England* (1855), iv.237 n. 3. The temporary banqueting house erected for the occasion was decorated with 'H' and 'K': Hall, *Chronicle*, p. 722.

29   *Cal. S. P. Ven., 1527–33*, 236.

30   Scarisbrick, *Henry VIII*, p. 149; David Starkey also suggests that Henry had had his eye on Anne from the winter of 1524–5: *Six Wives*, pp. 277–82.

31   Ibid., p. 282; see n.17, above.

32   Reginald Pole, *Pro Ecclesiasticae unitatis defensione* (Ingolstadt, 1587), f. lxxvi.

33   The etymology appears to be via the sense 'to give a blow'. W. von Warburg, *Französisches etymologisches Wörterbuch*, xii.294–5. I am grateful to Professor Peter Ricketts for his generous help on this matter.

34   Hall, *Chronicle*, p. 707. This could suggest that Henry began his pursuit of Anne soon after finishing with her sister.

35   The buck mentioned in the first letter suggests a date in the 'grease season', i.e. late summer and autumn.

36   See pp. 76, 140.

37   RO, SP1/66, ff. 39–45 [*LP*, v.276].

38   Confirmation of the year is provided by the reference to 29 Feb. [f. 42v] which dates the document to either 1527–8 or 1531–2. There is a reference to Henry at Hampton Court on 3 Dec. which might

suggest 1531, but the Beaulieu coincidence seems conclusive.

39 *Love Letters*, pp. 36–7 [*LP*, iv.4742].

40 For Suffolk's complicated exploitation of matrimonial law, see Gunn, *Brandon*, pp. 28–9, 95; Brewer, *Henry VIII*, i.95 n. 3.

41 *Love Letters*, pp. 27–8, 46, 39–40, 48 [*LP*, iv.3221, 3990, 4410, 4894].

42 *LP*, iv.4206: *Love Letters*, p. 48 [*LP*, iv.4894]; *Cal. S. P. Span., 1527–29*, p. 789.

Chapter 7 A Marriage Arranged

1 In general, for the following see Scarisbrick, *Henry VIII*, pp. 147–228.

2 *LP*, iv.3148, 3232.

3 Shakespeare reduces the episode to an emotional plea. For a modern account see Starkey, *Six Wives*, 240–2.

4 *Cal. S. P. Span., 1527–29*, pp. 789, 831; *LP*, iv.App.206.

5 Ibid., iv.4942; *Cal. S. P. Span., 1527–29*, p. 845; Hall, *Chronicle*, p. 754.

6 *LP*, iv.4858.

7 *Love Letters*, p. 46 [*LP*, iv.3990].

8 Ibid., p. 47 [*LP*, iv.4597, a dating which assumes that the 'book' he was working on was not the one taken to Rome by Fox and Gardiner: ibid., iv.4120]; *Love Letters*, pp. 46–7 [*LP*, 4539].

9 Ibid., pp. 36–7, 48 [*LP*, iv.4742, 4894].

10 Pocock, *Records*, i.120–35, 141–55.

11 For the mixed reaction to Henry's speech, see Hall's eyewitness comment: *Chronicle*, p. 755.

12 *Cal. S. P. Span., 1527–29*, pp. 845–6.

13 It may be at this time that Henry made an attempt to have renewed sexual relations with Katherine: *LP*, iv.4981.

14 *Love Letters*, p. 37 [*LP*, iv.4648].

15 *Ambassades de du Bellay*, 171 at p. 481 [*LP*, iv.5016].

16 Strickland, *Queens of England*, ii.205.

17 *Ambassades de du Bellay*, 178 at p. 518 [*LP*, iv.5063].

18 Hall, *Chronicle*, p. 756. Campeggio had been a widower when he entered the Church.

19 Cavendish, *Wolsey*, p. 35.

20 Ibid., pp. 259–62; cf. W. Forrest, *The History of Griselda the Second*, ed. W. D. Macray (Roxburghe Club, 1875).

21 BL, Sloane MS 2495, f. 2v. The Latin MS edited by C. Bémont under the title *Le premier divorce de Henri VIII, fragment d'une chronique* (Paris, 1917) agrees, but is not independent of the Sloane MS.

22 George Wyatt, in *Wolsey*, ed. Singer, p. 428. He does not mention Anne Zouche as the source; cf. ibid., p. 429.

23 *Ambassades de du Bellay*, 101 at p. 304 [*LP*, iv.4391].

24 Ibid., 114 at p. 320 [*LP*, iv.4440]; 124 at pp. 339–40 [*LP*, iv.4542].

25 *Love Letters*, pp. 30–2 [*LP*, iv.4403].

26 Ibid., pp. 43–4 [*LP*, iv.4383].

27 *St. Pap.*, i.298–9 [*LP*, iv.4409].

28 *Ambassades de du Bellay*, 132 at p. 363 [*LP*, iv.4649].

29 Cavendish, *Wolsey*, p. 35.

30 D. Knowles, 'The matter of Wilton', in *BIHR*, 31 (1958), 92–6.

31 Eleanor seems also to have been supported by those nuns opposed to any tightening of discipline.

32 *LP*, iv.4477; cf. ibid., vi.285; *House of Commons*, iii.627.

33 *LP*, iv.4477.

34 Cavendish, *Wolsey*, pp. 35–6.

35 The contemporary term was not 'faction' but 'friends'. For the phenomenon generally, see E. W. Ives, *Faction in Tudor England* (1979) and 'Henry VIII: the political perspective', in *Henry VIII*, ed. D. MacCulloch, pp. 28–34 and the bibliographies cited in each; also David Starkey, 'Representation through intimacy', in *Symbols and Sentiments*, ed. I. M. Lewis (1977), pp. 187–224; 'The age of the household', in *The Later Middle Ages*, ed. S. Medcalf (1981), pp. 225–90; 'From

feud to faction', in *History Today*, 32 (1982), 16–22.

36   Cf. G. R. Elton on the situation in the late 1530s: 'You could no more follow Cromwell if you were a convinced papist than you could attach yourself to Norfolk and Gardiner if you thought that there had been no true religion before Luther.' *Studies in Tudor and Stuart Politics and Government* (Cambridge, 1974–92), iii.55.

37   Mattingly, *Catherine of Aragon*, pp. 160–1, 288; J. E. Paul, *Catherine of Aragon and her Friends* (1966); David Starkey, *The Reign of Henry VIII* (1985), pp. 44–5.

38   *Ordinances for the Household*, p. 154.

39   *LP*, iii.2955; *Ordinances for the Household*, p. 154.

40   See pp. 12–14.

41   *LP*, iv.5497 shows the early in trouble with Wolsey, apparently for making overtures to the court; cf. ibid., iv.3748.

42   Ibid., iv.4081.

43   For the following see ibid., iv.3216, 4436–7; 4452; 4456; 4710; 6748(15).

44   Ibid., iv.4584; for the vulnerability of Wolsey, see also ibid., iv.4556.

45   RO, SP1/49, f. 175 [*LP*, iv.4584].

46   *Ambassades de du Bellay*, 188 at p. 543 [*LP*, iv.5210].

47   Ibid., iv.5624; *House of Commons*, i.634–7.

48   *LP*, v.311–12, 315.

49   Ibid.,   iv.6072(21),   6187(12); v.318(21).

50   Ibid., vi.462.

51   For   the   following,   see   ibid., iv.3213(18),   3869(29),   3964,   4005, 4081, 4335.

52   *St. Pap.*, i.302; *LP*, iv.4656.

53   Francis's mother and Anne's mother were half-sisters: E. W. Ives, *The Common Lawyers in Pre-Reformation England* (Cambridge, 1984), p. 377.

54   *St. Pap.*, vii. 145. NB also the appointment of George Boleyn as esquire of the body on 26 Sept. 1528: *LP*, iv.4779.

55   See pp. 34–6.

56   *LP*, iv. 1319, 1329. Although G. W. Bernard, *War, Taxation and Rebellion in*

Early Tudor England (Brighton, 1986), pp. 76–87, demonstrates that the dukes did not 'provoke refusals and disturbances' nor 'capitalise on troubles … to do down Wolsey', but they were clearly anxious to communicate with the king direct instead of via the cardinal.

57   Cavendish, *Wolsey*, pp. 43–4.

58   *Cal. S. P. Span., 1527–29*, pp. 109, 190–3.

59   *LP*, iv.3318.

60   *St. Pap.*, i.261 [*LP*, iv.3360].

61   Ibid., i.278–9; cf. ibid., i.267.

62   *Cal. S. P. Span., 1527–29*, p. 432.

Chapter 8   Anne Boleyn and the Fall of Wolsey

1   *Cal. S. P. Span., 1527–29*, pp. 432–3.

2   *Ambassades de du Bellay*, 132 at pp. 363–4 [*LP*, iv.4649].

3   This seems much more probable than that Anne bore a grudge over Henry Percy.

4   Cavendish, *Wolsey*, p. 12.

5   Ibid., pp. 64–7; Hall, *Chronicle*, pp. 733–4; see pp. 67, 84, 89–90. For the fate of Henry's solo initiative see Scarisbrick, *Henry VIII*, pp. 158–62, 202–6, and Starkey, *Six Wives*, pp. 294–313. *Pace* Starkey, there is no evidence of Anne's involvement other than the use of John Barlow, who was later associated with her. I see the fiasco as an instance of Henry's overconfidence in his own abilities (perhaps showing off to Anne) and I do not accept Cavendish's story that Anne was already intransigently hostile to Wolsey: see pp. 64–5.

6   Ellis, *Letters*, 3 ii.131 [*LP*, iv.4005].

7   *LP*, iv.4081; see, p. 106.

8   *St. Pap.*, i.289 [*LP*, iv.4335]. The movements of Henry and Anne necessarily date this letter before the sweat.

9   BL, Cotton MS Otho C x, f. 220. The MS is mutilated; for a full text see Burnet, *History*, i.104 [*LP*, iv.4480]; *LP*, iv.App. 197.

10 BL, Cotton MS Vit. B xii, f.4. The MS is mutilated; for a full text see Burnet, *History*, i.103–4 [*LP*, iv.4360].

11 The reference to Campeggio establishes the date as after Anne had returned to court following the sweat: *LP*, iv.4538, 4649. It was known on 28 June that Campeggio had not set off [ibid., 4430], by which time Anne and Henry were separated.

12 *Cal. S. P. Span., 1527–29*, p. 790.

13 Cavendish, *Wolsey*, p. 36.

14 *Cal. S. P. Span., 1527–29*, p. 847.

15 Except, perhaps, du Bellay: *Ambassades de du Bellay*, 162 at pp. 454–5 [*LP*, iv.4915], and 163 at p. 463 [*LP*, iv.4942].

16 *St. Pap.*, i.194–5 [*LP*, iv.3217]; *Ambassades de du Bellay*, 132 at p. 363 [*LP*, iv.4649].

17 Brewer, *Henry VIII*, ii.486.

18 Ibid.

19 *St. Pap.*, vii.106 [*LP*, iv.4977, p. 2159].

20 *Cal. S. P. Span., 1527–29*, p. 861.

21 *Ambassades de du Bellay*, 188 at p. 543 [*LP*, iv. 5210].

22 *Cal. S. P. Span., 1527–29*, pp. 885–6.

23 For Bryan's role see *St. Pap.*, vii.166 [*LP*, iv. 5481] and p. 128.

24 Ibid., vii.170 [*LP*, iv.5519]; cf. ibid., vii.167 [*LP*, iv.5481].

25 Ibid., vii.149 [*LP*, iv.5213]; *LP*, iv.5294, 5315, 5344, 5348.

26 *St. Pap.*, i.330 [*LP*, iv.5393].

27 Ibid., vii.143 [*LP*, iv.5152].

28 *Cal. S. P. Span., 1527–29*, p. 327.

29 Burnet, *History*, v.444 [*LP*, iv.5422]. Cramp-rings (allegedly so called because they were a prophylactic against cramp) were a frequent gift in this period.

30 *Cal. S. P. Span., 1527–29*, p. 877.

31 Burnet, *History*, iv.115–17 [*LP*, iv.5427]; iv. 79–92 [*LP*, iv.5428]; *St. Pap.*, vii.169–70 [*LP*, iv.5519]; Burnet, *History*, iv.93 [*LP*, iv.5523]. This last can be dated *c.*9 May and was sent on 13 May: *LP*, iv.5535, 5576.

32 Ibid., iv.5572 at p. 2461; Burnet, *History*, iv.112–13 [*LP*, iv.5576].

33 *LP*, iv.5302 [for the date see ibid., iv.5037, 5073], 5535 at p. 2450, 5572 at p. 2461.

34 Ibid., iv.5447, 5477; *St. Pap.*, vii.169 [*LP*, iv.5519].

35 The crucial letters were dated 21 Apr., received early May: *St. Pap.*, vii.166–9 [*LP*, iv.5481]; *LP*, iv.5476. For the scene with Campeggio's secretary: ibid., iv.5572 at pp. 2463–4. But Wolsey told Campeggio that the decision to press the pope was Henry's, in spite of his telling him the facts: ibid., iv.5584 at p. 2470.

36 Burnet, *History*, iv.94 [*LP*, iv.5523]; cf. ibid., iv.108–13 [*LP*, iv.5576]; *LP*, iv.5535 at p. 2450.

37 Du Bellay, *Correspondance*, i.14 at pp. 44–8 [*LP*, iv.5702], 15 at pp. 48–51 [*LP*, iv.5701]; *LP*, iv.5681 at pp. 2510–11, 5703, 5710, 5713, 5733.

38 Ibid., iv.5604.

39 *St. Pap.*, vii.167 [*LP*, 5481]; cf. *LP*, iv.5518; *St. Pap.*, vii.170 [*LP*, iv.5519].

40 Bryan's interview with Francis I must have been on the way out, since Suffolk left England while Bryan was still at Rome: *LP*, iv.5585, 5606.

41 Du Bellay, *Correspondance*, i.4 at p. 14 [*LP*, iv.5541]; *St. Pap.*, vii.182–4 [*LP*, iv.5635]. Anne's response is made clear by du Bellay, *Correspondance*, i.17 at p. 58 [*LP*, iv.5742 is inaccurate]. Suffolk had arrived by 18 May: *LP*, iv.5562.

42 *St. Pap.*, vii.183 [*LP*, iv.5635].

43 Du Bellay, *Correspondance*, i.17 at p. 58. The reference is to the notorious ostentation shown (and success gained) by Wolsey at the conference with Francis I at Amiens in 1527.

44 *LP*, iv.5723, 5741, 5771. For the following see also Ives, in *Cardinal Wolsey*, ed. Gunn and Lindley, pp. 286–315.

45 *LP*, iv.5750. For this highly individual character see ibid., ii.295, 3486, 3659, 3831, pp. 1459, 1460; iii.3680, 3681; iv.39, 955, 4560, 5459, 5806–9. See also G. Stein, *John Palsgrave as Renaissance Linguist* (Oxford, 1997). Murphy dates this

material as early as 1528: *Bastard Prince*, p. 76.

46 Ibid., iv.5749; cf. Guy, *Public Career of More*, pp. 106–7, 206–7.

47 Wolsey's own phrase.

48 Du Bellay, *Correspondance*, i.11 at p. 40 [*LP*, iv.5679].

49 *Cal. S. P. Span., 1529–30*, p. 133; Hall, *Chronicle*, p. 758; cf. du Bellay, *Correspondance*, i.7 at p. 19 [*LP*, iv.5582]. Gardiner also warned the envoys at Rome of the danger to Wolsey, though this could have been a diplomatic tactic: *LP*, iv. 5715.

50 Hall, *Chronicle*, pp. 758–9. The 'book' could have been the final version of Darcy's charges. Henry intended to leave Greenwich on 2 Aug., and had left by 4 Aug.: *LP*, iv.5965, 5825. The decision to issue the writs for a parliament was clearly made before the close roll entry date of 9 Aug.: ibid., iv.5837.

51 Ibid., iv.5816. The fact that the grant to Rochford is called a (signed) bill shows that it was very recent.

52 Ives, in *Cardinal Wolsey*, ed. Gunn and Lindley, pp. 293–4.

53 Ellis, *Letters*, 3 i.345 [*LP*, iv.5825]; cf. *LP*, iv.4428.

54 Ibid., iv.5749 at p. 2549.

55 *Cal. S. P. Span., 1527–29*, p. 927.

56 *LP*, iv.5700, 5710, 5712; du Bellay, *Correspondance*, i.17 at p. 58 [*LP*, iv.5742].

57 Du Bellay, *Correspondance*, i.17 at pp. 58–60 [*LP*, iv.5742].

58 Ibid., 16 at pp. 52–3 [*LP*, iv.5741]; *LP*, iv.5733.

59 Du Bellay, *Correspondance*, i.22 at pp. 64–5 [*LP*, iv.5862]. See p. 117.

60 Ibid., 17 at p. 58 [*LP*, iv.5742].

61 *LP*, iv.5801, 5891.

62 *LP*, iv.5713, 5893.

63 *LP*, iv.5881; du Bellay, *Correspondance*, i.24 at pp. 70–1, 26 at pp. 73–4 [*LP*, iv.5911, 5912].

64 *St.Pap.*, i. 337–8 [*LP*, iv.5875].

65 *LP*, iv.5882, 5883.

66 *St. Pap.*, i.340, 342 [*LP*, iv.5885, 5894].

67 Ibid., i.342 [*LP*, iv.5890].

68 Ibid., i.342–3 [*LP*, iv.5894]. Gardiner quoted the tag: 'we can more easily regret the past than put it right.'

69 This is clear from the following.

70 RO, SP 1/55 f. 120 [*LP*, iv.5918].

71 *LP*, iv.5883, 5923.

72 Du Bellay, *Correspondance*, i.24 at pp. 70, 72 [*LP*, iv.5911].

73 *Cal. S. P. Span., 1529–30*, p. 195.

74 Du Bellay, *Correspondance*, i.43 at pp. 109–10 [*LP*, iv.6019].

75 *St. Pap.*, i.344 [*LP*, iv.5936]. The date of the proposed interview has been lost through damage to the MS, but it must be 19 Sept.

76 Cavendish, *Wolsey*, pp. 92–7; *Cal. S. P. Span., 1529–30*, pp. 214, 235, 257; cf. Hall, *Chronicle*, p. 759.

77 *Cal. S. P. Span., 1529–30*, p. 222.

78 Ellis, *Letters*, 1 i.307–10 [*LP*, iv.5953]. The reading 'Grene[wich]' by Ellis and *LP* is incorrect.

79 There is a curious letter of 29 Aug. in which Tuke provides an encomium for Gardiner: *St. Pap.*, i.339 [*LP*, iv.5885].

80 *Cal. S. P. Span., 1529–30*, p. 234.

81 Ibid., pp. 276–7; Cavendish, *Wolsey*, p. 97; *LP*, iv.6035; du Bellay, *Correspondance*, i.37 at pp. 91–2 [*LP*, iv.5982].

82 Wolsey surrendered the great seal on either 17 or 18 Oct.: Guy, *Public Career of More*, p. 31 n.179; *LP*, iv.6017.

83 Du Bellay, *Correspondance*, i.43, 44 at pp. 110–12 [*LP*, iv.6011, 6018].

84 Ibid., 46 at p. 115 [*LP*, iv.6030]; *Cal. S. P. Span., 1529–30*, p. 303 [*LP*, iv.6026].

85 Ibid., pp. 295–6 [*LP*, iv.6026].

86 Cavendish, *Wolsey*, p. 137.

87 Du Bellay, *Correspondance*, i.44 at p. 113 [*LP*, iv.6019].

88 Ibid., 38 at p. 94 [*LP*, iv.5983].

89 Ibid., 41 *bis*, at pp. 104–5.

90 Ibid., 41 *bis*, at p. 105.

91 Ibid., 41 *bis*, at p. 105; *LP*, iv.5996.

Chapter 9   Stalemate, 1529–1532

1   *LP*, v.App.26.

2   *Cal. S. P. Span.*, p. 196.

3   Returned from Paris mid-Feb., in post by 21 Dec. 1530: ibid., pp. 467, 854.

4   Ibid., p. 366; cf. *St. Pap.*, vii. 370 [*LP*, v.1025].

5   Cf. the comments on the polite formality of Henry and Katherine: *Cal. S. P. Ven., 1527–33*, 584.

6   Ibid., 224.

7   Ibid., 241; Hall, *Chronicle*, p. 768.

8   Nicolas, *Privy Purse*, p. 13; *Cal. S. P. Span., 1529–30*, p. 446.

9   Cavendish, *Wolsey*, p. 137.

10   J. H. Baker, *Reports of John Caryll*, ii (Selden Soc. 116, 2000), 683–92.

11   Ibid., ii.691. Cf. E. W. Ives, 'Crime, sanctuary and royal authority under Henry VIII', in *On the Laws and Customs of England*, ed. M. S. Arnold et al. (Chapel Hill, NC, 1981), pp. 299–303.

12   Harpsfield, *More*, p. 193.

13   Du Bellay, *Correspondance*, i.46 at p. 115 [*LP*, iv.6030].

14   *Cal. S. P. Span., 1529–30*, p. 368; and p. 384 n. 16.

15   Ibid., pp. 449–50, 469; *LP*, iv.6094, 6181–2, 6262, 6411, 6436, 6447.

16   Ibid., iv.6579, 6688; *Cal. S. P. Span., 1529–30*, pp. 630, 819; cf. *Cal. S. P. Ven., 1527–33*, 637: 'Everyday I miss the cardinal of York.'

17   *LP*, iv.6112.

18   *St. Pap.*, i.352 [*LP*, iv. 6114].

19   Cavendish, *Wolsey*, p. 121.

20   *Cal. S. P. Span., 1529–30*, p. 450.

21   Ibid., p. 449; *LP*, iv.6076.

22   Ibid., iv. 6290; *Cal. S. P. Span., 1529–30*, pp. 436, 630, 711, 721.

23   Ibid., p. 819. Walsh left to arrest Wolsey on 1 Nov. 1530. For Norfolk's absence and recall on 29 Oct.: ibid., p. 788.

24   L. R. Gardiner, 'Further news of Cardinal Wolsey's end', in *BIHR*, 57 (1984),

99–107; *LP*, iv. 6720; *St. Pap.*, vii.211 [*LP*, iv.6733].

25   *Cal. S. P. Span., 1529–30*, pp. 805, 820; *Cal. S. P. Ven., 1527–30*, 642.

26   For a detailed study of the period 1529–32 see Guy, *Public Career of More*, although the following differs at a number of points.

27   Gunn, *Brandon*, p. 116.

28   Guy, *Career of More*, pp. 102–8.

29   For Norfolk's desperation to move Charles V and Clement VII: *Cal. S. P. Span., 1529–30*, pp. 510–11. This may be connected with Wolsey's doctor being still in Norfolk's hands on 1 Mar. but at Ghent by 23 Mar. 1531, representing the duke to the imperial government: *LP*, v. 120, 153, 283. In fairness to Norfolk, he did present to Henry a copy of the 14th-century chronicle of William of Nangis in which the king made a number of marginal notes, many relating to papal authority and the issue of consanguinity [BL, MS Royal 13 E iv]. I owe this reference to the kindness of Prof. J. P. Carley.

30   The source followed here is Cranmer's secretary, Morrice [*Narratives of the Reformation*, pp. 240–2], not the reworking by Foxe, *Acts and Monuments*, viii.7–8, with the king's supposed remark that Cranmer had 'the sow by the right ear'.

31   MacCulloch, *Cranmer*, pp. 36, 44–6.

32   *Narratives of the Reformation*, p. 242.

33   It is not clear why Henry had not followed similar earlier hints: MacCulloch, *Cranmer*, p. 46.

34   Du Bellay, *Correspondance*, i.22 at p. 65 [*LP*, iv.5862].

35   MacCulloch, *Cranmer*, p. 46, notes that Foxe suggests an earlier meeting in London, but Henry only returned to Greenwich on 24 October at the end of the summer progress: N. Samman, 'The Henrician Court during Cardinal Wolsey's Ascendancy' (University of Wales, Ph.D. thesis, 1988), p. 386. The difficulties about this meeting, raised by Jasper Ridley, *Cranmer*, pp. 24–8, are overcome by

dating it soon after Henry's return to Greenwich following the summer progress, i.e. the earliest practical moment. Cf. Scarisbrick, *Henry VIII*, p. 255; MacCulloch, *Cranmer*, p. 46.

36 MacCulloch, *Cranmer*, p. 47.

37 Ibid., p. 48; Ridley, *Cranmer*, pp. 29–31.

38 For the following see *Narratives of the Reformation*, pp. 52–7; George Wyatt, in *Wolsey*, ed. Singer, pp. 438–41; for the book campaign see *LP*, iv.5416. The latest possible date of the episode is before the court went on progress at the start of August.

39 *Narratives of the Reformation*, pp. 57–8; George Wyatt, in *Wolsey*, ed. Singer, pp. 422, 439. Wyatt was related to the Gainsfords.

40 William Tyndale, *Works*, ed. H. Walter, Parker Society (1848–50), i.118, 333. Cf. D. Daniell, *William Tyndale* (New Haven, 1994), pp. 222–49.

41 Tyndale, *Works*, i.240.

42 Ibid., i.206–7, 240.

43 *Cal. S. P. Span., 1529–30*, p. 708. Clement did threaten to excommunicate anyone furthering unilateral action in England: *LP*, iv.6256; repeated Jan. 1531: ibid., v.27.

44 *Narratives of the Reformation*, p. 56.

45 *The Obedience* remained on the banned list: *Tudor Royal Proclamations*, i.129.

46 He failed, and *The Practice of Prelates* (Antwerp, 1529) showed that Tyndale opposed the divorce: R. Marius, *Thomas More* (1985), pp. 387–9.

47 Foxe, *Acts and Monuments*, iv.656–8

48 Simon Fish, *The Supplication of Beggars*, in *English Historical Documents, 1485–1558*, ed. C. H. Williams (1967), p. 673.

49 In the 1570 edition, Foxe added another version of events in which a royal footman tells the king about the book and introduces two merchants who read the tract to Henry then and there. This elicited

the king's famous comment that 'if a man should pull down an old stone wall and begin at the lower part, the upper part thereof might chance to fall upon his head.' For this tale, too, there is good support since the names of the footman and the merchants can be substantiated in other sources [*LP*, iv.2839(24), 4595, App.78; v. p. 305]. T. S. Freeman argues that this story is not incompatible with the story about Anne and that [pace *Anne Boleyn* (1986), p. 163n] there is no confusion with her promotion of Tyndale's *Obedience*, which Foxe learned about only in 1579: Freeman in *Hist. Journ.*, 38, 802, 805–6, 809–10.

50 Herbert, *Henry VIII*, pp. 446–51.

51 Ives, in *Trans. Hist. Soc. Lancs. & Ches.*, 123, 7–8.

52 *House of Commons*, iii.664.

53 *Cal. S. P. Span., 1529–30*, p. 599.

54 G. D. Nicholson, 'The nature and function of historical argument in the Henrician Reformation' (University of Cambridge, Ph.D. thesis, 1977) and 'The act of appeals and the English reformation', in *Law and Government*, pp. 20–5.

55 Ibid., p. 21; MacCulloch, *Cranmer*, p. 55.

56 *Censurae academiarum* (T. Berthelet, 1531); *Cal. S. P. Span., 1529–30*, pp. 818, 821, 847.

57 *The Determinations of the most famous and excellent Universities of Italy and France, that it is unlawful for a man to marry his brother's wife; that the Pope hath no power to dispense therewith* (T. Berthelet, 1531).

58 *The Divorce Tracts of Henry VIII*, ed. E. Sturtz and V. Murphy (Angers, 1988), p. 265.

59 V. Murphy, in *Henry VIII*, ed. MacCulloch (1995), pp. 138–42.

60 Ibid., pp. 142–3, 154; Nicolson in *Law and Government*, p. 25; *LP*, iv.6088. See pp. 249–50.

61 *Cal. S. P. Span., 1529–30*, p. 601.

62 Ibid., pp. 758–9.

63   Ibid., p. 790.

64   Ibid., pp. 797–8, 803.

65   *Glasse of Truthe* (T. Berthelet, 1531); *Disputatio inter militem et clericum* (Berthelet, 1531); St. German, *New Additions* (Berthelet, 1531). Thomas Berthelet was the royal printer. For St. German see p. 149.

66   *Cal. S. P. Span., 1529–30*, p. 862.

67   J. J. Scarisbrick, 'The pardon of the clergy', in *Cambridge Historical Journal*, 12 (1956), modified by Guy, in *EHR*, 97, 481–503. See also G. W. Bernard and J. A. Guy, 'The pardon of the clergy reconsidered', in *JEH*, 37 (1986), 259–87. The convocation for the province of York was much smaller and normally met later, since its bishops were required at parliament.

68   *Cal. S. P. Span., 1531–33*, p. 3 [*LP*, v.24].

69   Ibid., pp. 16, 22–3, 26 [*LP*, v.40, 45].

70   Guy, in *EHR*, 97, 492–3, 495.

71   *Cal. S. P. Span., 1531–33*, p. 63 [*LP*, v.105].

72   By claiming this 'under God', Henry was also able to circumvent the traditional restriction of secular authority to 'temporal matters'.

73   *Cal. S. P. Ven., 1527–33*, 656 must suggest that the ambiguity was deliberate, for the Crown rejected the extra qualification 'as far as canon law allows'. Cf. Henry's tendentious reply to Bishop Tunstall: Scarisbrick, *Henry VIII*, pp. 278–80.

74   *Cal. S. P. Span., 1531–33*, pp. 63, 71, 75 [*LP*, v.105, 112].

75   Ibid., p. 152 [*LP*, v.238]; cf. Knecht, *Renaissance Warrior and Patron*, pp. 227–9.

76   *Cal. S. P. Span., 1531–33*, p. 26 [*LP*, v.45].

77   Ibid., *1529–30*, p. 511.

78   *LP*, v.340, 616; xiii.961. Note Exeter's praise of Katherine's strength of conviction in May 1531: ibid., v.238.

79   *Cal. S. P. Span., 1529–30*, pp. 279, 470, 514, 536, 587, 692; *1531–33*, p. 198 [*LP*, v.308].

80   Ibid., *1529–30*, p. 421; see above, p. 127.

81   See p. 76.

82   Muir, *Life and Letters of Wyatt*, p. 201. See p. 331.

83   *Cal. S. P. Span., 1529–30*, pp. 708–9. The reference to 'Norfolk' [p. 709] should read 'Suffolk': Friedmann, *Anne Boleyn*, i.120 n.2.

84   *Cal. S. P. Span., 1531–33*, p. 177 [*LP*, v.216].

85   Ibid., p. 214 [*LP*, v.340].

86   For the duchess see Wood, *Letters*, ii.360–72; *LP*, vi.474, 475.

87   *Cal. S. P. Span., 1531–33*, p. 814 [*LP*, vi.1164]; Friedmann, *Anne Boleyn*, i.233.

88   *Cal. S. P. Span., 1529–30*, p. 368.

89   Ibid., pp. 762, 819 [*Correspondence of Charles V and his Ambassadors*, ed. W. Bradford (1850), p. 323]; ibid., *1531–33*, pp. 44, 154 [*LP*, v.216, 238]. The ambiguity of the first reference is settled by Wood, *Letters*, ii.363, 368; it was the marriage with the son of the earl of Derby which the duchess preferred. Chapuys' gossip on the Howard marriages is contradictory, e.g. *Cal. S. P. Span., 1529–30*, 279, 360, in part because of his wish to detach Norfolk from Anne by suggesting the marriage of Surrey to Mary.

90   Friedmann, *Anne Boleyn*, i.128 n.1; *Cal. S. P. Span., 1531–33*, p. 154 [*LP*, v.238].

91   September 1530 found Anne trying to force courtiers to abandon Katherine: ibid., *1529–30*, p. 422.

92   Ibid., pp. 710, 852; literally: 'thus it will be, grudge who grudges.'

93   R. L. Greene, 'A carol of Anne Boleyn by Wyatt', in *Review of English Studies*, NS 25 (1974), pp. 437–9. It is not by Wyatt: Harrier, *Canon*, p. 54. Line 11 might well be a pre-echo of Anne's later motto: 'The Most Happy'.

94 Friedmann, *Anne Boleyn*, i.128 n.3.

95 *Cal. S. P. Span.*, *1531–33*, p. 3 [*LP*, v. 24]. Cf. Henry's reported response to the vandalizing of Katherine's barge: ibid., p. 693 [*LP*, vi.556].

96 *Cal. S. P. Span.*, *1529–30*, p. 600; ibid., *1531–33*, pp. 214, 239 [*LP*, v.340, 416]. Chapuys regularly refers to 'the young marquis', which from 10 Oct. 1530 should mean Henry Grey, marquis of Dorset (b. 1517) and not Henry Courtenay, marquis of Exeter (b. *c*.1498), although the references only make sense if the latter is meant. Chapuys began the practice in the last months of Grey's father's life, hence 'young marquis' = Exeter [ibid., *1529–30*, pp. 430, 600]; hence also the wife dismissed from court was Katherine's former attendant, Gertrude Courtenay, née Blount, not Frances Grey, the daughter of Charles Brandon and Mary Tudor. Cf. Friedmann, *Anne Boleyn*, i.146 n.3.

97 *Cal. S. P. Span.*, *1529–30*, p. 600.

98 Some of Anne's anger might be accounted for if she was also making shirts for Henry: Nicolas, *Privy Purse*, p. 97.

99 *Cal. S. P. Span.*, *1531–33*, p. 699 [*LP*, vi.556]. The evidence, however, is retrospective. For Norfolk on Boleyn, see ibid., *1529–30*, pp. 442–3.

100 *LP*, v.216; *Cal. S. P. Span.*, *1531–33*, pp. 152–3 [*LP*, v.238]. For Anne's open rejection of Katherine as queen, see ibid., p. 3 [*LP*, v.24; Friedmann, *Anne Boleyn*, i.129 n.1].

101 *Cal. S. P. Span.*, *1531–33*, pp. 175–7 [*LP*, v.287].

102 Scarisbrick, *Henry VIII*, pp. 276–8; Mattingly, *Catherine of Aragon*, p. 232; Guy, *Public Career of More*, pp. 175–6.

103 *LP*, v.216; vi.1464–6, 1468, 1470.

104 W. Schenk, *Reginald Pole* (1950), pp. 28–9.

105 *Cal. S. P. Span.*, *1531–33*, p. 322 [*LP*, v.563].

106 Ibid., *1529–30*, p. 586; *1531–33*, pp. 239–40 [*LP*, v.416]; *LP*, v.364(28).

107 But Bryan and Fox did pray for Henry to receive 'your heart's desire': Pocock, *Records*, ii.140 [*LP*, v.427].

108 *Cal. S. P. Span.*, *1531–33*, p. 152 [*LP*, v.238]; *LP*, v.1025. He did make a brief return visit in Sept.: ibid., v.401, 427.

109 Nicolas, *Privy Purse*, passim; *LP*, v.App.10.

110 RO, E101/420/1 [*LP*, iv.App. 256].

111 *Cal. S. P. Span.*, *1529–30*, p. 536.

112 Nicolas, *Privy Purse*, pp. 47, 50.

113 Ibid., p. 74.

114 George Wyatt, in *Wolsey*, ed. Singer, pp. 429–30.

115 *Cal. S. P. Span.*, *1529–30*, p. 634.

116 Ibid., *1531–33*, p. 35 [*LP*, v.64]. The probable cause of the quarrel was Anne's ill-treatment of a courtier: ibid., p. 33 [*LP*, v.61].

117 *LP*, v.216.

118 *Cal. S. P. Span.*, *1531–33*, p. 33 [*LP*, v.61].

119 Alternatively on the feast of SS. Philip and James: *LP*, v. p. 325.

120 *Cal. S. P. Span.*, *1531–33*, p. 153 [*LP*, v.238], but preferring Friedmann's reading: *Anne Boleyn*, i.148 n.3.

121 *Cal. S. P. Span.*, *1531–33*, p. 154 [*LP*, v.238]; RO, E36/252 ff. 419–20 [*LP*, v.p. 448].

122 Colvin, *King's Works*, iv.306–12; Hall, *Chronicle*, p. 774; see p. 247.

123 Ibid., p. 781.

124 *Cal. S. P. Span.*, *1531–33*, p. 198 [*LP*, v.308].

125 *LP*, v.337. Starkey has shown that Hall was wrong to say that Henry left for Woodstock [*Chronicle*, p. 781]. From Chertsey, he proceeded on a progress through Sussex and Hampshire in order, Starkey suggests, to cement support from local courtiers and gentry. In early August, Katherine was ordered to move to The More, and Mary to Richmond: Starkey, *Six Wives*, pp. 440–3.

126 *Cal. S. P. Span.*, *1531–33*, p. 291.

127 Ibid., pp. 222–4 [*LP*, v.361].

128   John Stowe, *Survey of London*, ed. C. L. Kingsford (Oxford, 1908), ii.36. 'King Henry and Queen Katherine dined' at the feast for the new serjeants-at-law at Ely House 'but in two chambers, and the foreign ambassadors in a third chamber'.
129   *Cal. S. P. Ven., 1527–33*, 682.

Chapter 10   The Turning-point, 1532–1533

1   Hall, *Chronicle*, p. 784.
2   *Cal. S. P. Span., 1531–33*, p. 354 [*LP*, v.696].
3   *LP*, Add.746.
4   *Cal. S. P. Span., 1531–33*, p. 278 [*LP*, v.512].
5   Pocock, *Records*, ii.144–5.
6   *Cal. S. P. Span., 1531–33*, pp. 263–4 [*LP*, v.478].
7   For the following see *Cal. S. P. Span., 1531–33*, pp. 353–4 [*LP*, v.696].
8   Ibid., p. 354: *'certain dards faytz a la biscayne'*. 'Une darde' was a short spear with a two-edged, leaf-shaped blade, which, given the source (or perhaps the fashion) of the weapons, suggests 'boar spear'. For the 1531 gift see Nicolas, *Privy Purse*, p. 101.
9   Chapuys says that the prohibition included Mary, but she did receive a gift: *LP*, v. p. 327.
10   *Dialogus de fundamentis legum Anglie et de consciencia* (1528), translated as *A dyaloge betwyxt a doctore of dyuynytye and a student in the lawes of England* (1530), ed. T. F. T. Plucknett and J. J. Barton (Selden Society, 91, 1974), pp. 315–40. See J. A. Guy, 'The Tudor commonwealth', in *Hist. Journ.*, 23 (1980), 684–7; *Public Career of More*, pp. 151–6; in *Moreana*, 21, 5–25; *Christopher St German on Chancery and Statute* (Selden Society, 1985), pp. 19–55.
11   St German, *Doctor and Student*, p. 315.

12   Ibid., p. 327.
13   Guy, in *Moreana*, 21, 8; *Public Career of More*, pp. 151–2, 156.
14   *LP*, iv.5366.
15   Lehmberg, *Reformation Parliament*, p. 114.
16   For the following see Guy, *Public Career of More*, pp. 180–201; Lehmberg, *Reformation Parliament*, pp. 131–53; M. Kelly, 'The submission of the clergy', in *Transactions of the Royal Historical Society*, 5th series, 13 (1965), 97–119; G. R. Elton, 'Thomas More and the opposition to Henry VIII', in *Studies*, i.155–72, although the interpretation below differs at certain points.
17   *Cal. S. P. Span., 1531–33*, pp. 272, 295 [*LP*, v.488, 546].
18   G. R. Elton, The evolution of a reformation statute', in *Studies*, pp. 85–6.
19   23 Henry VIII, c.20: 'our said sovereign lord the king, and all his natural subjects as well spiritual as temporal be as obedient, devout, Catholic and humble children of God and Holy Church as any people be within any realm christened.'
20   *Cal. S. P. Span., 1531–33*, p. 417 [*LP*, v.898]; cf. *St. Pap.*, vii.349 [*LP*, v.868, 831].
21   *Cal. S. P. Span., 1531–33*, p. 384 [*LP*, v.805].
22   *'sans vouloer mestre le chat entre les jambes d'autres'*.
23   Guy, *Public Career of More*, pp. 164–74.
24   Ogle, *Lollards' Tower*, p. 330.
25   Muller, *Gardiner*, pp. 45–6.
26   BL, Sloane MS 2495, ff. 15v–16; *Cal. S. P. Span., 1531–33*, pp. 427–8 [*LP*, v.941].
27   Ogle, *Lollards' Tower*, p. 340.
28   *LP*, v.479, 679.
29   Audley initially had the title of 'keeper of the great seal' rather than 'chancellor'.
30   *LP*, v.1069.
31   *LP*, v.1059.
32   Cf. John London, 'wherever I find occasion to oblige the king or any pertain-

ing to my lady marquess [Anne], I do my duty as Mr. Barlow and Mr. Taylor her servants can testify': *LP*, v.1366; cf.1034, 1632.

33 BL, Harleian MS 303, ff. 13–15v [cf. *LP*, iv.6542(23); v.1139(32), 1207(7)].

34 Colvin, *King's Works*, iv.147–9; W. H. Tapp, *Anne Boleyn and Elizabeth at the Royal Manor of Hanworth* (1953); Thurley, *Palaces*, p. 78.

35 *Lisle Letters*, i. p. xxxii [*LP*, ix.402]. M. St. Clare Byrne pointed out that the *LP* date is wrong, and proposed May/June 1530 to Summer 1532. The letter, however, clearly comes at the start of a summer progress and must refer to a royal visit to Waltham on a Monday in July/Aug., i.e. 8 Aug. 1532. The other possible date is 9 Aug. 1529, which seems too early [*LP*, iv.5825; v. pp. 314, 320–1, no. 1152].

36 *Cal. S. P. Span., 1531–33*, p. 481 [*LP*, v.1165].

37 *Cal. S. P. Span., 1531–33*, p. 489 [*LP*, v.1202].

38 Nicolas, *Privy Purse*, pp. 274–7; 222–3.

39 *LP*, v.1307.

40 MacCulloch, *Cranmer*, pp. 75–7.

41 *Cal. S. P. Span., 1531–33*, pp. 464, 488 [*LP*, v.1109, 1202]. For the conference, see P. A. Hamy, *Entrevue de François Premier avec Henry VIIIe à Boulogne* (Paris, 1898); *Cal. S. P. Ven., 1527–33*, pp. 822–4; *LP*, v.1485; *The Maner of the Tryumphe at Caleys and Bulleyn*, Wynkyn de Worde (1532), ed. A. F. Pollard, in *Tudor Tracts* (1903).

42 Hamy, *Entrevue*, pp. ix–xii [*LP*, v.1187]. Hamy, following *LP*, attributes this item to du Bellay. Friedmann, *Anne Boleyn*, i.165 corrects to La Pommeraye; du Bellay was in France: du Bellay, *Correspondance*, i. 280. *Cal. S. P. Span., 1531–33*, p. 494 [*LP*, v.1256].

43 Ibid., p. 528 [*LP*, v.1377]; Hamy, *Entrevue*, p. 143; *LP*, vi.134; Jourda, *Marguerite d'Angoulême*, p. 172; see pp. 32–3.

44 Francis's second son Henri would marry Catherine de' Medici at Marseilles in October 1533.

45 Hamy, *Entrevue*, pp. ix–xii [*LP*, v.1187].

46 *Cal. S. P. Span., 1531–33*, p. 525 [*LP*, v. 1377]; *Cal. S. P. Ven., 1527–33*, 808.

47 Hamy, *Entrevue*, pp. xi–xii [*LP*, v.1187]; *Cal. S. P. Span., 1531–33*, p. 511 [*LP*, v.1316].

48 Ibid., p. 511 [*LP*, v.1316]; Hamy, *Entrevue*, p. l.

49 *LP*, v.1373, 1600.

50 Ibid., v.1237; BL, Royal MS 7 C.xvi, f. 41v [*LP*, v.1376].

51 *Cal. S. P. Span., 1531–33*, p. 525 [*LP*, v.1377].

52 Ibid., p. 508 [*LP*, v.1292]; *Cal. S. P. Ven., 1527–33*, 802; *LP*, v.1274(3), (4); Hall, *Chronicle*, p. 790. The partisan nature of the ceremony was emphasized by the countess of Rutland being a daughter of Sir William Paston, a Norfolk neighbour of the Boleyns, and the countess of Derby being the stepsister of Anne's mother. The duke of Norfolk's estranged wife was intended to be present, but probably refused: *LP*, v.1239.

53 Anne was described as both 'marquis' and 'marchioness' of Pembroke. The point in the former title was that she held a newly created peerage in her own right, not (as was the case otherwise) by virtue of marriage. But for convenience I have used 'lady marquis' or the female form.

54 *Cal. S. P. Ven., 1527–33*, 802 gives thirty, 822 gives twenty; a French report, *LP*, v.1485, gives ten or twelve only.

55 *Cal. S. P. Ven., 1527–33*, 824.

56 Thus *The Maner of the Tryumphe*; cf. Hall, *Chronicle*, p. 793.

57 See pp. 105, 156; *Cal. S. P. Span., 1531–33*, p. 466 [*LP*, v.1109].

58 *LP*, v.1093, 1168.

59 Hall, *Chronicle*, p. 794.

60 The pamphlet states that the king 'purposeth to be at Canterbury the 8th

day of November': *The Maner of the Tryumphe*, p. 8.

61 The 'lady Mary' cannot be Henry's sister, who is always called 'queen of France'.

62 Colvin, *King's Works*, iii.349–51.

63 *Cal. S. P. Span., 1531–33*, pp. 556–7 [*LP*, v.1579].

64 This is the probability; Anne had conceived by the beginning or at least the middle of December; see p. 170.

Chapter 11   Wedding Nerves

1 Cranmer, *Letters*, p. 246.

2 *LP*, vi.230, 242.

3 *Cal. S. P. Span., 1531–33*, pp. 609, 625 [*LP*, vi.180, 296]; *Cal. S. P. Ven., 1527–33*, 870.

4 For the following see *LP*, v.1685; *Cal. S. P. Span., 1531–33*, pp. 566–7 [*LP*, v.1633].

5 *Cal. S. P. Ven., 1527–33*, 846; MacCulloch, *Cranmer*, pp. 75–8, 83–6; Ridley, *Cranmer*, pp. 52–3. Cranmer may have been approached prior to Warham's death.

6 Lehmberg, *Reformation Parliament*, pp. 161, 168.

7 *Cal. S. P. Span., 1531–33*, pp. 598–600, 602 [*LP*, vi.142, 160].

8 Ibid., p. 602 [*LP*, vi.160]. Chapuys seems to have believed that what was being proposed was a bill to approve the marriage to Anne.

9 Friedmann, *Anne Boleyn*, i.189 n.2, 190 n.1.

10 *Cal. S. P. Span., 1531–33*, p. 617 [*LP*, vi.212].

11 Ibid., p. 618 [*LP*, vi.235]; Lehmberg, *Reformation Parliament*, pp. 174–8. Cranmer presided at Convocation for the first time on 1 April but appears to have been preparing the divorce for some weeks previously: MacCulloch, *Cranmer*, pp. 84–9.

12 The annulment of Katherine's marriage postdated the public recognition of Anne, and was achieved at an archiepiscopal court at Dunstable, 10–23 May. It was followed on 28 May by a hearing which confirmed the legality of the union already effected between Anne and Henry.

13 *Cal. S. P. Span., 1531–33*, p. 625 [*LP*, vi.296].

14 Ibid., p. 629 [*LP*, vi.324].

15 Ibid., p. 643 [*LP*, vi.351]; *Cal. S. P. Ven., 1527–33*, 870.

16 Wriothesley states that Anne was proclaimed queen at Greenwich, but it is not clear whether he meant publicly or to the court. There is a similar crux about the proclamation of Jane Seymour, though his references to Katherine Howard and Katherine Parr suggest the latter: *Chronicle*, i.17, 44, 122, 143. Philip and Mary were publicly proclaimed on 25 July after their marriage at Winchester [ibid., ii.121] and also in London on 1 Aug., but Philip was not merely a consort: *Diary of Henry Machin*, ed. J. G. Nichols (Camden Society, 42, 1848), p. 67.

17 Parliament was prorogued by commission on 4 Nov., on the excuse of the king's absence in Calais; that problem had been realized in July, but the decision to prorogue was only taken during the week before 2 Oct.: *LP*, v.1187, 1406, 1514–15, 1518. The alleged reason would have justified a brief prorogation (the Calais meeting was over by 29 Oct.), but hardly for three months. Plague was possibly a factor. Lehmberg, *Reformation Parliament*, p. 217. An understanding with France had been reached by 1 Sep.: *LP*, v.1292.

18 *Cal. S. P. Span., 1531–33*, p. 699 [*LP*, vi.556].

19 Ibid., p. 405 [*LP*, v.850]. G. Redworth is unwilling to see any political significance: *Church Catholic*, pp. 41–2. Yet though Norfolk and Gardiner had different motivation, each loathed the

implications of the *Supplication*: 'misery acquaints a man with strange bedfellows.'

20 Ibid., pp. 476–7 [*LP*, v.1131].

21 Ibid., p. 699 [*LP*, vi.556]. Chapuys' report 'that ... the Lady taking a piece of material, as is the custom with pregnant women here to add to gowns which are too tight, her father said to her that she should take it out and thank God to find herself in such a condition' is often interpreted as criticism of Anne by Wiltshire. The advice not to disguise the pregnancy only makes sense if interpreted as proposed. The alternative reading in Friedmann, *Anne Boleyn*, i.158 n.1, amounts to much the same.

22 *Cal. S. P. Span., 1531–33*, pp. 487–9 [*LP*, v.1202]; Starkey, *Six Wives*, pp. 454–5.

23 *Cal. S. P. Ven., 1527–33*, 761; 25 Henry VIII, c.32; *LP*, v.1139(11), 1183, 657. This last should be dated post 8 June 1532, the date of the election of the abbot of Northampton: ibid., v.1139(23).

24 *Cal. S. P. Ven., 1527–33*, 792, 802; *Cal. S. P. Span., 1531–33*, pp. 509, 512, 613 [*LP*, v.1292, 1316; vi.212].

25 It is more likely that she was in her final illness. She died in June 1533; cf. *LP*, vi.693.

26 Vienna, Haus-, Hof- und Staatsarchiv, England Korrespondenz Karton 5, Konvolut 1532, ff. 81–2; Friedmann, *Anne Boleyn*, i.159–61; *LP*, x.864.

27 *LP*, v.1524, 1679; *Cal. S. P. Span., 1531–33*, p. 986 [*LP*, v.1256]; *Cal. S. P. Ven., 1527–33*, 803, 811, 816.

28 Ibid., 824; the Milanese envoy in France even called Anne 'the king's beloved wife': *Cal. S. P. Milan*, ed. A. B. Hinds (1912), 900.

29 *LP*, v.1538; *Cal. S. P. Ven., 1527–33*, 822; ibid., *1534–54*, 1035.

30 *LP*, xiii(1), pp. 317–18.

31 *Cal. S. P. Span., 1531–33*, p. 527 [*LP*, v.1377].

32 Ibid., p. 495 [*LP*, v.1256].

33 *LP*, v.1538.

34 BL, Harleian MS 303, f. 1; cf. *LP*, v.1370(1).

35 The patent was proclaimed by Gardiner.

36 Friedmann, *Anne Boleyn*, i.162–3.

37 MacCulloch, *Cranmer*, pp. 76–7.

38 *LP*, v.1493; *Cal. S. P. Span., 1531–33*, pp. 585, 599 [*LP*, vi.89, 142].

39 Ibid., 585–7 [*LP*, vi.89]; *LP*, vi.91.

40 *Cal. S. P. Span., 1531–33*, pp. 592–8 [*LP*, vi.142].

41 Ibid., p. 594 [*LP*, vi.142].

42 Sander, *Schism*, pp. 93–4; Harpsfield, *Pretended Divorce*, pp. 234–5; BL, Sloane MS 2495, ff. 13–14.

43 Harpsfield, *Pretended Divorce*, p. 235.

44 *Cal. S. P. Span., 1531–33*, p. 608 [*LP*, vi.180]. Starkey, *Six Wives*, p. 475, has shown that Henry slipped away from Greenwich on 24th, spent the night at Whitehall and returned to Greenwich on the 25th.

45 *LP*, v. p. 327; vi. p. 14; Brereton, *Letters and Accounts*, pp. 243, 248.

46 *LP*, viii.121.

47 Pocock, *Records*, i.25.

48 Elizabeth believed in a papal bull covering her mother's marriage and set Matthew Parker to search for it. He at first reported no success, but later found 'matter of that bull' and sent William Cecil 'some quires': Parker, *Correspondence*, pp. 414, 420. Even Cranmer did not know the exact date of the marriage: 'about St. Paul's Day'.

49 See p. 184.

50 Hall, *Chronicle*, p. 794, gives St. Erkenwald's Day, 14 Nov. 1532. On the date of a marriage ceremony *c.*25 Jan. 1533, Friedmann's arguments (*Anne Boleyn*, ii.338–9) are conclusive.

51 Sander, *Schism*, pp. 92–4.

52 Kelly, *Matrimonial Trials*, p. 40n. I am pleased that this conjecture is now

supported by MacCulloch, *Cranmer*, pp. 637–8.

53   Scarisbrick, *Henry VIII*, pp. 305–7. Cf. Francis I's complaint late in 1533, 'as fast as I study to win the pope, ye study to lose him': *LP*, vi.1427.

54   *Original Letters*, ii.552–3.

55   Cavendish, *Metrical Visions*, p. 41; cf. also BL, Sloane MS 2495, f. 2v.

56   *St. Pap.* vii. 454 [*LP*, vi.438].

Chapter 12   A Coronation and a Christening

1   *Cal. S. P. Ven.*, *1527–33*, 878.

2   Hall, *Chronicle*, p. 798.

3   e.g. *LP*, vi.396.

4   Ellis, *Letters*, 1 ii.32–3.

5   Edward Hall was one of the organizing committee [Kipling, in *Civic Ritual*, pp. 46–7], which makes his *Chronicle*, pp. 798–805, the most authoritative source. The following also relies on *The noble tryumphant coronacyon of Quene Anne*, Wynkyn de Worde (1533); Dublin, Trinity College MS 518, ff. 30–2; BL, Harleian MS 41 [*LP*, vi.561, 601]; RO, PRO 31/8 ff. 50v–54 [*LP*, vi.585]; Spelman, *Reports*, i.68–70 [*LP*, vi.583]; Wriothesley, *Chronicle*, i.18–22; *Cal. S. P. Ven.*, *1527–33*, p. 912; *Ordinances for the Household*, pp. 123–211; *LP*, vi.396, 562–3, 584, 701; Cranmer, *Letters*, pp. 245–6; cf. Anglo, *Spectacle*, pp. 246–61.

6   K. N. Palmer, *Ceremonial Barges on the River Thames* (1997), p. 5.

7   *LP*, vi.563.

8   Dublin, Trinity College MS 518, f. 30v; Wriothesley, *Chronicle*, i.18.

9   For Arundel and Saville, see *House of Commons*, i.337; iii.280.

10   Wynkyn de Worde in *The noble tryumphant coronacyon* gives 46 names; *LP*, vi.563 gives a figure of 63.

11   Also in securing exemptions; cf. *LP*, vi.746.

12   Cf. the engraving of Edward VI's coronation procession after a lost fresco from Cowdray: Society of Antiquaries, London.

13   *Actes de François Ier*, ii. 590, no. 6639.

14   The procession was half a mile long: *LP*, vi.661.

15   R. Marius, *Thomas More* (1985), pp. 438–40.

16   RO, PRO31/8 f. 51 [*LP*, vi.585].

17   *Cronica del Rey Enrico*, pp. 17–18 [*Chronicle*, ed. Hume, p. 14].

18   *Cal. S. P. Ven.*, *1527–33*, 912.

19   *LP*, vi.613.

20   Colvin, *King's Works*, iv.290–1.

21   For the length of the ceremony see Cranmer, *Letters*, p. 245, and *LP*, vi.601.

22   Ibid., vi.554; Hall, *Chronicle*, p. 804.

23   *Cal. S. P. Milan*, p. 911; cf. Colvin, *King's Works*, iv.290.

24   *Cal. S. P. Span.*, *1531–33*, p. 704 [*LP*, vi.653].

25   *LP*, vi.561.

26   Hall, *Chronicle*, p. 805. *The noble tryumphant coronacyon*, and Wriothesley, *Chronicle*, i.22, say that 18 took part.

27   De Carles, in Ascoli, *L'Opinion*, lines 111–27.

28   RO, SP1/76 f. 195 [*LP*, vi.613].

29   *Actes de François Ier*, ii.393, no. 5721, ii.416 no. 5829; *Cal. S. P. Ven.*, *1527–33*, p. 893; *Cal. S. P. Span.*, *1531–33*, pp. 721, 724 [*LP*, vi.720].

30   *Tudor Royal Proclamations*, i. 209.

31   *Cal. S. P. Span.*, *1531–33*, p. 794 [*LP*, vi.1125]; *St. Pap.*, i.408 [*LP*, vi.1252].

32   *Cal. S. P. Ven.*, *1527–33*, 923.

33   *LP*, vi.1009; *Cal. S. P. Span.*, *1531–33*, p. 756 [*LP*, vi.918].

34   De Carles, in Ascoli, *L'Opinion*, lines 148–64.

35   Hall, *Chronicle*, p. 805; *LP*, vi.895.

36   *Ordinances for the Household*, pp. 125–6; Dublin, Trinity College, MS 518, ff. 117–19.

37   *LP*, vi.890; J. W. Kirby, 'Building work at Placentia, 1532–33', in *Transac-*

tions of the Greenwich and Lewisham Anti-quarian Society, 5 (1954–61), 22–50.

38 LP, vi.948, 1004 [Lisle Letters, i.35].

39 Cal. S. P. Span., 1531–33, p. 788 [LP, vi.1069]; LP, vi.1070; Hall, Chronicle, p. 805.

40 De Carles, in Ascoli, L'Opinion, lines 168–76.

41 LP, vi.1166; Hall, Chronicle, p. 805.

42 LP, vi.1089; Wriothesley, Chronicle, i.22–3, which contradicts Chapuys: Cal. S. P. Span., 1531–33, p. 795 [LP, vi.1125]. For the christening, see also Hall, Chronicle, pp. 805–6; LP, vi.1111.

43 De Carles, in Ascoli, L'Opinion, lines 181–2.

44 Ibid., lines 183–5. The godmothers were Agnes, dowager duchess of Norfolk, Margaret, dowager marchioness of Dorset, and the godfather, Cranmer; the marchioness of Exeter was godmother at the confirmation which followed immediately on the baptism, but her name was Gertrude, not Elizabeth ['Ysabeau'], as de Carles assumed from the name given to the child.

45 Henry, earl of Worcester; John Dudley.

46 LP, vi.1111(4).

Chapter 13 A Royal Marriage

1 C. Morris, The Tudors (1955), p. 151.

2 Quoted Prescott, Mary Tudor, p. 307.

3 George Wyatt, Papers, p. 141; for a concurrent Catholic view, see BL, Sloane MS 2495, f. 2: 'King Henry gave his mind to three notorious vices, lechery, covetousness and cruelty, but the two latter issued and sprang out of the former.'

4 If Henry had other mistresses (for which there is no firm evidence), the record of childlessness becomes even more significant.

5 J. Dewhurst, 'The alleged miscarriages of Catherine of Aragon and Anne Boleyn', in Medical History, 28 (1984),

49–56, has significantly revised the number of Katherine's supposed pregnancies, although I disagree with his reduction of Anne's pregnancies to two (1533 and 1535/6), omitting that in 1534 (see pp. 191–2). The report of 24 June 1535 that Anne was visibly pregnant [LP, viii.919], redated 1533 or 1534 in Lisle Letters, i.10, belongs to 1533, as the court was at Hampton Court in 1534. The Milanese report in May 1535 that Anne was pregnant seems to refer to the events of the previous summer: Cal. S. P. Milan, p. 962.

6 Scarisbrick, Henry VIII, p. 485. Alternatively, the ulcer could have been varicose. For Francis I see Knecht, Renaissance Warrior and Patron, pp. 112, 544–5.

7 Burnet, History, iv.427, 430. The phrase in Henry's declaration that if Anne of Cleves 'brought maidenhead with her' he never 'took any from her by true carnal copulation', seems to suggest that he had attempted intercourse. He consulted his doctors several times about the inability to consummate, and Dr Chamber 'counselled his majesty not to enforce himself, for eschewing such inconveniences as by debility ensuing in that case were to be feared'. Chamber reported that Henry could not, in Anne's company, 'be provoked or stirred to that act': John Strype, Ecclesiastical Memorials (1822), I ii.460–1.

8 Thus Dr Butts, ibid., p. 461.

9 Cal. S. P. Span., 1536–38, p. 126 [LP, x.908], quoted from Friedmann, Anne Boleyn, ii.280 n.1. Cf. Chapuys' phrase, 'not capable of satisfying her': ibid., p. 122 [LP, x.909] and Henry's evidence about relations with Anne of Cleves: 'neither will nor courage'.

10 But for more speculative psychological discussion see L. B. Smith, Henry VIII: The Mask of Royalty (1971), pp. 64–6.

11 Cal. S. P. Span., 1531–33, p. 638 [LP, vi.351].

12 Ibid., *1534–35*, p. 67 [*LP*, vii.94]; *Lisle Letters*, ii.175 [*LP*, vii.556]. Dewhurst, in *Medical History*, 28, rejects this pregnancy, and suggests pseudocyesis, the exhibition of pregnancy-like symptoms as a result of psychological stress. Anne, however, had no reason to be under stress at this date, having produced a healthy female child eight months earlier. If she had 'a goodly belly' in late April (and the informant is her receiver-general), she would then be more than sixteen weeks pregnant, i.e. conceiving not later than the start of the year. Imperial sources at Rome had been informed by 23 Jan. 1534 that Anne was pregnant, allegedly by a letter from the newly arrived English ambassador in France. If this was Lord William Howard, the date of arrival must have been the beginning of December [*LP*, vi.1438], suggesting that Anne became pregnant in November 1533. This could just make good sense, but the chain of information is too long for complete confidence: *LP*, vii.96.

13 RO, SP1/88 f. 116 [*LP*, vii.1668]. Since Hayes' bill was for items delivered to 'Mr Secretary' (i.e. Cromwell) it must have been prepared post April 1534. It is unlikely that the detailed bill for a cradle for Elizabeth would be delayed so long. Alternatively, it could have been ordered for the expected birth in 1536. It was not for the future Edward VI: Cromwell would then have been addressed as 'lord privy seal'.

14 *St. Pap.*, vii.565 [*LP*, vii.958]; *Cal. S. P. Span.*, *1534–35*, p. 224 [*LP*, viii.1013].

15 That it was a miscarriage and not a stillbirth or neonatal death is indicated by the queen not having 'taken her chamber'.

16 *Cal. S. P. Span.*, *1534–35*, p. 264 [*LP*, vii.1193].

17 Ibid., *1531–33*, p. 760 [*LP*, vi.995].

18 *LP*, vi.1054.

19 *Cal. S. P. Span.*, *1531–33*, p. 788 [*LP*, vi.1069]; Friedmann, *Anne Boleyn*, i.213 n.1.

20 Cf. *LP*, vi.1054 with *Cal. S. P. Span.*, *1534–35*, pp. 292–3.

21 *LP*, vi.879, 891, 948, 963, 1004.

22 *Cal. S. P. Span.*, *1531–33*, p. 755 [*LP*, vi.918].

23 Ibid., p. 777 [*LP*, vi.1018].

24 Ibid., p. 800 [*LP*, vi.1125].

25 *LP*, vi.1065.

26 For the above see ibid., vi.1293, 1510, 1528; vii.83, 126, 556, 682, 888; *Cal. S. P. Ven.*, *1527–33*, p. 924; *Cal. S. P. Span.*, *1531–33*, p. 842 [*LP*, vi.1392].

27 The imperial envoy at Rome reported rumours about bad feeling between Anne and Henry, which were circulating in France on 20 Sept., but withdrew this on 3 Oct., having received Chapuys' letter dated 27 Aug.: *Cal. S. P. Span.*, *1534–35*, pp. 260, 268–9 [*LP*, vii.1174, 1228].

28 Ibid., p. 264 [*LP*, vii.1193].

29 Ibid., p. 280 [*LP*, vii.1257]. For the rest of the paragraph see ibid., pp. 293, 294–5, 299–301, 344 [*LP*, vii.1279, 1297, 1554]; *LP*, viii.263 at p. 104.

30 She too was a court beauty, much like the duchess of Milan in physique and looks: *LP*, xii.1187.

31 *Cal. S. P. Span.*, *1536–38*, p. 127 [*LP*, x.908]; *LP*, x.1047.

32 *Cal. S. P. Span.*, *1534–35*, p. 344 [*LP*, vii.1554].

33 Ibid., p. 354 [*LP*, viii.1]; *LP*, viii.121.

34 Anne owed her initial opportunity to her father, but from the start of Henry's interest, Thomas Boleyn owed more to Anne than vice versa.

35 *LP*, vii.454.

36 *Cal. S. P. Ven.*, *1534–54*, 54.

37 *Cal. S. P. Span.*, *1534–35*, p. 338 [*LP*, vii.1507]; ibid., p. 376 [*LP*, viii.48]; Friedmann, *Anne Boleyn*, ii.45 no.1.

38 *LP*, viii.909.

39 *Cal. S. P. Span.*, *1534–35*, p. 179 [*LP*, viii.949]. Greg Walker, who first drew attention to this, saw a problem in the dating. The feasts referred to are the Nativity of St. John Baptist (24 June) and Peter and Paul (29 June): *Plays of Persuasion* (Cambridge, 1991), p. 227.

40 For the above see also Ives, in *History Today*, 50, 48–53.

41 Prescott, *Mary Tudor*, pp. 45–57; Loades, *Mary Tudor*, pp. 76–103.

42 *Cal. S. P. Span.*, *1534–35*, p. 57 [*LP*, vii.214]. Cf. a male courtier's threat to Mary that 'were she his daughter, he would beat her to death, or strike her head against the wall until he made it as soft as a boiled apple': ibid., *1536–38*, p. 182 [*LP*, xi.7].

43 Ibid., p. 72 [*LP*, vii.296].

44 Ibid., p. 198 [*LP*, vii.871].

45 The bona fide argument was being canvassed in 1533 – see Cromwell's note: *LP*, vi.386 ii.

46 Hence Anne's orders to box Mary's ears if she insisted on using the style 'princess': *Cal. S. P. Span.*, *1534–35*, p. 34 [*LP*, vii.171].

47 *Cal. S. P. Span.*, *1534–35*, p. 573 [*LP*, ix.873].

48 Ibid., p. 72 [*LP*, vii.296].

49 Ibid., p. 224 [*LP*, vii. 1013]; Clifford, *Dormer*, pp. 81–2.

50 *Cal. S. P. Span.*, *1536–38*, p. 12 [*LP*, x.141]; ibid., p. 44 [*LP*, x.307].

51 Cf. the king's remarks in Nov. 1535: *Cal. S. P. Span.*, *1534–35*, p. 572 [*LP*, ix.862].

52 *LP*, vii.840.

53 *LP*, viii.196.

54 e.g. *Cal. S. P. Span.*, *1534–35*, p. 299 [*LP*, vii.1297].

55 *LP*, v.907.

56 *LP*, vii.754.

57 *LP*, vii.939.

58 *LP*, viii.565, 567.

59 On this see G. R. Elton, *Policy and Police* (Cambridge, 1972).

60 25 Henry VIII, c. 22.

61 26 Henry VIII, c.13.

62 Cavendish, *Metrical Visions*, p. 42.

63 Harpsfield, *More*, p. 264; see pp. 47, 156.

64 De Carles, in Ascoli, *L'Opinion*, lines 209–13.

65 Harpsfield, *More*, p. 264.

66 *Cal. S. P. Span.*, *1534–35*, p. 430 [*LP*, viii. 429], trans. Mattingly, *Catherine of Aragon*, p. 291.

67 e.g. *Cal. S. P. Span.*, *1534–35*, pp. 608–11 [*LP*, vii.1206].

68 Nov. 1533: *LP*, vi.1460; Wood, *Letters*, ii.362–3.

69 *LP*, viii.263 at p. 104.

70 *Cal. S. P. Span.*, *1534–35*, p. 217 [*LP*, ix.681].

71 Ibid., p. 484. [*LP*, viii.826]; *LP*, viii.985.

72 Knecht, *Renaissance Warrior and Patron*, pp. 304–5.

73 See p. 33; for the following see *Cal. S. P. Span.*, *1534–35*, pp. 327–9, 330–3, 335–8, 339–40, 345, 376 [*LP*, vii.1437, 1482, 1507, 1554; viii.48]; *St. Pap.*, vii.584–7 [*LP*, vii.1483].

74 *LP*, viii.174, at p. 61.

75 *LP*, viii.189, 263.

76 *LP*, viii.174 at p. 61; Friedmann, *Anne Boleyn*, ii.51.

77 *LP*, viii.336–8; *St. Pap.*, vii.584–90, 592–9, 602–3, 608–15 [*LP*, viii.339–41, 557, 793].

78 *LP*, viii.174.

79 *Cal. S. P. Span.*, *1534–35*, p. 452 [*LP*, viii.666].

80 Ibid., p. 476 [*LP*, viii.826].

81 Ibid., p. 493 [*LP*, viii.876].

82 *LP*, viii.985; ix.157; Burnet, *History*, vi.116.

Chapter 14 Influence, Power and Wealth

1 *LP*, ix.52.

2 See p. 202.

3 See p. 156.

4 *Cal. S. P. Milan*, 843.

5 *St. Pap.*, vii, pp. 481, 489, 557, and p. 208.

6 *Lisle Letters*, ii.468 [*LP*, ix.700].

7 See p. 260.

8 *Lisle Letters*, ii.147 [*LP*, vii.349].

9 BL, Cotton MS Vespasian F iii 16.

10 Hist. Mss. Comm., *Fifth Report*, p. 296b; *LP*, Add.746; ibid., 569 (possibly for one of her servants). See also *LP*, vii.125.

11 *Lisle Letters*, ii.152, 298, 299 [*LP*, vii.386, 1581, 1582].

12 *LP*, ix.463.

13 *LP*, ix.358, 450; cf. *LP*, v.1430.

14 *Cal. S. P. Span., 1531–33*, pp. 450–1 [*LP*, v.1058]; *LP*, v.1453; Redworth, *Church Catholic*, pp. 45–7.

15 *LP*, viii.1101, 1130; ix.21; S. J. Gunn, *Charles Brandon* (Oxford, 1988), pp. 115–42.

16 *LP*, ix.862.

17 LP, ix.478

18 *LP*, v.1450; vi.299 (cf. vii. p. 353); RO, E163/10/19 and 20.

19 *LP*, viii.1057; cf. v.1398. Letters between Anne and Cromwell are rare; she normally communicated by messenger.

20 *LP*, ix.357, 113.

21 *LP*, ix.723.

22 *LP*, v.367.

23 Hugh Latimer, *Remains*, ed. G. E. Corrie (Parker Society, 1845), p. 368 [*LP*, ix. 272].

24 *St. Pap.* vii.454–5 [*LP*, vi.438]; cf. Casale: *LP*, vi.670.

25 See p. 207.

26 *LP*, ix.85.

27 Ellis, *Letters*, 3 ii.249 [*LP*, v.1525].

28 *LP*, vii.594.

29 *Lisle Letters*, iv.841 [*LP*, ix.892].

30 *St. Pap.*, ii.302 [*LP*, x.185]; *LP*, x.186.

31 *Lisle Letters*, i.xxxviii, xxxviiia; ii.202, 202a [*LP*, vii.511–12, 734, 844]; *LP*, vii.409–14, 845.

32 *Lisle Letters*, ii.169–71.

33 Ibid., ii.202 [*LP*, vii.734].

34 Ibid., i.xxxviii [*LP*, vii.512].

35 Ibid., iv.841a [*LP*, x.416]; *LP*, ix.577.

36 Ibid., vi.837.

37 *Cal. S. P. Span., 1534–35*, p. 344 [*LP*, vii.1554]; *LP*, vii.1655.

38 Nicolas, *Privy Purse*, p. 88.

39 *LP*, vi.559, 917. She did get some employment: *LP*, xx.914.

40 *LP*, vii.1623.

41 *Lisle Letters*, ii.428 [*LP*, viii.1103]; *LP*, vii.922(9), 1352(8); viii.1007.

42 *LP*, vii.600, 641, App. 22; viii.81(2), 94; *Lisle Letters*, i.xxxiii [*LP*, vi.126].

43 *Lisle Letters*, i.519; *LP*, x.1009.

44 *House of Commons*, i.456; 'I think it much unkindness in the king to put such about me as I never loved...I would have had [those] of mine own privy chamber which I favour most': *Wolsey*, ed. Singer, pp. 454, 457.

45 See p. 335.

46 *Cal. S. P. Span., 1531–33*, p. 693 [*LP*, vi.556]; *LP*, xi.533, 590, 1155(5).

47 *House of Commons*, i.666–7.

48 Ibid., i.400–3. See pp. 262, 266, 268.

49 Ibid., iii.508–9.

50 *Lisle Letters*, i.346–7; *LP*, vii.543, x.1219.

51 D. L. Hamilton, 'The learned councils of the Tudor queens consort', in *State, Sovereigns and Society*, pp. 87–8; *LP*, vii.352. Katherine's auditor, Thomas Combes, remained in royal employ and so very probably continued to serve Anne., *LP*, viii. g149(36).

52 Latymer, 'Treatyse', ff. 22v–24 [Dowling, 'Cronickille', pp. 48–50].

53 *LP*, vii.415.

54 *Lisle Letters*, i.xxxii, xxxiii [dated June 1529 to August 1532 by the addressee, 'Lady Lisle', and the usages, 'my lady' and 'Lady Anne']. See p. 160.

55 Lady Lisle is not mentioned by name at the coronation but Lord Lisle served at the feast as chief panter; they arrived in Calais on 9 June: ibid., pp. 463–4, 469.

56 *Lisle Letters*, ii.182, 193, 207, 212a [*LP*, vii.613, 654, 795, 824].

57 Ibid., ii.109, 114 [*LP*, vii.25, 92].

58 Ibid., ii.299a [*LP*, ix.991].

59 Ibid., iv.826 [*LP*, viii.119].

60 Ibid., ii.421 [*LP*, viii.1084]; Katherine liked them, a memory of Spain.

61 Ibid., ii.302 [*LP*, viii.15].

62 Ibid., ii.307 [*LP*, viii.46].

63 For the following see ibid., iv.828, 829, 830a, 830, 833; ii.380; iv.835, 836; ii.492a, 497, 502a, 506; iii.658a, 658, iv.842; iii.668 [*LP*, viii.232, 353, 371,

378, 545, 664, 939, 1028, 1984; ix.898, 951, 1004, 1033; viii.110; x.499, 559, 573, 608].

64 Ibid., iii.658 [*LP,* x.499].

65 *LP,* Add.991.

66 BL, Harleian MS 303, nos. 4 and 5.

67 *LP,* vi.6.

68 25 Henry VIII c.25; BL, Harleian MS 303, ff. 16, 23v, 24 [*LP,* vii.419(25)].

69 Hamilton, in *State, Sovereigns and Society,* p. 89.

70 *LP,* vi.1189.

71 *Lisle Letters,* ii.147 [*LP,* vii.349]; cf. the appearance of even-handedness in the act for Katherine as princess dowager: 25 Henry VIII c.28.

72 *LP,* iii.2239; viii.962(1).

73 *LP,* vi.1189; vii.352.

74 *LP,* vi.1188. This is wrongly dated in *LP*; it follows the legislation that received the royal assent on 20 Mar. 1534.

75 *LP,* v.1274(3). A few of Anne's leases do survive in RO, E328.

76 RO, SC6 Hen. VIII, 6680 [*LP,* ix.477].

77 RO, SP 1/104 ff. 1v–16 [*LP,* x.914].

78 *LP,* ix.478.

79 Hist. Mss. Comm., *Rutland Mss.,* iv.272, 276–7.

80 RO, E101/421/13.

81 *LP,* vi.1194, 1382, 1589. No doubt the object was to enhance the appearance of Anne's attendants when on progress, etc.

82 RO, SP1/104 ff. 1v–16 [*LP,* x.914].

83 W. Loke, 'Account of materials furnished for the use of Anne Boleyn and Princess Elizabeth, 1535–6', in *Miscellanea of the Philobiblon Society,* vii (1862). The Lok bill covers the period 20 Jan. to 27 Apr. 1536, but the total, £124 15*s.* 2*d.,* disagrees with the equivalent figure in the list of debts, £123 10*s.* 6*d.:* RO, SP 1/104 f. 1v. The end of the bill is missing, and a minor deduction there could account for the difference; the bill does contain mistakes.

84 *Inventory,* no. 398; *LP,* viii.197. Lok was a keen reformer: see p. 273.

85 Wolsey, ed. Skinner, p. 461.

86 RO, SP 1/103 ff. 322–7 [*LP,* x.913].

87 BL, Harleian MS 303, no. 3.

88 See pp. 87–8.

89 Nicolas, *Privy Purse,* pp. 88–267.

90 Ibid., p.101.

91 Ibid., p.113.

92 The primary reference of 'farm' is to income, but the implication of 'place' was known by at least the mid-century.

93 Nicolas, *Privy Purse,* pp. 272–7. Apparently playing for crowns (worth 4*s.* 8*d.*).

Chapter 15 Image

1 Anglo, *Spectacle,* pp. 57, 186, 248–9, 258. Kipling, in *Civic Ritual,* p. 44.

2 Hall, *Chronicle,* p. 800.

3 BL, Add. MS 9835, f. 22 [*LP,* x.1016]; see p. 228.

4 For the following see pp. 173–81 and Kipling, in *Civic Ritual,* pp. 39–79. Cromwell's papers included a paper of preparations devised for the receiving of the Queen's Grace into London: *LP,* vii. 923 (xxxviii).

5 *Ballads from Manuscripts,* ed. F. J. Furnivall (Ballad Society, 1868–72), i.373–401, from BL, Royal MS 18A lxiv, ff. 1–16. This purports to be a copy of verses posted up or spoken during the course of the pageants, but the first two at least (by Leland on the river pageant and Anne's litter) and Leland's final piece on the coronation are probably additions, perhaps to prepare a presentation text to Anne. Omitting the 65 lines in these sections (35 plus 15 plus 12, all in Latin), Leland contributed 138 lines of Latin, Udall 310 lines of Latin, 221 of English. The source for the non-Udall/Leland material is Hall, *Chronicle,* pp. 800–2. Cf. Anglo, *Spectacle,* pp. 246–61.

6 He was possibly also a relative of Anne's secretary.

7 Kipling, in *Civic Ritual*, pp. 51–2.

8 The 10th mystery of the Rosary.

9 Kipling, in *Civic Ritual*, pp. 51–7.

10 *Ballads*, p. 389.

11 Ibid.

12 BL, Harleian MS 6561, f. 2.

13 *Pace* Kipling, in *Civic Ritual*, p. 77 n.56, this conclusion is not vitiated by the appearance of the falcon device in the illumined letters patent [BL, Harleian MS 303], granting the Pembroke title. The MS includes Anne's post-marital patents.

14 Anne's shield of arms was changed from quarterly 1 Ormonde; 2 Brotherton; 3 Rochford; 4 Warenne, to 1 Lancaster; 2 Angoulême; 3 Guienne; 4 quarterly Ormonde and Rochford; 5 Brotherton; 6 Warenne.

15 The imperial [i.e. closed] crown was used long before the Act of Appeals [cf. C. E. Challis, *The Tudor Coinage* (1978), pp. 49–51] but much emphasized subsequently.

16 Gospel of Luke, chapter 1, verse 35. Advantage was not taken of the coincidence of the coronation and the feast of Pentecost to exploit the descent of the Holy Spirit on Mary and the apostles: Acts of the Apostles, chapter 2, verses 1–4; see below, n.21.

17 *Ballads*, pp. 390–1.

18 Kipling, in *Civic Ritual*, pp. 54–7.

19 Lowinsky, *Florilegium*, pp. 180–1; see pp. 257–8.

20 Hall, *Chronicle*, p. 802.

21 It was also proposed for Jane Seymour's pageant.

22 The above follows John Stow [*Survey of London*, ed. C. L. Kingsford (Oxford, 1908), ii.41] in treating the Fleet Street Conduit and the Fleet Street Standard as a single installation. Wynkyn de Worde, *The noble tryumphant coronacyon*, p. 17, implies that the Standard was specially built of stone for the occasion. Hall, p. 802, refers only to the Conduit.

23 The Revelation of St John, chapter 21, verses 11, 18. A tower representing the heavenly Jerusalem was a standard feature in London entries, most recently for Charles V in 1522; Kipling in *Civic Ritual*, pp. 52–3. Jasper green was the traditional colour. When *The noble tryumphant coronacyon*, describes the exterior as 'gilt and azure' a blue-green is presumably intended.

24 For the following see plate 38, and n.30 below.

25 *Ballads*, p. 382.

26 Ibid., pp. 381–8.

27 Anglo, *Spectacle*, pp. 90–1, 187–202.

28 Somewhat harshly, Anglo describes the humanism as 'superficial': 'a self-conscious Latinity and a thin veneer of commonplace literary allusions covering what is, for the most part, a dull, trite and lamentably repetitious pageant series': ibid., p. 248.

29 For the following, see *Cal. S. P. Span., 1531–33*, pp. 704, 740, 754–5 [*LP*, vi.653, 805, 918].

30 Rowlands, *Holbein*, p. 88, argues that the bird was a falcon, but this seems iconographically extraneous. For the suggestion of an identification between Apollo and Henry VIII see D. Cressy, 'Spectacle and power', in *History Today*, 32 (1982), 18–19.

31 The Grace Thalia is not to be confused with the Muse Thalia; see above, p. 225.

32 Two Latin verses were probably displayed, not spoken.

33 The Greek and the Roman pantheon are confused here.

34 *Ballads*, p. 396.

35 Ibid., p. 398.

36 Hall, *Chronicle*, p. 802; Wynkyn de Worde, *The noble tryumphant coronacyon*, p. 16.

37 Ibid., p. 25.

38 Ibid., p. 17.

39 BL, Add. MS 9835, f. 22 [*LP*, x.1016].

40 Anglo, *Spectacle*, pp. 284, 290.

41 Ibid., p. 289

42 Ibid., pp. 319–20.

43 Ibid., pp. 327–39; *Chronicle of Queen Jane and Queen Mary*, ed. J. G. Nichols (Camden Society, 48, 1850), pp. 146–51.

44 Anglo, *Spectacle*, pp. 344–59.

45 J. Chartrou, *Les Entrées solennelles et triomphales à la Renaissance* (Paris, 1928), pp. 32–3.

46 Ibid., pp. 52–3.

47 Jourda, *Marguerite d'Angoulême*, i.58, based on the account by the Venetian ambassador, Sanuto.

48 At the entry of Francis I's second queen, Eleanor, into the city of Rouen in 1532, she was accompanied by the chariots of Mercury (drawn by serpents), Juno (drawn by peacocks) and Pallas Athene (drawn by the Muses and escorted by Apollo) [Chartrou, *Les Entrées solennelles*, pp. 82–3]. There is no evidence to suggest any link between Anne and Eleanor's entries, apart from the closeness of the dates.

49 Hall, *Chronicle*, p. 801.

50 *The noble tryumphant coronacyon*, p. 16.

51 Hall, *Chronicle*, p. 802.

52 See the use of the falcon badge on the 'mourning sword' of the City of Bristol (1594), the fireplace (1583), now in the library of Windsor Castle, and 'Queen Elizabeth's Virginals' (see pp. 256–7). Elizabeth also used it on her books: Neale, *Queen Elizabeth*, p. 9. cf. also her use of the phoenix (see p. 373 n. 29).

53 Hans Eworth (attr.), *Elizabeth I and the Three Goddesses*: H. M. the Queen, Hampton Court.

54 *Ballads*, p. 388.

55 Yates, *Astraea*, pp. 59–69; the quotation is from p. 61.

56 Ibid., pp. 78–9; R. Strong, *Gloriana* (1987), p. 43.

Chapter 16 Art and Taste

1 Gospel of Matthew, chapter 7, verse 20.

2 *LP*, vi.212.; see p. 31.

3 *The Inventory of Henry VIII*, ed. David Starkey, I: The Transcript (1998).

4 *Inventory*, no. 1134.

5 e.g. *Inventory*, nos 1046 'Queen Anne' and 1134 'late Queen Anne' can each be dated as a Boleyn item. However, court items specifically connected with Anne of Cleves are *Inventory*, nos 13422, 13543, the chapel ceiling at St James [Rowlands, *Paintings of Hans Holbein*, p. 237] and the oak bedhead in the Burrell Collection, Glasgow.

6 *Inventory*, no.141.

7 J. Williams, *Accounts of the Monastic Treasures Confiscated at the Dissolution*, ed. W. B. Turnbull (Abbotsford Club, 1836), p. 97; *Jewels and Plate*, p. 197. Plausibly, Trappers was a relative of the London goldsmith, Nicholas Trappes: Glanville, *Silver*, p. 78. For a further purchase from Trappers, see p. 252.

8 Thomas Rymer, *Foedera* (1739–45), vii(3).198. Cf. 'one Bason and Layer [small jug] of mother of pearl garnished with gold, enamelled with H and A knit together, and the king's arms on the top of the cover and H A embossed on the foot thereof, weight 34 ounces': *Inventory*, no. 163.

9 *Inventory*, no. 1046.

10 See p. 191.

11 *Inventory*, nos 674, 700, 790.

12 *Connoisseur Period Guides*, ed. R. Edwards and L. G. G. Ramsey, *The Tudor Period* (1956), pp. 69–70; *Jewels and Plate*, ed. Collins, p. 197, no.6. The immediate source is a pattern which circulated on the continent and was eventually published in a German pattern book of the 1540s, but the inspiration is Italian,

13 *Inventory*, no. 723. The other is no. 703.

14 *Inventory*, no. 10920.

15 *Inventory*, no. 178.

16 *LP*, vi.32. *Inventory* indexes these items (e.g. nos 1887–1890) and plate marked with only the Rochford arms (e.g. nos 1891–1895) as both deriving from Anne's brother, George, presumably after forfeiture. However, it is difficult to see why then only a minority (mostly silver) should be marked with the king's arms. It is more probable that items marked with both coats belonged to Anne. The remainder could have been hers or her brother's. The latter is assumed above. For Anne's use of the Rochford arms see pp. 242–3, 398 n.14.

17 For Holbein's jewellery designs see p. 400 n. 40.

18 Oskar Bätschmann and Pascal Griener, *Hans Holbein* (1997), p. 87, but Crown accounts relevant to the previous period are missing.

19 Ibid., p. 9, but cf. Rowlands, *Paintings*, p. 91.

20 Nicolas Bourbon, *Nugarum Libri Octo* (Lyons, 1538), Bk. 3 no. 8, p. 153; Bk. 6 no. 12, p. 338; Bk.7 no. 158, p. 427; Bk.8 no. 36, p. 450. *Paedagogion* (Lyons, 1536), p. 28.

21 National Gallery, no. 1314. For the following see Ives, in *Apollo*, 140 (1994), 39–40. Of the substantial literature see, principally, S. Foister, A. Roy and M. Wyld, *Holbein's Ambassadors* (1997); Rowlands, *Paintings*, pp. 85–7, 139–40; Elly Dekker and Kristen Lippincott, 'The scientific instruments in Holbein's Ambassadors: a re-examination', in *Journal of the Warburg and Courtauld Institutes*, 62 (1999), 93–125.

22 Possibly by the 9th: *LP*, vi.91, 110, 142, 160.

23 *Holbein's Ambassadors*, p. 14.

24 Ibid.

25 *LP*, vi.91.

26 *Holbein's Ambassadors*, p. 33. Dekker and Lippincott in *Journal of the Warburg and Courtauld Institutes*, 62, 108–9, are more sceptical. J. North argues that others of the instruments point to the 11 April date, notably the torquetum; *The Ambassadors' Secret* (2002), pp. 91, 97, 111, though I do not follow his overall analysis.

27 *Holbein's Ambassadors*, p. 16.

28 Johannes Walther, *Geistlich Gesangbuchli* (Wittenberg, 1524) but edited to place item II opposite item XIX.

29 See pp. 274–5.

30 de Selve left England too soon to have much detailed input to the painting, and his religious position is less clear, though he does seem to have written in favour of accommodation with the German reformers.

31 *Solomon and the Queen of Sheba*, H. M. the Queen Windsor Castle, Royal Library 12188. See Ives, in *Apollo*, 140, 38–9; Rowlands, *Paintings*, pp. 91–3, 150.

32 Ibid., pp. 83–4.

33 See p. 236 n. 36.

34 Matthew, 12: 42; Luke, 11: 31.

35 '*ut esses rex (constitutus) Domino Deus tuo*'.

36 28 Henry VIII, c.10.

37 '*beati viri tui et beati servi tui qui assistant coram te*' (happy are your men and happy are your servants who work around you'): I Kings, 10, 8.

38 Hilary Wayment, *The Windows of King's College Chapel, Cambridge* (1972), plates 61–3 [no. 4D]. The window could be as late as 1540–1 and Antonia Fraser, *Six Wives of Henry VIII* (1992) has suggested that Sheba may be a likeness of Katherine Howard. I reject this (a) because of the miniature and (b) because the symbolism would be irrelevant to Katherine.

39 See p. 43.

40 Ganz, *Die Handzeichnungen*, xxxix.2(e); xxxix.4(d); cf. xxxix.3(d) and (f), while xix.9 could be Anne's gryphon supporter.

41 Kupferstichkabinett, Oeffentliche Kunstsammlung, Amerbach-Kabinett, Basle: English Sketchbook [Ganz, *Die Handzeichnungen*, vi.7].

42 RO, SP1/88, f.116 [*LP*, vii.1668].

43 RO, E101/421/13 [*LP*, vii.9].

44 *Pace* Collins, *Jewels and Plate*, pp. 468–9; P. Glanville, *Silver*, pp. 170, 213; Rowlands, *Paintings*, p. 91; Starkey, *A European Court*, p. 135; Strong, *Lost Treasures*, pp. 80, 83, 86.

45 The women of the Basle cup are part-draped, not naked, and it is not certain Holbein intended more than two.

46 Collins, *Jewels and Plate*, pp. 468–9. These later descriptions also indicate that, as well as the three women round the foot of the fountain being naked, they had jewelled 'tirements' (head-dresses). Again this is not the case in the drawing of the cup and cover.

47 Kupferstichkabinett, Oeffentliche Kunstsammlung, Amerbach-Kabinett, Basle: English Sketchbook [Ganz, *Die Handzeichnungen*, xxiii.5]. She is not standing but clearly has a tirement on her head.

48 Kupferstichkabinett, Oeffentliche Kunstsammlung, Amerbach-Kabinett, Basle: English Sketchbook [Ganz, *Die Handzeichnungen*, vi.4].

49 For the following see Murdoch, *English Portrait Miniature*, pp. 29–33; Strong, *Artists*, pp. 34–44; also *Renaissance Miniature* (1984), pp. 30–44; H. Paget, 'Gerard and Lucas Hornebolt in England', in *Burlington Magazine*, 101 (1959), 396–402.

50 Tree-ring dating shows that the surviving portrait of William Carey must be a later copy, or even an enlargement of a miniature: J. Fletcher, 'A portrait of William Carey, and Lord Hunsdon's Long Gallery', in *Burlington Magazine*, 123 (1981), p. 304.

51 E. Auerbach, *Tudor Artists* (1954), p. 50.

52 He is credited with four miniatures of Katherine herself, one of Princess Mary, two of Brandon and one of Charles V, and possibly with a half-length panel painting of the countess of Salisbury, Mary's first governess and the mother of the Pole brothers: Strong, *Renaissance Miniature*, pp. 42–4, 189–90.

53 BL, Harleian MS 303.

54 *LP*, vii.1204.

55 Hever Castle, 'The Hours of Anne Boleyn' (*c*.1450); Christie's sale catalogue, *Valuable Printed Books and Manuscripts, 26 November, 1997*, pp. 12–17.

56 The 'Anne Boleyn' signature appears on the Hours f. 99v, but she was addressed as de Rochfort possibly from 1525 and certainly from 1529: see p. 285.

57 The absence of heraldic reference could suggest a commoner, but the inclusion of the feasts of St Hugh of Lincoln and St Edmund as red-letter days and Edward and Oswald in the litany is no more than compatible with a north Norfolk owner.

58 Hever Castle, *Hours of the Blessed Virgin Mary* (G. Hardouyn, Paris, n.d.). The conjectural date for the book, *c*.1528, is unlikely. I owe this information to the kindness of Mr Richard Allen.

59 Ibid., sig. f 1v.

60 'Hours of Anne Boleyn', f. 99v; Christie's, *26 November, 1997*, p. 12.

61 See p. 244.

62 BL, Royal MS 16E13.

63 Alnwick, the duke of Northumberland, Percy MS 465.

64 Ganz, *Die Handzeichnungen*, XXXVIII. 8.

65 I owe the suggestion about printing to Miss Janet Backhouse. Subsequent investigation showed that the ornaments imitated occur on the Alençon edition, *c*.1530: see p. 271.

66 Alnwick, Percy MS 465, f. 130.

67 Ibid., f. 2.

68 Ibid., f. 148.

69　BL, Harleian MS 6561. See Carley, in *Illuminating the Book*, fig. 155 and p. 268. For an extensive bibliographical analysis of the text see ibid., pp. 261–3, 266.

70　BL, Harleian MS 6561, f. 1v.

71　Ibid., f. 2r.

72　One would expect the monogram to refer more directly to Anne, and hence that 'S' and 'L' might make '*Servant*' or '*Serviteur Loyal*', but the *rex* makes it certain that the letters refer to the king.

73　Sold by Sotheby's, 7 Dec. 1982: *Western Manuscripts*, lot 62.

74　See pp. 249–50.

75　But letter ciphers were well known in France [I owe this information to the kindness of Margaret B. Freeman]. The attempt to use du Bellay's letter of 13 Apr. 1530 [Sotheby's, 7 Dec. 1982: *Western Manuscripts*, lot 62, pp. 72–3] to link the MS, the bishop, Anne and Henry, and the humanist Jacques Colin seems ill-advised. '*Je me trouveray...Madame*' refers to Francis I...at p. 142].

76　Alnwick, Percy MS 465, ff. 2; 12v, 61v, 130; 23, 117; 34; 44, 100v; 54; 88; 139.

77　Ibid., f. 54.

78　See pp. 252–5 and plate 44.

79　Alnwick, Percy MS 465, f. 139.

80　Ibid., f. 34.

81　Ganz, *Die Handzeichungen*, xxi.6(a),(f); xl.7(c); R. Strong, *The Cult of Elizabeth* (1977), p. 52. However, the Van Dyck of the 9th earl of Northumberland (National Trust, Petworth) includes a sphere which indicates 'wisdom'; cf. *Elizabeth*, ed. S. Doran, p. 201.

82　The Gospel of Matthew, chapter 26, verse 42; *Inventory*, no. 2530 is 'a pece' of gold inscribed *Fiat voluntas tua*.

83　R. Strong, *Gloriana* (1987), pp. 138–41 and below, n.84.

84　*Elizabeth*, ed. S. Doran, p. 201.

85　*LP*, vi.32; RO SP1/66 [*LP*, vi.276].

86　*Inventory*, nos 2619–2741, 3504–3620, but Katherine could have removed her books to Sudeley.

Chapter 17 Life at Court

1　M. Axton, *The Queen's Two Bodies* (1977), pp. 13–14

2　See also S. Thurley, *Palaces*, pp. 73–4.

3　Henry's only distant destinations were York and Hull in 1541.

4　See p. 265.

5　Thurley, *Palaces*, pp. 50, 78: 'almost certainly the only wife with a keen interest in architecture'.

6　*LP*, v.238.

7　*LP*, v.1299. 'Anne played a crucial part in the early development of Whitehall': Thurley, *Whitehall Palace*, p. 39.

8　Colvin, *King's Works*, iv(i).307; Thurley, *Whitehall Palace*, p. 39. BL, Sloane MS 2495, ff. 13–13v refers to 'York House in the high chamber over the West Gate'. The two palace gates extant in 1533 were the 'Holbein' Gate across King's Street and the Court Gate, set back from the street to the east. From the position of the royal apartments, the Holbein Gate was the further west of the two. Thurley, *Whitehall Palace*, pp. 10, 40.

9　*LP*, x.1231; Thurley, *Whitehall Palace*, pp. 38–51.

10　Thurley, *Hampton Court* (1988), p. 14. Cavendish indicates that Henry was given Hampton Court in 1525, though Wolsey continued to use it and to build there: Colvin, *King's Works*, iv(i).127; Thurley, *Hampton Court* (2003), pp. 57–8.

11　Thurley, *Hampton Court* (1988), pp. 8, 14.

12　Ibid., p. 28.

13　Ibid.

14　For the following see Thurley, *Palaces*, pp. 29, 41, 42, 46.

15　Thurley, *Hampton Court* (1988), pp. 15,16.

16　Thurley points out the need to match the level of the king's long gallery: ibid., p. 15. But at Whitehall the queen's new suite was again constructed on the same floor as the king's and with similar direct access to the king's privy gallery: Thurley, *Whitehall Palace*, pp. 50, 63.

17   M. Chatenet, *La Cour de France au 16ème siècle* (Paris, 2002), p. 163. I owe this reference to Professor R. J. Knecht.

18   Colvin, *King's Works*, iv(i).350; see p. 159.

19   Colvin, *King's Works*, iv(ii).105.

20   Ibid., iv(ii).82; see pp. 198–9.

21   Ibid., iv(ii).26.

22   Thurley, *Palaces*, pp. 102, 105.

23   Colvin, *King's Works*, iv(ii).241.

24   Ibid., iv(ii).104–5. Since the work was done after Henry had separated from Katherine, we can assume Anne's interest.

25   Ibid., iv(ii).82.

26   Ibid., iv(ii).105; 'Building work', in *Transactions of the Greenwich and Lewisham Antiquarian Society*, 5, 24.

27   Colvin, *King's Works*, iv(ii).148.

28   Thurley, *Palaces*, pp. 212–16.

29   Colvin, *King's Works*, iv(ii).133.

30   Ibid., iii.194; cf. Royal Commission on Historical Monuments, *City of Cambridge* (1959), i.128–30.

31   The heads elsewhere on the screen are antique and male. The screen was installed after Anne's death, but the expense and difficulty of making changes must explain why her symbols survived. This could mean that the 'Fall of the Angels' was not part of the original design.

32   R. W. Scribner, *For the Sake of Simple Folk* (Oxford, 1981), p. 158. The angels appear to be falling against a background of classical building which could represent Rome.

33   'Inventory of the wardrobe of Katherine of Aragon', in *Camden Miscellany*, iii. Camden Society, 61 (1855), p. 39 [*LP*, viii.209]. *LP*, v.1063.

34   Colvin, *King's Works*, iv(ii).105.

35   H.M. the Queen. A further clock associated with Anne was located at Windsor in 1547–8: *Inventory*, no. 13178.

36   RO, SP 1/103 ff. 322–7 [*LP*, x.913].

37   J. Caley, 'Extract from a MS in the Augmentation Office', in *Archaeologia*, 9

(1789), 248 [*LP*, viii.937]; RO, SP1/104 ff. 1v–16 [*LP*, x.914].

38   *LP*, v.696; RO, SP1/103 f. 320 [*LP*, x.912].

39   SP1/66 [*LP*, v.276]. In October 1532 he sent his jeweller twenty rubies and two diamonds reserved for Anne: *LP*, v.1376.

40   See p. 237.

41   *LP*, xii(2).1315.

42   The Bradford painting and the *Basilowgia* engraving; the BM medal has the double pearl necklace, but with a pendant cross.

43   The NPG pattern, the Hume ring and the Hoskins miniature; the ring does not allow the pendant to be seen.

44   Elizabeth's French hood is also decorated with a sequence of rubies and pearls which is very close to the necklace of the gable hood painting.

46   Dugdale, *Monasticon*, i.64 [see p. 232 for a Trappers piece of the same weight]; *Inventory*, no. 2914.

47   *Inventory*, no. 2863. The Lady Elizabeth received New Year's gifts of a little book of gold featuring the Annunciation and a brooch of gold with an antique, but it is not clear that these were given in Anne's lifetime. Roy 7Cxvi, ff. 21v, 27v.

47   See above, p. 217.

48   *Inventory*, nos 11320, 11318, 17036, 17034.

49   SP1/66 f. 42 [*LP*, v.276].

50   Ibid., ff. 43, 40v.

51   Sander, *Schism*, p. 25.

52   George Wyatt, in *Wolsey*, ed. Singer, pp. 442–3.

53   *Inventory*, no. 9219.

54   Ibid., nos 9226, 9225. To these we should add the cushion at Whitehall embroidered with Henry's cipher and honeysuckle, and possibly another bordered with honeysuckle, acorns and strawberry flowers: ibid., nos 9242, 9228. Whether the strawberry flowers are significant is not clear, but the symbolism of honeysuckle twining round an oak is obvious.

55 Ibid., no. 12061.

56 Ibid., no. 12054.

57 Ibid., no. 12057

58 *Inventory*, no. 12648. This was known as 'Queen Anne's bed' in Jane Seymour's lifetime: Roy 7Cxvi, f. 61v.

59 Glasgow Museums and Art Galleries; The Burrell Collection.

60 *Inventory*, no. 12162.

61 *Inventory*, no. 9365. The theme for Anne's bed at Whitehall was the falcon on the roses; the counterpane at the More was embroidered with 'H' and 'A' in diamond panels; the Windsor bed was embroidered with Rochford knots (though this was possibly confiscated from George Boleyn): ibid., nos 9770, 13383, 13147.

62 The Whitehall bed itself was 8 feet [2.43 m] wide and over 8 feet [2.5 m] long: ibid., no. 9770.

63 *Inventory*, no.11388.

64 e.g. Rogier van der Weyden: the *Bladelin Triptych* (Staatliche Museen, Berlin), the *Columba Altarpiece* (Alte Pinakothek, Munich), the *Medici Madonna* (Städelsches Kunstinstitut, Frankfurt), the *Annunciation Triptych* (Louvre).

65 *St. Pap.*, i.415 [*LP*, vi.1486]; *LP*, viii.440.

66 See p. 253.

67 RO, SP 1/103 ff. 322–7 [*LP*, x.913]. Conjecturally a device to straighten the fingers (about which the adult Elizabeth was very vain).

68 See pp. 198–9; *LP*, vii.509.

69 *LP*, x.1257 (ix); xi.117.

70 The decision to send Elizabeth to Hertford in December 1533 went through the council.

71 *St. Pap.*, i.426 [*LP*, ix.568]. The initiative seems to have been taken by Lady Bryan and communicated to Henry via Cromwell.

72 *LP*, ix.568; see above, p. 381 n. 53.

73 *Literary Remains of King Edward the Sixth*, ed. J. G. Nichols (1857), pp. xxxii–xxxiii.

74 See p. 352.

75 Parker, *Correspondence*, pp. 59, 400.

76 For Parker see pp. 266–7.

77 See p. 348.

78 John Harington, *Nugae Antiquae*, ed. H. Harington (1779), ii.147.

79 RO, SP 1/103 ff. 322–7 [*LP*, x.913].

80 London, Victoria and Albert Museum. The instrument has been dated by comparison with continental examples. It is not identifiable among the twenty in Henry's inventories.

81 London, Royal College of Music, MS 1070. For the following, see the authoritative study of the text by Edward E. Lowinsky, in *Florilegium*, pp. 161–235.

82 One item (apparently unique to the book) is a pastiche motet, *O salve genitrix Virgo*. This includes the line 'you outshine the roses' which, given identification of Anne with the Virgin, could be associated with her badge.

83 Cf. also the links between Hannah's prayer and the Virgin Mary's *Magnificat*.

84 Anne's text must have been derived from France since it leaves the name of Louis XII unchanged.

85 See p. 25.

86 Professor Warnicke points out that an item which occurs in MS 1070 was published in 1528: *Rise and Fall*, p. 249. A late 1520s date would tally with a possibly fanciful conjecture made by Lowinsky that two illuminations show birds which could be falcons, attacking what could possibly be pomegranates (Katherine of Aragon's badge). Once Anne had replaced Katherine, such a confrontation would have no point. However, even assuming the birds are falcons, they have neither crowns nor sceptres, and are not perching on roses. Birds pecking fruit are a standard decorative theme [Thurley, *Palaces*, p. 91]. See also Warnicke, ibid., pp. 248–9, and her rejection of Lowinsky's suggestions that the book includes likenesses of Anne and Katherine.

87 A longa in early notation equals two or three breves.

88 Lowinsky suggested that, ending as it does with a longa which could signify 'the

end', the notation referred to Anne executed. This is unlikely since even after her fall Anne was still normally called 'the queen'. An alternative speculation would see the minims referring to 1526 when Henry began to pursue Anne, 1527 when they were handfasted, and 1528 as the (anticipated) final year of waiting.

89 Cavendish, *Metrical Visions*, p. 36.
90 See pp. 24–5.
91 Josquin died in 1521.
92 Jean Mouton died 1522. Anne could also have met Loyset Compère (d. 1518) who contributed three liturgical items.
93 See pp. 273–4.
94 Knecht, *Renaissance Warrior and Patron*, pp. 460–1.

Chapter 18   The Advent of Reform

1 Foxe, *Acts and Monuments*, v.175.
2 The seminal exposition of M. Dowling, 'Anne Boleyn and reform', in *JEH*, 35 (1984), 30–46, has triggered considerable debate, e.g. Bernard, in *Hist. Journ.* 36, 1–20; J. S. Block, *Factional Politics and the English Reformation, 1520–1549* (1993), pp. 28–32, 59–64; Ives, in *Hist. Journ.* 37, 389–400, and in *François Ier et Henri VIII*, pp. 83–102; Warnicke, *Rise and Fall*, pp. 107–13, 152–4.
3 RO, SP70/7, ff. 1–11 [*Cal. S. P. For., 1558–59*, 1303 at p. 532] – hereafter: Ales, 'Letter'; Oxford, Bodl. MS Don. C. 42, f. 30. Dowling as 'Cronickille', pp. 23–65.
4 *Cal. S. P. Span., 1531–33*, p. 866 [*LP*, vi.1460].
5 Fox was very much of Anne's religious temper [see p. 144]. He supported the Ten Articles and the *rapprochement* with the German reformers, but resisted sacramentarian heresy: MacCulloch, *Cranmer*, pp. 45–7, 195–6, 216–17; Ridley, *Cranmer*, pp. 119, 121, 163; *LP*, viii.823. Fox helped Ales. Nicholas Hawkins, archdeacon of Ely, should probably be added to the list.

Intended for the see of Ely, he died early in January 1534 while returning from Spain: *LP* vi.661, 1546; vii.115 (2). Anne was very upset at the death of this reformer, who was close to Fox, a friend of Cranmer, visited Anne before leaving England and translated *The Glasse of Truth*: *LP*, v.1372, 1377; vi.661; vii.171; *St. Pap.*, vii p. 390 [*LP*, v.1564], ibid., p. 404 [*LP*, 1660].
6 Note the role of Goodrich, Skip and Capon in saving John Merbeck: Foxe, *Acts and Monuments*, v.482–4, 486, 490–2.
7 Wood, *Letters*, ii.188–9 [*LP*, vii.693].
8 *LP*, iv.4647, App. 197.
9 *LP*, vii.89; ix.189. Chapuys refers to the protection of 'Lutheran' clerics by Anne and her father in Mar. 1531 and May 1532, possibly Latimer in each case: *Cal. S. P. Span., 1531–33*, pp. 96, 445 [*LP*, v.148, 1013].
10 For the following see *LP*, v.333; viii.412, 466; ix.1091; x.19, 1182; cf. E. G. Rupp, *Studies in the Making of the English Protestant Tradition* (Cambridge, 1947), pp. 62–72.
11 Foxe, *Acts and Monuments*, v.250; Hall, *Chronicle*, p. 824.
12 *LP*, viii.722.
13 *The Zurich Letters*, ed. H. Robinson (Parker Society, 1842, 1845), i.200.
14 Foxe, *Acts and Monuments*, v.605.
15 *Cal. S. P. Span., 1536–38*, p. 91 [*LP*, x.699].
16 Bentley, *Excerpta Historica*, p. 263; Constantine, in *Archaeologia*, 23, 65; for the various versions of this speech see pp. 272, 419 n. 14.
17 Elton, *Reform and Renewal*, p. 23. The Tebold letters should conjecturally be ordered: 31 July 1535 Antwerp, dated by the return to England of Gabriel Donne; 9 Jan. 1536 Orléans, dated by the reference to 'last Lent' and the new pope; 4 Apr. Frankfurt, dated by the reference to Wolfe and the location of Charles V; post 12 Mar. Frankfurt or Tübingen (?), dated by the enclosure and the reference to the invasion of Savoy: *LP*, viii.1151; ix.522; viii.33; iv.6304; x.458.

18   For Poinz see *LP*, ix.182, 405; Foxe, *Acts and Monuments*, v.121–7; *House of Commons*, iii.147.

19   *LP*, x.942.

20   Ales, 'Letter', p. 532.

21   See p. 328 and *LP*, x.942.

22   See p. 388 n. 22; Cranmer, *Letters*, pp. 290–1; *LP*, ix.561.

23   *LP*, vi.700.

24   *LP*, viii.834, 1056. Whether or not Anne's letter about Vale Royal was effective is not clear. The successful candidate was John Harware, abbot of Hulton: Thornton, *Cheshire*, pp. 198, 206–7.

25   For the following see Latymer, 'Treatyse', ff. 30v–31 [Dowling, 'Cronickille', pp. 60–1]; Burnet, *History*, iv.221; *LP*, viii.989.

26   For the following see Wriothesley, *Chronicle*, i.90; *LP*, vii. App. 35; viii.989; ix.747, 1118; x.192; Knowles, *Religious Orders*, iii.352–3.

27   Latymer, 'Treatyse', f. 31 [Dowling, 'Cronickille', p. 61].

28   For the following see Knowles, *Religious Orders*, iii.218–20; *LP*, ix.954, 986. Knowles [p. 216] gives the date as autumn 1534.

29   On this see especially Dowling, in *JEH*, 35, 38–41.

30   *House of Commons*, i.626–9; Parker, *Correspondence*, pp. 2–3.

31   Ibid., pp. 1–2.

32   Ibid., pp. 4–5.

33   Ibid., p. ix.

34   Cranmer, *Letters*, p. 308.

35   Parker, *Correspondence*, pp. 59, 391, 400; see pp. 256, 286.

36   An alternative identification is Thomas Forman: Dowling, *Humanism*, p. 82.

37   Dowling, in *JEH*, 35, 36–7.

38   For Hilsey see *LP*, vi.433(iii). Shaxton and Latimer both resigned their bishoprics in 1539 because of the apparently reactionary *Statute of Six Articles*. Shaxton recanted heretical opinions in 1546 and died in 1556 as a suffragan bishop reconciled to Rome. Latimer was burned as a heretic in 1555.

39   L. Febvre, *Au coeur religieux du XVIe siècle* (Paris, 1957), p. 66.

40   Latymer, 'Treatyse', f. 31v [Dowling, 'Cronickille', p. 62].

41   Latymer, 'Treatyse', f. 32 [Dowling, 'Cronickille', p. 63].

42   BL, Royal MS 20. B xvii f. 1.

43   Latymer, 'Treatyse', ff. 31v, 32 [Dowling, 'Cronickille', pp. 62–3].

44   *LP*, vi.458.

45   *The newe Testament* (Antwerp, 1534) [BL, C23 a8].

46   Ibid., iv.3960.

47   BL, Sloane MS 1207, ff. iv, 3. The petition is only in draft, mixed up among other jottings. That it was actually presented can only be assumed.

48   Ellis, *Letters*, I ii.46.

49   A. G. Dickens, *The English Reformation* (1964), p. 131. A tradition exists that Anne Boleyn presented to her ladies miniature psalters or prayer books, and that one of these was given by her on the scaffold to a member of the Wyatt family. Tiny religious books were the height of female fashion at the time – but the tradition is only identifiable from the early eighteenth century and was not known to George Wyatt. Two such have been identified with this story: (i) BL, Stowe MS 956, formerly in the collection of the earl of Ashburnham, a metrical version of thirteen penitential psalms translated into English by John Croke. The frontispiece is a miniature of Henry VIII after the Holbein privy chamber pattern (i.e. post 1537). Hist. Mss. Comm. *Eighth Report*, iii (1881) suggested that the miniature was an addition; this is not taken up by BL, *Catalogue of Stowe Mss.* H. Tait, 'Historiate Tudor jewellery', in *Antiquaries Journal*, 42 (1962), 234–5, accepts dating by the image of the king. (ii) A MS owned by the earl of Romney in 1873, edited and described by his brother, Robert Marsham, in *Archaeologia*, 44 (1873), 259–72, English prayers and psalms in prose. Item 10 [pp. 270–1] is the prayer attributed to Thomas Cromwell on the scaffold [Foxe,

Acts and Monuments, v.403]. Neither book, therefore, can have been owned by Anne. Marsham, in a letter now pasted in Alnwick, Percy MS 465 (see pp. 241–2), claimed that the Ashburnham MS [now Stowe 956] was the same described by R. Triphook in his edition of George Wyatt, *Life of Anne Boleigne* (1817). [See also J. Rowlands, *The Age of Dürer and Holbein* (1988), p. 241.] There is no contemporary record of Anne giving gifts on the scaffold, which must cast doubt on the pendant supposedly given to a Captain Gwyn: Doran, *Elizabeth*, p. 11.

50 Erasmus, *Enchiridion Militis Christiani* (1503), quoted from *The Essential Erasmus*, ed. J. P. Dolan (New York, 1964), p. 37.

51 *Enarratio in Psalmum xxii* (Freiburg, 1530); *De praeparatione ad mortem* (Freiburg, 1533), translated as *A preparation to deathe* (Berthelet, 1538) [the quotation is from sig. Aiv]; *Explanatio Symboli* (Freiburg, 1533), translated as *A playne and godly exposytion or declaration of the commune crede* (Redman, 1533).

52 Carley, in *Illuminating the Book*, p. 277 n.50.

53 *La Saincte Bible en Francoys* (Antwerp, 1534) [BL, C18 c 9]. 'For as in Adam all die, so in Christ shall all be made alive' [1 Corinthians 15: 22]. 'The law was given by Moses [but] grace and truth [came] by Jesus Christ' [John 1:17].

54 *Les Choses contenu en ce present livre* (Paris, 1525?).

55 *Lecclesiaste Preschant que toutes chose sans dieu sont vanite* (Alençon, 1530?).

56 Carley, in *Illuminating the Book*, pp. 266–8.

57 Ibid., p. 272.

58 Ibid., p. 277 at n.43.

59 Carley also suggests that the translation enabled George to demonstrate his accomplishments, and reconciled court culture and piety: ibid. pp. 271–2. Cf. 'as much for public demonstrations of piety as for personal devotion' [Dowling, in *Henry VIII: European Court*, p. 108] and 'made

moderate reform a thing for English gentlemen' [Ives, in *François Ier et Henri VIII*, p. 102].

60 Shakespeare and Dowling, in *BIHR*, 55, 97; cf. *LP*, viii.197.

61 *LP*, x.827.

62 BL Royal MS 16 E 13.

63 In Clémont Marot, *Psaumes* (Antwerp, 1541).

64 C. A. Mayer, in 'Le "Sermon du bon pasteur", un problème d'attribution', in *Bibliothèque d'humanisme et Renaissance*, 27 (1965), 286–303, and 'Anne Boleyn et la version originale du "Sermon du bon pasteur" d'Almanque Papillon', in *Bulletin de la Société d'histoire du Protestantisme Français*, 132 (1986), 337–46.

65 BL Royal MS 16 E 13, ff. 15, 15v.

O ma dame Anne, O royne incomparable
Ce bon pasteur qui vous a aggreable
Vous doint ung filz qui soit l'ymaige vifve
Du Roy, son pere, et qu'il surcroisse et vive
Tant que vous deux le puyissiez veoir en l'age
Que l'homme doibt ou jamais estre saige.

66 Knecht, *Renaissance Warrior and Patron*, p. 317.

67 Latymer, 'Treatyse', ff. 28–9 [Dowling, 'Cronickille', p. 59].

68 E. W. Ives, 'A Frenchman at the court of Anne Boleyn', in *History Today*, 48 (1998), 21–6; M. M. Philips, 'The *Paedagogion* of Nicolas Bourbon', in *Neo-Latin and the Vernacular in Sixteenth-Century France*, ed. T. Cave (1983), pp. 71–82.

69 Bourbon produced two bestsellers: *Nicolai Borbonii Vanderoperani Nugae* (Paris, 1533) and *Nugarum Libri Octo* (Lyons, 1538).

70 Butts was the contact and Dinteville was Bourbon's patron [*Nugarum*, v.21, pp. 284–5, vii.113, p. 409] but the link was by letter if at all, for the poet was in England by May 1535 and the ambassador did not arrive until the autumn.

71 *Nugarum*, vii.90, p. 402.

72 Latymer 'Treatyse', ff. 28, 28v, [Dowling, 'Cronickille', p. 61]; for Butts, see also *Nugarum*, ii. pp. 86–8.

73 Cromwell: *Nugarum*, iv no. 81, p. 251, v no. 23, p. 286; Cranmer: vi no. 33, pp. 344–5, vii nos 9 and 10, p. 377; joint: iv no. 82, pp. 251–2.

74 Butts: ibid., vii no. 113, p. 409; Latimer: vii no. 36, p. 384; Holbein: iii no. 8, p. 153, vi no. 12, p. 338, vii no. 158, p. 427, viii no. 36, p. 450. Bourbon, *Paedogogion* (Lyons, 1536), p. 28.

75 Ibid., no. 119, p. 411.

76 Also: ibid., vii nos 14 and 15, p. 378, no. 64, p. 392, no. 90, p. 402, no. 109, p. 407; jointly with Henry, vii no. 110, p. 407.

77 Ibid., vii no. 109, p. 407.

Chapter 19   Personal Religion

1 See p. 240.

2 E. P. Wilson in *The Times*, 3 November 1997.

3 Alnwick, Percy MS 465, f. 148.

4 See p. 49.

5 See p. 269.

6 See pp. 32–3.

7 Lemaitre, in *François Ier et Henri VIII*, pp. 102–19.

8 Marguerite was also close to Claude: *Guillaume Briconnet et Marguerite d'Angouléme: Correspondance*, ed. C. Martineau and M. Veissière (Geneva, 1975), i.124, ii.64.

9 Ibid., i.75.

10 See pp. 239–40; if BL, King's MS 9 was Anne's and not Henry's, then there are three early traditional books: see pp. 6–7.

11 Carley, in *Illuminating the Book*, p. 271.

12 W. G. Moore, *La Réforme allemande et la littérature française* (Strasbourg, 1930), p. 185, quoted by Carley, in *Illuminating the Book*, p. 279 n.63.

13 M. D. Orth, 'Radical beauty: Marguerite de Navarre's illuminated Protestant catechism and confession', in *Sixteenth Century Journal*, 24 (1993), 383–425.

14 Carley, in *Illuminating the Book*, p. 279 n.65.

15 Bernard, in *Hist. Journ.* 36, 4; cf. 'dabbling with the new sects may for both Rochford and Anne have been more a matter of politics and radical chic than a matter of religious conviction', ibid., 20.

16 Latymer, 'Treatyse', ff. 31v, 32 [Dowling, 'Cronickille', pp. 62–3]; see pp. 6–7.

17 Ibid., f. 24 [Dowling, 'Cronickille', p. 50].

18 Alnwick, Percy MS 465, f. 3; cf. f. 9v: the world was intended for Adam 'for pleasure, voluptuousness and solace'.

19 Ibid., f. 13.

20 Ibid., ff. 147–8.

21 Ibid., f. 148.

22 Bray, *Documents*, p. 166.

23 Alnwick, Percy MS 465, f. 146v.

24 Ibid., f. 146.

25 Ibid., f. 145v.

26 Ibid., f. 40.

27 Lefèvre, *Épistres*, ed. Screech, p. 13.

28 Lefèvre, *Épistres*, ed. Bedouelle and Giacone, p. 366.

29 Alnwick, Percy MS 465, ff. 144v–45.

30 e.g. ibid., ff. 34 [Hydra], 38 ['the hand washeth the hand'], 7 [dropsy = diabetes], 15 ['crowns of the sun']. BL, Harleian MS 6561, 'Pistellis and Gospelles' has a scholarly note at f. 13: 'some read Bethania, but the word is corrupt, said for Betharia.'

31 Alnwick, Percy MS 465, f. 25v.

32 Ibid.

33 Ibid., f. 24.

34 BL, Harleian MS 6561, f. 74.

35 See pp. 353, 356. Screech argued strongly that 'without the framework of the mass, the choice of the scripture passages commented on in the exhortations would have no meaning': *Épistres*, ed. Screech, p. 13.

36 See pp. 307–10.

37 RO SP6/1 f. 9. Holy water was believed to have 'effectual power' to drive out demons and disease; holy bread was the communal loaf shared after mass in lieu of communion and was held to have apotropaic powers: E. Duffy, *The Stripping of the Altars* (New Haven, 1992), pp. 281, 125.

38 King Hezekiah destroyed the brass serpent made by Moses at God's command because sacrifices were being offered to it: 2 Kings, chapter 18, verse 4.

39 *LP*, x.371; Dowling, in *JEH*, 35, 44. I am not persuaded by her suggestion that Anne turned down the *Farrago* because of her 'precarious' position in 1536. The work must always have been unacceptable because of its full-blooded advocacy of the priesthood of all believers and its exposition in detail of the socially disruptive implications. I owe the information about Anne's ownership of Lambert's translations [BL C.37.a.22, items iv and v] to the generosity of J. P. Carley.

40 Cf. BL, Harleian MS 6561: f. 15 [*Épistres et Évangiles*, ed. Bedouelle and Giacone, pp. 25–6, 28–9] in which only one of the exhortations for Christmas Day makes any reference at all to Mary ['aujourd'hui nay d'une vierge'] and for St Stephen's Day stresses that Stephen is not honoured, but 'the Lord for the grace he gave Stephen' and 'the wisdom and spirit of God that did speak in him . . . It is God and our Lord Jesuchrist that we ought to call upon and not angels or any other creatures, and it is he to whom we ought to commend our souls': ff. 16v–17 [*Épistres*, ed. Bedouelle and Giacone, pp. 30–2].

41 *LP*, xii(2).1304.

42 Foxe, *Acts and Monuments*, v.36–7; Brigden, *Reformation in London*, pp. 205–7; Carley, in *Hist. Journ.*, 38, 814–15. Cromwell was also appealed to. Patmore's case was dealt with by a panel packed with reformers: *LP*, viii.1063.

43 Alnwick, Percy MS 465, f. 30.

44 Latymer, 'Treatyse', ff. 25–7 [Dowling, 'Cronickille', pp. 51–4].

45 Ibid., ff. 27v–28 [Dowling, 'Cronickille', pp. 54–5]; *LP*, ix.186.

46 Foxe, *Acts and Monuments*, v.135.

47 Wyatt, *Wolsey*, ed. Singer, p. 443.

48 For the legislation see Elton, *Reform and Renewal*, pp. 123–6; and 'An early Tudor poor law', in *Studies*, ii. 137–54.

49 Marshall translated the *Plain and Godly Exposition of the Common Creed* which Erasmus had written for Thomas Boleyn, with the special intention of making it suitable for circulation among the less educated: McConica, *English Humanists*, p. 137; see p. 270.

50 Dowling, *Humanism*, p. 239. Marshall's work was a translation of the *Forma Subventionis Pauperum*.

51 Elton, *Reform and Renewal*, pp. 62–3, 76, 122–5; *Studies*, ii.151–3, 245, 250.

52 27 Henry VIII, c.25. The proposed legislation was emasculated during passage.

53 For the difficulties with courtly verse see pp. 71–6.

54 HMC, *Salisbury* i.9–10; Dowling, *Humanism*, p. 131.

55 Robert Wakefield, *Kotser Codicis* (Berthelet, 1532); McConica, *English Humanists*, pp. 133–4.

56 BL, Royal MS 20 B xvii [see pp. 268–9]. There may have been an element of professional and courtly competition here, for in 1530, Palsgrave, Mary Tudor's protégé, produced a guide to French, and in 1532 Giles du Guez dedicated another to Princess Mary: Russell, *Cloth of Gold*, p. 126 n. 1.

57 *LP*, iv.6768; Wood, *Letters*, ii.191 [*LP*, viii.710].

58 Dowling, in *JEH*, 35, 34.

59 Latymer, 'Treatyse', f. 28v [Dowling, 'Cronickille', p. 56]; Beckynsaw died in 1559.

60 *LP*, vii.964.

61 Latymer, 'Treatyse', f. 28v [Dowling, 'Cronickille', p. 56]; *LP*, x.345; Dowling, in *JEH*, 35, 34.

62 John Strype, *Life and Acts of Matthew Parker* (Oxford, 1821), pp. 16–18.

63 *Nugarum*, vii.15, p. 378.

64 Ibid., vii. p. 368.

65 Ibid., vi. p. 330.

Chapter 20   The Rival, 1535–1536

1 *LP*, ix.310, 555, 571, 579, 639.

2 *Cal. S. P. Span., 1534–35*, p. 529 [*LP*, ix.58]. *Lisle Letters*, ii.451. The consecration dates in *Handbook of British Chronology*, ed. F. M. Powicke and E. B. Fryde (3rd edn, 1986), give Hilsey 18th and Fox and Latimer 26th.

3 *LP*, ix.121, 203, 252, 272–3, 342.

4 Ibid., ix.729(6), (7), (8); W. Seymour, *Ordeal by Ambition* (1972), pp. 41–2.

5 For the progress, see *LP*, viii.989; ix.460, 525, 620. The visit to Wolf Hall lasted from at least 4 to 10 Sept. inclusive (not the three days of tradition), and as it was a main stop for the progress (not a by-progress), Anne would have been there: *LP*, ix.271, 326.

6 Wriothesley, *Chronicle*, i.43.

7 *LP*, vii.9(ii).

8 Hamy, *Entrevue*, p. liv.

9 *LP*, ix.620, 639.

10 Clifford, *Dormer*, pp. 40–1.

11 *House of Commons*, i.53.

12 *LP*, ix.566 [dated by 594], 525, 555, 571.

13 *Cal. S. P. Span., 1536–38*, pp. 39–40 [*LP*, x.282].

14 Ibid., p. 28 [*LP*, x.199]; *LP*, x.495; Friedmann, *Anne Boleyn*, ii.202–3: '*La chose m'est bien difficile a croyre, oyres quell soit venue de bon lieu.*'

15 *LP*, ix.566; *Cal. S. P. Span., 1534–35*, p. 550 [*LP*, ix.594].

16 *LP*, vi.1164; Friedmann, *Anne Boleyn*, i.233; *LP*, ix.566.

17 *LP*, ix.862 and p. xxxii.

18 Mattingly, *Catherine of Aragon*, pp. 302–4.

19 Friedmann, *Anne Boleyn*, ii.121.

20 *Cal. S. P. Span., 1534–35*, p. 551 [*LP*, ix.594]; Wriothesley, *Chronicle*, i.32; *LP*, ix.378, 838, 964, 965, 969, 980, 987. See p. 33.

21 Ibid., ix.674; *Cal. S. P. Span., 1534–35*, p. 484 [*LP*, viii.826].

22 Ibid., *1536–8*, p. 97 [*LP*, x.699].

23 Ibid., *1536–8*, pp. 19, 28 [*LP*, x.141, 199]. Hall, *Chronicle*, p. 818, says that Anne wore yellow, Chapuys that Henry did.

24 *Cal. S. P. Span., 1534–35*, p. 595 [*LP*, ix.1035].

25 Ibid., p. 28 [*LP*, ix.199].

26 *LP*, x.200; *Cal. S. P. Span., 1536–38*, p. 67 [*LP*, x.427].

27 Ibid., p. 39 [*LP*, x.282]. The claim [Warnicke, *Rise and Fall*, pp. 196–8] that Anne miscarried possibly as early as 23 Jan. and that the failure of Chapuys to mention this in a supposed letter of 3 Feb. shows that the news must have been deliberately concealed is based on wrong dating by *Cal. S. P. Span., 1536–38*, and is without merit. For what Chapuys knew on 29 Jan. see p. 298. *Cal. S. P. Span., 1536–38* should be corrected as follows: pp. 34–5 '7 Mar.' *not* '3 Feb.' [*LP*, x.429]; pp. 39–42a '10' *not* '17 Feb.' [*LP*, x.282]; pp. 42b–45 '17 Feb.' [*LP*, x.307]; pp. 68–70 '18' *not* '10 Mar.' [*LP*, x.494].

28 Wriothesley, *Chronicle*, i.33.

29 The queen was at least $4\frac{1}{2}$ months from 'taking her chamber'. The sex would be especially difficult to tell if, as can happen, there was any retention.

30 Sander, *Schism*, p. 132; the mass of flesh appears in Berkshire Record Office, Trumble MS 5, f. 6 which is associated with Sander: Dowling, 'Cronickille', p. 40.

31 Warnicke, *Rise and Fall*, ch. 8. Cf. D. M. Loades, *Mary Tudor: A Life* (Oxford, 1989), p. 97; J. A. Guy, *Tudor England* (Oxford, 1988), pp. 141–2; P. M. Gross, *Jane the Quene, Third Consort of King Henry VIII* (Lampeter, 1999), p. 31. Miscarriage was accepted: D. Cressy, *Birth, Marriage & Death* (Oxford, 1997), p. 47; hence, until deformity can be proved, speculation of the 'what if' variety remains fatuous.

32 J. Loach, 'The usurped and unjust empire of women', in *JEH*, 42 (1992), 287.

33 *LP*, xiii (i), 493.

34 Warnicke, *Rise and Fall*, ch. 8.

35 *Cal. S. P. Span., 1536–38*, p. 28 [*LP*, x.199]. Friedmann, *Anne Boleyn*, ii.203.

36 See p. 327.

37 Chapuys' despatch detailing Henry's words is dated 29 Jan., but he did not report the miscarriage until his next letter. Since Henry could not have spoken of failure to have sons as long as Anne's pregnancy continued, his remark must have been passed on by the Exeters before they learned why Henry had said it.

38 Carewe, but why did Chapuys not identify him (as he usually did)?

39 Epistle to the Galatians, chapter 3 verse 1.

40 *Cal. S. P. Span., 1531–33*, p. 28 [*LP*, vi.1528].

41 H. A. Kelly, 'English kings and the fear of sorcery', *Medieval Studies*, 39 (1977), 235.

42 Neale, *Queen Elizabeth*, p. 17.

43 *Cal. S. P. Span., 1536–38*, pp. 39–40 [*LP*, x.282].

44 Ibid., p. 59 [*LP*, x.351].

45 Lehmberg, *Reformation Parliament*, pp. 221–8, 237 and n. 4. Shrovetide 1536 was from Sunday 26 Feb. to Thursday 2 Mar. The provisions of the dissolution bill became public knowledge on or before 3 Mar. Henry was meticulous in being readily available at parliament time.

46 *LP*, x.283, 450.

47 George Wyatt, in *Wolsey*, ed. Singer, pp. 443–4.

48 Sander, *Schism*, p. 132.

49 Clifford, *Dormer*, p. 79.

50 See pp. 313–14.

51 *LP*, x.352.

52 *LP*, x.670 at p. 269.

53 e.g. *Cal. S. P. Span., 1536–38*, p. 106 [*LP*, x.752] and his subsequent housing of Jane: see p. 327.

54 *Cal. S. P. Span., 1536–38*, pp. 81, 84–5 [*LP*, x.601]. For Eliot see also A. Fox, 'Sir Thomas Eliot and the humanist dilemma', in A. Fox and J. A. Guy, *Reassessing the Henrician Age: Politics and Reform, 1500–1550* (Oxford, 1986), pp. 59–60.

55 *Cal. S. P. Span., 1534–35*, p. 520 [*LP*, viii.1106];

56 *LP*, x.670 at p. 269.

57 *Cal. S. P. Span., 1536–38*, pp. 84, 106 [*LP*, x.752].

58 Friedmann, *Anne Boleyn*, ii.200 [*LP*, x. 901].

59 Elton, 'The good duke', in *Studies*, i.234.

60 Wyatt, Poems, CVII, p. 112.

61 *LP*, x.495.

62 George Wyatt, in *Wolsey*, ed. Singer, p. 444.

63 For the following see Ives, in *History Today*, 50, 48–53.

64 *Cal. S. P. Span., 1536–38*, p. 85, 106–7 [*LP*, x.601, 752].

65 Ibid., p. 107 [*LP*, x.782]. Cf. his remarks to Cromwell, ibid., pp. 81–2 [*LP*, x.601].

66 *Cal. S. P. Span., 1536–38*, pp. 84–5 [*LP*, x.601]. Chapuys was told this story by both Lady Exeter and Thomas Elyot.

67 George Wyatt, in *Wolsey*, ed. Singer, p. 443; Berkshire RO, Trumble MS 5, f. 6.

68 See pp. 85–6.

69 Strickland, *Queens of England*, ii.273.

70 *LP*, x.909; Strickland, *Queens of England*, ii.274–5.

Chapter 21   The Response, January-April 1536

1   *Cal. S. P. Span., 1536–38*, p. 106 [LP x.752]. I have been unable to locate G. Walker's source [*Hist. Journ.* 45, 13] for attributing to me the statement that Henry approached Stokesley on 27 April. Chapuys' report makes it certain that this was a private enquiry, probably by Geoffrey Pole or someone on behalf of Anne's enemies.

2   *Cal. S. P. Span., 1536–38*, p. 124 [*LP*, x.908].

3   Lehmberg, *Reformation Parliament*, pp. 57, 218.

4   *LP*, x.597(3), (4).

5   Lehmberg, *Reformation Parliament*, p. 230; *Cal. S. P. Span., 1536–38*, p. 102 [*LP*, x.699].

6   *LP*, x.243 (24). For this decision in the autumn of 1535 see *LP*, ix. 779.

7   *LP*, x.715. Chapuys' letter to Granvelle [ibid., 753] attributes Carewe's success to the support of Francis I; his letter of the same date to Charles portrays the election as a defeat for Anne and her brother: *Cal. S. P. Span., 1536–38*, p. 106 [*LP*, x.752]. The letter to Granvelle is correct; Francis had requested the order for Carewe in 1533 and had been promised it in 1535; *LP*, vi.555, 707; viii.174.

8   *LP*, x.741, 749. Stafford was, however, close to Edward Fox, *DNB*, vii.555.

9   *Cal. S. P. Span., 1536–38*, pp. 81–2 [*LP*, x.601].

10   See pp. 282–3. For the following see Ives, in *Hist. Journ.*, 37, 395–400.

11   RO SP1/103 f. 79. The material on the sermon consists of two hostile summaries and a set of interrogatories: RO SP6/1 ff. 7–11v; SP6/2 ff. 11–13; SP1/103 ff. 78–84. There are related MSS: RO SP/2 f. 18 sqq and SP6/6 ff. 70 sqq.

12   RO SP6/1 f. 8.

13   RO SP6/2 f. 12.

14   RO SP6/1 f. 9.

15   RO SP1/103 ff. 79v, 80; 6/1 f. 7v.

16   RO SP6/1 f 8v.

17   Ibid.

18   Lehmberg, *Reformation Parliament*, p. 226; D. Knowles, *Religious Orders in England*, iii (Cambridge, 1959), pp. 293–303.

19   Hugh Latimer, *Sermons*, ed. G. E. Corrie (Parker Society, 1844), p. 123. Knowles' objections are to a precision Latimer probably did not intend.

20   For the following, see Hoyle, in *Hist. Journ.*, 38 (1995), 284–99.

21   See p. 286–7.

22   RO SP6/1 f. 11.

23   Lehmberg, *Reformation Parliament*, p. 227. But the reference to Henry 'giving' could mean that the measure was the poor law: ibid., 232 n. 1.

24   RO SP 6/1 ff. 8, 9v; 6/2 f. 12v; Fletcher and MacCulloch, *Tudor Rebellions*, p. 131; see also n. 30 below.

25   RO SP6/1 f. 8v, 'I shall bring into your coffers ten thousand talents.' Cf. Vulgate *Liber Hester*, chapter 3, verses 8–9: 'dixitque Aman regi Asuero . . . si tibi placet decerne ut pereat et decem mila talentorum adpendam arcariis gazae tuae' ['if it please you, give a decision that this people should perish and that I should pay 10,000 talents for the archers into the treasury'].

26   RO 6/1 8v.

27   LP, x.445; *Tudor Constitutional Documents*, ed. J. R. Tanner (Cambridge, 1930), pp. 61–3.

28   Hoyle, *Pilgrimage*, pp. 79–80.

29   *Cal. S. P. For., 1558–59*, 1303. Dated 1 Sept. 1559 but relying on observations before he left England in 1539, Alexander Ales wrote that 'Cromwell, Wriothesley and certain others . . . hated the queen because she had sharply rebuked them . . . that under the guise of religion they were advancing their own interests [and] that they had put everything up for sale.'

30 For Singleton see Brigden, *London and the Reformation*, pp. 259, 349–52.

31 Latymer 'Treatyse', ff. 28v, 29 [Dowling, 'Cronickille', p. 57].

32 Ibid., ff. 28v, 29.

33 *LP*, x.705; MacCulloch, *Cranmer*, pp. 151–2, 155–6.

34 Ibid., p. 155 [*LP*, x. 705].

35 Latymer, 'Treatyse', ff. 29–30 [Dowling, 'Cronickille', pp. 57–9].

36 This could be queried as a possible Elizabethan gloss, but see p. 264.

37 'Lewdness' does not carry a primarily sexual implication.

38 From first reading to royal assent was a matter of only six weeks.

39 The redirection of assets was an even greater threat than granting exemptions alone because it blocked subsequent dissolution.

40 *Cal. S. P. Span.*, 1536–38, pp. 83–4 [*LP*, x.601]. Hoyle, *Pilgrimage*, p. 80 suggests that the preaching campaign could have had some effect and that the need to regularize disposal of land explains the April writs for a new parliament.

41 Or future protection for those who escaped in 1536.

42 *LP*, xii(i).786.

43 Jane Seymour is more likely but the undated letter of the prioress referring to the offer having already been made by the queen [*LP*, x.383], mentions a report which is either that dated 12 May [ibid., x.858] or else earlier, and Jane only married on 30 May and was openly shown as queen on 2 June, ibid., x.1047; see also ibid., x.916, 1166; dissolution began at Catesby on 27 June; ibid., x. 1215.

44 *LP*, xi.860; cf. ibid., 1250.

45 *Cal. S. P. Span.*, 1536–38, p. 75 [*LP*, x.575].

46 *LP*, x.670 at p. 269.

47 *Cal. S. P. Span.*, 1536–38, pp. 54, 89, 91, 93, 98 [*LP*, x.351, 699].

48 Ibid., pp. 91–8 [*LP*, x.699].

49 Ibid., p. 98 [*LP*, x.699].

50 Ibid.

51 Ibid., pp. 53, 99 [*LP*, x.351, 699], *LP*, x.308.

52 Ibid., x.308; *Cal. S. P. Span.*, 1536–38, p. 80 [*LP*, x.601].

53 *LP*, x.720.

54 *LP*, x.54, 410, 688.

55 *LP*, x.887.

56 *LP*, x.688, 752; *Lisle Letters*, iii.686 [*LP*, x.748]; *Cal. S. P. Span.*, 1536–38, pp. 99–102, 105 [*LP*, x.699, 752].

57 *LP*, x.760.

58 *LP*, x.700.

59 *Cal. S. P. Span.*, 1534–35, p. 484 [*LP*, viii.826] and ibid., 1536–38, p. 81 [*LP*, x.601].

60 Ibid., p. 130 [*LP*, x.908].

61 M. St Clare Byrne [*Lisle Letters*, i.161; ii.170–1, 333–43] and David Starkey [thesis, pp. 321–3] have argued that Cromwell set out to cut down 'the effective interference' of the privy chamber circle, and that he asserted full control over the signature of bills by the king. A close reading of the fifty and more Lisle letters between Oct. 1533 and Apr. 1536 which are concerned with patronage, suggests a different conclusion. Cromwell was important as the administrator whose workload might impose delay on the processing of grants, or who might (as duty bound) raise queries about the king's interests. In his initial months as secretary he used such possibilities to establish his claim to a share of the gratuities paid by applicants: *Lisle Letters*, ii.148, 151–2, 159–60, 168, 171, 183–5, 191 [*LP*, vii.350, 385, 386, 461, 474, 502, 522, 614, 620, 627, 652]. He also responded to the competitive pressure of factions at court: ibid., ii.259, 260a, 264 [*LP*, vii.1165, 1182, 1224]. His delay in paying out monies in his charge on the king's verbal orders via Norris may have been similarly motivated: ibid., ii.202, 202a [*LP*, vii.734, 844] and pp. 164–71. The privy chamber, and especially Norris in his capacity as groom of the stool, continued throughout this period to exercise an independent role;

court experts thought Sir Henry still the man to go to, and he did continue to promote bills for the king to sign [e.g. the affair of Leonard Mell: ibid., ii.379, 412, 415, 451, 463, 467, 473, 496; iv.836 [*LP*, viii.663, 1002, 1027, 1028; ix.642, 682, 767, 905]]. For the influence of Rochford, see ibid., i.104, 104b; ii.155a, 182, 207, 283, 411; iii.556, 677 [*LP*, vi.1515; vii.436, 613, 795, 1273, 1396; viii.977; ix.87; x.675].

62   *Cal. S. P. Span.*, 1536–38, p. 137 [*LP*, x.1069].

63   Ibid., pp. 16, 35, 60, 70 [*LP*, x.141, 351, 429, 494].

64   Ibid., pp. 85–6, 107 [*LP*, x.601, 699, 782].

65   Ibid., p. 108 [*LP*, x.782].

66   Ibid., p. 106 [*LP*, x.752].

67   Ibid., p. 108 [*LP*, x.782].

68   '*à fantasier et conspirer le dict affaire*': ibid., p. 137 [*LP*, x.1069].

Chapter 22   The Coup, April–May 1536

1   Wyatt, *Poems*, CXLIII: 'Who list his wealth and ease retain'.

2   Wriothesley, *Chronicle*, i.189–91.

3   Lehmberg, *Later Parliaments of Henry VIII*, pp. 15–16.

4   De Carles, in Ascoli, *L'Opinion*, lines 495–508.

5   Constantine, in *Archaeologia*, 23, 64.

6   Oxford, Bodl. Ashmole MS 861, f. 332.

7   *Wolsey*, ed. Singer, pp. 451, 456.

8   Hall, *Chronicle*, p. 819.

9   The tide at London Bridge on 1 May 1536 was high at 10.15 a.m., low at 4.19 p.m. and high at 10.39 p.m. I owe this information to Proudman's Oceanic Laboratory.

10   *Cal. S. P. Span.*, 1530–38, p. 108 [*LP*, x.782]; see p. 166.

11   *LP*, x.753. On the first of Chapuys' four days, the council sat from morning to 9 or 10 p.m. and there were apparently other important meetings that week: ibid, 1536–38, p. 105 [*LP*, x.752]. Other matters to discuss with Sampson were his move to Chichester and the expected receipt of Pole's attack on his *Regii sacelli decani oratio*: *LP*, x.7, 420, 619, 753, 818, 1146–7.

12   *St. Pap.*, vii.683–8; *LP*, x.726, 725. While agreeing with David Starkey that the words quoted do not imply that Anne was already pregnant [plus the fact that Henry would then not have rejected her], I do not accept his dismissing them as a mere summary of a statement by Chapuys: Starkey, *Six Wives*, pp. 561–2.

13   *LP*, x.760 (2).

14   If Henry had been hiding moves against Anne behind a front of normality, these documents could easily have been delayed. See n. 17 below.

15   George Bernard has pointed out that indications of royal authentication are not usually recorded on patents. Silence is, therefore, no evidence of royal noninvolvement, as argued in Ives, *Anne Boleyn* (1986), pp. 361–2. I also accept that the king must have known of the prosecution at some stage: Ives, in *EHR*, 107, 669–71. But the absence of authentication in the *Baga de Secretis* calendar is equally congruent with ex officio initiation by the chancellor and since an oyer establishes a court of trial, not enquiry, I conclude as above.

16   *DKR*, iii (ii). 226–68. The *Baga* for Henry VIII consisted of 12 pouches containing 19 bundles, each referring to a single defendant or group of defendants. Two are not treason cases: the trials of Lord Dacre of the South and of the accessories to Katherine Howard's offences.

17   De Carles, in Ascoli, *L'Opinion*, lines 481–4, 495–6.

18   For the following see *DKR*, iii (ii), 230–4, 240–1, 267–8.

19   The Boleyn case was the only instance where peers were proceeded against by oyer and terminer. The earlier trials of Buckingham and Lord Dacre of the North were triggered by indictment. In and after 1537 the process with accused peers was by a commission to receive indictments, a grand jury hearing and finally a commission to the high steward. To 1537, sensitive treason prosecutions of commoners were begun by a commission of oyer and terminer followed by a grand jury indictment (except in the case of the Abbot of Barling in 1537 where indictment came first and perhaps, in 1509, in the case of Edmund Dudley, who was tried by the London authorities). After 1537 procedure was the same as for peers.

20   Ralph Morice, 'Anecdotes of Archbishop Cranmer', in *Narratives of the Reformation*, p. 255.

21   Ives in *Anne Boleyn* (1986), p. 362, and Bernard in *EHR*, 107, 670, raised the possibility of royal instructions being given by word of mouth. Recognition of the irrelevance of a premature commission now rules out that possibility.

22   See p. 337.

23   Kingston's letter with Anne's key revelations about Norris and Weston was written on the morning after her arrest: see below, n. 28.

24   28 Henry VIII, c.10; Lehmberg, *Later Parliaments of Henry VIII*, pp. 25–8.

25   Prescott, *Mary Tudor*, pp. 82–3; Loades, *Mary Tudor*, pp. 98–103.

26   *Lisle Letters*, iii.677, 684, 687, 689 [*LP*, x.675, 738, 748, 779].

27   Ibid., iii.690 [*LP*, x.789].

28   The most probable explanation for the postponement is that the king wished to review the behaviour of Anne's household – cf. his own assertion of discipline in 1519. For what followed see the damaged BL MSS: Cotton Otho Cx, ff. 209v, 222, 223, 224v, 225 [*Wolsey*, ed. Singer, pp. 458–9, 453–5, 460–1, 456–7, 451–3], the undamaged Harleian MS 283, f. 134

[*Wolsey*, ed. Singer, pp. 459–60] and (also undamaged) RO, SP1/103 ff. 313–14 [*LP*, x.902]. Internal evidence suggests the following sequence: (1) Wednesday morning 3 May: Otho Cx, f. 225; (2) Thursday morning 3 May: ibid., f. 209v; (3) and (4) Tuesday 9 May to Thursday 11 May: ibid., ff. 222, 224v; (5) Tuesday morning 16 May: SP1/103 ff. 313–14; (6) later Tuesday 16 May: Harleian 283, f. 134; (7) Thursday morning 18 May: Otho Cx, f. 223. MSS are referred to subsequently by the pagination in *Wolsey*, ed. Singer.

29   Ibid., pp. 451–3.

30   Although Kingston reported it to Cromwell at Westminster on Wednesday morning [ibid., pp. 451–3], Baynton [ibid., pp. 458–9] knew of it at Greenwich – 'the communication that was last between the queen and Master Norris' – on what must be Wednesday or Thursday morning since he was unaware of the arrests of Brereton and Weston: see p. 326.

31   Ales, 'Letter', at p. 527.

32   *Wolsey*, ed. Singer, pp. 456–7, does not, as is often supposed, support the idea that Anne knew of Smeton's arrest on the Sunday night. At most it establishes that she learned he was in the Tower 'that night', i.e. Monday, and also possibly Norris, but the mutilated passage may refer to Kingston, and not to Anne.

33   G. Walker argues that the king was told of Smeton's confession on Sunday afternoon and that the decision to postpone the Calais journey indicates that he 'now suspected that the queen might be guilty' but 'had not entirely lost faith in her potential innocence': Walker, in *Hist. Journ.*, 45, 18–21. If so, why did Henry delay confronting Norris for twenty-four hours and what occurred to confirm his suspicions and so challenge Norris during a sudden unscheduled ride to London? The strong probability must be that information reached him during the joust and he reacted immediately. That news must be of the Smeton confession since the only other story

known at that time was Anne's public quarrel with Norris. The delay in getting Norris into the Tower until dawn on Tuesday and the interviewing of Anne only on Tuesday morning point in the same direction.

34   Nicolas, *Privy Purse*, passim, implies he was of an age with Weston; Cavendish, *Metrical Visions*, pp. 36–7; Lowinsky, in *Florilegium*, pp. 192–200. The assumption [ibid., p. 199] that one of the proverbs entered in BL, Royal MS 20 Bxxi refers to Anne is pure conjecture. Lowinsky takes Bourbon's hostile epigrams entitled '*In Marcum*' as applying to Smeton, suggesting a slight figure, a good dancer, avarice and a good opinion of his own capacity [ibid., pp. 193–4, 233–4]. Some of these verses antedate the author's visit to England: e.g. the verse quoted, ibid., p. 193, was first published in *Nicolai Borbonii Vandoperani Nugae* (Paris, 1533), sig. g iv. The poems relating to Bourbon's visit are concentrated in *Nugarum*, Books iv–viii, which appeared for the first time in 1538, and the only two of these which are addressed to a 'Mark' are to an incompetent doctor: *Nugarum*, v.84, 85, p. 302; *Florilegium*, p. 234.

35   Constantine, in *Archaeologia*, 23, 64 says 'May Day in the morning', but Antony Antony gives 6 p.m. [see p. 419 n. 6]. The latter is more likely since the king was clearly not told until the end of the joust. See pp. 320, 415 n. 33.

36   *Cal. S. P. Span., 1536–38*, pp. 107–8 [*LP*, x.782]. Roland Bulkeley reported the same day that Norris was the principal and Wiltshire, Rochford, Smeton and sundry ladies were accessories: RO, SP1/103 f. 218 [*LP*, x.785].

37   *Wolsey*, ed. Singer, pp. 458–9.

38   Constantine, in *Archaeologia*, 23, 64.

39   *Cronica del Rey Enrico*, pp. 80–1 [*Chronicle*, ed. Hume, pp. 60–1].

40   If the evidence of Antony Antony, who was possibly in the Tower at the time, is rejected in favour of Constantine [see p. 418 n. 68], then Smeton could not

have confessed at Stepney, but this would have allowed time for torture to be applied, as Constantine suspected, and then for his confession to reach the king at Greenwich at the end of the joust.

41   Burnet, *History*, iv.570; *Wolsey*, ed. Singer, p. 454.

42   See p. 316.

43   On the following see *Cal. S. P. Span., 1536–38*, pp. 124–5, 127 [*LP*, x.908]. This reads as though Henry had composed his tragedy before Anne's arrest, which seems hardly likely. But the ambassador was clearly puzzled, for he suggested that the king was referring to poems which Anne and George Boleyn had laughed at. For the full text: Friedmann, *Anne Boleyn*, ii.176 n.1, 267 n.2.

44   *Cal. S. P. Span., 1536–38*, p. 121 [*LP*, x.909].

45   *Wolsey*, ed. Singer, p. 451 and Oxford, Bodl. Ashmole MS 861, f. 332. The other possibility is that he knew nothing of what was going on. Anne certainly did not know until late morning on Tuesday 2 May that she was to be accused: *Wolsey*, ed. Singer, p. 452.

46   *Lisle Letters*, iii.698 [*LP*, x.919].

47   Cranmer, *Letters*, pp. 323–4.

48   BL, Cotton MS Cleo. E iv, ff. 109v–110 [*LP*, xiii(1).981(2) at pp. 362–3]. Retha M. Warnicke has argued that Bryan was a key figure in the alliance against Anne: in *History*, 70, 4–6, 13–14; *Rise and Fall*, pp. 207, 299. The evidence presented to link him with the Seymours is suspect [see p. 292]; in Jan. 1536 French sources say that Bryan was hostile to Katherine [*LP*, x.175]; Bryan was away from court during the crisis – returning in early April, having been 'long absent', and leaving after 14 and before 28 April: *Lisle Letters*, iii.671, 673, 686 [*LP*, x.635, 669, 748]; it is important to distinguish his sudden recall and interrogation in May 1536 from his interrogation, apparently in June, in connection with the legitimacy of Mary [*LP*, x.1134(3)]. That Bryan

became the alternate chief gentleman of the privy chamber and acquired spoils *after* the fall of Norris [Starkey, thesis, pp. 240–3] cannot be used to establish his factional alignment *before* that event.

49   *Lisle Letters*, iii.684, 694 [*LP*, x.738, 855] and Antony [see p. 418 n. 68].

50   Antony says at 9.00 a.m. [see p. 418 n. 68].

51   *Lisle Letters*, iii.695; iv.846 [*LP*, x.865, 920]; *LP*, iv.895; Nicolas, *Privy Purse*, pp. 97, 112, 168.

52   Ales, 'Letter', pp. 525–7.

53   Ascoli, *L'Opinion*, pp. 274–8. The author evidently did not know that Katherine was already dead.

54   *Cronica del Rey Enrico*, pp. 68–76 [*Chronicle*, ed. Hume, pp. 55–9].

55   Sander, *Schism*, p. 133.

56   Spelman, *Reports*, i.71. Bishop Burnet, who saw Spelman's original (now lost), noted that the rest of the page was torn off, which has given rise to the belief that part of the report has been lost [Burnet, *History*, i.316]. Any loss must have happened before the Yelverton MS copy [BL, Hargrave MS 388], which is now the only authority, was written early in Elizabeth's reign, for this shows no sign of any awareness of missing material at the relevant point: f. 187v. The Yelverton MS rearranged the original alphabetical order of topics into a chronological one [*Reports*, i.xxiii–iv, xxxii–iii], with the Boleyn material having originally appeared under the heading *Corone*. But there is no sign of lost or defective material in any of the sections which could have appeared on the other side of the torn page. Therefore either the half-page torn off coincided exactly with a complete report on the opposite side, or one side was blank (neither probabilities), or both sides were blank – hence the removal. To end a report 'etc.' is standard legal practice, and there are numerous examples in Spelman.

57   There are too many Lady Wingfields for comfort. The identification is made on

the evidence of Chapuys that Sir Richard's widow, who had married Harvey, 'came to court in attendance on' Anne: *Cal. S. P. Span., 1529–30*, p. 586; *House of Commons*, ii.310; iii.501, 645; RO, E101/421/13 [*LP*, vii.9]; *LP*, vii.1672. Anne and Henry stayed at Stone Castle in Nov. 1532: Nicolas, *Privy Purse*, p. 274.

58   Russell, *Cloth of Gold*, p. 203; *LP*, v.1711 (which dates from before Buckingham's execution).

59   Wood, *Letters*, ii.74–5 [*LP*, v.12]. The dating depends on the fact that Anne was called Lady Rochford after her father became earl of Wiltshire, 8 Dec. 1529, until she became marchioness of Pembroke, 1 Sept. 1532. *LP*, v.12 gives a date of 1531.

60   There was a possible Kent connection since Stone is only twenty miles from Hever.

61   Harvey died on 5 Aug. 1532 [*House of Commons*, ii.311], so Anne's letter would have been written later in August. Lady Wingfield's absence cannot have been protracted since she received New Year's gifts on 1 Jan 1532 and 1533: *LP*, v.686; vi.32.

62   e.g. *LP*, xi.533–4, 539.

63   See p. 140; S. J. Gunn, *Charles Brandon* (Oxford, 1988), pp. 118–19, 162; E. Paul, *Catherine of Aragon and her Friends* (1966), pp. 34–47, 126–8, 131–3. For the Wingfields and Brandon, see *House of Commons*, iii.638–41.

64   'Estate and household management in Bedfordshire, *c*.1540', ed. A. G. Dickens, in *The Gostwicks of Willington*, Bedfordshire Historical Record Society, 36 (1956), p. 45.

65   *LP*, vii.9; no dates are recoverable from *LP*, vii.1672.

66   De Carles, in Ascoli, *L'Opinion*, lines 882–5. In the poem the initial accusations include Rochford, so that the 'one woman' is the initial informant. If, however, Rochford was not an original suspect and if he made any such remark at the trial it must

refer to whoever accused him of incest. *Cal. S. P. Span., 1536–38*, p. 126 [*LP*, x.908].

67 This exists in an Italian version [Hamy, *Entrevue*, p. ccccxxxi] but is quoted here from the Portuguese version [Bentley, *Excerpta Historica*, pp. 261–2].

68 Oxford, Bodl. Fol. Δ 624, Herbert of Cherbury, *Henry VIII* (1679), facing p. 384, contains jottings by Thomas Tourneur from the journal of Antony Antony. I am indebted to Mr Gary Hill for this and other references to Antony Antony, and to the argument that Antony did not expand his comment with any mention of Lady Rochford's jealousy or later fate.

69 Burnet, *History*, i.316. Since the bishop did not have Chapuys' letter, we must assume he was relying on evidence now missing – possibly Antony Antony.

70 Warnicke, *Rise and Fall*, pp. 214–19. For a critique see Ives, in *Hist. Journ.*, 34, p. 199.

71 For the association of the Parkers with Katherine and Mary see Warnicke, in *History*, 70, 6–7; *Rise and Fall*, p. 30. Carley, in *Illuminating the Book*, pp. 267–8, effectively dismisses the long-held view that Lord Morley was on close terms with Anne; see p. 271.

72 *Wolsey*, ed. Singer, pp. 453–4; see pp. 328–9, 359.

73 Ellis, *Letters*, 1 ii.67 [*LP*, x.1010]; *LP*, xi.17. One may also wonder whether the incrimination of Lady Rochford in the crimes of Katherine Howard may not have owed something to revenge.

74 *Lisle Letters*, iii.703a; iv.847 [*LP*, x.953, 964].

75 See p. 214. Less probably, 'Mistress Margery' could be Margaret Shelton, the queen's cousin.

76 *Wolsey*, ed. Singer, p. 458.

77 *Lisle Letters*, iv.863 [*LP*, x.1165]. Margaret Shelton also remained at court: ibid., v.1086 [*LP*, xiii (1).24]

78 *Wolsey*, ed. Singer, p. 458. It was Fitzwilliam who obtained Norris's (with-

drawn) confession, who helped to interrogate Anne, and who was noted as not having the time to read correspondence 'since these matters begun': Constantine, in *Archaeologia*, 23, 64; *Wolsey*, ed. Singer, p. 456; *Lisle Letters*, iii.695 [*LP*, x.865].

79 To avoid her husband knowing: *LP*, xiii (1).450.

80 *Wolsey*, ed. Singer, p. 452.

81 *LP*, x.873; xi.29. By 9 May the story had already reached the French court that Anne had been found *in flagrante* with Smeton: *Cal. S. P. Span., 1534–36*, p. 571.

82 De Carles in Ascoli, *L'Opinion*, lines 349–50.

83 Pocock, *Records*, ii.574–5.

84 De Carles, in Ascoli, *L'Opinion*, lines 409–96. Alexander Ales was also aware of this version for he too reports an investigation over some days: 'Letter', pp. 526–7.

85 Carles, in Ascoli, *L'Opinion*, lines 437–44.

86 *LP*, xi.29.

87 De Carles, in Ascoli, *L'Opinion*, lines 349–84.

88 See the letters cited at 415 n. 28.

89 *Wolsey*, ed. Singer, p. 451.

90 Ibid., pp. 452–4, 457.

91 Where possible, Singer supplies the lacunae from Strype.

92 Antony says 5 May, no time stated: p. 418 n. 68.

93 Antony says Friday 5 May [see p. 345] but Constantine, who spoke to Brereton before his arrest, says Thursday before 2.00 p.m. [*Archaeologia*, 23, 65].

94 *Wolsey*, e.d. Singer, p. 455.

95 Wyatt, *Poems*, CXLIX, lines 49–56.

96 If, as Lowinsky suggested, Smeton was preparing Royal College of Music MS 1070 for Anne, he may well have found the idea of such a gift from a person of his status greeted with scorn: see p. 258.

97 *Wolsey*, ed. Singer, pp. 456–7. When Anne entered the Tower she knew only of the arrests of Norris and Smeton and assumed Norris had accused her. This

supports the conjecture that the first intention was a rapid trial accusing Smeton as principal and Norris as accessory [see p. 326]. Her concern for the whereabouts of both the king and her brother suggests that she was looking for allies, but alternatively might indicate that she suspected that George was in danger as an accessory: ibid., pp. 451–2. She seems never to have been questioned about Weston and Brereton.

98 'I have much marvel that the king's council comes not to me': ibid., p. 454, dated Tuesday–Thursday, 9–11 May.

99 '[Rochford] desired me [Kingston] to know at what time he should come afore the king's council, for I think I shall not come forth till I come to my judgement': ibid., p. 454.

100 Ibid., p. 452.

Chapter 23   Judgement

1 For the following see Wriothesley, Chronicle, i.189–226 and the letters listed p. 415 n. 28; RO, C193/3 f. 80.

2 Marius, More, p. 510.

3 De Carles was much impressed by this feature of English criminal procedure: in Ascoli, L'Opinion, lines 717–32, 774–6.

4 For the jury see House of Commons, i.307–8, 342–3; ii.52–3, 60–1, 409–10, 646–8; iii.54–6, 430–1, 597–9; LP, iv.1136(16); 1939(8); 5623(10), 6187 (12); G. E. C., Peerage, vi.624–7; Brereton, Letters and Accounts, p. 105: John Stow. Survey of London, ed. C. L. Kingsford (Oxford, 1908), i.133.

5 Wriothesley, Chronicle, i.37; Antony Antony in Bodl.Fol.Δ 624, facing p. 385; Cal. S. P. Span., 1536–38, p. 125 [LP, x.908]; E. O. Benger, Memoirs of the Life of Anne Boleyn (1827), p. 404. Antony refers to the making of 'a halfe pace [sic] and scaffold' for the people to stand upon. 'Halfpace' is a confusing term and possibly

means a raised platform for Anne to sit on: Thurley, Palaces, p. ix. The stands reported by Benger cannot have been genuine if 'the king's hall' was the hall in the royal apartments, since this was demolished in the 17th century: Colvin, King's Works, iii (1).266. Alternatively, did the trial take place in the hall in the White Tower?

6 Given the small number of available peers, the Crown was in no position to attempt much 'packing'. It had to rely on the peculiar loyalty peers were expected to give the king – or on their personal respect and fear of him. For the trial of Anne and Rochford see Wriothesley, Chronicle, i.37–9; de Carles, in Ascoli, L'Opinion, lines 821–1046; Friedmann, Anne Boleyn, ii.238; Cal. S. P. Span., 1536–38, pp. 125–7 [LP, x.908]; Ales, 'Letter'; Antony Antony in Herbert, Henry VIII (1679), facing p. 385 [see above, p. 418 n. 68]; Spelman, Reports, i.59, 70–1.

7 Ales goes too far in presenting Anne as a silent martyr. He does, however, suggest that Richard Pollard ['Master Polwarck'] led for the Crown, not Christopher Hales. A. G. Pollard was later in the forefront of government prosecution of rebels after the Pilgrimage of Grace.

8 Wolsey, ed. Singer, pp. 451, 457.

9 Wriothesley, Chronicle, i.37–8.

10 Ibid., i.38.

11 Spelman, Reports, i.71.

12 De Carles has Anne presenting a mixture of defence, rebuttal of judgement and defiance, plus a plea for those condemned with her. This last, and a request for time to prepare her soul, is found in Chapuys: Cal. S. P. Span., 1536–38, p. 127 [LP, x.908].

13 De Carles, in Ascoli, L'Opinion, lines 1002–12.

14 Accounts of the executions of May 1536 can be identified as follows: (1a) An Italian account by 'P. A.', possibly a Venetian diplomat in England, dated 1 June 1536: in Hamy, Entrevue, pp. ccccxxxi–ccccxxxvi, also printed version (Bologna,

1536); (1b) A Portuguese translation of (1a), dated 1 June, in Bentley, *Excerpta Historica*, pp. 261–5. (2a) An imperial account, printed in Thomas, *The Pilgrim*, pp. 116–17; (2b) A Spanish version of (2a) at Vienna: *LP*, x.911(1). (3) A French account, printed partially in Ascoli, *L'Opinion*, p. 273, and partially in Hamy, *Entrevue*, pp. ccccxxxvii–ccccxxxviii, possibly derived from (2a). (4) de Carles [see pp. 60–1]. (5) *Les regretz de Millort de Rocheffort*, printed in Ascoli, *L'Opinion*, pp. 274–8. (6) Constantine, in *Archaeologia*, 23, 64–6. (7) Wriothesley, *Chronicle*, i.39–40. (8) *Chronicle of Calais*, pp. 46–7.

15 *Wolsey*, ed. Singer, p. 460.

16 Constantine, in *Archaeologia*, 23, 64. The badly mutilated conclusion to one letter [*Wolsey*, ed. Singer, p. 455] may suggest that Norris confessed the facts of his conversation with Anne but denied the alleged implication. It can be reconstructed as '[whoever tries to take advantage of] anything of my confession, he is worthy to have [my place here; and if he stand to] it, I defy him.'

17 Constantine, in *Archaeologia*, 23, 65; Ives, in *Trans. Hist. Soc. Lancs. & Ches.*, 123, 31–2. We may note Chapuys' opinion: 'condemned on presumption and circumstances, not by proof or valid confession' [*'ont este condampnez par presumption et aucuns indices, sans preuve ne confession valid'*]. He did, however, have civil law procedure in mind, which required eyewitnesses or the confessions of the accused: *Cal. S. P. Span., 1536–38*, p. 125 [*LP*, x.908].

18 Cf. the opinion of John Hussey: *Lisle Letters*, iii.698 [*LP*, x.919]. The suggestion [Warnicke, *Rise and Fall*, pp. 214–22] that 'the men identified as Anne's lovers were known for their licentious behaviour and that some of them were also suspected of having violated the Buggery Statute' is wholly meretricious. For a detailed rebuttal of the supposed 'evidence' for this, see Ives, in *Hist. Journ.*, 34, 198–9. In particular, their scaffold statements do not bear the interpretation claimed.

19 Two grand juries of sixteen, a petty jury of twelve, a jury of twenty-six peers for Anne and twenty-five for Rochford.

20 The 'divers other days and places' always applies at the location alleged in the main charge, e.g. Norris accused of intercourse at Westminster on specific days is accused also of 'divers . . . at Westminster', never elsewhere in Middlesex. Brereton is the exception, with the original offence at Hampton Court and 'divers . . . at Westminster'.

21 The indictment referred to Anne's adultery as treasonous but the fact that the Treasons Act of 1352 did not cover adultery by a queen is indicated by inclusion of the offence in subsequent legislation: 33 Henry VIII, c.21.

22 The suggestion [*LP*, x.908 at pp. 377–8] that the poisoning charge was supported by Anne's gift to Norris of certain *médailles* is based on wrong punctuation and conflates two separate items [*Cal. S. P. Span., 1536–38*, p. 126; Friedmann, *Anne Boleyn*, ii.277 n.1].

23 Spelman [*Reports*, i.71] reported a charge of slandering the royal issue 'which is made treason by the statute of the twenty-sixth year of the present king'. There is some doubt about what statute was intended. The suggestion adopted above is that he conflated two separate charges: imagining the king's death (restated as treason by 26 Henry VIII, c.13, Dec. 1534) and slandering the royal issue (treason by 25 Henry VIII, c.22, Mar. 1534).

24 *Lisle Letters*, iv.845a [*LP*, x.866].

25 The condemnation of Norris etc. also meant that Anne could not cite their denial of misconduct as corroboration. By contrast, the accessories to Katherine Howard were indicted only after the queen had confessed and Culpeper and Dereham been condemned.

26 Wyatt, *Poems*, CXLIX.

27 For Brereton, see Brereton, *Letters and Accounts*, and Ives, in *Trans. Hist.*

Soc. Lancs. & Ches., 123, 1–38. For a dismissive verdict on Brereton see Thornton, *Cheshire*, pp. 195–213.

28 Ives, in *Trans. Hist. Soc. Lancs. & Ches.*, 123, 28–30.

29 Cavendish, *Metrical Visions*, pp. 33–5; the first and penultimate stanzas are omitted here.

30 The force of this was recognized by George Wyatt, in *Wolsey*, ed. Singer, pp. 445–6.

31 For the following see Ales, 'Letter', pp. 528–9.

32 This charge was specifically mentioned in the indictment.

33 *Cal. S. P. Span., 1536–38*, pp. 126, 127–8; [*LP*, x.908].

34 *Wolsey*, ed. Singer, p. 454.

35 See p. 303.

36 Walker, in *Hist. Journ.*, 45, 26.

37 See p. 21.

38 *Reginae Utopiae falso adulterii crimine damnatae, et capite mulctatae Epitaphium*: Etienne Dolet, *Epigram* (Lyons, 1538), Book iii, p. 162. '*Utopiae*' plays on the ambiguity of *ou-topos* (no place) and *eu-topos* (happy place).

39 *Cal. S. P. Span., 1536–38*, p. 125; RO, PRO31/8 f. 85 [*LP*, x.908, 965].

40 *Cal. S. P. Span., 1536–38*, pp. 137–8 [*LP*, x.1069].

41 *Narratives of the Reformation*, p. 255.

42 *Cal. S. P. Span., 1536–38*, p. 121 [*LP*, x.909]; *Wolsey*, ed. Singer, p. 459.

43 *Cal. S. P. Span., 1536–38*, p. 128 [*LP*, x.908]; de Carles, in Ascoli, *L'Opinion*, lines 788–808; *Lisle Letters*, iii.695 [*LP*, x.865].

44 *LP*, x.902, xi.381. Not from St Omer: RO, PRO31/8 f. 85 [*LP*, x.965]. That the executioner was at the Tower for the Friday morning implies either that any messenger who left after the sentence on Monday had a quick journey to Calais and the executioner an equally prompt crossing, or that advance warning had been given.

45 *LP*, xi.381A.

46 RO, C193/3 f. 80.

47 J. A. Froude, *History of England from the Fall of Wolsey* (1912), ii.161–2, 167. Froude [p. 161] rejected all parallels between Henry VIII and Leontes in Shakespeare, *A Winter's Tale*, but the parallels are there: E. W. Ives, 'Shakespeare and History: divergencies and agreements', in *Shakespeare Survey*, 38 (1985), 24–5.

48 Pollard, *Henry VIII*, pp. 276–7.

49 Muir, *Life and Letters of Wyatt*, p. 28.

50 Bernard, in *EHR*, 106, 609–10. To say 'some were guilty' is to agree that others were unjustly condemned, and if so, why?

51 Wriothesley, *Chronicle*, i.36–7; *Cal. S. P. Span., 1536–38*, p. 129 [*LP*, x.908].

52 Du Bellay, *Correspondance*, ii.453 at p. 506 [*LP*, xi.860]; cf. *LP*, xi.1250.

53 *Cal. S. P. Span., 1536–38*, p. 128 [*LP*, x.908].

54 Wyatt, *Poems*, CXLIII; 'grate' = grating.

55 For this see the letters at p. 415 n. 28; the reference to George is from *Wolsey*, ed. Singer, p. 461.

56 Some of his offices were held jointly with his son, his land grant of Fobbing was entailed on his male heirs, and in Kent, Anne was his heir: RO SP1/102 ff. 155–6; *LP*, v. g506(16). Retreat occurred re his Irish claims e.g. *St. Pap*, ii.436, 475–6 [*LP*, xii (1).1066, (2).963]; *LP*, xii 2 964(2)1310 i (20), ii (9); he also disposed of some English property: ibid. xiii (1) 1080, g734(24).

57 *LP*, xi.926, xii.(1) 1199, 1207(20), 1227(4), xiii.(1) 680, 783; xi 139(i), (iii) xi.17, 1277, xii (2) 580, 722, xiv (2) 782, pp. 318–20, 322; xii. (2) 911, 1012, 1060; *Lisle Letters*, v.10 [*LP*, xiii (1) 24].

58 Ibid., v.184 [*LP*, xiii (1) 1419].

59 *LP*, xiv(1).854. The story that he lost most of his estate [ibid., xi.320] refers to the office of Privy Seal: see p. 362.

60 *Wolsey*, ed. Singer, p. 460: 'this day at dinner the queen said that she should go to Antwerp and is in hope of life.'

61 *Wolsey*, ed. Singer, p. 461.

62 *LP*, x.896; Kelly, *Matrimonial Trials*, pp. 250–9, considers a whole range of possible reasons, without being able to reach a firm conclusion. That divorce papers existed see *LP*, xiii(i).1225.

63 *Wolsey*, ed. Singer, pp. 464–5; Wriothesley, *Chronicle*, i.41.

64 *Cal. S. P. Span.*, *1536–38*, p. 121 [*LP*, x.909]. Spelman says the divorce was on the ground of a pre-contract: *Reports*, i.59.

65 *Wolsey*, ed. Singer, p. 459. Sergeant, *Anne Boleyn*, p. 266; M. L. Bruce, *Anne Boleyn* (1972), pp. 326–75; Starkey, *Six Wives*, pp. 580–1.

66 Kingston wrote [original spelling], 'The kyng's grace showed me that my lord of Cantorbury should be her confessar and was here thys day with the quene and not in that matter Sir the tyme ys short for the kyng supposeth the gentelmen to dy to morow.' Starkey [*Six Wives*, p. 58] punctuates: 'and was here this day with the queen and not in that matter. Sir …' [i.e. not concerning her confession]. I accept the traditional reading: 'and was here this day with the queen. And note in that matter, Sir, the time is short.' Why should Henry explain his divorce difficulty to Kingston?

67 MacCulloch, *Cranmer*, p.158 points out that Cranmer was extremely unlikely to break the seal of the confessional.

68 25 Henry VIII, c.21. The only 'confession' required from Anne was an oath confirming her blood relationship to Mary.

69 28 Henry VIII, c.7.

70 *Cal. S. P. Span.*, *1536–38*, p. 121 [*LP*, x.909]. Divorcing Anne because he had married in defiance of the immutable law of God did, however, preserve Henry's assurance that he had a hot line to the Almighty.

71 28 Henry VIII, c.7.

72 There is no evidence of any lengthy illness. He attended the opening of parliament, but on 8 July was reported by Chapuys to be seriously ill. He died on 23 July. Murphy, *Bastard Prince*, pp. 174–5; Loach, *Edward VI*, p. 160.

73 *Wolsey*, ed. Singer, p. 461; *Cal. S. P. Span.*, *1536–38*, p. 131 [*LP*, x.908]. Her oath impressed even the hostile Chapuys.

74 *LP*, xi.381A.

75 *Wolsey*, ed. Singer, pp. 460–1.

76 RO, C193/3 f. 80, dated 18 May.

77 Anne's complaint is often taken to support the statements of Chapuys [*Cal. S. P. Span.*, *1536–38*, p. 131 [*LP*, x.908]] and de Carles [in Ascoli, *L'Opinion*, lines 1150–65] that her execution was postponed from Thursday to Friday. Friedmann [*Anne Boleyn*, ii.290–2] attributed this either to delaying for the executioner or the decision to clear foreigners from the Tower and minimize the number of spectators by not publicizing the time. Starkey shares that view: *Six Wives*, p. 582. However, Kingston's letter shows that when Anne complained, he was in course of writing that the time of execution still had not been fixed. Also Kingston's concern was not to limit but to ensure a respectable audience: 'If we have not an hour certain as it may be known in London, I think here will be but few and I think a reasonable number were best.' The natural construction is that Anne and her ladies (and via one of the latter, Chapuys) had misunderstood procedures; Kingston always warned victims early on the day. Starkey is wrong to suggest that the letter belongs to Friday 19 May since the time of execution was not noon. Wriothesley [*Chronicle*, i.41] gives 8 a.m., Chapuys 9 a.m. [*Cal. S. P. Span.*, *1536–38*, p. 130 [*LP*, x.908]], Antony Antony 'about 9 o'clock afore noon' [see p. 418 n. 68]. Chapuys' report about a delay was probably because the servant he sent to observe was, so Kingston said, excluded 'honestly' on the Thursday.

78 Chapuys reported that Anne spent her last night chattering '*le plus plaisamment du monde*', saying, *cum al.*, that she would be called 'Anne the Headless'. Also that she said her fate was not divine judgement, except for her treatment of

Mary: Friedmann, *Anne Boleyn*, ii.293 [*LP*, x.1070]. De Carles has her comforting her ladies [in Ascoli, *L'Opinion*, lines 1183–1217]. Kingston implies she was with her almoner.

Chapter 24 Finale

1 For sources covering the execution of Anne see p. 419 n. 14 above. She was beheaded on a new scaffold 'before the house of Ordnance', i.e. on what is now the parade ground north of the White Tower: *Lisle Letters*, iii.698 [*LP*, x.919]; Antony Antony in Herbert, *Henry VIII* (1679), facing p. 385. The current scaffold site was invented to please Queen Victoria: G. Parnell, 'Diary of a death at daybreak', in *BBC History Magazine*, 2 (2001), 14.

2 *Lisle Letters*, iii.918 [*LP*, x.918]; Wriothesley, *Chronicle*, i.41; *Wolsey*, ed. Singer, p. 461 [but Antony Antony says that foreigners were present].

3 Plus most of the council: *Cal. S. P. Span., 1536–38*, pp. 130–1 [*LP*, x.908]; Wriothesley, *Chronicle*, i.41.

4 The story that Anne's own ladies attended her on the scaffold appears to be derived from stories about her giving them keepsakes. See above, p. 406 n. 49.

5 See the imperial account (2a), p. 419 n. 14.

6 For Anne's speech see also George Wyatt, *Papers*, p. 189; *Wolsey*, ed. Singer, p. 448; Hall, *Chronicle*, p. 819; Foxe, *Acts and Monuments*, v.134; Antony Antony, in Herbert, *Henry VIII* (1679), facing p. 385.

7 *Lisle Letters*, iii.698 [*LP*, x.920].

8 Erasmus, *A Preparation to Death* (Redman, 1543), sig. fvij [see above, p. 270]. The text above is modified to read 'overpowered' for 'overcome' and 'instant by instant' for 'instantly'.

9 Source after source stresses the suddenness and speed of the execution; the headsman 'did his office very well': Spel-man, *Reports*, i.59. A French report was 'before you could say a paternoster': Hamy, *Entrevue*, p. ccccxxxvii. I am unaware of English evidence to confirm the executioner's costume described in G. Abbott, *Lords of the Scaffold* (1991), p. 61.

10 *LP*, xi.381. Thus Antony Antony and the imperial account; the Italian account suggests that the box was by the scaffold. The Crown redeemed Anne's jewels and apparel from Kingston for £100: ibid., xi. 381A.

11 *Cal. S. P. Span., 1536–38*, p. 129 [*LP*, x.908].

12 *LP*, x.878.

13 *LP*, vii.611; x.785, 820, 870.

14 *LP*, x.873; xi.29.

15 *Lisle Letters*, iii.698, 702 [*LP*, x.919, 943], p. 173.

16 Ibid., iii.713 [*LP*, x.1047].

17 *LP*, x.926.

18 *Lisle Letters*, iv.848a [*LP*, x.1000].

19 *LP*, x.g.1256(4); BL, Royal MS 7F xiv, f. 100.

20 Oxford, Bodl. MS Jesus College, 73, f. 249. The original for this appears to be the now mutilated BL, Cotton MS Otho C x [*LP*, x.1134]. Cf. Herbert, *Henry VIII*, p. 573. I owe this Bodleian reference to the kindness of Professor Richard Hoyle.

21 Cf. Benger, *Memoirs* p. 377, suggesting that Jane must have been attractive 'since we hear of no other fascination she possessed'.

22 *LP*, x.1212.

23 *LP*, x.968. Cf. Reginald Pole, 2 Oct. 1553: 'the misery of that period, and all that ensued subsequently, came through a woman': *Cal. S. P. Ven., 1534–54*, p. 424.

24 For the following see Prescott, *Mary Tudor*, pp. 76–83; Loades, *Mary Tudor*, pp. 98–103. *Cal. S. P. Span., 1536–38*, pp. 183–5; *LP*, vii.1036; x.1134, 1150.

25 *LP*, x.1268.

26 *LP*, xi.222; cf. vii.1036.

27 *LP*, xi.202(3), (14).

28 R. W. Hoyle [in *Pilgrimage*, pp. 14–16, 67–70, 159–66, 414–18] has undermined the claim that the rebellion

'was at heart the work of a political faction' [Elton, in 'Politics and the Pilgrimage of Grace', in *Studies*, iii, 214] but it remains true that neither Hussey nor Darcy showed the backbone Henry was entitled to expect. They, and many of the gentry drawn in, shared the popular horror of heresy and opposition to the dissolution and were probably responsible for the political dimension of the northern demands, in particular, for the legitimization of Mary.

29 For Heron and Tempest see *House of Commons*, ii.350; iii.430–1.

30 *Lisle Letters*, iii.748 [*LP*, xi.107]. He did not adhere to his determination, became chamberlain to Prince Edward and 'allegedly' took to drink [Loach, *Edward VI*, p. 9]. He probably escaped in 1536 because his step-daughter had recently married Edward Seymour.

31 That Cromwell was Wyatt's patron is clear from *Poems*, CLX. Cf. *House of Commons*, iii.669–70.

32 Wyatt, *Poems*, CXLIX.

33 Constantine, in *Archaeologia*, 23, 64; *LP*, x.926; Ales, 'Letter', pp. 530–1.

34 The inscription is unnumbered but can be found at the bottom right of no. 31 on the west wall of the main chamber of the first floor. It was first identified by Mr B. A. Harrison, a yeoman warder and an authority on the Tower inscriptions. The Martin Tower contains a fire-damaged carving which has been read as 'boullen', in which case it could refer to George Boleyn; alternatively, and on inspection more probably, it can be read as 'bouttell': Royal Commission on Historical Monuments, *London* (1924–30), v.83. I am indebted to Mr Peter Hammond for drawing my attention to these inscriptions, and for a rubbing of that in the Martin Tower, and to Mr Harrison.

Bibliographical
Abbreviations

THE following lists the abbreviated and full titles of works referred to. Unless otherwise stated, both here and in the notes the place of publication is London.

ABBREVIATION	EXPLANATION
Actes de François 1er	*Catalogue des Actes de François 1er* (Paris, 1887–1910).
Ales, 'Letter'	Alexander Ales, letter to Queen Elizabeth, 1 Sept. 1559, in RO, SP70/7 ff. 1–11, translated and calendared in *Calendar of State Papers Foreign, 1558–59*, 1303.
Ambassades de du Bellay	*Ambassades en Angleterre de Jean du Bellay*, ed. V. L. Bourilly and P. de Vassière (Paris, 1905).
Anglo, *Great Tournament Roll*	S. Anglo, *The Great Tournament Roll of Westminster* (Oxford, 1968).
Anglo, *Spectacle*	S. Anglo, *Spectacle, Pageantry and Early Tudor Policy* (Oxford, 1969).
Ascoli, *L'Opinion*	G. Ascoli, *La Grande-Bretagne devant L'Opinion Française* (Paris, 1927).
Ballads	*Ballads from Manuscript*, ed. F. J. Furnivall. Ballad Society (1868–72).
Benger, *Memoirs*	E. O. Benger, *Memoirs of the Life of Anne Boleyn* (1827).
Bentley, *Excerpta Historica*	S. Bentley, *Excerpta Historica* (1831).
Bernard in *EHR*, 106	G. W. Bernard, 'The fall of Anne Boleyn', in *EHR*, 106 (1991).
Bernard in *EHR*, 107	G. W. Bernard, 'The fall of Anne Boleyn: a rejoinder', in *EHR*, 107 (1992).
Bernard in *Hist. Journ.* 36	G. W. Bernard, 'Anne Boleyn's religion', in *Hist. Journ.* 36 (1993).

Bernard *Nobility*

The Tudor Nobility, ed. G. W. Bernard (1992).

BIHR

Bulletin of the Institute of Historical Research.

BL

British Library.

BM

British Museum.

BNF

Bibliothèque Nationale de France.

Bodl.

Oxford, Bodleian Library.

de Boom, *Marguerite d'Autriche*

G. de Boom, *Marguerite d'Autriche–Savoie et la Pré-Renaissance* (Paris and Brussels, 1935).

Bray, *Documents*

Documents of the English Revolution, ed. G. Bray (Cambridge, 1994).

Brereton, *Letters and Accounts*

Letters and Accounts of William Brereton, ed. E. W. Ives. Record Society of Lancashire and Cheshire, 116 (1976).

Brewer, *Henry VIII*

J. S. Brewer, *The Reign of Henry VIII* (1884).

Brigden, *London and the Reformation*

S. Brigden, *London and the Reformation* (Oxford, 1989).

'Building work', in *Transactions of the Greenwich and Lewisham Antiquarian Society*, 5

J. W. Kirby, 'Building work at Placentia, 1532–33', in *Transactions of the Greenwich and Lewisham Antiquarian Society*, 5 (1954–61), 22–50.

Burnet, *History*

Gilbert Burnet, *History of the Reformation*, ed. Nicolas Pocock (Oxford, 1865).

Cal. S. P. For.

Calendar of State Papers, Foreign Series, Elizabeth I, ed. J. Stevenson et al. (1863–1950).

Cal. S. P. Milan.

Calendar of State Papers . . . in . . . Milan, ed. A. B. Hinds (1912).

Cal. S. P. Span.

Calendar of Letters . . . and State Papers . . . between England and Spain, ed. G. A. Bergenroth et al. (1862–1954).

Cal. S. P. Ven.

Calendar of State Papers . . . in . . . Venice, ed. Rawdon Brown et al. (1864–1940).

de Carles, in Ascoli, *L'Opinion*

Lancelot de Carles, '*De la royne d'Angleterre*', in Ascoli, *L'Opinion*.

Carley in *Illuminating the Book*

J. P. Carley, 'Her moost lovyng and fryndely brother sendeth gretyng', in *Illuminating the Book*, ed. M. P. Brown and S. McKendrick (1998).

Cavendish, *Metrical Visions*

George Cavendish, 'Metrical Visions', in *The Life of Cardinal Wolsey and*

	Metrical Visions, ed. S. W. Singer (1825).
Cavendish, *Wolsey*	George Cavendish, *The Life and Death of Cardinal Wolsey*, ed. R. S. Sylvester. Early English Text Society, 243 (1959).
Chronicle, ed. Hume	*Chronicle of King Henry VIII of England* (see below, *Cronica del Rey Enrico*), ed. M. A. S. Hume (1889).
Chronicle of Calais	*Chronicle of Calais*, ed. J. G. Nichols. Camden Society, 35 (1846).
Clifford, *Dormer*	Henry Clifford, *Life of Jane Dormer* (1887).
Colvin, *King's Works*	H. M. Colvin, *The History of the King's Works* (1963–82).
Constantine, in *Archaeologia*, 23	'A memorial from George Constantine', ed. T. Amyot, in *Archaeologia*, 23 (1831).
Cranmer, *Letters*	*Miscellaneous Writings and Letters of Thomas Cranmer*, ed. J. E. Cox. Parker Society (1846).
Cronica del Rey Enrico	*Cronica del Rey Enrico Otava de Inglaterra*, ed. Marquis de Molins (Madrid, 1874).
de Iongh, *Margaret of Austria*	Jane de Iongh, *Margaret of Austria* (1954).
Dewhurst, in *Medical History*, 28	J. Dewhurst, 'The alleged miscarriages of Catherine of Aragon and Anne Boleyn', in *Medical History*, 28 (1984).
DKR iii(ii)	*Reports of the Deputy Keeper of Public Records*, iii: Appendix ii (1842).
Dowling, in *JEH*, 35	M. Dowling, 'Anne Boleyn and reform', in *JEH*, 35 (1984), 30–46.
Dowling in Starkey, *European Court*	M. Dowling, 'Anne Boleyn as patron', in Starkey, *European Court*.
Dowling, 'Cronickille'	'William Latimer's Cronickille of Anne Bulleyne', ed. Maria Dowling, in *Camden Miscellany*, xxx (Camden Soc. 4th ser. 39, 1990).
Dowling, *Humanism*	M. Dowling, *Humanism in the Age of Henry VIII* (Beckenham, 1986).
du Bellay, *Correspondance*	*Correspondance du Cardinal Jean du Bellay*, ed. R. Scheurer (Paris, 1969).
Dugdale, *Monasticon*	William Dugdale, *Monasticon* (1817–30).
EHR	*English Historical Review*.

Elizabeth, ed. Doran — *Elizabeth*, ed. S. Doran (Greenwich, 2003).

Ellis, *Letters* — H. Ellis, *Original Letters Illustrative of English History* (1824–46).

Elton, *Reform and Renewal* — G. R. Elton, *Reform and Renewal* (Cambridge, 1973).

Elton, *Studies* — G. R. Elton, *Studies in Tudor and Stuart Politics and Government* (Cambridge, 1974–97).

Fletcher and MacCulloch, *Rebellions* — A. Fletcher and D. MacCulloch, *Tudor Rebellions* (4th edn, 1997).

Foxe, *Acts and Monuments* — John Foxe, *Acts and Monuments*, ed. S. R. Cattley (1837).

François Ier et Henri VIII — *François Ier et Henri VIII: deux princes de la Renaissance*, ed. C. Giry-Deloison (London and Lille, 1996).

Freeman in *Hist. Journ.*, 38 — T. S. Freeman, 'Research, rumour and propaganda: Anne Boleyn in Foxe's 'Book of Martyrs', in *Historical Journal*, 38 (1995).

Friedmann, *Anne Boleyn* — P. Friedmann, *Anne Boleyn: a Chapter of English History, 1527–1536* (1884).

Gairdner, in *EHR* — J. Gairdner, 'Mary and Anne Boleyn', and 'The Age of Anne Boleyn', in *EHR*, 8 (1893), 53–60; 10 (1895), 104.

Ganz, *Die Handzeichnungen* — P. Ganz, *Die Handzeichnungen Hans Holbein des Jüngeren* (Berlin, 1911).

G. E. C., *Peerage* — G. E. Cockayne, *Complete Peerage*, ed. V. Gibbs (1910–49).

Giustinian, *Four Years at the Court of Henry VIII* — Sebastian Giustinian, *Four Years at the Court of Henry VIII*, ed. R. Brown (1854).

Glanville, *Silver* — P. Glanville, *Silver in Tudor and Early Stuart England* (1990).

Gunn, *Brandon* — S. J. Gunn, *Charles Brandon* (Oxford, 1988).

Guy, *More* — J. A. Guy, *Thomas More* (2000).

Guy, in *EHR*, 97 — J. A. Guy, 'Henry VIII and the *praemunire* manoeuvres of 1530–31', in *EHR*, 97 (1982), 481–503.

Guy, in *Moreana*, 21 — J. A. Guy, 'Thomas More and Christopher St German', in *Moreana*, 21 (1984).

Guy, *Public Career of More* — J. A. Guy, *The Public Career of Sir Thomas More* (Brighton, 1980).

Hall, *Chronicle* — Edward Hall, *The Union of the Two Noble and Illustre Famelies of York and Lancaster*, ed. H. Ellis (1809).

Hamy, *Entrevue*

P. A. Hamy, *Entrevue de François Premier avec Henri VIIIe à Boulogne* (Paris, 1898).

Harpsfield, *More*

Nicolas Harpsfield, *The Life and Death of Sir Thomas More*, ed. E. V. Hitchcock and R. W. Chambers. Early English Text Society, 186 (1932).

Harpsfield, *Pretended Divorce*

Nicholas Harpsfield, *A Treatise on the Pretended Divorce between Henry VIII and Catherine of Aragon*, ed. N. Pocock. Camden Society, 2nd series, 21 (1878).

Harrier, *Canon*

R. C. Harrier, *The Canon of Sir Thomas Wyatt's Poetry* (Cambridge, Mass., 1975).

Henry VIII, ed. MacCulloch,

The Reign of Henry VIII: Politics, Policy and Piety, ed. D. MacCulloch (1995).

Herbert, *Henry VIII* (1679)

Edward Herbert, *The Life and Raigne of King Henry the eighth* (1679).

Herbert, *Henry VIII*

Edward Herbert, *The History of England under Henry VIII* [ed. White Kennett] (1870).

Hist. Journ.

Historical Journal.

Hist. Mss. Comm.

Historical Manuscripts Commission.

Holbein's Ambassadors

S. Foister, A. Roy and M. Wyld, *Holbein's Ambassadors* (1997).

House of Commons

The House of Commons, 1509–58, ed. S. T. Bindoff (1982).

Hoyle, in *Hist. Journ.*, 38

R. W. Hoyle, 'The origins of the dissolution of the monasteries', in *Historical Journal*, 38 (1995).

Hoyle, in Bernard, *Nobility*

R. W. Hoyle, 'Henry Percy, sixth earl of Northumberland and the fall of the house of Percy 1527–37', in Bernard, *Nobility.*

Hoyle, *Pilgrimage*

R. W. Hoyle, *The Pilgrimage of Grace* (Oxford, 2001).

Inventory

The Inventory of Henry VIII, ed. David Starkey, i (1998).

Ives, in *Hist. Journ.* 37

E. W. Ives, 'Anne Boleyn and the early reformation: the contemporary evidence', in *Hist. Journ.* 37 (1994).

Ives, in *Apollo*, cxl

E. W. Ives, 'The queen and the painters; Anne Boleyn, Holbein and Tudor royal portraits', in *Apollo*, cxl (1994).

Ives, in *François Ier et Henri VIII*

E. W. Ives, 'Anne Boleyn and the "Entente Évangelique"', in *François Ier et Henri VIII.*

Ives, in *History Today*, 50

E. W. Ives, 'Marrying for love', in *History Today*, 50 (2000).

Ives, in *Cardinal Wolsey*, ed. Gunn and Lindley

E. W. Ives, 'The fall of Wolsey', in *Cardinal Wolsey, Church, State and Art*, ed. S. J. Gunn and P. G. Lindley (Cambridge, 1991).

Ives, in *EHR*, 107

E. W. Ives, 'The fall of Anne Boleyn reconsidered', in *EHR*, 107 (1992).

Ives, in *Hist. Journ.*, 34

E. W. Ives, 'Stress, faction and ideology in early-Tudor England', in *Hist. Journ.*, 34.

Ives, in *Trans. Hist. Soc. Lancs. & Ches.*, 123

E. W. Ives, 'Court and county palatine in the reign of Henry VIII', in *Transactions of the Historic Society of Lancashire and Cheshire*, 123 (1972), 1–38.

JEH
Jewels and Plate

Journal of Ecclesiastical History
Jewels and Plate of Queen Elizabeth I, ed. A. J. Collins (1956).

Jourda, *Marguerite d'Angoulême*

Pierre Jourda, *Marguerite d'Angoulême* (Paris, 1930).

Kelly, *Matrimonial Trials*

H. A. Kelly, *The Matrimonial Trials of Henry VIII* (Palo Alto, Calif., 1975).

Kipling, *Triumph of Honour*

G. Kipling, *The Triumph of Honour* (The Hague, 1977).

Kipling, in *Civic Ritual*

G. Kipling, 'Anne Boleyn's royal entry into London', in *Civic Ritual and Drama*, ed. A. F. Johnston and W. Hüsken (Amsterdam, 1996).

Knecht, *Renaissance Warrior and Patron*

R. J. Knecht, *Renaissance Warrior and Patron: The Reign of Francis I* (Cambridge, 1994).

Knecht, *Francis I*
Knowles, *Religious Orders*

R. J. Knecht, *Francis I* (Cambridge, 1982).
D. Knowles, *Religious Orders in England*, iii (1959).

Latymer, 'Treatyse'

William Latymer, 'Treatyse' on Anne Boleyn, in Oxford, Bodleian Library, MS Don. C.42.

Law and Government

Law and Government under the Tudors, ed. C. Cross et al. (Cambridge 1988).

Lefèvre, *Épistres*, ed. Bedouelle and Giacone

Jacques Lefèvre d'Étaples, *Épistres et Évangiles pour les cinquante et deux dimanches de l'an* (Pierre de Vingle, ?Lyons, 1532), ed. G. Bedouelle and F. Giacone (Leiden, 1976).

Lefèvre, *Épistres*, ed. Screech

Jacques Lefèvre d'Étaples, *Épistres et Évangiles pour les cinquante et deux*

	dimanches de l'an (Simon du Bois, ?Paris, 1525–6), ed. M. A. Screech (Geneva, 1964).
Lehmberg, *Later Parliaments of Henry VIII*	S. E. Lehmberg, *The Later Parliaments of Henry VIII* (Cambridge, 1977).
Lehmberg, *Reformation Parliament*	S. E. Lehmberg, *The Reformation Parliament, 1529–36* (Cambridge, 1970).
Lemaitre, in *François Ier et Henri VIII*	Nicole Lemaitre, 'Les évêques réformateurs français', in *François Ier et Henri VIII*.
Lisle Letters	*The Lisle Letters*, ed. M. St Clare Byrne (Chicago & London, 1981).
Loach, *Edward VI*	J. Loach, *Edward VI*, ed. G. Bernard and D. Williams (New Haven, 1999)
Loades, *Mary Tudor*	D. M. Loades, *Mary Tudor: A Life* (Oxford, 1989).
Love Letters	*Love Letters of Henry VIII*, ed. H. Savage (1949).
Lowinsky, in *Florilegium*	E. E. Lowinsky, 'A music book for Anne Boleyn', in *Florilegium Historiale*, ed. J. G. Rowe & W. H. Stockdale (Toronto, 1971), pp. 160–235.
LP	*Letters and Papers, Foreign and Domestic, of the Reign of Henry VIII*, ed. J. S. Brewer et al. (1862–1932).
MacCulloch, *Cranmer*	Diarmaid MacCulloch, *Thomas Cranmer* (1996).
The Maner of the Tryumphe	*The Maner of the Tryumphe at Caleys and Bulleyn*, Wynkyn de Worde (1532), ed. A. F. Pollard, in *Tudor Tracts* (1903).
Marius, *More*	R. Marius, *Thomas More* (1985).
Mattingly, *Catherine of Aragon*	G. Mattingly, *Catherine of Aragon* (1950).
McConica, *English Humanists*	J. K. McConica, *English Humanists and Reformation Politics* (Oxford, 1965).
Muir, *Life and Letters of Wyatt*	K. Muir, *The Life and Letters of Sir Thomas Wyatt* (Liverpool, 1963).
Muller, *Gardiner*	J. A. Muller, *Stephen Gardiner and the Tudor Reaction* (1926).
Murdoch, *Portrait Miniature*	J. Murdoch et al., *The English Portrait Miniature* (1981).
Murphy, *Bastard Prince*	B. A. Murphy, *Bastard Prince* (Stroud, 2001).
Murphy, in *Henry VIII*, ed.	V. Murphy, 'The literature and

propaganda of Henry VIII's first divorce', in *Henry VIII*, ed. MacCulloch.

Narratives of the Reformation   *Narratives of the Days of the Reformation*, ed. J. G. Nichols. Camden Society, 77 (1859).

Neale, *Queen Elizabeth*   J. E. Neale, *Queen Elizabeth* (1934).

Nicolas, *Privy Purse*   *Privy Purse Expenses of King Henry VIII*, ed. N. H. Nicolas (1827).

The noble tryumphant coronacyon   *The noble tryumphant coronacyon of Quene Anne*, Wynkyn de Worde (1533), ed. A. F. Pollard, in *Tudor Tracts* (1903).

NPG, *Portraits*   National Portrait Gallery, *Catalogue of Tudor and Jacobean Portraits*, ed. R. Strong (1969).

Nugarum   Borbonius [Nicolas Bourbon], *Nugarum Libri Octo* (Lyons, 1538).

Ogle, *Lollards' Tower*   A. Ogle, *The Tragedy of the Lollards' Tower* (1949).

Ordinances for the Household   *Ordinances and Regulations for the Royal Household*, ed. Sort, Gough, Topham and Brand (Society of Antiquaries, 1790).

Original Letters   *Original Letters relative to the English Reformation*, ed. H. Robinson. Parker Society (1846–7).

Paget, in *BIHR*, 54   Hugh Paget, 'The youth of Anne Boleyn', in *BIHR*, 54 (1981).

Parker, *Correspondence*   *Correspondence of Matthew Parker*, ed. J. Bruce and T. T. Perowne. Parker Society (1853).

Parker, *Drawings*   K. T. Parker, *The Drawings of Hans Holbein . . . at Windsor Castle* (1945).

Pocock, *Records*   *Records of the Reformation: the Divorce, 1527–33*, ed. N. Pocock (Oxford, 1870).

Pollard, *Henry VIII*   A. F. Pollard, *Henry VIII* (1951).

Prescott, *Mary Tudor*   H. F. M. Prescott, *Mary Tudor* (1952).

Quinn in *Irish Historical Studies*   D. B. Quinn, 'Henry VIII and Ireland, 1509–34', in *Irish Historical Studies*, 12 (1961), 318–44.

Redworth, *Church Catholic*   G. Redworth, *In Defence of the Church Catholic* (Oxford, 1990).

Ridley, *Cranmer*   J. Ridley, *Thomas Cranmer* (Oxford, 1962).

RO   London, Public Record Office.

Rowlands, in *British Museum Yearbook*	J. Rowlands, 'A portrait drawing by Hans Holbein the younger', in *British Museum Yearbook*, 2 (1977).
Rowlands, *Paintings*	J. Rowlands, *Holbein: The Paintings of Hans Holbein the Younger* (Oxford, 1985).
Russell, *Cloth of Gold*	J. G. Russell, *The Field of Cloth of Gold* (1969).
Sander, *Schism*	Nicolas Sander, *The Rise and Growth of the Anglican Schism*, ed. D. Lewis (1877).
Scarisbrick, *Henry VIII*	J. J. Scarisbrick, *Henry VIII* (1968).
Sergeant, *Anne Boleyn*	P. W. Sergeant, *Anne Boleyn: a Study* (revised ed, n.d.).
Shakespeare and Dowling, in *BIHR*, 55	J. Shakespeare and M. Dowling, 'Religion and politics in mid-Tudor England', in *BIHR*, 55 (1982).
Smith, *Henry VIII*	L. B. Smith, *Henry VIII: The Mask of Royalty* (1971).
Southall, *Courtly Maker*	R. Southall, *The Courtly Maker* (Oxford, 1964).
Spelman, *Reports*	*The Reports of Sir John Spelman*, ed. J. A. Baker. Selden Society, 93, 94 (1977–8).
Starkey, thesis	D. R. Starkey, 'The King's Privy Chamber, 1485–1547' (unpublished Ph.D. thesis, University of Cambridge, 1973).
Starkey, *European Court*	D. Starkey, *Henry VIII, a European Court* (1991).
Starkey, *Six Wives*	D. Starkey, *Six Wives: The Queens of Henry VIII* (2003).
State, Sovereigns and Society	*State, Sovereigns and Society*, ed. C. Carlton et al. (Stroud, 1998).
Sterling, *Master of Claude*	Charles Sterling, *The Master of Claude, Queen of France* (New York, 1975).
St German, *Doctor and Student*	Christopher St German, *Doctor and Student*, ed. T. F. T. Plucknett & J. J. Barton (Selden Society, 91, 1974), pp. 315–40.
St. Pap.	*State Papers, King Henry VIII*, (1830–52).
Strickland, *Queens of England*	Agnes Strickland, *Lives of the Queens of England* (1868).
Strong, *Artists*	*Artists of the Tudor Court*, ed. R. Strong (Victoria and Albert Museum, 1983).
Strong, *Lost Treasures*	R. Strong, *Lost Treasures of Britain* (1990).

Strong, *Gloriana*	R. Strong, *Gloriana* (1987).
Strong, *Renaissance Miniature*	R. Strong, *The English Renaissance Miniature* (2nd edn, 1984).
Thomas, *The Pilgrim*	William Thomas, *The Pilgrim*, ed. J. A. Froude (1861).
Thomson, *Wyatt and his Background*	P. Thomson, *Sir Thomas Wyatt and his Background* (Stanford, Calif., 1964).
Thornton, *Cheshire*	T. Thornton, *Cheshire and the Tudor State, 1480–1560* (2000).
Thurley, *Hampton Court* (1998)	S. Thurley, *Henry VIII's Hampton Court* (1988).
Thurley, *Hampton Court* (2003)	S. Thurley, *Hampton Court* (New Haven and London, 2003).
Thurley, *Palaces*	S. Thurley, *The Royal Palaces of England* (New Haven, 1993).
Thurley, *Whitehall Palace*	S. Thurley, *Whitehall Palace* (New Haven and London, 1999).
Tudor Royal Proclamations	*Tudor Royal Proclamations*, ed. P. L. Hughes and J. F. Larkin, i (1964).
Walker, in *Hist. Journ.*, 45	G. Walker, 'Rethinking the fall of Anne Boleyn', in *Hist. Journ.*, 45 (2002).
Warnicke, in *History*, 70	Retha M. Warnicke, 'The fall of Anne Boleyn: a reassessment', in *History*, 70 (1985), 1–15.
Warnicke, *Rise and Fall*	R. M. Warnicke, *The Rise and Fall of Anne Boleyn* (Cambridge, 1989).
Wolsey, ed. Singer	*The Life of Cardinal Wolsey by George Cavendish*, ed. S. W. Singer (2nd edn, 1827).
Wood, *Letters*	*Letters of Royal and Illustrious Ladies*, ed. M. A. E. Wood (1846).
Wriothesley, *Chronicle*	Charles Wriothesley, *A Chronicle of England, 1485–1559*, ed. W. D. Hamilton. Camden Society, 2nd series, 11 & 20 (1875, 1877).
George Wyatt, *Papers*	*The Papers of George Wyatt*, ed. D. M. Loades. Camden Society, 4th series, 5 (1968).
George Wyatt, in *Wolsey*, ed. Singer	George Wyatt, 'The Life of Queen Anne Boleigne', in *The Life of Cardinal Wolsey by George Cavendish*, ed. S. W. Singer (1827).
Wyatt, *Poems*	Sir Thomas Wyatt, *Collected Poems*, ed. J. Daalder (Oxford, 1975).
Yates, *Astraea*	F. A. Yates, *Astraea: The Imperial Theme in the Sixteenth Century* (1975).

INDEX